JOHN GOODWIN
AND THE PURITAN REVOLUTION

1 Portrait of John Goodwin aged 47 in 1641, first published in *A Treatise of Justification* (1642), and later republished in *Divine Authority of the Scriptures* (1647), *The Obstructors of Justice* (1649) and *Redemption Redeemed* (1651). From the Fairclough Collection of the University of Leicester Library.

John Goodwin
And The Puritan Revolution

RELIGION AND INTELLECTUAL CHANGE
IN SEVENTEENTH-CENTURY ENGLAND

John Coffey

THE BOYDELL PRESS

© John Coffey 2006

All Rights Reserved. Except as permitted under current legislation
no part of this work may be photocopied, stored in a retrieval system,
published, performed in public, adapted, broadcast,
transmitted, recorded or reproduced in any form or by any means,
without the prior permission of the copyright owner

The right of John Coffey to be identified as
the author of this work has been asserted in accordance with
sections 77 and 78 Copyright, Designs and Patents Act 1988

First published 2006
Transferred to digital printing
Printed in paperback 2008

ISBN 978-1-84383-265-2 Hardback
ISBN 978-1-84383-42-81 Paperback

The Boydell Press is an imprint of Boydell & Brewer Ltd
PO Box 9, Woodbridge, Suffolk IP12 3DF, UK
and of Boydell & Brewer Inc.
668 Mt Hope Avenue, Rochester, NY 14620, USA
website: www.boydellandbrewer.com

A catalogue record for this book is available
from the British Library

This publication is printed on acid-free paper

Contents

Illustrations	page vi
Preface	vii
Abbreviations	ix
Introduction: 'A Man by Himself'	1
1 'A Tryar of Men's Doctrines', 1594–1632	13
2 'Goodwin of Colman-Street', 1633–39	44
3 'The Anti-Cavalier', 1640–43	66
4 'A Bitter Enemie to Presbyterie', 1643–45	97
5 'The Grand Heretick of England', 1645–48	131
6 'Champion of the Army', 1648–51	168
7 'The Great Spreader of Arminianism', 1647–53	199
8 'A Man of Strife', 1652–59	233
9 'Infamous Firebrand', 1660 & Beyond	266
Conclusion: 'A Harbinger of the Lockean Age'	291
Appendix: Anonymous Works Attributed to Goodwin	298
A Goodwin Bibliography	308
Index	327

Illustrations

1 Portrait of John Goodwin aged 47 in 1641, first published in Goodwin's *Treatise of Justification* (1642). From the Fairclough Collection of the University of Leicester Library. — *ii*
2 *The Cittie of London*, map attributed to the late sixteenth-century engraver, Augustus Ryther. This edition published by Cornelis Dankerts in 1645. By permission of the British Library Crace Collection of Maps. — 46
3 Satirical Caricature of John Goodwin from John Vicars, *Coleman-Street Conclave Visited* (1648). From the Fairclough Collection of the University of Leicester Library. — 162
4 John Goodwin and Hugh Peters seated in Cromwell's hellish council, frontispiece to *The Devils Cabinet Councell* (1660). By permission of the British Library. — 269

PREFACE

This volume is a sequel of sorts to my first book, *Politics, Religion and the British Revolutions: The Mind of Samuel Rutherford* (Cambridge, 1997). Like Samuel Rutherford, John Goodwin was a zealous and learned Protestant divine, and a prolific pamphleteer during the 1640s and 1650s. Both men addressed major contemporary controversies over armed resistance, predestination and free will, and religious toleration. Both were resident in London in the critical years of the mid-1640s. It is not clear if they ever met face to face, but they were certainly familiar with each other's work. Yet Rutherford and Goodwin represent radically different versions of early modern Protestantism. Rutherford was a Scot; Goodwin was English. Rutherford was a Covenanter; Goodwin a supporter of the regicide and the republic. Rutherford was a high Calvinist; Goodwin a champion of Arminianism. Rutherford was a formidable proponent of divine right Presbyterianism; Goodwin a leading Independent. Rutherford defended traditional Reformed notions of religious uniformity and coercion; Goodwin became one of England's leading tolerationists. Together they introduce us to the major religious controversies in mid-seventeenth-century Britain. This intellectual biography of Goodwin is a contribution to ongoing debates over Puritanism, the English Revolution and intellectual change.

During research and writing for this book, I have incurred many debts, both institutional and personal. The British Academy provided vital support by awarding several small research grants that enabled me to visit libraries and archives in London, Cambridge, Oxford, Manchester and Norwich. The University of Leicester granted study leave in the first semester of 2002-03, and invested in Early English Books Online, a resource which transformed my research. Crucially, the Arts and Humanities Research Board awarded me a research leave grant for the second semester of 2002-03, during which I completed the first draft of the book. Without its generosity, and the assistance of the British Academy and the University of Leicester, this study would have taken much longer to finish. I also owe a considerable debt to librarians and archivists at the British Library, the National Archives, the Dr Williams Library, Friends House Library, Cambridge University Library, the Bodleian, John

Preface

Rylands Library, Leicester University Library, the Guildhall Library, and the Norfolk Record Office.

My personal debts are many. I have benefited from the advice, encouragement and generosity of various friends and colleagues, including Alister Chapman, Gordon Campbell, Michael Davies, Alan Ford, David Gentilcore, Mark Goldie, Crawford Gribben, Ian Harris, Ann Hughes, Neil Keeble, William Lamont, David Loewenstein, Paul Lim, J. Sears McGee, Herbert McGonigle, Anthony Milton, Ellen More, John Morrill, Steve Rowlstone, Tom Schwanda, John Spurr, Daniel Strange, Chad van Dixhoorn, Tom Webster and Sonoko Yamada. At Leicester, Peter Musgrave has been a kind and considerate Head of School. At Boydell and Brewer, Peter Sowden has been a patient and understanding editor. Finally, my greatest debt is to my family. My wife Cate has listened with wry amusement to my protestations that the book is 'nearly finished' – she will be glad to see it published. Our young sons, Ethan and Ben, have been a source of constant joy and delight. The book is dedicated to Cate, with much love and affection – I owe more to her than words can say.

ABBREVIATIONS

BL	British Library
Bodl.	Bodleian Library
CCJ	Common Council Journal
CJ	*Commons Journals*
CLRO	Corporation of London Record Office
CSPD	*Calendar of State Papers Domestic*
CUL	Cambridge University Library
DNB	*Dictionary of National Biography*
GL	Guildhall Library, London,
HMC	Historical Manuscripts Commission
HP	Hartlib Papers, Sheffield University Library
Kirby, 'Parish'	'The parish of St Stephen's, Coleman Street, London: A study in radicalism c. 1624–1664', University of Oxford B. Litt. dissertation, 1968.
Kirby, 'Radicals'	'The radicals of St. Stephen's, Coleman Street, London, 1624–1642', *Guildhall Miscellany*, 3 (1969–71), 98–119.
LJ	*Lords Journals*
More, 'New Arminians'	'The new Arminians: John Goodwin and his Coleman Street congregation in Cromwellian England', University of Rochester PhD dissertation, 1979.
More, 'Congregationalism'	'Congregationalism and the social order: John Goodwin's gathered church, 1640–60', *Journal of Ecclesiastical History*, 38 (1987), 210–35.
NA	National Archives
NRO	Norfolk Record Office
ODNB	*Oxford Dictionary of National Biography*
SP	State Papers
Walwyn	*The Writings of William Walwyn*, ed. J. R. McMichael and B. Taft (Athens, GA, 1989)

ABBREVIATIONS

Wing   Donald Wing, *Short-Title Catalogue of Books Printed in England, Scotland, Ireland, Wales, and British America and of English Books Printed in Other Countries, 1641–1700*, revised edition, 4 vols (New York, 1982–98).

For Cate

Introduction

'A Man by Himself'

John Goodwin was one of the most prolific and controversial writers of the English Revolution. Between 1640 and 1663, he published around sixty books and pamphlets, and had almost as many written against him. The journalist and propagandist, Marchamont Nedham, once compared Goodwin to a neighbour's dog, barking furiously at every passer-by. He offered a list of Goodwin's 'Duels'.

> The single persons he hath been in the field with in Print, as his Adversaries, and whom he used accordingly when he got them under the Presse, are these, viz. Mr Gataker, Mr Walker, Mr Roborough, Dr Williams, Bishop of Ossory, Mr Pryn, Sir Francis Nethersole, Mr John Geree, Mr Herbert Palmer, Dr Thomas Goodwin, Mr Resbury, Dr Hammond, Dr Burgess, Dr Hill, Dr Jenkins, Mr Edwards, Mr Barlow, Mr A Steward (in particular Books printed) besides several members of his own Church.[1]

These gladiatorial contests were fought out in three arenas of controversy: the theological, the ecclesiastical and the political. In terms of theology, Goodwin's *Treatise of Justification* (1642) was the culmination of several years of controversy over his ideas among London Puritans, and his major work on the *Divine Authority of the Scriptures* (1647) also attracted hostile criticism. But it was his conversion to Arminianism in the late 1640s that caused the greatest consternation among the godly – no fewer than ten books were published in response to Goodwin's Arminian magnum opus, *Redemption Redeemed* (1651). In matters ecclesiastical, Goodwin defended Congregationalism against Presbyterians to his right (mainly in the 1640s) and Baptists to his left (in the 1650s). Although he endured a difficult relationship with Calvinist Independents like John Owen, he was widely regarded as one of the foremost apologists for Independency. After the Restoration, he penned stinging condemnations of the 'prelatick' Church of England. Finally, as a political pamphleteer, Goodwin was one of the first clergymen to go into print in defence of the civil war, the army revolt, Pride's Purge, the regicide and the Protectorate. He was also one of the English Revolution's leading tolerationists, speaking for

---

1 Marchamont Nedham, *The Great Accuser Cast Down, or A Publick Trial of Mr John Goodwin of Coleman-street London* (1657), sig. b2v.

liberty of conscience at the Whitehall Debates in 1648, and publishing almost a dozen tracts against the magistrate's power in religion.

As vicar of St Stephen's, Coleman Street, Goodwin was responsible for a strategic parish. It was a hotbed of Puritan activity, and both Christopher Hill and Valerie Pearl dubbed it 'the Faubourg St Antoine of the English Revolution'.[2] Ensconced in one of the capital's most influential pulpits, Goodwin attracted a remarkable array of hearers during twenty-seven years of ministry – London mayors like Sir Morris Abbot and Sir Isaac Pennington; aristocrats like Lady Mary Vere; intellectuals like Samuel Hartlib; political activists like John Lilburne; merchants like William Kiffin; and medical practitioners like Dr Nathan Paget and the herbalist Nicholas Culpepper.

Goodwin's critics were agreed that he was an estimable figure. To the Presbyterian clergy, he was a godly colleague who had strayed from the true path and become their most formidable intellectual foe. Goodwin was arguably the number one target of Thomas Edwards's *Gangraena* (1646), which described him as 'the Great Red Dragon of Coleman Street', 'the great lying Oracle of the Sectaries', and 'this great Goliah of the Sectaries'.[3] To John Vicars he was 'that Grand Imposter, the Schismaticks Cheater-in-Chief', 'a White-Devill', the 'monstrous Metropolitan of Coleman-street Conclave'.[4] Another Presbyterian called Goodwin 'the master-Sectary of the City', 'sins Solicitor, Satans brewer, a walking Amsterdam, the turnkey to every untruth, the City-Ishmael, the Attorney for a toleration, and the very Pandor to the lusts of the people'.[5] Marchamont Nedham, writing on behalf of Cromwell's Protectorate, denounced him as 'this Wandring Star of Error and Falshood', 'this Hyper-phantastical Metropolitan of Bell-Alley'.[6] For the Anglican Royalist, Anthony Wood, Goodwin was 'that infamous and blackmouth'd Independent'.[7]

Some critics were more willing to acknowledge Goodwin's gifts and piety. The Scottish Presbyterian, Samuel Rutherford, writing against the tolerationists, considered Goodwin 'undoubtedly the learnedst and most godly man of that way'.[8] Thomas Barlow, future bishop of Lincoln, told Goodwin: 'I always find, in the prosecution of your Arguments, that perspicuity and acuteness which I often seek, but seldom find, in the writings of others'.[9] The Calvinist Independent, John Owen, began his critique of Goodwin by admitting that 'his worth, pains, diligence, and opinions, and ... contests' had 'delivered him from being the object of any ordinary thoughts or expressions. Nothing not great, not considerable, not some way eminent,

---

2 C. Hill, *Economic Problems of the Church from Archbishop Whitgift to the Long Parliament* (Oxford, 1956), 255; V. Pearl, *London and the Outbreak of the Puritan Revolution* (Oxford, 1961), 183.
3 Thomas Edwards, *Gangraena* (1646), ii. 31, 39, 136. All three parts of the work contain references to Goodwin, but over half of Part Two is an anti-Goodwin diatribe.
4 John Vicars, *Coleman Street Conclave Visited* (1648), frontispiece, 2.
5 [Anon], *Moro-Mastix: Mr John Goodwin Whipt with his own Rod* (1647), 3, 9.
6 Marchamont Nedham, *The Great Accuser Cast Down*, 44, 102.
7 Anthony Wood, *Athenae Oxonienses*, ed. P. Bliss, 4 vols (Oxford, 1813–20), iii. col. 964.
8 Samuel Rutherford, *A Free Disputation against Pretended Liberty of Conscience* (1649), 362.
9 *The Genuine Remains of That Learned Prelate Dr Thomas Barlow* (1693), 122.

is by any spoken of him'.[10] The Presbyterian historian, Edmund Calamy, grandson and namesake of one of Goodwin's clerical foes, confessed that 'He had a clear Head, a fluent Tongue, a penetrating Spirit, and a marvellous Faculty in Descanting on Scripture; and with all his faults, must be owned to have been a considerable Man, by those who will take the Pains to peruse his Writings'.[11]

Historians on Goodwin

Goodwin's significance has not gone unnoticed by historians. John Hunt, the Victorian authority on English religious thought, believed that 'A thorough life of John Goodwin would be a history of all the changes, both in Church and State, which were witnessed between the first assembling of the Long Parliament and the Restoration of Charles. In his almost forgotten tracts there is scarcely a subject either in politics or theology, on which he has not written.'[12] William Haller remarked that 'a study of the career of John Goodwin is an important chapter in the intellectual history of the Puritan Revolution, which still remains, and deserves, to be written'.[13] Perez Zagorin concurred: 'a full up-to-date study of Goodwin's life is badly needed'.[14]

Despite such pleas for 'a full up-to-date study', this monograph is the first substantial book on Goodwin to appear in print since Thomas Jackson's *Life of John Goodwin* in the nineteenth century.[15] Jackson was an English Methodist minister who celebrated Goodwin as one of the great precursors of Wesleyan Arminianism. His biography was based on a wide-ranging study of the original pamphlet literature. It first appeared in 1822, but in 1872, a year before his death at the age of ninety, Jackson produced a revised and extended edition, running to 450 pages.

Jackson's *Life* promoted two images of its subject that have dominated subsequent studies – Goodwin as isolated controversialist and Goodwin as liberal hero. On the one hand, his biography was essentially a study of Goodwin's controversies, and it perpetuated the myth that Goodwin was an isolated man. This particular myth originated in Goodwin's own lifetime, and it was not without foundation. Even by the standards of a highly polemical age, Goodwin participated in numerous 'Duels', and his amalgamation of Arminianism, congregationalism, and republicanism left him estranged from the major ideological blocs of his day. He was excluded from the Westminster Assembly, he was never asked to preach before Parliament, and even in the 1650s he was not part of Cromwell's inner circle of godly chaplains.

---

10 *The Doctrine of the Saints Perseverance* (1654), in *The Works of John Owen*, ed. W. H. Goold, 24 vols (1850–53), xi. 13.
11 Edmund Calamy, *An Account of the Ministers ... Ejected by the Act of Uniformity*, 2 vols, second edition (London, 1713), i. 53.
12 J. Hunt, *Religious Thought in England*, 3 vols (London, 1870), i. 260.
13 W. Haller, *The Rise of Puritanism* (New York, 1938), 391.
14 P. Zagorin, *A History of Political Thought in the English Revolution* (1954), 81.
15 T. Jackson, *The Life of John Goodwin* (London, 1822).

However, this image of an isolated Goodwin was also constructed for polemical purposes. Goodwin himself rather liked the thought of being a prophet in the wilderness, a latter-day Jeremiah standing for truth against hordes of false teachers. He admitted that he had 'a temper very creative of enemies'.[16] In one book he claimed that God and his conscience had forced him 'to contend (in a manner) with the whole Earth round about me'.[17] In another work, he called himself 'a man of contention to the whole world' (though he went on to boast about the many supportive letters he had received from other ministers and university students).[18] The myth of Goodwin's isolation also suited his enemies, who were keen to dismiss him as a 'singular' figure, an unpredictable maverick. Presbyterians and Calvinists branded him 'that Ishmael of Coleman-street, whose hand being against all men, hath provoked all men'.[19] They referred, of course, to the biblical Ishmael, the son of Abraham by his concubine, and rival to the true son Isaac. It was prophesied that 'he will be a wild man; his hand will be against every man, and every man's hand against him' (Genesis 16:12). This view of Goodwin was set in stone by the historian Edmund Calamy, who wrote: 'He was a Man by himself; was against every man, and had every man almost against him'.[20] His comment has been enormously influential. It is the one statement quoted in practically everything written about Goodwin since the eighteenth century. Yet it is fundamentally misleading.

Goodwin was not an eccentric individualist who picked fights with everyone around him. Still less was he a 'wild man' fundamentally at odds with the godly. Although Nedham was right to say that Goodwin had fought many 'Duels', a vociferous crowd of supporters cheered him on from the sidelines. Among those who rallied to his defence in the mid-1640s was a certain Marchamont Nedham.[21] If Goodwin had operated as a lone ranger, his critics would not have taken him so seriously. He mattered precisely because he spoke for others besides himself and his congregation. By offering a thoroughly contextualised account of Goodwin's life and thought, this book aims to show that he was emphatically not 'a man by himself', but an important player in a variety of networks and alliances.[22]

For if Goodwin had many enemies, he also had devoted followers. At St Stephen's, Coleman Street, he claimed (hyperbolically, of course) that many parishioners were willing to pluck out their eyes for him.[23] The adulation heaped on Goodwin frustrated critics like George Walker, who grumbled that 'the rude

---

16 *The Unrighteous Judge* (1649), 1.
17 *Catabaptism*, 'Epistle Dedicatory', sig. c3v.
18 *The Banner of Justification*, 'To the Reader'.
19 Henry Hickman, *Patro-scholastiko-dikaiösis, or, A Justification of the Fathers and the Schoolmen* (1659), 21. See also *Moro-Mastix*, 9.
20 Calamy, *An Account*, i. 53.
21 M[archamont] N[edham], *Independencie no Schisme* (1646), 5–6, 8.
22 Thus what I am attempting is analogous to the effort of modern Hobbes' scholarship, which has demonstrated that Hobbes was not as isolated and unacceptable to contemporaries as his clerical critics suggested. See Quentin Skinner, *Visions of Politics*, iii: *Hobbes and Civil Science* (Cambridge, 2002), 264–70.
23 John Goodwin, *The Saints Interest in God* (1640), sigs. a4v-a5r.

multitude of his Disciples' proclaimed him 'the great light of Gods Church, revealed in these last times'.[24] Although Goodwin's Independency led to his ejection in 1645, loyal parishioners continued to petition on his behalf, and a substantial number remained by his side in the gathered church. One of them, Daniel Taylor, wrote a verse to accompany his minister's portrait, in which he acclaimed the subject as a man in whom were gathered the 'gifts and graces' and 'perfections rare' of 'ten thousand persons'.[25] To his congregation, Goodwin was 'our dearly beloved Pastor';[26] 'a great Master in Israel' and 'the best of men';[27] 'a deep Divine, a Teacher of Teachers'.[28] William Walwyn, who knew the congregation well, declared that 'Mr Goodwin is the apple of their eie'.[29]

Modern scholarship has done much to reconstruct a picture of Goodwin's relationship with his parish and his gathered church. The work began in the late nineteenth century, when Edwin Freshfield published extracts from the records of St Stephen's, Coleman Street, and it was continued by Dorothy Williams whose article on the parish appeared in 1959.[30] However, the real breakthrough came with David Kirby's 1968 Oxford B.Litt. thesis and his subsequent article on the parish of St Stephen's, Coleman Street. Kirby's work was marred by minor factual errors, but it contained a great wealth of detail on the parish and laid the foundations for later studies.[31] Ellen More contributed further to our understanding of Goodwin and his supporters in her 1979 Ph.D. dissertation, 'The new Arminians: John Goodwin and his Coleman Street congregation in Cromwellian England'. This thesis and the two substantial articles that grew out of it have been the main reference points for subsequent historians. Although More devoted several chapters of the thesis to Goodwin's ideas, her chief contribution lay in providing the fullest study of the gathered church. Her carefully researched article on Goodwin's congregation remains a valuable source of information.[32] Meanwhile, the goings on at St Stephen's, Coleman Street were examined by a number of historians working on the religious history of seventeenth-century London, notably Paul Seaver, Murray Tolmie and Tai Liu,[33] while the political activism of Goodwin's parishioners

---

24 George Walker, *A Defence*, 27.
25 See *Treatise of Justification*, frontispiece.
26 Robert Smith et al., *An Apologeticall Account of some Brethren of the Church whereof Mr John Goodwin is Pastor* (1647), 2.
27 See [John Vicars], *To His Reverend and Much Respected Good Friend Mr John Goodwin* (1645), 6.
28 See Edwards, *Gangraena*, ii. 39.
29 *Walwyn*, 427.
30 E. Freshfield, 'Some remarks upon the Book of Records and History of the Parish of St Stephen, Coleman Street, in the City of London', *Archaeologia*, 50 (1887), 17–57; D. A. Williams, 'London Puritanism: the Parish of St Stephen's, Coleman Street', *The Church Quarterly Review*, 160 (1959), 464–82.
31 Kirby, 'Parish'; Kirby, 'Radicals'.
32 E. More, 'New Arminians'; 'John Goodwin and the origins of the new Arminians', *Journal of British Studies*, 22 (1982), 50–70; 'Congregationalism'.
33 See P. Seaver, *The Puritan Lectureships: The Politics of Religious Dissent, 1560–1662* (Stanford, 1970), 257–64, 281–83, M. Tolmie, *The Triumph of the Saints: The Separate Churches of London, 1616–49* (Cambridge, 1977), 111–17; T. Liu, *Puritan London* (London, 1986).

and supporters was scrutinised by historians of City politics, including Valerie Pearl, James Farnell, Robert Brenner and Keith Lindley.[34]

This book draws on the research of these historians, while also extending our knowledge of Goodwin's friends and enemies. Recent scholarship on early modern print culture has explored the relationship of writers to patrons, licensers, printers, booksellers and readers, thus setting a challenge to intellectual historians who focus on the ideological context of texts, but ignore wider questions about the sponsorship, production, circulation and reception of books.[35] Although this book is essentially an intellectual biography of Goodwin, it does try to avoid a purely intellectualist approach to the history of ideas by attending to political factionalism, social networks, religious passions and the role of publishers. Goodwin will emerge, not as a disembodied mind thinking lofty thoughts, but as a flesh and blood participant in the rough and tumble of his times.

Although Goodwin always remains at the centre of the picture, he is never 'a man by himself'. In trying to tell the story of his parish, his gathered church, his Independent and Arminian allies, his publishers, printers and readers, one runs the risk of overstretching. But understanding Goodwin's milieu is vital for understanding his ideas. Only by building up a richly layered set of contexts can we gain a rounded appreciation of our author. Consequently, this is a densely peopled book, peppered with references to Goodwin's contemporaries, both famous and obscure. Although Goodwin will be our central focus, we will regularly fan out from him to explore the various networks of people whose lives and works intersected with his. Our protagonist emerges, not as an isolated pugilist, but as a well-connected and influential figure.

Jackson's *Life of Goodwin* also promoted a second image of his protagonist – Goodwin as liberal hero. In the first edition, he praised Goodwin as the first Englishman to argue for 'universal liberty of conscience', 'the elder brother' of Milton and Locke.[36] In the second, he declared that alongside Milton, Locke and Jeremy Taylor, Goodwin had championed 'full religious liberty' and helped to make Britain a free nation. It was time that he occupied his rightful place 'among the enlightened divines and philosophers of the country'.[37]

The picture of Goodwin as liberal hero proved popular with other Nonconformists and with church historians. The leading light of American Methodism, Daniel Whedon, declared that 'the free thought of the nineteenth

---

34 See V. Pearl, *London and the Puritan Revolution*; J. E. Farnell, 'The usurpation of honest London householders: Barebone's Parliament', *English Historical Review*, 82 (1967), 24–46; R. Brenner, *Merchants and Revolution: Commercial Change, Political Conflict, and London's Overseas Traders, 1550–1653* (Princeton, NJ, 1993); K. Lindley, *Popular Politics and Religion in Civil War London* (Aldershot, 1997).

35 See A. Hughes, *Gangraena and the English Revolution* (Oxford, 2004); A. Johns, *The Nature of the Book: Print and Knowledge in the Making* (Chicago, 1998); J. Peacey, *Politicians and Pamphleteers: Propaganda during the English Civil Wars and Interregnum* (Aldershot, 2004); J. Raymond, *Pamphlets and Pamphleteering in Early Modern Britain* (Cambridge, 2003).

36 Jackson, *Life of John Goodwin*, iii, 139.

37 Jackson, *Life of John Goodwin* (1872), viii–xii.

century ... is proving the Nemesis which Awards to John Goodwin his rightful place among the loftiest names of the period of the Commonwealth'.[38] Later Nonconformists wrote brief lives of Goodwin that were notably Whiggish. For Henry Clark, Goodwin was 'a pioneer in the cause of religious liberty' and 'one of Congregationalism's greatest men'; for W. W. Biggs, he was 'in advance of his time', a 'prophet of political freedom', and 'the great apostle of liberty'.[39] In the judgement of John Hunt, 'no man of that age had more advanced views, both in religion and what concerned civil government'.[40] Another Victorian hailed Goodwin as 'a Locke before Locke', on account of his tolerationism.[41]

Twentieth-century scholarship elaborated this Whig approach. William Haller republished Goodwin's *Anti-Cavalierisme* and *Theomachia* in his *Tracts on Liberty in the Puritan Revolution*.[42] Goodwin (alongside Milton and the Levellers) was one of the chief protagonists in Haller's compelling books on the rise of Puritanism and the Puritan Revolution. For Haller, Goodwin was 'the most important exponent among Puritan divines of rationalistic reaction to the intransigent dogmatism of the Presbyterian reformers'. 'No one represented more clearly the influence of Christian humanism in its Protestant phase upon the Puritan revolutionary movement'. Goodwin, 'humanist, Platonist, disciple of Acontius', was the champion of 'the free exercise of reason' and 'the separation of powers between church and state'.[43] William Clyde's study of *The Struggle for Freedom of the Press* gave Goodwin equally high marks for his 'powerful and enlightened' defence of unlicensed printing.[44] W. K. Jordan's work on *The Development of Religious Toleration in England* declared that Goodwin 'gave to religious toleration the ablest and most systematic defence which it was to receive during the period under survey'.[45] The Jesuit historian of toleration, Joseph Lecler, agreed that Goodwin was 'one of the most determined defenders of religious freedom' with a particularly clear conception of 'the separation of church and state'.[46] Gerald Cragg declared that 'no man of his period held such enlightened views regarding civil government and religion'.[47]

Most recently, Perez Zagorin has devoted a number of pages to Goodwin in his study of *How the Idea of Religious Toleration Came to the West* (2003).[48]

---

38 D. D. Whedon, 'Memorabilia of John Goodwin', *Methodist Quarterly Review*, 51 (October 1869), 486–505, quotation at 487.
39 Henry William Clark, *The Life of John Goodwin* (London, 1913), 7; W. W. Biggs, *John Goodwin* (London, 1961), 4, 17, 20.
40 Hunt, *Religious Thought in England*, i. 259.
41 M. Fuller, *The Life, Letters and Writings of John Davenant* (London, 1897), 61.
42 W. Haller, ed., *Tracts on Liberty in the Puritan Revolution*, 3 vols (New York, 1933–34), ii. 217–69; iii. 3–52.
43 W. Haller, *The Rise of Puritanism*, 195–96; Haller, *Liberty and Reformation in the Puritan Revolution* (New York, 1955), 76, 251, 253.
44 W. M. Clyde, *The Struggle for the Freedom of the Press from Caxton to Cromwell* (St Andrews, 1934), 258. Extracts from one of Goodwin's tracts were republished in Appendix F.
45 W. K. Jordan, *The Development of Religious Toleration in England*, 4 vols (London, 1932–40), iii. 376–412.
46 J. Lecler, *Toleration and the Reformation*, 2 vols (Eng. Trans: London, 1960), ii. 456–461.
47 G. Cragg, *From Puritanism to the Age of Reason* (Cambridge, 1950), 17.
48 Zagorin, *How the Idea of Religious Toleration Came to the West* (Princeton, NJ, 2003), 208–13.

Zagorin had surveyed Goodwin's political ideas fifty years before in his *History of Political Thought in the English Revolution*, written partly under the supervision of W. K. Jordan.[49] He now reasserted the traditional Whig picture of Goodwin: 'his critique of dogmatism, insistence on human fallibility, and faith in free inquiry as a religious virtue distinguished him as one of the most forceful and liberal proponents of toleration during the revolution'.[50]

Zagorin's own student, Ellen More, adopted and developed this image of Goodwin. Disregarding the rising tide of revisionism in Stuart historiography, her dissertation began with the resounding declaration that the Puritan Revolution was the first modern revolution, one that changed the land of William Prynne and John Foxe into the England of Samuel Pepys and John Locke. Goodwin was an agent of this transformation, because he stood for the values of the new age – tolerance, rationality, optimism about human reason, free choice and popular sovereignty. 'His conclusions do not look back to Perkins or Sibbes', wrote More, 'but to the liberal and latitudinarian theology of the early English Enlightenment'. In his defence of liberty of conscience, as in much else, 'he was a harbinger of the Lockean age to come'. His followers were 'self-made men', practical and enterprising, who 'foreshadowed the individualism and commitment to individual interest in the eighteenth century'.[51]

Other studies of Goodwin have made similar claims. Dale Zimdars concluded that Goodwin was 'a forerunner of the "Age of Reason"', though he added the important rider that 'unlike many who followed, his fundamental understanding of existence remained theocentric'.[52] William Strickland argued that Goodwin was 'ahead of his time'. He had modified Puritanism with the assistance of Christian humanism and Arminianism, resulting in 'a more liberal, rational, tolerant, and individualistic approach'. He had contributed to democratic principles by emphasising ideas of contract, free debate and the separation of church and state.[53] John Burgess made a study of the political reading of the Bible in the Puritan Revolution, and depicted Goodwin as a 'rationalist' who provided 'a crucial link' to Locke.[54] Tom Webster's brief article on Goodwin and 'the crisis of Calvinism' presented Goodwin as a 'theological maverick' whose 'rational humanism' was part of the 'intellectual revolution' of the seventeenth century.[55]

---

49 Zagorin, *A History of Political Thought in the English Revolution*, 81–86.
50 Zagorin, *How the Idea of Toleration*, 213.
51 More, 'New Arminians', 1, 164, 332–33, 335.
52 D. E. Zimdars, 'John Goodwin and the development of rationalism in seventeenth-century England', unpublished Ph.D. thesis, University of Chicago (1967), 189.
53 W. J. Strickland, 'John Goodwin as seen through his controversies, 1640–60', unpublished Ph.D. thesis, Vanderbilt University (1967), 1, 224, 231–32.
54 J. Burgess, 'The problem of Scripture and political affairs as reflected in the Puritan Revolution: Samuel Rutherford, Thomas Goodwin, John Goodwin and Gerrard Winstanley', unpublished Ph.D. thesis, University of Chicago (1986), ch. 4. See also J. Brauer, 'Types of Puritan piety', *Church History*, 56 (1987), 39–58.
55 T. Webster, 'Strange bedfellows: Oliver Cromwell, John Goodwin and the crisis of Calvinism', *Cromwelliana*, (1990), 7–17.

INTRODUCTION

This book both corroborates and corrects these grand claims about Goodwin as 'a harbinger of the Lockean age'. On the one hand, it warns against the tendency to modernise and even secularise his thought, and to focus on some aspects of his career at the expense of others. Haller and his successors were fascinated by Goodwin's writings on politics and toleration, but less interested in (and less reliable on) his theology. They highlighted his humanism, not his scholasticism; his scepticism, not his dogmatism. While delighting in his radical heterodoxy, they slighted his conservative orthodoxy. They focused on his battle with the Presbyterians in the 1640s but ignored his polemics against Baptists and Socinians in the 1650s. They praised his 'enlightened' high-mindedness, but turned a blind eye to his rancour and ruthlessness. They neglected the tensions and inconsistencies in his thought, and had little to say about his early life and his later career.

Thankfully, some studies have offered a more balanced picture of Goodwin. William Hinson produced a solid account of Goodwin's theological works, though he was unaware of some of Goodwin's anonymous books and had little to say about his contexts.[56] Margaret Sommerville provided a probing analysis of Goodwin's political thought and his natural law reasoning as part of a wider analysis of 'Independent thought, 1603–49'. She emphasised that while Goodwin rejected the enforcement of orthodoxy, he still believed in the enforcement of morality.[57] The most recent study of Goodwin is by Professor Sonoko Yamada, who has written two monographs and two articles on Goodwin. Unfortunately, with the exception of a helpful article on Goodwin's millenarianism, her work is only available in Japanese.[58]

This book continues the project of painting a fuller and more rounded picture of Goodwin, one that does justice to the complexity of the man. It emphasises that he remained to the end a self-consciously godly, biblical, Reformed theologian. But it shares the concern of earlier studies with questions of intellectual and religious change. It will argue that Goodwin reflected some of the most powerful trends in seventeenth-century intellectual life – the rise of Arminianism; the development of toleration; the growing stress on reasonable religion; the defence of individual judgement; and the optimism about new knowledge. It will try to explain how and why Goodwin refashioned Protestant religion. Although Goodwin was not a first-rank thinker comparable to Hobbes or Locke, and although his writings never

---

56 W. J. Hinson, 'The theological thought of John Goodwin, 1593–1665', unpublished Ph.D. thesis, University of Edinburgh (1953).
57 M. Sommerville, 'Independent Thought, 1603–49', unpublished Ph.D. thesis, University of Cambridge (1981), esp. 171–93.
58 Sonoko Yamada, *Igirisu Kakumei no Shukyo Siso [John Goodwin: His Thought and Career in the 1640s]* (Tokyo, 1994); Yamada, *Igirisu Kakumei to Arminius Shugi [John Goodwin and the Doctrine of Universal Redemption]* (Saitama, 1997); Yamada, 'John Goodwin against the Cromwellian Church Scheme', in Hideo Tamura, ed., *Oliver Cromwell and the English Revolution*, (Saitama, 1999); Yamada, 'Two ways toward the Millennium', in H. Tamura, ed., *The Millennium in the English Revolution* (Tokyo, 2000). An English translation of the last article is published in *Hiroshima Law Journal*, 23 (1999). I am indebted to Professor Yamada for pointing me towards several primary sources which refer to Goodwin.

attained classic status like the works of Bunyan and Milton, he serves a valuable case study in intellectual change.

Above all, Goodwin can help us to explore the evolution of English Puritanism. Educated at Queens' College, Cambridge, in the days of John Preston, and appointed vicar of one of London's flagship Puritan parishes in 1633, Goodwin had an impeccable godly pedigree. To the end of his days, he cherished the language and the piety of Puritanism and saw himself as a Reformed theologian. But he also became notorious for his defence of free will, reason, independent judgement and toleration. How this could be so is one of the major themes of this book. It picks up on the puzzle recently highlighted by John Spurr:

> The existence of Arminian puritans is another of the great paradoxes of puritan history ... there were eminent seventeenth-century figures, men like John Milton and John Goodwin, and a whole branch of the Baptist movement, the 'General Baptists', who were Arminian and undoubtedly puritan.[59]

This runs against the widespread assumption (among both professional historians and the educated public) that all Puritans were Calvinists. The assumption is so deep rooted that it is not unusual to see Puritans defined as 'experimental predestinarians'.[60] At times, this definition of Puritanism as militant Calvinism also becomes linked to the stereotype of Puritans as intellectual reactionaries, fanatical zealots, irrational enthusiasts and intolerant bigots. This study points towards a richer and more dynamic understanding of English Puritanism. It enables us to see how radical new ideas emerged out of the confluence of reformist Protestantism, Renaissance humanism, and political revolution. As Gerald Cragg once suggested, 'It may be that Goodwin helps us to understand the secret of the weakness of Calvinism in the critical years before and after the Restoration'.[61] He helps us to see how the traditional Puritanism of the early seventeenth century started to evolve towards the radical Whig Dissent of the eighteenth.

But if Goodwin helps us to understand the revolution within Puritanism, he also adds something to our picture of 'the Puritan Revolution'. Although the term was widely used from the 1870s to the 1960s, it has fallen out of favour.[62] The Marxist Christopher Hill wanted to abandon the phrase because it placed religion at the heart of the English Revolution and obscured its affinities with the French and Russian Revolutions.[63] Yet revisionist historiography heavily underlined the

---

59 J. Spurr, *English Puritanism, 1603–89* (London, 1998), 68.
60 The phrase originates with R. T. Kendall, *Calvin and English Calvinism to 1649* (Oxford, 1979), 8.
61 Cragg, *From Puritanism to the Age of Reason*, 17.
62 It was first popularised by S. R. Gardiner in *The First Two Stuarts and the Puritan Revolution, 1603–1660* (1876), and *The Constitutional Documents of the Puritan Revolution, 1625–1660* (Oxford, 1889). It was later used by D. M. Wolfe, *Milton in the Puritan Revolution* (New York, 1941); W. Haller, *Liberty and Reformation in the Puritan Revolution*; and V. Pearl, *London and the Outbreak of the Puritan Revolution*. But the last major book to employ the term in its title (or rather its subtitle) was D. Underdown, *Pride's Purge: Politics in the Puritan Revolution* (London, 1971).
63 See C. Hill, 'Irreligion in the "Puritan" Revolution', in J. F. MacGregor and B. Reay, eds, *Radical Religion in the English Revolution* (Oxford, 1984), 191–211.

centrality of Puritans to the political upheaval of the mid-seventeenth-century, leading John Morrill to write in 1985 that 'Historians have begun to rediscover the Puritan Revolution.'[64] This book contributes to that rediscovery by examining the role of one key figure and his associates. At each turning point in the revolutionary years, Goodwin stepped in with influential pamphlets. He defended the Civil War in *Anti-Cavalierisme* (1642), the army revolt in *The Army Harmlesse* (1647), Pride's Purge in *Might and Right Well Met* (1649), the regicide in *The Obstructors of Justice* (1649), and the Protectorate in *Dis-satisfaction Satisfied* (1653). He finally turned on the Cromwellian regime in *Basanistai* (1657). He thus provides a striking case study in how a radical Puritan responded to each major turning point in the crisis, and helps us to understand the mentality of the men who were at the heart of the English Revolution. Historians have written extensively on Levellers, Diggers and Ranters, but if we wish to understand the people who stood alongside Oliver Cromwell through all the upheavals between 1640 and 1657, Goodwin is clearly a more helpful guide than John Lilburne, Gerrard Winstanley or Abiezer Coppe.

A thorough intellectual biography of Goodwin fills in another section on the map of English intellectual history in this period. As Michael Hunter has suggested, 'only through a full understanding of individual cases – which does not preclude alertness to the broader factors underlying them – will we grasp the true intellectual life of this (or any other) period'.[65] As I hope to show, Goodwin gives us a new perspective on Anglicans, Presbyterians and Levellers, and helps us to understand Baxter, Owen, and Milton a little better. Goodwin was a significant reference point on their mental maps of the ideological terrain. If we think of the major figures of the English Revolution as peaks in a mountain range, some have been scaled (or at least assayed) by countless climbers, while others remain untouched. If Cromwell is the Everest of this range, Goodwin is merely a medium sized peak, but he has attracted considerable attention precisely because of his challenging angularity. If we conquer Goodwin we get a new perspective on the surrounding fells. To stretch the metaphor, intellectual biographies like this one give us a better sense of the lie of the land, and of the period's ideological supply lines and battle lines.

Goodwin is worth studying because he is not easily pigeonholed. Standing at the crossroads between Puritanism and Arminianism, Renaissance and Reformation, he provides a revealing 'way in' to different aspects of seventeenth-century

---

[64] J. Morrill, 'Sir William Brereton and England's wars of religion', reprinted in P. Gaunt, ed., *The English Civil War* (Oxford, 2000), 184. A number of other historians have retrieved the term: B. Worden, 'Classical republicanism and the Puritan Revolution', in *History and the Imagination: Essays in Honour of Hugh Trevor-Roper* (London, 1981), 182–200; D. Wootton, 'Leveller Democracy and the Puritan Revolution', in J. H. Burns and M. Goldie, eds, *The Cambridge History of Political Thought, 1450–1700* (Cambridge, 1991), 412–42; W. Lamont, 'The Puritan Revolution: a historiographical essay', in J. G. A. Pocock et al., eds, *The Varieties of British Political Thought, 1500–1800* (Cambridge, 1993), 119–45.

[65] M. Hunter, *Science and the Shape of Orthodoxy: Studies of Intellectual Change in Late 17th-Century Britain* (Woodbridge, 1995), 2.

thought and a fascinating case study in the interaction of different intellectual traditions. Although rooted in the Reformed tradition, he drew heavily on humanist thinkers like Acontius and Grotius, and in certain respects looks forward to the early Enlightenment Protestantism of John Locke. Providing a compelling account of such a complex figure is no easy task. But the sources available for such a study are abundant.

Sources

As the first comprehensive intellectual biography of Goodwin, this book is grounded on a close reading of all of Goodwin's known works. In the course of his career, he published six thousand pages in quarto, six hundred pages in folio, as well as several small books in duodecimo. These are my core sources, and this is the first book to be based on a thorough reading of all his published writings. One of the major challenges I have faced is the problem of attribution. A dozen anonymous books and pamphlets have been attributed to Goodwin over the years, and I have gone beyond previous studies by providing a brief critical assessment of the authorship of each of these disputed works in the Appendix. In a number of cases, I have identified works by Goodwin that illuminate important moments in his career.

In addition to exploring Goodwin's own works, I have also drawn heavily on the voluminous pamphlet literature by Goodwin's contemporaries, including his critics and members of his congregation. In keeping with the contextual approach to the history of ideas championed by scholars like Quentin Skinner, I pay close attention to the intellectual and political context in which Goodwin was operating, and try to understand his books and pamphlets as interventions in particular controversies.[66] This is most obviously true of his writings on toleration and politics, but it also applies to his theological works.

In order to chronicle Goodwin's career as fully as possible, I have consulted a variety of archival records that shed valuable light on Goodwin's time in Norfolk, Cambridge and London, and on his post-Restoration career. But Goodwin's fame or notoriety rested above all on his writings. He was, complained Marchamont Nedham, an 'absolute Pen-and-Inkhorn Prince'.[67] Our main task, therefore, is to understand and interpret his many publications.

---

[66] See Q. Skinner, *Visions of Politics*, vol. i: *Regarding Method* (Cambridge, 2003), esp. ch. 6: 'Interpretation and the understanding of speech acts'.

[67] Nedham, *The Great Accuser*, 83.

1

'A Tryar of Mens Doctrines'
1594–1632

Unlike many other seventeenth-century divines, John Goodwin never found a contemporary biographer. His supporters were dispersed after the Restoration, and a career of incessant controversy did not fit neatly into the genre of conventional 'godly lives'. However, we can build up a detailed picture of his early life, and identify some of the sources of his later intellectual development. Even in his youth, Goodwin had become 'a tryar of mens doctrines'.

Early Life (Norfolk, 1594–1612)

Goodwin was born in the parish of Helloughton, Norfolk in the final decade of the sixteenth century. The parish records note: 'Johannes Goodwin filius Jo: Goodwin baptis. xiii die Maii 1594'. In the margin a pointing hand has been drawn (probably in the later seventeenth century), indicating the significance of this 'Johannes Goodwin'.[1] Although Goodwin was a fairly common name in Norfolk, we can be sure that this is our man. His portrait, drawn in 1641, noted that he was forty-seven years old.[2] Moreover, Helloughton was next to East Rainham, where Goodwin became minister in the 1620s under the patronage of the Townshend family.

Goodwin's father and grandfather – both called John – had also been employed by the Townshend family. The grandfather, John Goodwin I (d.1605) was a distinguished surveyor, who had worked in a number of counties, and was Special Surveyor of Lands to Queen Elizabeth. He had been admitted a citizen of Norwich in 1566, and became Town Clerk in 1578. In addition to these responsibilities, he was also employed on the Townshend estates at Rainham. His son, John Goodwin II (d. 1636), appears to have spent his entire life at Helloughton in the service of the Townshend family. His name crops up frequently in the Townshend estate

---

1 NRO PD 368/1, Helloughton Parish Records, 1594.
2 The portrait was published in his *Imputatio Fidei, or A Treatise of Justification* (1642).

papers, as a surveyor and bailiff.³ Our subject, John Goodwin III, was his eldest son, but Goodwin of Helloughton was to have eight more children in the following quarter of a century. William – who is later mentioned in his older brother's will – was born in 1599, Edward in 1601, Mary in 1602, and Margaret in 1604. Then between 1612 and 1620, John had four more children, possibly the offspring of a second marriage.⁴

The Townshends were distinguished local gentry. Sir Roger Townshend (1543?–90), had been educated at Trinity College, Cambridge. He held court offices under Elizabeth and was knighted for his services in the Armada campaign. His son John Townshend (1564–1603), was also educated at Trinity, and knighted after participating in the Cadiz expedition of 1596. The grandson, Roger Townshend junior (1596–1637), was just a couple of years younger than Goodwin, and the two would have known each other from childhood.⁵

Norfolk had a reputation as a centre of advanced Protestantism, but our evidence suggests that the young Roger Townshend was exposed to both the godly and the profane. His father died of wounds sustained in a duel on Hounslow Heath in 1603, which hardly suggests a paragon of godly virtue. His wife, however, was the daughter of Sir Nathaniel Bacon of Stiffkey, an eminent Puritan gentleman.⁶ We know that Roger was tutored by Giles Fletcher (1585/86–1623), a distinguished poet educated at Trinity College, Cambridge.⁷ When Fletcher dedicated his book *The Reward of the Faithful* (1623) to Townshend, he also expressed gratitude to 'the worthy Lady your mother', and 'the religious knight, Sir Nathaniel, your second Father'.⁸ Between them, mother and uncle ensured that the young Roger had a godly upbringing and a classical education. The tutor they secured for Roger was both learned and devout.

Under the influence of his mother, his grandfather and his tutor, Townshend developed a deep and serious faith. According to Thomas Fuller, he was 'a religious Gentleman, expending his soul in piety and charity, a lover to God, his Service, and

---

3 *Dictionary of Land Surveyors and Local Map-Makers of Great Britain and Ireland, 1530–1850*, 2 vols, second edition, ed. S. Bendall (London, 1997), ii. 205–06. For further references see *The Papers of Nathaniel Bacon of Stiffkey*, ed. V. Morgan, J. Key and B. Taylor (Norwich, 2000), 211–12; Historical Manuscripts Commission, *Report on the Family and Estate of the Townshend Family, Marquesses Townshend 14th–20th Century* (1986), 5, 19, 26, 33, 40, 52, 53, 55, 56, 72, 82, 103, 125, 129, 186. Previous accounts of Goodwin's early life have sometimes conflated Goodwin's father and grandfather, and confused both with John Goodwin of Bucklersby, an instrument-maker, inventor of the circumferentor and mathematician. The *Dictionary of Land Surveyors* helpfully disentangles the three men.
4 NRO PD 368/1, Helloughton Parish Records.
5 See the *ODNB* articles on Sir Roger Townshend (c. 1544–90) and Sir John Townshend (c. 1567/8–1603). See also J. M. Rosenheim, *The Townshends of Rainham: Nobility in Transition in Restoration and Early Hanoverian England* (Middleton, CT, 1989), 9–15.
6 See J. Venn and J. A. Venn, *Alumni Cantabrigienses ... Part I from the Earliest Times to 1751*, 4 vols (Cambridge, 1922–27), ii. 355.
7 See the will of Jane, Lady Townshend (20 July 1617) in J. Durham, *The Townshends of Rainham* (Cambridge, 1922), 34. On Fletcher, see *ODNB*.
8 G. Fletcher, *The Reward of the Faithful* (1623), sig. A3v.

Servants'.⁹ As an adult, he was an active patron of Puritan preachers and of promising young men, such as Thomas Cawton, born in Rainham in 1605. Cawton's biographer tells us that Townsend not only funded his education, but also took a personal interest in his academic and spiritual development, praying with him and correcting his verses. When Cawton went to Queens', Townshend ensured that Goodwin was his tutor.[10]

The close relationship between Goodwin and Roger Townshend is the key to Goodwin's early life. It probably helped to secure him an excellent education, ensured his return to East Rainham in the mid-1620s, and played a part in his selection as minister of St Stephen's, Coleman Street in 1633. But the influence of Goodwin's own family is also important. His grandfather (who died when Goodwin was ten or eleven) was a highly accomplished man, and his father was a trusted servant of the Townshend family. The precision that marks Goodwin's theological writings may owe something to the fact that he came from a family of surveyors. His taste for cutting sarcasm may also be a family trait; Thomas Goodwin was alleged to have claimed that John's 'scoffing' and 'unmannerly jeering' were learned from his father.[11] Goodwin's strong attachment to Rainham suggests that he enjoyed a strong relationship with both his father and his patron. Thanks to them, he would have been well prepared for starting university in 1612. Even if his family's faith was conventional rather than zealous, Goodwin was inclined to listen to the voices of the godly. At Cambridge, he would hear them loud and clear.

Education (Queens' College, Cambridge, 1612–25)

Goodwin matriculated at Queens' College in July 1612.[12] Easter was the most common term for entering university, and ran from April to July. Goodwin was a sizar, which meant that unlike students from a gentry background he worked his way through college in return for reduced fees. While a sizar was the lowest rank of student, it was perfectly respectable and represented value for money. Since Goodwin turned eighteen in May 1612, he was one of the older boys in his cohort. Of the future New Englanders who attended Oxford or Cambridge around this time, 45 matriculated under seventeen, 24 were seventeen, 13 were eighteen, and 25 were older.[13]

Soon after he had entered the college, Goodwin contributed an acrostic Latin poem to an anthology of Greek and Latin verse published by the University in memory of Prince Henry.[14] Henry, who was the heir to the throne and the great

---

9 T. Fuller, *The Worthies of England* (1662), ii. 272.
10 *The Life and Death of that Holy and Reverend Man of God Mr Thomas Cawton* (1662), 1–3.
11 See William Jenkyn, *The Blinde Guide* (1648), 55.
12 CUL Cambridge University Archives, Matriculation Book, vol. i (1544–1613), f. 490r; *Alumni Cantabrigienses*, ii. 238.
13 See S. E. Morison, *The Founding of Harvard College* (Cambridge, MA, 1995 [1935]), 61–62; see also J. Twigg, *A History of Queens' College, Cambridge, 1448–1986* (Woodbridge, 1987), 95.
14 *Epicedium Cantabrigiense, In obitum immaturum, semperq[ue] deflendum, Henrici, Illustrissimi Principis Walliae* (Cambridge, 1612), 48–49. The author is described as 'I. Goodwin Coll. Reginalis'.

white hope of patriotic English Protestants, had died tragically of typhoid fever at the age of eighteen. Goodwin then, was writing about a prince who was his contemporary, cut down in the prime of his youth. If Henry had lived, the course of English history and of Goodwin's own life might have been very different. As it was, Goodwin would eventually salute the execution of Henry's younger brother, Charles I. In 1612, this was unimaginable, and the young student must have been delighted to appear in an anthology alongside such distinguished names as George Herbert and Thomas May. The collection also included two lengthy poems in Latin and Greek by 'G. F. T. C.' – almost certainly Giles Fletcher of Trinity College. More intriguingly still, there is a short poem by 'R. T. T. C. Gen.', probably none other than Roger Townshend, Trinity College, Gentleman.[15] If this is the case, one can surmise that Goodwin and Townshend were writing under the supervision of Fletcher.

Indeed, there is a good case for suggesting that Giles Fletcher was a key intellectual influence on the young Goodwin. He was at Cambridge throughout Goodwin's student days, and was made Reader in Greek grammar in 1615, and Reader in Greek language in 1618. His short epic poem, *Christ's Victory* (1610), has been described as the missing link between Spenser and Milton.[16] Although Fletcher's own poetic voice is quite distinctive, he shared the cultured Protestant faith of these other poets, and strove to integrate the classical and the biblical heritages. In the dedication to the Master of Trinity College, Fletcher wrote that England was 'the beautie of all Europe, in which both true Religion is faithfully professed without superstition, and…true Learning flourishes without ostentation'.[17] This twinning of devotion and erudition was characteristic of Fletcher, who like Herbert and Donne was both poet and pastor. Ordained in 1613, he was a parish minister from 1617 until his death. Although his piety was Trinitarian and Reformed, he was far from being anti-episcopal or nonconformist. If Townshend and Nathaniel Bacon were important patrons, so were the Bishop of London and Lord Francis Bacon.[18]

From the College Bursar's Books, it seems that Goodwin was normally resident in the college for four terms of about nine weeks each, though the sums he paid for his food and lodging per quarter varied from four shillings to fourteen shillings, eleven pence.[19] Separate tuition fees would have been arranged with the tutor. Although John Goodwin senior was probably able to contribute to the costs of his university education, it is likely that either Roger Townshend himself or Nathaniel Bacon footed some of the bill.

---

15 *Epicedium Cantabrigiense*, 12–14, 97–99 (Fletcher), 38 (Townshend).
16 *Seventeenth-Century Verse and Prose*, vol. i: *1600–1660*, ed. H. C. White, R. C. Wallenstein, R. Quintana (New York, 1951), 195.
17 Fletcher, *Christ's Victory, and Triumph in Heaven and Earth, Over and After Death* (Cambridge, 1610), sig. ¶2v.
18 See his dedication to the Bishop of London in Nathaniel Pownall, *The Young Divines Apologie* (1612); and his reference to Francis Bacon in *The Reward of the Faithful*, sig. A3v.
19 CUL, Queens' College Archives, Bursar's Books, no. 24 (c. 1614). The fluctuating costs were probably related to the amount of menial work the sizar had performed each term.

Queens' was one of the largest Cambridge colleges; in 1621 it had around 230 students and 19 fellows.[20] The President in 1612 was Humphrey Tyndall, a former chaplain to the Earl of Leicester, and a conventional conformist Calvinist. The fellowship also included George Mountain, a future Archbishop of York. However, two men stood out among the rest. The first, John Davenant (1572–1641), had been a fellow of the college since 1597, and Lady Margaret Professor of Divinity since 1609. In 1614, he became President of Queens'.[21] Davenant was the very model of a moderate English Calvinist, and was eventually appointed Bishop of Salisbury in 1621. Goodwin referred respectfully to Davenant in his own theological writings, calling him in 1642 'the late Bishop of Salisburie (a learned man, doubtlesse, though a Bishop)'.[22] The second major figure at Queens' was John Preston, who was set to become England's leading godly divine, 'the Puritan pope of all England'.[23] Preston had been elected a fellow of Queens' in 1609, at the age of twenty-two, but the decisive turning point in his life came when he heard a powerful sermon by John Cotton at around the same time that Goodwin entered the University. Preston underwent a classic Puritan conversion experience, and threw himself behind the godly cause, quickly becoming one of the most popular tutors in the University.[24]

Over the next decade, he and Davenant formed a formidable double-act. In 1614, it was Preston who masterminded Davenant's succession as Master, riding to Court in order to secure a free election in which Davenant would triumph. In return, Davenant 'had bin his constant & faithfull friend, & given countenance upon all occasions to him & all his pupils'.[25] Thomas Fuller, who studied at Queens', tells us that it was 'commonly said in the Colledge, that every time, when Master Preston plucked off his Hat, to Doctor Davenant the Colledge Master, he gained a Chamber or Study for one of his Pupils'. 'He was the greatest Pupil-monger in England in mans memory', Fuller declared, 'having sixteen Fellow-Commoners (most heirs to fair estates) admitted in one year in Queens-Colledge, and provided convenient accommodations for them'.[26] The boom in student numbers prompted the college to raise over £800 for a new building.[27]

It would be convenient to report that Goodwin was one of Preston's many pupils. There is, however, no evidence of this, and the College Bursar's Book for around 1614 lists 'Goodwin' under William Cox, who had studied at Queens' since 1601 and been made a fellow in 1610.[28] It may be that Preston's preference

---

20 Twigg, *A History of Queens' College*, 445, 450.
21 For further information on Davenant and his Mastership see W. G. Searle, *The History of Queens' College, Part ii: 1560–1662* (Cambridge, 1871), 405–44.
22 *Treatise of Justification*, ii. 99.
23 P. Collinson, 'Puritan Emmanuel', in S. Bendall, C. Brooke, and P. Collinson, eds, *A History of Emmanuel College, Cambridge* (Woodbridge, 1999), 220.
24 T. Ball, *The Life of the Renowned Doctor Preston, writ by his Pupil, Master Thomas Ball*, ed. E. W. Harcourt (London, 1885), 16–18.
25 Ball, *Life of the Renowned Doctor Preston*, 36–39, 71.
26 Fuller, *Worthies of England*, ii. 291.
27 Twigg, *A History of Queens' College*, 132.
28 CUL Queens' College Bursar's Books, book 24 (c. 1614), n.f. On Cox, see *Alumni Cantabrigienses*, i. 409.

for 'heirs to fair estates' worked against someone like Goodwin. But it is more likely that Goodwin's father and patron deliberately chose Cox as his tutor.[29] Since Cox was not (as far as we know) a member of the 'spiritual brotherhood' of godly divines, this may indicate that Goodwin's family was not particularly Puritan. Thomas Goodwin, who arrived at Cambridge at around the same time from King's Lynn, was sent not to the well-known Christ's Puritan (William Chappel), but to William Power.[30]

Although the University's statutes laid down basic guidelines for the undergraduate curriculum, most teaching took place in the colleges and individual tutors were allowed considerable scope in shaping the programme of study followed by their students. Sizars were expected to complete the bachelor of arts degree in four years, during which time their studies would cover the two parts of the medieval curriculum: the *trivium* (Latin grammar, rhetoric and logic), and the *quadrivium* (arithmetic, geometry, music and astronomy). Students were immersed in the works of classical authors, above all Aristotle. Instruction followed the time-honoured format of tutorials, lectures and disputations. Students attended academic disputations in their second year, and participated in them in their third and fourth years at the same time as studying moral, natural and metaphysical philosophy. The idea was that all students would be trained in the liberal arts and philosophy, and introduced to a unified and integrated body of knowledge, organised according to the same scholastic method.[31] The curriculum reflected the continuing vitality and dominance of scholastic Aristotelianism.[32] John Preston was an ardent admirer of Aristotle, and had been 'drawne on very farr into ye study of ye schoolmen', including Scotus, Ockham and Aquinas. When King James visited the University in March 1615, Preston delighted the canine-loving monarch by arguing that dogs could make syllogisms.[33]

However, the continuing dominance of scholastic Aristotelianism did not mean that the curriculum was stuck in the Middle Ages. The logic and rhetoric of the French Reformed intellectual Peter Ramus had been taken up with some enthusiasm in the late sixteenth century.[34] Moreover, as Mordechai Feingold has demonstrated, there was considerable interest in science and mathematics at both Oxford and Cambridge. Queens' had lecturers in geometry and arithmetic; Edward Davenant (fellow from 1615–25) was a highly regarded mathematician who corresponded with the learned Archbishop Ussher on astronomy; and John Mansell

---

29 On the relationship between father and tutor see J. Morgan, *Godly Learning: Puritan Attitudes towards Reason, Learning and Education, 1560–1640* (Cambridge, 1986), 286–92.
30 See M. Lawrence, 'Transmission and transformation: Thomas Goodwin and the Puritan project, 1600–74', unpublished Ph.D. thesis, University of Cambridge, (2002), 60–61.
31 M. Feingold, ed., *Before Newton: The Life and Times of Isaac Barrow* (Cambridge, 1990), 6–8; Twigg, *A History of Queens' College*, 98.
32 See W. T. Costello, *The Scholastic Curriculum at Early Seventeenth-Century Cambridge* (Cambridge, MA, 1958).
33 Ball, *Life of the Renowned Doctor Preston*, 9–10, 13, 18–27.
34 See M. H. Curtis, *Oxford and Cambridge in Transition, 1558–1642* (Oxford, 1959), 118–19, 252–56; D. McKim, *Ramism in William Perkins' Theology* (New York, 1987).

(Davenant's successor as President) had defended Copernicanism in his MA exercises in 1601.[35] The resurgence of neo-scholasticism in the late sixteenth century had not displaced the humanist elements in the curriculum. Cambridge students were exposed to classical texts in the original languages, and learned to read Greek as well as Latin.[36] With the impact of the new Renaissance learning, rhetoric tended to replace logic as the principal theme of undergraduate studies, and students were introduced to Cicero, Terence and Quintilian.[37] As James McConica has emphasised with reference to Oxford, 'a cosmopolitan Protestant and humanist culture' was arrayed around the still largely Aristotelian curriculum.[38]

A typical day for a Cambridge undergraduate commenced with morning chapel at 5a.m., followed by a simple breakfast of bread and beer at 5.30 or 6a.m. Thereafter, lectures and study filled the hours before lunch at 11a.m., which was followed by an hour or so of recreation. From 1pm, the student would engage in two or three hours of personal study (or attend public disputations in the schools), followed by free time. The evening meal usually began at 5p.m. or 6p.m., and was followed by another period of free time. Finally, at around 7–8p.m., the tutor would gather his students for an hour of discussion and evening prayer.[39] The fact that a student's day began with chapel and ended with group prayer should not be overlooked. Tutors were spiritual mentors as well as academic teachers, and since the university produced the Church of England's clergy, the focus on spiritual formation was integral to its function.[40]

For Goodwin, as for so many of his contemporaries, university prepared him for a godly ministry. He cannot have escaped the influence of John Preston. For a brief period in the 1610s, Preston's catechetical sermons turned Queens' College Chapel into one of the hottest venues in Cambridge. Local people and students from other colleges would flock to hear the celebrated preacher, so that 'the fellows, for the crowd & multitude, could not get through & come to chapple to their places'. Critics sniffed about the influx from outside and the unprecedented crowding. They suggested that 'it was not safe for any man to be thus adored & doted on, unless they had a minde to cry up Puritanisme, wch would in a short tyme pull them downe'. Eventually, an order was issued restricting admission to members of Queens'.[41] Preston then started preaching on Sunday afternoons at St Botolph's church, where he 'occasioned such a throng & crowd as was incredible'.[42] Equally popular was Richard Sibbes, whose Sunday afternoon lectures at Holy Trinity Church were so popular that a new gallery had to be added in 1616 to

---

35 M. Feingold, *The Mathematicians' Apprenticeship: Science, Universities and Society in England, 1560–1640* (Cambridge, 1984), 35, 39, 60, 80, 102, 184–85.
36 See M. Todd, *Christian Humanism and the Puritan Social Order* (Cambridge, 1987), ch. 3.
37 V. Morgan and C. Brooke, *A History of the University of Cambridge* (Cambridge, 2004), 512–13.
38 J. McConica, 'Humanism and Aristotle in Tudor Oxford', *English Historical Review*, 94 (1979), 291–317 (316).
39 See Morison, *The Founding of Harvard College*, 63–64.
40 See Morgan and Brooke, *A History of the University of Cambridge*, 326.
41 Ball, *Life of the Renowned Doctor Preston*, 40–42.
42 Ball, *Life of the Renowned Doctor Preston*, 43–48.

accommodate the crowds. It was the preaching of Sibbes that had transformed the ministry of John Cotton, who in turn impacted Preston, and it is no surprise that Sibbes and Preston became close associates.[43]

Besides listening to famous preachers, Goodwin could also draw on the support of other godly students. Thomas Cawton's biography gives us a glimpse of this subculture. Cawton, we are told, 'kept no company with bad company'. Instead, when any youths from Norfolk or elsewhere arrived at the University who had been 'well educated under godly Parents, or a godly ministry', Cawton would arrange to meet them, introduce them to 'the society of some pious Schollars', and take them to hear lectures by Preston and Sibbes. In this way, he was 'disingaging them from the company and acquaintance of vain and debauched Schollars, of which that Colledge was then full'.[44] In an effort to curb the activities of the ungodly, Preston refused to countenance stage plays in which students played female parts.[45] But the college theatre was one of the liveliest in Cambridge, and Queens' plays were performed before both James I and Charles I, though not in the college itself. Among them were 'plays attacking Puritanism and Puritan hostility towards the theatre', such as Robert Ward's *Fucus Histriomastix* of 1622/23.[46]

Cambridge University then, was not without its temptations, and students were caught in a culture war between the 'godly' and the 'debauched'. Sir Simonds D'Ewes claimed that as a student at St John's in 1618–19 he had to live like a recluse in order to avoid the dissipation: 'swearing, drinking, rioting and hatred of all piety and virtue under false and adulterate nicknames, did abound there and generally in all the University. Nay the very sin of lust began to be known and practised by very boys.'[47] Goodwin avoided scandal, but he was not averse to some light entertainment. In later years, when accused of being an avid card player, Goodwin flatly denied the charge, but added: 'In my younger days, I confess I did pass some of my precious hours in the vanity'. Yet he also insisted that he had done so 'without scandal, or any observation of excess or inordinateness in my addiction or practise that way'.[48]

Goodwin's contemporaries at Cambridge included the next generation of godly ministers.[49] At Queens' itself, he was an exact contemporary of Samuel Fairclough (BA 1615), who after taking up a lectureship at King's Lynn became rector of Kedington from 1629 until his ejection in 1662. In other colleges, there were students who would later be appointed to the Westminster Assembly, including Simeon Ashe and Anthony Tuckney (who both matriculated at Emmanuel in 1613),

---

43 M. E. Dever, *Richard Sibbes: Puritanism and Calvinism in Late Elizabethan and Early Stuart England* (Macon, GA, 2000), 38–39, 40, 52.
44 *Life and Death of ... Mr Thomas Cawton*, 9–11.
45 Ball, *Life of the Renowned Doctor Preston*, 32.
46 Twigg, *A History of Queens' College*, 106–09.
47 *The Autobiography and Correspondence of Sir Simonds D'Ewes*, ed. J. O. Halliwell, 2 vols (London, 1845), i. 141–42. See also Thomas Shephard's autobiographical reminiscences in *God's Plot: Puritan Spirituality in Thomas Shephard's Cambridge*, ed. M. McGiffert (Amherst, MA, 1993), 43.
48 *A Fresh Discovery of the High Presbyterian Spirit* (1655), 69.
49 The following information is derived from *Alumni Cantabrigienses* and the *ODNB*.

Stephen Marshall (Emmanuel, 1615), Edmund Calamy (Pembroke, 1616), John Arrowsmith (St John's, 1616), Richard Vines (Magdalene, 1619), Jeremiah Whitaker (Sidney Sussex, 1616), Herbert Palmer (St John's, 1616), John Lightfoot (Christ's, 1617), and Thomas Hill (Emmanuel, 1618). Of the five leading Westminster Independents, four matriculated at Cambridge in the 1610s: Thomas Goodwin (Christ's, 1613), Sidrach Simpson (Emmanuel, 1616), Jeremiah Burroughes (Emmanuel, 1617), and William Bridge (Emmanuel, 1619). Henry Jessey (St John's, 1618) was another future minister who was well known to Goodwin in the 1640s and 1650s, while Paul Best (Jesus, 1606, fellow of Catherine Hall, 1617) would provoke calls for persecution with his anti-Trinitarian preaching in the mid-1640s. William Fenner (Pembroke, 1612), took his BA and MA in the same year as Goodwin and was made a fellow of Pembroke in 1618. Goodwin would later promote his works of practical divinity.[50] Of the one hundred Cambridge men who migrated to Puritan New England before 1646, around half overlapped with Goodwin, and a dozen were almost exact contemporaries. They included the notorious Hugh Peter (Trinity, 1613), a close ally of Goodwin in the 1640s.[51]

We cannot be sure how many of these men Goodwin knew in Cambridge, but Francis Bremer has observed that 'examples of cross-college friendships and gatherings are abundant'. 'At Cambridge', he writes, 'clerical friendships were formed which became the basis of a congregational communion that would influence the seventeenth-century history of England and New England'.[52] In 1639, Thomas Goodwin would call John 'my ancient friend', and he appears to have known John's father.[53] Thomas grew up in King's Lynn, a few miles from Rainham and Helloughton, and the two Goodwins may have been related.

These godly networks would also have included students destined for a lay career. They included future Parliamentarian politicians like Miles Corbet (Christ's, 1612). At Queens', Goodwin was acquainted with a number of well-to-do students who were to enjoy distinguished political careers. Henry Slingsby (matriculated 1618) and Arthur Capel (1619) would side with the King in the Civil War, though both had been pupils of John Preston. Other future royalists at Queens' included Spencer Compton, second Earl of Northampton (matriculated 1614) and Sir Orlando Bridgeman (1619).[54] By contrast, other Queens' students became firm Parliamentarians in 1640s. They included William Strickland (1614), Christopher Yelverton (1619), the New Englander George Fenwick (1619), as well as Philip

---

50 See CUL Cambridge University Archives, Supplicats, where Goodwin and Fenner are to be found listed on the same page for 1619.
51 Morison, *The Founding of Harvard College*, Appendix B: 'English University Men who Emigrated to New England before 1646'.
52 Bremer, *Congregational Communion: Clerical Friendship in the Anglo-American Puritan Community, 1610–92* (Boston, 1994), 21, 17. The whole of chapter 1 ('The Cambridge Connection') provides abundant evidence of Puritan networks in the University.
53 *The Works of Thomas Goodwin*, 11 vols (Edinburgh, 1861–65), xi. 534; Jenkyn, *The Blinde Guide*, 55.
54 See articles on these figures in the *ODNB*.

Stapleton (1617), who became a prominent Presbyterian politician and military commander, before being impeached by the army in 1647.[55]

But the most important contemporary whom Goodwin got to know at Queens' was Oliver St John. A few years younger than Goodwin, St John matriculated in August 1615, and studied under the tuition of John Preston. He entered Lincoln's Inn in 1619, and was called to the bar in 1626. In the 1630s, he was to defend the Puritan minister Henry Burton, act as counsel for John Hampden and Lord Saye in the Ship Money case, and marry a cousin of Oliver Cromwell. Unsurprisingly, he became one of the leading Parliamentarian grandees in the 1640s, and a key leader of the Independent party.[56] As we shall see, Goodwin and his congregation were closely aligned with the Saye-St John faction in the mid-1640s.

During these formative years at Cambridge, then, Goodwin was being introduced to the godly networks that would play a central role in the Puritan Revolution. But Puritanism in the early Stuart period was hardly revolutionary. The Presbyterian campaign for the reform of the Church of England had been broken by Elizabeth I and Archbishop Whitgift in the 1590s, and under James I and Archbishop Bancroft (1604–10) there had been a large number of clerical suspensions for nonconformity.[57]

Faced by firm resistance to ecclesiastical reform from both monarch and archbishop, the godly concentrated their energies on inculcating Protestant theology and piety. Although they still felt uncomfortable with the half-reformed nature of the established church, they also became part of its mainstream Reformed consensus. Indeed, the leading historian of Jacobean Puritanism, Patrick Collinson, has contended that at times 'Puritanism' all but disappeared into the 'Religion of Protestants'.[58] This in itself is testimony to the strongly Reformed character of a Church whose bishops were mostly Calvinist in theology and deeply committed to preaching and Protestant evangelism.[59]

Queens' College provides an excellent example of how this Reformed consensus worked. John Preston can reasonably be described as a moderate Puritan. Early in his career at Queens', he nearly lost his place after being accused of being a 'Non-Conformist', and 'an enimy to formes of Prayer'. Although he was to achieve great eminence in the 1620s, he never occupied episcopal office. John Davenant, by contrast, is perhaps best described as a conformist Calvinist.[60] Yet the differences between the two men were slight, and they were close allies during their twelve years together at Queens'. With Davenant in charge, and Preston at his side, the

---

55 For further information about these figures see the *ODNB* and M. F. Keeler, *The Long Parliament, 1640–41: A Biographical Study of its Members* (Philadelphia, 1954).
56 *Alumni Cantabrigienses*, iv. 5; *ODNB*.
57 Compare Patrick Collinson's *The Elizabethan Puritan Movement* (Oxford, 1967) with Collinson's *The Religion of Protestants: The Church in English Society, 1559–1625* (Oxford, 1982).
58 See P. Collinson, *The Puritan Character* (Los Angeles, 1989, 59. See Collinson, *The Religion of Protestants*, ch. 2.
59 See Collinson, *The Religion of Protestants*, ch. 2.
60 See A. Milton, *Catholic and Reformed: The Roman and Protestant Churches in English Protestant Thought, 1600–1640* (Cambridge, 1995), 7–8, 26.

college flourished as a centre of Reformed Protestantism.[61]

Politically, the legacy of Goodwin's Cambridge years is less clear. Under James I, England was at peace, and there was only one parliament between 1610 and 1621, the short-lived 'Addled' Parliament of 1614. Although political life was not without its tensions, contemporaries were firmly supportive of monarchy. John Preston was to become a chaplain to Prince Charles in 1621, at a time when the godly still looked to princes for assistance. Not surprisingly, university teachers emphasised the authority of kings. Writing in 1649, Goodwin looked back on the conservative political ideas he encountered in his student days:

> Between thirty and forty years since, when I was a young student in Cambridge ... such doctrines and devises as these: ... that the interest of the people extends only to the nomination or presentation of such a person unto God, who they desire might be their king, but that the regal power, by which he is properly and formally constituted a king, is, immediately and independently in respect of any act of the people derived unto him by God – these, I say, or such like positions as these were the known preferment-divinity of the doctorate there, and as the common air, taken in and breathed out by those who lived the life of hope in the king and sought the truth in matters of religion by the light of his countenance.[62]

Yet Goodwin can hardly have failed to notice that there were alternatives to this designation theory, alternatives propounded by absolutists on the one hand and defenders of popular sovereignty on the other. Calvinist resistance theorists like Beza, Hotman, 'Junius Brutus', Buchanan and David Paraeus had argued that the power of kings (not merely their nomination) came from the people, and that inferior magistrates could raise arms against tyrants.[63] Indeed, Goodwin may have been present when the absolutist David Owen refuted Paraeus and the 'Antimonarchians' in 'a Determination in the Divinity Schooles in Cambridge' on 9 April 1619.[64]

Although we can build up a rich picture of the University at this time, we have little personal information on Goodwin himself. He received his BA in 1616,[65] after his successful participation in public disputations, and was admitted a fellow of the college in 1617, shortly after commencing three further years of study for the MA.[66] Elections to fellowships were made by majority vote among the fellows, so he must have been held in high regard by men like Davenant, Preston and Cox. Competition for fellowships was stiff, for fellows enjoyed a reasonable standard of living. In addition to a basic stipend, they received payments for lectures and

---

61 Ball, *Life of the Renowned Doctor Preston*, 36–39.
62 ὑβριστοδίκαι. *The Obstructors of Justice* (1649), 28–29.
63 See J. Sommerville, *Royalists and Patriots: Politics and Ideology in England, 1603–40* (Harlow, 1999), chs. 1–3; M. Todd, 'Anti-Calvinists and the republican threat in early Stuart Cambridge', in L. L. Knoppers, ed., *Puritanism and its Discontents* (Cranbury, NJ, 2003), 85–105.
64 Owen's speech was published in Latin as *Anti-Paraeus* (1622), and translated into English at the start of the Civil War: *Anti-Paraeus* (1642).
65 CUL Cambridge University Archives, Subscriptiones, vol. i (1613–38), 59.
66 *Alumni Cantabrigienses*, ii. 238.

college offices. Dividends from college profits could be substantial, and in 1624–25 each fellow received a dividend payment of £18 18s 6d. The fees of graduated students were also divided among the fellows, and fellows received tutorial fees. As a new Fellow, Goodwin would have been required to donate £3 6s 8d to the library, purchase a silver spoon for 13s 4d, and treat the fellowship to a feast. For many, including Goodwin, a fellowship was a first step towards a career in the church.[67]

Goodwin completed his MA degree in 1619.[68] By the early seventeenth century, the MA degree had been transformed into 'a course of independent study aimed at expanding and elaborating the foundations of knowledge previously acquired'.[69] Students engaged in public disputing and some lecturing, and graduated after successfully negotiating a series of public disputations.[70] As a fellow, Goodwin would have combined his MA studies with the tutoring of undergraduates. Tutors acted in *loco parentis*, and were responsible for managing their students' finances, advising them, educating them and providing spiritual direction.

Goodwin was already displaying an independent streak. When accused in 1654 of having been a critic of orthodoxy for the last twenty years, Goodwin replied that he had been 'a Tryar of mens Doctrines and opinions' for twice that time.[71] By this reckoning, his taste for posing awkward questions and exploring unconventional answers dated back to his days as a student in the mid-1610s. John Vicars later wrote, 'That even when [Goodwin] was a student in the University of Cambridge, his contemporaries there with him, have reported and witnessed of him, that he ever loved to maintain and defend strange opinions among them'.[72] Thomas Cawton's biographer was anxious to assure his readers that Cawton had 'sucked in none of [Goodwin's] evil Principles, which even then he endeavoured to infuse into his Pupils, though it were afterward that he discovered himself more fully in setting his Hereticall Doctrines more openly to sale'.[73]

Of course, Presbyterians may have read Goodwin's later radicalism back into his college days. But this was an exciting time to be doing advanced theological study, and Goodwin must have been caught up in the drama of the theological controversies raging in the Reformed churches. In both England and the Netherlands, the firmly 'Calvinist' theology of the Reformed churches was coming under increasing attack from 'Arminians'. As early as the 1590s, Cambridge University had been wracked by controversies over predestination. On the one side, the Puritan theologian William Perkins (whom Goodwin later called 'That great light of our Church')[74] had propounded a high Calvinist theology emphasising double predestination, limited atonement and supralapsarianism. Repelled by this

---

67 Twigg, *A History of Queens' College*, 74–79.
68 *Alumni Cantabrigienses*, ii. 238.
69 Feingold, *Before Newton*, 7–8.
70 Twigg, *A History of Queens' College*, 98.
71 *A Fresh Discovery of the High Presbyterian Spirit* (1655), 55.
72 John Vicars, *The Picture of Independency* (1645), 8.
73 *Life and Death of ... Mr Thomas Cawton*, 3.
74 *Impedit ira Animum, or Animadversions* (1641), 56.

concoction, Davenant's predecessor as Lady Margaret Professor of Divinity, Peter Baro, had explicitly repudiated not just the high Calvinism of Perkins, but also the very concept of absolute predestination. Predestination, Baro argued, was conditional. God had decreed that he would save whomsoever freely responded to his grace in repentance and faith. Baro was effectively driven out of Cambridge in 1596, and his follower William Barrett left the university in the following year. But Cambridge anti-Calvinism was not extinguished. John Overall, Regius Professor of Divinity from 1595 to 1607, denied the doctrine of the inevitable perseverance of the saints. His successor, John Richardson, appears to have held Arminian views on both perseverance and election, and resigned in 1617 as a result of increasing anti-Arminian pressure.[75]

Cambridge anti-Calvinists were still an embattled minority, and Goodwin's theological mentors were firmly supportive of unconditional predestination. However, as Jonathan Moore has shown, Davenant and Preston did soften the high Calvinism of Perkins in response to the promptings of Archbishop Ussher.[76] Ussher was concerned that the uncompromising theology of Perkins caused others to react against the Augustinianism of Calvin and the mainstream Reformed tradition. His solution has been labelled 'hypothetical universalism'. Denouncing the 'extreme absurdity' of limited atonement, he argued that Christ's death was sufficient for all and had rendered all men salvable. However, the universality of this atonement was only hypothetical, because Christ did not intend to apply this 'all-sufficient remedy' effectually to the whole world. Christ had made *atonement* for all, but had only *interceded* for the elect – he had *paid* for the whole world, but *prayed* only for the chosen. Thus Ussher was able to assert a general atonement and maintain the core Calvinist doctrine of absolute predestination.[77]

A much more radical reaction to Beza and Perkins came from the Dutch theologian, Jacob Arminius, who broke decisively with traditional Reformed thinking. He taught that predestination was conditional and based on divine foreknowledge – God had predestined those whom he foresaw would freely respond to his grace. Individuals possessed the free will to accept or reject divine grace, and believers could fall from grace. The teachings of Arminius caused a sensation at Leiden University, where he clashed with the Calvinist theologian Fransiscus Gomarus.[78] Following the death of Arminius in 1609, his followers signed a formal Remonstrance to the States of Holland, stating their theological position. The Remonstrants were attacked by Contra-Remonstrants, and the Dutch Reformed Church descended into a theological civil war. Eventually, a national synod was

---

75 See N. Tyacke, *Anti-Calvinists: The Rise of English Arminianism, c. 1590–1640* (Oxford, 1987), ch. 2, 'Cambridge University and Arminianism'.
76 J. D. Moore, '"Christ is dead for him": John Preston (1587–1628) and English Hypothetical Universalism', unpublished Ph.D. thesis, University of Cambridge (2000). The paragraphs that follow summarise Moore's meticulous exposition of the theology of Ussher, Davenant and Preston.
77 Moore, '"Christ is dead for him"', 152–59.
78 The standard work on Arminius is C. Bangs, *Arminius: A Study in the Dutch Reformation* (Nashville, 1971). On his theology, see also R. Muller, *God, Creation and Providence in the Thought of Arminius* (Grand Rapids, 1991).

called in Dordrecht in November 1618 to settle the issue once and for all.[79]

The synod was dominated by Contra-Remonstrants, but there were representatives from other European Reformed churches, including an English delegation led by John Davenant. When the young Simonds D'Ewes heard Davenant lecture in 1618, 'he most clearly confuted the blasphemies of Arminius, Bertius, and the rest of the rabble of Jesuited Anabaptists'.[80] However, at Dort, he led the English delegation in its dissent from the doctrine of limited atonement.[81] The synod stopped short of endorsing the high Calvinism of Gomarus, but condemned the views of 'Arminius and his party'. The Dutch Arminians were deprived of their livings, and formed their own Remonstrant churches.[82]

Back in Cambridge, Davenant developed his hypothetical universalism in a series of lectures probably delivered shortly after Dort,[83] and published posthumously in 1650.[84] In these lectures (which Goodwin would surely have attended), Davenant tried his very best to acknowledge Arminian concerns within a moderate Calvinist framework. He declared that 'God in sending a Redeemer' had demonstrated 'that common love of the human race, which we call philanthropy, and that special and secret love, which we call good pleasure'. Stung by the Remonstrants' 'odious imputation of illusion in the general propounding of the Evangelical Promises', he went to great lengths to emphasise the natural capacity of even the non-elect to repent and believe. He insisted that there was 'an universal capacity of salvation in all persons living in the world'. Christ had made atonement for the whole world, and in some sense it was actually applied to all men, for all experienced 'sundry initial preparations to conversion, merited by Christ', such as illumination, conviction of sin, and fear of punishment. Salvation, Davenant declared, 'neither is, nor ought to be conceived by us to be altogether impossible in any person living'. God desired the salvation of all, Christ had died for all, and some measure of saving grace was given to all though many resisted it. As Jonathan Moore notes, this was a far cry from Perkins and constituted 'a much "softer" Calvinism'. 'The whole thrust of such a system', suggests Moore, 'swings in a potentially Arminian or semi-Pelagian direction'.[85] Yet Davenant continued to insist that God had predestined particular persons to salvation not on the basis of his foreknowledge of their free response (as Arminians asserted) but simply on the basis of his own free choice. Davenant's uneasy marriage of Calvinist and Arminian motifs can also be found in the writings of John Preston. On the one hand, Preston 'stood in a most rigorous tradition of predestinarian theology, and ... his sermons

---

79 P. Benedict, *Christ's Churches Purely Reformed: A Social History of Calvinism* (New Haven, 2002), 305–10.
80 *Autobiography and Correspondence of Sir Simonds D'Ewes*, i. 120.
81 Davenant's role at Dort is illuminated in Anthony Milton, *The British Delegation and the Synod of Dort (1618–19)* (Woodbridge, 2005).
82 Benedict, *Christ's Churches Purely Reformed*, 310–13.
83 Moore, '"Christ is dead for him"', 160, notes that Anthony Milton favours a date in the early 1620s, shortly before Davenant became Bishop of Salisbury.
84 John Davenant, *Dissertationes Duae* (1650).
85 Moore, '"Christ is dead for him"', 160–78.

are replete with predestinarian language and themes'. On the other, he rejected limited atonement and softened double predestination.[86]

The moderate Calvinism of Ussher, Davenant and Preston is of vital importance for understanding Goodwin's theological development. After his conversion to Arminianism, Goodwin sometimes appears to suggest that he had been a high Calvinist, but his preaching in the 1630s and early 1640s echoes Davenant's stress on divine philanthropy and human capacity.[87] An undated letter from Goodwin to Davenant, which survives in the Bodleian Library, suggests a friendly familiarity between the student and his mentor. Written in Latin in Goodwin's elegant hand, it was followed by a long list of sentences from every book of the Greek New Testament (folios 5r–19v), an academic exercise demonstrating Goodwin's command of the classical languages. He also offered some playful spiritual reflection on mortality and immortality based around an anagram on his teacher's name: 'John Davenante/Have I not an end?/Yes sure thou ha'st, who thereon thinkest ever,/And daily di'st, that die thou maiest never./ I have not an end'.[88]

But however much Goodwin valued his teachers, Davenant and Preston had left him with an intellectual problem. To their critics (both high Calvinists and Arminians), their position appeared riddled with logical contradictions. Moderate Calvinists claimed that God desired the salvation of the whole world but had predetermined that only the elect should be saved; that Christ had made sufficient atonement for everyone, but never intended this sacrifice to be effectual for the non-elect; that men had only themselves to blame for their damnation, but that as reprobates their doom had been sealed by God's eternal decree. Goodwin lived with the tensions inherent in this position for many years, but eventually he would find them unbearable. His conversion to Arminianism in the late 1640s can be understood, at least in part, as an attempt to resolve the contradictions inherent in hypothetical universalism.

Goodwin was to remain full time at Queens' until 1625, but he was ordained on 17 December 1620 by Samuel Harsnett, the new Bishop of Norwich.[89] Ironically, in light of Goodwin's later theology, Harsnett was one of the oldest English anti-Calvinists, a man who had been reprimanded by Archbishop Whitgift as long ago as 1584 for preaching against double predestination.[90] At this stage, however, Goodwin would have disagreed profoundly with Harsnett's Arminianism, and the fact that it was combined with high church leanings made it all the more unacceptable. But his ordination by Harsnett shows that he was willing to conform, even if his attitude to episcopacy may have been less than enthusiastic. Many years later, he claimed that the most he had ever expected from 'Lord-Bishops' was

---

86 Moore, '"Christ is dead for him"', 80 and passim.
87 See chapters 2 and 3 below.
88 Bodl. MSS Rawl. G. 117, f. 4r.
89 NRO DN/VSC 2/3A, Consignation Books for the Diocese of Norwich, 1633, f. 36.
90 See Tyacke, *Anti-Calvinists*, 164–65. The sermon was finally published in 1656: *A Fourth Sermon* appended to Richard Stewart, *Three Sermons* (1656).

'the refraining of themselves from troublesome and vexatious practices against godly, innocent, and well deserving men, from countenancing vanity and profaneness'.[91]

Goodwin's ordination may have reflected a new seriousness in his spiritual life. He later recalled that he had shaken off his card-playing habit 'ten years at least' before the start of his London ministry (which began in 1633).[92] If there was a fresh intensity to his faith, it perhaps reflected the growing sense of crisis among Europe's Protestants. Goodwin was part of what Hugh Trevor-Roper called 'the generation of the 1620s, of the Protestant débâcle'.[93] In continental Europe, the Bohemian nobility had risen in revolt against the Hapsburgs and elected a Calvinist prince, Frederick of the Palatinate, as their new monarch. Their revolt inaugurated what was to become the Thirty Years War (1618–48). By accepting the throne, against the wishes of his father-in-law James I, Frederick threatened Hapsburg dominance and the delicate balance of power between Catholics and Protestants within the Holy Roman Empire. In 1620, imperial forces crushed the Bohemian revolt at the Battle of the White Mountain, and the Palatinate was sacked. For many Protestants, especially the Reformed, this catastrophe marked the final onslaught in the war between Christ and Antichrist. English Puritans, including Sir Roger Townshend, lobbied hard for military intervention on behalf of the Palatinate.[94] But James I, who saw himself as a Christian peacemaker, would not go to war.

Although the king's stance was deeply controversial among his subjects, he was strongly supported by the High Church 'Arminians', including Samuel Harsnett, Lancelot Andrewes, and William Laud. The rise of the Arminians to positions of power and influence accelerated. The godly now feared that the true Reformed faith was under attack from without and within. In central Europe, it was being dismembered by the Catholic Hapsburgs. In England, it was being subverted by crypto-Catholic Arminians. In the years to come, Laudians and Puritans would clash repeatedly, as High Church bishops insisted on clerical conformity. In 1620, John Preston himself was questioned by Andrewes, the Bishop of Ely, who had been told that Preston was 'an enimey to formes of Prayer'. Preston denied the charge, and was forced to defend set forms of prayer before a large crowd of listeners in a sermon at St Botolph's church. He retained his fellowship, but Andrewes warned the king that though Preston should not be made a martyr, he was 'very dangerous'. Although Preston was made chaplain to Prince Charles a year later, he continued to favour English military intervention abroad, and was opposed to a Catholic marriage for Charles.[95]

When Davenant was appointed Bishop of Salisbury in 1641, his successor as President was John Mansell, 'a capable college administrator' who seems to have

---

91 *Triumviri* (1658), 219.
92 *Fresh Discovery*, 69.
93 H. Trevor-Roper, *Religion, the Reformation and Social Change* (London, 1967), 293. See also 245–48.
94 HMC, 11th Report, Appendix 4: *The Manuscripts of the Marquess Townshend* (London, 1887), 20–21.
95 Ball, *Life of the Renowned Doctor Preston*, 52–68.

maintained 'the Calvinist Protestant tradition of his predecessors'.[96] Following the appointment, Goodwin joined the other fellows in signing a letter of thanks to the king for allowing a free election.[97] Preston was among the signatories, but he had lost his leading patron. According to his biographer, 'The fellows for the most parte were not his friends, envied his numbers, & great relations'. Goodwin may have been an exception to this rule, but as a junior fellow he was in no position to 'shelter' Preston as Davenant had done. In 1622, Preston was elected Master of Emmanuel. 'It was strange newes at Queens, and all ye college were much affected with it, woundering extreamely that so great a transaction should be caryed with so much secrecy'. But when Preston moved the few hundred yards across town, 'a very great company' from Queens' processed with him to Emmanuel, and enjoyed a great banquet before returning home.[98] Goodwin no doubt was among them, and we can guess that he felt saddened by Preston's departure. Whatever the nature of their relationship, Goodwin's early ministry was thoroughly Prestonian. He was a moderate Puritan in his churchmanship and a moderate Calvinist in his theology.

With Preston and Davenant gone, the college was a less dynamic and less conducive environment for the likes of Goodwin. But in the early 1620s, Queens' still had its fair share of gifted, godly students, some of whom may have been tutored by Goodwin. Peter Hobart (matriculated 1621, migrated to Magdalene 1623) was from a Puritan family in Hingham, Norfolk, and may have been another Townshend protégé; he was to serve as pastor of Hingham, Massachusetts for over forty years. Other students included the celebrated historian of the English church, Thomas Fuller (matriculated 1621, BA 1625); the future Independent divine, Sidrach Simpson (BA 1622, MA 1625); Thomas Ball, biographer of John Preston and editor of his works (BA 1622, MA 1625); and Thomas Edwards (BA 1622, MA 1625). Twenty years later, Edwards and Goodwin were to fall out in spectacular fashion. Even in the 1620s, Edwards was known for his fiery temper. As Fuller recalled, 'I knew Mr Edwards very well, my contemporary in Queens' Colledge who often was transported beyond due bounds with the keenness and eagerness of his spirit'.[99] The long acquaintance of Edwards and Goodwin added spice to their later dispute. Ann Hughes speculates that 'when Edwards complained (eight times in fifteen pages [of *Gangraena*]) of Goodwin's sneers ... he was perhaps also recalling ancient slights'. When Goodwin questioned Edwards's command of Latin, he may have been 'remembering a difficult and mediocre student from twenty years before'.[100]

Another Puritan in the college was Herbert Palmer (1601–47) who was elected to a fellowship in 1623, and was subsequently to become a prominent Westminster Divine and Master of Queens' from 1644. In the mid-1620s, Palmer was in contact with John Cotton, one of the most influential godly divines. In a letter to Palmer,

---
96 Twigg, *A History of Queens' College*, 44.
97 The letter is printed in Searle, *The History of the Queens' College*, 449–50.
98 Ball, *Life of the Renowned Doctor Preston*, 70–87, quotations at 71, 86, 87.
99 T. Fuller, *The Appeale of Injured Innocence* (1659), Part iii, 58.
100 A. Hughes, *Gangraena and the Struggle for the English Revolution* (Oxford, 2004), 24.

dated 8 November 1626, Cotton concluded, 'Com*m*ende me heartily to M^r. Goodwin, Mr. Perne, Mr. Arrowsmith'. Although this could refer to John or Thomas Goodwin,[101] there can be little doubt that John was well known to Cotton and thoroughly integrated into the spiritual brotherhood.

Queens' reflected the broad spectrum of clerical opinion within the Church of England, and alongside Puritans the college housed future Laudians like John Towers (Bishop of Peterborough, 1639), William Roberts (Bishop of Bangor, 1637), Anthony Sparrow (Master of Queens' after 1662, and Bishop of Norwich, 1676), and Edward Martin, who was a chaplain to Laud in 1627, and Master of Queens' from 1631 to 1644. Under Martin, the college would turn decisively towards Laudian Arminianism. When the Parliamentarians purged the university in the early 1640s, Queens' was practically emptied of its fellows, who almost all refused to take the Solemn League and Covenant.[102]

Goodwin and Palmer, by contrast, were active apologists for Parliament's armed resistance in 1642–43. Of course, civil war was far from anyone's mind in the 1620s, and there is no evidence of great ideological tensions at Queens'. But the Parliaments of 1621 and 1624 were the scene of heated debates over the rise of Arminianism and the Thirty Years War. The godly were already convinced that the battle with popery was reaching a crescendo. Through much of James's reign, moderate Puritans had been close to the heart of the Church of England. By the mid-1620s, however, their star was waning, and even John Preston was to fall out of favour at court. As Goodwin entered the parish ministry, the prospects for the godly were looking bleaker.

Humanism, Scholasticism and Intellectual Sources

Before examining Goodwin's early ministry in Norfolk, we should consider the legacy of his education, and the sources and methods he was to employ in his later writings. At Cambridge, he had encountered both humanism and scholasticism, and both are evident in his own works.

The *studia humanitatis* involved a five-fold syllabus, and Goodwin's writings display a fair grasp of each element: grammar or the study of the classical languages; rhetoric; classical poetry; the study of history; and the study of civil and moral philosophy.[103]

His familiarity with the classical languages is clear from many of his publications, and his humanist education gave him an eye for grammatical infelicities. Henry

---

101 *The Correspondence of John Cotton*, ed. S. Bush jr. (Chapel Hill, NC, 2001), 118. Bush argues that the Goodwin in question was John, since he (like Palmer) was a fellow of Queens'. This may well be the case, though by late 1626, Goodwin was spending most of his time in Rainham, and it is just as likely that Cotton was referring to Thomas Goodwin, who was based next door at St Catherine Hall along with Andrew Perne and John Arrowsmith.
102 Twigg, *A History of Queens' College*, 53–54, 446.
103 See Q. Skinner, 'Hobbes and the studia humanitatis', in *Visions of Politics, vol. III: Hobbes and Civil Science* (Cambridge, 2002), ch. 2.

Hammond was taken to task for 'a double grammaticall crime', and treated to a tutorial on the relationship between antecedents and relatives. Goodwin wished that Hammond had paid attention to a 'common and known Rule in the Grammar Syntaxts' nicely illustrated by a quotation from Terence.[104] Thomas Edwards was upbraided for his 'grammaticall infirmities', and sent away to read Cicero, Sir Philip Sidney and Joseph Hall.[105]

More significantly, Goodwin's major theological works show him to have been a careful exegete of biblical texts. *A Treatise of Justification* and *Redemption Redeemed* both contain reams of painstaking exegesis, and Goodwin rests his case on his close reading of Scripture, especially the Greek New Testament. Throughout his works, he interacts with the leading biblical commentators of the period, especially with those whom he calls 'our best Protestant Expositors'.[106] Again and again, Goodwin quotes sixteenth and early seventeenth-century Reformed commentators like Calvin, Peter Martyr Vermigli, Martin Bucer, David Paraeus, Wolfgang Musculus, Franciscus Junius, Rudolf Gaulter, Henry Ainsworth and Hugo Grotius. Although these commentators have been dubbed 'pre-critical', recent scholarship reminds us that they were shrewd readers of the biblical text who skilfully employed the tools of humanist exegesis.[107] Goodwin explained that he himself followed the standard exegetical procedure of these learned 'Expositors', who examine 'the scope and context' of the text, 'the different sences or significations of words', and 'the Scripture dialect and phrase', before answering objections to their reading, and demonstrating its 'harmony' with other passages of Scripture.[108] He was also well aware of humanist textual scholarship which highlighted the complex transmission history of the biblical manuscripts. More than other Puritan divines, Goodwin recognised that the received text was a product of human history as well as divine inspiration.[109]

Goodwin's command of the second element of the humanist curriculum, classical rhetoric, was widely recognised. John Owen noted Goodwin's 'prompt facility' with language, his 'great store' of words and expressions, his 'luxuriant eloquence' and 'satirical sarcasms'.[110] In his very first polemical pamphlet, a reply to George Walker, Goodwin showcased a gift for satire that would serve him well during two decades of polemical encounters. Although he began by pleading his 'ignorance in Rhetorick', he soon subjected his fellow minister to merciless ridicule

---

104 *Obstructors of Justice*, 134–36.
105 *Anapologesiastes Antapologias* (1646), sigs. C4r, Dv-D2r.
106 *Triumviri*, 'Preface to the Reader', sig. P2r.
107 See R. A. Muller and J. L. Thompson, eds, *Biblical Interpretation in the Era of the Reformation* (Grand Rapids, 1996).
108 *An Exposition of the Nineth Chapter of … Romans* (1653), sig. b2v.
109 See especially *The Divine Authority of the Scriptures Asserted* (1647), 11–16. On Protestant controversies over the textual history of the Bible see R. Muller, *Post-Reformation Reformed Dogmatics: The Rise and Development of Reformed Orthodoxy*, 4 vols (Grand Rapids, 2003), ii. ch. 6; and J. Levine, 'Matter of fact in the English Revolution', *Journal of the History of Ideas* (2003), 317–335.
110 *The Doctrine of the Saints Perseverance* (1654), in *The Works of John Owen*, ed. W. H. Goold, 24 vols (1850–53), xi. 14.

laced with classical allusions.[111] Walker was chastised for a cavalier abuse of phrases and expressions that 'would astonish William Lilie, and put Tully and Quintilian halfe besides their Rhetoricall witts'.[112] He was said to have shrouded his doctrine in 'a thick and darke cloud of words', just as Venus had hid her son Aeneas. Like 'the Tyrant Mezentius' who had tormented his victims by tying them to the carcasses of dead men, Walker had bound Goodwin to rotting heretics by 'his necromanticall bringing up the dead Corpses of Socinus and Arminius'. He had contrived 'a Gorgonean fiction' that called to mind Apuleius's *Golden Ass* and Ovid's *Metamorphoses*.[113]

As such allusions suggest, Goodwin displayed a thorough knowledge of the third aspect of humanistic studies: classical poetry. Given the probable role of Giles Fletcher in his early education, this is hardly surprising. Although there is no evidence that Goodwin continued to write classical verse after his early Latin poems, his published writings were peppered with literally hundreds of pithy quotations from the classical poets. Among those he cited were Homer, Plautus, Virgil, Horace, Ovid, Cato, and Terence. In his reply to Walker, a quotation from Ovid's *Metamorphoses* was emblazoned on the title page. The text itself was interspersed with around thirty short quotations from the poets, generally deployed to satirise his opponent.[114]

Goodwin's engagement with the study of classical history was much less extensive. Perhaps surprisingly, his political writings referred little to the ancient Greeks and Romans, though in some early sermons he did allude to ancient tyrants. His political examples were largely biblical, while his arguments were mainly derived from Scripture and natural law contract theory. In this respect, he stands in contrast with John Milton, who drew much more heavily on classical history. When supporting the commonwealth, he explicitly appealed to the example of the 'ancient Romans' who had laid aside government by kings, and he quoted long passages of historical examples from Milton and his own disciple, John Price.[115]

Goodwin's attitude towards the fifth element of humanist studies, moral and civil philosophy, was ambivalent. On the one hand, he praised pagan virtue. In sermons to his parish, he commended heathens like Socrates and Thales for their 'decorum' and 'patience' in the midst of great afflictions. He warned his flock that 'Socrates, Plato, Fabricius, and their fellows, will be more severe Judges against Christians, then Paul, Peter, and John'.[116] *The Divine Authority of the Scriptures* (1647) contained a number of references to the 'Heathen Philosophers', including Pythagoras, Plato, Aristotle, Plutarch, Cicero, and Seneca.[117] But whilst Goodwin admired 'the greatest masters of morality' in the pagan world, he argued that their morality fell below the high standard set by Scripture. Plato allowed 'that unnaturall

---

111 *Impedit ira Animum, or Animadversions*, 10, 57.
112 *Animadversions*, 1, 82.
113 *Animadversions*, 6–7, 73, 103.
114 See for example, *Animadversions*, 94.
115 *Obstructors*, 78–81.
116 *The Returne of Mercies* (1641), 305–09.
117 *Divine Authority*, 68, 75, 78–80, 114, 116, 152–54, 215, 273–74, 317–18, 331, 373–74.

pollution which they call *pederastia*; Aristotle made a virtue of vices such as jesting and pride; and Seneca commended Cato's suicide. In contrast to the Scriptures, 'the Philosophers ointment, hath many dead flies in it'. Natural reason fell far short of biblical revelation. 'The tallest and best-grown men, that ever sprang from the root of Plato, Aristotle, Seneca, Plutarch, or any other of those ancient Fathers of secular learning, were but a race of dwarfes, or pygmies in reall worth', compared to 'that heroique progeny' of the Gospel.[118]

This did not stop Goodwin appealing to the classical authors in 1648–49 to justify the revolution.[119] If he made no effort to develop a fully-fledged republican theory of government, this was mainly because the job was being done already by laymen like Nedham and Milton, whose writings he commended. His own task was to respond to the counter-revolutionary arguments of other divines, whether Anglican or Presbyterian. Unlike some other regicides, he was enthusiastic about both the execution of Charles I and the destruction of dynastic monarchy, and he implied that this form of government was inherently flawed. His republican sympathies were nourished (at least in part) by ancient history and civil philosophy.[120]

His taste for humanist philosophy also extended to modern authors. Although he never mentioned Montaigne, he had read that other sceptical French humanist, Charron. In a tolerationist work of 1644, Goodwin cited the French edition of *De la Sagesse*: 'I well remember a saying in *Charron*; That every humane proposition hath equall authoritie, if reason make not the difference'.[121] He also knew the *Essays* of Francis Bacon, 'that late great Scholar and States-man', who had been a patron of his former tutor, Giles Fletcher.[122] And he was much impressed by George Hakewill's *Apologie of the Power and Providence of God in the Government of the World* (1627). Hakewill had cited recent scientific achievements to confute the notion that man's intellectual powers were in decline. As Nicholas Tyacke observes, 'his book was chiefly significant as a solvent of traditional attitudes ... For the non-specialist the book opened up the prospect of new mental worlds to conquer'.[123] Goodwin appealed to Hakewill for precisely this reason – to prove that traditional opinions could be rejected if they were found wanting 'upon due examination'.[124] Humanist scholarship gave him the confidence to challenge conventional wisdom.

The humanist strain in Goodwin should not lead us to overlook his scholasticism. It is true that on occasion, Goodwin mocked his conservative Presbyterian adversaries for multiplying meaningless scholastic distinctions, and meddling with 'subtilties, niceties, or curiosities'.[125] But at Cambridge, he had been drilled in the art of scholastic disputation, and in his writings he would

---

118 *Divine Authority*, 78–79, 331.
119 See *Right and Might Well Met* (1649), title page, 34–35, 43; *Obstructors*, title page, 31–32, 38, 123, 144.
120 On Goodwin's 'republicanism', see chapter 6.
121 *M.S. to A.S.* (1644), 81.
122 *Right and Might Well Met*, 19.
123 Tyacke, *Aspects of English Protestantism* (Manchester, 2001), 248–49.
124 *Treatise of Justification*, sigs. cr–cv.
125 *M.S. to A.S.*, 70.

periodically refer to 'the old axiome in Metaphysiques', or the 'rule of the Schoolmen', or 'a rule in Aristotle'.[126] He rebuked one critic for 'that poore trick in *Logick*, which they call *Petitio principii*, or begging the Question'.[127] While he declared that 'I pretend to no great knowledge in any other Science, but to that which is the glory of all the rest (Divinity, I mean)', he went on to explain that he could 'understand many Principles and Maximes of reason, besides those which I have learned from the Scriptures; As that every whole is more than any part of it; That no effect can possibly exceed the virtue or efficacy of the totall cause thereof; That one part of any contradiction is verifiable of every thing ... with many others of affinity with these'.[128] His scholastic method is apparent in all his major works, not least in *A Treatise of Justification* (1642). Here Goodwin constructed numerous syllogistic arguments against the notion that Christ's righteousness is imputed to the believer. He also devoted sixty pages to expounding the doctrine of justification in terms of the Aristotelian theory of causality.[129]

Goodwin's employment of scholastic logic was thoroughly conventional, and he never displayed any awareness or interest in the 'new philosophy' associated with Descartes. As he explained in 1651, 'My whole Estate in Philosophy is not (I confess) very great. That modicum which I have, is generally of the ordinary and best-known stamp'.[130] Recent scholarship has emphasised that scholastic modes of reasoning were employed by all kinds of theologians in early modern Europe: Dominican, Jesuit, Jansenist, Lutheran, Calvinist, Arminian and Socinian. Scholastic method did not in and of itself predispose someone to a particular theology. Whereas some older scholarship contrasted the 'humanist' Calvin to the 'scholastic' later Calvinists, the work of Richard Muller and others has effectively demolished this false dichotomy.[131] Although Calvin was a humanist scholar, he also made extensive use of scholastic concepts and categories.[132] The same can be said of Arminius.[133] Scholasticism provided intellectual tools that were used by radically different theologians. Although scholasticism would soon be eclipsed by new styles of academic writing, Goodwin belonged firmly to the scholastic era.

Goodwin's grasp of humanist studies and scholastic logic reflect his wide reading. The authors quoted on the title pages of his various works give a fair idea of his range (and of the names that impressed contemporary readers). There were references from classical sources (half a dozen quotations from Seneca, three from Ovid, two each from Juvenal and Homer, and others from Virgil, Thucydides and Euripides); the Fathers (ten quotations from Augustine, three each from Ambrose

---

126 *Treatise of Justification*, i.141; *Divine Authority*, 209, 318.
127 *Animadversions*, 81.
128 *Calumny Arraigned or Cast* (1645), 29–30.
129 *Treatise of Justification*, ii. ch. iv, 61–121.
130 *Confidence Dismounted* (1651), 16.
131 See especially his *magnum opus*, *Post-Reformation Reformed Dogmatics*.
132 See R. Muller, *The Unaccomodated Calvin* (Oxford, 2000); C. Trueman and R. S. Clark, eds., *Protestant Scholasticism: Essays in Reassessment* (Carlisle, 1999).
133 See R. Muller, *God, Creation and Providence in the Thought of Jacob Arminius: Sources and Directions of Scholastic Protestantism in the Era of Early Orthodoxy* (Grand Rapids, 1991).

and Chrysostom, two from Tertullian and Cyprian, and others from Ignatius, Origen, Lactantius, Jerome, Hilary and Basil); medieval theologians (three from Bernard, another from Brawardine); one post-Reformation Roman Catholic (the commentator Cornelius à Lapide); and Protestant theologians (four from Calvin, three from Luther and Musculus, and others from Zwingli, Paraeus, Chamier, Oecolampadius, and Grotius).

Goodwin's own book collection was not particularly large, for in 1641 he explained that the testimonies he could assemble were limited because of 'my short Librarie', 'my poore Library'.[134] Nevertheless, the plentiful citations in his works suggest that his personal library must have contained a substantial number of biblical commentaries and theological works. Moreover, in Cambridge, Rainham and London, Goodwin would have had access to other collections. At Rainham, for example, he could take advantage of Sir Roger Townshend's impressive library, which we shall consider below. In London, he would have enjoyed access to the library of Sion College, a kind of member's club for the London clergy. Although this was surely closed to him after his ejection in 1645, his own parishioner Dr Nathan Paget was assembling a remarkable book collection, which would eventually include around six hundred Latin theological and philological works, and an even larger number of English books.[135] Paget and other private collectors known to Goodwin may have enabled him to check references and explore new works. For most of his writing, however, Goodwin's own 'poore Library' was probably sufficient.

Since Goodwin was first and foremost a theologian, the sources cited in his works are overwhelmingly religious. Yet, characteristically, he justified his concentration on 'the Science of Divinity' with a quotation from a classical source: 'when the streame of endevours is divided, the waters of knowledge run but shallow in a plurality of channels'.[136] His primary source, of course, was the Bible. He normally referred to the Authorised Version, but constantly checked it against the Hebrew and Greek original. When he became Arminian, he complained of the Calvinist bias of the AV translators.[137] He occasionally quoted from the Geneva Bible, or cited marginal notes from 'the larger Bible of the last Translation'.[138] In one sermon, he corrected an error in the marginal note 'of some of your larger Bibles of the former Translation', which suggests that his hearers still consulted their Geneva Bibles and possibly even brought them to church.[139]

Although all of his own works were in English, Goodwin was familiar with a wide range of theological writing in Latin and Greek. Besides the Scriptures, he referred frequently to the early Church Fathers. Predictably, Augustine was quoted far more than any other patristic authority, and Goodwin called him 'that Star of

---

134 *Animadversions*, 43, 92.
135 *Bibliotheca Medica viri clarissimi Nathanis Paget* (1681), 20–52. Paget's intellectual and religious tastes were arguably more eclectic and heterodox than Goodwin's. See C. Hill, 'Nathan Paget and his library', in *Milton and the English Revolution* (London, 1977), Appendix iii.
136 *Calumny Arraigned*, 30.
137 See Απολvιρωσις Απολvιρωσεως, *Redemption Redeemed* (1651), 283; *Exposition*, 260.
138 See A *Door Opening unto the Christian Religion (1662)*, 397.
139 Πληρωμα ιο πνευματικον. Or *A Being Filled with the Spirit* (1670), 136–37.

the first magnitude in the Christian Firmament', and 'the first born amongst the Fathers, though not in time, yet in worth, and Name'.[140] He had obviously read a wide variety of Augustine's works including the *Confessiones, Soliloquia, De Fide et Symbolo, De Civitate Dei, Retractationes, De Correptione et Gratia,* and *De Dono Perseverantiae.* Although Goodwin's eventual rejection of absolute predestination placed him at odds with the later Augustine, it was easy to find quotations within the Father's vast canon to support Arminian views of free will, universal atonement, the defectibility of the saints, and prevenient (rather than irresistible) grace. No other Father ranked with Augustine in importance for Goodwin, but in *Redemption Redeemed* he cited a host of Latin and Greek Fathers. Goodwin provided his own translations of the sources, and reproduced the original Greek and Latin in the margin.[141]

Goodwin referred much less to medieval theologians or to post-Reformation Roman Catholics. However, he had no principled objection to citing Catholics. When John Geree chided him for quoting Thomas Aquinas, Goodwin responded contemptuously:

> it is very well known, that many Popish writers, in such points, which are eccentricall to the Controversies on foot between them and the Protestants, and where they have their judgements at liberty, are as acute, solid, and sound, as Protestant writers themselves.[142]

On another occasion, in a dispute with Samuel Chidley, Goodwin 'began to commend what he had read of the Papists works, concerning the Nature and Essence of God'.[143] This was anathema to the separatist Chidley, but it is a reminder that mainstream Reformed anti-popery did not rule out the appreciative reading of Roman Catholic theologians.[144] Thus on occasion one finds Goodwin quoting Leo the Great, Gregory the Great, the Venerable Bede, Haymo the Franciscan, Anselm of Canterbury, Bernard of Clairvaux, Thomas Aquinas and Duns Scotus.[145] In his *Exposition of Romans 9*, he referred on a number of occasions to the commentaries on Paul's epistles by the Douai theologian, Estius.[146] But significantly, his knowledge of the Jesuit theologians Molina, Fonseca and Lessius seems to have been secondhand, mediated by the English Protestant, Dr Prideaux.[147] The relative paucity of references to Roman Catholic sources reflected the low opinion in which Goodwin and his readers held post-Reformation Catholicism.

Unsurprisingly, the great bulk of Goodwin's quotations came from Protestant divines. He quoted Luther and his lieutenant Melancthon quite often, and pointed

140 *Redemption Redeemed*, 378, 524.
141 *Redemption Redeemed*, chs. 15 (the issue of perseverance) and 19 (the extent of redemption).
142 'A Reply to Mr Geree's Might Overcoming Right' in *Obstructors of Justice*, 109–10.
143 David Brown, *Two Conferences between some of those that are called Separatists and Independents* (1650), 15.
144 See A. Milton, 'A qualified intolerance: the limits and ambiguities of Early Stuart anti-Catholicism', in A. F. Marotti, ed., *Catholicism and Anti-Catholicism in Early Modern English Texts* (London, 1999), 85–115.
145 See *Treatise of Justification*, i. 47–48, 105, 193, 212; *Redemption Redeemed*, 541–45.
146 *Exposition*, 82, 114, 328, 343, 387.
147 *Innocency and Truth Triumphing Together* (1645), 45.

out Melancthon's leanings towards freewill theology.[148] Goodwin also cited the leading exponent of Lutheran orthodoxy, Chemnitius, but in general he displayed little familiarity with later Lutheran writers.[149] He always regarded himself as a Reformed divine. The index to his *Exposition* of Romans 9 gives a good idea of how often he resorted to particular authorities: Calvin (13 citations); Grotius (7); Bucer (6); Paraeus (5); Musculus (4); Peter Martyr (3); Beza, Chamier (2); Ainsworth, Mede, Mollerus, Oecolampadius, Piscator, Ursinus (1).[150] The picture is confirmed by Goodwin's anti-Baptist treatise, *Catabaptism* (1655): Calvin (13 citations); Musculus (6); Bullinger (5); Ursinus (2); Beza, Gualter, Martyr, Zwingli (1).[151] Calvin was first among equals, and Goodwin observed that other Reformed theologians were 'generally looked upon as Followers of His Doctrine'.[152] Goodwin quoted Calvin more than any other Reformed theologian, and thought more highly of him than of Beza.[153] He cited a wide variety of Calvin's writings, but drew most deeply on the *Institutes* and the biblical commentaries. Goodwin never ceased to regard Calvin as a great theologian, but he became convinced that the Reformed should move beyond the French Reformer on such matters as predestination, church government, and toleration. After describing Calvin as 'a great Presbyterian', he added that he preferred 'one greater then Calvin (I mean the Apostle Paul)'.[154]

While the names of Calvin and other continental Reformed divines carried much weight, the Elizabethan and early Stuart periods had also seen a flowering of theological writing by English Reformed divines. Recent scholarship has emphasised that before the rise of the Laudians there was a Reformed consensus among English divines.[155] Calvinist theology was not the exclusive preserve of Puritans, but was defended at the highest levels of the English Church by Archbishops Whitgift and Abbot. Thus it is no surprise to find Goodwin drawing on the theological writings of conformist episcopal divines like Bishop Davenant, Bishop Downham, and Bishop Prideaux ('a great light of the *Church*, yet living and shining').[156] Alongside these men, and usually undifferentiated from them, Goodwin cited the works of Puritan systematic theologians like Perkins, Ames, Wotton, Baxter and Gataker.

Of course, Goodwin's familiarity with mainstream Reformed theology is not what made him distinctive. His intellectual radicalism stemmed (at least in part) from his reading of radical Protestant sources. Thomas Edwards tried to link Goodwin with sixteenth-century spiritualists like David George and Sebastian Franck,[157] but Goodwin showed little or no interest in Anabaptist thought or in

---

148 *Hagiomastix*, 68–69.
149 *Redemption Redeemed*, 384–87; 549–52.
150 *Exposition*, 'A Table of some particular Heads'.
151 *Cata-Baptism* (1655), 'A Table of the particulars contained in the preceding Discourse'.
152 *Redemption Redeemed*, 552.
153 *Redemption Redeemed*, 525.
154 *Innocency and Truth*, 39.
155 See especially Tyacke, *Anti-Calvinists*; Tyacke, *Aspects of English Protestantism*; Milton, *Catholic and Reformed*; Lake, 'Calvinism and the English Church, c.1570-c.1635', *Past and Present*, 114 (1987).
156 *Animadversions*, 15.
157 Thomas Edwards, *Gangraena* (1646), ii. 44, iii. 116.

perfectionist mysticism. He was dismissive of 'Enthusiasme' and 'revelations eccentrick to the Scriptures',[158] and disparaged 'that fanatique Spirit of Suencfeldius',[159] and 'that famous Mountebank Paracelsus'.[160] But he was fascinated by the more academic writings of sixteenth-century Italian humanist reformers and seventeenth-century Dutch Arminians. William Haller and Ellen More suggested that two key influences on Goodwin's intellectual development were Sebastian Castellio and Jacobus Acontius, who had both written against theological dogmatism and heresy persecutions.[161] Goodwin never mentioned Castellio or cited his *De Haereticis* (Basle, 1554), but his parishioner Nathan Paget did own copies of Castellio's tolerationist works,[162] and his friend Samuel Hartlib was an admirer of both Castellio and Acontius.[163] Moreover, Goodwin did refer to Beza's *De Haereticis* (Geneva, 1554), a direct reply to Castellio, and he was certainly familiar with *Strategematum Satanae* (1565), the classic tolerationist work by another Italian Reformed humanist and critic of religious persecution, Jacobus Acontius. In 1644, he cited the 1631 Latin edition published at Oxford, and praised the author as 'a man of much piety and worth, who fled for his conscience, took sanctuary at this Kingdome'.[164] In 1648, Goodwin wrote the preface to an English translation of Acontius. Another likely source was *In Haereticis coercendis quatenus progredi liceat* (Basle, 1577), compiled by yet another Italian Reformed humanist, Mino Celsi. This work was packed with citations from Castellio and Acontius, and Thomas Edwards was convinced that Goodwin's arguments for toleration had been 'stollen out of Minus Celsus Senensis'.[165]

As well as being fiercely critical of the execution of Servetus, Castellio was also hostile to the Calvinist doctrine of absolute predestination. Thus it comes as no surprise that the Dutch Arminians republished his complete works in 1611–12, and that some Calvinists in the Netherlands even denounced Castellio as the real founder of Arminianism.[166] Although Goodwin rarely quoted Arminian works, he was clearly very familiar with the Dutch Arminian controversy, and confessed to reading Arminius and his followers.[167] He was particularly fond of Hugo Grotius, the Dutch legal theorist, Arminian theologian and Christian apologist. Goodwin often cited the Dutchman's great works: his *De Veritate Religionis Christianae* (1622), *De Jure Belli ac Pacis* (1625), and *Annotationes in Vetus et Novum Testamentum* (1642). Moreover, as we shall see, he endorsed the controversial governmental

---

158 *Innocency and Truth*, 80.
159 *Treatise of Justification*, ii.175.
160 *Anapologesiastes*, 11.
161 W. Haller, *The Rise of Puritanism* (New York, 1938), 194–96; E. More, 'John Goodwin and the New Arminians', *Journal of British Studies*, 22 (1982), 50–70.
162 *Bibliotheca Medica viri clarissimi Nathanis Paget*, 28, 31.
163 See for example, HP 30/4/82A: 'Castalio is an author full of excellent notions and likest to Acontius of any. But because hee is branded by Calvin as an heretike therefore hee is so little regarded'.
164 *Innocencies Triumph* (1644), 12.
165 Thomas Edwards, *The Casting Down of the Last and Strongest Hold of Satan* (1647), 197.
166 H. Guggisberg, *Sebastian Castellio, 1515–1563: Humanist and Defender of Religious Toleration in a Confessional Age* (Aldershot, 2003), 242–44.
167 *Hagiomastix* (1647), 104.

theory of the atonement developed by Grotius in his *Defensio fidei Catholicae de satisfactione Christi adversus Faustum Socinum* (1617). In his tolerationist and Arminian writings, Goodwin played a major role in transmitting 'libertine' Reformed ideas to seventeenth-century England. J. W. Allen once suggested that 'The straight line from Castellion through Acontius to Coornhert, Arminius and Simon Episcopius, may be said to end in England'.[168] If so, Goodwin was one of the key intellectuals at the end of the line.

Goodwin's curiosity about radical Protestantism is confirmed by his admission (in 1647) that ever since his arrival in London he had searched for Socinian books, but with little success.[169] Yet while Goodwin defended Socinians against persecution, and even implied at times that they were among the 'saints', he resisted the lure of anti-Trinitarianism. He had embraced the tolerationism of Castellio, Acontius and Celsi, and the freewill theology of the Dutch Arminians, but he drew the line at Socinianism.

Early Ministry (East Anglia, 1625–33)

Although Goodwin had been ordained in 1620, he remained a fellow of Queens'. Meanwhile, his friend Roger Townshend was emerging as a significant figure in county politics. He had been made a baronet in 1617, and had come into a substantial inheritance on the death of Sir Nathaniel Bacon in 1622. Townshend had recently appointed the newly ordained Emmanuel Puritan, Samuel Whiting, as his chaplain,[170] but he also wished to have his boyhood companion by his side at Rainham. In 1623, he invited Goodwin to return to East Rainham as parish minister. Initially, Goodwin seems to have accepted the invitation, and then changed his mind. In a letter to Townshend written on 7 October 1623, posted from South Creake (near Rainham) to Stiffkey (the Bacon family home), he referred cryptically to an accident involving 'ye losse of my horse' which had forced him to reconsider his plans. He had resolved to rest content with his college fellowship, rather than attempt to better it.[171]

Goodwin's renewed commitment to Queens' did not last long, and the prospect of being close to his extended family must have been appealing. His younger brother William had already started a family in Helloughton. By April 1624, we find Goodwin acting in the capacity of curate at St Mary's, East Rainham, as he returns a transcript of the parish register to the Archdeacon.[172] He was finally instituted as rector on 31 August 1625, with Roger Townshend cited as his patron. It was also noted that he was replacing William Armstead who had resigned.[173]

---

168 J. W. Allen, *A History of Political Thought in the Sixteenth Century* (London, 1964), 102.
169 *Hagiomastix*, 110–11.
170 Morison, *The Founding of Harvard College*, 406–07.
171 NRO MF/RO 27/3, Papers sent to Members of the Bacon and Townshend Families at Stiffkey, ff. 425–27.
172 NRO ANW 13 Archdeacons' Parish Register Transcripts, East Rainham, 1624.
173 NRO DN/REG 16, Institution book 22, f. 10v.

Armstead (or Armitsted) was a graduate of Christ's College, who had been rector of Rainham since 1622, and it is not clear whether he had found another living or was forced out.[174] In his 1623 letter, Goodwin hoped that Townshend had 'dispatched wth Mr Armstead for me (notwithstanding my absence) or else that you may yet doe it'.[175] Whether he was lobbying for Armstead's removal, or simply asking for him to be dispatched on business is unclear.

In the end, it took more than Townshend to dislodge Goodwin from Queens' – his farewell to academia was necessitated by his marriage sometime in the mid-1620s.[176] Since fellows were supposed to be single, Goodwin's days as a don were coming to an end. He did not vote in the hotly contested election of the new chancellor in 1626, an election that resulted in victory for the royal favourite, the Duke of Buckingham.[177] However, he hung on to his fellowship at Queens' until 1627. The college 'Journale' records that in 1626 he paid just £2 18s 10d rather than the usual £9 for an entire year's residence, suggesting that he was still in residence for part of the year. In 1627 he was recorded as paying nothing, and in 1628 he was no longer listed among the fellows.[178] Thomas Edwards, who was a fellow of Queens' at the time, later attacked his former colleague for 'his juglings and indirect walkings between his Fellowship in the Colledge and a wife (both against the Statutes, and I think against his oath)'.[179] Edwards was hardly an unbiased witness, but the college records speak for themselves: despite his marriage and his appointment as curate and then rector at East Rainham, Goodwin was reluctant to sever his ties with Queens'. Although he was to be a pastor for the rest of his life, he also yearned to be a scholar and a theologian. Finally, however, on 31 August 1625, he was instituted as rector of St Mary's, Rainham, following the resignation of William Armstead.[180]

Goodwin had returned to his home turf, and he had a sympathetic and increasingly influential patron. Throughout the 1620s, Townshend was constructing the splendid Rainham Hall under the direction of Inigo Jones, a project that was structurally completed by 1632. Sir Roger became a JP in 1625, a knight of the shire in 1627, a deputy lieutenant, and then sheriff in 1629–30. Through him, Goodwin probably got to know figures like William Hevingham, who served as a deputy-lieutenant and a sheriff in Norfolk in the 1630s and was to become a militant Parliamentarian MP in the 1640s.[181] Townshend had also married Mary

---

174 *Alumni Cantabrigienses*, i. 40 does not record what Armitsted did between leaving Rainham in 1625 and his death in 1638–39.
175 NRO MF/RO 27/3, ff. 425–27.
176 I have been unable to discover the date of Goodwin's marriage, but the East Rainham parish records show that his son, also John Goodwin, was born in October 1627.
177 The voting figures can be found in J. B. Mullinger, *The University of Cambridge*, 3 vols (Cambridge, 1873–1991), vol. iii, appendix A.
178 CUL Queens' College, 'Journale', Bk vi (1622–91), ff. 16, 20, 24, 28.
179 Edwards, *Gangraena*, ii. 84.
180 NRO DN/REG 16, vol. 22, f. 10v; NRO DN/VSC 2/3A, Visitation Consignation Books for the Diocese of Norwich, 1633, f. 36.
181 See *ODNB*; R. W. Ketton-Cramer, *Norfolk in the Civil War* (1970).

Vere, daughter and coheiress of Lord Horace Vere and Lady Mary Vere. Horace Vere was one of the leading advocates of English intervention in the Thirty Years War, and his wife was a patroness of godly clergy, including John Preston, James Ussher, William Ames, John Dod and John Davenport (the current vicar of St Stephen's Coleman Street in London).[182] According to Davenport, Townshend was a man of 'strong compliance with the best affected patriots' in the parliaments of the 1620s.[183]

Because it was only a small parish, the duties at East Rainham were not particularly onerous. The parish register records just a handful of baptisms, marriages and burials each year. Goodwin baptised his eldest son John on 4 October 1627, but he buried his daughter Anne on 7 May 1628. Another son, Edward, was baptised on 13 November 1629, but Samuel (baptised in October 1631) was buried in January 1632. Finally, another daughter, Mary, was baptised in February 1633, shortly before the family moved to London.[184]

Goodwin probably acted as an unofficial chaplain to the Townshends, and he may have used Sir Roger's impressive library, acquired in part from Nathaniel Bacon in 1622. The library contained a wide range of books in English, Latin, French, Greek, Italian and Spanish, covering law, theology, science, philosophy, belles-lettres, history, travel, medicine and the classics. As one would expect, it included a substantial number of works by British Reformed divines like Knox, Hall, Dent, Bayly, Dering, Perkins, Baynes, Gataker, Travers, Dod, Whately and Denison, as well as continental Calvinists such as Philippe du Plessis Mornay, whose defence of Christianity had been translated by Philip Sidney. It also boasted classical works by Plato, Aristotle, Xenophon, Ariosto, Juvenal, Cicero, Suetonius and Tacitus, and a few books by humanist writers such as Charron and Machiavelli.[185]

Despite the distractions of library and family, Goodwin was perhaps under-employed in East Rainham, and he set his sights on making a broader impact in the county as a whole. Having a sympathetic patron clearly helped, for during his eight years at Rainham (1625–33) Goodwin was involved in active ministry in Great Yarmouth, King's Lynn and Norwich. As Thomas Edwards later noted, Goodwin had oscillated 'between the two towns of Raynum and Lyn, between Raynum and Yarmouth, Raynum and Norwich, between Raynum and London, between his two Churches and Livings'.[186]

The corporation of Great Yarmouth was in the early stages of a heated battle with the dean and chapter of Norwich over which of them possessed the right of

---

182 See *ODNB* articles on Horace and Mary Vere.
183 *Letters of John Davenport, Puritan Divine*, ed. I. M. Calder (New Haven, 1937), 64. On the patronage of Townshend and Lady Mary Vere see also K. Shipps, 'Lay patronage of East Anglian Puritan Clerics in Pre-Revolutionary England', Ph.D. thesis, Yale University (1971), 147–49.
184 NRO PD 369/1 Parish Records for East Rainham, 1627–33. See also NRO ANW 13, Archdeacons' Parish Register Transcripts, East Rainham, 1624–31.
185 'An Inventory of Books in the Possession of Sir Roger Townshend, ca. 1625', in R. J. Fehrenbach and E. S. Leedham-Green, eds, *Private Libraries in Renaissance England* (Binghamton, NY, 1992), i. 79–135.
186 Edwards, *Gangraena*, ii. 84.

ecclesiastical patronage in the town.[187] At least some of the corporation had strong Puritan sympathies, and the town's MP in 1628 was to be Miles Corbet, a future regicide. In 1625, the Corporation had appointed as minister an Emmanuel graduate, John Brinsley, who had been Joseph Hall's assistant at the Synod of Dort. But Brinsley's appointment was being contested by the dean and chapter, and would eventually be overturned. It was in this context that the Great Yarmouth Assembly agreed in November 1626 to 'send for Mr Goodwyn to come to preache amongst us in our charge, for tryall ... for our preacher'. Two churchwardens were appointed to ride to see him.[188] Although Goodwin did go to preach at Great Yarmouth, he continued to hold on to his rectory at Rainham. This was partly to do with the pull of his family and his patron, but the continuing struggles between the Corporation of Great Yarmouth and the ecclesiastical authorities in Norwich were another deterrent. The dispute rumbled on through 1627 and 1628, until eventually in September 1629 Mr Whitfield was appointed as minister.

With Great Yarmouth embroiled in controversy, another Norfolk town soon courted Goodwin. On 31 July 1629, the Mayor, Aldermen and Common Council of King's Lynn elected 'Mr Goodwyn preacher of Gods word att Rainham to be preacher att St Nicholas Chappell'. Their first choice had been Thomas Goodwin, but he had declined the offer in order to remain in Cambridge. John was 'to have the fee of ffifty pounds anno and five pounds for a dwellinge house or a convenyent dwelling house to be provided for hym'. Goodwin was expected to preach twice every Sunday, and also on the anniversary of the King's accession, the fifth of November, and on three feast days (St John's, St Michael the Archangel's, and 'the feast daye of the Birth of our Lord God'). The reference to these feast days suggests that the town council was not a hotbed of militant Puritanism, but they were still eager to attract an outstanding godly preacher. On 10 August, Goodwin was present in person to accept the invitation to become vicar of St Nicholas, and he 'promised that within a concenyent tyme next after the approbacon of this election by the L:Bishopp of Norwich he will resigne the benefice he hath nowe and nott hereafter take an other else where, orells this election shall be void'.[189]

However, once again Goodwin could not let go of East Rainham. In April 1630, the King's Lynn Common Council agreed to write a letter to the Bishop of Norwich 'to procure his favour for the countyewance of Mr John Goodwyn Preacher of Gods Word to be lecturer here as he hath been, so as he give over his benefice wch he hath att Rainham and come to dwell here'. Whether for family reasons or because Sir Roger did not want to lose him, Goodwin was still living at Rainham and commuting to King's Lynn. Unwilling to relinquish this arrangement, he was removed from his position within a year of taking it up. In September, the

---

187 C. J. Palmer, *The Perlustration of Great Yarmouth*, 3 vols (Great Yarmouth, 1872–75), i. 36; J. Browne, *History of Congregationalism and Memorial of the Churches in Norfolk and Suffolk* (London, 1877), 129ff.
188 NRO Y/C 19/6, Great Yarmouth Assembly Book (1625–42), f. 47r.
189 KL/C 7/9, King's Lynn Hall Book (1611–37), ff. 307r-v. See also W. Richards, *The History of Lynn*, 2 vols (Lynn, 1812), ii. 992–4.

Common Council elected a successor, John Arrowsmith, who had been a fellow of Catherine Hall in Cambridge and was later to become a Westminster Divine.[190]

According to Thomas Edwards, Goodwin also preached in Norwich during his Rainham years. No records have been found that shed light on his Norwich ministry, though Thomas Edwards implies that it involved more than occasional preaching appointments; as with his engagements at Yarmouth and Lynn, Goodwin was flirting with (or being courted by) another parish while he was still rector of Rainham.[191] It has often been suggested that he was also a preacher at St Mary's in Dover at this time, though this was almost certainly another John Goodwin, a graduate of St John's College, Oxford.[192]

It would appear that our Goodwin lived almost his entire life between Norfolk, Cambridge and London, and there is no evidence that he ever travelled outside England. East Anglia was England's Puritan heartland, and it gave Goodwin the best possible preparation for an influential godly ministry. Even before he went to London, he was a well-connected man. In the 1640s, he would find himself working alongside people he knew from Cambridge or Norfolk – Independent preachers like Jeremiah Burroughs, Hugh Peter and Thomas Goodwin; and Puritan politicians like Sir Simonds D'Ewes, Oliver St John and Miles Corbet. Of course, he would also find himself at odds with old acquaintances, for men like Thomas Edwards, Thomas Hill and Anthony Tuckney were appalled at the wayward course of Goodwin's pilgrimage. Yet for all their differences, these Puritans would divert the course of English politics and religion in the 1640s, creating that remarkable upheaval that is not unjustly called the Puritan Revolution.

---

190 KL/C 7/9, ff. 319v, 329v; Richards, *History of Lynn*, ii. 994. Shipps, 'Lay patronage', 148, 309–10, suggests that the Bishop of Norwich finally suspended Goodwin from the lectureship on grounds of nonconformity, but I have been unable to substantiate this account.
191 Edwards, *Gangraena*, ii. 84.
192 See J. Foster, *Alumni Oxonienses: The Members of the University of Oxford, 1500–1714*, 4 vols (London, 1891–92), ii. 38; J. Bavington Jones, *Annals of Dover* (Dover, 1938), 206–7.

2

'GOODWIN OF COLMAN-STREET'
1633–39

In his own lifetime, John Goodwin's name would become synonymous with the London parish of St Stephen's, Coleman Street. He was vicar of the parish from 1633 to 1645, and again from 1649 to 1660, and it also became the base for his gathered church. It was here that he made his reputation as a preacher, propagandist and controversialist. Although he published nothing in the 1630s, it is during the early years of his London ministry that we can first hear his distinctive voice. He was already gaining a reputation for theological singularity, ecclesiastical nonconformity and political subversion. But at this stage, he was also set against lay preaching, sectarianism and Independency. His intellectual journey was under way, but it had a long way to run.

St Stephen's, Coleman Street

August 1633 witnessed the death of the Calvinist Archbishop of Canterbury, George Abbot, and the election of his successor, the high church Arminian, William Laud. In the very same month, the vicar of St Stephen's Coleman Street disappeared from his parish. Eluding the five pursuants sent to catch him, he escaped to the Netherlands, where he joined a growing community of exiled English Puritans. John Davenport had been appointed vicar in 1624, after giving assurances of his conformity with canons and liturgy of the Church of England. He had become a key figure in the London Puritan scene, serving as one of the Feoffees for Impropriations, and working closely with the great Puritan preacher Richard Sibbes to edit the sermons of John Preston for publication. But Davenport became increasingly disturbed by the rise of the Laudians, the dissolution of the Feoffees in February 1633, and the growing pressure for clerical conformity. After consulting with other disillusioned Puritan ministers, including Thomas Hooker and John Cotton, he decided that the compromises required of parish ministers were now intolerable.[1] As has been recently demonstrated,

---

1 Davenport's decade at St Stephen's is recorded in *Letters of John Davenport, Puritan Divine*, ed. I. M. Calder (New Haven, 1937), 13–43.

Davenport was in trouble 'for preaching against some points of Arminianisme against his Majestys Prohibicion', and especially for denying that Christians could fall from grace'.[2]

When Davenport formally resigned his charge, his parish was required to search for a new minister. St Stephen's was one of only thirteen London parishes in which the vestry had control of the advowson and could elect their own minister. The independence that came with this privilege made these parishes strategic centres of Puritanism. As Paul Seaver has noted, 'In effect these parishes provided working models of a congregationalist polity within the Established Church. They also provided a haven for some of the most famous nonconformist preachers of the day'.[3] The vestry of St Mary, Aldermanbury, a few blocks away from Coleman Street, elected a series of eminent Puritan divines as vicar (including John Stoughton and Edmund Calamy), and at St Anne, Blackfriars, the famous William Gouge had been vicar since 1608. St Stephen's was another flagship Puritan parish, and under Davenport it had given substantial support to the Feofees, the colonisation of New England, and collections for the relief of Protestants in the Palatinate. It provided more resistance to the Forced Loan of 1627 than anywhere else in the City, and was the site of protests against the Duke of Buckingham in 1628.[4]

In deciding on a new minister, the vestry were no doubt guided by the advice of leading Puritan ministers and dignitaries. Goodwin was already well known in the Puritan heartland of East Anglia and at Cambridge University, and he was well connected to networks of godly clergy. More importantly, perhaps, his patron, Sir Roger Townshend, was the son-in-law of Lady Mary Vere and Sir Horace Vere. Lady Vere took a keen interest in St Stephen's; in 1624 she had been instrumental in persuading the Bishop of London and the Archbishop of Canterbury that John Davenport was a conformable minister, worthy of becoming vicar of the parish.[5] It seems likely that Lady Vere recommended Goodwin to the leading parishioners, or at least strongly supported his candidacy.

However it came about, a meeting of the vestry on 3 December 1632 agreed that Goodwin and William Bruce should be considered as candidates for election as vicar. On the following day, a meeting of seventy-nine parishioners agreed that Goodwin 'shalbe and is ffreely elected and chosen viccar of this parish'. On 6 December, the vestry agreed the terms of his appointment. He was to be granted a basic stipend of £11 10s, plus an additional sum of £39 and the rent from a house amounting to £12 per annum. Goodwin acknowledged that the basic salary was 'his right the benefit of the viccaridge', while 'the rest of the Amyties and profits' were 'to be the bountye and love of the parishioners wch they have granted unto him for the tyme of his residency with them'.[6]

---

2 See D. Como, 'Predestination and political conflict in Laud's London', *Historical Journal*, 46 (2003), 287.
3 P. Seaver, *The Puritan Lectureships: The Politics of Religious Dissent, 1560–1662* (Stanford, CA, 1970), 138.
4 Kirby, 'Parish', 12–26; Kirby, 'Radicals', 103–07.
5 See Kirby, 'Radicals', 100; *ODNB* articles on the Veres; and *Letters of John Davenport*, 17–19.
6 GL MS4458/2, 'Vestry Minute Book of St Stephen's, Coleman Street, 1622–1726', ff. 86–87.

2 The Cittie of London, map attributed to the late sixteenth-century engraver, Augustus Ryther. This edition published by Cornelis Dankerts in 1645. Coleman Street is just north of centre, leading from Moorgate towards the heart of the City. By permission of the British Library.

Goodwin had landed in a burgeoning metropolis, one that had grown from around 200,000 people in 1600 to more than a quarter of a million by 1633. London had expanded geographically beyond the walls of the old City into new suburbs like Whitechapel and Stepney. It was now one of Europe's greatest cities, and accounted for around 7% of England's population. It dwarfed Norwich and Bristol, which with 10–20,000 inhabitants were the nation's next largest towns. The population was particularly concentrated within the walls of the City itself, which extended in an arc on the north bank of Thames, from the Tower of London in the east to the Fleet River in the west. Ninety-seven parishes and 70,000 people were jammed into this relatively small area.[7]

The parish of St Stephen's, Coleman Street covered just thirteen acres, and its main street was only two hundred and fifty yards long.[8] According to John Stow, Coleman Street was 'a faire and large street, on both sides builded with divers faire houses'.[9] It was the home of wealthy merchants and prominent citizens, and

---

7 See E. A. Wrigley, 'A simple model of London's importance in changing English Society and economy, 1650–1750', *Past and Present*, 37 (1967), 44–45; V. Harding, 'The population of London, 1550–1700', *London Journal*, 15 (1990), 111–28; and Harding, 'City, capital and metropolis: the changing shape of seventeenth-century London', in J. F. Merritt, ed., *Imagining Early Modern London* (Cambridge, 2001).

8 In what follows I am indebted to David Kirby's description of the parish: Kirby, 'Parish', ch. 1; Kirby, 'Radicals', 98–99.

9 John Stow, *The Survey of London* (1633), 293.

during the first half of the seventeenth century no fewer than eight Lord Mayors of London had homes on the street.[10] But the crowded alleys off Coleman Street (Bell Alley, Swan Alley, White's Alley, Nun's Court) contained 'small tenements, in great number'.[11] Over one hundred tenements had been erected since 1600, and these were crammed with people, especially the poor. By the late 1650s, the vestry minutes record that the parish was finding it increasingly difficult to provide for the sheer numbers of poor inhabitants. Already by the 1630s, Coleman Street was one of the most densely populated parishes in the City. By 1631, St Stephen's had 1400 communicants, and by 1642 there were estimated to be around four hundred families. It was one of only four City parishes with more than two hundred houses – 278 were listed for the 1641 poll tax.[12]

Thus if St Stephen's provided exciting new opportunities, it also involved a dramatically increased workload. The parish had approximately seventy or eighty baptisms per year, twenty-five or thirty marriages, and sixty or seventy burials.[13] Goodwin's curate, Francis Bright, would have performed some of these ceremonies,[14] but a vicar's life in this teeming urban parish was a busy one. Goodwin had the pleasure of baptising five of his own children between 1635 and 1641: Thomas (baptised on 17 December 1635), Samuel (23 March 1637), Sara (September 1639); Jonathan (9 December 1640); and Jeremy (22 October 1641). However, Sara only lived a few months, and Goodwin buried her on 27 December 1639. Jeremy survived for just a week, and was buried on 2 November 1641.[15]

The parish was governed by its general and select vestries. The general vestry met in April and December to elect parish officials and common councilmen, and was called on other occasions to discuss important parish business. Up to one hundred male householders were eligible to participate, though attendance was usually less than sixty. Effective power was held by the select vestry, which was composed of leading citizens, the churchwardens and the minister. Twenty-five to thirty were eligible to attend, but there were usually less than twenty present at meetings.[16]

Goodwin's select vestrymen in the 1630s were prosperous, influential and strongly supportive of his godly ministry.[17] Sir Thomas Wroth (1584–1672) was a prominent backer of colonisation projects in both Virginia and New England, and had been MP for Bridgewater in 1627–28. He was the brother-in-law of Sir Nathaniel Rich, the prominent Essex Puritan, and when his wife (and Rich's sister) died in 1635, Wroth published a moving encomium for her, praising her

---

10 Sir Steven Soame, Sir Henry Rowe, Sir Thomas Bennet, Sir Thomas Campbell, Sir Thomas Middleton, Sir Morris Abbot, Sir Edmund Wright, Isaac Penington.
11 Stow, *Survey*, 293.
12 See Kirby, 'Parish', 2–3; 'Radicals', 98–99.
13 This is my tally of the number of baptisms, marriages and burials in 1635. See GL, MS4449/1, St Stephen's, Coleman Street, parish register, 1558–1636.
14 Kirby, 'Parish', 48.
15 GL, MS 4449/1 and 4449/2 for births and burials before and after 1636 respectively.
16 Kirby, 'Parish', 3–4; 'Radicals', 99–100.
17 See Kirby, 'Parish', 34–39; 'Radicals', 109–111.

piety.[18] Wroth then married the sister of Sir Edward Dering, who was to become a leading sponsor of the bill for root and branch reform of the church in 1641.[19] Wroth's literary interests (as a translator of the *Aeneid*) and his godliness must have made him a congenial colleague for Goodwin.[20] Sir Morris Abbot (1565–1642) was the younger brother of George, Archbishop of Canterbury, and Robert, John Davenant's predecessor as Bishop of Salisbury. Sir Morris was one of London's grandest citizens: a past governor of the East India Company and MP for Kingston-upon-Hull in 1621 and 1624, he was knighted in 1625 and appointed Lord Mayor in 1638. Theophilus Eaton (1590–1658) was a younger man and had only been appointed to the select vestry in 1631, but he was to be the governor of the Puritan colony of New Haven in New England for almost two decades. Isaac Penington (1587–1661) had moved to the parish in 1632, and was one of its wealthiest citizens. A member of the East India and Levant Companies, he would emerge as the political leader of the City radicals in the 1640s. Owen Rowe's career (1593?–1661) was to be closely tied to that of Penington throughout the English Revolution. In the 1630s, Rowe was already a committed Puritan, and he seriously considered emigration to New England.[21]

Other leading parishioners had been actively involved in Puritan ventures. Several, including Caldwell Farrington and Samuel Aldersley had assisted the Feofees for Impropriations. Others were heavily committed to the Puritan colonisation projects of the 1620s and 1630s. Sir Richard Saltonstall and Samuel Aldersey were two of the three founders of the New England Company, and two other Adventurers in the Company, George Foxcroft and Theophilus Eaton moved to the parish in the 1630s. Foxcroft was to become a prominent member of Goodwin's gathered church. Saltonstall, Aldersey, Foxcroft and Eaton were also founders of the Massachusetts Bay Company, and Aldersey was its Treasurer. Five of the Company's original thirty-three subscribers were from the parish of St Stephens (Davenport, Saltonstall, Aldersey, Robert Crane, Edmund White). The parish curate from 1625–29, Francis Bright, was one of the first ministers to emigrate to New England, though he returned soon afterwards and was to assist Goodwin as a curate and reader until 1640. Another prominent figure, Thomas Barnardiston, was a friend of John Winthrop and an Adventurer in the Providence Island Company. Eaton and Owen Rowe had both invested in the Massachusetts Bay Company, and Daniel Taylor had relatives in Bermuda and Massachusetts.[22]

The parish was also home to Puritans involved in the book trade. The bookseller, Henry Overton, had taken up his freedom in the Stationer's Company in

---

18 *Sir Thomas Wrothe his Sad Encomion upon his Dearest Consort, Dame Margaret Wrote* (1635).
19 See N. Tyacke, *Aspects of English Protestantism* (Manchester, 2001), p. 127; *ODNB*.
20 See Sir Thomas Wroth, *The Destruction of Troy, or The Acts of Aeneas. Translated out of the Second Booke of the Aeneads of Virgill, that Peerelesse Prince of Latine Poets* (1620).
21 Rowe and the other figures listed all have entries in the *ODNB*.
22 Kirby, 'Parish', 37–43; 'Radicals', 110–111; Bremer, *Congregational Communion: Clerical Friendship in the Anglo-American Puritan Community, 1610–92* (Boston, 1994), 102; R. Brenner, *Merchants and Revolution: Commercial Change, Political Conflict, and London's Overseas Traders, 1550–1653* (Princeton, NJ, 1993) 536–37.

1629, and owned a bookshop at the entrance to Pope's Head Alley off the great thoroughfare of Lombard Street.[23] He had already been hauled before the Ecclesiastical Commission in 1630 for publishing unlicensed books, and was acting as an intermediary between the congregationalists Henry Jessey and John Winthrop in 1633. Rice Boye was part of a secret press syndicate that published works by Puritan dissidents like John Bastwick, Henry Burton and William Prynne.[24]

Some remarkable intellectuals also resided in Coleman Street. The German Reformed intellectual, Samuel Hartlib, was resident in the street in the early 1630s.[25] In his 'Ephemerides' he refers a number of times to 'Good[w]in of Colman-street', thus distinguishing him from Thomas ('Good[w]in of Cambridge'). Thomas Goodwin had been vicar of Trinity Church in Cambridge until 1634, when he resigned over his refusal to conform and moved to London. Here he was to remain until 1639, and throughout this time he was in close contact with John. A very different figure, the physician and occultist, Robert Fludd, had established a laboratory in Coleman Street, and lived there until his death in 1637.[26]

As one of London's leading preaching centres, St Stephen's also attracted hearers from outside the parish. 'Gadding' to taste the sermons of the City's star divines was a popular Sabbath pursuit. William Kiffin, a young apprentice who later became a wealthy merchant and a leading Baptist, recorded how in the early 1630s he used to tour the City 'to hear some of them they called Puritan ministers'. Among his favourite was John Goodwin.[27] Nehemiah Wallington, the London wood-turner, and Robert Woodford, the steward of Northampton, also attended Goodwin's preaching.[28] He attracted more prominent figures too, including Lady Mary Vere. According to Tom Webster, St Stephen's was perhaps her favourite London parish in the late 1630s.[29]

Goodwin's Teaching

We know less than we would like to know about Goodwin's preaching and teaching in the 1630s. We do know that he preached often. In 1645 he claimed that hundreds of his parishioners would testify 'that scarce any Minister in or about the City, or throughout the whole kingdome, have been more diligent, laborious, frequent or constant, in the work of the Ministery'. 'For severall years together', he wrote, 'I

---

23 H. R. Plomer, *A Dictionary of the Booksellers and Printers who were at work in England, Scotland and Ireland from 1641 to 1667* (London, 1907), 142. 24 Kirby, 'Parish', 49–51; 'Radicals', 113.
24 Kirby, 'Parish', 49–51; 'Radicals', 113.
25 HP 46/6/13B.
26 See *ODNB*.
27 *Remarkable Passages in the Life of William Kiffin*, ed. W. Orme (London, 1823), 3–5, 9.
28 P. Seaver, *Wallington's World: A Puritan Artisan in Seventeenth-Century London* (London, 1985), 127; J. Fielding, 'Opposition to the Personal Rule: the Diary of Robert Woodford, 1637–41', in P. Gaunt, ed., *The English Civil War* (Oxford, 2000), 114.
29 T. Webster, 'Introduction', *The Diary of Samuel Rogers, 1634–38*, ed. T. Webster and K. Shipps (Woodbridge, 2004), xlv.

preached constantly thrice, often four times; sometimes five or six times in a week unto them'.[30]

Goodwin's sermons bore all the hallmarks of the Puritan style. At Cambridge, he had been raised on the preaching of John Preston and Richard Sibbes, who were famous as 'affectionate theologians'.[31] In 1639 he wrote the introductory 'Epistle' to one of Sibbes's published commentaries, praising the author as 'so great and worthy an agent in the factorage of Heaven'.[32] In a later preface to a book of sermons by the Puritan preacher, William Fenner, he would explain that the 'two soveraign ingredients' of Gospel preaching were '*light* and *heat*, eminencie of knowledge in the things of God, together with strength and fervencie of zeale'.[33]

Although there are no surviving shorthand notes on Goodwin's sermons, he did publish four books of sermons in 1640–41, some of which date from the 1630s. These give us a clear sense of his preaching style. Goodwin followed the classic Puritan sermon structure of Doctrine, Reason and Use.[34] He began with exegesis of the text, expounding 'the coherence, sense and meaning of words' so as to bring out the doctrine. He then provided a series of reasons, proofs and grounds which substantiated the doctrine. Finally, he turned to the uses of the text, applying it to his hearers by way of instruction, encouragement, reproof and exhortation.[35] In common with other Puritan divines, Goodwin preached at length. He complained that when the preacher's hourglass ran out, some hearers began 'to sweate, and to faint, and sometimes to nestle this way, and that; as if their seats by this time were growne too hot for them'.[36]

Goodwin's preaching aimed at fostering serious godliness among the laity. His ideals for his flock are vividly portrayed in a sermon at the funeral of Mrs Abbot, who died aged just twenty-six in 1640. Abbot was the daughter of a wealthy Puritan merchant, John La Motte, and Goodwin praised her as a paragon of godliness. She had no time for 'riches of furniture', 'costly vanity of apparell' or for 'fashion' ('that great Goddesse of her sex worshipped with so much devotion'). She 'loathed and abhorred ... Those cages of uncleane birds the common Theaters or Play-houses'. By contrast, 'All her delight was in the saints on earth ... Those that could speak the language of Canaan'. Despite her affluent status, she rejoiced in the fellowship of 'the lower sort'. She was a woman of 'very tender bowels, and of overflowing compassions, to those that were in misery'. Moreover, she delighted in the Lord's Day, and in prayer, and was steeped in the Scriptures, so much so

---

30 *Innocencies Triumph* (1644), 14–15.
31 See M. Dever, *Richard Sibbes* (Macon, GA, 2000), ch. 6: 'An "Affectionate" Theologian'.
32 Richard Sibbes, *An Exposition of the Third Chapter of the Epistle of St Paul to the Philippians* (1639), sigs. A2r-A2v. Goodwin may also be responsible for the chapter divisions in Sibbes's most famous work, *The Bruised Reed*. See *The Works of Richard Sibbes*, ed. A. B. Grosart, 7 vols (1862–64), i. 34, 100.
33 William Fenner, *Practicall Divinitie* (1647), 'To the Reader', sig. A2.
34 On the structure of Puritan sermons see the classic work of P. Miller, *The New England Mind: The Seventeenth Century* (New York, 1939), ch. 12.
35 See for example *The Saints Interest in God* (1640), where the doctrine is expounded in chapters 1–2, the reasons given in chapters 3–4, and the uses in chapters 5–9.
36 *God a Good Master* (1640), 123–24.

that she 'was able (ordinarily) to supply the defect of a Concordance'.[37]

This is a classic portrayal of the godly person, those whom Patrick Collinson has called the 'super-Protestants' of early Stuart England.[38] Goodwin himself knew that few were like Abbott, and he complained of 'the coldnesse, and deadnesse, and general indifferencie, that is found in farre the greatest part of the world'. Such nominal religion was an 'abomination' to God.[39]

Although Goodwin's published sermons reveal him to be a typical Puritan preacher, a couple of revealing firsthand accounts suggest that he was distinctive as well. Samuel Rogers, who became chaplain to Lady Mary Vere at the end of 1637, first heard Goodwin preach in January 1638: 'Master Goodwin, obscure, voluminous, preaches;/about faith; I hear only two errors;/nor even after such prayers,/might I have heard such confused chaos'.[40] The comment indicates that at least some of Goodwin's hearers were discomforted by his involved arguments and unconventional theology. Lady Vere, however, was clearly an ardent admirer of Goodwin, and Rogers attended the monthly communions at St Stephen's in 1638, repeatedly testifying to the spiritual refreshment he experienced.[41] On 1 July, for example, he wrote: 'Saboth; and sacrament at Coleman: broken to pieces with joy; drunk with comfort; this is a day of rejoicing, and strength'. Following communion, Rogers went for dinner to the home of 'Mr Roules' (possibly Goodwin's parishioner, Owen Rowe), where he experienced 'A sweet communion of Saints'.[42] On 7 October, he was again at St Stephen's, where he commented: 'Ravished by Mr Goodwins prayer (but odde preacher) and at sacrament'.[43] Rogers' brief remarks indicate that St Stephen's under Goodwin was a spiritual hothouse environment, where the godly came to meet with God and each other. And contrary to the stereotype of Puritanism as a religion of the Word that elevated the sermon far above the communion, 'the Sacrament of the Supper' was a monthly high point, at which in Goodwin's words, Christ 'presents himselfe, and his dearest love unto us in those elements of bread & wine: whereunto uniting himselfe sacramentally, they goe down together, bread and wine into the body, and Christ into the soule'.[44] On such occasions, Goodwin stoked the flames of godly zeal through eloquent and fervent prayer, even if some thought his preaching 'odde'.

Thomas Goodwin offers us another view of Goodwin's preaching. 'Goodin of Colman-street was able to point out Wicked Men bravely', he told Hartlib in 1634, and possessed 'an excellent Faculty of Answering of objections'. His preaching,

---

37 *Christs Approbation of Maries Choice* (1640), appended to *The Christians Engagement for the Gospel* (1640), 320–30.
38 P. Collinson, 'Puritanism as popular religious culture', in C. Durston and J. Eales, eds, *The Culture of English Puritanism, 1560–1700* (Basingstoke, 1996), 46.
39 *Christs Approbation of Maries Choice*, 282, 293, 295–96.
40 *Diary of Samuel Rogers*, 136.
41 *Diary of Samuel Rogers*, 140 (4 February), 151 (3 June), 154–55 (1 July), 157 (5 August), 159 (2 September), 162 (7 October), 165 (4 November).
42 *Diary of Samuel Rogers*, 154.
43 *Diary of Samuel Rogers*, 162.
44 *The Christians Engagement*, 237.

in other words, was both spiritually convicting and intellectually rigorous. Apparently, he had 'been a great while to proove the truth of the Gospel', presumably meaning that he was giving a series of sermons or lectures in Christian apologetics. John was also a gifted expositor and exegete of the Scriptural text, and Thomas thought he would make a good commentator: 'Hee should be provoked to write short notes vpon the Bible. Herin hee was excellent'. Finally, a cryptic remark: 'Hee would hardly pierce to the bottomes of grace'.[45] Here was a hint that Goodwin was not the kind of preacher who emphasised the total depravity of natural man, or the absolute necessity of irresistible grace.

It would be a serious mistake, however, to conclude that Goodwin was a moralist who neglected to preach the classic Reformation doctrine of justification by faith through grace. What was controversial about Goodwin was the *way* in which he preached this message. In the first place, Goodwin became well known for teaching that since salvation came by faith alone, it did not necessarily have to be proceeded by a period of personal brokenness and repentance. The relationship between repentance and faith, law and grace were the subject of intense debate among the godly in the 1630s. For some, like Thomas Hooker, the law had an essential role in leading someone to Christ. Only when the sinner realised the depth and gravity of his sin, only when he was reduced to hopeless despair, would he be ready to reach out in faith for the gift of salvation. This time of 'humiliation' might last for weeks, months or even years.

Other Puritan divines, like the two Goodwins, were concerned about the pastoral implications of this teaching. To begin with, it seemed to introduce a new kind of 'works righteousness' into Protestantism by the back door; those who saw 'preparation' as essential for their conversion might fall into the trap of thinking that God's favour had to be earned by spiritual self-flagellation. Secondly, 'preparationism' could exacerbate the common Puritan problem of spiritual despair, by implying that conversion experiences were invalid unless preceded by humiliation. Thomas Goodwin, for one, confided to Hartlib in 1634 that '[Thomas] Hooker is a severe and Cruel Man like John Baptist, vrges too much and too farre the Worke of Humiliation'.[46] He told Hartlib that it was 'very necessary' to refute error on conversion, humiliation, faith, sanctification, obedience to the law, and the Christian life, and 'hee would entreat Mr Goodin of Colman-street' to take on the task.[47]

Goodwin of Coleman Street rose to the challenge in the 1630s, and his critique of 'preparationism' was one of the most distinctive features of his preaching. Although for some it was controversial, for others it came as a blessed relief. The young William Kiffin, for example, was troubled by his reading of Thomas Hooker's sermon, 'The Soul's Preparation for Christ'. Kiffin concluded that 'there was reason to question the truth of the work of grace in my soul'. Still aged only seventeen, he was in danger of being tormented by a lack of assurance. It was at this point that

---

45 HP 29/2/63A – Ephemerides, 1634.
46 HP 29/2/56A – Ephemerides, 1634.
47 HP 29/2/56A – Ephemerides, 1634.

John Goodwin first arrived in London. Kiffin attended his ministry and found it 'very profitable'. Goodwin 'shewed that the terrors of the Law were not of necessity to be preached to prepare the soul for Christ; but rather in the nature and tendency of them, did drive the soul farther from Christ'. He convinced Kiffin that 'God had not tied himself to any one way of converting a sinner; but ... took several ways to bring a soul to Jesus Christ'.[48]

Goodwin's distinctive positions in the 1630s can be pieced together from two documents: 'A satisfactory letter' to a correspondent held in the British Library, and a short paper written for the benefit of some of his parishioners, which was later published by a friend in 1641 under the title, *Christ Lifted Up*.[49] In responding to queries from his correspondent, Goodwin explained why he denied that 'the preaching and pressing the Lawe upon the conscience for the humbling and terrifying of a sinner, be absolutely necessary before the preaching of the Gospell'. Crucially, he argued, preparationism undercut the freeness of the Gospel. God's promises were 'absolutely and purely free, exacting nothing by way of any preceding condition of any man'. God offered salvation to whoever believed, and there were no preceding conditions attached. It was not right for a preacher to encumber 'the Doore of Life, with Condicions and Qualificacions wch [God] himselfe hath left open and free'.[50] Indeed, God was perfectly able to work instant conversion 'in the middest of the greatest and deepest unpreparednesse'.[51]

Drawing on his pastoral experience, Goodwin warned that 'sorrows and horrors of conscience, and apprehensions of the wrath of God and feare of being damned for sinne ... leade to death and despaires, and not to life'. Sinners convinced that God was against him would find it hard to believe that he wanted to save them; they needed to recognise that God was on their side, and desired their salvation.[52]

Thus as well as recognising the freeness of God's Grace, people also had to see 'the fullness of that Grace'. Here Goodwin stressed the universality of divine love. It extends, he insisted, 'to all sinnes', so that no sin was unforgiveable, and 'to all psons of what ranke or condicion soever, or of what number soever'. John 3:16 sounded 'that note of universality' – 'whosoever believeth in him shall not perish'. Justifying faith was a simple matter of believing the Gospel promise that God would save 'whosoever believeth'. In Scripture, God confirmed 'the generall truth or promise of the Gospell' (i.e. believe and you shall be saved), but he did not 'confirme any promise made to any particular man' (i.e. you are one of the elect).[53] Instead of seeking assurance that they were numbered among the chosen, they should put their trust in the general promise of the Gospel that whosoever believed would be saved.

---

48 *Remarkable Passages in the Life of William Kiffin*, 9.
49 'A satisfactory letter of Mr John Goodwin, Minister in Coleman-street; At the Request of a Friende. Concerning Points in Religion', BL Harleian MS 837/2, ff. 50r–61v; *Christ Lifted Up or The Heads of the Chief Controverted Points, Preached by Mr John Goodwin, Pastor of Colman-street London* (1641).
50 'A satisfactory letter', ff. 51r, 54v.
51 *Christ Lifted Up*, point 1.
52 'A satisfactory letter', ff. 52r–53v.
53 'A satisfactory letter', ff. 57v–60.

This then was Goodwin's response to the pervasive presence of legalism and despair within the Puritan subculture. Like Richard Sibbes, he wanted to emphasise free grace not works, simple faith not legal preparation, assurance rather than self-doubt.[54] Goodwin's preaching, therefore, sounded a positive note that contrasted sharply with the bleak emphasis on legal preparation, double predestination and self-scrutiny that echoed from some Puritan pulpits. Goodwin emphasised 'that note of universality' in the Gospel, taught the possibility of immediate conversion, and assumed that assurance should flow from faith. His was a message designed to calm the tortured souls who sought counsel from Calvinist pastors.

Goodwin still believed in absolute predestination, but by suggesting that individuals were wasting their time in prying into God's list of the elect and the reprobate, he undermined 'experimental predestinarianism'. Predestination was an important doctrine insofar as it reminded Christians that they were saved by pure grace, but the person searching for salvation should not be preoccupied by whether he was among the elect or the reprobate. Gospel preaching had to focus on God's promise of salvation rather than on his inscrutable decree.

Goodwin then, was known for his challenge to preparationism and legalism, and his emphasis on free grace offered to all men. This was controversial, but it was well within the bounds of Reformed orthodoxy. Indeed, in response to later claims that he had set the City on fire by denying the necessity of humiliation, Goodwin retorted that his teaching had 'cooled and composed' the City, and was embraced by most of the ministers.[55]

What did arouse great controversy within London's Puritan community was Goodwin's articulation of the doctrine of justification. Many Reformed divines taught that God's justification of the sinner involved two divine acts: firstly, remission of a person's sins; secondly, the imputation of Christ's righteousness to the believer. Goodwin, however, denied the imputation of Christ's righteousness, and taught that justification 'consists wholly in forgiveness of sinnes'.[56]

His teaching was partly inspired by a need to challenge antinomianism. Having made a name for himself as a preacher of 'free grace' he was open to charges of denigrating God's law and the need for obedience and repentance. As David Como's researches have revealed, the London Puritan community had been rocked by a serious antinomian controversy in 1629–31.[57] In Massachusetts Bay, the fledgling Puritan colony was also thrown into turmoil in the mid-1630s by its own 'free grace controversy'.[58] Goodwin was well aware of the problem, and he sought to

---

54 See J. Knight, *Orthodoxies in Massachusetts: Rereading American Puritanism* (Cambridge, MA, 1994). Knight overdraws the contrast between 'preparationists' like Perkins and Hooker and 'spiritists' like Sibbes, Preston and Cotton. But the distinctiveness of Sibbes is also emphasised by R. N. Frost, '*The Bruised Reed* by Richard Sibbes', in K. Kapic and R. Gleason, eds, *The Devoted Life: An Invitation to the Puritan Classics* (Downers Grove, IL, 2004), 79–91.
55 *A Fresh Discovery of the High Presbyterian Spirit* (1655), 64.
56 *Christ Lifted Up*, point 3.
57 D. Como, *Blown by the Spirit: Puritanism and the Emergence of an Antinomian Underground in Pre-Civil War England* (Stanford, 2004), esp. ch. 3.
58 See now the fine study by Michael Winship, *Making Heretics: Militant Protestantism and Free Grace in Massachusetts, 1636–1641* (Princeton, NJ, 2002).

sail between the Scylla of legalism and the Charybdis of antinomianism. By refuting the widely accepted notion of the imputation of Christ's righteousness he was killing off a doctrine much loved by those whom Como calls 'imputative' antinomians. For if Christ's active obedience (i.e. his perfect life) really was imputed to the believer, some reasoned, then the Christian was not merely a forgiven sinner but a perfect saint in the eyes of God. Goodwin undermined this logic by attacking its premise, and he had some success in countering the antinomians. The young William Allen, who had just arrived in London in the mid-1630s, later told Richard Baxter that he was led into antinomianism at this time by 'the Opinion of the Imputation of Christ's Righteousness' and 'never fully recovered my self till I heard Mr. John Goodwin'.[59]

In denying the imputation of Christ's righteousness to believers, Goodwin claimed to be in good company. There was, indeed, a good deal of Protestant diversity over the doctrine of justification, and the imputation of Christ's righteousness to the believer had been denied by Piscator and the leading London Puritan minister, Anthony Wotton.[60] However, Wotton had been bitterly accused of 'Socinianism' back in the 1610s by George Walker, the rector of St John the Evangelist, Watling Street. As Peter Lake explains, 'The Walker and Wotton Affair' became 'a *cause celebre* in godly circles in the capital', and Walker gained a reputation as 'a doctrinal attack dog of quite outstanding tenacity and viciousness'. His charges against Wotton were eventually considered by a jury of eminent Puritan divines, including Lewis Bayly, William Gouge and John Downham (on Walker's side), and Thomas Gataker, James Balmford and William Hickes (on Wotton's). The ministers declared that though they disagreed with Wotton on some points, 'yet we do not hold the difference to be so great and weighty as that they are to be justly condemned of heresy and blasphemy'. The compromise infuriated Walker, who stormed out of the meeting and continued to campaign on the issue for years to come. But as Lake shows, it provides a remarkable insight into 'doctrinal dispute and damage limitation' within London Puritanism.[61]

When Goodwin arrived in London in the early 1630s, Walker was still rector of St John the Evangelist, near St Paul's Cathedral. As a veteran heresy-hunter, he soon sniffed the burning rubber of error half a mile away in Coleman Street. Goodwin later suggested that Walker's quarrel with him dated from 'an ancient meeting betweene us in Cheap-side' around 1637 or 1638, when Walker had taken offence because Goodwin failed to show due reverence to his discourse, 'but either smiled or laughed at it'. Although Goodwin could not remember smirking,[62] he soon found himself being accused of Socinianism and Arminianism. In many ways, the Walker–Goodwin dispute was a re-run

---

59 *Reliquiae Baxterianae* (1696), Appendix iv, 98.
60 See A. E. McGrath, *Iustitia Dei: A History of the Christian Doctrine of Justification* (Cambridge, 1998), 232–34.
61 P. Lake, *The Boxmaker's Revenge: 'Orthodoxy', 'Heterodoxy' and the Politics of the Parish in Early Stuart London* (Manchester, 2001), 200, 221–46.
62 *Animadversions*, 4.

of the Walker–Wootton dispute two decades earlier. Once again, the church authorities and the godly ministers attempted to restore 'order and the appearance of consensus ... through an essentially co-operative process of control, advice and censorship'.[63]

In his annual account to the King in 1638, Archbishop Laud reported that there had been a 'distraction, both among the ministers and the people, occasioned at first by some over-nice curiosities, preached by one Mr Goodwin ... concerning the imputation of Christ's righteousness'. But the disturbance had been settled by the intervention of the Bishop of London and his Chancellor, who had convened 'the parties dissenting' and extracted 'a promise of forbearance'.[64] Neither Goodwin nor Walker would have accepted that they were arguing about 'some over-nice curiosities', so it is hardly surprising that in the following year Laud was forced to admit that his promise of peace had been a little premature. Goodwin had 'preached again in the same way, and the same perplexity is like to be caused again thereby in the city'. But Juxon was confident that he could settle things quietly again, and Laud would give him 'the best assistance I can'.[65]

Laud's account confirms that these doctrinal disputes were not confined to clerical circles; they also generated 'heat' and 'perplexity' among the laity, thus confirming Laudian suspicions about chaotic Puritan populism. Apparently, Laud was not alone in blaming Goodwin for restarting the fight. Although many critics accepted that his doctrines were not heretical, they objected to his 'singularity, or vaine glory'.[66] Goodwin's notoriety as a controversialist had begun.

Nonconformity, Separatism and Semi-separatism

As if being embroiled in theological controversy was not enough, Goodwin was also to encounter trouble over ecclesiastical conformity. He later complained about 'the Ceremonial and superstitious injunctions of the late Prelaticall power, when men thought better of themselves for standing at the Creed, joining in Gloria Patri ... bowing at the Name Jesus, cringing before an Altar, &c'.[67]

Within two years of coming to St Stephen's, Goodwin was in trouble with the church hierarchy. As Laud reported in 1635:

> There have been convented in this diocese Dr [John] Stoughton, of [St Mary] Aldermanbury, Mr [Sidrach] Simpson, curate and lecturer of St Margaret's, New-Fish-street, Mr Andrew Moline, curate and lecturer of St Swithin, Mr John Goodwin, vicar of St Stephen's, Coleman-street, and Mr [John] Viner, lecturer of St Laurence, in the old Jury, for breach of the

---

63 Lake, *Boxmaker's Revenge*, 244.
64 *The Works of the Most Reverend Father in God, William Laud*, 7 vols, ed. W. Scot and J. Bliss (Oxford, 1847–60), v. 356, 362.
65 *Works of William Laud*, v. 362.
66 'Epistle to the Reader', *Christ Lifted Up*.
67 *Innocency and Truth*, 78.

canons of the church in sermons, or practice, or both. But because all of them promised amendment for the future, and submission to the Church in all things, my lord [Bishop Juxon] very moderately forbare other proceeding against them.[68]

The Laudian language of moderation was the velvet glove concealing the iron hand of ecclesiastical pressure. Goodwin was reported once again in 1636, for administering communion on Easter Day to parishioners who were sitting rather than kneeling,[69] and in March 1637 the visitation of London rebuked him for 'not wearing of the surplice'.[70] In November 1637, a survey of the London clergy once again reported him for administering communion 'to divers strangers sitting'.[71] In Laudian eyes, this entailed two offences – refusal to enforce kneeling at communion, and failure to exclude non-parishioners ('strangers') from parish communion. Although the charges did not result in Goodwin's removal, the situation was becoming increasingly uncomfortable. Around this time, Goodwin may have written down his objections to one Laudian practice, in a document that was eventually published in 1641 as *Arguments against Bowing at the Name of Jesus*.[72]

As the pressure grew on England's Puritans, so did their sense of desperation and militancy. It is vividly displayed in a letter written in 1635 by Sir Thomas Wroth to Goodwin's fellow Puritan divine, Dr John Stoughton. Wroth was clearly writing from outside London, and he sent his letter via Sir Nathaniel Rich, a godly nobleman, and Lady Elizabeth Cleere, Goodwin's most prominent female parishioner. After asking Stoughton to pass on his greetings to Goodwin, Wroth lamented the terrible state of the nation, declaring that things were going 'from worse to worse'. Events had reached a critical juncture:

> Now is the time to shew our courage. If now we stand to our captain Christ Jesus, and forsake him not, we are to be well paid for our service. It will argue some patience if we suffer *usquam ad rerum amissionem*, but will be a great evidence of true Christian resolution if we suffer *usque ad sanguinis effusionem*, for preservation of faith and good conscience.[73]

Some scholars have seen in this a dark hint of bloody civil war,[74] but it is perhaps better to see it as a prediction of martyrdom. Militant Puritans like Alexander Leighton and William Prynne had already suffered bloody punishments for their opposition to the Caroline regime, and Wroth believed that the saints had to steel themselves for further trials. The very survival of 'faith and good conscience' was at stake.

Faced with such prospects at home, more and more Puritans started to contemplate emigration. During the course of the 1630s, thousands of the godly

---

68 *Works of William Laud*, v. 333.
69 NA SP 16/339/53 Information concerning the Diocese of London, 1636.
70 NA SP 16/351/100 Account of the Visitation of the Diocese of London, March 1637.
71 NA SP 16/371/39 Information concerning the Diocese of London, November 1637.
72 For the authorship of this anonymous tract see Appendix.
73 NA SP 16/297/39 Letter from Sir Thomas Wroth to Dr John Stoughton dated 12 September 1635. Cited in Kirby, 'Parish', 51–52; K. Shipps, 'Lay patronage of East Anglian Puritan Clerics in Pre-Revolutionary England', Ph.D. thesis, Yale University (1971), 201.
74 Kirby, 'Parish', 51–52; Shipps, 'Lay Patronage', 201.

left for Ireland, the Netherlands, the Caribbean and North America. In 1636–37, Theophilus Eaton and John Davenport recruited a group of settlers from the parish to found a new plantation in New England. Altogether fourteen families from St Stephen's chose to join them, including that of Nathaniel Rowe, the son of Owen Rowe.[75] Goodwin's reaction to the venture is unknown, but he later lamented the days when England 'hunted away almost a little Nation of Saints to New-England'.[76]

As the crackdown on England's Puritans intensified, it seemed as if Eaton and Davenport had made the right choice. In May and June 1637, three leading Puritan critics of the Laudian regime were tried before Star Chamber. The lawyer William Prynne, the doctor John Bastwick, and the divine Henry Burton had each published vitriolic attacks on the high church bishops, and they were sentenced to branding, mutilation, the pillory, a £5000 fine and life imprisonment. On 30 June, the three men had their ears cut off and their cheeks branded with the letters 'S.L.' for 'seditious libeller'. A large crowd of Londoners, which must have included many of Goodwin's followers and possibly Goodwin himself, witnessed their sufferings and their impassioned speeches from the pillory. Isaac Pennington wrote to his brother: 'these proceedings cause much dejection among many good loyal subjects, make men fly and many more think of providing for their safety in other places'.[77]

A growing number of Puritan clergy were now attracted to the semi-separatist congregationalism advocated by Dutch exiles like William Ames and New Englanders like John Cotton. In the late 1630s, various godly ministers were deprived of their livings and emigrated to America and the Netherlands, where they joined congregational churches. Jeremiah Burroughes, William Bridge, Sidrach Simpson, Joseph Symonds pastored congregations in Rotterdam, while John Archer and Philip Nye led an English church in Arnhem.[78] Goodwin knew most of these men from Cambridge and Norfolk, and in London he was in regular contact with Symonds. In 1639, Thomas Goodwin also departed for the Netherlands, having become convinced of the need to gather pure covenanted churches of the godly.

Distressed by his departure, John Goodwin wrote to Thomas on 25 October begging him to reconsider. Describing himself as 'your old friend', John admitted that he 'deerely longed after your bosome'. By leaving, however sincerely, Thomas had opened a 'fountain of blood ... in the womb of our Churches here'. Although John wanted to be conciliatory he rebuked Thomas for removing his light from 'an English Table' and placing it under 'a Holland Bushell'. He was unconvinced by Independent claims that they had discovered the biblical model of church government and worship, and rejected their insistence on 'the absolute necessity

---

75 Kirby, 'Parish', 49. See also *Letters of John Davenport, Puritan Divine*, ed. I. M. Calder (New Haven, 1937), 5–7.
76 *M.S. to A.S.* (1644), 17.
77 CSPD, 1637, 311. Quoted in K. Sharpe, *The Personal Rule of Charles I* (New Haven, 1992), 764.
78 See K. Sprunger, *Dutch Puritanism: A History of English and Scottish Churches of the Netherlands in the Sixteenth and Seventeenth Centuries* (Leiden, 1982), 162–74, 226–32.

of one and the same government or discipline in all particulars whatsoever for all Churches, in all times and places, a full and peremptory determination of all things whatsoever appertaining to the worship of God'. His friend's ecclesiology (with its congregational polity, ruling elders, office of widows and prescriptive regulative principle) was simply wrongheaded: 'I doe as clearly apprehend error and mistake throughout the greatest part of your way, as I doe in this conclusion, that twice two makes four'.[79]

In 1644, Goodwin was to admit that he had got his sums wrong when he admonished Thomas: 'once I was so wise to think that six and seven made just nineteen; but now am become so weake, as to judge they onely make thirteene'[80] But in 1639, he was convinced that the burden of proof lay on those who had separated, and he asked them to justify their action 'by a high hand of pregnant and expresse Scriptures ... letter for letter, word for word, and tittle for tittle, to the proofe of all you maintaine against us'.[81]

Thomas's response was indignant. Although he acknowledged John as 'My ancient friend and dear brother in the Lord', he also complained that the letter was full of 'provocation', and was upset that it had been 'dispersed everywhere abroad', bringing the congregational exiles into disrepute among the godly. He staunchly defended the congregational model one that 'God hath ordained', insisting that New Testament churches should be composed of 'visible saints'. Church covenants were useful because they 'knit fast the agreement' of the body, but John had misunderstood them. They were not intended to form 'a wall of partition ... from all saints and churches else, whom we love, pray for, hold communion with, and honour as the spouse and churches of Christ'.[82]

If Thomas Goodwin continued to see the Church of England as a true church, other Puritans were more radical in their separation. The area around Coleman Street was a hotbed of separatist and semi-separatist activity. In a diocesan report of 1636, the parish of St Stephen's was singled out for 'much disorder and unconformity' within the City.[83] So severe was the problem that around 1638, Goodwin recruited Thomas Edwards to preach against the sects. As Edwards explained in *Gangraena* (1646):

> *About 8. yeares agoe when Errors on the right hand tooke with many, I did at a Lecture in the City at* Aldermanbury, *and* Coleman-street *preach against Apostasie and falling to Errors on the right hand, and more particularly at* Coleman-street, *(many in that parish being then leaning that way) gave some considerations against Errors on the right hand, and warned the people of the White Devill, quoting a saying of Master* Cartwright *out of the Proverbs, and Master* Brightman

---

79 *A Quaere concerning the Church Covenant ... Sent with a Letter thereunto annexed from J.G. to T.G.* (1643), 9–13.
80 *Theomachia* (1644), Epistle to the Reader, sig. A2. This makes it impossible to accept More's claim ('New Arminians', 43–52) that the exchange with Thomas Goodwin indicates John's 'emerging congregationalism'.
81 *A Quaere*, 14.
82 'Two Letters which passed between the Reverend Mr John Goodwin and the Author, concerning a Church Covenant', in *The Works of Thomas Goodwin*, 11 vols (Edinburgh, 1861–65), xi. 526–40.
83 NA SP 16/339/53, Information concerning the diocese of London, 1636.

out of the Revelations against leaving the Church of England, and Master John Goodwin *was then well pleased with my Sermon that he gave me great thanks.*[84]

Despite the efforts of Edwards and Goodwin, separatism continued to grow. The most notable conventicle in the parish was led by the cobbler Samuel How. Having once been part of Henry Jacob's semi-separatist church, How became leader of the separatist congregation founded by John Canne in 1633, and attracted many admirers including John Lilburne and William Kiffin.[85] How had acquired a formidable knowledge of the Bible by reading it while he mended shoes. As Roger Williams wrote many years later, 'by searching the holy Scriptures, [How] grew so excellent a Textuary or Scripture learned man, that few of those high Rabbies that scorne to mend or make a Shoe, could aptly and readily from the holy Scripture, outgo him'.[86] How's outstanding piety and mastery of Scripture made him 'the most famous lay preacher of the Laudian decade'.[87]

The growth of this populist, plebeian Puritanism represented a serious challenge to the learned Puritan divines who had inadvertently unleashed it by promoting lay piety and Bible reading. As Gerald Aylmer explains, 'although some of the most radical puritans (e.g. John Goodwin and John Milton) were intellectual mandarins to their fingertips, there was an anti-academic, anti-intellectual strain in popular puritanism'.[88] When Goodwin announced from his pulpit that an unlearned man could not be a public teacher of God's Word, How's admirers were aggrieved, and challenged Goodwin to prove his allegation by choosing a text for their hero to preach on. Goodwin cunningly chose 2 Peter 3.16: 'they that are unlearned and unstable wrest [St Paul's writings] as they do all the other Scriptures to their own destruction'. This was (to say the least) an unpromising starting point for the cobbler, but news of his upcoming performance spread quickly in London's Puritan underground. His sermon was preached 'in the Nags-head Taverne neare Coleman Street in the presence of aboue a hundred people, among which was five Ministers [including Goodwin] (some of them silenc't ones)'.[89]

This was one of the great set piece occasions in early Stuart Puritanism – it dramatised the tension between clergy and laity, learning and charisma, establishment and sect. How turned in a barnstorming performance, arguing in favour of the 'sufficiencie of the Spirit's teaching, without humane learning'. The sermon over, Goodwin replied 'with much passion'. According to How himself, the vicar of Coleman Street accused the cobbler of blasphemy, and then fumed

---

84 Thomas Edwards, *The Third Part of Gangraena* (1646), 'The Preface'.
85 See Lilburne, *A Copy of a Letter written by John Lilburne, Close Prisoner in the Wards of the Fleet* (1640), pp. 4, 7; and Kiffin's commendation in How, *Sufficiency of the Spirits Teaching* (1655), 'Postscript'.
86 Roger Williams, *The Hireling Ministry None of Christs* (1652), in *The Writings of Roger Williams*, ed. P. Miller, 7 vols (New York, 1963), vii. 167.
87 Tolmie, *The Triumph of the Saints: The Separate Churches of London, 1626–1649* (Cambridge, 1977), 36.
88 G. Aylmer, *The State's Servants: The Civil Service of the English Republic, 1649–1660* (London, 1973), 279.
89 *The Vindication of the Cobler* (1640).

that he had 'made a Calf (meaning a false and unsound exposition)' and 'danced about it'. Goodwin's remarks were reported around the City, exposing How to 'derision, contempt, and table-talk'.[90] One disgruntled critic later complained that Goodwin had used his leverage with the City's publishers to ensure that 'all Presses were stopt' against How, who was forced to print his tract in Holland.[91] How used the Amsterdam separatist press run by the future Leveller leader Richard Overton. When imported back to London, the published sermon was a roaring success, and eventually went through more editions than anything written by Goodwin himself.[92] A broadsheet entitled *A Vindication of the Cobler* was published in 1640, complete with a poem in his honour (possibly by Overton), reminding Oxbridge-trained divines that 'The *Spirits Teaching* flowes not from your quill'.[93]

By the close of the 1630s, Goodwin was besieged on every side. Summoned before Bishop Juxon, denounced by George Walker, estranged from Thomas Goodwin, and challenged by Samuel How, he must have felt exposed. He was still, of course, a respected, moderate, mainstream Puritan divine, one of the godly brotherhood. But under immense pressure from Laudianism, the godly were in serious danger of splitting up. As Goodwin lamented in a sermon around this time, 'many daily and sad experiences teach us that Saints on earth are not Angels in heaven'. Instead of being 'knit together in the same minde', the godly were 'little other then divided and scattered upon the face of the whole earth about them'.[94]

Contending for the Faith

Yet in the midst of these trials, Goodwin was defiant. His militant attitudes can be gauged from two sets of sermons which he eventually published in 1640. In his dedicatory epistle to *The Christians Engagement for the Gospel*, Goodwin explained that 'this little piece had stucke in the birth some yeares together, and was well neere stifled'.[95] This would date these sermons to the mid-1630s, and suggest that publication was blocked by Caroline censorship. A second book was entitled, *The Saints Interest in God: Opened in Severall Sermons preached Anniversarily upon the Fifth of November*. Since Goodwin's introductory epistles were dated 7 August 1640, these sermons must have been preached on 5 November celebrations in the 1630s, probably in the final years of that decade.[96] Although Goodwin may have edited them for publication, these two sets of sermons provide us with the best

---

90 Samuel How, *The Sufficiencie of the Spirits Teaching, without Humane-Learning* (1640), 'To the Reader'.
91 See the comment by 'C. D.' in Samuel How, *The Sufficiency of the Spirit's Teaching ... The Fifth Edition Corrected* (1689), v–vi.
92 New editions were printed in 1644, 1655 (with a postscript by Kiffin), 1683 and 1689. The sermon was even republished in Boston in 1772 and in London in 1792.
93 *The Vindication of the Cobler*. The 1655 edition of How's *Sufficiency of the Spirits Teaching* reprints the poem and attributes it to 'R.O.'.
94 *The Christians Engagement*, 120–21.
95 *The Christians Engagement*, 'The Epistle Dedicatory'.
96 *The Saints Interest*, 'Epistle Dedicatory' and 'To the Reader'.

insight into his public preaching during the final years of Laudian ascendancy.

The sermons contained in *The Christians Engagement* expounded and applied the third verse of the epistle of Jude: 'earnestly contend for the faith which was once delivered unto the saints'. The text was a loaded one at a time when zealous Protestant Christians believed that their Reformed faith was being betrayed by apostates and assaulted by Antichrist. Although Goodwin avoided naming names, his audience can have been in doubt as to his targets.

Goodwin had stern words for those who felt that the current religious situation was confusing, 'that God may be truly served, and men saved in any Religion whatsoever'. God 'hateth and abhorreth' such easy-going relativism. Theological controversies might seem puzzling to the laity, but there was no need to cast up their hands in despair. The person who was 'no Philosopher' could still tell truth from error. As one of the Marian martyrs had rightly declared, 'shee could dye for the truth, but could not dispute for it'. If an opinion or tenet had established and upheld by sober, holy men, there was 'a strong presumption' in its favour. 'The complaints, and teares, and sorrowes, of godly men for the losse of truth, or corruptions at any time', were usually a sure guide to truth and error. '*Vox populi*, the voyce of the people, bee not always *vox Dei*, the voyce of God: yet *vox populi Dei*, the voyce of the people of God is (for the most part) the voyce of God'.[97]

Although Goodwin did not specify the 'corruptions' or erroneous 'opinions and tenets' he was attacking, it seems certain that he was referring to the Laudians' high church worship and 'Arminian' theology. His references to 'the free grace of God' and 'the simplicitie of the Gospel' were coded condemnations of the Laudians' stress on free will and 'the beauty of holiness'.[98] For Puritans like Goodwin, Laudianism was a form of crypto-popery polluting the pure Reformed faith of the Church of England from within.[99] His sermons constituted a coded call to arms against Archbishop Laud and all his works. He urged his hearers to throw themselves into 'this holie warre'.[100]

At this stage, of course, the language of war was metaphorical. Goodwin explained that the godly should fight the good fight by propagating the Gospel, arguing for the truth, living innocent lives and praying. Magistrates and influential men 'must countenance the truth, the teachers, abettors, and professors of it', and 'men must confesse the truth when they are examin'd or call'd to it, whatsoever it cost them'. If the godly did not do these things, 'this faith of ours will be laid waste and utterly destroyed by the enemies of it', and God would withdraw his presence from the nation. But if the godly were obedient, they might lose estates, friends, credit, liberties and even their lives, but they would share in 'that great victorie of the Lambe over the Beast'.[101]

---

97 *The Christians Engagement*, 126–27, 119, 107–8, 153, 155.
98 *The Christians Engagement*, 115, 166.
99 See C. Hibbard, *Charles I and the Popish Plot* (Chapel Hill, NC, 1983).
100 *The Christians Engagement*, 193.
101 *The Christians Engagement*, 194–212, 165, 169, 180–81.

The second set of sermons from this period, *The Saints Interest in God*, was even more aggressive in its attack on crypto-popery. Preached on 5 November, the anniversary of the discovery of the Gunpowder Plot, these sermons gave powerful expression to English Protestant nationalism. Goodwin called 'that Deliverance' of 1605 'a mercy so transcendently glorious'. It demonstrated that England was a land with a unique providential status: 'What other construction can all the world make of such his dealings with us, but that he delights to have his praises sung, and his name magnified by the English Nation, more than all Lands besides?' In 1605, 'your God stepped in between the Match and the Powder'. In 1588 too, the English were saved by direct divine intervention.[102]

For Goodwin, the remembrance of such great moments of divinely wrought salvation was what would sustain the saints during the gloomy days of the 1630s:

> So, suppose we be now in the Wildernesse, we see no meanes of support, of subsisting before us, we have not those visible, those sensible testimonies of Gods presence with us, as sometimes we have had, yet God hath given us meat, to feed and live upon: those 36 Barrells of Gunpowder, wherewith God furnished us out of the Cellar at our enemies cost, let us drinke downe then, they will breed good blood, spirit, and courage.[103]

November the fifth then, was a Protestant sacrament, when the godly fed on the memory of past deliverance. 'Let us season the flesh of the Traitors, the Gunpowder, the Barre, the Billets', he exclaimed, 'that they may keep fresh and sweet; and so doubtlesse they will be a nourishment of an high and excellent spirit'.[104]

Since God was on their side, the saints should be strong and courageous. Goodwin was scathing about godly people who 'walke with dejected countenances, and with hands hanging down' because of troubled times. 'What if the face of Rulers should be clouded', he declared, 'should we not rejoyce neverthelesse, if the light of Gods countenance shine upon us?' The Lord was setting a trap for his enemies, using his church as a 'snare' to lure them in; like a lion he would 'breake out of the thicket upon them, and teare them to pieces suddenly'.[105]

This was a warning to 'that cursed confederacy' that had set its face against the godly: 'that service of the devill, persecuting Saints…is a worke that never prospered in the hands of any, from the beginning of the world to this day'. The church was the apple of God's eye, and 'The touching of it hath cost the blood of the greatest Monarchs, of many Kings and Princes of the earth'. Men 'that persecute the Saints of God' were effectively calling on God to destroy them by fire and sword. Goodwin also warned his hearers that many persecutors were men of 'honour and reputation' 'for Morall honesty and Justice'. Decius and Trajan had raised 'cruell stormes of persecution against Christians', but they were 'two of the best and most moderate, and just Emperors otherwise'. When 'the Roman State of old' wished to despoil Ptolemy of his 'great wealth and treasury', it gave the job to

---

102 *The Saints Interest*, 2, 9, 159, 163.
103 *The Saints Interest*, 166.
104 *The Saints Interest*, 169.
105 *The Saints Interest*, 181–82, 187, 246.

Cato, 'the great Patron of Justice in their State', so that 'the notorious baseness of the fact might be a little over-shadowed by the credit and authority of the man that was the principall actor in it'.[106]

Here was preaching that verged on sedition. Once again, Goodwin had carefully avoided any direct reference to the bishops or the king, but this was a thinly veiled warning to both. Throughout these sermons, monarchs, emperors and rulers appeared as persecutors of the people of God, and Goodwin's hearers can hardly have failed to see the comparison between the pious and austere Charles I and other morally upright oppressors like Decius, Trajan, and Cato. Conscious of how far he had gone, Goodwin stressed that the godly were not seditious:

> they are no enemies to the Civill peace, and society of men; they are no disturbers of the publique affaires of States and Kingdoms: Nay, they pray for the People and State wheresoever they live; and they have intelligence with Heaven, with the King of Kings, who makes earthly crownes to flourish upon the heads of Princes, and who watcheth over Kingdomes and Nations for good, for the wealth and peace of the places where they lived.[107]

This denial of sedition hardly improved matters, for here was a decidedly conditional view of royal power. The really important king was not Charles I, but 'the King of Kings', and the godly had a hotline to his throne. If earthly princes persecuted the saints, the very future of their crowns was insecure. At this stage, there is no reason to think that Goodwin was fomenting rebellion, though he may have spoken with the Scottish Covenanter uprising in mind. He preached about direct divine intervention rather than armed uprisings by the godly. But his political attitudes were miles apart from those of his old college president, John Davenant, Bishop of Salisbury, 'Charles's tame Calvinist'.[108] Despite being close to Davenant in his theological outlook, Goodwin was far from tame.

Revisionist historians have sometimes suggested that without the impetus provided by the Scottish Covenanter revolution, English Puritans would not have resisted Charles I.[109] Although we can only speculate on this counterfactual thesis, one wonders if it underestimates the depth of Puritan rage against the Laudian and Caroline regime. Goodwin's sermons need to be treated with care since they were published after the crucial 1640 watershed, but if the published text was essentially the same as the text preached in the 1630s, it shows that the mood of London Puritans had turned very ugly indeed. We have seen that in the face of episcopal pressure, Goodwin was willing to make tactical withdrawals. But these should not be mistaken for timidity. Convinced that a great confrontation with the forces of Antichrist was looming, Goodwin knew that the godly had to be wise as serpents in the meantime. However embattled Puritans felt, their theology told

---

106 *The Saints Interest*, 258, 273, 319, 323–24, 326–27.
107 *The Saints Interest*, 330–31.
108 C. Russell, *The Fall of the British Monarchies* (Oxford, 1991), 18.
109 The argument is present in C. Russell, *The Causes of the English Civil War* (Oxford, 1992), but is more explicit in J. Adamson, 'England without Cromwell', in N. Ferguson, ed., *Virtual History: Alternatives and Counterfactuals* (London, 1997), esp. 101–09.

them that they were 'a people confederate with the great and terrible Lord of Hosts'.[110] Although they were a minority, they were well placed to strike when the opportunity arose. When Pym and Pennington led Parliament and the City of London into war with the king, Goodwin was on hand to act as their clerical cheerleader.

---

110 *The Saints Interest*, 263.

3

'THE ANTI-CAVALIER'
1640–43

By the close of the 1630s, Goodwin was a well-known and well-connected London minister. Firmly established as one of the City's leading Puritan preachers, he was a respected if controversial figure. Yet despite having reached his mid-forties, he had not published a single book or pamphlet. In part this was because he was preoccupied with a busy ministry in a teeming urban parish. More importantly, it was a reflection of early Stuart controls on the press.[1] In dedicating a book of sermons to John Pym, Goodwin explained that 'this little piece had stucke in the birth some yeares together, and was well neere stifled', but had now been published thanks to the 'influence of that happy constellation, wherein your selfe shine as a starre, in much glory'.[2]

During the 1640s, England (and London in particular) was to witness a spectacular rise in the number of new books and pamphlets. Whereas the average press output for the 1630s was just 624 items per annum, 848 titles were published in 1640, 2042 in 1641, and an astonishing 4038 in 1642.[3] The central European Reformed philosopher, Jan Amos Comenius, reported from London in 1641 that 'there are truly not more bookstalls at Frankfurt at the time of the fair than there are here every day'.[4] It is little wonder that Goodwin himself referred in May 1641 to 'the late overflowing of the Presses'.[5] Undeterred by the complaint 'that the world is still pesterd with more bookes',[6] Goodwin was swept along by the new craze for publication. In 1640–41 he published four small volumes of his sermons, combining spiritual counsel with political purpose. In 1641–42, his controversy with George Walker over the doctrine of justification found its way into print, as Goodwin responded to Walker's attack with a direct rebuttal and a major work,

---

1 The degree of censorship under the Caroline regime is much debated, and is ably assessed in A. Milton, 'Licensing, censorship and religious orthodoxy in early Stuart England', *Historical Journal*, 41 (1998).
2 *The Christians Engagement for the Gospel* (1640), dedication.
3 J. Raymond, *Pamphlets and Pamphleteering in Early Modern Britain* (Cambridge, 2003), 163–65.
4 Quoted in A. Johns, *The Nature of the Book* (Chicago, 1998), 66.
5 *The Returne of Mercies* (1641), 'To the Reader', sig. A8r.
6 *God a Good Master and Protector* (1640), 'To the Reader'.

his *Treatise of Justification*. Finally, Goodwin published a series of inflammatory anti-royalist pamphlets, the most influential being *Anti-Cavalierisme*. In his two key books of this period, Goodwin articulated a vision of reformation that was to resonate through all his subsequent writings: *A Treatise of Justification* envisaged a new age of discovery, when individuals would throw off their servility to institutional authorities and set forth on quests for unknown continents of knowledge; *Anti-Cavalierisme* announced that the Civil War was nothing less than England's war of liberation from civil and religious bondage.

This was an inspirational vision. Throughout this period, the parish of St Stephen's Coleman Street was a hotbed of agitation, as Goodwin's parishioners emerged as John Pym's most ardent supporters. In the second half of this chapter, we will turn to the politics of Goodwin and his followers, but we will begin by examining his theological writings.

Reforming Reformed Theology

Goodwin was first and foremost a pastor and theologian, and his publications are the product of a mind steeped in Scripture and the Reformed tradition. But even at this stage, Goodwin was subtly modifying Reformed theology. His published sermons reveal a Calvinist with a number of decidedly un-Calvinist emphases.

Despite an occasional emphasis on the utter sovereignty of God and the puny insignificance of man,[7] Goodwin often struck a softer note. Although he taught that God had made an 'absolute' covenant with the elect, he was emphatic about the universality of God's 'conditional' covenant with the whole of mankind. 'There is no creature under heaven', he wrote, 'but God hath thus far conditioned or covenanted with it, that if it will believe and accept of Jesus Christ from his hand, he will receive it and be a God to it'.[8] Goodwin seemed to imply that God's grace was not irresistible. 'Though God be of an omnipotent and irresistible power, yet can he not compel any creature whatsoever, indued with understanding and will, to receive and owne him against their will, because it is by an act of the will that he is, and must be received'.[9] This statement was not incompatible with Calvinism, which taught that God irresistibly wooed the elect; he did not force himself on them against their will. But the stress in Goodwin's sermon was not on the irresistibility of the wooing, but on the act of the human will.

Secondly, Goodwin displayed a profound concern with justifying the ways of God to man. High Calvinists typically insisted that God was a law unto himself before whose inscrutable decrees men must simply prostrate themselves. Puny sinners could not complain that God was unjust in decreeing the reprobation of the majority of mankind. Goodwin felt uncomfortable with this. Instead, he wished to show that God was justified in the condemnation of sinners. In *God a Good*

---

7 *The Returne of Mercies*, 196, 204–05.
8 *The Saints Interest in God* (1640), 79–86.
9 *The Saints Interest*, 88.

Master, he argued that God was determined to show that those who perished were 'without excuse' and had only themselves to blame for their fate. God was not a 'hard master', and through 'the effectual proffer and tender of Christ' he had provided a way of salvation.[10]

Finally, Goodwin placed an unusual emphasis on the universality of God's love. Men could trust God, because of 'the love that hee beares unto his creature man, being the workemanship of his owne hand'. The 'Scripture often expresseth' the 'bountifull disposition in God', and taught that he loved the whole world (John 3:16).[11] Goodwin urged his hearers to 'behold as in a Glasse with open Face, that Philanthropie, that sweet and gracious, and soule-indearing disposition in God, wherein he inclines to that poore creature of his called Man'.[12]

As we shall see, each of these emphases was taken up and developed in Goodwin's later Arminian works. Goodwin the Arminian continued to use the language of Goodwin the soft Calvinist: he talked of God being 'justified' in the 'condemnation of sinners'; of sinners being left 'without excuse'; of 'the note of universality' in the Gospel; of God's 'bountifull disposition'; and of divine 'Philanthropie'. In 1640–41, Goodwin obviously believed that the doctrine of absolute predestination was compatible with human agency, divine justice, and the universality of God's love (though none of his extant writings explain how this was so). He later concluded that these things could only be preserved by a doctrine of conditional predestination. Goodwin himself saw his pilgrimage as a journey towards theological consistency, for he contended that almost all Calvinists contradicted their Calvinism when they preached.

In the early 1640s, however, Goodwin was less concerned with the doctrine of predestination, than with the doctrine of justification. His long-running dispute with George Walker received fresh impetus from a 'conference' between the two men held some time in late 1640 or early 1641. The 'conference' was held at the house of Walker's brother (another minister) and conducted in the presence of 'divers others'. But it was 'managed in a tumultuous and issuelesse manner', and the perplexed audience asked Goodwin 'to leave something in writing'. Goodwin left a short paper he had written on Romans chapter 4, a paper that would eventually form the second chapter of his *Treatise of Justification*. Several months later, he received 'a Tract in writing' by an anonymous author, which answered his paper on Romans 4 and chastised him for heresy and blasphemy. In response, Goodwin wrote to Walker, asking him if he was the author, and requesting that he 'disavow' 'the rough Turkie dialect, as, Socinian, Arminian, lyar, lying Sophister, impudent fellow, Heretique, Blasphemer ... ' When Walker failed to respond, Goodwin sent him a substantial manuscript 'Reply', which according to the victim was 'full of lyes, absurdities, contradictions, blasphemies, and intollerable scoffes and reproaches'.[13]

10 *God a Good Master*, 67–72.
11 *God a Good Master*, 34–35, 37.
12 *The Saints Interest*, 102.
13 There are three separate accounts of the course of the dispute: *A Defence of the True Sence and Meaning of the Words of the Holy Apostle* (1641), 'To the Reader'; *Impedit ira Animum, or Animadversions* (1641), 'Preface', 1–3, 14–15; George Walker, *Socinianisme in the Fundamentall Point of Justification* (1641), 'The Epistle to his Reverend Brethren'.

Up until this stage, everything had circulated in manuscript, and there had been no intention to publish. But Goodwin's 'Reply' provoked the outraged Walker into print. He published a long work on the controversy entitled *Socinianisme in the Fundamentall Point of Justification Discovered* (1641), which condemned 'Socinian John' as 'a dangerous seducer'. Goodwin had revived a grievous heresy first taught by Peter Abelard ('a pestilent and blasphemous Heretick'), championed by the arch heretics Servetus, Faustus Socinus, and Arminius, and finally brought to England '28 yeares agoe' by the 'perverse' Anthony Wotton. Indeed, Goodwin had 'stollen the most part of his conclusions' from Wotton's *De Reconciliatione* (1624).[14]

Goodwin's followers responded swiftly. Condemning *Socinianisme* as 'a confused medley',[15] they attempted to set the record straight by publishing Walker's original answer to Goodwin's paper on Romans 4, together with Goodwin's 'Reply'. The resultant volume was in two parts, comprising Walker's *Defence of the True Sence and Meaning of the Words of the Holy Apostle* and Goodwin's *Impedit ira Animum, or Animadversions* (1641).[16] *Animadversions* was a merciless lampoon of the unfortunate Walker. Rather than rant, Goodwin announced that he preferred 'to make merry with my Antagonist'.[17] Walker was portrayed as an absurd figure, a self-styled warrior for orthodoxy who 'buckles on his harnesse, and meanes to fight stoutly for his beloved Dalila'.[18] He was depicted dumping dunghills of abuse at Goodwin's door, and was compared to an angry man with a thorn in his finger 'which makes him rage'. Taking up Walker's reference to Peter Abelard, 'that was gelded for his incontinencie', Goodwin jested that if the law of England inflicted castration for 'incontinencie of tongue', 'Mr Ws manhood would be one of the first that should suffer'.[19]

Such no-holds-barred satire was unprecedented among the Puritan ministry, though it did have antecedents in the notorious Marprelate tracts of the 1580s. In resorting to such mockery, Goodwin revealed the depth of his indignation and frustration at Walker's insistent charges of heresy and blasphemy. He took grave exception to the claim that he was following in the footsteps of 'the Heretick Socinus, the Arminians &c'. For Goodwin, this kind of name-calling was 'Popish Mountebankerie'. Walker was 'crucifying the truth betweene those two Malefactors, Socinus and Arminius'. Socinus was 'an accursed Denier of Christs satisfaction', whereas Goodwin emphasised the necessity of 'atonement by blood'. Arminians generally taught that justifying faith 'includes obedience to the Law of God'.[20]

Goodwin insisted that his own position was consonant with both Scripture and Protestant orthodoxy. The dispute centred on the Apostle Paul's statement

---

14 Walker, *Socinianisme*, 4–9. The Wotton–Walker dispute had also flared up once again with a flurry of pamphlets by Gataker and Walker in 1641–42.
15 *A Defence*, sig. A3.
16 In *Imputatio Fidei, or a Treatise of Justification* (1642), ii. 187, Goodwin confirms that his answer to Walker was 'now Printed by some … at the unreasonable importunity of my Antagonists *Socinianisme Discovered*.
17 *Animadversions*, preface, 13.
18 *Animadversions*, 32.
19 *Animadversions*, 74–5, 66, 79, 93.
20 *Animadversions*, 6–18.

that 'faith was imputed for righteousness'. Walker advanced a 'tropicall or Metonymicall' reading of Paul's words, according to which 'faith' was a trope for 'the active obedience or righteousness' of Christ. Goodwin thought that this was fanciful, for if that was what Paul meant he could have said so quite clearly without resorting to strange metonyms. Theologians had wisely followed Augustine's rule, 'that a literall, and proper sense in Scripture is still to be preferr'd, where there is no necessity of rejecting it, or substituting a tropicall, or improper in the stead'. 'The proper nature, and direct signification' of Paul's words was that faith itself was imputed as righteousness, because God justified sinners on account of their faith. Goodwin had no doubt that this was in accord with the Reformation principles of *sola fides* and *sola gratia*. Justification was by faith alone, not by works of the law (for the believer was justified by faith in Christ's atoning death, not by his own works nor by Christ's works imputed to him). Goodwin also insisted that faith was not meritorious, but was merely instrumental in justification. Although the believer's faith had no saving merit in itself, God in his grace accepted it and imputed it for righteousness, forgiving the believer's sins on the basis of his faith in Christ's atoning death.[21]

At the close of his *Animadversions*, Goodwin vowed never to 'anti-pamphlet' with Walker again. Instead, he concentrated on completing his sober and scholarly *Treatise of Justification*, on which he had been working since the late 1630s.[22] Published in January 1642, the book was Goodwin's first major work, and almost five hundred pages in quarto. It boasted a fine engraved portrait of 'Johannes Goodwin. S: Theol: Cantabrig: Aetat 47: 1641'. Goodwin, his beard neatly trimmed, sat in sober clerical garb, holding a book in one hand while making a precise point with the other. As David Masson remarked, his portrait presents him as 'a man of calm general appearance' with 'a nose rather fine and ironical, and a face altogether suggesting ability and opinionativeness blended with ingenuousness and composure'.[23] Underneath was an adulatory verse by 'D.T.' (Goodwin's parishioner, Daniel Taylor). The portrait said a great deal about the image Goodwin wished to project. Here was a man to be taken seriously – learned, mature, earnest, gifted and intellectually acute.

'The Preface to the Reader' amounted to a manifesto for further reformation in doctrine. Goodwin set out a conception of the theologian's task strikingly different to that held by conservative clergy like Walker. By complaining about 'noveltie', he remarked, such men sounded just like papists, who levelled the same charge against 'that glorious light brought into the church by Luther'. Theologians were wrong to see themselves merely as conservers of well-established traditions; they should be intellectual voyagers traversing the oceans in search of new worlds. If America, the world's fourth great continent, lay undiscovered for so many ages, then 'many truths' 'may be yet unborne'. The church needed new Luthers to sail like Columbus into unknown regions. Goodwin justified such openness to innovation by appeal

---

21 *Animadversions*, 21ff, 63, 44–45.
22 *Treatise of Justification*, sig. d4v.
23 D. Masson, *The Life of Milton*, 7 vols (London, 1877–94), ii. 583.

to Hakewill's catalogue of human discoveries, but he also invoked eschatology. The prophet Daniel had prophesied that in the last days, 'many shall runne to and fro, [that is shall discourse and beate out the secrets of GOD in the Scripture with more libertie and freedom of judgement ...] and knowledge [by this means] shall be increased'. God was angry because the English had done 'so little' to raise 'the line of Evangelicall Knowledg' since 'our first Reformers'. Protestants had swallowed the 'ignoble Principle' of the Church of Rome, 'to beleeve as the church beleeveth'. But surely there should be 'more light in the aire' at the noonday of the Reformation than at its daybreak![24]

The strength of Goodwin's plea lay in its fusion of Renaissance ideals and radical Reformation visions. He brought together the humanist insistence on free discourse and independent inquiry with radical Protestant millenarianism. 'Libertie and freedom of judgement' were vital in order to complete the Reformation, discover new truths and restore primitive Christianity after the disastrous era of popish apostasy. In the early 1640s, this dream was shared by a number of Puritan intellectuals imbued with humanist values, including Lord Brooke, John Milton and Thomas Gataker.[25] It was a thrilling prospect. London in 1641 attracted some of the most brilliant intellectuals in the Reformed world with the promise of millennial reform. The ecumenist Scotsman John Dury, the German scientist Samuel Hartlib, and the Czech educationalist Comenius had each been profoundly influenced by the millenarianism of Johannes Alsted and Joseph Mede, and entertained the thought that London would be at the centre of a great flowering of Reformed thought.[26]

Goodwin believed that recovering the biblical doctrine of justification by faith was a vital part of this larger intellectual project. Justification was the 'corner stone' of the house of faith, and it was imperative that theologians reconstructed the biblical doctrine with great precision. Those who taught that God justified believers by imputing the righteousness of Christ to them had made a grave error. Goodwin promised to refute them by 'the authority of Scripture', 'the grounds of reason', and the 'consent of Authors'.[27]

Most important was the exegesis of Scripture. Once again, Goodwin's central claim was that when one interpreted the words of Apostle Paul in a 'proper' and 'literal' (as opposed to 'tropical') sense, his teaching became crystal clear. Paul had taught that God imputed (or counted) the sinner's faith for righteousness, so that in response to this faith God declared the sinner justified.[28] Justification consisted

---

24 *Treatise of Justification*, sigs. b3v–c2, e2v–e3.
25 See Robert Greville, *The Nature of Truth* (1641) and Milton's *Areopagitica* (1644). On Gataker, see Lake, *The Boxmaker's Revenge*, 235.
26 H. Trevor-Roper, 'The three foreigners', in *Religion, the Reformation and Social Change* (London, 1967), ch. 5. For a fuller account of the enterprises of Hartlib and his associates see C. Webster, *The Great Instauration: Science, Medicine and Reform 1626–60* (London, 1975); and M. Greengrass, M. Leslie, T. Taylor, eds, *Samuel Hartlib and Universal Reformation: Studies in Intellectual Communication* (Cambridge, 1994).
27 *Treatise of Justification*, sig. d3r–v, i. 17.
28 *Treatise of Justification*, i. 36–41.

simply in the remission of sins, which was secured by Christ's 'passive obedience' (his death on the Cross).[29] Thus the righteousness of the justified sinner was 'negative' (he was not guilty), rather than positive (for he was not clothed in Christ's works of righteousness).[30] Justification was a single act of God, by which he pronounced that the believing sinner was forgiven of his sins, or acquitted from condemnation.

Goodwin was also worried that 'the Antinomian Sect amongst us' would use the notion of the imputation of Christ's righteousness to 'justify their non-necessitie of personall sanctification or inherent holynesse'. If one was clothed in Christ's perfect righteousness, where was the need for sanctification? Indeed, Goodwin feared that the doctrine fostered blasphemous presumption. Was it not outrageous 'robbery' for 'a silly worme (a sinfull and contemptible creature) to take this robe of unmeasurable Majesty upon it, and to conceit it selfe as great in holinesse and righteousnesse as Jesus Christ himselfe'. Christ's righteousness was 'incommunicable' – the benefit of his righteousness was communicated to Christians through his sinless sacrifice on the Cross, but his righteousness itself was 'still his personall propriety'.[31] Of course, conservative Puritans like Walker did not draw antinomian conclusions from their doctrine, but as David Como has shown, an influential strain of 'imputative' antinomianism had developed within early Stuart Puritanism.[32]

Goodwin argued that he was simply defending 'the common interpretation anciently received and followed by the principall lights, (I meane the Fathers) of the Church of God, from the primitive times, and for 1500 yeares together (as far as my reading and memorie together will assist me), was never questioned or contradicted. Neither did the contrary opinion ever looke out into the world (at least was never contended for) till the yesterday of the last age'. To substantiate the claim, Goodwin quoted early church Fathers, medieval Schoolmen, sixteenth-century Protestants, and early Stuart divines. Aware of the importance of having Calvin's support, he spent eight pages examining the writings of the Reformer.[33] Whether Calvin and other Reformed writers really were on his side was highly debateable, but even if the majority report among Reformed divines favoured double imputation, there was an articulate and respected dissenting minority.

Having set forth his doctrine of justification in Part I of his *Treatise*, Goodwin used Part II to 'disarme our Enemies'. He analysed the various fine distinctions employed by the theologians, and offered a scholastic dissection of the 'severall causes' of justification – efficient, final, material and formal. He took on the proof texts of his opponents (four from the Old Testament, and nine from the New) and explained why they did not support the imputation of Christ's active righteousness.

---

29 *Treatise of Justification*, i. 17, 75.
30 *Treatise of Justification*, i. 76.
31 *Treatise of Justification*, i. 57, 108–111.
32 See David Como, *Blown by the Spirit: Puritanism and the Emergence of an Antinomian Underground in Pre-Civil War England* (Stanford, CA, 2004), esp. ch. 6: 'John Eaton, the Eatonists, and the "Imputative" Strain of English Antinomianism'.
33 *Treatise of Justification*, i. 44–54, 119–27; ii. 108–110.

And he answered a series of objections to the imputation of faith for righteousness.

Besides bolstering his position, Part II also revealed Goodwin's unconventional views on two other key doctrines. On original sin, Goodwin declared that 'The sinne of Adam is no where in Scripture said to be imputed to his posterity'. All men were born sinners, but Adam's sinful act was not imputed to them. Men were condemned 'not *for* Adams transgression, as *by* Adams transgression'. Because Adam, 'the fountaine and spring-head of all his posteritie', was poisoned and corrupted, he 'could not but sent forth streames of like corruption and defilement with the fountaine it selfe'. Thus the descendants of Adam inherited his polluted nature, and consequently his 'guilt and punishment'. By reformulating the doctrine of original sin, Goodwin aimed to make it more rational and equitable, as well as more congruent with his doctrine of justification.[34]

Goodwin also departed from the mainstream of Reformed thought on the atonement. Most Protestant theologians taught that God's just sentence on sinners had been executed on the crucified Christ. Goodwin took issue with this. 'The sentence or curse of the Law', he wrote, 'was not properly executed upon Christ in his death, but this death of Christ was a ground or consideration unto God, whereupon to dispence with his Law, and to let fall or suspend the execution of the penalty or curse therein'.[35] Although Goodwin did not reveal his source, he was advocating the governmental theory of the atonement developed by Grotius in his critique of the Socinians. Socinus had portrayed Christ as little more than a martyr and exemplar, and Grotius wrote in defence of 'the Catholic Faith' that Christ had been punished for man's sins. However, he did not reiterate the orthodox Reformed claim that Christ had borne the equivalent punishment that sinners deserved and hence cancelled their debts. God was not so much a creditor demanding the exact payment of debts, but a governor concerned to uphold the moral law. Christ did not suffer the penalty owed by the sinner (i.e. eternal death), but his death did vindicate the law and satisfy divine justice. It enabled God to forgive sins while still upholding the law.[36]

Goodwin used one of Grotius's own examples to illustrate the point. The ancient lawgiver Zaleucus caused 'one of his owne eyes to be put out, that one of his Sons eyes might be spared'. Zaleucus 'did not precisely execute the Law' (which would have required that his son lose both eyes), but by taking punishment on himself, he 'gave a sufficient account or consideration, why it should for that time be dispenced with, and not be put into execution'.[37] In the same way, Christ had died so that man would not be punished for his sins. His death was not the equivalent punishment due to sinners (since he did not suffer millions of eternal deaths), but it allowed God to forgive sinners and to uphold the moral law without

---

34 *Treatise of Justification*, ii. 13–16.
35 *Treatise of Justification*, ii. 33.
36 Hugo Grotius, *Defensio fidei Catholicae de satisfactione Christi adversus Faustum Socinum* (1617); English translation: Hugo Grotius, *A Defence of the Catholic Faith concerning the Satisfaction of Christ* (1692).
37 Grotius, *A Defence of the Catholic Faith*, 108–109.

executing it. In sparing transgressors, God 'manifestly dispenceth with the Law', wrote Goodwin, 'and doth not execute it'.[38]

In a recent essay on Goodwin and other Arminians, Mathew Pinson has argued that Goodwin 'betrayed an understanding of atonement and justification which had moved a great distance from Reformed orthodoxy and even beyond Arminius himself – and was much like that of Hugo Grotius'.[39] This was very much the view of Goodwin's critics, and it is not far off the mark. Goodwin's enthusiasm for Grotius is particularly significant, and it makes his later conversion to full-blown Arminianism less surprising. The Grotian theory of the atonement was more compatible with the doctrine of universal redemption than was the traditional penal theory (which left the puzzle of why unrepentant sinners should be punished in hell when Christ had borne their punishment on the cross). Throughout his writings, Goodwin echoes Grotius's stress on God's philanthrophy, his 'love to mankind', and this characteristically Arminian emphasis would gradually erode his Calvinism.[40]

It is misleading, however, to describe the *Treatise of Justification* as 'Arminian', let alone 'Socinian'. The Arminian controversy centred on the doctrine of predestination not the doctrine of justification, and a variety of Calvinist divines endorsed an understanding of justification similar to Goodwin's. Goodwin's comments on Arminius in the *Animadversions* were hostile, and he clearly adhered to the Calvinist doctrine of absolute predestination.[41] Although Grotius's doctrine of the atonement was controversial, it was still a theory of penal substitution, and was endorsed by a number of moderate Calvinists (including Richard Baxter). Moreover, Goodwin was emphatic in defending the Deity of Christ against the Socinians.[42]

Surprisingly, *A Treatise of Justification* did not attract a response from George Walker. But Walker's old ally Henry Roborough, rector of St Leonards, Eastcheap, did publish a lengthy reply to both the *Treatise* and the *Animadversions* entitled *The Doctrine of Justification Cleared* (1643). In an introductory epistle to the ministers of London, Roborough urged them to 'interpose your selves to the setling of our brother'. He fully supported Walker's charges against Goodwin, and insisted that 'all Orthodox Divines' had taught the imputation of Christ's righteousness against Papists and Arminians.[43]

Roborough had the final word in this controversy, and Goodwin's critics claimed that he had been vanquished.[44] However, Richard Baxter later wrote that 'John Goodwin (not yet turned Arminian) preached and wrote with great diligence about Justification against the rigid sence of Imputation, who being answered by Mr

---

38 *Treatise of Justification*, ii. 33–36.
39 J. Matthew Pinson, 'The diversity of Arminian soteriology: Thomas Grantham, John Goodwin and Jacobus Arminius', http://generalbaptist.net/resources/FWBBC/arminian_soteriology.htm
40 See Grotius, *A Defence of the Catholic Faith*, 3, 63.
41 See for example, *Treatise of Justification*, i. 63; ii. 179–81.
42 *Treatise of Justification*, i. 112.
43 Roborough, *Doctrine of Justification*, sig. A3v, 1.
44 See Thomas Edwards, *Gangraena* (1646), ii. 70; William Jenkyn, *The Blinde Guide* (1648), 13.

Walker and Mr Roborough, with far inferiour strength, his book had the greater success for such answerers'. Goodwin's *Treatise* was among the small number of books that Baxter recommended to his readers on this subject.[45] Indeed, one of Baxter's critics noted with chagrin 'how highly he magnifies J. Goodwin, with others of his notion, and how slightingly he mentions Dr. Twisse, and all our Protestant Divines that differ from him'.[46] However, Baxter recognised that 'because J. G. turned to the Arminians, prejudice cryed down his Doctrine of Justification, (and it was not all to be approved)'.[47]

Despite this, Goodwin's *Treatise* continued to be read and recommended for several decades after its publication. In *Ecclesiastes* (1647), the standard reading list for preachers compiled by John Wilkins, Goodwin's *Treatise* was on the shortlist of key works on justification, and was only displaced in the eighth edition of 1679.[48] Clement Barksdale, an Anglican royalist divine who translated Grotius and was a close ally of Henry Hammond, naturally deplored Goodwin's Parliamentarian polemics, but was so pleased with *A Treatise of Justification* that he wrote a verse praising Goodwin's 'Learning and his Temper'.[49]

Baxter's moderate Calvinism, Wilkins's latitudinarianism, and Hammond's pious Anglicanism have all been credited (or blamed) with promoting a shift away from Reformed orthodoxy. In their stress on the reasonableness of Christianity and the importance of holy living, these divines have been depicted as key figures in the rise of a Christianity that elevated reason above revelation, works above faith, human agency above divine grace, and right living above right doctrine. In *The Rise of Moralism*, Christopher Allison argued that the doctrine of justification played a pivotal role in this theological sea-change, and he included Goodwin among the moralisers.[50]

Allison's thesis, however, needs to be treated with caution. In the first place, it reflects a widespread tendency in twentieth-century scholarship to exaggerate the 'liberalism' and 'rationalism' of seventeenth-century theologians. Secondly, by lumping so many disparate figures together, Allison papered over the cracks that separate them. Isabel Rivers, by contrast, detects a fundamental difference between 'Anglican moralism' and the Puritan 'religion of grace' defended by Baxter, though she too may overemphasise the moralism and rationalism of the Anglicans.[51]

Goodwin himself had no doubt that his *Treatise of Justification* upheld the Reformation principles of *sola fides* and *sola gratia*. For him, as for Luther,

---

45 Richard Baxter, *A Treatise of Imputed Righteousness* (1675), 21, 47.
46 William Eyre, *Vindiciae Iustificationis Gratuitae* (London, 1654), sig. A3r.
47 Richard Baxter, *A Breviate of the Doctrine of Justification* (1690), sig. A2r.
48 John Wilkins, *Ecclesiastes: Or, A Discourse Concerning the Gift of Preaching* (1647), 76. Goodwin's Treatise is also listed in the editions of 1653, 1656, 1669 and 1675.
49 [Clement Barksdale], *Nympha Liberthris, or The Cotswold Muse* (1651), 85.
50 C. F. Allison, *The Rise of Moralism* (London, 1966), 164–66.
51 I. Rivers, *Reason, Grace and Sentiment: A Study in the Language of Religion and Ethics, 1660–1780*, vol. i: *Whichcote to Wesley* (Cambridge, 1991). For an alternative reading of Anglican theology, which stresses its traditional accent on sin and the need for atonement, see W. M. Spellman, *The Latitudinarians and the Church of England, 1660–1700* (Athens, GA, 1993).

justification was a forensic act of God, whereby he imputed righteousness to the sinner by pronouncing him forgiven on account of faith alone. Goodwin rejected outright the Roman Catholic claim that justification was the process by which men were made just by being infused with inherent righteousness. The process by which the sinner became holy was sanctification, and was not to be confused with justification. Furthermore, Goodwin insisted that faith was not to be regarded as a work which fulfilled God's new law, or as something with 'inherent dignity, or merit'. It was simply the condition of justification, 'which justifyeth him' not 'by virtue of its inherent worth', but 'by the free and gracious acceptation of it by God'.[52]

Despite this, the dispute damaged Goodwin's reputation. When the Westminster Assembly of Divines was established in 1643, Walker was appointed as a voting member (and Roborough as a scribe), but Goodwin was excluded. Suspicions of unsoundness were hard to dispel, though it should be noted that Goodwin's position on justification was also defended by a minority in the Westminster Assembly, including such eminent figures as Thomas Gataker, Richard Vines and William Twisse.[53] Unlike Walker, many Puritan divines viewed this position as within the bounds of orthodoxy. Goodwin's cause may have been harmed more by his satirical response to the older man, which was probably viewed as a serious breach of ministerial etiquette. Accusing another minister of heresy and blasphemy was apparently acceptable; ridiculing a fellow divine was beyond the pale. Goodwin would pay a heavy price for defending himself against the most inflammatory of theological charges.

The Road to Civil War

As well as publishing works of theology, Goodwin issued three small books of sermons between August and December 1640, and another in May 1641. These publications were works of practical divinity, but they were also interventions into the contemporary crisis inaugurated by the recall of Parliament. Their dedicatory epistles offer an insight into the alliances that Goodwin had formed with key figures in the Puritan-Parliamentary movement. *The Saints Interest in God* was dedicated to Alderman Isaac Pennington and 'the rest of my loving Parishioners', who were 'a teachable, wise, and tractable people'. The bond between the pastor and his flock was 'precious', and Goodwin testified that they 'rejoiced in my light' and in 'the truth, life and power which you have seen, tasted and felt in my Ministry.'[54]

---

52 *Treatise of Justification*, 148.
53 See C. van Dixhoorn, 'Reforming the Reformation: Theological Debate in the Westminster Assembly, 1643–1652', (unpublished Ph.D. dissertation, University of Cambridge, 2004), ch. 5. See *Minutes of the Westminster Assembly of Divines*, ed. A. F. Mitchell and J. Struthers (London, 1874), 154–60. Thomas Gataker, however, chose not to publish the sermons on justification he had begun to preach in April 1640, and they were only published posthumously by his son. See Thomas Gataker, *An Antidote against Errour concerning Justification* (1679), sig. B.
54 *The Saints Interest in God*, sigs. A4r–a5v.

Goodwin's fame across the City helped to make Coleman Street one of the key organising centres of political and religious radicalism. The most prominent godly parishioners played a vital role in the Parliamentarian movement. Pennington was elected as a City MP for both the Short and the Long Parliaments of 1640, and would quickly emerge as the most important leader of the City's radicals between 1640 and 1643. William Spurstow was MP for Shrewsbury, and he too would help to forge the radical alliance in the City and Parliament. Sir Thomas Wroth was once again MP for Bridgewater, and during the 1640s he would be a steadfast supporter of Parliament and of the political Independents in particular.[55]

Goodwin had also formed relationships with key Puritan politicians. On 14 October 1640, just a few weeks before the Long Parliament assembled, he dedicated *God a Good Master* to Elizabeth Hampden of Westminster, mother of John Hampden, who had been imprisoned in 1627 for refusing to pay the Forced Loan and had sparked controversy in the mid-1630s by refusing to pay Ship Money. Hampden had been one of the most influential MPs in the Short Parliament, and he would be a key ally of Pym in the Long Parliament. Goodwin had clearly become a valued spiritual counsellor to Elizabeth, and he thanked her for her 'respects, and many expressions of love' towards him.[56]

Once the Long Parliament opened in November 1640, John Pym quickly emerged as the leader of the Parliamentary opposition to the policies of the 1630s. On 4 December 1640, Goodwin dedicated *The Christians Engagement for the Gospel* 'To the Worshipful and Much Honoured John Pymme Esquire'. He noted that Pym had 'beene knowne to my selfe, heretofore by some particular acquaintance', but confessed that the 'discontinuance and decrease' of their relationship was due to Goodwin's own 'negligence in addressing my selfe to you'. However, he knew Pym well enough to declare, 'I know you are in for the Gospell, with all your heart, and with all your soule'. He assured Pym that he and the other worthies in Parliament were engaged in a 'great work ... the rescue, and advancement of the Gospell'. Their 'worthy Senate' had 'opened a doore of hope to a Land and People brought very low'. Alluding to Ezekiel's apocalyptic vision of the valley of dry bones, Goodwin declared that Pym and his colleagues were breathing life into the dry bones and initiating a national renewal that would continue apace 'till the throne, and kingdome of Jesus Christ bee lifted up on high'.[57]

The millenarian tone of the dedicatory epistle highlights the great hopes Goodwin had invested in the Long Parliament and in Pym. Although the sermons in *The Saints Interest* and *The Christians Engagement* had originally been preached in the 1630s, their publication was Goodwin's contribution to the new drive for reformation. The Gunpowder Plot sermons in *The Saints Interest* fed the fierce anti-popery that would fuel the Parliamentarian cause, while *The Christians Engagement* urged the godly to contend for the faith and participate in 'that great victorie of the Lambe over the Beast'.

---

55 See *ODNB* articles. Kirby, 'Parish', 53–54 notes that several other MPs had links to the parish.
56 *God a Good Master*, 'Epistle Dedicatory'.
57 *The Christians Engagement*, 'Epistle Dedicatory'.

God a Good Master was a fast-day sermon on Isaiah 58, the classic biblical text concerning true fasting. Goodwin declared that 'wherever a city, nation, or people, did humble themselves before God (especially with prayer and fasting) ... the windowes of Heaven were opened upon it, and the blessings and mercies sued for, powred doune upon them'.[58] But England had no hope unless:

> the whoredomes of Jezabel, the abominable Idolatries, and superstitions of that mother of abominations be taken from between our breasts, except the blood, wherewith the land now for many yeares together hath beene polluted, be some wayes purged and attoned, except there be some short worke made ... with the Agents and Factours for the Sea of Rome amonst us ... the rich give over his trade of grinding the faces of the poore, & live upon that which is their own ... except the great profaneness of the land, cease from the hearts and mouthes of men: in a word, except there be a reformation.[59]

Goodwin warned that if the English were impenitent, they would 'turne the God of all grace, into a consuming fire'. Failure to serve God accounted for 'all the wrath and indignation of the Almightie that is powred out in fire and blood upon the earth, upon the heads of Kings and Princes, of Kingdomes and Nations, of Cities and People'. But if the English embraced the service of God, they could be assured that God was a good master who would hear their prayers and have mercy.[60]

This sermon, published shortly before the opening of the Long Parliament, articulated a Puritan programme of moral and religious reformation – an attack on popish idolatry, Romish conspiracy, profaneness, and the oppression of the poor. It had a politically radical edge, above all in its willingness to contemplate the wrath of God poured out 'upon the heads of Kings and Princes'. Regicide was not on Goodwin's mind in 1640, but basic concepts of blood guilt and divine judgement on monarchs were already in place.

It is hardly surprising then that Goodwin's parishioners played an important role in the radicalisation of City politics during the autumn of 1640. Isaac Pennington, re-elected to Parliament in November 1640, quickly became the leading voice of the City radicals. According to Clarendon, Pennington was 'a man in highest confidence with the party [of Pym and Hampden], and one who insinuated all things to the Common Council which he was directed should be started there'.[61] Brenner has suggested that 'It may have been through Goodwin that Pennington established his ties with John Hampden and John Pym', a conjecture based on Goodwin's dedicatory epistles in 1640.[62]

The early days of the Long Parliament were euphoric ones for the godly. In late November, the Puritan martyrs William Prynne and Henry Burton were welcomed into the City by ecstatic crowds. Prynne was soon to become one of

---

58 *God a Good Master*, 84.
59 *God a Good Master*, 116–17.
60 *God a Good Master*, 120, 108.
61 Edward Hyde, Earl of Clarendon, *The History of the Rebellion and Civil Wars in England*, ed. W. D. Macray, 6 vols (Oxford, 1888), Bk. iii, § 92.
62 R. Brenner, *Merchants and Revolution: Commercial Change, Political Conflict, and London's Overseas Traders, 1550–1653* (Princeton, NJ, 1993), 323.

Goodwin's bitterest foes, but as John Vicars later recalled Goodwin's followers had (with other Puritans) 'brought him home from banishment, as it were in the triumphing Chariot of your love and praises!'[63] Galvanised by such visible signs of the turning of the tide, the City radicals sprang into action. On 11 December, Pennington presented Parliament with a 'root and branch' petition signed by 15–20,000 Londoners, demanding the abolition of episcopacy.

Although Parliament was unwilling to accede to such radical demands at this stage, it did need the City's money to pay the Scottish army. Because the aldermen were reluctant to advance much money, Parliament quickly began to go directly to common hall for its loans using Pennington as its middleman. This was a tactical triumph for the radicals, because common hall was 'the only City institution in which the London parliamentary militants, still a militant minority on the common council (not to mention the court of aldermen), were politically dominant'. On 23 January 1641, Pennington made it clear that the freemen would only lend the House £60,000 if they put pressure on the king to dismiss delinquents from his court and execute the condemned Catholic priest John Goodman. Parliament responded by asking the king to crack down on papists and execute Goodman. It also ordered a commission to destroy altars in churches and gave a first reading on 5 February to Pennington's bill for abolishing superstition and idolatry and settling true religion.[64]

When Parliament debated the root and branch bill on 8 February, a number of MPs tried to prevent its consideration on the grounds that it had been 'tumultuarily brought'. Pennington leapt to the citizens' defence, and two days later he responded to a request for more money by saying that 'they were much discouraged by some malevolent speeches'. As arguments over finances continued, Pennington told Parliament on 1 March that the citizens would deliver their promised funds if a delegation of ten MPs were sent to the City. Besides the four City MPs, the list included Hampden, Pym, Denzil Holles, Nathaniel Fiennes, Sir Walter Earle and Sir Henry Vane the younger.[65] Goodwin must have known several of these men personally, and the City radicals also had connections with militant MPs like Simonds D'Ewes, Sir Thomas Barrington, Sir Henry Marten and Sir Arthur Haselrig.

It was Haselrig who made the crucial move in the campaign for the execution of the Earl of Strafford. After the opening of his treason trial on 22 March, the radical citizens circulated a petition calling for his execution and the reform of the church, and Haselrig made his motion for Strafford's attainder. On 21 April, a crowd of up to 10,000 Londoners walked to Westminster to present their petition against Strafford to Parliament. Pennington was one of those who presented it, and many other Coleman Street parishioners must have been among the crowd or at least among the 20–30,000 signatories. This mass mobilisation combined with strictly conditional offers of financial assistance placed considerable pressure on

---

63 John Vicars, *To his Reverend and Much Respected Good Friend, Mr John Goodwin* (1645), 3.
64 Brenner, *Merchants*, 329–31.
65 Brenner, *Merchants*, 331–36.

Parliament, which eventually approved the attainder. With great reluctance, the king agreed to the attainder on 10 May, and on 12 May Strafford was executed before a vast crowd on Tower Hill.[66] It seems likely that Goodwin was present to witness the death of the delinquent. Throughout the revolutionary era he showed no compunction about the death of Parliament's enemies whether in battle or on the scaffold. This ruthless streak combined with a powerful ideological vision of reformation would make him a genuine revolutionary.

Strafford's execution was simply the most dramatic of the Long Parliament's actions in its first year. By August 1641, after a burst of legislative activism, Parliament had passed a Triennial Act, imprisoned Archbishop Laud in the Tower, ended Ship Money, forest fines, and other controversial measures, and abolished the Star Chamber and the Courts of High Commission. But City radicals like Pennington wished to go further still, and in the second half of 1641 they continued to throw their weight behind a programme of reform in both the City and Westminster. On 8 August, Pennington persuaded the Commons to order the destruction of altar rails and the removal of the Laudian communion tables. In September, he supported Cromwell's motion that the House legalise the actions of parishioners who took it upon themselves to hire Puritan lecturers.[67]

However, the willingness of Pennington and other London radicals to push for ecclesiastical change frightened social and religious conservatives, and Pym was concerned at alienating potential supporters. In November 1641, shortly after Parliament had re-adjourned after its summer recess, a number of leading English Puritan clergy met at the house of Edmund Calamy. Thomas Edwards, who was among those present, described it as 'a full and great meeting'. The congregational way was represented by the returned exiles, Thomas Goodwin, Nye, Burroughs, Simpson and Bridge. John Goodwin was also present, and may already have been aligned with the Congregationalists. The ministers were 'sensible how much our differences, and divisions might distract the Parliament, and hinder the taking away of Episcopall government'. Determined to present a common front, they agreed on three short-term policies to enhance the credibility of their campaign against the bishops: they would continue using the Book of Common Prayer; they would persuade their sectarian allies to take a lower profile; and they would avoid publicising their differences over church government. All the ministers also signed an agreement to preach against Anabaptists and Separatists.[68]

November 1641 proved to be a critical turning point on the road to Civil War. In the wake of a Catholic rebellion in Ireland, horrific stories began to circulate of atrocities and massacres against Protestant settlers. Parliament responded with a drive to raise finances for a relief force. On 14 November, Goodwin preached an anti-popish fundraising sermon which was immediately published by William Larner under the title *Irelands Advocate*. He urged his hearers

---

66 Brenner, *Merchants*, 337–41.
67 Brenner, *Merchants*, 351–52.
68 See T. Webster, *Godly Clergy in Early Stuart England* (Cambridge, 1997), 330–31. See also Goodwin's *Anapologesiastes Antapologia* (1646), 252.

to make 'liberall contributions by way of lending ... to redeeme the lives and liberties and estates of your poore Brethren the Protestants in Ireland'. The situation was desperate – 'that faction of Hell, the Romish party' had an army of 30,000 men that was growing daily, while the settlers were 'few in number ... naked, and unarm'd ... as a flock of Kids, before an Host, or Army of Lyons'. Their defencelessness was Strafford's fault, who at least 'hath made some part of atonement for that and other outrages, with his head'. The 'bloody, barbarous' Irish were devoid of 'all mercie, pittie, and compassion', and would respect 'neither age, nor sex, neither young-men, nor Maids, neither old-men, nor Babes, but all are one before the rage of their cruelty'. They were determined to destroy Protestantism in order to advance their 'breaden God' and 'the Catholique cause', and had already committed 'barbarous villainies and outrages'.[69]

Now was the time for England's Protestants to reveal their true selves. By making 'free and liberall contributions' they would discourage the rebels, and prevent the rebellion spreading to England. 'Ireland is not unfitly termed a back doore into England', Goodwin remarked, and it would not do 'to have the Pope keeper of the keyes of your back doore'. Goodwin did not want to hear excuses: 'Wife and Children, and charge, and poverty, and want of moneys, and occasions of disbursements otherwise, with a thousand other such insinuations as these, must with Sathan himselfe be commanded to get them behind us'.[70] Goodwin's exhortations caused his hearers to dig deep into their pockets. The parish collected the great sum of £1170 for the relief of the Irish Protestants.[71]

Amidst the general panic induced by news of the rebellion, Pym introduced the Grand Remonstrance to Parliament on 8 November. It was a lengthy indictment of government policy between 1625 and 1640, with a particular accent on the popish plot against English Protestantism. Although it was eventually passed on 23 November, it deeply divided the Commons, with 159 votes for and 148 against. Two days later, the City's conservative magistrates (who dominated the Court of Aldermen and the Common Council) laid on a spectacular celebration to welcome the king on his visit to the City. In response the City radicals drew up another petition signed by some 15,000 Londoners, which declared that despite 'the King's late entertainment in the City', the citizens were still loyal to Parliament. They called for the removal of bishops and Catholic peers from the House of Lords, demanded parliamentary control over the militia, and called for the overhaul of City government. On 11 December, the petition was presented to the Commons by Pennington. Their campaign had a major impact on the Common Council elections, held on 21 December. A host of new men were elected, ardent supporters of Pym and Pennington, who wasted no time in demanding a vote for all the City's freemen. Emboldened by this success, Pennington presented yet another monster petition, signed by 30,000 Londoners, calling for root and branch reform of the church. Among those organising the drive for signatures was Deputy Daniel Taylor,

---

69 *Irelands Advocate* (1641), 26–29.
70 *Irelands Advocate*, 30–35.
71 GL MS4458/1, f. 145.

one of Goodwin's most devoted supporters.[72]

By now the dangerous divide between the king's supporters and the Parliament's supporters was becoming ever clearer. The king rejected the Grand Remonstrance, and on 5 January 1642 he came to the house with a troop of soldiers to arrest five treasonous MPs including Pym. The politicians had had prior warning and they escaped from Westminster and took refuge in the City. One of the parishes to which they fled was Coleman Street.[73] Given the fervent support given to Pym by both Goodwin and Pennington, it is hardly surprising that some of Goodwin's parishioners were involved in sheltering the fugitive MPs. Two key figures in the parish were the new merchants, Owen Rowe and James Russell, who were both appointed to the City's Militia Committee.[74]

The Militia Committee attracted strong criticism from conservative Londoners on the Court of Aldermen and Common Council, but in the spring and summer of 1642, the radicals achieved what Brenner calls 'a full-scale constitutional revolution to break the old form of oligarchic rule'.[75] They removed the power of veto from the Court of Aldermen and ended the Lord Mayor's power to convene and dissolve Common Council meetings. From the summer of 1642, Common Council was firmly in charge of City government, and power had been shifted from oligarchic cliques to the generality of the City freemen. Among the 'new men' elected to Common Council were three Coleman Street parishioners: Samuel Avery, Caleb Cockcroft and James Russell.[76] When the archroyalist Lord Mayor, Sir Richard Gurney tried to block the changes, Rowe and Russell took a leading role in his dismissal, by petitioning the House of Lords and giving evidence before Parliament. On 12 August 1642, Common Hall elected Isaac Pennington the new Lord Mayor.[77] Goodwin's parishioners had played a vital role in the radical capture of the City government.

When Civil War finally broke out in August 1642, Goodwin's godly parishioners sided overwhelmingly with Parliament. Among them were several MPs who had backed 'root and branch' reform of the church and worked with John Pym. Besides Pennington, they were William Spurstow (MP for Shrewsbury), and the Wiltshire MP Sir John Evelyn, who was lodging in Coleman Street in 1641.[78] Of the other prominent parishioners for whom we have information, almost every one sided with Parliament. It is significant that no fewer than five parishioners who were members of the East India or Levant companies—Thomas Barnardiston, Caleb

---

72 A. Woolrych, *Britain in Revolution, 1625–1660* (Oxford, 2002), 199–204, 208–09; Brenner, *Merchants*, 361–71; V. Pearl, *London and the Outbreak of the Puritan Revolution: City Government and National Politics, 1625–43* (London, 1961), 132–40.
73 Clarendon, *History of the Rebellion*, Bk. iv, § 162.
74 Brenner, *Merchants*, 370–71.
75 Brenner, *Merchants*, 372.
76 K. Lindley, *Popular Politics and Religion in Civil War London* (Aldershot, 1997), 193 n.175. On Rowe and Russell, see Pearl, *London*, 324–25.
77 Brenner, *Merchants*, 372–73.
78 Kirby, 'Parish', 53–54. For Evelyn's Coleman Street residence see T. C. Dale, *The Poll Tax for London 1641* (1935), 3.

Cockcroft, Caldwell Farrington, Pennington and William Spurstow – backed Parliament in 1642, even though the majority of East India-Levant merchants were royalist. Of these traditional merchants, only Pennington was politically radical, but the fact that they were Parliamentarians at all is significant.[79] Furthermore, two of the three Merchant Adventurers who backed the radicals' takeover of City government in 1642 were members of Goodwin's parish – Russell and Cockcroft. The third was William Walwyn, a man who must have already been well known to Goodwin's followers. There were two other Merchant Adventurers in Goodwin's parish – Samuel Avery also supported Parliament, and Andrew Kendrick, who initially aligned himself with the royalists before becoming Parliamentarian.[80] The fact that these men went against the majority of their colleagues among the traditional merchant elite provides striking evidence that a commitment to zealous Protestantism could incline people towards Parliament even when their social position might have made them likely royalists. Having sat under Goodwin's ministry, these men would have been left in little doubt as to which side God was on. It seems certain that Goodwin spent the spring and summer of 1642 persuading his parishioners to do their godly duty by backing Parliament, and his success confirms recent scholarship on the role of Puritan clergy as Parliamentarian recruiters.[81]

Goodwin's less socially prominent godly followers also sided with Parliament. Men of the middling sort, like Mark Hildesley, John Price and Daniel Taylor, were zealously Parliamentarian, though they would only occupy political offices after the Independent coup of 1648. Significantly, these figures also identified Goodwin's gathered church in 1645, whereas the leading men of the parish did not. Thus there does seem to be a rough correlation between social status and ideological commitments – socially prominent members of the merchant elite did back Parliament, but only Pennington, Russell and Cockcroft were politically radical, and even they remained in the parish in 1645 rather than joining Goodwin's gathered church; men of more modest social standing like Price and Taylor were committed political radicals who came to form the backbone of Goodwin's Independent congregation and were personally close to Leveller leaders like Walwyn.

By the outbreak of Civil War, Goodwin's followers had forged important alliances in the City and at Westminster. In the City, they were linked with radical new merchants like Maurice Thompson and Robert Tichborne, who would remain close to Goodwin's followers throughout the 1640s. They were already also familiar with the future Leveller leaders, Walwyn, Lilburne and Richard Overton. Walwyn and Overton, for example, had signed the same citizens' petitions as Richard Price, and another signatory was Henry Robinson, a leading tolerationist in the mid-1640s. As both Brenner and Lindley have shown, future radicals and political Independents dominated the City's militant politics in 1641–42, and relationships

---

79 Brenner, *Merchants*, 379–81.
80 Brenner, *Merchants*, 384–87.
81 See M. Stoyle, *Loyalty and Locality: Popular Allegiance in Devon during the English Civil War* (Exeter, 1994).

formed at this time were to last throughout the 1640s.[82] Many of Goodwin's followers were longstanding members of the Honourable Artillery Company, which had long been associated with Puritanism and was now under the firm leadership of Philip Skippon, a godly Parliamentarian who had fought under Sir Horace Vere. Men like Rowe, Hildesley, Taylor, Nathaniel Lacy and Overton were familiar with practising military drill at the Artillery Garden, and were now ready to defend their City if necessary. Goodwin himself may have enrolled or preached before the Company in 1642–43.[83] At Westminster, Pennington had worked closely with Pym and other Puritan MPs like D'Ewes, Hampden, St John, Cromwell, Haselrig, Miles Corbet and Sir Henry Vane the younger. Goodwin certainly knew Pym, Hampden, St John and Corbet, and he was probably familiar with other MPs and with the leading Puritan aristocrats in the House of Lords like Saye and Sele, Brooke and Warwick.

Perhaps the most revealing piece of evidence about the emerging alliances among militant Parliamentarians dates from September 1642, shortly after the outbreak of the Civil War. Parliament had already announced its intention to call a synod of divines to debate a new ecclesiastical settlement, and the New England Congregationalists – Cotton, Hooker and Davenport – were approached to participate. The signatories to the letter comprise a roll call of the militant core of the Puritan-Parliamentarian movement: the Earl of Warwick, Lord Saye and Lord Brooke; Nathaniel Fiennes, Oliver Cromwell, Arthur Haselrig, Oliver St John, Henry Marten, Valentine Walton and Miles Corbet. Also among the signatories were two of Goodwin's parishioners, Isaac Pennington and William Spurstow.[84]

Many of the signatories were supporters of the Additional Sea Adventure to Ireland in 1642, which raised funds to send an independent military force to relieve Irish Protestants. The project was spearheaded by City militants, backed by godly aristocrats and new merchants, and by Independent ministers like Jeremiah Burroughs and Hugh Peter, with whom Goodwin was now closely associated.[85] Several of Goodwin's followers supported the fund, and his parishioners invested heavily in the Irish Adventurers scheme: Pennington advanced £1000, John LaMotte £600, Thomas Barnardiston £200, Goodwin and Hildesley £100 each.[86]

---

82 Lindley, *Popular Politics*, 391.
83 See G. A. Raikes, *The Ancient Vellum Book of the Honourable Artillery Company being the Roll of Members from 1611–1682* (1890), 64, 69 (for 'John Goodwin'). On the role of Puritans within the Company see Pearl, *London*, 170–73.
84 The letter can be found in T. Hutchinson, *The History of the Colony of Massachusetts Bay*, 2nd edn (London, 1765), 116. It is reprinted in *The Correspondence of John Cotton*, ed. S. Bush jr (Chapel Hill, NC, 2001), 362–65. The New Englanders chose not to attend the synod, largely because this allowed them to openly espouse the congregational way. See F. Bremer, *Congregational Communion: Clerical Friendship in the Anglo-American Puritan Community, 1610–1692* (Boston, MA, 1994), 134–35.
85 Brenner, *Merchants*, 400–10.
86 See J. R. Prendergast, *The Cromwellian Settlement of Ireland* (Dublin, 1922), 401–48, which prints the lists of investors in both the Irish Adventurers and the Additional Sea Adventure.

Anti-Cavalierisme

Goodwin's most important contribution to the cause was his pamphlet, *Anti-Cavalierisme, or Truth Pleading as well the Necessity as the Lawfulness of this Present War*. The case for Parliament's resistance had already been powerfully articulated in Henry Parker's *Observations* (July 1642), but *Anti-Cavalierisme* added something fresh to the case for war. It was essentially a sermon in print, and it possessed a homiletic energy and directness lacking in more theoretical writings. As William Haller noted, 'Goodwin was not a statesman or a political philosopher. He was a preacher' who 'set out to rouse the people to resistance as a duty'.[87] Published by Henry Overton, the tract was collected by Thomason on 21 October 1642, just two days before the first major encounter of the Civil War, the battle of Edgehill.

Anti-Cavalierisme opened by demonising Parliament's enemies, 'that bloody and butcherly Generation, commonly knowne by the name of Cavaliers'. Having managed to take possession of the king, they were now set on a series of 'desperate designes': to destroy Parliament, to root out the saints, to spoil goods and possessions, to resurrect clerical 'Hierarchie', to restore 'Popish error and superstition', and finally 'to make rubbidge' of the king himself. This was a moment of great crisis which called for total mobilisation. Men should volunteer their bodies for war, open their 'Purses and Estates', use their 'heads' to contrive ways of proceeding, and pray from their hearts for 'the Armies of the Lord'.[88]

Having issued his rallying cry, Goodwin then set out two motives for Parliamentarians: the first was that their cause was just (pp. 5–36), the second was that it was supremely important (pp. 35–51). Parliament's cause was just, because it was essentially defensive. It supporters were fighting 'in the defence of your Lives, your Liberties, your Estates, your Houses, your Wives, your Children'; in defence of Parliament; in defence of 'his Majesties royall person, honour and estate'; and 'in defence of the true Protestant Religion'. Goodwin reiterated the point that Parliament's quarrel was not with the King, but with 'that accursed retinue of vile persons that are gathered about him, as Ivie about an Oake'. Parliamentarians had no intention of 'offering violence to the person of the King, or attempting to take away his life', and believed that kings should be 'secure from the violence of men'. Their lives were 'as consecrated Corne, meet to be reaped and gathered only by the hand of God himselfe'.[89] Unsurprisingly, these lines were flung back in Goodwin's face after the regicide, and they already looked pretty implausible after Edgehill, when the King was in some danger from Parliamentarian fire. Indeed, it was hard to avoid the impression that Goodwin was paying lip service to Charles I while undermining his standing at every turn. The tract argued explicitly for armed resistance against kings, and cited provocative examples of idolatrous monarchs like Ahab, Nebuchadnezzar and Jeroboam.[90]

---

87 W. Haller, *The Rise of Puritanism* (New York, 1938), 373.
88 *Anti-Cavalierisme* (1642), 1–5.
89 *Anti-Cavalierisme*, 5, 10–11.
90 *Anti-Cavalierisme*, 11, 18, 21.

Goodwin did not shy away from the objection that it was unlawful to 'resist the King the Lords anointed'. To counter this objection, Goodwin appealed to the natural law contract theory which had served Protestant resistance theorists so well in the sixteenth century.[91] Firstly, he explained that governments were not natural, God-given institutions. They were the 'creation, or creature of man'. God allowed human societies to establish whatever form of government they choose, whether democratic, aristocracy or kingly. Kingly government was not by divine right, as was suggested by royalist divines intent on 'swelling the Prerogative of Kings to a monstrous and most unnaturall proportion'. And kings were not the only ones to be obeyed – 'inferiour Magistracy' and 'subordinate Rulers' were also worthy of obedience. Secondly, obedience and submission to rulers was 'never intended by God to be universall, but with limitation'. Government was created by the people, and they could not confer any power upon rulers 'to doe unjustly'. In setting up political authority, 'reasonable men' would not have given 'a power to injure, or to wrong either them or their posterity'. If a people made a contract 'inconsistent with reason and common sence', such an act would be 'a meere nullitie'. And if a king violated the terms of his contract, and started to make unlawful commands, he could be resisted. Such resistance would initially be passive – thus the early Christians had resisted unlawful commands, and patiently accepted the punishment that followed. But sometimes 'the unlawfull command of a King' was such that it could not be resisted other than by 'taking up Armes'. Thus David, though a private individual, had gathered 'a strength of men and armes to him, whereby to make resistance against [King] Saul'. Parliamentarians were now in a situation just like David – their very lives were threatened by Irish cutthroats, who 'either have, or pretend to have a Warrant or Commission from the King … to make prey and spoile of you'. In such a plight, armed resistance was justified.[92]

Royalists, of course, had another objection: 'who shall be Judge in this case, Whether the command or commission of a King … be unjust, or no?' Goodwin replied that in cases like this, the 'unlawfulnesse' of the king's command was 'written with such Capitall Letters, that he that runs may read it'. Moreover, if it was unlawful for 'inferiours to examine and enquire into the commands of Kings, and other their Superiours', then the people must regard their rulers as 'equall with God', infallible and incapable of error. This was 'blasphemy'. Kings and other rulers were fallible men, and their people had both a liberty and a duty 'of examining the Commands of Superiours'. The apostles themselves had urged their hearers to examine their doctrines. If this was true of the apostles, who received direct inspiration from heaven, how much more was it true of kings, who enjoyed no such privilege? The Old Testament indicated that God was angry with 'those who have swallowed the commands of Kings', and it illustrated how an uncritical people could ruin a ruler by failing to warn him when he went astray. 'When men or

---

91 See Q. Skinner, *The Foundations of Modern Political Thought*, vol. ii: *The Age of Reformation* (Cambridge, 1978), 318–48; J. Sommerville, *Royalists and Patriots: Politics and Ideology in England, 1603–1640* (Harlow, 1999), ch. 2.
92 *Anti-Cavalierisme*, 6–18.

women shall make Idols of Kings and Princes, and great men, and fall downe before them ... what doe they else but shake the very foundations of their lives ... and call for the fire of God's jealousie from heaven to consume them?'[93]

There was a further objection to the justice of Parliament's war. Did not the primitive Christians suffer the tyranny of Emperors, and refuse to arm themselves against persecution? Had not the early Church Father Tertullian explicitly rejected armed resistance as unchristian? Goodwin devoted fourteen pages to answering this objection. He suggested that the early Christians were relatively few in number, and they had no authorisation from any lawful authority in the empire to resist by force of arms. Their case was 'farre differing from ours, who are invited, countenanced, encouraged, and some waies commanded by as great and as lawfull an Authority as this state hath' to take up arms against 'the rage and violence of that malignant and bloodthirsty generation'. The 'Parliamentary Assembly is the whole body of the Nation', wrote Goodwin, and as such it certainly had the authority to command resistance.[94]

Goodwin capped his reply to Tertullian with a remarkable, if somewhat bizarre, argument about sacred history. If lawful resistance had been taught by the Church, he reasoned, it would have 'caused an abortion in Antichrists birth', and he would have been unable to ascend to 'that *Cathedram pestilentiae*, that chaire of papall state'. Men's consciences had been 'cowed' as they were indoctrinated by 'doctrines and tenents, excessively advancing the power of superiours, over inferiours, and binding Iron yokes and heavy burthens upon those that were in subjection'. By permitting this ideology of domination and submission to flourish, God had enabled sacred history to move forward into its darkest phase. Now however, the situation was reversed. The reign of Antichrist was coming to a close and his downfall was 'drawing neere'. Christians were rediscovering old truths, such as 'the just bounds and limits of Authoritie' and 'the just and full extent of the lawfull liberties of those that live in subjection'. God was liberating men 'from the bands and fetters of those enslaving Doctrines and apprehensions, wherewith they had been formerly oppressed and made servile above measure'. And he was doing so in order to facilitate the destruction of tyranny and oppression. Indeed, 'the commonalitie of Christians', 'Christians of inferiour ranke and qualitie', would be instrumental in the destruction of Antichrist, as predicted in Revelation chapter 18. The days of martyrdom were passing, and the day of liberation was dawning.[95]

Having answered objections to armed resistance, and established that the Parliamentarians fought for a just cause, Goodwin then told his hearers and readers that their cause was 'of the highest and deepest concernment', both in 'this world' and 'the world which is to come'. In this world, the survival of everything men held dear depended on the success of the cause – estates, liberties, wives and children, representative government and lives. If Parliament lost, his hearers could say goodbye to their estates. Even worse, they would take 'your liberties'. 'Our

---

93 *Anti-Cavalierisme*, 18–22.
94 *Anti-Cavalierisme*, 22–28.
95 *Anti-Cavalierisme*, 30–36.

liberties are not so high prised with us as matter of estate is', observed Goodwin. People took liberty for granted because it was so plentiful. But if they lived 'under the great Turke, or in the State of Persia; yea or in France it selfe', they would soon see why liberty was so precious. In these states, 'the poore subject is yoked with an Iron yoke of bondage'. England was in danger of becoming just like that. The 'Malignant partie' were ready with 'bands, chaines, and fetters ... and Irons that will enter into your soules'. Only if people stood up for the Parliamentary cause could they save themselves from perpetual slavery.[96]

As if the threat to estates and liberties was not enough, 'wives and children' were in jeopardy too. Goodwin asked his audience to imagine 'the honour and chastitie of your wives, & daughters plundred by the barbarous lusts of those brutish men', to picture 'your young children ... taken by the hand of an inhumane monster, and dashed in peeces against the stones, or torne one limbe from another, or tossed upon the point of the Pike or Speare'. The 'honourable Senate of both Houses of Parliament' was also vulnerable. The two Houses had defended liberty and true religion, and were at work to make England 'a land of righteousnesse'. They were the object of enemy rage, and 'if Cavaliers Swords drinke Senators blood' it would 'make your memoriall an infamy and reproach throughout all generations'. If Parliament was defeated, Goodwin warned, 'your lives themselves' could be lost. The enemy was bloodthirsty, and would not draw back from indiscriminate slaughter. Finally, a Cavalier victory would spell the end of vital, evangelical religion. The pure ordinances of worship would be outlawed, and the saints would see an end to 'excellent ravishments and raptures of spirit'. A godly ministry would be replaced by one 'that is low, and cold'. 'If the cause should suffer or miscarry, it would bee as a sword that would passe through all the righteous soules throughout the land'.[97]

The stakes could not be higher. Although the price of failure was terrible to contemplate, this was a day of unparalleled 'opportunitie'.[98] If the English threw themselves behind Parliament, the future was bright indeed:

> Your light will be like the lightning which (as our Saviour saith) shineth from the East even unto the West: the heate and warmth and living influence thereof, shall pierce through many kingdomes great and large, as France, Germany, Bohemia, Hungaria, Polonia, Denmarke, Sweden, with many others ...[99]

This was not just another political crisis. It was a climatic moment in redemptive history, when God was working to liberate the world from temporal slavery and spiritual bondage. Goodwin even dared to compare it to the saving work of Christ himself:

---

96 *Anti-Cavalierisme*, 36–39.
97 *Anti-Cavalierisme*, 39–47.
98 *Anti-Cavalierisme*, 50.
99 *Anti-Cavalierisme*, 50.

> The opportunitie and occasion is so rich and glorious, that it calls to remembrance (as sometimes the shadow doth the substance) the great opportunitie that was before the Lord Jesus Christ, for the salvation of the world.[100]

This was a breathtaking vision. It invested the Parliamentarian cause with immense spiritual significance, and located the present crisis within the grand sweep of sacred history. Goodwin's sermon brought together natural law theory and apocalyptic speculation, visceral war propaganda and ideas of liberty. It mixed up the temporal and the spiritual, the constitutional and the religious. For Goodwin, the civil war was being fought for civil liberty as well as pure religion.

Alongside the preface to *A Treatise of Justification, Anti-Cavalierisme* can be seen as Goodwin's great programmatic statement of 1642. As J. W. Allen observed, it was 'an astonishing production' because of its 'visionary idealism'.[101] The coming crisis would see the destruction of Antichristian tyranny and the liberation of the people of God. In the new age, slavery would give way to liberty; exorbitant tyranny to circumscribed authority; implicit faith to critical examination; servility to equality. And whereas the rule of Antichrist had smothered intellectual inquiry, the new freedom would allow men to recover long lost truth and explore new continents of knowledge. *Anti-Cavalierisme* helps us to understand Goodwin's passion for the civil war, and his ardent support for the hardline war party. This was a conflict with a transcendent, eschatological purpose, and Goodwin had no compunction in prosecuting it. Whereas many saw the war as a tragedy, for Goodwin it was to be a war of liberation.

Quentin Skinner has recently declared that 'From the Parliamentary perspective, the civil war began as a war of national liberation from servitude'. 'If there was any one slogan under which the two Houses finally took up arms', he writes, 'it was that the people of England never, never, never shall be slaves'.[102] He argues that the Parliamentarians were particularly impressed by the 'neo-classical' definition of liberty as the antithesis of slavery – a free people were not subject to the will of another, they were their own masters.[103] Skinner does not cite Goodwin, and for good reason, since aside from a few allusions, *Anti-Cavalierisme* referred little to classical sources or the example of republican Rome. But as we have seen, Goodwin talked repeatedly about 'slavery', 'bondage', 'domination' and 'subjection', about 'Iron yokes', 'enslaving Doctrines', and 'Irons that will enter into your souls'. He also defined liberty in the 'neo-classical' terms Skinner has so carefully delineated. His audience were 'free men and women' who had enjoyed 'the disposal of your selves and of all your wayes'; however, they could lose their liberty by

---

100 *Anti-Cavalierisme*, 51.
101 J. W. Allen, *English Political Thought, 1603–60*, vol. i (London, 1938), 475.
102 Q. Skinner, 'Classical liberty and the coming of the English Civil War', in M. van Gelderen and Q. Skinner, eds, *Republicanism: A Shared European Heritage*, 2 vols (Cambridge, 2002), ii. 28.
103 Skinner has developed this point in 'John Milton and the politics of slavery' and 'Classical liberty, Renaissance translation and the English Civil War', in his *Visions of Politics*, 3 vols (Cambridge, 2002), ii. 286–343. See also his 'A third concept of Liberty', *Proceedings of the British Academy*, 117 (2002), 237–68.

becoming subject to the 'arbitterments and wills' of 'domineering' royalists who would 'make themselves Lords over you'.[104] Goodwin may have imbibed this definition of liberty from the classical tradition and theorists like Henry Parker, but his language was biblical, and invoked the narrative of the ancient Hebrews, enslaved in both Egypt and Babylon. As Michael Walzer explained in his book *Exodus and Revolution*, the biblical story of national liberation from Egyptian bondage was of immense importance to English Puritans.[105] Again and again in the 1640s, the godly told their story as the story of the ancient Exodus. The classical meshed with the biblical to form a powerful political narrative legitimising Parliament's revolt against the king, the army's revolt against Parliament, and the Leveller and republican revolt against Cromwell. The Roman story and the Jewish story came together in English imaginations.

The idea of liberation from slavery was particularly important to radical Puritans, who wanted to free themselves from ecclesiastical as well as political domination. Indeed, Goodwin drew an explicit analogy between church and state, religion and politics – in both realms, he argued, it was wrong to submit unquestioningly to the dictates of authorities. Individuals had a liberty and a duty to examine the commands of their rulers and the doctrines of their clergy.[106] This powerful stress on liberty, equality and independent consciences would guide Goodwin throughout the rest of the decade.

Anti-Cavalierisme was one of Goodwin's most influential pamphlets. The first edition was soon sold out; a second issue was printed at the end of 1642, and a third appeared early in 1643.[107] Herbert Palmer and the London Puritan ministers commended its rejoinder to early Christian pacifism; Jeremiah Burroughes echoed its argument that Antichristian tyranny would be pulled down by the people; and even Henry Parker seems to draw on its refutation of Tertullian.[108] It was the first in a series of resistance tracts by Puritan divines, including William Bridge, Charles Herle, Herbert Palmer, Jeremiah Burroughs and Philip Hunton. Opposing them were royalist clergy such as Henry Ferne, Griffith Williams, Henry Hammond, John Bramhall and Peter Heylyn. Although Parker was the pre-eminent Parliamentarian theorist, several royalist writers were persuaded that Goodwin's tract was a dangerous piece of propaganda. Hammond explained that he had answered Goodwin 'at large, because it is said, many have been satisfied in the lawfulnesse of their present course by those Answers and Objections which that booke hath helpt them to'. Hammond pointed out the irony that for someone who insisted that Parliament was not opposing the King, Goodwin spent an awful lot of

---

104 *Anti-Cavalierisme*, 38–39.
105 M. Walzer, *Exodus and Revolution* (New York, 1985).
106 *Anti-Cavalierisme*, 18–20.
107 Wing G1146, G1146A, G1147.
108 See [Herbert Palmer], *Scripture and Reason Pleaded for Defensive Armes* (1643), 50–51; Jeremiah Burroughs, *A Brief Answer to Dr Ferne's Book* (1643), 16; Henry Parker, *Jus Populi* (1644), 66–67.

time justifying resistance to kings. Did Goodwin really favour 'a Republique'? As for his discourse on the rise and fall of Antichrist, Hammond was sure that Goodwin was the first to ever broach such an argument. 'Here is a great secret of new Divinity', he teased, 'that God hides truths ... on purpose to help Antichrist to his throne'. Goodwin clearly thought the age of martyrdom was passed, and that Christians 'must set up a new trade of fighting, destroying, resisting, rebelling'.[109] Dudley Digges also expressed amazement at Goodwin's populist apocalypticism – he printed the key passage in full just to prove to sceptical readers that Goodwin really had said things 'so strange'.[110] In *The Grand Rebellion* (1643), Griffith Williams, Bishop of the Irish diocese of Ossory, condemned Goodwin and others for producing 'lying Pamphlets, so stuffed with Treason, to animate Rebellion'. 'The Anti-Cavalier' was among the 'ignorant fellowes' who asserted that kingly government was a human creation. He was 'an incendiary of warre' who dishonoured the Fathers like Tertullian, and threw dirt in the faces of the martyrs.[111] Other royalists responded to Goodwin's arguments, though without mentioning him by name. Henry Ferne, for example, tackled each of the three Old Testament cases of armed resistance cited in *Anti-Cavalierisme*: Jonathan, David and Elisha.[112]

Although *Anti-Cavalierisme* gave Goodwin a national profile, he was first and foremost a London preacher, and he fully appreciated the strategic importance of London. In a prologue to a fast-day sermon preached before the Lord Mayor, the Sheriffs and other City officials, he declared that London was the prize the Cavaliers coveted more than anything else: 'your selves in particular, and this your City, are the great hatred and wrath and indignation of these men'. London was vital for five reasons. First, it was known for its 'purity of religion', and had become 'a Sanctuary' and 'place of refuge' for the godly. It was 'the great Bullwark against those Prelaticall invasions wherewith the Kingdom was so sorely infested and annoyed of late'. If London had not stuck in the prelates' throat, they would have swallowed the whole kingdom with ease. Second, the City was 'the chiefe protection and safeguard of that Honourable Assembly and Court of Parliament'. Third, the metropolis had 'begotten and brought forth all that opposition' against the prelates and Cavaliers. Fourth, it was 'the great *remora* and barre' to the popish cause. Were it not for London, the Laudians 'might have Organs and Altars, Cringings and Crouchings, they might have Copes and Surplisses, Wafers and Tapers Crucifixes and Crosses, Pilgrimages and Pictures, with all Accoutrements, and the whole prophane glory of the Romish Sinagogue'. Finally, the City was 'the great Magazine of wealth, riches & treasure in the Kingdom, the garden of Hesperides, where the trees grow that beare the golden apples'. Was it any wonder that London was the principal target of 'the rage, malice, hatred and cruelty' of the popish Cavaliers'?[113]

---

109 Henry Hammond, *Of Resisting the Lawfull Magistrate under colour of Religion*, 2nd edition (Oxford 1644), 10, 18–19, 22–23, 25. Pages 10–33 were devoted to refuting the arguments of *Anti-Cavalierisme*. The first edition was published in London, 1643, and a third edition in London, 1647.
110 [Dudley Digges], *The Unlawfulness of Subjects Taking Up Armes* (1644), 107–10.
111 Griffith Williams, *Vindiciae Regum, or the Grand Rebellion* (1643), 49, 60, 79, 95.
112 Henry Ferne, *The Resolving of Conscience*, 2nd edition (1643), 4–5.
113 *The Butchers Blessing* (1642), 1–6.

The importance of London's money and manpower was underlined in the early months of the Civil War. In July and August 1642, the capital provided ten thousand volunteers for the Parliamentary army, and radicals held most of the key offices at the head of the City's trained bands. Pennington was one of six colonels in charge of the trained bands, and in mid-November they marched from the City to turn back the royalist advance at Turnham Green. The City radicals were openly critical of Parliament's lacklustre war effort and demanded better funding, equipment, leadership and organisation. Fired by Goodwin's conviction that this was a war of liberation, his parishioners laboured to promote it. Pennington was one of twelve commissioners appointed to oversee the collection of the weekly assessment in the City; James Russell was appointed to Parliament's commission for customs set up to support the navy, and also sat on a committee to collect plate, money and horses from the City; Daniel Taylor became part of a commission of militants tasked with rooting out and registering royalists; Mark Hildesley worked alongside William Walwyn on the volunteer committee for raising a new City cavalry; Owen Rowe was put in charge of the Magazine at the Tower, from where he supplied Parliament's forces with arms.[114]

The depth of the parishioners' commitment to the cause can be gauged by their contribution to the City's loan to Parliament in November 1642. Altogether they contributed £1130 19s 0d, a sum surpassed by only one parish – the equally radical St Dunstan's in the East. The godly vestrymen who had worked most closely with Goodwin gave sacrificially to the cause – Rowe £100, Cockcroft, Foxcroft and Russell £80 each, and Hildesley and Avery £50.[115]

Despite their remarkable successes, the City radicals had cause for alarm in late 1642. Crypto-royalist sentiment was strong within London, and the king's forces were raiding the outskirts of the metropolis. Although Pennington was Lord Mayor, the majority of aldermen and common councilmen were moderate Parliamentarians, more interested in reaching an accommodation with the King than in winning the war. The City radicals could not afford to be complacent. On Thursday 1 December 1642, they sent a delegation of 'four score and fifteen citizens' to Westminster where they presented a petition to Parliament expressing their disappointment at the course of events. The delegation was accompanied by Goodwin, Jeremiah Burroughs and Hugh Peter. As Brenner suggests, the petition was a dramatic outworking of the ideology of the radical Puritan preachers.[116] The petitioners complained that they had expended 'very great and vast summes' for the Parliamentarian cause, and had raised many men for the army, but were 'little nearer their end'. They were disturbed by the failure to carry out 'exemplary punishment of Delinquents', and by the constant calls for 'accomodation'. They

---

114 Brenner, *Merchants*, 428–38; *Calendar of the Proceedings of the Committee for the Advance of Money, 1642–56*, 3 vols (London, 1888), i. 2–3, 7. Rowe's later activities are detailed in i. 368 and iii. 1495–96.
115 NA SP16/492/76: The names of those at St Stephens who lent money to Parliament in November 1642. See Kirby, 'Parish of St Stephen's', 58–59.
116 Brenner, *Merchants*, 435–42; Pearl, *London*, 253–54.

called for 'the vigorous and effectual prosecution of this Warre' and a clear declaration from Parliament 'against this dangerous accommodation'.[117]

The petition engendered a fierce debate in Common Council, and on 14 December, conservative common councilmen presented Parliament with their own 'petition for peace'. Despite its conciliatory tone, its was rejected by the king, who demanded that Pennington and other City militants be tried as traitors.[118]

Charles's intransigence played into the radicals' hands, and in January they returned to Parliament with their petition, supported by war party MPs like Miles Corbet. On 30 March 1643, the radicals presented a Petition and Remonstrance to Common Council and to Parliament, which was unapologetic in its advocacy of popular sovereignty and parliamentary supremacy. The new petition was strongly supported by Pennington, and by future followers of Goodwin including Richard Price the mercer and his nephew Richard Price the scrivener.[119]

In April 1643, Parliament agreed to the radicals' demands by establishing a subcommittee to sit at Salters Hall to raise a volunteer army under the authority of the Militia Committee, which was already a stronghold of the radicals. As Pearl and Brenner have explained, this was a triumph for the radicals, for it gave them their own financial and military power base in the City. As the confidence of the London radicals increased, the Common Council ordered that Cheapside Cross should be destroyed on account of 'the idolatrous and superstitious figures there set about'. On 28 April, Common Council removed more power from the City's aldermen, by ruling that their deputies should be chosen from among elected common councillors rather than appointed by the aldermen themselves.[120]

The radicals' advance in the City would have delighted Goodwin, but the military situation was still disturbing. Royalist troops were enjoying considerable success, and the Parliamentary army appeared ineffectual. It was in this context that Goodwin published his reply to Bishop Griffith Williams, *Os Ossarianum, or A Bone for a Bishop to Pick* (11 April 1643). Goodwin began with an excoriating attack on 'statizing Prelates', who had 'drunk away their Christian wits ... in the intoxicating cup of the Romish whore'. 'Prelates, especially of later times', he wrote, 'have beene the Grand Corrupters of the loyalty of Kings unto God'. The blame for the 'Grand Rebellion', as Williams called it, should be placed squarely on the shoulders of men like Dr Corbet, late Bishop of Norwich, who had preached at Paul's Cross 'investing Kings with all the Royalties of Heaven'. Such men, 'through importune flatteries and Idolatrous admiration and adoration of Regall power, bereave [Kings and Princes] of all memory and thought of their being *but men*, compelling them to own and claime to themselves Prerogatives above the Moon, such as parallel, if not transcend, the Prerogatives of God himselfe'. 'And he certainly

---

117 *The True and Original Copy of the First Petition Which was Delivered by Sir David Watkins, Mr Shute, who were accompanied with Mr Burrowes, M. Peters, Mr. Goodwin and fourscore and fifteene men* (1642), n. p.
118 See *The True and Original Copy*; Brenner, *Merchants*, 442–43.
119 Brenner, *Merchants*, 443–48; *Walwyns Just Defence*, in *Walwyn*, 395.
120 Brenner, *Merchants*, 448–51.

is the greatest endammager, if not destroyer of Kings, that placeth their Thrones too neere the Throne of God'.[121]

Royalist divines were quite wrong to teach that God's favoured form of government was monarchy. 'It can never bee proved,' Goodwin asserted, 'that Kings were originally ordained by God to rule'. If kingly rule was the highest divine ideal, why was the first king mentioned in the Bible the ruthless tyrant, Nimrod, while the second was 'Pharoah King of Egypt'? 'God never imposed the government of Kings upon any Nation', argued Goodwin, 'but hath left all Nations free to erect amongst themselves what government they please, whether Aristocraticall, Democraticall, and however mixt, so it be just and lawfull, as well as Regall'. God had established the *institution* of government, but the *form* of that government was of the people's choosing and it was they who invested power in the ruler. Monarchy was a legitimate form of government, but far from recommending it to the people, God had 'left them purely to themselves'.[122] Brenner may go too far in labelling City radicals like Goodwin and Burroughs 'moderate republicans', but ever since the late 1630s these men had been willing to speak disparagingly about kings and princes. If regicide had not yet crossed Goodwin's mind, he was in no doubt that there were legitimate alternatives to England's monarchical form of government.

On the question of armed resistance, Goodwin denied that he had advocated resistance by private individuals, and he defended himself against the charge that he was 'an incendiary of Warre' who promoted 'violent resistance'. He had never intended 'to make it lawfull to draw a sword, when the shutting of a doore may be a sufficient security'. If this was what Williams meant by 'violent resistance', it was clearly supported by the Scriptures.[123]

Ultimately, Goodwin argued, disputes about 'resistance' and 'authority' could only be settled by the properly constituted authorities, not by divines. The lawful power of the King of England or the Parliament could not be discovered by searching the Scriptures, but by consulting 'the English Lawes'. If the laws were open to dispute, one must consult the lawyers, and if they were unable to provide a definitive answer, 'recourse must be had to ... the Supreme Judicatorie ... the high Court of Parliament'.[124]

This argument confirms Glenn Burgess's claim that even Goodwin – who at times portrayed the civil war as a crusade against Antichrist – accepted that a legitimate war required secular authorisation. His apocalyptic case for war was combined with an 'inferior magistrates' theory of resistance and an appeal to 'the English Lawes'.[125] As a trained theologian, Goodwin felt most comfortable with biblical and natural law arguments for resistance, but he was also quite willing to

---

121 *Os Ossorianum, or a Bone for a Bishop to Pick* (1643), 3–5.
122 *Os Ossorianum*, 28–36.
123 *Os Ossorianum*, 8–9, 37, 42.
124 *Os Ossorianum*, 60–61.
125 G. Burgess, 'Was the English Civil War a War of Religion? The evidence of political propaganda', *Huntingdon Library Quarterly*, 61 (2000), 173–201 (187–90 on Goodwin). Burgess bases his analysis of Goodwin on *Anti-Cavalierisme*, but my reading of *Os Ossorianum* confirms his argument.

invoke the neo-Roman and legalistic arguments popularised by men like Henry Parker and William Prynne.

If Goodwin's pamphlets were less influential than those of Parker and Prynne, he was certainly one of the most important clerical propagandists on the Parliamentarian side. Griffith Williams felt it necessary to publish an instant reply to *Os Ossorianum*, a mock serious compilation of its author's 'grave' and 'charitable' expressions and rhetorical devices.[126] Goodwin himself was proud of his contributions to the Parliamentarian cause. 'I have once and againe in Print', he wrote, 'asserted the Parliamentary cause against the Oxfordian; yea (as far as I yet understand) I was the first amongst all my Brethren who serve at the Altar, that rose up in this kind, for the Parliament'. In the pulpit too, he had 'for many moneths together ... (almost) uninterruptedly ... laboured by preaching to advance the service'. He had vigorously promoted every initiative recommended by Parliament, and had given sacrificially from his own estate to the City's collections for the war effort. Thousands could testify that he had commended Parliament 'without ceasing' in his public prayers, and it was well known that 'many young men and others' had been 'armed with courage and resolution by me for the warres', through his preaching, conference and persuasion. And as if his work in the City was not enough, he had also 'been as diligent and faithfull an Agent' for Parliament in his home county of Norfolk, 'and that not without some considerable successe'.[127]

Of course, by the spring of 1643 most people had already taken sides in the civil war. But political pamphleteering still served a valuable purpose, as a means to keep up morale. In the spring and early summer, the Parliamentary forces suffered a series of humiliating defeats. In response to the crisis, Henry Overton published John Price's *A Spirituall Snapsacke for the Parliament Souldiers* (24 May 1643). Price reassured the troops that they had 'A GOOD CAUSE' backed by godly, learned, orthodox divines—witness '*Goodwins* Anticaval:'. 'You fight for God', Price continued, 'who hath bound Kings in chaines and Nobles in fetters of Iron, Psal. 149.8. Who hath rebuked Kings and destroyed mighty Princes in the behalf of those that fought for him'. This anti-monarchical text was to be much quoted in 1649, but Price was quick to tell the Parliamentary soldiers that however paradoxical it might sound, 'You fight for the recovery of his Royall Person out of the hands of these miscreants, and reinstate Him in his Royall Throne and Dignity'. Yet ultimately, it was the populist note that prevailed in Price's tract. While other reformations had been begun by kings, 'this Reformation is from the people'.[128]

Price's pamphlet was dedicated to the Earl of Essex, whom the author hoped would become both 'a Moses' and 'a Joshua' to the English people, leading them out of Egypt and into the Promised Land.[129] But with the loss of Bristol in late July,

---

126 Griffith Williams, *Os Ossis & Oris, or a Collection of the Most Remarkable Passages in a Book intituled Os Ossorianum* (13 April 1643).
127 *Calumny Arraigned* (1645), 21–22.
128 J[ohn] P[rice], *A Spirituall Snapsacke for the Parliament Souldiers* (1643), 6, 7–9, 11–12.
129 P[rice], *A Spirituall Snapsacke*, sig. A2v.

Essex's image as England's Joshua was seriously damaged, and City radicals and war party MPs campaigned openly for his dismissal and the reconstruction of the army. On 20 July, a petition signed by 20,000 Londoners was submitted to the Commons, calling for the creation of a new army made up of 10,000 volunteers. The petition was backed by war party MPs, including Pennington.[130]

But the triumph of the radicals would have to wait. For all their great successes, the City militants represented a small minority of Londoners. They had achieved a constitutional revolution in the City in 1641–42, and had reached the apogee of their influence in 1642–43. But there was now widespread resentment at the burden of war, and from late 1643 to 1648, City politics was to be dominated by moderate Parliamentarians who favoured a Presbyterian settlement of the church and a negotiated peace with the king. Goodwin and his radical parishioners had played a central role in London politics between 1640 and 1643, but for the next few years were in eclipse. In the fall of 1643, the moderate Parliamentarian Sir John Wollaston replaced Pennington as Lord Mayor. Pennington had been made Lieutenant of the Tower in July 1643, and he continued to sit on Common Council (and the Court of Aldermen) along with Rowe and Russell. But their influence over City politics was much reduced, and the moderates controlled both Common Council and the Militia Committee.[131] Even in the parish of Coleman Street itself, the radicals would lose out to their rivals. For Goodwin, the mid-1640s were to be difficult years.

---

130 Pearl, *London*, 270–71.
131 Brenner, *Merchants*, 459–93; Pearl, *London*, 271–75.

4

'A BITTER ENEMIE TO PRESBYTERIE' 1643–45

In his *Areopagitica*, published in November 1644, John Milton declared that 'God is decreeing to begin some new and great period in his Church, even to the reforming of Reformation itself'. The Lord would reveal himself 'first to his Englishmen', and London would be at the heart of the new reformation. 'This vast City', wrote Milton, was 'the mansion-house of liberty', for besides its anvils and hammers fashioning instruments for a just war, there were 'pens and heads there, sitting by their studious lamps, musing, searching, revolving new motions and ideas wherewith to present, as with their homage and their fealty, the approaching Reformation'.[1]

From 1640 to 1645, Milton lived in Aldersgate Street, just ten or fifteen minutes walk from Coleman Street. He was a friend of Samuel Hartlib, Isaac Pennington junior and Doctor Nathan Paget, who were well known to Goodwin too.[2] Goodwin and Milton also shared the same printer, Matthew Simmons, who saw a significant number of their pamphlets through the press.[3] It is almost certain that the preacher and the poet knew each other personally – Goodwin may have been one of the thinkers Milton had in mind, 'sitting by their studious lamps'. Milton's biographer, Dom Wolfe, once described the two men as 'philosophical brothers'.[4] The ideals and rhetoric of *Areopagitica* are certainly reminiscent of Goodwin's preface to *A Treatise of Justification*. Like Milton and the Hartlib circle,

---

1 *The Complete Prose Works of John Milton*, ed. D. M. Wolffe et al. (New Haven, 1953–82), iii. 552–54.
2 See B. Lewalski, *The Life of John Milton* (Oxford, 2000), 172–73, 409–10. Another member of the Hartlib circle, Benjamin Worsley, lived in Coleman Street in the mid-1640s. In 1646, Robert Boyle wrote to Worsley about his fresh discovery in the art of husbandry, 'as new as any of the religions minted in your heretical [*Coleman*] street'. *Correspondence of Robert Boyle*, ed. M. Hunter et al., 6 vols (London, 2001), i. 42.
3 During the 1640s, Simmons printed or published at least six of Milton's works, including several of his divorce tracts, *The Tenure of Kings and Magistrates* (1649) and *Eikonoklastes* (1649). He also printed at least nine of Goodwin's tracts, including *Innocency and Truth* (1645), *Hagiomastix* (1647), *Sion College Visited* (1648), and *Right and Might Well Met* (1649).
4 D. M. Wolfe, *Milton in the Puritan Revolution* (New York, 1941), 91.

Goodwin was not itching to turn London into Calvin's Geneva or Knox's Edinburgh. His was a more expansive and dynamic vision of increasing knowledge, new light and 'studious expeditions' into uncharted territory.[5]

During the turmoil of the first Civil War, this progressive Reformation vision would collide with a conservative Reformation represented by the Presbyterian clergy who dominated the Westminster Assembly of Divines and London's Sion College. Goodwin, who was not appointed to the Assembly, quickly emerged as 'a bitter enemie to Presbyterie'.[6] Having established a gathered church while he was still a parish minister, his views on Independency became increasingly emphatic, leading to his ejection in 1645. And he started to articulate a radical defence of religious toleration, one designed to undermine the Presbyterian drive for uniformity.

The Origins of the Gathered Church

The evolution of Goodwin's ecclesiology in these years is difficult to trace. We can say with certainty that he was not an Independent in October 1639, for his letter to Thomas Goodwin revealed his scepticism about congregationalist polity, with its popular ordination of pastors, offices of ruling elders and widows, and formal church covenant. None of the works he published in 1640–43 dealt with the nature of the church, and his first openly congregationalist statements came in 1644. Thomas Edwards claimed that Goodwin only embraced Independency after his pride was wounded by his exclusion from the Westminster Assembly.[7] William Walwyn wrote that he got to know one of Goodwin's followers during Pennington's year as Mayor (1642–43), 'before Mr John Goodwin had gathered his Church, or at least, before this Mr [Richard] Price was a Member of it'.[8] Since both Edwards and Walwyn were well informed about Goodwin and his followers, it seems clear that Goodwin's gathered church only became public knowledge after mid-1643.

However, other evidence suggests that Goodwin was moving in a congregationalist direction before 1643. Marchamont Nedham later claimed that 'within a few monneths after [his letter to Thomas Goodwin], he [i.e. John Goodwin] changed his Judgement from the Presbyterian way wherein he then stood, and professed himself for this way which he had so confidently decried, and took up the practice of it, and gathered a Separate Church in Coleman Street'.[9] Nedham was writing in the late 1650s in order to discredit Goodwin, but his information probably came from the Independent Philip Nye who knew Goodwin well.[10]

---

5 On the ideals of the Hartlib circle see C. Webster, *The Great Instauration: Science, Medicine and Reform, 1626–1660* (London, 1975); and M. Greengrass, M. Leslie and T. Raylor, eds, *Samuel Hartlib and Universal Reformation* (Cambridge, 1994).
6 R. Baillie, *Letters and Journals*, ed. D. Laing, 3 vols (Edinburgh, 1841–42), ii. 181.
7 Edwards, *Gangraena* (1646), ii. 57–58.
8 *Walwyn*, 395.
9 Nedham, *The Great Accuser Cast Down* (1657), 'To the Reader'.
10 See *Triumviri* (1658), sig. a3v, where Goodwin detects Nye's hand in Nedham's polemic.

Goodwin was certainly associated with Henry Burton and Nathaniel Homes, both of whom were openly advocating a congregationalist ecclesiology by mid-1641.[11] Goodwin was also enjoying renewed friendship with the congregationalists who had returned from exile in the Netherlands and New England – men like Thomas Goodwin, Jeremiah Burroughs, Sidrach Simpson and Hugh Peter, all of whom he had probably known at Cambridge. Significantly, letters from the Rotterdam congregationalist John Bachelor in 1641 suggest that the leading congregationalists acknowledged Goodwin's parish church as a true church, because it already conformed closely to two of their key ideals: St Stephens (like St Mary's Aldermanbury) had many visible saints and chose its own pastor.[12]

What does seem clear is that prior to 1643, Goodwin was already accepting godly followers into some kind of membership. This may not have involved anything as formal as the signing of a church covenant, but at the very least it was a verbal agreement in which a person asked Goodwin to be their pastor and Goodwin consented. Among the earliest members of the church we can probably include the stationer John Bellamy. Writing in 1646, John Price reminded Bellamy that he had once belonged to 'a select company', where he had spoken the 'language of Canaan', and enjoyed 'the glory of Christian society, and brightness of such a fellowship':

> you betook your self to a very precious select company of Christians who met together in a coursary manner according to agreement, for the mutual comfort & edification of one another by prayer, exhortation and the exercise of one anothers gifts, in which company, none more free frequent, and forward, then Master Bellamy, and indeed according to their acknowledgements exceeding and excelling them all ... who with much griefe of soule assert these things.[13]

Bellamy and Price had been close friends, and it does seem that Price was voicing the pain of Goodwin's company at the loss of such a godly member. If Bellamy did belong to Goodwin's circle of followers, it must have been prior to 1643, for in April of that year he published Roborough's attack on Goodwin's *Treatise of Justification*.[14] In the same year he also published Goodwin's embarrassing 1639 letter to Thomas Goodwin denouncing the congregationalists for separatism.[15] It was the start of a busy career as a Presbyterian propagandist.[16]

---

11 See their sermons to Parliament in May and June 1641: Nathaniel Homes, *The New World, or the New Reformed Church* (1641); Henry Burton, *Englands Bondage and Hope of Deliverance* (1641). I owe these references to Steve Rowlstone, whose work on Henry Burton will do much to clarify the development of his thought.
12 See Thomas Edwards, *Antapologia* (1644), 48.
13 John Price, *The City Remonstrance Remonstrated* (1646), 18–19.
14 Henry Roborough, *The Doctrine of Justification Cleared* (Printed by R.C. and are to be sold by John Bellamy and Ralph Smith, 1643), sig. *3v, where Roborough signs his dedicatory epistle 3 April 1643.
15 *A Quarie concerning the Church-Covenant practiced in Separate Congregations* (Printed for John Bellamie and Ralph Smith, 1643).
16 See the many references to Bellamy in A. Hughes, *Gangraena and the English Revolution* (Oxford, 2004).

In his reply to Price, Bellamy endeavoured to blur the boundaries between the gathered church and the conventional voluntary religion of the godly. Downplaying the significance of his time in Goodwin's fellowship, he said that he had 'often met with sundry select Companies of godly Christians in holy duties'.[17] Yet while this particular 'select company' met together in a 'coursary manner', Price also adds that they met 'according to agreement', suggesting a more formal arrangement between the members and their pastor.

The existence of a membership prior to 1643 is confirmed by other sources. When the young shoemaker, Luke Howard, came to London from Dover in late 1642, he was soon 'received as a Member' by Goodwin.[18] The Cornhill linen draper Thomas Lamb also became a member of Goodwin's flock before 1643, though he lived in another parish. Years later, his wife wrote to Richard Baxter explaining that 'the Ministry he [i.e. Lamb] was nourished and bred up in was, *Mr John Goodwin's*, for Twelve or Thirteen Years, where he joined a member, and afterward by common Consent, and Prayer, and Fasting was ordained an Elder over that Flock'.[19] Since Lamb separated from Goodwin's Independent congregation around May 1653, his wife was dating the start of his membership to the very early 1640s. Lamb himself explained that he had 'lived under [Goodwin's] ministry almost twenty yeares' (i.e. from around 1633 to 1653),[20] which confirms that Goodwin took regular hearers from beyond the parish and accepted them as 'members' of his gathered church. What we can say with certainty is that by late 1642 at the latest, Goodwin had created a gathered church with some kind of admission to a formal membership which included both parishioners and non-parishioners.[21]

He later explained that 'in Independency', pastors did not gather churches; rather, 'the Churches gather their Pastors'.[22] He himself had established meetings in his house because non-parishioners wanted him to become their shepherd. Initially, Goodwin probably did not think of such meetings as gatherings of a distinct 'church'. As Patrick Collinson (and John Bellamy) remind us, voluntary religious meetings were part and parcel of the Puritan subculture; they should not be seen as necessarily separatist or as independent congregations in embryo, even if their critics accused them of being such.[23] But in Goodwin's case, informal

---

17 John Bellamy, *A Justification of the City Remonstrance* (1646), 29.
18 Luke Howard, *Love and Truth in Plainness Manifested* (1704), 5. Howard explains that he helped to build the City's fortifications, and we know that 'frantic work on the construction of fortifications' was being undertaken in the autumn of 1642 (K. Lindley, *Popular Politics and Religion in Civil War London* [Aldershot, 1997], 238).
19 *Reliquiae Baxterianae* (London, 1696), Appendix iii, 50.
20 Thomas Lamb, *Truth Prevailing against the Fiercest Opposition* (1655), 95.
21 Contra More, 'New Arminians', 62–63, who declares that the congregation's existence predated Lamb's being made a 'member' in 1639 or 1640, and that by '1640 at the latest' it was a fully functioning gathered church complete with elected elders. This seems to me to read too much into Barbara Lamb's account.
22 *Anapologesiastes Antapologia* (1646), 137.
23 P. Collinson, *The Religion of Protestants: The Church in English Society, 1559–1625* (Oxford, 1982), ch. 6.

meetings between the pastor and his godly hearers did eventually develop into a gathered church. Goodwin later claimed that he had chosen 'the congregational way' because of 'a sense of mine owne defectivenesse' and a desire to 'build up my selfe in holinesse'. In these meetings of the truly godly he found great spiritual sustenance, and concluded that 'that way of Church-government which hath the richest sympathy, and most direct and full compliance with the edification of the Saints in holinesse, is ... the way which Jesus Christ hath sealed'.[24]

Presbyterians and Independents

As Goodwin was reforming his own parish, the Parliamentarians were embarking on the reform of the national church. In June 1643, Parliament passed an ordinance calling an Assembly of Divines at Westminster, and the Assembly met for the first time on 1 July 1643. At the same time, Parliament was in negotiations with the Scottish Covenanters, who wanted a Presbyterian church settlement in both kingdoms.

The alliance was sealed in August 1643 by the Solemn League and Covenant, a document containing a clause on religion that would cause endless wrangling between Presbyterians and Independents. The signatories were to agree to endeavour 'the preservation of the reformed religion in the Church of Scotland' and 'the reformation of religion in the kingdoms of England and Ireland, in doctrine, worship, discipline and government, according to the Word of God, and the example of the best reformed Churches'.[25] For the Scots, this necessitated a Presbyterian settlement, but for Independents it left open the possibility of a congregationalist settlement. Presbyterians assumed that 'the best reformed Churches' were the major churches in Scotland and continental Europe, but Independents could make a strong case for the purity of the New England churches. Moreover, Independents insisted that what mattered most was that the new ecclesiastical reformation was 'according to the word of God'. As Goodwin put it, 'this one little clause ... is to the Covenant, as the rudder is to the Ship'.[26] Within months, this difference of outlook was to emerge within the Westminster Assembly.

The strongest supporters of the Scottish alliance, according to David Scott, were the politicians 'associated with the most godly of the peers – the Earl of Manchester, Viscount Saye, and Lord Wharton – and John Pym, Sir Henry Vane junior and Oliver St John in the Commons'. In early 1643, this network also included the Earl of Essex, John Hampden, Sir Philip Stapleton and Isaac Pennington. This group opposed a quick accommodation with the king, and at least some of its members favoured parliamentary sovereignty. All supported the Scots alliance, and portrayed the war as a campaign to defend English Protestantism.[27] Goodwin's anti-cavalier publications in 1642–43 clearly fitted the

---

24 *Innocency and Truth Triumphing Together* (1645), 29–30.
25 S. R. Gardiner, ed., *Constitutional Documents of the Puritan Revolution* (Oxford, 1979), 268.
26 *Anapologesiastes*, 111.
27 D. Scott, *Politics and War in the Three Stuart Kingdoms, 1637–49* (Basingstoke, 2004), 41–42.

agenda of the Saye-Pym-St John faction. Besides being Pennington's pastor, he had dedicated books to Hampden and Pym, and been at college with both St John and Stapleton. In 1645, St John was to marry the widow of Caleb Cockcroft, another of Goodwin's parishioners.[28]

Given his connections with prominent godly politicians and clergy, Goodwin must have had high expectations of being appointed to the Assembly, which promised to be the most significant gathering of Reformed divines since Dort. On 6 January 1643, when the Commons had first passed an act for the calling of the Assembly, it resolved 'That Mr Jo. Goodwyn, of Coleman Street, London, be named in this bill'.[29] This was no doubt in recognition of his service to the Parliamentarian cause, but opposition to Goodwin's appointment seems to have built up thereafter. When the Assembly divines were confirmed later in the year, Goodwin was not named. First to be nominated was Herbert Palmer, Goodwin's former colleague at Queens'. Goodwin's successor at King's Lynn, John Arrowsmith, was another appointment, as were the congregationalists recently returned from the Netherlands – Thomas Goodwin, William Bridge, Jeremiah Burroughs, William Greenhill and Philip Nye. The London Puritan ministry was also well represented by figures like William Gouge, Edmund Calamy, Lazarus Seaman, and Simeon Ashe. Goodwin's exclusion was all the more galling because one of those appointed was his nemesis, George Walker.[30]

A last ditch effort to include Goodwin was made on 30 October 1643, when he was nominated by the House of Lords to be added to the list of Assembly members. Also recommended were Nathaniel Homes, who established an Independent congregation with Henry Burton in 1643, and Thomas Horton, professor of divinity at Gresham College. It seems more than likely that the nominations of Goodwin and Homes were an attempt to strengthen the hand of the Independents in the Assembly in anticipation of forthcoming debates over church government. The driving force behind the nominations may well have been Viscount Saye, an Independent sympathiser who was a member of the Assembly and one of fifteen peers present in the Lords on the day in question.[31] The Commons promised to send its answer to the proposal,[32] and Saye (if he was the sponsor) had surely primed St John and other MPs to back the nominations.

The Presbyterians, however, were determined to prevent further Independent appointments, and they wasted no time in attacking the nominees. On 7 and 8 November, the Westminster Assembly heard disturbing reports of freelance ordinations being carried out by Independent divines. Dr Stanton had recently met with a newly ordained minister, Mr Anderson. When asked who had ordained him, Anderson confessed that 'he was ingaged to keepe silence by ministers in the citty: Dr [Nathaniel] Homes, Mr Goodwin in Coleman street. Imposition of

---

28 See *ODNB*, article on Oliver St John.
29 *CJ*, 6 January 1643.
30 See R. S. Paul, *The Assembly of the Lord* (Edinburgh, 1985), 546–53.
31 *LJ*, vi. 283.
32 *LJ*, vi. 290, 308; *CJ*, iii. 299.

hands & prayer, another ordained with him'. John White had also spoken with Anderson, who had failed to produce 'his orders'. White told the Assembly that the action of Goodwin and Homes was 'a high presumption & fit to be remonstrated to the Houses'. He proposed that the Assembly 'make the House of Commons acquainted with this businesse ... concerning the liberty & presumption that some men take to give orders unto men that come for benefices and thereby <abuse> the assembly'. Edmund Calamy weighed in to complain of the 'fame of a ministry that doth openly preach against this assembly'. The Commons should be informed about 'the liberty that many take in the city and other places in gathering of churches at this time to anticipate the worke of the parliament and assembly'.[33]

As R. S. Paul has noted, these accusations placed the Westminster Independents in a tricky position: 'They did not approve of irregular ordination, and yet in strict Congregational ecclesiology a pastor could be ordained by the presbytery of a local congregation with or without the assistance of presbyters from other churches'.[34] On 9 November, the Dissenting Brethren hit back. According to Lightfoot, William Bridge 'brought in a paper under the hands of Dr. Holmes and Mr John Goodwin, whereby they disclaimed their ordaining of Mr. Anderson; which cost some time, more than we had well to spend'.[35] As Paul suggests, Homes and Goodwin 'had apparently disclaimed any intention of "ordaining" Anderson and claimed that their certificate had simply been a way of recognizing him in terms of his ability and worthiness to be a minister'. The Dissenting Brethren demanded that the Assembly publicly vindicate Homes and Goodwin, and after some acrimonious exchanges the matter was quickly dropped.[36] The Westminster Independents were clearly very keen to recruit two more allies to the Assembly, and they explicitly cited the Lord's nomination of the two men. In the end, however, the Presbyterian protest had its desired effect. The nominations were shelved, and the Commons response to the Lords is unrecorded. The Upper House later nominated Horton again, but Goodwin and Homes were non-starters.[37] Goodwin was to spend the 1640s in the vicinity of Coleman Street, a couple of miles away from the most significant clerical gathering in the history of Protestant Britain.

He would no doubt have heard reports of the Assembly's meetings, and would have known, for example, that in September the divines engaged in days of heated dispute over the doctrine of justification. Although the majority had sided with Walker, a minority led by Richard Vines had staked out a position almost identical

---

33 John Lightfoot, *The Journal of the Proceedings of the Assembly of Divines*, in *The Whole Works of the Rev. John Lightfoot* (London, 1824), xiii. 42–46; 'Minutes of the Westminster Assembly', Session 91 (8 November 1643), f. 170r. Transcribed in C. van Dixhoorn, ' Reforming the Reformation: Theological Debate at the Westminster Assembly, 1643–1652', unpublished Ph.D. thesis, University of Cambridge (2004), iii. 263, 271–72. I am grateful to Chad van Dixhoorn for drawing my attention to this significant material.
34 Paul, *Assembly of the Lord*, 183–84.
35 Lightfoot, *Journal*, 46. See also the sketchy minutes for 9 November transcribed in van Dixhoorn, 'Reforming the Reformation', iii. 272–74.
36 Paul, *Assembly of the Lord*, 184–85.
37 *CJ*, iii. 376 (24 January 1644).

to that of Goodwin's *Treatise of Justification*.³⁸ To be excluded from such a critical debate among his fellow divines over his favourite doctrine must have been intensely frustrating for Goodwin. His exclusion from the Westminster Assembly was a critical turning point in his career. From this point on, he was – to use President Johnson's indelicate expression – 'outside [the tent] pissing in'. By excluding Goodwin, the Presbyterians had created a formidable foe, one who would quickly emerge as the leading clerical voice of radical Puritanism in the City and the London press. As one Presbyterian told Goodwin: 'some observe that ever since your self could not get to be part of the Assembly, you have been labouring to assemble a partie'.³⁹ This ignores earlier indications of Goodwin's radicalism, but his non-involvement in the Assembly certainly liberated him from the constraints of collegiality. Had he participated in the Assembly, he would no doubt have cooperated closely with Thomas Goodwin and the other Westminster Independents, and may have pursued a more cautious and conservative course during the 1640s. Excluded, he was to advance a radical Independency that went well beyond the position of the Dissenting Brethren.

By the autumn of 1643, Goodwin was firmly committed to congregationalism. In October, Henry Overton published an anonymous pamphlet entitled *Satisfaction concerning Mixt Communions Unsatisfactory*, which expressed disquiet at the 'promiscuous Communions' in the parish churches. The tract emphasised the need for ministers to the 'rightly called', congregations to be 'rightly gathered', the ordinances to be 'rightly administered', and 'right Discipline exercised'. In 'most Parishes', it complained, 'there is no discipline at all'. A 'common Parochiall Church' was not the same as 'a truely reformed Church'.⁴⁰ Even if Goodwin did not write this, he surely endorsed it. He had become convinced that the bold new era of reformation would involve a radical reform of the church.

The vestry minute book of St Stephen's shows how Goodwin went about implementing his vision. In June 1642, the general vestry agreed in principle to remove the font 'up to Goodwin's deske', though it was not until March 1643 that a formal order was issued to place 'a new ffont ... as neare Mr Goodwins seate as may conveniently'.⁴¹ St Stephen's was the first parish in the City to do this, and it demonstrates Goodwin's zeal for reformation.⁴² The vestry had agreed to Goodwin's request for a godly minister to assist him in his work as early as April 1642, perhaps because he wanted to spend more time with those, like Thomas Lamb, who he had gathered from other parishes. The first candidate to be interviewed was Mr Yates, but he had certain scruples about the direction in which the parish was moving and attention turned to Robert Smyth, who was in place by December 1643.⁴³ Yates was later to identify with the Presbyterian cause, whereas Smyth

---

38 See van Dixhoorn, 'Reforming the Reformation', ch. 5.
39 *Moro-mastix* (1647), 11.
40 *Satisfaction concerned Mixt Communions Unsatisfied* (1643), 2–3, 9.
41 GL MS4458/1 ff. 121, 122.
42 Lindley, *Popular Politics*, 260.
43 GL MS4458/1 ff. 121, 122, 126.

seems to have become a member of Goodwin's gathered church.[44]

Lamb later recalled that at the time when the nation took the Solemn League and Covenant in September 1643, 'Mr Goodwin, with my self and divers of the Church' entered into their own 'most solemn Vow and Covenant ... wherein we agreed to go one before another in the work of reformation'. 'Shortly after', and because of this 'Vow and Covenant' – 'with other reasons in conjunction' – Goodwin 'thought himself bound in conscience to withdraw from them [i.e. his parishioners], and actually did so, and made this solemn Vow and Covenant, one argument that induced him thereunto'. Lamb was quite clear that Goodwin had decided to 'separate from the national Church, and gather a particular [church]'.[45]

In the autumn of 1643, Goodwin pressed the vestry of St Stephen's to restrict admission to communion. At two meetings in mid-December, the general vestry agreed to establish six men to assist Goodwin in deciding who was 'worthy ... to partake of the sacrament'. The assistants included George Foxcroft, William Montague and Robert Smyth (who all signed declarations by Goodwin's gathered church after 1645), and James Russell, Richard Ashurst and Samuel Avery (who did not). The vestry agreed that individuals who were 'found worthy by Mr Goodwin' and his assistants 'shall submit to have their names writ downe in a booke kept for that purpose by which they shalbe accounted members of this church and congregation'.[46]

This was a radical redefinition of church membership along congregational lines. Instead of being a 'member' of a church by virtue of being an inhabitant of the parish, one was added to a membership book by virtue of being 'found worthy' by the pastor and his assistants (a nascent eldership). The resultant 'congregation' would be a church of visible saints. As Ellen More observed, this 'parochial Independency' would 'infuse the St Stephen's parochial framework with the internal life of a gathered church'.[47] Writing in October 1644, William Prynne commented that 'Mr Goodwin delegate[d] the power of determining who should be fit persons to receive the Sacrament, and to become members of his independent Congregation, to eight select substitutes'. Prynne may have been misinformed on the number of 'select substitutes', but he well understood the implications of what Goodwin was doing.[48]

It was a move that divided Goodwin's godly parishioners. In July 1644, Edwards claimed that after Goodwin's conversion to Independency, 'the known godly' of Coleman Street were no longer admitted to communion 'by vertue of their relation of membership they hold in the Parish church'. He also suggested that 'so many godly persons' of the parish 'could not be received in by him [Goodwin] as Churchmembers ... without yeelding to some rules and conditions, which they being

---

44 'Robert Smyth' was first on the list of signatories to the congregation's *Apologeticall Account* (1647). As Goodwin's ministerial assistant, Smyth would have been the natural choice to draft this defence of their pastor.
45 Lamb, *Truth Prevailing against the Fiercest Opposition* (1655), 2; sigs. a3v, br
46 GL, MS 4458/1, f. 125.
47 More, 'New Arminians', 63–64.
48 William Prynne, *A Full Reply* (1644), 24.

members of Christ (and some of them none the meanest) could not condescend unto'.[49] Goodwin himself claimed that he had been willing to compromise with his parishioners, and had consented to their choosing another minister to preach and administer to the sacrament to them, even offering to pay for this out of mine own allowance'.[50] Moreover, 'many' of those initially excluded were soon admitted to the sacrament, not 'by virtue of their ... Membership in this Parish-Church', but by virtue of 'their known, or supposed godlinesse'. The only godly persons not admitted were those who 'disclaimed their Relation both to this Pastor and Church ... by separating themselves both from him, and those of the said Parish who owned him, and joyned themselves unto him in an orderly way'.[51]

The key stumbling block for these parishioners seems to have been Goodwin's insistence that his extra-parochial flock be admitted to membership alongside the godly from the parish. As he later explained in answer to Edwards, the only condition of membership (besides godliness) which he had required of his parishioners was 'that they would acknowledge the persons, who had joyn'd themselves unto him as a Pastor, fellow members of the same particular Church with themselves'.[52] The requirement reflected Goodwin's disdain for parish boundaries, which were 'drawne by the hand of blindnesse', in 'times of ignorance and superstition'. In his mind, they were just as unbiblical as the names of parishes called after 'Popish Saints'. Goodwin criticised the Presbyterian ministers for restricting membership of their churches to 'those that are parochialized with them'.[53]

Although some 'faithfull and conscientious' parishioners 'did condescend to all that was required', other godly parishioners made things very difficult for Goodwin. They 'multiplied rules and conditions, to order, umpire, and limit him ... in his proceedings'. According to his own account, Goodwin was willing to compromise on these matters, but agreement was scuttled when 'towards the very end and close' of negotiations with the parish, his critics refused to acknowledge the outsiders as 'fellow members of the same particular church with themselves', 'in the due sense and construction of the words'. Faced with their intransigent stance, Goodwin had only three options. His first option was 'to abandon' his extra-parochial flock, 'those who in the cleerest and most regular way had chosen him for their Pastor, and he engaged himself unto them accordingly'. Goodwin ruled this out, because to turn his back on men like Thomas Lamb would be 'a kinde of unnaturall impietie'. The second option was 'to have a Pastorall Relation to two distinct Churches at once', his remodelled parochial church and his gathered church. Goodwin thought that this involved 'a manifest and unchristian incongruitie'. The final option, which he took, was to stand his ground and 'to leave them, who for the present condescended not to that proposition, to their further thoughts, and considerations, what to doe for their own accommodation and contentment, in point of Church-affairs'. These parishioners may have been godly, but because

---

49 Thomas Edwards, *Antapologia* (1644), 53–54, 96.
50 *Innocencies Triumph* (1644), 18–19.
51 *Anapologesiastes*, 53–54.
52 *Anapologesiastes*, 228.
53 *Anapologesiastes*, 185.

of their unwillingness to accept his extra-parochial flock, they were no longer considered members of the church, and were left to look for another pastor. Alienating them was preferable to abandoning his most ardent followers from outside the parish. In the end, Goodwin explained, he 'chose to walk with those whose hearts and affections he had cause to judge clave fastest unto him in the Lord'.[54]

This was not an ideal situation, and the fallout from his decision would cause many months of turmoil in the parish, culminating in Goodwin's ejection. In December 1643, however, Goodwin had managed to get the backing of the vestry, and he was determined to ride out the criticism. His problem was that from the beginning, Presbyterians outside the parish were willing to assist disaffected parishioners by attacking Goodwin's reputation. On 7 December, Robert Baillie reported that the Westminster Assembly was taking action against him: 'John Goodwin, accused by Mr. Walker and Dr. Homes òf Socinianisme, and others, are appointed to be admonished for their assaying to gather congregations'.[55]

The growing divisions and mutual suspicions among Parliamentarians did not go unnoticed by the Royalists. In late 1643, the royalist Captain Thomas Ogle (who was a prisoner in Winchester House) endeavoured to prise the Independents away from the Presbyterian majority. In a letter to the King's advisor, the Earl of Bristol, outlining his plans, Ogle explained that the Independents' 'jelosy of the Scots Press[bytery] remayns greater then ther displesur against the Einglish prelat'. Ogle's information came from the keeper of Winchester House, Thomas Devenish, who was probably already a member of Goodwin's congregation.[56] Devenish gave Ogle to believe that the Independents would be willing to strike a deal with the King in return for a guarantee of religious toleration. According to Devenish, Ogle also contacted Philip Nye and Goodwin himself, 'whoe as they are very eminent and have great interest in the most active people, soe wee found them – and theire principles lead them to itt – to be very desirous of theire liberty'. If they were given assurances of toleration, they might be willing to use their influence among 'the cyttysons' to engineer a royal victory. Devenish allowed Ogle to visit Oxford to present his scheme to the King in person, who responded by writing to both Devenish and Lieutenant-Colonel Mosely who was to surrender the town of Aylesbury into royalist hands. In January 1644, Ogle wrote to Goodwin inviting him to come to Oxford to clinch the deal. He told the pastor to 'bringe the remonstrance with yow which your brother N[ye] toold me of, and a list of the mil[itia] and com[manders] C[ity] of L[ondon], with an estimate of your strength in booth Ar[mies]'. He also requested £100 or £200 to cover his expenses, in the knowledge that 'your credit is

---

54 *Anapologesiastes*, 227–28.
55 Baillie, *Letters and Journals*, ii. 111.
56 Devenish signed the congregation's declaration in 1647.
57 'A Secret Negotiation with Charles the First, 1643–44', ed. B. M. Gardiner, *Camden Miscellany*, 8 (1893), 6, 26, 32–33. Gardiner mistakenly assumes 'Mr. Goodwin' to be Thomas Goodwin, but the *Lords Journal* and Baillie's *Letters and Journals*, ii. 137 refer unmistakeably to John. This is confirmed by Goodwin's connection with Devenish and his 'great interest in the most active people', 'the cyttysons'. The best account of the plot and its exposure is still that of S. R. Gardiner, *History of the Great Civil War*, 4 vols (London, 1893), i. 266–75. Gardiner, however, repeats B. M. Gardiner's mistake concerning the identity of 'Mr. Goodwin'.

soe good amongst your con[gregation] that yow may have 200li for the askinge'.[57]

Unfortunately for Ogle, the Independents had hatched an elaborate plot. Keeping Parliament informed at every stage, they would lure the King into a secret deal, and then expose his scheming to public view. According to William Walwyn, Goodwin's follower Richard Price the scrivener acted as a double agent, going to negotiate with Charles I in person, 'with knowledge, if not direction of their Church'. Price's goal was 'to betray the King ... under pretence of giving up Alisbury unto him, in lieu of Liberty of Conscience (that was the gold upon the bait)'. Walwyn wondered 'how many untruths' Price had had to tell his monarch.[58] On 26 January 1644, Lord Philip Wharton revealed Ogle's plot to the House of Lords, and the correspondence of Ogle and the King was read to the House. It was another damaging blow to the King's credibility. The Lords were told 'that My Nye and Mr John Goodwin did refuse to meddle in the business'. The House agreed that Goodwin, Nye, Devenish and Mosely 'should have thanks given and a reward for their faithfulness in the carriage of this business'.[59]

Goodwin's prominence in the incident underlines both his Independent credentials and his political clout. By late 1643, he was already regarded as the most politically significant Independent minister in the City, with Nye his counterpart at Westminster. Five years later, the royalist periodical *Mercurius Pragmaticus* could still describe Goodwin and Nye as 'the two politic pulpit-drivers of Independency'.[60]

Despite their demonstration of loyalty to the Parliamentarian cause, the Independents were becoming increasingly estranged from their Presbyterian brethren. The year 1644 saw a decisive parting of ways. It began with the issuing of an *Apologeticall Narration* by five 'Dissenting Brethren' – William Bridge, Jeremiah Burroughes, Thomas Goodwin, Philip Nye and Sidrach Simpson. They declared themselves in favour of a congregational system of church government which would offer 'a middle way' between 'Brownism' and 'the authoritative Presbyterial government'.[61]

One of the most aggressive responses to the *Apologeticall Narration* came from the Scottish Presbyterian, Adam Steuart. Steuart's *Considerations and Annotations upon the Apologeticall Narration* was published at the end of February and it provoked Goodwin's first Independent book, *M.S. to A.S, With a Plea for Libertie of Conscience* (3 May 1644). Goodwin came out emphatically in favour of the 'Congregational' way, 'mis-called Independency'. The churches had become 'so corrupt', that the only solution was 'a thorough reformation'. This was not a time to 'reform but in part, by halves, imitating Hen. 8. towards the Pope, *cutting off the head of Prelacie, and sitting down in their chair*'. If Erastian Episcopacy was a 'half-reformation', so was Presbyterianism, for as John Davenport had remarked 'in his way to New-

---

58 *Walwyn*, 400.
59 *LJ*, vi.394.
60 *Mercurius Pragmaticus*, 12–19 December 1648, quoted in *The Clarke Papers*, ed. C. H. Firth, Camden Society, new series, 4 vols (1891–1901), ii. 75.
61 *An Apologeticall Narration* (1644).

England', a classical presbytery was 'but thirteen Bishops, for one'. The Apologists had taken up a minority position, but in doing so they stood in the line of Wyclif, Hus and Luther. Moreover, the congregational way was gathering increasing support. Steuart claimed to speak for all the Reformed churches, but there were in fact 'many churches' in London, Holland and New England that did not accept his 'Classicall Presbyterie'. And Goodwin rejoiced that Parliament had refused to condemn the Apology, and had continued to honour Mr. Nye.[62]

M.S. to A.S. did not set out a detailed congregational model, but Goodwin made it clear that he now viewed congregationalism as *the* biblical pattern for the church. Each congregation should possess 'entirenesse of Government or jurisdiction', and should not be subject to the compulsory dictates of synods or assemblies. 'Subjection unto strangers' was 'a matter of punishment and sorrow'. Self-government, by contrast, was 'a sweet priviledge & benefit to a particular Church', just as it was to 'Towns and Corporations'. The members' meetings of congregational churches also served an important pedagogical function, for they allowed private Christians to see and hear 'all the carriages, debates, and judiciarie proceedings in the Church'. In the Presbyterian system, by contrast, congregations were at the mercy of presbyteries and synods that could corrupt entire regions if they miscarried.[63]

Goodwin was particularly disturbed by the Presbyterian defence of the magistrate's coercive power in matters of religion. Indeed, this was the major burden of his tract, and *M.S. to A.S.* counts as his first defence of religious toleration. 1644 was to witness the publication of a series of classic tolerationist works by writers like Walwyn, Milton and Roger Williams, but the book that Goodwin may have read by this stage was Henry Robinson's *Liberty of Conscience*, which Thomason acquired on 24 March.

Goodwin poured scorn on the Scottish Presbyterian claim that the magistrate had no *directive* power in matters of religion (since this belonged to the church and its assemblies), but that he did have *coercive* power (to enforce the authoritative teaching of the church). Presbyters were setting themselves up as 'Judex', he argued, and reducing the civil magistrate to 'Carnifex': 'the one must give the sentence, the other must do the execution'. This was to ask the magistrate 'to pull out his own eyes', and place implicit faith in the judgements of the clergy. A Protestant Assembly, however, should not expect to have its conclusions 'swallowed without chewing', and a Protestant Parliament should follow truth rather than majority votes. If it judged the minority in the Assembly to be in the right, it could support their conclusions.[64]

Goodwin flatly denied that magistrates had 'coercive power in matters of religion'. He faced up squarely to 'the Grand Pillar and supporter' of the anti-tolerationist position: 'What? would you have all Religions, sects, and schisms tolerated in Christian Churches? Should Jewes, Turks (and Papists especially,) be

---

62 *M.S. to A.S. With a Plea for Liberty of Conscience* (1644), 9–19.
63 *M.S. to A.S.*, 72–77.
64 *M.S. to A.S.*, 32–38.

suffered in their Religions?' Goodwin responded by distinguishing between two types of 'toleration' – which elsewhere he labelled 'an Ecclesiastique or Church toleration' and 'a civill or state Toleration'. Ecclesiastical toleration was unjustified, for the church had a duty to refute false religion. However, Christians should support a civil or state toleration – 'a non-suppressing of such Religions, Sects, and Schismes, by a strong hand, as by fineing, imprisoning, disfranchising, banishment, death, or the like' – provided that the adherents and proponents of the false religion 'be otherwise peaceable in the State, and every waies subject to the Laws, and lawfull power'.[65]

This was a radical position, for it ran against an established Reformed consensus in favour of the magistrate's use of coercion against false religion.[66] Goodwin was arguing that it was illegitimate for the state to fine, imprison, disenfranchise, banish or execute peaceable religious dissenters, whether they were Jews, Roman Catholics, or Protestant heretics and sectarians. Yet just a few pages earlier, Goodwin had written that he did not object to the magistrate 'fighting with superstition, heresie, schisme, corruptions in manners' so long as he was 'farre enough out of this danger of fighting against God'.[67] As so often in early modern tolerationist literature, there were reservations.

M.S. to A.S. marshalled most of the tolerationist arguments that Goodwin was to develop in his later writings. He focused much of his fire on the claim that the Old Testament 'Kings of Judah' provided a warrant for contemporary religious coercion. Like Roger Williams, he argued that God had given them 'a larger power in matters of Religion' than rulers 'under the Gospel' because they were 'types' of Christ's future rule. Their power was an aspect of the temporary judicial law of Israel, not of its permanently binding moral law.[68]

But Goodwin also advanced ten positive arguments in favour of civil toleration. First, God had appointed the Word not the sword as the means of overcoming false religion (2 Cor. 10:5). Second, God had commanded ministers of his word to show meekness towards unbelievers (2 Tim. 2:24–25). Third, and here Goodwin used a distinctively Calvinist argument, repentance was 'a speciall gift of God', and it would be 'unreasonable' to punish a man for not doing what only the power of God could do. Fourth, 'External compulsion in matters of Religion' produced hypocrites rather than true believers. Fifth, if Christian magistrates had greater power in matters of religion than pagan magistrates, then (perversely) it would be better to live under the pagan, who lacked the power to persecute. Sixth, 'Frequent experience' showed that more often than not, magistrates persecuted the godly. Seven, those who championed the magistrate's power in religion were usually very confident that it would be used as they wished. Eight, ascribing such power to the

---

65 *M.S. to A.S.*, 53–54, 105.
66 See Coffey, *Persecution and Toleration in Protestant England* (Harlow, 2000), ch. 2.
67 M.S. to A.S., 50. William Prynne, *The Sword of Christian Magistracy Supported* (1647), 152 quoted this statement, noting that 'John Goodwin himself' agreed that magistrates could use their sword against dissenters.
68 *M.S. to A.S.*, 49–53.

magistrate would hinder further reformation, because people would be afraid to think differently to the magistrate. Nine, the victims of this power would not be 'men of loose or no conscience', but conscientious men who would adhere to sincerely held beliefs even in the face of persecution. Finally, coercive power in religion 'tends to defile and pollute the consciences of men' – a conscience which conformed with 'the State-Religion' 'against the graine of its owne judgement and inclination' would either lose its sensitivity or descend into 'grievous agonies' of self-recrimination.[69]

With its radical challenge to traditional Protestant ideas about conscience and the magistrate's power in religion, *M.S. to A.S.* provoked an immediate reaction from the Presbyterians. On 6 May, the Westminster Assembly singled out the book for criticism, asking a committee to report 'what they find in the said booke that may reflect either upon this Assembly or the Commissioners of Scotland'.[70] The Scots commissioners were particularly disturbed. In the month of its publication, Robert Baillie wrote to his correspondent in the Netherlands that the author was 'John Goodwin of Coleman Street ... a bitter enemie to Presbyterie, and is openly for a full liberty of conscience to all sects, even Turks, Jews, Papists, and all to be more openly tolerate than with yow. This way is very pleasant to very many here'. Goodwin wanted 'to take from the magistrate all power of taking any coercive order with the vilest hereticks', and denied that the magistrate could employ any coercion against 'Turk, Jew, Papist, Socinian, or whatever, for his religion'. Baillie recognised that the five Apologists 'will not say this; but "M.S." is of as great authoritie here as any of them'.[71] Adam Stewart himself eventually published a prolix and tedious two-part reply to the tract,[72] but a more incisive response was provided by another Scot, George Gillespie, one of the Covenanter clergy attending the Westminster Assembly. Gillespie grouped *M.S. to A.S.* with two other notorious tolerationist works of 1644, *The Bloudy Tenent of Persecution* by Roger Williams and *The Compassionate Samaritan* by William Walwyn.[73]

Despite being lumped together with radicals like Williams and Walwyn, Goodwin continued to associate with the conservative Westminster Independents. This probably explains why he issued a second edition of his controversial tract in July, under a new title, *A Reply of the Two Brethren to A. S.* Goodwin (still writing anonymously) explained that he was issuing this 'corrected, and inlarged' edition in response to the demands of friends. He had blotted out 'some sharp expressions', added some new material, and made unclear things clearer. The vast majority of the tract was identical to the first edition, but Goodwin had inserted several pages in which he added a surprising rider to his earlier case for toleration. He suggested that he only wanted toleration for orthodox Protestants, not for those who denied

---

69 *M.S. to A.S.*, 54–61.
70 Westminster Assembly, session 212: see van Dixhoorn, 'Reforming the Reformation', v. 53.
71 Baillie, *Letters and Journals*, 3 vols, ii. 180–81, 184.
72 A[dam] S[teuart], *Zerubbabel to Sanballat and Tobiah, or the first part of the Duply to M.S. alias Two Brethren* (1645); A[dam] S[teuart], *The Second Part of the Duply to M.S. alias Two Brethren* (1645).
73 George Gillespie, *Wholesome Severity reconciled with Christian Liberty, or The True Resolution of a Present Controversie concerning Liberty of Conscience* (1645).

the fundamentals of the faith:

> The least venting of any opinion against fundamentals; as *Judaisme*, denying Christ to be the true Messias; *Arrianisme* and *Socinianisme*, opposing the Deity of Jesus Christ; *Arminianisme*, that questions the person of the Holy Ghost: *Papisme*, holding Justification by works; or that *Anabaptisme* that denies the derivation of Adams originall corruption to us, and the power of Christs grace to be conveyed to us without any spirituall power of our free will (falsly supposed to be in us) or of the like opinions, ought to be suppressed by due proportion ...[74]

Besides containing a very odd definition of Arminianism, this statement appeared to contradict the basic thrust of Goodwin's argument in *M.S. to A.S.*, where he had emphatically denied the magistrate any coercive power in matters of religion. The best explanation for the revision is that Goodwin had come under pressure from old friends like Thomas Goodwin and Jeremiah Burroughs, who feared that the talk of a 'universal' toleration was undermining prospects of a rapprochement with the Presbyterians. Both men went out of their way to emphasise that the Apologists were firmly opposed to 'the Toleration of all Religions', and Goodwin's unqualified arguments must have troubled them.[75] It may even be that the tract was re-titled *A Reply of the Two Brethren* because Burroughs or another conservative Independent had written the new sections. The revisions certainly show that Goodwin still wanted to work closely with the conservative Independents, and still resisted the logic of his own arguments. The conservative Independent William Bartlet quoted this passage from *The Reply* in 1647, to refute the 'slander' that Independents favoured an unlimited toleration.[76] By that stage, however, Goodwin had abandoned the caution of 1644, and was firmly on the side of radical tolerationists. It may be significant that in later tracts he cited *M.S. to A.S.* rather than the second revised edition.[77]

Goodwin's increasingly strident Independency was now causing serious ructions in his own parish. At a meeting of the vestry on 15 August 1644, a parish committee was established for 'settling the differences betwixt the parish and Mr Goodwin'. Goodwin made 'two propositions', and the vestry agreed 'that one of the two should be accepted'.[78] Unfortunately, the minutes do not record the propositions, nor do they elaborate on 'the differences'. However, there was clearly growing resentment at the way in which Goodwin had spurned his old parishioners in favour of his new 'members'. Disgruntled parishioners claimed that Goodwin had

---

74 *A Reply of the Two Brethren to A. S.* (1644), 24.
75 See Thomas Goodwin, *The Great Interest of States and Kingdoms* (1645), 53; Burroughs, *Irenicum, to the Lovers of Truth and Peace* (1645), 18–47.
76 William Bartlet, *A Model of the Congregationall Way* (1647), 126.
77 See *Anapologesiastes*, 224, 229–30.
78 GL MS 4458/1, f. 129. A list of twelve names follows this minute and includes two members of Goodwin's gathered church (Hildesley and Montague). More assumes that this was the committee appointed to settle 'the differences betwixt the parish and Mr Goodwin', but a note below explains that they were 'chosen feoffees in trust for the landes of the poore'.
79 Prynne, *Full Reply*, 21, 24.

neglected his preaching and refused to administer communion and even some baptisms 'for a yeares space or more'.[79] Goodwin was hauled before the Committee of Plundered Ministers, and although forty-five parishioners signed a counter-petition on his behalf, the situation was increasingly fraught.[80]

As ecclesiastical tensions rose in Westminster and the City, the military conflict between Parliamentarians and Royalists continued in the country. In May, Henry Overton published another morale-boosting tract by John Price, dedicated 'To all the Persecuted Members of Jesus Christ, especially the Exiles, and Plundered, of Bristol, Exeter, Westchester, Oxford etc'.[81] In July, the Scots helped the Parliamentary army to win an important victory at Marston Moor. But August saw serious setbacks for Parliament in the south-west, culminating in the surrender of six thousand troops at Lostwithiel on 2 September. Parliament called a day of fasting and humiliation. Goodwin took the opportunity to offer his own explanation of why God was angry in two sermons preached at St Stephen's. The sermons caused controversy, and Goodwin decided to publish them under the title *Theomachia: or the Grand Imprudence of Men Running Hazard of Fighting Against God*.

His text was from Acts chapter 5, where the Jewish leader Gamaliel urges his coreligionists not to suppress the Christians, 'lest yee be found even fighters against God'. Goodwin warned that while God might be merciful to those who mistook truth for error and opposed it by preaching (*per modum Doctoris*), he would 'take up armes' against those who tried to suppress truth by 'an Authoritative power, whether Ecclesiastique or Civill' (*per modum Judicis*). This was provocative stuff, for Goodwin was blaming the recent defeats of the Parliamentary armies on militant Presbyterians intent on suppressing 'the *Congregational Way*'. The hardline Presbyterians were contemporary equivalents of Achan, whose sin had brought divine judgement and military disaster on Israel at the battle of Ai.[82]

Goodwin married this Protestant providentialism to Erasmian scepticism.[83] The militant advocates of the Presbyterian way were acting 'as if it self were the Lord of infallibility'. But in taking their own rectitude for granted, they were running a great risk. 'It is extreme madnesse in men', declared Goodwin, 'to run the hazard we speak of, I mean, of fighting against God'. Wise men (like Gamaliel) would not call in the power of the state against 'any Way, Doctrine, or Practice whatsoever, until they have proof upon proof, demonstration upon demonstration, evidence upon evidence'.[84] Such sceptical arguments for toleration had already surfaced in his *M.S. to A.S.*, and they were to be developed at length in *Hagiomastix*.

Besides being potentially hazardous, the use of religious coercion was also incompatible with human reason and Christian religion. 'Error cannot be healed

---

80 *Innocencies Triumph*, 15.
81 J[ohn] P[rice], *Honey out of the Rock* (1644).
82 θεμαχια *[Theomachia], or The Grand Imprudence of Men running the Hazard of Fighting against God* (1644), 5, 12–13, 20–21.
83 On the use of sceptical arguments for toleration by Christian humanists like Erasmus and Acontius see G. Remer, *Humanism and the Rhetoric of Toleration* (University Park, PA, 1996).
84 *Theomachia*, 24, 19, 18.

or suppressed but by the manifestation of the truth'. The way that would triumph would be the one 'which shall be able to *out-reason*, not that which shall *out-clubbe* all other wayes'. Indeed, Christ himself had 'sufficiently furnished' his church to win the battle against error even though he only given it 'the sword of the Spirit' (the word of God), 'without any concurrence of any heterogeneall or external power'. For its first three hundred years, the church had flourished 'with farre better successe, then they were able to do afterwards, when they had an arme of flesh and a sword in it, to assist them'.[85]

If Goodwin's main task was to strip the civil magistrate of authority in religion, he also wanted to undermine the authority of synods in general and the Westminster Assembly in particular. Goodwin's heterodox tendencies had been openly discussed in the Assembly in early September, when Daniel Cawdry reported on 'what he heard Mr John Goodwin about the mortality of the soule'.[86] Although the Assembly's minutes do not record Cawdry's report, it seems clear that he was associating Goodwin with the mortalist heresy, the subject of fierce controversy since the publication of Richard Overton's *Mans Mortallitie* in January 1644.

Indignant, Goodwin now launched a direct assault on Presbyterian pretensions. Councils and synods, he argued, were prone to assume their own infallibility, commanding 'all mens judgements and consciences to bow downe at the feet of their determinations'. But God would only bless assemblies where men gathered 'with humilitie and meeknesse ... candidly and impartially to argue and debate ... and not to exercise a *dominion over their Faith* ... by an authoritative commanding them out of their present judgement, what ever it be, to doe homage to the results of their debates, whether they see the light and truth in them or no'. When God wished to communicate a new truth, Goodwin maintained, he rarely chose to reveal it to majorities, or to the learned, or to 'Councels, Synods, and Conventions of men eminent in their qualifications'. Indeed, God might well conclude that 'there are too many learned and wise men in a great Councel, for him to reveale the truth'. Instead, he normally choose to reveal himself to the young, the humble, 'Mary a woman', and 'particular men'.[87] The history of the Reformation taught this lesson clearly:

> That light of Evangelicall truth, wherein the Reformed Churches rejoyce at this day, yea, and triumph over Antichristian darkness, did not break out of the clouds of Councels and Synods unto them, but God caused it to shine upon them, from scattered and single stares, as Luther, Calvin, Zuinglius, Martyr, &c.[88]

By undercutting the coercive authority of magistrates and synods, Goodwin aimed to create space for godly individuals to make their own choices about their spiritual lives. He argued that the rigid parochial system directly impeded the

---

85 *Theomachia*, 33, 30, 34–35.
86 'Minutes of the Westminster Assembly', Session 277: 3 September 1644, f. 169r. Transcribed in C. van Dixhoorn, 'Reforming the Reformation', v. 258. I owe this reference to the kindness of Chad van Dixhoorn.
87 *Theomachia*, 43–47.
88 *Theomachia*, 45.

saints' 'growth in grace', for it denied men the 'libertie to choose what Pastor they please'. The wealthy could easily move house to their preferred parish, but for the poor this was often impossible. A voluntary system, by contrast, would allow people to choose their own pastor regardless of their parish. Presbyterians thought this would cause confusion and strife, but in the Low Countries peace prevailed even though 'scare every 5th, nay, not every 8th person (as I have been credibly informed)' was a member of the public Reformed church. If a single parish could contain 'sundry members of twenty severall Companies' like Merchant Taylors and Grocers, why could it not contain members of different churches too?[89]

Theomachia highlighted Goodwin's radicalisation. He was now abrasively critical of the Westminster Assembly. The real spiritual action, he implied, was not taking place in St Margaret's church in Westminster, but in the City, where godly individuals like himself were (in Milton's words) 'musing, searching, revolving new motions and ideas'. Milton's *Areopagitica*, published a month after *Theomachia*, echoed Goodwin's sermons and developed this radical Protestant vision. Another radical Puritan and close friend of Milton, Roger Williams, later praised Goodwin's 'excellent labour' in his *Theomachia*.[90]

It is hardly surprising that *Theomachia* stirred a strong reaction from Presbyterians. One critic, probably the Scottish Westminster divine George Gillespie, declared that Goodwin was widely judged to be 'an irreligious Polititian, adiephorist, neutralist, Nullifidian'. His hostility to synods was reminiscent of the Dutch Arminians, and his denial of the magistrate's power in religion 'giveth a sore Blowe to the Parliaments Power'. 'Shall every one in Israel do in Religion what seemeth good in his own eyes?', asked the author. 'Hath the magistrate no coercive power in matters of religion?' Goodwin's radical tolerationist position contradicted the Apologists. The 'Genealogie of this doctrine' with its stress on fallibility and uncertainty could be traced to 'an Origination and Descent from *Socinians* and *Arminians*'.[91]

The irascible Puritan Erastian, William Prynne, had no compunction about 'scratching' the brethren, and he warned that Goodwin's Independency had already caused chaos:

> yea Mr Goodwins present case in his own Parish, miserably divided, disordered by his Independent way, which hath induced him to refuse to administer the Lords Supper, (yea Baptisme to some children of Parishioners) for a yeares space or more, though they offer to be examined by him; esteeming them none of his Flocke, (preaching but seldome to them, though he receive their tithes) and instead to gather an Independent congregation to himselfe, out of divers Parishes and his owne, to whom he prescribes a Covenant ere they be admitted members of it; preaching, praying, administering the Sacrament to them alone in private conventicles, neglecting his Parishioners: which hath engendered such discontents

---

89 *Theomachia*, 25–26, 23, 31.
90 'The Bloody Tenent yet more Bloody', in *The Complete Writings of Roger Williams*, 7 vols (New York, 1963), iv. 92.
91 [George Gillespie], *Faces About: or A Recrimination Charged Upon Mr John Goodwin* (1644), pp.
92 Prynne, *A Full Reply*, 21.

and rents in the Parish, even among the well-affected and truely religious, that he must either desert it or his Independent way.⁹²

Prynne was particularly disturbed by Goodwin's claim that the people were 'a secular root' out of which it was impossible for 'a spiritual extraction' to be made. Prynne agreed that the power of magistrates derived from the people, but he deplored the suggestion that the (ungodly) people could not transfer power in matters of religion to their appointed magistrates.⁹³ By undermining at the inclusive universality of the parochial community, and Parliament's power in ecclesiastical affairs, Goodwin had struck at two of Prynne's most cherished principles.

Goodwin believed that Prynne was incensing Parliament against him, and trying to get him removed from his parish. In *Innocencies Triumph* (26 October 1644), he defended his reputation, reminding his readers that he had endeavoured with all his might to 'vindicate the Authority, power and priviledges of Parliament'. He was simply concerned to defend 'the most sacred and incommunicable royalties and priviledges of Heaven'. The magistrate should use his power to protect the godly, but he had no power to impose, punish or coerce in matters of religion.⁹⁴

Goodwin also responded to Prynne's charges concerning his parish ministry. He flatly denied that he had neglected his parishioners. Hundreds of them would testify that 'scarce any Minister in or about the City ... have been more diligent, laborious, frequent or constant, in the work of the Ministery'. For several years, he had 'preached constantly thrice, often four times; sometimes five or six times in a week unto them'. The only reason he did not preach more was 'because they do not come so oft to hear me'. Moreover, he had never preached to his Independent congregation 'apart from my parishioners'. He had prayed with his gathered church, and 'now and then debated a question in mine own house', but his doors were always open for any parishioners who wished to join in. As for tithes, he had not received any, and was only given a 'voluntary Contribution', which in the past year amounted to 'very little above 20*l*. His parsonage was impropriate in the hands of his parishioners, and his vicarage was only endowed with £11 per annum. He did receive the half-yearly rent on a small house let for £12–14 per year, but £12 10s of this was deducted to pay for the rent of his house. What remained was barely sufficient 'for the maintenance of a Minister, his Wife, and seven children (most of them very small) in such an expensive place as this City is'. Indeed, 'the Church-warden who gathereth that slender allowance which my Parishioners amongst them think me worthy of' reckoned that the parishioners had 'sav'd their purses harm lesse for a long time'.⁹⁵

As for his gathered church, he had not 'gone about from place to place' seeking recruits, he had simply received individuals from other parishes who had asked to enter 'a Church relation' with Goodwin as their pastor. This had been done with 'the consent of my Parishioners in a publick Vestry'. Those who joined his

---

93 Prynne, *A Full Reply*, 22–24.
94 *Innocencies Triumph*, 2–13.
95 *Innocencies Triumph*, 14–16. Unfortunately, the Churchwardens Accounts for the parish do not survive for the years 1640–55, so it is impossible to cross-check Goodwin's account.

congregation did not have to sign a church covenant, but simply had to express their desire to join and be judged 'meet for such a relation'. Goodwin admitted that he had stopped administering the sacrament to his parishioners, but so had 'very many godly Ministers in and about the Citie'. He did not want to use the old Book of Common Prayer, but he had been willing to allow his parishioners to appoint another minister to administer the sacrament (and even pay him out of his own allowance). As for refusing baptism to parishioners, Goodwin had only done this on two or three occasions in eleven years of ministry at St Stephen's.[96]

The row between Goodwin and Prynne mirrored the struggle for power at Westminster. In September 1644, the Independents Cromwell and St John had steered an Accommodation Order through the Commons directing a parliamentary committee to explore ways of accommodating 'tender consciences'. However, nothing was done to give effect to the Order, and on 18 September the House thanked a group of City clergy who had petitioned for the suppression of 'erroneous opinions, ruinating schisms, and damnable heresies'. In early November, the Assembly recommended Presbyterianism as the only fitting government for the Church, and on 15 November, the Commons passed a resolution 'that no person be permitted to preach who is not an ordained minister'. When peace propositions were adopted and sent to the king on 20 November, they recommended reformation of the Church in line with whatever Parliament decided in consultation with the Assembly.[97]

For Goodwin, these were disturbing developments. He vented his intense frustration in an anonymous pamphlet, *A Paraenetick of Humble Addresse to the Parliament and Assembly for (not Loose, But) Christian Libertie* (30 November 1644).[98] It expressed astonishment at the current threats to the Christian liberty of the Independents. If this had been the doing of the bishops, it could have been more easily borne. But it was the work of 'our Brethren, our Companions once in the same iron yoke and furnace of affliction', who 'have sat and wept together by the Rivers of Babylon'. Were the Independents to be treated as 'vassals' in 'this yeare of Jubilee ... when all other liberties are vindicated?' Parliament had lately considered 'the just and mercifull accommodation of tender consciences', so Independents were 'amazed and astonished' at the 'sudden prejudice' they had received from both Parliament and Assembly. Back in December 1643, Parliament had promised to preserve 'the Rights of particular Congregations', but where was that promise now? 'We have fought, and adventured purse and person upon this expectation of Liberty' wrote Goodwin. 'Christ bought our liberties for us with his blood, wee have bought them over again at your hands with our own blood'. Parliament had bobbed 'Apples of liberty and toleration' before the mouths of its loyal supporters, but failed to deliver: 'What jot or tittle of toleration have you yet brought forth?' Parliament and Assembly were now intent on banning 'preaching without ordination', and there were ominous rumblings of 'Fines, Prisons, Exile, prohibiting

---

96 *Innocencies Triumph*, 16–20.
97 Gardiner, *History of the Great Civil War*, ii. 75–78.
98 For Goodwin's authorship, see Appendix.

the exercise of our Way and our Ministry'. This was a grotesque betrayal of the men who had shed their blood for Parliament in expectation of 'Liberty, first of the Kingdome, then of the Conscience in the Protestant Religion, that they might not be inslav'd in either'. If the ghosts of dead war heroes returned to haunt MPs they would cry, 'Give us our lives againe; we laid them downe for your liberties, performe the like for us'.[99]

This was a startling assault on the integrity of Parliament and the Westminster Assembly. Both institutions were in danger of betraying the cause of liberty, and departing from the way of Christ. 'Would Christ,' asked Goodwin, 'have such desperate Experiments practised upon his members to kill them, if you cannot cure them of their lesser errours; to fine them, prison them, banish them?' Opponents of the congregational way were courting disaster. 'If our Way be of God, you cannot overthrow it', Goodwin warned, 'You may shew your selves fighters against God'. In the end, '*Tandem vincet veritas*, Truth shall overcome'. The 'Congregationall way' did not resort to worldly weapons or coercion: 'the members of this societie grow up freely unto it ... they meddle with their own things, and are not busie with others'. There were many, however, who followed 'the way of man', and relied on 'the fleshly arme of numbers and multitudes, of power and authoritie'. Independents were 'heartily grieved' at the differences between them and their brethren, but on issues so important 'we cannot yeeld'.[100]

Goodwin elaborated his views in a lengthy reply to Prynne, *Innocency and Truth Triumphing Together* (8 January 1645). Although he was honoured to confront 'so noble an Antagonist', he chided Prynne for advocating a 'compelled or inforced' reformation, when real reformation must be 'voluntary and free'. God alone had dominion over conscience, and no human institution had the authority to dictate to believers. Prynne was teaching 'servility or subjection in judgement and conscience to the decisions or determinations of men in matters of conscience or Religion'. Independents, by contrast, taught that the individual believer should search the Scriptures and think for himself. He could choose to submit to the regulations of an Independent church 'by free and voluntary consent', but he could also withdraw whenever 'he cannot with peace of his conscience walk any longer with them'. Independency, then, was the one form of church government that allowed room for individual conscience, because it rejected compulsion and imposition.[101] This 'voluntary principle' was one of the foundation stones of congregationalism, and it became an equally important element of the concept of 'religious liberty'.[102]

In response to the charge that Independency was a novel position rejected by most ministers, Goodwin retorted that it was the original apostolic pattern. Men

---

99 *A Paraenetick or Humble Addresse to the Parliament and Assembly for (Not Loose, But) Christian Liberty* (1644), 2–9.
100 *A Paraenetick*, 11–14.
101 *Innocency and Truth* (1645), 1, 27, 6–7.
102 See G. Nuttall, *Visible Saints: The Congregational Way, 1640–1660* (Oxford, 1957), ch. 3; T. Larsen, *Friends of Religious Equality: Nonconformist Politics in Mid-Victorian England* (Woodbridge, 1999).

were witnessing its 'discoverie (or recovery rather)', 'the birth (or resurrection rather)'. Independency was like Ulysses returned from his travels. After twenty years of absence, even his own wife Penelope had failed to recognise him at first; so was it any wonder that Independency seemed strange after 1500 years? Independents found themselves standing alone like Athanasius at the Council of Nice, 'opposing (in a manner) the whole Christian world now turned Arrian'.[103]

Goodwin also stood by his insistence that 'a spiritual extraction' could not be derived from 'a secular root'. The 'generalitie of men' in 'every State Politique or Kingdome' were 'naturall men' and 'unsanctified persons', whom 'God hath not indued ... with spirituall wisdome and understanding'. To give these men (or the rulers they set up) control over religion, 'were to give a power unto the blind, to lead not the blind onely, but even the seeing also'. Goodwin was not questioning the enfranchisement of 'naturall men', but he emphatically rejected Prynne's claim that the people ('a secular root') could empower the magistrate to establish and enforce religious uniformity ('a religious extraction').[104] The logic of this argument, as later works demonstrated, was that state itself was a secular extraction with authority restricted to secular matters. Yet Goodwin was still holding on with one hand to the view that magistrates had a duty to act as 'nursing Fathers' to the church, and 'to further the honour and service of the true God, and his people in the worship of him'. In an ambiguous phrase, he stated that Independency 'trembles' to use 'confiscation of goods, imprisonment, banishment, death' in matters of religion, but 'denies not a power of restraint from opposing the received faith, with publick disturbance and offence'.[105]

When Goodwin posted a copy of *Innocency and Truth* to his old friend, John Vicars, he received a sharp reply that was quickly put into print. Vicars was not impressed by Goodwin's bitter attack on Prynne, a man of 'never-dying name and fame'. Goodwin was in no position to criticise others, since he himself had fallen into Socinianism and other 'damnable' errors. In a published reply to Vicars, Goodwin's follower Daniel Taylor leapt to the defence of his pastor: 'I could give you such a lively and bright description of him, as would dazle your eyes to look upon, and make you blush with shame to have grappled with such a person as he is'. Taylor expressed his respect for both Prynne and Vicars, but warned them that they were losing their way. *Innocency and Truth* had 'found joyfull and bountifull entertainment in the judgements of sober and intelligent men'.[106]

The row between Prynne and Goodwin, Vicars and Taylor, illustrated the bitter rifts that were now dividing old friends and allies. Worried by the polarisation, John Price weighed in with his own contribution to the debate, *Unity our Duty* (31 January 1645). In contrast to the writings of Goodwin and Taylor, this was a remarkably irenic tract, an eloquent plea for godly unity. As tensions in the parish

---

103 *Innocency and Truth*, 42–47.
104 *Innocency and Truth*, 84–85, 89–90.
105 *Innocency and Truth*, 50–53.
106 John Vicars, *To his Reverend and Much Respected Good Friend Mr John Goodwin ... An Answer Thereunto* (1645), 1–4 (Vicars' letter), 4–8 (Taylor's reply).

of St Stephen's reached breaking point, Price was making a last ditch appeal for reconciliation, albeit one that laid the blame for the strife on Presbyterian intolerance. 'The Saints should be each others shelter', wrote Price; it was a catastrophe when 'our brethren turnes Dragons', and become 'brethren without bowels, without naturall affection to brethren'. Yet 'intelligent men' agreed that if only Presbyterians and Independents would hear one another 'with meekenesse and patience', the outcome would be 'reconciliation'.[107]

By this time, however, both Independents and Presbyterians were far too busy shouting at each other to listen. Poor Prynne was now inundated with replies to his work. Besides Goodwin's two tracts, there were also anonymous works entitled *Certaine Brief Observations* (1644) and *A Moderate Answer to Mr Prins Full Reply* (1645). Prynne believed that Goodwin had written these tracts too, and Goodwin had to explain that he was not the author.[108] When Prynne published his long counterblast against his Independent critics, *Truth Triumphing Over Falshood* (1645), he accused Goodwin of attacking the authority of Parliament, and suggested that as a 'meer Divine' he was unqualified to pronounce on Parliamentary prerogatives.

Goodwin responded in *Calumny Arraigned* (31 January 1645), collected by Thomason on the same day as Price's *Unity our Duty*. The two men were clearly pursuing a hard cop-soft cop strategy, hitting Presbyterians with one hand while offering an olive branch with the other. Goodwin accused Prynne of 'brain-dead' slanders and passionately defended his own loyalty to Parliament. Stung by Prynne's attack on 'meer divines', Goodwin also hit back against the lawyers. Prynne was obsessed with dredging up 'old obsolete, exolete Records, fetch'd out of the darkest times of Popery'. But such records were 'no Oracles to be consulted about the mind of Christ'. On matters of fact concerning laws, divines would defer to lawyers; but on normative questions about whether laws were 'lawfull in point of conscience, and justifiable in the sight of God', 'the meere Divine is the only competent Judge in the case'. 'The meere Lawyer, with his bookes and records', declared Goodwin, 'must stand by'.[109]

This jurisdictional dispute reveals much about Goodwin's sense of his high calling and his cavalier attitude towards questions of legality. He had no doubt that the language of theologians was to take priority over the language of lawyers.[110] Mere lawyers were simply pedantic recorders and collectors of legal fact, but divines could make rational moral judgements about what laws were just and what laws were unjust. Natural law trumped positive law every time they were in conflict. Whatever the laws of the land said, it was simply unlawful for civil magistrates 'to make any such [penal] Lawes or Statutes in matters of Religion'. Goodwin admitted

---

107 J[ohn] P[rice], *Unity our Duty* (1645), 2, 4–9.
108 On the authorship, see Appendix.
109 *Calumny Arraigned and Cast, or a Briefe Answer to William Prynne* (1645), 2–3, 29–32.
110 On the legal and theological languages of political theory in the seventeenth century, see G. Burgess, *The Politics of the Ancient Constitution: An Introduction to English Political Thought, 1603–1642* (London, 1992), ch. 5.
111 *Calumny Arraigned*, 33–36.

that he had argued this in his sermons, just as he had argued for the justness of Parliament's cause 'in the present warres'.[111] His insistence on the priority of natural law over positive law allowed him to dismiss legal obstacles to religious toleration and armed resistance to kings.

Goodwin's opposition to Parliament's coercive power in matters of religion had landed him before the Committee for Plundered Ministers in 1644. Prynne, who was present at the hearings, alleged that the Committee had questioned Goodwin for 'Antiparliamentary passages' in *Theomachia*. He also alleged that Goodwin had been censured or sequestered for making similar remarks again from the pulpit and in print while 'under examination', and for neglecting his parishioners (in favour of his covenanted church) while continuing to receive their tithes. Goodwin claimed that this was a travesty of the truth. He was not guilty of the things charged to him, and if he had been sequestered no one had told him about it.[112]

As the dispute with the Presbyterians deepened, the Independent coalition became more organised. It brought together a disparate collection of radical Puritans – congregationalists, separatists, Baptists, Seekers, and sympathisers – who for all their differences were united in opposition to religious uniformity. The coalition drew on a variety of talents and professions: Westminster politicians (Lord Saye and Sele and Sir Henry Vane), military commanders (Cromwell), ministers (Goodwin and Hugh Peter), lay pamphleteers (Price, Lilburne and Walwyn), political activists (Hildesley), publishers (Henry Overton), printers (Matthew Simmons) and licensers like John Bachelor whose role in licensing *Theomachia* and other Independent tracts infuriated Presbyterians.[113] By early 1645, such figures were involved in a concerted campaign against Presbyterian uniformity. In the City itself, Goodwin's congregation played a central role in organising Independent protests. William Walwyn testified that at this time, 'I held daily meetings, and intimate Discourse with Mr John Goodwin, Mr Henry Burton, Mr Hugh Peters, Mr Hilsly, Mr Lilburn, and others, and continued so after with the best respect'.[114]

The effectiveness of the network is attested by its coordinated pamphlet war against the Presbyterians. Goodwin's own sallies were seconded by other activists. When Gillespie (or another Scottish divine) attacked *Theomachia* in *Faces About*, he was soon answered by 'an unworthy Auditor' of Goodwin, whom Thomason noted was 'supposed to be Ezeck: Woodward'. Woodward, an educationalist and member of the Hartlib circle, commended Goodwin as a 'Iuditious-pious-Divine'.[115] Prynne's anti-Goodwin pamphlets were answered by William Walwyn, who praised Goodwin

---

112 *Calumny Arraigned*, 5–7, 38–40.
113 John Vicars, for example, complained of the cosy relationship between 'the Licenser [Bachelor] and the Licentious Author [Goodwin]' in *The Schismatick Sifted, or the Picture of Independency* (1646), 28–29. Bachelor's activities are explored in Hughes, *Gangraena and the English Revolution*, 239–41; J. Peacey, *Politicians and Pamphleteers: Propaganda during the English Civil Wars and Interregnum* (Aldershot, 2004), 149–53.
114 *Walwyn*, 386.
115 P. P. [Hezekiah Woodward], *As You Were* (1644), 1–3.
116 *A Helpe to a Right Understanding* (1645), in *Walwyn*, 137–39.
117 *A Copie of a Letter written by John Lilburne Leut. Collonell to William Prynne Esq.* (1645), 2.

as a 'faithfull servant of God, and sincere lover of his Country'.[116] Lilburne also replied to Prynne in a bitterly anti-clerical pamphlet against 'the Blacke-Coats in Synod'.[117]

The early months of 1645 were critical in the Presbyterian–Independent struggle. At Westminster, there was a realignment of factional politics. Essex and the Saye-St John group had now split apart, and were becoming identified with the two sides in the struggle over the church. Essex was a strong supporter of a uniform national church, and his faction were now called 'Presbyterians'. Saye and St John, by contrast, were in favour of toleration for the gathered churches, though few members of their faction actually belonged to a separated congregation. Whereas Essex favoured a continuing alliance with the Scots and a generous peace deal with the king, the Saye-St John group was determined to win outright victory in the war and impose a settlement that would reduce the king's power. They succeeded in steering a Self-Denying Ordinance through Parliament, which excluded all members of Parliament from military offices. Essex was ousted from his command of the army, though Cromwell managed to hold on to his post. The army was also 'new modelled'. A national force of 22,000 men was created under the command of General Fairfax. From its creation in April 1645, the New Model Army was closely identified with the Independents.[118]

Despite these heartening developments at Westminster and in the army, things were going from bad to worse in Goodwin's parish. On 3 May 1645, the Committee for Plundered Ministers agreed to consider Goodwin's case, together with a 'petition of divers of the parishioners', later in the month.[119] At a general vestry on 12 May 1645, a final attempt was made to reconcile the two sides. It was agreed 'by generall consent of the parishioners', that Goodwin and the vestry should each nominate six persons 'to consider and compose the present difference between Mr Goodwin and his people within the space of a month if it may be'. Goodwin chose Owen Rowe, Doctor Nathan Paget, Mr Ashurst, and three known members of his gathered church (Hildesley, Montague and Price). The parish nominated such prominent men as Samuel Avery and Thomas Barnardiston.[120]

Unfortunately, the vestry minutes do not explain the substance of the dispute, and we have no clear sense of how much support he still had within the parish. Although some of his parishioners were fiercely critical of his Independency, others were core members of the gathered church, and Goodwin probably had the sympathy of parochial Independents like Pennington and Rowe who were to back his return in 1649. In the end, what finished him was the coordinated campaign of disgruntled parishioners (both godly Presbyterians and others not godly enough to pass Goodwin's sacramental tests) and political Presbyterians at Westminster led by Prynne and Edward Leigh who chaired the Committee of Plundered Ministers. On 22 May 1645, the Committee finally ordered that 'the vicarage of St Stephens Coleman Streete London be sequestred from John Goodwin Vicar thereof to the use of some godly & orthodox divine'.[121] Three days later, according

---

118 Scott, *Politics and War in the Three Stuart Kingdoms*, 87–91.
119 BL Add MS 15, 669, Proceedings of the Committee for Plundered Ministers, f. 66, 68v.
120 GL MS 4458/1, f. 134.
121 BL Add MS 15,669, Proceedings of the Committee for Plundered Ministers, f. 75v.

to Thomas Edwards, Goodwin prayed before his gathered church, 'O Lord make the Parliament friends to the Saints'.[122] Years later, Goodwin expressed disgust at the treatment he had received at the hands of the Parliament and the Committee. He listed his grievances:

> ... that some of my Writings (as I was inform'd) very narrowly escaped the double doom of the hands of the common Hangman, and of the fire; that I was (to my no small trouble) time after time summoned before the Consistory (sirnamed, the Committee for Plundred Ministers,) and this by the procurement, abetment, and contrivance of some of the Members themselves of the Authority I speak of, that here I was coarsly handled, disgracefully entreated, my Accusers, though but few and less considerable, countenanced, my Friends, who appeared with me, and for me, neglected; and that at last I was compelled to drink the cup, prepared only for Malignant Ministers ... being not only sequestred from my Living (the best means I had for the support of my self, wife, and seven children) but denyed the liberty so much as of preaching in my wonted place.[123]

In Goodwin's own view then, he was pulled from his vicarage by the Committee of Plundered Ministers, not ousted by his parishioners, many of whom remained friendly. This is not how historians have told the story, but there is no hard evidence to support Tolmie's claim that Goodwin's fate was sealed because Pennington and other 'eminent godly puritans' in the parish, 'threw their influence against Goodwin'.[124] Both Pennington and James Russell did cooperate with the establishment of Presbyterian classes in the mid-1640s,[125] but they (along with Owen Rowe) were firm supporters of the Independent regime in 1649. Goodwin had certainly encountered much opposition in the parish, but without the pressure from Westminster he may well have retained his place. Instead, on 1 August 1645, the general vestry elected 'by their whole consent' a new vicar – the Presbyterian William Taylor.[126]

Goodwin's Gathered Church

Goodwin's ejection might have dealt a severe blow to his public profile and influence. The fact that it did not owes much to his gathered church. To begin with, the congregation was a large one, despite having strict rules of admission. As Goodwin revealed in 1647, new members were required to fulfil five conditions:

> We allow none to be capable of our Membership, till we have had [1] a sufficient trial of their Conversation, [2] and have heard the confession of their faith, [3] and the evidences of the truth of their conversion, [4] and till they have entred into a solemne Covenant, [5] and have the joint assent of the whole Congregation.[127]

---

122 Thomas Edwards, *Gangraena* (1646), i. 40.
123 *Peace Protected* (1654), 7.
124 Tolmie, *The Triumph of the Saints: The Separate Churches of London, 1626–1649* (Cambridge, 1977), 113.
125 See W. A. Shaw, *A History of the English Church during the Civil Wars and under the Commonwealth*, 2 vols (London, 1900), ii. 402, 432.
126 GL MS 4458/1, f. 135.
127 *Independencie Gods Veritie* (1647), 6.

We can reconstruct the membership by using a variety of sources: the three public declarations issued by the church in 1647, 1652 and 1661; the parish records of St Stephen's; the wills of members; and contemporary pamphlets, particularly Walwyn's *Just Defence* (1649), which names fourteen of Goodwin's followers, including five who were not signatories to any of the congregation's declarations.[128] The public declarations are the most important source, for they identify the church's leading men. *An Apologeticall Account of some Brethren* (1647) defended Goodwin's reputation and was signed by sixteen male members of the church.[129] *The Agreement and Distance of Brethren* (1652), outlined the congregation's theological position, and was signed by fourteen men, including Goodwin.[130] The third document was *A Declaration* (1661), condemning the Fifth Monarchist rising. Of the six signatories, only one had signed a previous declaration.[131] Altogether, these three published statements yield thirty names, including Goodwin's. Using other contemporary sources, Ellen More identified the names of a further twenty-one men and women who had been 'members' of the church.[132] This yielded a list of fifty people (forty-six men and four women) who were members of the congregation at some time between 1640 and 1660.

More's list can be corrected and supplemented. Given that the surviving evidence tells us little about women or the poorer sort, it is quite possible that the names identified constituted only a minority of the membership. At least half the members are likely to have been female.[133] Some of the congregation's women – Elizabeth Foxcroft, Barbara Lamb, Elizabeth Overton and Mrs Goodson – emerge from the historical record as more than mere ciphers.[134] But others are known only by their names. The poor are even harder to trace. The wills of members make charitable bequests to both the 'poor of Coleman Street parish',

---

128 Henry Brandreth, Henry Overton, Captain Nathaniel Lacy, David Lordell and Thomas Chaplain.
129 Robert Smith, Mark Hildesley, Robert Saunders, Thomas Devenish, William Montague, William Allen, Joseph Gallant, Thomas Lamb, Daniel Taylor, James Paris, Thomas Norman, Bartholomew Lavender, Richard Preice, Thomas Morris, John Price and Richard Arnald.
130 Those who had signed *An Apologeticall Account* were: Allen, Arnald, Lamb, John Price and Taylor. The eight new names (in order of appearance) were: George Foxcroft, William Godfrey, Hamond Brend, John Dye, Joseph Hutchinson, Thomas Tassel, George Cook and Samuel Sowthen
131 Joseph Hutchinson. The new names were (in order of appearance) Richard Pryor, John Weekes, John Wightman, George Backlar and Edward Addenbrook.
132 Captain Thomas Alderne, George Appletree, Richard Atkins, Henry Brandreth, Mistress Mary Browne, Thomas Chaplain, Tobias Conyers, Thomas Firmin, Mrs Goodson, Mrs Sarah Goodwin, Luke Howard, Nathaniel Lacy, Mrs Barbara Lamb, Samuel Lane, David Lordell, Henry Overton, Isaac Penington Jr, Richard Price, Edmund Rozier, Thomas Rudyard and Lawrence Steel.
133 The parish register of St Stephen's names the wives of leading members: Dorothy Alderne, Sara Cook, Sara Dye, Elizabeth Foxcroft, Sarah Lavender, Elizabeth Overton, Martha Price, Elizabeth Smyth(?), Rebecca Taylor, Dorothy Weekes. The parish register also records the death of Mrs Joseph Gallant in 1662.
134 We will come across Foxcroft and Lamb in future chapters. Elizabeth Overton took over her husband's publishing business for a short while after his death, publishing William Bartlet, *Soveraigne Balsome* (1649). Mrs Goodson was married to a naval officer, and separatist, William Goodson, who refused to share communion with Independents, occasioning two conferences between Goodwin's Independents and Samuel Chidley's separatists. See the *ODNB* entry for William Goodson, and also David Brown, *Two Conferences between some of those that are called Separatists and Independents* (1650), 9–22.

and 'the poor of Mr Goodwin's church'. Thomas Alderne left the substantial sum of £40 to be distributed among 'the poorest people of Master Goodwin's Church',[135] and when the congregation were permitted to use St Stephen's church again in 1649, it was agreed that public collections for the poor should be 'divided equally' between the parish and the gathered church.[136] This suggests that Goodwin's congregation contained a significant number of poorer people, who remain anonymous. Twenty people seceded from the congregation to form a Baptist church in 1653, but we only know the names of the leaders of the schism (William Allen and Thomas Lamb).[137] At its heights, Goodwin's gathered church probably attracted several hundred people. Thomas Edwards complained that Goodwin and other Independents preached to 'great Congregations'.[138] When Goodwin debated John Simpson before an audience of 'thousands' in All-hallows Church in 1650, he declared that 'there are some hundreds of persons here present, who have been constant hearers of my Doctrine in these controversies'.[139]

Between 1645 and 1647, the congregation seems to have met in 'one room' of the buildings hired by Goodwin in Swan Alley.[140] Given the size of his following, this must have been a substantial meeting room, and it is no surprise to find Goodwin challenging the claim that Presbyterians met in 'publick Assemblies', while Independents held 'private' or 'separated Assemblies'. Goodwin retorted that though Independent meeting rooms were 'not so capacious and vast' as parish churches, they were no less public. The fact that they occupied just one acre rather than the two acres of the average parish church did not make them 'private' or 'separated'. The public enjoyed 'liberty of access' to attend and 'partake' in these assemblies. Though the sacrament was restricted to members, Independent gatherings were 'more cordiall, open, and free, then many of your Assemblies doe afford'.[141] Eventually, Goodwin's congregation would be granted the use of St Mary Abchurch, and they would return to St Stephen's Coleman Street in 1649. But for Goodwin parish churches were no more than conveniences. The early church had met in 'private houses' and 'upper chambers', and there was nothing sacred about the 'consecrated places' favoured by Presbyterians.[142]

Geographically, the congregation was drawn from across the City of London, but its core was based in the Coleman Street parish. Of the thirty men who signed the public declarations, twelve lived in the parish of Coleman Street.[143] Key figures in Goodwin's inner circle lived in the parish, including John Price, Daniel Taylor, Mark Hildesley, and Henry Overton. As More explains, 'Goodwin's gathered church retained a parochial character'.[144] However, the majority of the congregation

---

135 NA PROB 11/265, Will of Thomas Alderne.
136 GL MS 4458/1, f. 161.
137 See chapter 8.
138 Edwards, *Gangraena*, ii. 132. See also *Moro-mastix*, p. 7.
139 *Truths Conflict with Error* (1650), 77.
140 *Cretensis, or a Brief Answer to an Ulcerous Treatise ... intituled, Gangraena* (1646), 37.
141 *Anapologesiastes*, 131
142 *Anapologesiastes*, 163.
143 Goodwin, Cook, Dye, Foxcroft, Gallant, Hildesley, Lavender, Montague, Price, Sowthen, Smyth, Taylor.

probably came from outside the parish – of the twenty-nine men who signed its public declarations, sixteen do not appear in the St Stephen's parish records.[145]

The majority of the members for whom we have occupational data were engaged in domestic trade as shopkeepers, manufacturers or both. Nine of these were freemen of companies concerned with the outfitting or cloth trades, including five haberdashers (Thomas Chaplain, Joseph Hutchinson, Thomas Lamb, Daniel Taylor and John Wightman), a merchant tailor (John Price), a dyer (John Weekes), and a draper (Thomas Rudyard). Others engaged in domestic trade were a tavern keeper (Mark Hildesley), a brewer (Richard Arnald), a baker (William Montague), a confectioner (Hamond Brend), a silkman (Samuel Sowthen), a provisioner (Henry Brandreth), a shoemaker (Luke Howard) and a bookseller (Henry Overton). In addition, the congregation boasted four merchants involved in overseas trade: Thomas Alderne, William Allen, George Cook and George Foxcroft (both of the East India Company). There were also several 'professionals': a schoolmaster (Joseph Gallant), a barber-surgeon (Bartholomew Lavender), a scrivener (Richard Price), and two ordained ministers (Robert Smyth in the 1640s; Tobias Conyers in the 1650s). Henry Brandreth was classified as gentlemen. Finally, several members of the congregation were involved in military affairs, either as officers in the Parliamentarian armies (Major Robert Saunders, Captain Nathaniel Lacy), or perhaps as captains in the London trained bands (Captain Chaplain, Captain Stacy, Captain Alderne). Thomas Devenish was keeper of Winchester House.[146]

This constitutes a rather impressive list, and includes men of some social standing. The majority of Goodwin's named followers clearly 'inhabited the milieu of the middling London trader', though some were much more prosperous than others. The churchwardens' accounts for St Stephens in the 1630s allow us to gauge their relative wealth. The records of the tithe money given by individuals are particularly illuminating. In 1639–40, Hildesley contributed 11s, slightly less than the wealthiest men in the parish such as James Russell (14s) and Thomas Barnardiston (12s 6d). Of the other future members of the gathered church, Montague contributed 9s 8d, Foxcroft 6s, Gallant 4s, but Overton paid only 2s 9d, Lavender 2s, and Price just 1s 5d.[147] The differentials in wealth are confirmed by a listing of payments given over a four-year period 'towards ye repair of the church'. George Foxcroft was named among the wealthiest parishioners (Avery, Barnardiston, Cockcroft and Russell) who each paid £5 4s. Hildesley gave £1 14s 4d, Overton, Montague and Lavender £1 14s, while John Price, Gallant and Chaplain each contributed 17s 4d.[148] The wills of members confirm that Gallant and Price were men of relatively modest means, while Henry Overton, Daniel Taylor, Thomas

---

144 More, 'Congregationalism', 215.
145 Edward Addenbrooke, William Allen, Richard Arnald, George Backlar, Hamond Brend, Thomas Devenish, William Godfrey, Joseph Hutchinson, Thomas Lamb, Thomas Morris, Thomas Norman, James Paris, Richard Price, Richard Pryor, Thomas Tassel, John Wightman.
146 More, 'Congregationalism'. Walwyn refers to Captain Chaplain in *Walwyns Just Defence* (1649), in *Walwyn*, 388.
147 GL MS 4457/2, ff. 354–356.

Alderne, Mark Hildesley, Thomas Lamb and William Allen all had gross assets of more than £500. As More observes, 'Such a high proportion of the relatively well-to-do [in the congregation] places Goodwin's followers at a social distance from those attached to many other gathered churches in Civil War London'.[149]

The prosperity and standing of Goodwin's followers provided him with a firm base throughout the 1640s and 1650s. His gathered church saw him through the difficult years of 1645–49, and all the members whose wills date from the 1640s or 1650s left bequests to their pastor. They helped to finance and advertise his numerous publications. In 1648, a critic complained that Goodwin's 'disciples' had been out on the streets of the City distributing the title page and dedicatory epistle of a forthcoming pamphlet by 'Bishop John'.[150]

However, we must not exaggerate the social status and political influence of Goodwin's congregation in 1645. The most prominent members of his parish did not join the gathered church. At no time during the 1640s or 1650s did the congregation contain any members of Parliament, and before 1649 few held office above the level of the parish. The congregation's political influence came through pamphleteering, petitioning, and personal connections with war-party politicians like Cromwell and Haselrig. Men like Richard Arnold, Richard Price and John Price earned a reputation as 'spies' and 'agents' who gathered intelligence at Westminster Hall, the Exchange and London's many churches and taverns.[151] They functioned as Goodwin's eyes and ears in the City and beyond while also working for Independent grandees. As faithful servants of the grandees, Goodwin's followers were often at odds with the Levellers. But as representatives of London's middling sort, they shared Leveller concerns and were able to cooperate with Lilburne on and off from 1645 to December 1648. As Brenner has observed, Goodwin's gathered church 'seems to have played a central leadership role' in 'the more radical wing of London political independency'.[152]

The most important lay leaders of the congregation were Daniel Taylor and John Price, who both lived in the parish. It was Taylor who had written the laudatory verse to accompany Goodwin's portrait in 1641, and had gone into print to defend his pastor against John Vicars in 1645. Ellen More describes Taylor as 'the hub of various relationships among members, spiritual, social and economic', and notes that his will cites 'twelve of Goodwin's followers as brethren, friends and as business associates'.[153] When Goodwin preached Taylor's funeral sermon in 1655, the 'Epistle Dedicatory' was a pen portrait of the model godly layman. Taylor was 'an highly accomplisht man', who loved to read theological books in his 'spare hours', and was well able 'to argue the most thorny and abstruse points in Divinity'. He never accepted anything on faith, but examined everything for himself. He 'maintained

---

148 GL MS 4457/2, ff. 356v–359.
149 More, 'Congregationalism', 220.
150 *Sion College: What it is and Doeth* (1648), 13.
151 See *Walwyn*, 386, 400, 411.
152 Brenner, *Merchants*, 537, 539.
153 More, 'Congregationalism', 224.

a constant and close trade of communion with God', showed respect for those who disagreed with him, and avoided 'ostentation or vanity' in his dress. Goodwin had the highest opinion of his 'counsel and advice'.[154]

The other key figure in the congregation was John Price, and it would not be misleading to see him as Goodwin's right-hand man. Critics called him Goodwin's 'beloved Disciple', his 'precious Second', his 'puppet incendiary', and 'a chip of the old block'.[155] He lived in Swan Alley where Goodwin had his study, and was 'a shopkeeper in the Exchange'.[156] Next to Goodwin, Price was the congregation's most active pamphleteer. Altogether he wrote some thirteen tracts between 1642 and his death in 1654. Like Goodwin, he published mainly with Henry Overton in the 1640s (though also with Matthew Simmons and Thomas Paine), and with Henry Cripps and Lodowick Lloyd after 1649. He was a scourge of the City's Presbyterian clergy and the Leveller, William Walwyn. One critic was not surprised at his bitter rhetoric, 'when I consider who hath had the Tutoring of you: like master, like schollar'.[157] Price worked at Goodwin's behest and under his supervision – in one tract he thanked his pastor for 'your favourable acceptance of my present pains, and candid construction of engaging my self therein'.[158] In places he even culled passages from Goodwin's tracts and silently inserted them into his own text.[159] As we shall see, Price also worked as a political activist and represented the congregation at meetings of the Independent politicians.

Goodwin held Price and Taylor in such high esteem that he allowed them to deputise for him in the pulpit.[160] As William Walwyn remarked, Goodwin had clearly 'chang'd his mind' since his famous altercation with the preaching cobbler Samuel How in 1639.[161] Lay preaching had now become a significant feature of radical Puritanism in the City and the army, but Goodwin had little time for enthusiasts and tub-preachers. Why then did he change his tune? His critics argued that his prime motive was to free up time for writing anti-Presbyterian polemics.[162] But there were weightier reasons. Firstly, as an Independent Goodwin was trying to recreate a primitive church along New Testament lines, and he believed that 'prophesying' by 'members' was 'a practise recorded in Scriptures'.[163] Secondly, the experience of the gathered church had convinced Goodwin that Taylor and Price had the gift of teaching. Finally, his controversy with the Presbyterians had made

---

154 *Mercy in her Exaltation* (1655), 'The Epistle Dedicatory', sigs. a2v–a4r.
155 Edwards, *Gangraena*, iii, 160; C[ornelius] B[urges], *Sion College: What it is and Doeth* (1648), 21; William Jenkins, *The Blinde Guide*, 100; Christopher Love, *A Modest and Clear Vindication ... of the Ministers of London from the Aspersions of John Price* (1649), 5.
156 *The Pulpit-Incendiary Anatomized* (1648), 15.
157 *The Pulpit-Incendiary Anatomized*, 15.
158 J[ohn] P[rice], *Independency Accused* (1645), sig. A2r.
159 See for example *The Pulpit Incendiary* (1648), 39–41, which borrows extensively from *Anti-Cavalierisme* (1642), 38–39.
160 See Edwards, *Gangraena*, iii. 160; Vicars, *Coleman-street Conclave Visited* (1648), 36.
161 *Walwyn*, 418.
162 See Edwards, *Gangraena*, iii. 160; Vicars, *Coleman-street Conclave Visited*, 36.
163 *Anapologesiastes*, 163.

him increasingly critical of domineering clergy. Goodwin was determined to be a different kind of minister, one who empowered the laity by teaching them to judge for themselves and to exercise their spiritual gifts.

The bookseller and stationer Henry Overton was another key member of the church, and he worked closely with both Goodwin and Price. He owned a shop on the corner of Pope's Head Alley and Lombard Street, and worked with a number of printers, particularly Matthew Simmons. Overton's catalogue covered a wide range of publications, from news accounts and official Parliamentary publications to a pamphlet puffing the benefits of *Warm Beer* (1641). But the bulk of the works Overton published and sold were religious. After 1644, he became one the leading publishers of Independent books, including works by John Cotton, Richard Mather, Henry Burton, Nathanael Homes, Samuel Eaton, John Ellis, Henry Jessey, William Dell, Walter Cradock and Paul Hobson. He also published two influential defences of toleration penned by MPs: the anonymous *Ancient Bounds, or Liberty of Conscience* (1645) by Francis Rous;[164] and Sir Simonds D'Ewes, *The Primitive Practise for Preserving Truth* (1645).[165] Given the closeness of the relationship between Goodwin and his flock, it seems very likely that Overton discussed with his pastor the books he was going to publish. Thus his catalogue of publications tells us much about the values of Goodwin's congregation and the alliances it was forming during these critical years. In addition, Overton published no fewer than twenty-one books and pamphlets by Goodwin between 1640 and his death in 1648, from *The Saints Interest in God* (1640) to *Neophutopresbuteros* (1648). He also published several pamphlets by John Price.

Despite Goodwin's ejection from the vicarage of St Stephen's, his followers maintained a strong working relationship with their old friends in the parish. Indeed, the vestry minutes for the late 1640s reveal that Goodwin's congregation continued to make a full contribution to the running of the parish. No fewer than seven members attended a general vestry on 4 July 1645, and five were present on 1 August 1645, when the general vestry chose William Taylor as Goodwin's successor.[166] Even Goodwin seems to have attended a meeting of the general vestry on 12 August, at which the terms of Taylor's appointment were confirmed. Mark Hildesley and William Montague sat regularly on the select vestry after 1645 and both were auditors of the parish accounts. In December 1645, Hildesley was even chosen as one of the four common councilmen from the parish – for the next decade, he would be the congregation's most politically distinguished figure. Other members of the gathered church (Price, Cook, Overton, Gallant and Steel) were

---

164 Rous's authorship is persuasively demonstrated by J. Sears McGee, 'Francis Rous and "Scabby or Itchy Children": the problem of toleration in 1645', *Huntingdon Library Quarterly*, 67 (2004), 401–22. I am grateful to Professor McGee for allowing me to see a draft of this paper. The coauthor ('J.S.') was Joshua Sprigge.

165 See J. S. McGee, 'Sir Simonds D'Ewes and "the Poitovin Cholick": Persecution, toleration and the mind of a Puritan member of the Long Parliament', *Canadian Journal of History*, 38 (2003), 481–91.

166 GL MS 4458/1 ff. 134–35: the seven were Cooke, Foxcroft, Gallant, Hildesley, Montague, Overton and Price. Five of these attended on 1 August (the absentees being Cooke and Gallant).

present at general vestries in 1646 and 1647.[167]

However, the influence of Goodwin and his congregation spilled out beyond the parish and the City. Thomas Edwards had been 'informed from severall hands' that Goodwin had become an itinerant 'Baptizer generall, baptizing in Stepney Parish, Hackney, severall parishes of London, and baptizes sometimes three or foure in a day, going from one place to another'.[168] By agreeing to baptize the children of godly supporters across the City and beyond, Goodwin was cultivating an extended network of sympathisers across London. Although the references are scattered and non-specific, it seems clear that he made a number of trips outside London and maintained active contacts in Norfolk. His followers were also active outside London. *Gangraena* alleged that John Price had recently visited Bury St Edmunds, where he preached in a house, and vented Goodwin's latest ideas – 'dangerous and hereticall opinions' on divine grace and the natural ability of the non-elect to repent and believe.[169] In 1647, John Lilburne complained that Goodwin's congregation had used its influence to undermine Leveller petitioning in Buckinghamshire and Hertfordshire.[170] The congregation's reputation had even spread to New England. When a group of petitioners approached the General Court of Massachusetts to ask for a reform of church polity, one expressed a preference for 'that particular government which Mr John Goodwin in Colemanstreet was exercised in'.[171]

By the mid-1640s then, Goodwin had emerged as the leading champion of Independency in the City of London. His congregation was large, active and influential, and he was a fierce critic of Presbyterian uniformity. He was on the verge of becoming 'the Grand Heretick of England'.

---

167 GL MS 4458/1 ff. 135–51.
168 Edwards, *Gangraena*, ii. 119.
169 Edwards, *Gangraena*, ii.161.
170 Lilburne, *Jonah's Cry out of the Whales Belly* (1647), 5.
171 Edward Winslow, *New Englands Salamander* (1647), 3.

5

'THE GRAND HERETICK OF ENGLAND' 1645–48

Goodwin's sequestration was indicative of an escalating civil war among the godly. The initial panic over gathered churches was now being displaced by an even greater alarm over heresy. The Puritan clergy bewailed the rapid rise of Antinomianism, Arminianism, Anti-Scripturism, Socinianism, Familism and other pernicious errors. Heresiographers rushed into print with voluminous catalogues of contemporary sects and heresies.[1] In Fast Sermons to Parliament, the Presbyterians implored the magistrate to crush heresies and schisms, and introduced a Blasphemy Ordinance in Parliament prescribing capital punishment for anti-Trinitarians and imprisonment for Arminians and other heretics. The City Presbyterians declared open season on sects and heresies, and identified Goodwin as Public Enemy No. 1. As the Leveller Humphrey Brooke commented, the Presbyterians styled Goodwin 'The Grand Heretick of England'.[2]

Stung by such bitter attacks, Goodwin responded in three major ways. Firstly, he sought to demonstrate his own soundness by combating heresy through preaching and writing. He lectured against Antinomians, Anabaptists and Seekers and devoted months of sermons to a critique of the Anti-Scripturists, which resulted in a major work of apologetics, *The Divine Authority of the Scriptures Asserted*. Secondly, in a series of tracts culminating in *Hagiomastix*, Goodwin challenged the Blasphemy Ordinance with sceptical arguments, and developed his tolerationist critique of the use of force in religion. Finally, Goodwin threw his weight behind the New Model Army. With the political Presbyterians dominant in both the City and Westminster, the army emerged as the one reliable protector of the radical Puritan minorities. In Goodwin's eyes, the army was the agent of England's deliverance from Presbyterian slavery.

---

1 See E. Pagitt, *Heresiography: or A Description of the Hereticks and Sectaries of these latter times* (1645); R. Baillie, *Dissuasive from the Errours of the Time* (1645); T. Edwards, *Gangraena* (1646); J. J. Bastwick, *The Utter Routing of the Whole Army of Independents and Sectaries* (1646); S. Rutherford, *A Survey of the Spirituall Antichrist* (1648).
2 Humphrey Brooke, *The Charity of Church-men* (1649), in W. Haller and G. Davies, eds, *The Leveller Tracts, 1647–53* (New York, 1944), 342.

In all three of these ventures, Goodwin was making significant modifications to the received Reformed tradition. His apologetics set out to highlight the reasonableness of Christianity – in the process, he ended up abandoning Calvinism, exposing problems with the textual history of the Bible, and teaching that faith must be based on evidence. In his tolerationist writings, he sided with Castellio and Acontius against Calvin and Beza, exalting individual liberty of conscience and denying that the magistrate had any coercive powers in matters of religion. In politics, he developed the ideas of *Anti-Cavalierisme*, articulating a vision of the civil war as a war for civil and religious liberty.

The Godly's Civil War

In June 1645, the New Model defeated the king's forces in the most decisive battle of the first Civil War, at Naseby in Northamptonshire. As David Scott remarks, Naseby and its aftermath 'confirmed the Independents and their army as the most powerful force in British politics'.[3]

Goodwin and his congregation continued to work closely with the political Independents in the army and at Westminster. Writing a year later in May 1646, Thomas Edwards declared that the Independent ministers were taken up 'with the resort of great persons to their houses, and with the consultations they are admitted unto till midnight about great affairs; and particularly *Cretensis* [Goodwin] of late, as tis talked everywhere in London'.[4] But City politics were under Presbyterian control, and at Westminster the Essex faction could garner enough votes to push through a Presbyterian settlement of the church.

Despite their differences, Presbyterians and Independents were still able to cooperate on common projects to promote godliness. At some time before 1646, Goodwin joined with two Presbyterians (Calamy and Gouge) and three other Independents (Caryll, Burroughes and Greenhill) to recommend Hezekiah Woodward's book on children's education.[5] In 1645, both Goodwin and Calamy contributed commendatory epistles to William Fenner's *A Divine Message to the Elect Soul*.[6]

Although militants on each side knew where they stood, some moderates were left feeling confused. One 'godly learned Minister' wrote to a member of Goodwin's church explaining he had been 'respectfull and reverent ... towards the Congregationall Way', and had been studying *Theomachia* and *Innocencies Triumph*. However, he needed answers to some troubling questions, for 'I dare not be guilty of that which hee [i.e. Goodwin] so much pleads against, *blind obedience, implicit*

---

3 D. Scott, *Politics and War in the Three Stuart Kingdoms* (Basingstoke, 2004), ch. 3, quotation at 97.
4 Thomas Edwards, *Gangraena* (1646), ii. 132.
5 The book was circulated in manuscript and published several years later by the Presbyterian bookseller Thomas Underhill: Hezekiah Woodward, *Of the Childs Portion, viz: Good Education* (1649), title page.
6 Significantly, Goodwin's epistle was retained in three further editions of the book published in 1647, 1651 and 1676.

faith. Was it credible that 'all the Christian Churches in the world suffer'd the government of Christ ... to be destroy'd?' 'If the subject matter of Political administration be merely humane matters', as Goodwin asserted, why did the Congregationalists wait until 1644 to say so? Why were they silent in 1640 to 1642, when the politicians 'had their hands thrust deep into Church-affaires, and things spirituall?' Did not the New England Congregationalists suppress sects and heresies? Moreover, was there not clear biblical evidence, especially in the Old Testament, for the forcible suppression of false religion? Did not Calvin and John Cotton support the execution of blasphemers?[7]

These were good questions, and tricky ones. Goodwin commissioned John Price to publish an answer entitled *Independency Accused ... and Acquitted* (12 August 1645).[8] On the issue of the Church's apostasy, Price argued that the congregational polity had been maintained in the first two centuries, but that in the third century smaller churches had been subordinated to greater churches, 'at which time Antichrist had made much progresse towards his usurpation'.[9] As for the role of the civil magistrate in religion, Price was anxious not to appear too radical. He justified the iconoclasm of the early 1640s by saying that 'The ruining of Babylon' was acceptable, but 'the compulsion of Sion' was not. He was very reluctant to 'accuse our brethren abroad' (the New Englanders). Although contemporary rulers did not have the religious authority of Old Testament kings, they did have 'a coercive power in matters of religion, in things that are of a morall and capitall consideration, such as are prophane swearings, cursings, blasphemies, and such things'. They could punish three kinds of offences: crimes 'against the light of nature and conscience'; 'cursed apostasie from Christ, professedly denying him to be God, or come in the flesh'; and thirdly, 'such as are turbulent, violent, mutinous and factious'. Goodwin himself, according to Price, had never pleaded for toleration of such false prophets or blasphemers as were condemned to death in Deuteronomy 13. The magistrate could punish 'a prophane, wilfull, wicked blasphemer and curser of God', but it was quite a different matter to punish 'one who through ignorance misconceiveth of God, either in respect of his Attributes, or in respect of the Trinity'. Price would not make a judgement about which category Servetus fell into, and he was not willing to criticise John Cotton or Thomas Goodwin.[10] At this stage then, the Goodwin congregation was still anxious not to break too sharply with mainstream Reformed tradition or the conservative Congregationalists. Over the next two years, however, the militant Presbyterian attack on heresy would force Goodwin into an emphatically radical position.

As a Presbyterian church settlement came ever closer to reality, Goodwin issued *Twelve Considerable Serious Cautions ... about a Reformation* (17 February

---

7 J[ohn] P[rice], *Independency Accused by Nine Severall Arguments written by a Godly, Learned Minister to a Member of Mr John Goodwins Congregation, and Acquitted by Severall Replyes to the said Arguments by a Member of the same Church* (1645), 1–3, 9–12, 14–19, 27–29.
8 P[rice], *Independency Accused*, sig. A2r.
9 P[rice], *Independency Accused*, 4–6.
10 P[rice], *Independency Accused*, 11, 12–14, 19–23, 25, 29–31.

1646). The tract warned against 'the hot-pressers of Reformation' who were clamouring for coercive uniformity in religion. Goodwin reminded his readers that the Solemn League and Covenant bound them above all else to pursue reformation 'according to the word of God'. Such a biblical reformation, he argued, must not harm any of God's children, and it must not obstruct 'the propagation of the truth'. It must not feel bound to imitate 'the best Reformed churches' except insofar as they comported with the word of God, and it must not place the interests of the ministers above those of the people. It must be a 'tender and nursing-mother unto all, not a bloody cruel stepmother to any Churches of Christ'. It must not punish the conscientious who expressed doubts about doctrines like the Trinity, and it must not slander the saints. It must promote free trade in religion, giving 'liberty to the Spirit of God to do with his own what he pleaseth; and must not confine him to his market, or compel him to traffique only with Councels and Synods for his heavenly commodities'. False reformation condemned 'sober, learned, pious and conscientious men' as 'hereticall' on the advice of 'a very small parcel of men' who had set themselves up as guardians of orthodoxy.[11]

A fortnight after collecting Goodwin's tract, George Thomason acquired *Gangraena, or a Catalogue and Discovery of many of the Errours, Heresies, Blasphemies and Pernicious Practices of the Sectaries*. The author was Thomas Edwards, and he painted a lurid picture of a nation sliding into religious anarchy. Edwards illustrated his case with a wealth of salacious and shocking anecdotes, backed up by letters from godly ministers and other informants. Posing as an expert heresiographer, he catalogued 176 errors, heresies and blasphemies, 28 pernicious practices, and 16 sorts of sectaries.[12]

Prominent among his targets was his former friend (and teacher?), John Goodwin, who was now cast out from the Church of England and numbered among the 'Sectaries'. He alleged that Henry Burton had denounced Goodwin's errors on justification as 'damnable' and 'not to be endured', and was planning to preach against Goodwin's errors, until persuaded by another Independent that it would be a 'scandal' to the Congregational cause if 'two such famous men as you two fall out'.[13] Edwards also condemned Goodwin for misrepresenting learned authors, preaching against Parliament, scoffing at religion, producing books with swelling titles, and playing cards and bowls on Sabbaths and public thanksgiving days.[14] Most hurtfully of all, he responded to Independent tales of divine judgement on Presbyterians by claiming that two of Goodwin's children had been killed 'by the plague of pestilence' at the very time when Goodwin himself was 'upon the making his house a meeting place for the Sectaries'.[15]

Gangraena part I provoked various replies from authors like Walwyn and Saltmarsh. Goodwin himself responded in *Cretensis, or a Briefe Answer to an Ulcerous Treatise* (19

---

11 *Twelve Considerable Serious Cautions* (1646), 1–8.
12 Edwards, *Gangraena*, i. 15.
13 Edwards, *Gangraena*, i. 25, 128.
14 Edwards, *Gangraena*, i. 45, 54, 55, 67, 73.
15 Edwards, *Gangraena*, i. 128.

March 1646), described by Stevie Davies as 'a witty and urbane tract'.[16] Goodwin joked that Edwards's tall tales (such as the story of the shrinking nude woman) made 'the tale of *Gargantua* and *Don Quixote* with his windmills to look like Gospels in comparison of it'.[17] Yet beneath the satire, Goodwin was deadly serious. Edwards had slandered the saints, and Goodwin was determined to defend their reputation.

Goodwin devoted the bulk of the tract to defending his own reputation. His supposed 'error' on justification was a truth defended by godly theologians like Paraeus, Wootton and Gataker. The suggestion that he and his congregation were addicted to cards or loose on the Sabbath was nonsense. As for the claim that he had played bowls on a Thanksgiving Day for the victory at Naseby, Goodwin confessed that after 6p.m. he had gone to the 'garden-house of a friend', and indulged in a gentle game for about half an hour with both Presbyterians and Independents. This was an 'innocent transgression'. Did not the Presbyterian clergy go to watch fireworks on the evening of November the fifth? Had not a Westminster divine gone fishing on the afternoon of a thanksgiving day? Edwards, like the Pharisees, 'doth straine out gnats, and swallow camels'. If he did not stop his slanders, Goodwin threatened to publish a manuscript documenting his 'juglings' between two livings in Surrey and Essex. With regard to the tale about his children, Goodwin himself had been 'far absent for severall weeks, when God took them away'. Goodwin's followers had met in his meeting room several times without any children dying, and they only died 'upon my deserting and disuse of it'. Although the children were 'very dear' to Goodwin, he reflected that God had perhaps taken them away because he could no longer provide for them after his ejection. And he noted that 'three Grave men (and two of them Great) who were principall Actors in my troubles and ejection' had been taken away by death shortly afterwards.[18]

The rest of the tract detailed Edwards' forgeries, slanders and misrepresentations of Goodwin's allies like Jeremiah Burroughs, Joseph Symonds, William Kiffin and John Lilburne. It seems clear that Goodwin had consulted these figures in the course of preparing his tract. For example, he refuted the charges against Lilburne by confirming that neither of his eyes had been put out with a pike, and that 'the man protested he never plaid a game at cards since his coming to London'.[19]

The Presbyterians responded by intensifying their accusations of heresy. Josiah Ricraft, whom Goodwin had identified as an informant of Edwards, published *A Nosegay of Rank-smelling Flowers, such as Grow in Mr John Goodwins Garden* (6 May 1646). Styling himself 'an enemy to the Hydra of Anarchy', he trawled through Goodwin's writings against Walker and Edwards, assembling a collection of Goodwin's 'Rhetoricall railings', 'wilful lyes and falshoods', 'absurdities', 'contradictions', and 'blasphemies'. Ricraft complained of Goodwin's 'Billings-gate language', and 'the bruitish carriage of those his associates of Swan-Alley' in 'the Diocese of Coleman Street'.[20]

---

16 S. Davies, *Unbridled Spirits: Women of the English Revolution, 1640–1660* (London, 1998), 100.
17 *Cretensis, or A Briefe Answer to an Ulcerous Treatise ... intituled, Gangraena* (1646), 47.
18 *Cretensis*, 22–38,
19 *Cretensis*, 38–50, quotation on 48.
20 Josiah Ricraft, *A Nosegay of Rank-Smelling Flowers* (1646), 5–24.

In *The Second Part of Gangraena* (28 May 1646), Edwards replied to his critics, who compared to the Apologists were 'hairy, rough, wilde red men, especially Cretensis' or 'Goliah Goodwin'. One hundred pages of the book were given over to a point-by-point rebuttal of *Cretensis*.[21] Goodwin, as Ann Hughes remarks, was 'Edwards' anti-hero', and 'the single most important target of *Gangraena*'.[22] Goodwin's own 'company is an unclean Conventicle', wrote Edwards, 'where the spirit of Errour and pride prevailes in most ... Socinian, Arminian, Popish, Anabaptisticall, Libertine Tenets being held by himself and many of his people'. Goodwin had lived up to his billing as 'the great Red Dragon of Coleman street' by breathing fire against Presbyterians everywhere. He had 'an hereticall wit', and had held 'some strange opinions' for 'many yeers'. He was 'an Hermophradite and a compound of Socinian, Libertine, Anabaptist, &c'. He had shied away from Presbyterian discipline, and settled for 'the Independent way, as that wherein he might with more safety enjoy his opinions'.[23]

Instead of weeping at the heresies of his brethren, Goodwin had excused them. 'Antitrinitarians, Antiscripturists, Arrians, Socinians, Perfectists,' wrote Edwards, 'are canonised for Saints'. If the Antitrinitarian MP, Paul Best, was punished by Parliament, 'he shall be a Martyr too as well as a Saint in *Cretensis* Kalender, and be reckoned the Protomartyr of the Sectaries'.[24] No one in the entire kingdom had 'a more hereticall head and heart'. If he lived just seven more years, 'he will prove as arch an Heretick, and as dangerous a man as England ever bred', the equal of those sixteenth-century heresiarchs, David George, Sebastian Frank, and Socinus.[25]

By presenting Goodwin as an arch heretic, Edwards was hoping to discredit the entire Independent cause. He presented the more conservative Westminster Independents (like Burroughs and Greenhill) as worried men, who had been feeding information to Goodwin because they were scared of alienating the burgeoning sects. The choice, Edwards implied, was stark: sectarian rule or Presbyterian settlement.[26]

Gangraena was the product of deep frustration among the Presbyterian clergy. Although the King surrendered himself into the hands of the Scots on 5 May, things were not going according to plan. In April 1646, the Commons revealed its hostility to clerical authority and religious uniformity in stern responses to the Scottish Commissioners and the Westminster Assembly. MPs were willing to endorse a Presbyterian settlement, but they favoured state control of ecclesiastical affairs and provision for 'tender consciences'. A coalition of Erastians and Independents was calling the shots at Westminster.[27]

---

21 Edwards, *Gangraena*, ii. 30–140.
22 A. Hughes, *Gangraena and the English Revolution* (Oxford, 2004), 125, 353.
23 Edwards, *Gangraena*, ii. 10–11, 16, 30–32.
24 Edwards, *Gangraena*, ii. 37.
25 Edwards, *Gangraena*, ii. 44.
26 Edwards, *Gangraena*, ii. 95.
27 S. R. Gardiner, *History of the Great Civil War*, 4 vols (London, 1893), iii. 92–95.

Goodwin relished Parliament's snub to the Assembly's ambitions. How could any reasonable man have thought that 'the two Honourable Houses of Parliament, would ever absolutely, and without liberty, and opportunity of appeale, subject the soules, bodies, Liberties, Estates' of the English people, 'to the wills and pleasures of such a generation ... proud, ignorant, covetous, ambitious, cruell, domineering?'[28]

Foiled in the Commons, the Presbyterians turned to the City for support. At the prompting of the Earl of Essex's party and the Presbyterian clergy, the Common Council presented a Remonstrance to both Houses on 26 May, demanding 'the neerest conjunction and uniformity in Religion' with Scotland, and the resumption of peace negotiations with Charles. The Remonstrance was welcomed by the Lords, but ignored by the Commons.[29] Despite its mixed reception, the Remonstrance worried the Independents. According to John Price, 20,000 copies had been printed and distributed 'in all the Parts of this Kingdome, and beyond the seas', causing 'divisions' among Puritan Parliamentarians in many counties.[30] The Independents wasted no time in launching a counter-attack. Isaac Pennington criticised the Lord Mayor in the Commons, and Hugh Peter and Jeremiah Burroughs preached against the Remonstrance. On 2 June Henry Overton published an Independent petition urging the House to prevent the enslavement of 'the freeborn people of this kingdom'. The petition divided MPs, with the Commons voting very narrowly in favour of returning thanks.[31]

Overton also published *A Moderate Reply to the Citie-Remonstrance* by John Price (12 June 1646). It expressed the Independents' 'utter dislike' of the '*Malignant Remonstrance*', and accused the Common Council of misrepresenting Londoners. The Remonstrance was portrayed as an assault on Parliament and 'the Parliaments friends', the Independents. In an ominous move, Price accused the King of treachery. He cited a recent pamphlet, *Truth it's Manifest*, which 'positively affirmes that his Majestie himselfe sent a Commission from Scotland, sealed with the Scots broad Seale, unto the Irish Rebells, to authorize them in the bloudy work'. 'Doe you hear of any reall remorse upon his heart?', Price asked, 'any relentings for the innocent bloud that hath been spilt by his meanes?' He defended the actions of the City's marshall, Roger Quartermayne (one of Goodwin's 'disciples'),[32] who had recently been removed from his post by the Lord Mayor and Alderman after issuing a Parliamentary proclamation without informing the Mayor. 'God sent Saviours for London', declared Price, but the City had despised its deliverers.[33]

By this stage, the First Civil War was effectively over. The royalist capital of Oxford had been surrendered to parliamentary forces on 24 June, and mopping-

---

28 *Anapologesiastes Antapologia* (1646), 132–33.
29 Scott, *Politics and War*, 120.
30 J[ohn] P[rice], *The City-Remonstrance Remonstrated* (1646), 7.
31 See Lindley, *Popular Politics and Religion in Civil War London* (Aldershot, 1997), 382–86.
32 According to John Vicars, *Coleman-Street Conclave Visited* (1648), 32–34; John Vicars, *Speculum Scripturale Schismaticorum, or a Scripture Looking-Glasse* (1649).
33 [John Price], *A Moderate Reply to the Citie-Remonstrance* (1646), quotations at sigs. A2v, A4v, B2v, D2r–D3v.

up operations were almost complete. For the Independents, this was a remarkable triumph. As David Scott has written, 'victory in the English Civil War went not so much to Parliament, as to a faction within it – the Independents. It was effectively their army that won the war – a victory rooted in their political dominance at Westminster'.[34] Yet the godly were more divided than ever. *A Moderate Reply* provoked a tense exchange of pamphlets between Price and John Bellamy.[35] The two men were 'long acquainted and intimate friends', but their friendship lay in ruins.[36]

Goodwin's friendship with Thomas Edwards had gone the same way. Edwards had jeered at the non-appearance of Goodwin's long-promised reply to *Antapologia*, which had been registered with the stationers many months before (on 2 July 1645) but had still not hit the bookstalls.[37] Galled by the mockery, Goodwin finally completed the book in July 1646.[38] *Anapologesiastes Antapologia* (27 August 1646) contained a preface in which Goodwin defended himself against *Gangraena's* charges. He was not, he insisted, a friend of heresy. He opposed the use of force against heretics, partly because magistrates might suppress truth by mistake, but also because force was not 'the Christian and lawfull way' to suppress heresy. Yet he was utterly committed to confuting heretics by argument from the word of God. Indeed, from 1644 to 1646, he had devoted his 'week-day Lectures' to a sustained critique of the Antinomians, Anabaptists and Seekers. He had also preached 'for severall moneths together of late' against 'the error of the AntiScripturists (more dangerous and pestilentiall then all the rest)'.[39]

Although critics talked of his volte-face 'from Presbytery to Independencie', Goodwin maintained that there had been an underlying consistency in his beliefs throughout his ministry. He had always abhorred:

> The persecution of Saints, the rough handling of tender consciences, the lifting up of Religion upon a swords point, violenced conformities, uniformities inforced, quenchings of Proceedings in the knowledge of Truth, binding up of judgements and consciences in Synodicall decrees, the making of Churches of whole Nations and Kingdomes, the choosing of Church-Officers by the qualifications of wealth and Secular Greatnesse, the standing upon Ceremonies, to the prejudice of substance, (as when the Gospel must not be preached, because such and such hands have not been imposed) the lording over the heritage of Christ ... [40]

The main body of the book was 250 pages long, and its eight chapters took aim at the various weaknesses of *Antapologia* and its author, condemning him for 'trampling the honour and reputation of the Apologists under foot, and prophaning their excellency'. Goodwin admitted that this was all rather 'wearisome', though

---

34 Scott, *Politics and War*, 97–98.
35 John Bellamy, *A Vindication of the Humble Remonstrance* (1646); J[ohn] P[rice], *The City-Remonstrance Remonstrated* (1646); John Bellamie, *A Justification of the City Remonstrance* (1646).
36 Bellamie, *A Justification*, sig. A3r.
37 Edwards, *Gangraena*, ii. 58–62.
38 'The Preface to the Reader' was signed July 17 1646.
39 *Anapologesiastes*, 'The Preface to the Reader', sig. A4v–ar.
40 *Anapologesiastes*, 'Preface', sig. c.

he hoped that he had put to rest the ridiculous claim that *Antapologia* was 'unanswerable'.[41]

Despite its rather tedious method, the book did shed light on Goodwin's brand of Independency, with its stress on private judgement and its disdain for clerical authority. Goodwin condemned Edwards for treating the decrees of the Westminster Assembly as oracles, as if we had 'arriv'd at the beautifull Haven of Papal infallability'. Edwards and his like had taken it upon themselves to define orthodoxy and impose it on others: 'Never was this poore ignorant world more abused with a word, then at this day with the word, *Orthodox*. *Romana Ecclesia* amongst the Papists was never more imperious and tyrannicall in making truth of what she pleased, then *Ministri Orthodoxi* now are amongst Protestants'. Throughout sacred history, God had revealed his secrets to 'single persons, not Councells'. The 'light of Evangelicall Truth ... did not breake forth out of the clouds of Councels and Synods', but from 'scattered and single stares, as Luther, Calvin, Melancthon, Martyr &c'. Even 'the great and rare inventions of the world' were made by 'particular and single men' rather than by multitudes of experts.[42]

The champions of high Presbytery, however, were unwilling to tolerate innovative minds. They wanted a reformation that would give them the right 'to order the judgements and Consciences of men as they please', and to command magistrates 'to smite' their rivals. They also hoped to revive 'the Leviticall Law of paying tithes'. But true reformation, wrote Goodwin, would see 'the breaking of the yoke of tyranny and oppression, as well spirituall as corporall, from off the necks of the Saints'.[43] Tellingly, Goodwin commended the Dutch, who were 'known to be very indulgent ... and to give Toleration upon Toleration, I mean to tolerate severall kinds of Religion, and Church-Governments amongst them'. As a result of their policy, the Netherlanders enjoyed 'tranquillity and peace ... above the proportion of any Kingdome or State round about them'. 'The greatest danger and mischief that ever befell the [Dutch] State' arose not from their tolerated minorities but from their established clergy ('the Presbyterians'!) 'who were at daggers drawn' in the 1610s as they fought for 'the Interest and favour of the Civill Magistrate'. While Goodwin was enthusiastic about Dutch tolerance of religious minorities, he was noticeably more reticent about New England, rebuking the Massachusetts Puritans for punishing and banishing Familists and Anabaptists as 'disturbers of the Civill peace'.[44] Increasingly, his radical Independency was diverging from that of the conservative Congregationalists.

Indeed, at this stage Goodwin's congregation was working closely with radical activists in the City like John Lilburne and William Walwyn. Walwyn had been on friendly terms with Goodwin's followers since the 1630s, when he 'discoursed much' with them 'upon what they and I heard him preach'. However, he had always been somewhat critical of Goodwin's teaching, judging that he 'perplex'd'

---

41 *Anapologesiastes*, 80, 253.
42 *Anapologesiastes*, 57, 102, 140–44.
43 *Anapologesiastes*, 112, 148–49.
44 *Anapologesiastes*, 70, 115, 94.

his audience, and 'spent much time ... to make plain things difficult to be understood'. When Goodwin's followers 'fell to congregate in a Church-way, they gave me good respect', but were 'not a little troubled, that I closed not with them', or some other gathered church. Thomas Lamb had sighed: 'O, Mr Walwyn, that you had a good opinion of Churches'. When Walwyn dared to criticise Goodwin's writings, he found himself 'slandered to death' by Lamb. Shortly before the creation of the New Model Army, Richard Arnold had 'groundlessly reported' to Cromwell that Walwyn 'held correspondence with Oxford'. However, Walwyn was in regular contact with Goodwin and Hildesley at the time, and other members of the congregation expressed their gratitude to him for his tracts against Prynne and Edwards. In May 1646, Goodwin's Church even 'disbursed fifty shillings towards the printing of ten thousand' copies of Walwyn's anti-Edwards tract, *The Word in Season*.[45]

By this point, Lilburne and Walwyn had emerged as the leaders of their own political movement, soon to be known as the Levellers. In July 1646, they set out their stall in *A Remonstrance of Many Thousand Citizens*, a pamphlet that called for the abolition of the monarchy and the House of Lords, and for radical economic and legal reform.[46] For the City Independents, including Goodwin, this was rash and potentially damaging. The Levellers were lending support to Presbyterian allegations that Independency threatened the established order. Indeed, in the third part of *Gangraena*, published in December 1646, Edwards used Leveller activities to make precisely this point. The City Independents were determined to proceed cautiously, and work closely with their allies at Westminster. When the Levellers promoted a pro-toleration petition in 1646, they garnered substantial support from the Baptist and Separatist congregations, but were frustrated by the Congregationalists: 'Master Goodwins people, and some other of the Independent Churches being against the season, it was never delivered'. When a second petition was 'agreed to by all sorts of conscientious people, that were opposite to persecution', 'multitudes' endorsed the Leveller view that it should be presented immediately, but once again the City Independents insisted that this was not 'the season'. At a final meeting, probably held in the Windmill Tavern in Lothbury, tempers boiled over, and Walwyn was accused of being 'an Atheist and denier of the Scriptures, a loose and vitious man'. The Levellers' critics seized upon the accusation, and 'thereupon some leading people of master John Goodwins, set themselves down as a Committee', gathering evidence from informants about Walwyn's heterodoxy and drawing up a list of 'articles' against him.[47]

The heresy investigation was probably intended to discredit the Levellers, but it also demonstrated that Independents were tough on heterodoxy. But although 'the violent party' (to use Walwyn's phrase) was led by Goodwin's right-hand man, John Price, the Leveller still had friends within Goodwin's church, who were

---

45 *Walwyns Just Defence*, in *Walwyn*, 425–27, 386, 427.
46 *A Remonstrance of Many Thousand Citizens* (1646), in D. Wolffe, ed., *Leveller Manifestoes of the Puritan Revolution* (New York, 1944), 109–30, quotation at 109.
47 *Walwyns Just Defence*, in *Walwyn*, 387–88.

convinced that he was 'really honest and conscientious', 'amongst which Mr Henry Brandriff, Captain Chaplain, Mr Weekes and others'. These men kept him informed about the proceedings against him. Eventually, a meeting was called at the Dolphin in Cornhill, where Walwyn was to have the charges read to him and be asked to respond. Price and his allies failed to appear, and the charges against Walwyn were laid aside, if only for a season.[48] The likelihood is that Goodwin had called off the dogs, recognising that the dispute could damage the Independent coalition.

The Blasphemy Ordinance

The truth was that Independents could ill afford to fall out amongst themselves. With the end of the Civil War, the Presbyterians were increasingly confident that they could disband the army and crackdown on heresy and schism. While a majority wanted lay control of ecclesiastical matters, few MPs had any sympathy for religious radicals.[49] On 2 September 1646, two Presbyterian MPs introduced an ordinance for the suppression of blasphemy and heresy.[50] It listed a series of theological errors divided into two categories—the most serious were to be punished by death, the less serious by imprisonment. Among the capital crimes were denial of the Trinity, the atonement and resurrection of Christ, and the authority of Scripture. Offences in the second category, by contrast, were only to be punished with imprisonment. This category included a much wider range of errors, reflecting the Presbyterians' usual bugbears: universalism (the doctrine all will be saved), Arminianism, Catholic doctrines (purgatory, use of images), mortalism, antinomianism, rejection of the sacraments, denial of infant baptism, anti-sabbatarianism, attacking Presbyterianism as Antichristian etc.[51]

Although the ordinance was sent to a committee of the whole House, and would not reach the statute books until 1648, it still induced panic among radical Puritans. Had it been put into effect, the prisons of England would have been bursting at the seams, and Socinians like Paul Best might have gone to the stake. Its publication produced a storm of protest, including Goodwin's anonymous short tract, *Some Modest and Humble Queries concerning a Printed Paper* (22 September 1646). Goodwin's thirty-eight queries had two main thrusts. Firstly, they attacked the principle of religious coercion. It was against 'the spirit of Christ', who came to save men, not to destroy them; against 'the mind of Christ', who had not appointed infallible judges of disputes among brethren; and against 'the will of

---

48 *Walwyns Just Defence*, in *Walwyn*, 388–89.
49 See Gardiner, *History of the Great Civil War*, iii. 138–39.
50 See *An Ordinance presented to the Honourable House of Commons* (1646). Although introduced in September 1646, the Ordinance was only passed in May 1648. The final version is reprinted in C. H. Firth and R. S. Rait, eds, *Acts and Ordinances of the Interregnum*, 3 vols (London, 1911), i. 1133–36.
51 The final Blasphemy Ordinance of 1648 follows the earlier draft Ordinance of 1646 very closely, though it lists the entire Protestant canon of Scripture in order to specify what 'the holy Scripture' is. See *An Ordinance* (1648), 4–5.

Christ', which made no provision 'for Civill Magistrates to compell men, upon paine of death, to call them Rabbi or Masters'. As Lactantius said, men ought to defend truth, 'not by slaying others, but by dying our selves for it'. Christians who used the 'Stratagems' of physical force were copying the 'Idolatrous Heathen' and 'the Papacy', which relied on the same 'props'. They assumed their own infallibility, and quenched the Holy Ghost by telling him, 'reveale nothing more unto others, then thou hast revealed on to us'.[52]

Secondly, Goodwin critiqued the specific provisions of the ordinance, complaining that the list of errors was ill conceived. Did Luther deserve death or imprisonment for teaching consubstantiation? Should Calvin have been punished for denying strict Sabbatarianism? Were deniers of infant baptism or presbytery a greater problem that the godless? Were not some so-called heretics 'as full of grace and goodnesse, as precious in the sight of God, as fruitfull in every good worke, as serviceable to the State, and Commonwealth' as their critics? Could a jury of 'twelve simple Countrimen' or 'an ordinary Judge of Assize' be competent adjudicators in the case of 'a studious, learned, and conscientious man' 'in the abstruse and disputable points of Religion'? What exactly was erroneous about the proposition that 'a man by nature hath free will to turn to God'? What was meant by 'impugning the word of God'? In what sense was it wrong to say that 'God seeth no sin in the justified'? Why was it an error to teach that 'a man is bound to beleeve no more, then by his reason he can comprehend'? Was one bound to believe an opinion for which one could see no reason? What was meant by 'publishing Doctrines with obstinacy'? Who were to be the 'judges or determiners' of heresy and orthodoxy?[53]

The Presbyterian clergy could not afford to ignore Goodwin's queries, particularly as they were 'cried up' 'above all other pieces that have been published in this kind'.[54] They were answered by a leading Westminster divine in *A Vindication of a Printed Paper*.[55] The author zeroed in on his sceptical defence of toleration. By casting doubt on the provisions of the ordinance, Goodwin was guilty of 'wickednesse and blasphemy'. The ordinance had stated that it was heresy to teach 'that there is no God' 'that he is not Almighty', 'that Christ is not God', or 'that Christ is not Man'. One did not need to be infallible to recognise that these were gross heresies, just as a physician did not need to be an infallible judge of 'all drugs, or potions', to recognise 'rank poyson'. The author called on Goodwin's congregation to excommunicate their pastor, so that 'you may learne not to blaspheme thus any more'.[56]

The *Vindication* provoked Goodwin into writing his most important and most controversial tolerationist work, *Hagiomastix, or the Scourge of the Saints Displayed*

---

52 *Some Modest and Humble Queries concerning a Printed Paper* (1646), 1–2.
53 *Some Modest and Humble Queries*, 2–12.
54 *A Vindication of a Printed Paper* (1646), sig. A2v.
55 On the authorship, see Thomas Edwards, *The Casting Down of the Last and Strongest Hold of Satan, or a Treatise against Toleration* (1647), 115.
56 *A Vindication of a Printed Paper*, 4–6.

(5 February 1647). At 170 pages, it was more than a mere pamphlet, for as Joad Raymond notes, 'Books of more than a hundred pages aspired to a more elevated status'.[57] Goodwin made it clear from the outset that his disagreement with the militant Presbyterians was an argument over the *extent* of the magistrate's power. Tolerationists were under attack because 'they dare not calculate the power of the Magistracie, for the Meridian of the torrid zone of High Presbyterie'. Congregationalists could live with the moderate Presbyterian settlement being proposed by Parliament, but not with the High Presbyterianism of the City clergy. This 'Procrustian Race' demanded complete conformity. 'Gangraena's Gang,' wrote Goodwin, 'breath out nothing but fire, fury and fiercenesse'.[58]

Against this 'Procrustian' programme, Goodwin set out his revisionist vision of a progressive, innovatory reformation. As in his *Treatise of Justification*, he reminded his readers of Daniel's prophecy that in the last days, knowledge would increase as men threw off popish servility and learned to think for themselves:

> In the times of Popery, men generally stood still, made no Inquiries beyond the lips of their Teachers, and knowledge then was at a stand, and advanced not. But since God hath been pleased to put in into the hearts of men to conceive and think, that there may be Tracts or Regions of knowledge, beyond the line of the travailes, and discoveries of their Teachers, and have made many studious expeditions themselves to find them out, knowledge hath increased; yea and will increase daily more & more, if we relapse not into the lethargie of Popish slothfulnesse and servilitie, and suffer our Teachers to exercise a Dominion over our Faith.[59]

As well as delivering this counterblast against clerical pretensions, *Hagiomastix* tackled once again the Presbyterians' biblical arguments for enforced uniformity. They appealed to the Old Testament, Goodwin complained, as if 'they prove a thing to be Christian, because it is Jewish'. But the judicial law ordering capital punishment for false teachers was no longer binding in the church age.[60] Goodwin was equally dismissive of the claim that Romans 13 taught the magistrate's power in religion. Not one magistrate in a hundred throughout history had had 'any sufficiency of means to discern between Heresie and sound Doctrine'. Romans 13 only gave magistrates the power to punish 'that kinde of evill ... whereof Magistrates, or Magistrates in generall, as well Heathen, as Christian, are competent judges ... as that which is contrary to the light and law of nature, as Whoredome, Adultery, Murder, Theft, Injustice, Sedition, Treason'. The power of magistrates was radically circumscribed and restricted to purely civil matters – sins against natural law and the Second Table of the Decalogue, or acts 'prejudiciall or destructive to the peace, safety, or wellfare of their state'. It was a mistake to 'thinke that Magistrates have any whit the more power for being Christians, or the lesse for being Pagans'. There was no difference whatsoever between the powers of Christian

---

57 J. Raymond, *Pamphlets and Pamphleteering in Early Modern Britain* (Cambridge, 2003), 82.
58 *Hagiomastix, or The Scourge of the Saints* (1647), 'To the Reader', §12–14.
59 *Hagiomastix*, 'To the Reader', §18.
60 *Hagiomastix*, 43–54, quotation at 44.

and pagan magistrates, for 'the Authority and power of supreme Magistrates is uniforme, standing and fixed (at least in respect of God)'.[61] This was a strikingly minimalist (and naturalistic) account of the magistrate's power, one that Goodwin would develop in the Whitehall Debates and subsequent writings.

But the central line of argument in *Hagiomastix* was sceptical. Goodwin sought to undermine the epistemological foundation of persecution by emphasising human fallibility. Although High Presbyterians were 'confessedly fallible', they were acting as if they enjoyed papal infallibility. When they spoke of 'damnable Heresie', they declared that heresy was contrary to the 'manifest' Word of God, and 'certainly' known. To Goodwin this was sheer presumption on the part of fallible men, and to underline the point he repeatedly printed the word CERTAINTIE in capital letters. Unlike the Old Testament prophets or the New Testament apostles, the Presbyterian clergy did not have the benefit of 'immediate revelation from God' to tell what was heresy and what was not. Like everyone else, they had to rely on their fallible rational faculties to read the Scriptures correctly. God's infallibility was an incommunicable attribute, though the promoters of the Blasphemy Ordinance seemed to think otherwise. They were men 'borne to Sovereignty' and wound not stoop to 'the servility of disputing'.[62]

Hagiomastix's sceptical case for a general toleration that would protect even anti-Trinitarians was anathema to Thomas Edwards, George Gillespie and Samuel Rutherford, each of whom eventually wrote substantial replies. In June, Edwards published his major contribution to 'the great Controversie of the times', *A Treatise against Toleration*. The book was essentially a reply to Goodwin. Edwards referred repeatedly to *M.S. to A.S.*, *Some Modest and Humble Queries* and *Hagiomastix*, and boasted to the 'Independents and Sectaries' that he had conquered 'your great Rabbi and Oracle'. He dealt with most of Goodwin's major arguments, and pointed out that for all his scepticism, Goodwin's own writings abounded with claims to 'his absolute certaintie, and full demonstrative knowledge of many Points of Religion'[63]

The Scottish Covenanters adopted a different tack, portraying Goodwin's scepticism as all too real. For Gillespie, *Hagiomastix* reflected 'the academical, yea, Pyrrhonian demur and dubitation, by which some call in question the most received doctrines in the Christian church'. Scepticism was 'the epidemical disease of the sectaries of this time', and Goodwin was 'one of the fomenters' of it. But Gillespie was also shocked by Goodwin's claim that the magistrate could only punish errors 'contrary to the very light of nature'. As Gillespie realised, this implied a more far-reaching toleration than could be supported on Goodwin's sceptical grounds, for it would protect those whom even Goodwin was certain were in the wrong, including men who rejected Christianity altogether.[64]

---

61 *Hagiomastix*, 58–64, 118, 25.
62 *Hagiomastix*, 19–34, 66, 87.
63 Edwards, *The Casting Down of the Last and Strongest Hold of Satan*, 197, 114–21.
64 Gillespie, 'A Treatise of Miscellany Questions' (1648), in *The Works of George Gillespie*, 2 vols (Edinburgh, 1646), ii. 54, 60, 65, 67–68.

These points were developed further by Samuel Rutherford in his four-hundred page treatise, *A Free Disputation against Pretended Liberty of Conscience* (1649). Although Rutherford had other tolerationists in his sights besides Goodwin, including Henry Robinson and Jeremy Taylor, the book can be read as an extended reply to *Hagiomastix* and the various arguments Goodwin had mounted against religious coercion – chapters were devoted to fundamentals and non-fundamentals, the relevance of Old Testament judicial law, Zechariah 13 (the subject of *An Appendix to Hagiomastix*), the Parable of the Wheat and the Tares, Gamaliel and Romans 13. But like Gillespie, Rutherford dreaded scepticism and subjectivism most of all, and he reasserted the traditional belief that 'a conscience void of knowledge is void of goodnesse'. With an eye on Goodwin, he penned a satirical Independent prayer: 'Lord open my eyes, and increase my knowledge, grant that thy Holy Spirit may bestow upon my dark soule more scepticall, conjecturall, and fluctuating knowledge … let me Lord, have the grace of a circular faith, running like the wheel of a wind-mill'.[65]

Goodwin's critics even tried to initiate Parliamentary proceedings against him, on the grounds that *Hagiomastix* denied Scripture to be the word of God. As John Vicars explained, Thomas Underhill, a Presbyterian Stationer, 'endeavoured to have [Goodwin] and his Blasphemous Book to be called into question, and him severely punished, (as justly he deserved) by the Parliament'.[66] Goodwin himself testified that 'some of my accusers made it their most affectionate request, that my late book might be burnt by the common Hangman'.[67] According to William Walwyn, the offending passage of the book was read before Colonel Edward Leigh's Parliamentary committee by one of Goodwin's critics, with the result that *Hagiomastix* was 'called a most impious, blasphemous Book, and ordered to be seized, all of them immediately'. Walwyn himself claimed to have been present on the committee, and to have given 'timely notice of the order' to Henry Overton, who managed to save copies of the book before it was confiscated. The irony of the situation was not lost on Walwyn – it was 'a strange providence' that Goodwin's followers should find their pastor accused of denying the Scriptures after having 'scandalized' Walwyn for the exact same error.[68]

According to John Vicars, the actions of Leigh's committee made Goodwin very nervous: 'hereupon Mr Goodwin begins to sweat and swagger, and (being rub'd upon his gall'd back) to kick and winch most notoriously in print'.[69] In a brief pamphlet entitled, *A Candle to see the Sun* (18 February 1647), Goodwin declared that his intention in writing *Hagiomastix* was not 'to deny the Scriptures to be the word of God, or at least to scruple others about believing them to be so

---

65 Samuel Rutherford, *A Free Disputation against Pretended Liberty of Conscience* (1649), 5, 81. The windmill reference was likely an allusion to John Vicars's satirical cartoon of Goodwin with a windmill above his head (discussed later in this chapter).
66 Vicars, *Coleman-street Conclave Visited*, 27.
67 *A Postscript or Appendix to a Treatise lately published by Authority, Intituled Hagio-mastix* (1647), sig. A3v.
68 *Walwyns Just Defence*, in *Walwyn*, 389.
69 Vicars, *Coleman-street Conclave Visited*, 27.

(both of which are the great abominations of his soule)'. Many hundreds of people in the City could testify that during the thirteen years of his London ministry, Goodwin had devoted more effort to arguing for the authority of the Scriptures than any minister in the City.[70]

His orthodoxy was attested by his own congregation, who issued *An Apologeticall Account of some Brethren of the Church whereof Mr John Goodwin is Pastor* (25 February 1647). The collective statement was signed by sixteen male members of the church, including Robert Smyth (his ministerial assistant), Mark Hildesley (a City politician), Robert Saunders (a Parliamentary Major) and Thomas Devenish (keeper of Winchester House). They had to come to Goodwin's defence because the the author of the *Vindication* had urged them to excommunicate their pastor. They testified that Goodwin was an exemplary and impeccably orthodox pastor, whose teachings 'refresh the very root of our soules'. His accusers had perpetrated 'a deed of darkness against him, whom God hath made more precious to us than our lives'.[71]

Neither Goodwin nor his congregation, however, could stop the flow of heresy accusations. Wednesday 10 March had been appointed as 'a day of publike humiliation for the growth and spreading of Errors, Heresies and Blasphemies', and the Presbyterians were determined to make the most of it. *Hell Broke Loose* (9 March 1647), briefly catalogued the errors of men like Roger Williams, Paul Best, John Saltmarsh and Samuel Gorton, who had preached 'in Colemanstreet before many', presumably at Thomas Lambe's General Baptist church. But Goodwin was also cited for his errors on free will, justification and the Scriptures.[72]

Another short pamphlet, *Moro-mastix: Mr John Goodwin whipt with his own Rod*, declared that Goodwin himself was the real 'scourge of the Saints'. As 'the master-Sectary of the City', those he 'canonizeth' included 'a saint of the new Edition, a Gangraen'd saint; saint Oates, saint Gorton, saint Lilburn, saint Seeker, saint Dipper, saint Antiscripturist'. The author of the tract had been an eyewitness of a disputation over tithes at Christ Church, and he insisted that Goodwin had been trounced. Yet he also complained that the 'Vapours of Heresies' that 'arise out of Mr Goodwins brain', had infected 'the ayre of London'. Indeed, 'were it possible to get a Bill of spiritual mortality, I fear we should find few Parishes cleer of the pest of his opinions'.[73]

In the face of these continuing assaults, Goodwin returned to the fray with *A Postscript or Appendix to ... Hagiomastix* (2 April 1647), in which he reiterated his credentials as a godly, orthodox minister, stoutly committed to the authority of the Bible and the doctrine of the Trinity.[74] He devoted twenty-eight pages to an exposition of Zechariah 13:3, concerning the slaying of false prophets, a favourite text with

---

70 *A Candle to See the Sunne* (1647), 1–4.
71 *An Apologeticall Account of some Brethren of the Church whereof Mr John Goodwin is Pastor* (1647), 1–10.
72 *Hell Broke Loose: or a Catalogue of Many of the Spreading Errors, Heresies and Blasphemies of these Times, for which we are to be Humbled* (1647), 4.
73 *Moro-mastix* (1647), 3–4, 8–9, 12.
74 *A Postscript*, sigs. A2v, Br.

supporters of the Blasphemy Ordinance. Goodwin contended that Protestant expositors had generally understood the text metaphorically, to mean that false prophets should be destroyed by confutation and argument (not by fire or sword).[75] Indeed, the real point of Zechariah 13, thought Goodwin, was eschatological. God still had 'precious thoughts towards his ancient people, the nation of the Jews'. The chapter should be read as a prophecy of how false prophets would be decisively confuted as God illuminated the minds of his ancient people.[76] Goodwin's expectation of a latter day glory was very much alive. It was an expectation shared by a wide array of Puritans in the 1640s, from radical Independents like John Milton to high Presbyterians like Samuel Rutherford. But in contrast to Rutherford, Goodwin believed that the imminent restoration of all things would be realised through freedom of conscience and theological experimentation.

The Army and the Independents

The power struggle between Presbyterians and Independents turned on the fate of the New Model Army. Once the Civil War had ended, the political Presbyterians (led by Holles and Stapleton in the Commons) set about trying to disband the New Model. Angered, the soldiers were rapidly politicised.[77] They began their own petitioning movement, and in April and May 1647, the regiments elected agitators to represent their interests. Instead of backing down, Holles and his allies redoubled their efforts. Major Robert Saunders, probably a member of Goodwin's church, was summoned before the Commons for distributing a pamphlet critical of Parliament.[78] Fearing that the Presbyterians would strike a deal with Charles I, Cornet Joyce abducted the king from Holmby House on 2 June. *A Declaration from Sir Thomas Fairfax and the Army* issued in mid-June asserted that the New Model was 'no mere mercenary army'. It made a series of radical demands: a purge of Parliament to remove MPs who abused their power, fixed term parliaments and reapportionment of seats; and religious toleration. Some agitators even lobbied for the army to march on London.[79]

Throughout these tense months, Goodwin's congregation was working as part of an Independent coalition that included Westminster politicians, officers and soldiers, Levellers and other City radicals. Presbyterian critics tended to lump them all together as 'the Sectarian Party'. Even in 1649, a supporter of the Presbyterian MPs complained of 'those spiritually proud Sectaries, and fiery Salamanders of contention, Master *John Goodwin*, together with his most seditious brother *John Lilburne, Overton*, and divers others of that rotten rout'. In one

---

75 *A Postscript*, 1–20.
76 *A Postscript*, 21–24.
77 See M. Kishlansky, *The Rise of the New Model Army* (Cambridge, 1979).
78 See I. Gentles, *The New Model Army, 1645–53* (Oxford, 1992), 159. The pamphlet was *A New Found Stratagem* (1647).
79 A. Woolrych, *Britain in Revolution, 1625–1660* (Oxford, 2002), 351–65, 369–72.

breath he denounced 'lying *Lilburnes* base Pamphlets, Goodwins abhominably blasphemous *Hagio Ma:*'.[80]

But as we have already seen, relations with the Levellers were strained. On 13 February, John Lilburne had written a letter to Goodwin himself, acknowledging his debt to 'his much honoured and much respected friend', and expressing gratitude to Goodwin and his congregation 'for your large kindnesses manifested unto me in this present imprisonment in supplying my necessities'. But although he was 'more obliged to you personally, than to all the Congregations in and about London', he had a serious grievance. Some of Goodwin's people, Lilburne complained, had been working behind the scenes 'to crush all petitions that tended to my deliverance'. Lieutenant Colonel John Sadler had come 'to the Randevous at Saint Athones, and there in the name of diverse knowing men of Mr John Goodwines Congregation, improved all his interest utterly to destroy the Petitioner'. Goodwin's people had even tried 'to destroy' petitions from Buckinghamshire and Hertfordshire for the release of the Leveller leaders. Through the Independent minister Christopher Feake, Lilburne had learnt that the Levellers' Hertfordshire petition would have attracted ten times more subscriptions 'if it had not been for the base, unworthy, undermining dealing of some of Mr John Goodwins Congregation'. The prime movers behind these sinister manoeuvres, thought Lilburne, were Goodwin himself, Sir Henry Vane the younger, and Oliver St John.[81] But Lilburne still hoped that Goodwin would listen to his plea:

> By reason of those many engagements, by which I stand obliged to your selfe, for your so stout and deep engagement for the publick welfare of all those that thirst after either morall, or religious righteousnesse ... [I] earnestly entreat you to spare so much time from your weighty employments, as to do mee the favour to let me speake a few words with you, and if you please to bring Mr Price along with you.[82]

Lilburne's letter suggests that (unlike the Levellers) Goodwin's congregation was working closely with Independent grandees like Vane and St John. In late 1647, an agitator in Fairfax's regiment claimed that Lord Saye's son (Nathaniel Fiennes) had been 'informing a Member of Mr Goodwin's Church' about developments within the Army Council.[83] Unfortunately, such references are few and far between, and Goodwin's behind-the-scenes politicking is largely hidden from sight. But the congregation's influence was far-reaching.

Despite being much more disciplined and on-message than the Levellers, Goodwin's church was not unanimously critical of Walwyn. Henry Brandreth assured Walwyn that there was 'no real enmity, but only causles doubts and jealousies' towards him. If only he would vindicate his belief in the Scriptures in print, he would find that Goodwin's people 'should be as good and as loving friends as ever'. In March or April 1647, Walwyn published *A Still Small Voice from the Scriptures*,

---

80 *Hinc Illae Lachrymae, or the Impietie of Impunitie* (1649), 2, 10, 13.
81 John Lilburne, *Jonah's Cry out of the Whales Belly* (1647), 5–6.
82 Lilburne, *Jonah's Cry*, 6.
83 Francis White, *The Copy of a Letter sent to his Excellencie Sir Thomas Fairfax* (1647), 2.

Witnessing them to be the Word of God.[84] Without mentioning names, the tract delivered some sharp jabs against Price and 'superstitious' men who 'watch, spy, accuse and informe' on other Christians. However, he commended 'ingenious men' (like Brandreth) 'with whom I have daily converst, that know I doe acknowledge and believe there is a God, and that the Scriptures are the Word of God'. In contrast to Goodwin, who tried to prove the divine authority of the Bible by assembling evidences and arguments, Walwyn contrasted the earth, wind and fire of rational arguments that aimed to shake the house of unbelief to pieces, with 'the soft still voyce' of God that wrought deep and genuine faith.[85] Despite its veiled critique of Goodwin and Price, the tract appears to have satisfied most of Walwyn's critics, and for 'a good while after this', he had 'much respect from many of them, and not an ill look from any'. Thomas Devenish thanked Walwyn for publishing the book, and even said that 'he should make it his rule'.[86]

Whatever their differences, the Levellers and the Goodwin Independents were thrown together in the summer of 1647 by the political crisis over the army. In May and June, there were 'joynt meetings and debates' between Levellers and Independents concerning the petitioning movement and the threat posed by Leigh's committee. Price and Walwyn 'often' visited Oliver Cromwell in his house in Drury Lane, enjoying 'aboundance of friendly discourse'. Goodwin's followers once again enjoyed Walwyn's hospitality and comradeship, coming to his house 'day by day' to 'sit and discourse friendly and cheerfully, and seriously of the present affairs, and refresh themselves in my Garden'. The fruits of this renewed cooperation emerged in early June, when 'we all, both his [i.e. Price's] Friends and mine, joyned in a Petition, the last and most sharp of any'.[87]

Goodwin himself vindicated the New Model in an anonymous pamphlet entitled *The Army Harmelesse* (16 July 1647).[88] He maintained that 'the late and present proceedings of the Army' were 'not only unquestionably just, but emphatically honourable also'. Yet 'Anti-Armists' were a noisy brigade, and 'the Friends of the Army' had to answer them.[89]

Goodwin identified three principles that would justify the army revolt. Firstly, the army had acted in accordance with 'that great and Soveraigne Law', *salus populi suprema lex*. Secondly, the army's action was also supported by 'that great Law of Nature, which obligeth every part or member of the body, to sympathize in taking the same care one of another'. And thirdly, 'the Army stood bound in duty, and by the band of their Covenant, to maintain and defend the lawful rights and Liberties of the Subject'. These three principles – *salus populi*, the natural law of sympathy for other members of the body, and the army's covenant – formed the basis for a justification of its actions.[90]

---

84 *Walwyns Just Defence* in *Walwyn*, 388–89.
85 *A Still and Soft Voyce*, in *Walwyn*, 269–72.
86 *Walwyns Just Defence*, in *Walwyn*, 389.
87 *Walwyns Just Defence* in *Walwyn*, 391–92.
88 For a defence of Goodwin's authorship see Appendix.
89 [John Goodwin], *The Army Harmlesse* (1647), 2–3.
90 *The Army Harmlesse*, 5–10.

Goodwin maintained that the army had stepped in at a moment of χρισις (crisis). At this singular 'juncture of time' the hand of wicked men had been 'stretched out to lay hold on their prey'. These men were driven by 'their beloved lusts of oppression, tyranny and domination', and like 'an hungry Lion' they had their victim between their teeth. With a silent nod in the direction of John Lilburne, Goodwin declared that there had been 'numerous Arbitrarie and illegal, yea causeless and reasonablelesse imprisonments of the persons, sequestrations of the estates, and many grievous and unjust molestations otherwise of the free-born subjects of the Nation'. But the defining act came when Parliament had burned the petitions presented to it, and branded peaceable petitioners 'Enemies to the State'. The burning of petitions removed the normal means for achieving 'the healing of Greivances', and presaged 'a season of tyrannie and blood'. Seeing that the 'safety and well being of the people of their Land, was now laid upon the Altar', the army had justifiably taken action. Had it disbanded, this would have been 'a constructive surrender and delivering up of this Nation into the hand of a more cruel servitude and vassalage then ever it served since it was a Nation'. Men in power were clearly preparing 'a yoke of iron for the neck of the Nation', and intended to create 'that Lordly paradise of a perpetual and unaccountable domination'. Fairfax's army was 'the sole hope of recovery, under God, to the drooping and dying freedoms of this Nation'. Morally, the army had little choice but to intervene in 'a day of danger and extremity'. The Nation was facing 'a death of their liberties', and the army was the only 'probable means' of deliverance. For its bold actions, it would be honoured 'throughout all Generations'.[91]

To those who objected that the army was guilty of 'disobedience to authority, and resistance against the higher powers', Goodwin responded by pointing out that the army was willing to disband, and had simply given good reasons for the disbandment to be postponed. Moreover, Scripture showed that in exceptional circumstances even God's good commandments could be lawfully transgressed. Finally, 'the Law of Lawes, the Law of Necessity' often overruled 'ordinary or standing Law' – 'all other Lawes must keepe silence before it, and bow downe to it as their Soveraigne'.[92]

The obvious objection was: 'Yea but who shall Judge of a case of necessity?' Goodwin replied that 'cases of necessity they are for the most part very easie to be judged and discerned'. Ordinarily, 'men in places, civill Judicature and Magistracy' were 'the most competent Judges of such 'cases of necessity'. But the people were not obliged to follow 'blind Magistrates'. It was by no means impossible for 'inferiours' to see that the commands of 'superiours' were unlawful. Even if an inferior misjudged the case, mistaken non-obedience was better than uncritical submission.[93]

In the present case, the Parliament had set its face against the 'really conscientious and peaceable in the Land; to whom the Army by reason of their

---

91 *The Army Harmlesse*, 4–13.
92 *The Army Harmlesse*, 15–17.
93 *The Army Harmlesse*, 18–26.

union and power, were a little Sanctuary'. In his benediction for both institutions, Goodwin alluded to Israel's Exodus from Egypt, casting the New Model Army as England's deliverer and Parliament as the pursuer. The 'Lord of Hosts' had 'greatly delighted' in the army, looking on it 'out of the cloudy and fiery pillar, when he took off the chariot wheels of the Egyptians ... whilst they were in hot pursuit of his people Israel'.[94]

As in 1642, so in 1647, Goodwin believed that he was living through England's liberation from slavery. *The Army Harmlesse* was a piece of Protestant casuistry, but it also fused two main lines of argument developed by Parliamentarians and Levellers since 1642. In the first place, it appealed to the common law idea of the individual liberties of 'the free-born subjects of the Nation'. Such liberties had been undermined, Goodwin suggested, by arbitrary arrests and imprisonments, and by Parliament's aggressive assault on petitioning. But the tract also employed the neo-classical argument that this attack on individual rights and liberties would reduce 'free-born subjects' to a condition of 'servitude and vassalage', subjecting them to the 'domination' and 'lusts' of 'Lordly' rulers. And this neo-classical theme of freedom from slavery was underwritten by the biblical epic of the Exodus.

On the very day that Thomason acquired Goodwin's pamphlet, the army's General Council met to discuss the way forward. It debated Ireton's Heads of Proposals, which offered hope for both political reform and a negotiated settlement with the king. On 20 July, eleven leading Presbyterian MPs including Holles withdrew from the House. Parliament quickly restored control of the City trained bands to the old Militia Committee. This capitulation to the army angered the City Presbyterians. Thousands gathered in riotous demonstrations, and there were mass petitions asking the Common Council to retain control of the trained bands. But the Presbyterian counter-revolution was futile. On Saturday 7 August, Fairfax's regiments marched from Hyde Park to Cheapside, 'with colours flying, trumpets playing, and drums beating'. The Lord Mayor and three aldermen were impeached for treason; the Independent Robert Tichborne was appointed Lieutenant of the Tower; and the City's eleven miles of Civil War fortifications were destroyed.[95]

Throughout this great political drama, Goodwin's followers continued to be actively involved in the local affairs of St Stephen's parish. As many as ten members of the gathered church had attended one or more meetings of the general vestry during 1646–47,[96] and Hildesley and Montague had sat on the select vestry.[97] In September 1647, Hildesley was added to the City's Militia Committee, where he joined Pennington, Rowe and Russell.[98] It is likely that Goodwin retained the sympathy of leading political Independents in the parish like Pennington and Rowe, and they may have supported a parishioners' petition calling for Goodwin's return

---

94 *The Army Harmlesse*, 27, 28–29.
95 Woolrych, *Britain in Revolution*, 373–80.
96 GL MS 4458/1, ff.
97 GL MS 4458/1, ff. 147–151. The ten who attended vestry meetings were (roughly in order of prominence): Hildesley, Gallant, Montague, Price, Overton, Alderne, Smith, Steel, Stacy, Cooke.
98 *CJ*, v. 288–90 (2 September 1647).

as lecturer (rather than vicar). In October 1647, the House of Lords read 'the Petition of the Inhabitants of Steven Coleman Street, desiring, That Mr. John Goodwin may be admitted to be their lecturer, and preach every Lord's-day'. The House ordered 'that the Order mentioned in the said Petition be procured, and then this House will give further Direction', but nothing came of the proposal.[99]

Despite this setback, Goodwin's congregation was given permission to meet at St Mary's Abchurch. This probably occurred some time after Joseph Symonds was appointed as minister on 1 March 1647.[100] Symonds had been on friendly terms with Goodwin's parishioners during his time as a London minister in the 1630s. Deprived of his living in 1639, he had migrated to the Netherlands.[101] Two of his new parishioners were members of Goodwin's gathered church: Richard Price, the scrivener, and Thomas Morris. Price was clearly a substantial figure in the parish. He was an auditor of the parish accounts in 1646, and between 1645 and 1647 he was paid for legal work on the parish's behalf.[102]

The churchwarden's accounts for 1648–49 tell us that several other Independent divines assisted Joseph Symonds.[103] One was Sidrach Simpson, the Westminster Independent who knew Goodwin from Queens' College, and had worked alongside Symonds in the congregational church at Rotterdam in the late 1630s.[104] Symonds was clearly the main minister, for in Michaelmas quarter 1648, he was paid £25 to Simpson's £10, though Simpson eventually succeeded him as rector in 1649.[105] Other preachers who were paid for occasional sermons included John Canne, Thomas Brooks and Vavasour Powell, whose congregation was meeting in the parish church in 1650.[106] More strikingly, Goodwin himself was listed among the parish's 'ministers'. He was paid £10 for the Christmas quarter 1648, and for the midsummer and Christmas quarters 1649. Indeed, it seems that the preaching at St Mary's was shared out between a number of ministers, with Symonds, Simpson, Goodwin and Canne taking different quarters in 1648–49. Payment for the ministers came from two distinct sources: tithes and gifts. Thus in the Michaelmas

---

99 *LJ*, ix. 488 (19 October 1647).
100 W. A. Shaw, *A History of the English Church during the Civil Wars and under the Commonwealth*, 2 vols (London, 1900), ii. 338.
101 See J. Venn and J. A. Venn, *Alumni Cantabrigienses ... Part I from the Earliest Times to 1751*, 4 vols (Cambridge, 1922–27), iv. 77; *The Diary of Samuel Rogers*, ed. T. Webster and K. Shipps (Woodbridge, 2004), xlviii, 154–55; NA SP 16/297/39, Letter from Sir Thomas Wroth to Dr Stoughton, 1635, which sends greetings to 'Mr Symmons and Mr Goodwin'. Surprisingly, Symonds has no entry in the *ODNB*.
102 GL MS 3891/1, Churchwarden's Accounts, St Mary Abchurch (not foliated, see 1645–47). The accounts and parish register also mention Edmund Rosier, who was to collaborate with Goodwin's people in 1649 against Walwyn.
103 For what follows see GL MS 3891/1, Churchwarden's Accounts, St Mary Abchurch (not foliated, 1648–49).
104 G. Nuttall, *Visible Saints: The Congregational Way, 1640–1660* (Oxford, 1957), 11–12.
105 See *ODNB* on Simpson.
106 See *Three Hymnes, or Certain Excellent new Psalmes, composed by those Three Reverend, and Learned Divines, Mr. John Goodwin, Mr. Dasoser [sic] Powel, and Mr. Appletree. Sung in their respective Congregations, at Stephens Coleman-streete, London, and at Mary Abchurch, on Thursday the 8. of October, 1650* (1650).

quarter 1648, £18 was received in tithes, and slightly over £10 'upon mens ffree guift for the ministers'. Goodwin was highly critical of tithes, and had engaged in a public disputation in Christ Church parish against them around 1646; it seems clear that his payment would have come from 'ffree guift', though other Independents may have been willing to receive tithe money.[107]

The terms on which Goodwin and his congregation were accommodated within Mary Abchurch were very favourable, for when Goodwin was reinstated at St Stephens in November 1649 he insisted that his gathered church be given 'the same libertie and accommodation ... as with readiness was granted to them by the people in Abchurch Lane'. His congregation joined with the parishioners for worship and preaching, but they met separately and privately in the parish church for communion, collections, and consultation over 'their other affaires'. In these meetings, they were 'intire of themselves', and they would not admit others to communion 'without their admission and fre consent'.[108]

Symonds, in other words, seems to have succeeded where Goodwin had failed by remodelling his parish along thoroughly congregational lines. Mary's Abchurch had become an Independent stronghold. It was not only the base for several key Independent preachers, but for several congregations as well – including Goodwin's, Simpson's and Powell's. Once again, we see that Goodwin was not a man by himself, but was integrated into an effective network. The other ministers were no doubt disturbed by Goodwin's growing Arminian tendencies, but they knew that Independents had to pull together to counter the Presbyterian threat.

Goodwin himself continued to promote a distinctly radical version of the Independent cause. In *Independencie Gods Veritie: or the Necessitie of Toleration* (14 October 1647), he stated the case for Independency and toleration in 'one single sheet' (i.e. eight quarto pages).[109] The primitive church, he argued, was 'divided into distinct Congregations', but they were 'like birds that sing divers notes yet make one harmony'. The church should not be 'tied in one Knot, and kneaded in one lump'. Those who tried to enforce conformity did 'tyranize over mens Consciences', forgetting that God could only be served by 'a willing mind' and that those who acted against their consciences sinned. Christ was 'the only ruler of the Church', though the temporal magistrate had the power 'to punish all grosse crimes'.[110]

Presbyterians, however, 'bestow on the temporal Magistrate, the Office belonging only to Christ'; they 'constraine tender consciences'; and they admit 'unconverted' persons to church membership. Independents, by constrast, sought to erect their congregations on the biblical model 'without any assistance from the Kingdomes of the world'. 'Independency', argued Goodwin, 'is the only lint that can stanch our wounds ... for the very name of Presbytery, is hatefull to the people'.[111] The tide of history was against the Presbyterians:

---

107 *Hagiomastix*, 'To the Reader', §16.
108 GL MS 4458/1, f. 158.
109 On the authorship, see Appendix A.
110 J[ohn] G[oodwin], *Independencie Gods Veritie, or The Necessity of Toleration* (1647), 3–6.
111 *Independencie Gods Veritie*, 6–7.

> We know well that the originall of our late Warre was the Bishops assuming to themselves that power, which Christ never gave them, to wit, of compelling men to yield obedience of what ever they imposed; and men now, are grown more various in their opinions than ever before, and will be as easily perswaded to forsake their meat, as to relinquish their Tenets; and moreover, it is come to that passe, but by what meanes I will not question, that every man esteemeth it as properly his own, as any Immunity contained in Magna Charta, to use his conscience without controule; and when they shall be debarred of what they have so long injoyed and so much covet to keep, what they may attempt let the wise judge; therefore there is not only a reason, but also a necessity of Toleration.[112]

This remarkable passage placed the struggle for religious liberty at the heart of the contemporary crisis. For Goodwin, the age of imposed uniformity and hierarchical control was giving way to an age of individual conscience and religious pluralism.

The Divine Authority of the Scriptures

For all this, Goodwin had no intention of abandoning traditional Protestantism. Throughout the political crisis of 1647, he had been working on *The Divine Authority of the Scriptures* (18 December 1647). It was his second major theological treatise, and reproduced the engraved portrait of the author first displayed in *A Treatise of Justification*. The book originated as sermons, and Goodwin explained that he 'was necessitated, to print them ... as I Preached them', with 'very little alteration'.[113]

The primary purpose of *Divine Authority* was announced in its subtitle: to undermine 'that King of Errours and Heresies, Antiscripturisme, who hath already destroyed the faith of many'. Among some of the godly, confidence in the authority of the Bible was shaken by endless wrangling over its interpretation, and growing awareness of the problems of translation and textual scholarship. Troubled by the difficulties of a religion of the Word, many began to place greater weight upon the Spirit or Reason or both. In their different ways, radical Puritans like William Walwyn, Gerrard Winstanley, George Fox, Samuel Fisher and Clement Wrighter exemplified this crisis of confidence in traditional Puritanism, where the laity listened respectfully as the Word was expounded by orthodox and learned divines.[114] It was anxiety about this phenomenon, and Walwyn's scepticism about Goodwin's apologetics, that had provoked accusations of anti-scripturism against the Leveller in 1646. Despite a patching up of differences, there was 'a great falling out' again in August 1647, when the Levellers were once more aspersed as 'Atheists, Non-Scripturists, Jesuites'.[115] Goodwin then, felt that he was addressing a pressing problem for his constituency. His arguments were tailored to appeal to committed (if troubled) Christians.[116]

---

112 *Independencie Gods Veritie*, 8.
113 *The Divine Authority of the Scriptures Asserted* (1647), sig. a4v.
114 Christopher Hill, 'Samuel Fisher and the Bible', in *The World Turned Upside Down* (London, 1972), ch. 11.
115 *Walwyn*, 393.
116 See *Divine Authority*, 77, 126, 134, 149, 230–31.

Divine Authority had a second purpose too, for it would be a showcase for Goodwin's recommended approach to the problem of heresy. In contrast to the heresiographers, he believed that theological error must be undermined by argument and intellectual persuasion, not by coercion or clerical authority. Indeed, Goodwin blamed the rise of anti-scripturism on his old bugbear, implicit faith. Too many people believed things on the authority of their teachers; 'men supposed learned and Orthodox'; 'Ancestors and fore-fathers'; 'the determinations of the State'; or 'the generall profession' of their nation. As a result of their 'negligence', their failure to enquire into the grounds of biblical authority, they were extremely vulnerable to 'contrary reasonings, arguments and inducements'. The solution to the crisis of faith lay not in appeals to synodical authority or the magistrate's sword, but in waking up lazy minds with rational arguments and persuasive evidence. Goodwin was going to provoke his audience to expend some 'labour of minde' so that they could give 'a substantiall, rationall, or solid account' of their faith.[117]

Thirdly and finally, *Divine Authority* would vindicate Goodwin's own orthodoxy. The book was a powerful demonstration that Goodwin was on the side of the angels, a warrior for truth who would stop 'the plague from spreading further'.[118] Far from tolerating error, he was determined to confute it. As he later explained, while the Presbyterians were busy fulminating against heresy and appealing to the magistrate to do their job for them, he had been devoting much of his ministry to the refutation of four great contemporary errors, 'Antinomianisme, Anabaptisme, Anti-Scripturisme, Querisme or Seeking'.[119]

Indeed, *Divine Authority* reveals that Goodwin was a far more orthodox figure that the outcry against him would suggest. His understanding of the Scriptures was 'pre-critical'. The emerging higher critical scholarship that was to be brought into the open by Thomas Hobbes, Isaac la Peyrère, Benedict Spinoza and Richard Simon had not impinged on his consciousness.[120] He entertained no doubts about the Mosaic authorship of the Pentateuch, the great ages of the patriarchs, or the young age of the earth.[121] He thought that Matthew had begun writing his Gospel just eight years after Christ's ascension.[122] He was also traditional in his defence of the Trinity, the Incarnation and the everlasting torments of hell.[123]

Yet there were several features of Goodwin's book that would only fuel the controversy over his theology. First and foremost, *Divine Authority* contained an aggressive ethical critique of the high Calvinist God. We shall explore this in detail in chapter 7. Suffice it to say that Goodwin's Presbyterian critics immediately seized on the key passages and rightly concluded that he had become an Arminian.

---

117 *Divine Authority*, sigs. a3r-v.
118 *Divine Authority*, sig. a3r.
119 *Sion-Colledg Visited* (1648), 29.
120 See the excellent account of the emergence of this critical scholarship in N. Malcolm, *Aspects of Hobbes* (Oxford, 2002), ch. 12: 'Hobbes, Ezra, and the Bible: The history of a subversive idea'.
121 *Divine Authority*, 41–42, 48–53.
122 *Divine Authority*, 18.
123 *Divine Authority*, 205–14.

Secondly, Goodwin continued to stand by his controversial claims in *Hagiomastix*: the Scriptures were not the foundation of Christian religion; and neither English translations nor the extant Greek and Hebrew manuscripts were the word of God. Goodwin did admit that 'in a sense ... even the English Scriptures, or English Translation it self (and much more the Originalls) may be called the Word of God'. And he insisted that 'Translations of Scripture, are great benefactours unto the world', and perfectly adequate to point men to salvation. Yet both contemporary translations and the surviving Hebrew and Greek copies differed amongst themselves and must also differ in certain respects from the original biblical texts (which were no longer extant). The impeccable Word of God could not be identified with imperfect texts. Rather, translations and copies were the cup that contained the wine of the Gospel. 'The true and proper foundation of Christian Religion' was not 'inke and paper' but 'the substance' of the Gospel.[124]

Such statements exposed Goodwin to the charge that he was troubling the minds of ordinary believers. Other ministers complained that he openly discussed apparent contradictions in the text, incommensurable interpretations among learned men, and the difficulties of refuting Arianism from Scripture. One minister had concluded that Goodwin was 'a wicked man', whose preaching was designed 'rather to make unbelievers and Atheists, then to work Faith in men'.[125] Of course, raising intellectual problems was all part of Goodwin's strategy as a teacher – he wanted to foster independent minds, and took delight in teaching people *how* to think (not merely *what* to think). Yet by discussing problems of textual transmission so openly, he did perhaps sow seeds of doubt in some minds. The radical Clement Writer was familiar with Goodwin's preaching and writing, and was described by Edwards in 1646 as 'an anti-Scripturist, a Questionist and Sceptick, and I fear an Atheist'.[126] When Writer later published his ideas on Scripture, he praised Goodwin as 'a man both of great learning and deep judgement' who had exposed the problems of received texts 'much more ... than any of our dissenting Brethren'.[127] Men like Writer were more impressed by the problems Goodwin highlighted than by the solutions he proposed.[128]

The third controversial feature of *Divine Authority* was its method. Goodwin placed great faith in the power of rational argument. Following well established convention, he divided his arguments into two categories: 'intrinsecall' (31–227), and 'extrinsecall' (227–376).[129] *Internal arguments* were based on both the form

---

124 *Divine Authority*, 3–24.
125 *Gangraena*, iii. 115–116.
126 *Gangraena*, i. 96.
127 Clement Wrighter, *Fides Divina, the Ground of True Faith Asserted* (1657), 14–23.
128 John Owen later accused Brian Walton, the erudite editor of the Polyglot Bible, of providing ammunition for 'Fanatick Antiscripturists' like Writer. See J. Owen, *Of the Divine Originall, Authority, Self-Evidencing Light, and Power of the Scriptures ... Also a Vindication of the Purity and Integrity of the Hebrew and Greek texts of the Old and New Testaments; in some Considerations on ... the late Biblia Polyglotta* (1659).
129 On 'intrinsic' and 'extrinsic' evidences see R. Muller, *Post-Reformation Reformed Dogmatics*, 4 vols (Grand Rapids, MI, 2003), ii. 269–81.

and the content of the Scriptures themselves. With regard to the form of the text, Goodwin averred that the Scriptures were distinctive, authoritative, richly textured, very ancient and admirably harmonious. With regard to substance, he emphasised the Bible's ethical purity, its 'heart-searching property', its power to comfort and transform, its wisdom and mystery. *External arguments* were drawn from human history and experience. The authority of the Bible was confirmed by its remarkable preservation, its success against enormous odds, its fulfilled prophecies, judgements on its enemies, and confirmatory evidence from other civilisations. While Goodwin admitted that some of his arguments might meet with 'dis-satisfaction or discontent', he believed that he had assembled a compelling cumulative case for biblical authority.[130] The arguments presented had 'a sufficient potencie of reason and argument to persuade, where there is no barre of wilfull neglect, frowardnesse, or resistance in the way'.[131]

Goodwin's evidentialist apologetic was not startlingly original. There was a long tradition of Christian apologetics that extended back through Thomas Aquinas to Origen and Justin Martyr, and recent Reformed thinkers like Philippe du Plessis Mornay and Hugo Grotius had written major apologetic works.[132] But as Goodwin noted in *Hagiomastix*, the general view among orthodox Reformed divines was that 'Arguments and Proofes' were only 'probable, not demonstrative', and were 'not sufficient to perswade men to a firme assent unto them'. Divines like Ursinus, Rivet and Musculus, 'only allow the supernaturall and immediate worke of the Spirit ... as an Argument demonstratively and infallibly conclusive'.[133] The Calvinist emphasis on man's natural depravity thus led to the conclusion that the human mind was enlightened not by rational arguments but by the witness of the Spirit.[134] This was the position that was to be articulated at length by John Owen.[135] Edward Leigh, the MP and lay theologian, had presented evidences for biblical authority in *A Treatise of Divinity* (1646), but he was quick to point out that 'none of these arguments can undoubtedly perswade the heart *certitude fidei*' that Scripture was the word of God, 'till we be taught it of God, till the holy Spirit of God have inwardly certified and sealed it'.[136] Goodwin did not share Calvinist misgivings about the force of rational argument: 'mine own Judgement, I confesse, rather inclines another way'.[137] As the Scottish Presbyterian George Gillespie noted, Goodwin had 'called in question' 'the common resolution of sound Protestant writers ... that these arguments and infallible characters in the Scripture itself,

---

130 *Divine Authority*, sig. a4v.
131 *Divine Authority*, 376–77.
132 Du Plessis Mornay, *Traité de la Verité de la Religion Chrestienne* (1579; English translation 1587); Hugo Grotius, *De Veritate Religionis Christianae* (1622).
133 *Hagiomastix*, 32–33.
134 See R. Muller, *Post-Reformation Reformed Dogmatics*, ii. 255–85.
135 See Owen, *Of the Divine Originall* (1659) and *The Reason of Faith* (1677). See also S. Rehnmann, *Divine Discourse: The Theological Methodology of John Owen* (Grand Rapids, 2002), ch. 5: 'Belief and evidence'.
136 Edward Leigh, *A Treatise of Divinity* (1646), 23–24.
137 *Hagiomastix*, 32–33.

which most certainly prove it to be the word of God, cannot produce a certainty of persuasion in our hearts, but this is done by the Spirit of God within us'.[138]

Goodwin's rational apologetic harmonised with his newfound Arminianism and his tolerationism. Whereas many profoundly Augustinian Calvinists emphasised the weakness of human reason, the necessity of irresistible grace, and the (analogous) need for the magistrate's coercion in religion, Goodwin stressed the natural capacity of human reason, the sufficiency of universal grace, and the use of persuasion rather than coercion. God worked by rational persuasion not by physical compulsion, and the church should do the same.

The Presbyterian Backlash

Divine Authority certainly impressed some readers. Richard Baxter recommended it in several works, with the proviso that 'some of his Positions I judg unsound'.[139] John Wilkins placed it at the top of his list of books on biblical authority in the 1651 edition of *Ecclesiastes*.[140] But the book failed to silence Goodwin's critics. On 14 December 1647, fifty-two of the City's Presbyterian clergy (including 13 Westminster divines) signed *A Testimony to the Truth of Jesus Christ*. The heart of their collective statement was a lengthy list of 'abominable Errours, damnable Heresies, and Horrid Blasphemies' illustrated by quotations from radical pamphlets. The errors identified were against Scripture (Goodwin), God and the Trinity (Paul Best and John Biddle), Election, Reprobation and Original Sin (Laurence Saunders), Christ's Mediation (Best, Richard Overton, Paul Hobson), General Redemption (Henry Hammond, Saunders), Free Will (Goodwin, Saunders), Faith and Justification (Goodwin, Hammond), Moral Law (Tobias Crisp, John Eaton, Robert Towne), Ordinances (John Saltmarsh), Baptism (John Tombes, Saltmarsh), Lawful Oaths (Roger Williams), Marriage (John Milton), the Future State (Overton, Avery), and Toleration (Walwyn, Best, Williams).[141] The proponents of error were certainly a motley crew. Henry Hammond (the only Anglican on the list) complained bitterly that he had been lumped 'with the broachers of all the blasphemies and heresies of this age'.[142]

Goodwin too felt sorely aggrieved. His fellow Puritan ministers in the City had turned on him, publicly denouncing him as a teacher of error. Old foes like George Walker had been joined by respected figures like William Gouge and Edmund Calamy; Goodwin's successor at St Stephen's, William Taylor; and his former pupil, Thomas Cawton. In his reply, *Sion-Colledg Visited* (1 February 1648),

---

138 Gillespie, 'A Treatise of Miscellany Questions' (1648), in *The Works of George Gillespie*, ii. 106.
139 Richard Baxter, *The Saints Everlasting Rest* (1650), 250. See later recommendations in Baxter, *The Reasons of the Christian Religion* (1667), 453; Baxter, *A Christian Directory* (1673), 924.
140 John Wilkins, *Ecclesiastes, or A Discourse concerning the Gift of Preaching* (1651), 95. Goodwin's book was still listed in the 1679 edition.
141 *A Testimony to the Truth of Jesus Christ* (1647).
142 Henry Hammond, *A Vindication of Three Passages in the Practical Catechisme* (1648), 12–13.

Goodwin claimed that he himself was 'the chiefe' target of the 'the 52 hands'. The *Testimony* may never have been published 'had not the two and fifty prudently judged it expedient that my Name should be blasted'. It had been issued hard on the heels of his *Divine Authority*, 'to blast the credit, and way-lay the acceptation of it with the generality of men'. It was also an act of overdue revenge for 'The sore wound given to their Cause by *Hagiomastix Displayed* &c'.[143]

Goodwin may have had an over-inflated sense of his own importance, but many Presbyterians did regard him as their most formidable critic. It was a role Goodwin was happy to fulfil, and he chastised the Presbyterian clergy for trying to extirpate heresy with abusive language 'without so much as levying one word of an argument'. Their reputation was in decline because they were determined to 'stigmatise the Truths of God', 'pull downe with both your hands the precious names and reputations of the faithfull servants of God', and 'exasperate and incense the sword of the Magistrate against such as are peaceable in the Land'. Instead of acting 'as if the Chaire of Papal Infallibility were of late translated from Rome to Sion-Colledge', they should recognise that the progress of reformation had fatally wounded clerical authority.[144] In a resonant Miltonic statement, Goodwin declared that the days when the laity would submit to the pronouncements of the clergy were over:

> The night is too farre spent for them to think, that men even of ordinary judgement or consideration, will now measure or judge of Error and Truth, only by their Magisteriall votes ... Indeed when it was midnight, the grosse darknesse of Popish ignorance and superstition as yet spread upon the face of the nation, it was enough for a Province of Priests, or Clergy-men, gravely met together in the Name and Authority of their Sacred Unction, to stigmatize what opinions they pleased, for Errors and Heresies ... But the Day-spring from on high hath now (blessed be God) visited this nation, and men have put away those childish things from them, to believe as the Church (i. As the Clergy) beleeveth: to call Error, whatsoever 52. Church-men ... shall baptize by the name of Error ...[145]

This was radical anti-clericalism coming from the mouth of an ordained minister. As his critic William Jenkyn observed, in *Sion-Colledg Visited* Goodwin set aside his usual custom of signing off as 'Minister of a Church in Colemanstreet', and described himself simply as 'John Goodwin, a servant of God and men'. Jenkyn wondered if Goodwin now recognised any distinction between ministers and laity.[146]

Yet for all his anti-clericalism, Goodwin did not relish being lumped together with Best, Walwyn, Gorton, Overton and other radicals. This was partly because he had substantive doctrinal disagreements with some of these figures over the Trinity, justification, or baptism. But there was also an element of elitism too, as revealed by his dismissive comment about 'the obscurity and inconsiderablenesse'

---

143 *Sion-Colledg Visited*, 27–29.
144 *Sion-Colledg Visited*, 7, 19, 4.
145 *Sion-Colledg Visited*, 9.
146 William Jenkyn, *Allotrioepiskopos: The Busie Bishop or The Visitor Visited* (1648), 3.

of the other authors condemned in the *Testimony*.¹⁴⁷ Indeed, Goodwin's relationship to the 'radicals' of the 1640s was as ambivalent as that of another Cambridge-educated Reformed humanist, John Milton. Like Milton, Goodwin was both allied to sectarian radicals and fundamentally distinct from them, set apart by his reputation as a serious scholar.

Milton and Goodwin were more comfortable working with respected intellectuals like Samuel Hartlib. It was Hartlib who recruited Goodwin and John Dury to recommend an English translation of Acontius. *Satan's Stratagems*, containing the first four books, was published in February 1648, and the translator wrote dedications to Parliament and to General Fairfax and Lieutenant-General Cromwell. Goodwin provided 'The Epistle to the Reader', and a commendatory letter by the ecumenist John Dury was also added. It was published by John Macock and sold by both John Hancock and Giles Calvert. The enterprise bore witness to the coalition of intellectuals, printers, booksellers, military commanders and sympathetic politicians ranged against the imposition of a rigid religious uniformity.¹⁴⁸

Goodwin's introductory epistle argued that these were days in which heresies and 'many ancient Truths' jostled for men's attention. In a reference to the *Testimony*, he complained that 'men make no scruple or Conscience to binde up God and Belial, Christ and the Devil together in one and the same bundle of condemnation'. To make things worse, such men armed themselves 'with the material sword' against heresies rather than with the Word of God. 'If men would call more for light, and less for fire from heaven', wrote Goodwin, 'their warfare against such enemies would be much sooner accomplished'. He recommended Acontius highly: 'I have not met with any Author comparable to this now in thine hand, for a Christian genius and dexterity, in teaching that desireable and happy Art' of combating heresy with spiritual weapons.¹⁴⁹

Satans Stratagems confirmed what Goodwin had been arguing since *Theomachia* and had articulated most fully in *Hagiomastix*. Acontius built on the work of the great Christian humanist Erasmus, and provided a twofold solution to the problems of theological dogmatism, internecine conflict and persecution.¹⁵⁰ In the first place, he encouraged Protestant Christians to cultivate intellectual humility and civility, and distinguished a minimalist core of fundamental doctrines necessary for salvation from secondary doctrines on which diversity was permissible. His list of fundamentals amounted to a minimalist creed that even Socinians could endorse.¹⁵¹ Secondly, writing only a decade after the execution of Servetus, Acontius sided with Castellio against Calvin by denying the magistrate 'the power of punishing Heretiques'.¹⁵²

---

147 *Sion-Colledg Visited*, 28.
148 Jacobus Acontius, *Satans Stratagems* (1648). Dury's letter is addressed to Samuel Hartlib, and (like Goodwin's Epistle) it is dated 9 February 1647/48, suggesting that both Dury and Goodwin were replying to an urgent request by Hartlib for commendations.
149 Goodwin, 'The Epistle to the Reader', in Acontius, *Satans Stratagems*, sig. a4-A.
150 See G. Remer, *Humanism and the Rhetoric of Toleration*, ch. 2.
151 Acontius, *Satans Stratagems*, 81.
152 Acontius, *Satans Stratagems*, Book iii, 90–111.

Francis Cheynell, the orthodox Calvinist nemesis of William Chillingworth, quickly picked up the scent of *Satan's Stratagems*. 'I confess I was amazed at it', he later wrote, 'but could not learne who was the Translatour of it. We were at the time required to look after all books that were pernicious or dangerous and I did complaine to the reverend Assembly sitting at Westminster'. In his report to the Assembly, Cheynell criticised Acontius's enumeration of the fundamentals of the faith – there was no mention of 'the Godhead of Jesus Christ, or the Godhead of the holy Ghost', and Acontius declined to use 'the Orthodox expressions of the Ancient Church, in the first foure generall Synods', delivering his creed 'in such general expressions, that as we conceive the Socinians may subscribe it, and yet retaine the worst of their blasphemous errours'. The Assembly responded to Cheynell's report by appointing a committee to report on the book, but its members were surprised that one of their own, John Dury, had commended the book. The unfortunate Dury was co-opted onto the committee and forced to admit that 'he had given too faire a Testimony to that subtill peace'. He had failed to see that 'Acontian Syncretisme' went beyond his own ecumenical schemes by including Socinians within 'the lines of Christian Communication'.[153] The translation of the first four books was eventually reissued (along with Dury's commendation) under the title *Darkness Discovered* (1651), but the censuring of Dury deterred Hartlib from publishing the rest of the translation.[154] In 1654, Dury wrote to Hartlib suggesting that he 'suspend' 'the printing of Acontius', because its publication 'may preiudice the business I now have in hand'.[155] Unlike Goodwin, Dury always believed that one needed to win friends in order to influence people.

In the same month as Cheynell reported to the Assembly (March 1648), John Vicars and William Jenkyn joined the Presbyterian counter-offensive by publishing highly personalised attacks on Goodwin in response to *Sion-Colledg Visited*. A third response by Cornelius Burgess was published in May, entitled *Sion College: What it is and what it Doeth*. Together these tracts constituted a three-pronged assault on Goodwin's 'visitation': Vicars supplied the vitriol, Jenkyns provided the considered theological response, and Burgess explained what Sion College was really like.

Vicar's pamphlet, *Coleman-Street Conclave Visited*, announced its intentions on its frontispiece. A satirical portrait of Goodwin depicted him holding a copy of what Vicars called 'his most hereticall' and 'horrid' *Hagiomastix*. Since that notorious tract was indelibly associated with scepticism, Goodwin was pictured with a windmill hovering above his head, its sails blown by 'Error' and 'Pride'. A weathercock

---

153 Francis Cheynell, *The Divine Trinunity of the Father, Son, and Holy Spirit* (1650), 443–45, 453–56.
154 When the Cambridge latitudinarian, Dr John Worthington, recalled the controversy over the book, he suggested that 'the rest [of the translation] was also finished but not printed, and I think Mr Hartlib had it'. *The Diary and Correspondence of Dr John Worthington*, ed. J. Crossley, 2 vols (London, 1847–86), II.i. 143–44.
155 HP 4/3/32A. Further references to the publication of *Satans Stratagems* can be found in HP 13/213B (where Sir Cheney Culpepper regrets that 'Acontius is soe ill relished' but tells Hartlib that 'Mr Dury can never bestryde a better cause & author'); and HP 9/11/21A (where W. Hamilton draws the attention of Hartlib and Dury to Cheynell's attack on Acontius in his *Divine Triunity*).

3 Satirical caricature of John Goodwin, reprinted from *John Vicars, Coleman-Street Conclave Visited* (1648).

stood on top of the windmill, both representing his instability in judgement. Vicars explained that Goodwin was 'continually coyning and contriving, in his busie-brain and hereticall-heart, one blasphemous Errour or another'. A hand from the clouds offers him a copy of *MoroMastix* to cure his ills. But the proud Independent scornfully spurns the book, and complains that he is always being misrepresented: 'In all the Grists I Grinde in Errors Mill,/Unhappie I, I am mistaken still'. In reality, Vicars explained, Goodwin was the 'Patron of Heresy, and Shame of Divinity'.[156]

If anything, Vicars' tract outdid even *Gangraena* in its apoplectic vehemence. It accused Goodwin of the 'most detestable and damnable Pelagian, Arminian, Papisticall, and Socinian Heresies'. He had abused innocent men like Walker, Prynne, and Edwards, and poured scorn on the whole of Sion College. He had promoted 'a Toleration of all opinions', undermined the authority of Scripture, taught that heathens could be saved by natural light, exalted reason and free will, rejected predestination and reprobation and denied the imputation of Christ's righteousness to the believer. He was an 'abominable abuser of the Word of God'. The 'proud Priest of Coleman-street' had inspired his followers with 'a spirit of bold and blasphemous Atheisme' – only recently, his follower Mr Quarterman of Southwark had dropped down dead seven days after declaring that 'there was no more holynesse in the Scriptures than in ... a hundred Dogs-tayles'. If Goodwin failed to repent of his crimes, warned Vicars, he would face 'the flaming light of hel-fire'.[157]

---

156 Vicars, *Coleman-street Conclave Visited*, 'To the Reader'.
157 Vicars, *Coleman-street Conclave Visited*, title page, 2–4, 15, 16, 36, 40.

Vicars' pamphlet underlines Goodwin's position as the Presbyterians' leading literary foe. On page after page, Vicars fixates on Goodwin's *size*. He is compared to the giant Goliath, the emperor Belshazzar, the High Priest Caiaphas, and 'bloody Nero'; he is 'That Grand Imposter', 'the Schismatics Cheater in Chief', 'this most huge Gargantua', the 'monstrous Metropolitan', 'this Hungry Helluo Errorum, this greedy Heliogabolus'; he is 'the Arch-Master of impudencie and impiety' who employs the 'Grand-Engine' of equivocation; he is addicted to 'his own big-bragadochio and Wave-like-swelling and swaggering Writings, full-fraught with Six-footed Terms'.[158] The fact that Goodwin loomed so large in the mind of the Presbyterians is remarkable, for he was utterly outnumbered among the London clergy, fifty-two of whom had recently condemned his errors. Yet by 1648 the Presbyterians were painfully aware of their own impotence in the face of the New Model Army and the political Independents at Westminster. Vicars complained that Goodwin had escaped prosecution for *Hagiomastix* because he and other 'irreligious and rotten builders' had secured 'such potent props' in Parliament.[159] The Independents had might on their side, and as their most eloquent clerical voice, Goodwin now seemed truly monstrous.

The young minister of Christ Church, William Jenkyn, who had also signed the *Testimony*, joined the fray with his *Allotrioepiskopos: The Busie Bishop or The Visitor Visited*. Jenkyn wished that Goodwin had not ventured from 'his darker diocese' in 'Errour-alley' to attack Sion College, but he was determined to repel the assault with a swift counterattack.[160] He focused on the two most controversial features of what he called 'your late book, against the Authority of the Scriptures' – its denial that Scripture was the foundation of the Christian religion, and its affirmation of natural man's capacity to do supernatural good.[161]

Goodwin would offer an extended theological response to Jenkyn in due course, but in the meantime his right-hand man, John Price, launched a direct assault on the 'Sion-Colledge Preachers' in *The Pulpit Incendiary*. Price and his friends had been gathering intelligence on the sermons and prayers of 'our Citie Preachers', especially in their morning lectures, during February, March and April of 1648. He had come across numerous examples of Presbyterian clergy praying and preaching against 'the Parliament, Army, and the People of God'. The guilty men included Edmund Calamy, Thomas Cawton, 'Mr Taylor in Colemanstreet', and 'that pertinatious Mr Jenkyn'. These Presbyterian ministers were 'fomenters of trouble', and all the City's recent woes had been 'hatched at Sion Colledge'.[162]

The actions of the Sion College preachers were jeopardising England's Exodus. Having escaped from 'the Pope and his Hierarchy', and the 'Lordly domineering and tyrannizing spirits' of their oppressors, and experienced 'excellent ravishments and raptures of the spirit' and 'an open and a free trade to Heaven', were the godly now about to regress? God had brought them 'unto the very edge of Canaan', but

---

158 Vicars, *Coleman-street Conclave Visited*, 27.
159 Vicars, *Coleman-street Conclave Visited*, 27.
160 Jenkyn, *Allotrioepiskopos*, sig. A3, 17.
161 Jenkyn, *Allotrioepiskopos*, 6, 19–27 (Scripture), 27–55 (natural man's capacity).
162 [John Price], *The Pulpit Incendiary* (1648), 1–21.

the Presbyterians were now planning to 'return again to the bondage of Pharoah'. Price urged his readers not to exchange 'that libertie which we now enjoy', for an 'everlasting bondage' and worse than 'Turkish slavery' under new 'Task-masters' and 'oppressions'.[163]

But as well as condemning the Presbyterians, Price also pleaded with them as brothers:

> Consider the deare relation wherein we stand each to other in Jesus Christ, have we not the same Lord, the same Faith, the same Baptisme? Did we not all lie together as it were in the same womb of the Almightie's gracious purpose? Are we not all the price of the same ransome, the redeemed of the same Saviour? Doth not the same Spirit of Jesus breathe in our hearts? the same blood of Jesus run in our veins? Are we not all brethren in the faith? and shall brethren reproach brethren? brethren raile against brethren? What! brethren without bowels, without naturall affection to brethren?[164]

Here was an important reminder that despite the ferocious polemics, Independents and Presbyterians could still recognise each other as 'the redeemed'. Price admitted that they disagreed about toleration and the magistrate's role in religion. But when contrasted with their 'Cavaleerish' enemies, their commonality became apparent. They shared the same religious culture, and the same longing for moral reformation and spiritual renewal.[165] This plea for mutual toleration and 'joynt operation', muddled as it was with bitter condemnation, fell on deaf ears, and Christopher Love published a trenchant answer to Price.[166]

The third Presbyterian pamphlet against Goodwin, *Sion College: What it is and Doeth* was by 'C.B.', whom Goodwin believed to be the Westminster divine Cornelius Burgess.[167] It described Goodwin as 'an Apostate member' of the College, who was driven by ambition to become 'Contradictor in chief to all your Brethren in points of greatest weight'. The author explained the origins and purposes of Sion College, and indignantly denied the charge made by Price that it was guilty of plotting against Parliament.[168]

The Second Civil War

As this war of words raged among the godly, the Second Civil War broke out in country. In April and May 1648, a series of royalist uprisings occurred in Wales and parts of southern England, including Kent, Surrey and Essex. Meanwhile, the

---

163 [Price], *The Pulpit Incendiary*, 24, 34, 39–41.
164 [Price], *The Pulpit Incendiary*, 59.
165 [Price], *The Pulpit Incendiary*, 43.
166 Christopher Love, *A Modest and Clear Vindication ... of the Ministers of London from the Aspersions of John Price* (1649).
167 Νεοφυτοπρεσβύτερος *[Neophutopresbuteros], or The Yongling Elder or Novice-Presbyter* (1648), 111–12, 121, 126–27. Goodwin does not mention Burgess by his full name, but suspects that the author is a former minister of Magnus parish who has since held a lectureship.
168 C[ornelius] B[urgess], *Sion College: What it is and Doeth* (1648), 1, 20, 21.

Scottish Parliament agreed to an Engagement with the king which would lead to an invasion of England. By the end of May, there were fears of an imminent assault on London. For Goodwin and other radical Independents, the future of their radical Reformation was in the balance.

In the midst of the crisis, the New Model Army performed brilliantly, quelling rebellion in Wales and Kent, and laying siege to the royalist stronghold of Colchester in June. But Independents believed, with some justification, that the army was being let down by inadequate support. As Austin Woolrych observes, 'the City government was downright unfriendly, the Lords were equivocal, and the Commons were wavering'.[169] Indeed, Parliament seemed to be given firm backing to the Westminster Assembly's Presbyterian programme. On 2 May, Parliament had finally passed the draconian Blasphemy Ordinance that Goodwin had fought so hard against. To make matters worse, London itself was now 'a prime centre of royalist conspiracy and insurrection'. In April 1648, there were riots involving thousands of royalist apprentices, running through Fleet Street and the Strand, shouting 'Now for King Charles'. When the Second Civil War broke out, large numbers of Londoners left to join the royalist risings, and 'The City had become such a hotbed of royalism that at the height of the fighting the army was forced to steer clear of it'. The Tower and its garrisons were controlled by political Presbyterians, as was the City government, and the pulpits were mostly occupied by clergy linked to Sion College.[170] To Independents, these institutions appeared more worried by the army than by the royalist threat. On 19 June, the City government failed to prevent gangs of apprentices from attacking wagons carrying military supplies for the army through London. The radical Independent minority were caught between a royalist populace and a political Presbyterian City government.

It was against this background that Goodwin issued his reply to his three Presbyterian assailants in *Neophutopresbuteros, or the Yongling Elder* (June 1648). The bulk of the tract was devoted to rebutting Jenkyn's charges of anti-scripturism and Pelagianism.[171] Goodwin also suggested that Jenkyn had probably been 'the principall hand' behind the *Testimony* issued in December. He and his collaborators were 'forgers of testimonies', who had got fellow ministers like John Downame to endorse an early draft of the document mentioning 'only some of the wildest and most absurd opinions', before deviously inserting the 'errors' of Goodwin and Hammond.[172] Goodwin dealt with Vicars, 'with his Pictures, Poetry, and Windmills', in a single dismissive paragraph, suggesting that he should learn to bridle his tongue.[173] Burgess took a little longer, but Goodwin insisted that what he and Price had written about Sion College was accurate, and that Price could produce 'very competent and substantiall witnesses' to support all his reports of seditious Presbyterian preaching.[174]

---

169 Woolrych, *Britain in Revolution*, 413.
170 I. Gentles, 'The struggle for London in the Second Civil War', *Historical Journal*, 26 (1983), 286–91.
171 *Neophutopresbuteros*, 1–119.
172 *Neophutopresbuteros*, sigs. A3r–A4v.
173 *Neophutopresbuteros*, 120.
174 *Neophutopresbuteros*, 120–138.

When Jenkyn finally issued a reply to *Neophutopresbuteros* in November, he condemned it as 'this last and worst of your pamphlets' in which 'the Reader beholds you vomiting your excrements of scurrility and wrath in every page'.[175] Jenkyn supplied his readers with anti-Goodwin gossip from the London Puritan scene. Back in the 1630s, he alleged, 'Famous Doctor Stoughton' had observed 'how Master Goodwin was wont to torture Scripture for the defending of his error'. 'Mr. C.' of St Magnus (presumably Cornelius Burgess), had agreed that Goodwin's exposition clouded the Scriptures, comparing him to a horse that entered 'a very clear streame', but left it 'very thick and muddy' by 'pawing with his feet'. A Scottish clerical Commissioner to the Westminster Assembly (i.e. Rutherford or Baillie), had burst out on reading *Sion College Visited*: 'Goodwin is a beast'. John Downame, whom Goodwin claimed was duped into signing the *Testimony* against him, had expressed to a number of ministers 'his abhorring of Mr Goodwins opinions mentioned in the Catalogue'. Even his fellow Independents were turning against Goodwin. William Bridge had told fellow ministers that some Independents were resolved to confront Goodwin about his errors on the Scriptures, and 'quit communion with him' if he refused to stop maintaining them. Jenkyn himself had heard 'sundry of the Independent judgement' disowning Goodwin, denouncing his views on Scripture 'and his other opinions, propagated in the alley against grace, with the height of abhorrence, and with much professed detestation'. Some observers of Goodwin's ministry were even claiming 'That they never heard or perceived that ever God blessed it with the turning of any one sinner toward God'.[176]

This image of Goodwin as an arch-heretic with a God-forsaken ministry was diametrically opposed to Goodwin's image of himself as a godly, learned, orthodox Protestant divine. In October 1648, for example, he preached a sermon at St Mary's Abchurch against judicial astrology, a bugbear of traditional Puritanism. Manuscript notes of the sermon survive among the papers of the royalist astrologer, Elias Ashmole, and may have been forwarded to him by Goodwin's former disciple, Nicholas Culpeper.[177] Culpeper and Ashmole had both been present at the inaugural meeting of the Society of Astrologers at Gresham College in February 1647,[178] and Culpeper's growing interest in astrology may have alienated him from his pastor and turned him into a churchless Seeker.[179] Other radicals and Independents shared Culpeper's fascination, and many consulted the astrologer William Lilly

---

175 William Jenkyn, *The Blind Guide, or the Doting Doctor* (1648), 116.
176 Jenkyn, *The Blind Guide*, 4, 6, 8, 10.
177 Bodl. Ashmolean MS 436, no. 8, 'Sermon by Mr John Goodwin at Abchurch 1648, Octobr 22 M.' The sermon notes are lodged rather incongruously among various astrological charts.
178 See B. Woolley, *The Herbalist: Nicholas Culpeper and the Fight for Medical Freedom* (London, 2004), 251–52.
179 According to *Mercurius Pragmaticus*, 4–11 September 1649, Culpeper 'Admitted himselfe of John Goodwins Schoole (of all ungodliness) in Coleman-street. After that hee turn'd Seeker, Manifestarian, and now hee is arrived at the Battlement of an absolute Atheist'.

during the political crises of the 1640s.[180] Goodwin was disturbed by the growing popularity of the art, and his sermon was an uncompromising attack on astrological prediction, which usurped the divine prerogative by claiming 'to declare today what shallbe tomorrow, and to spie the historie of men yet unborne'. Men who employed astrology to predict the future did 'most palpablie & desperately ... stand up in competition with the holy one of Israel'. Goodwin wanted to drive home this point, because 'ye Cittie wee live in is (as Jerusalem of old) full of the manner and wayes of Eastern Nations who generally small and great went wandering after these Soothsayers and Starr Prophets ... competitors with his prophets'.[181]

Goodwin did not bother to reply to Jenkyn, who apart from some new gossip had merely gone over old ground. Indeed, in the two-and-a-half years between *Neophutopresbuteros* (June 1648) and *Redemption Redeemed* (February 1651), only one of his tracts was concerned with theological matters. He was now preoccupied with just two things: the writing of his Arminian *magnum opus*, and the revolutionary events of 1648–49.

---

180 On the popularity of astrology in this period, not least among Independents and radicals, see K. Thomas, *Religion and the Decline of Magic* (London, 1971), chs. 10–12, esp. 442–48. Thomas suggests (435–40) that Calvinists were astrology's strongest critics, while Arminians and Laudians were more inclined to be sympathetic. Goodwin, however, was denouncing astrology at the same time as he was rejecting Calvinism.
181 Bodl. Ashmolean MS 436, no. 8, 'Sermon by Mr John Goodwin', ff. 47–48.

6

'CHAMPION OF THE ARMY' 1648–51

1648 to 1651 were the climactic years of the English Revolution. They marked the height of Goodwin's political career, and the apotheosis of his political theology of liberation. In his mind, the English were completing their Exodus from Egypt, crossing the Red Sea and entering the Promised Land. He found himself in the vanguard of a revolutionary minority, which purged Parliament, executed the King, abolished the House of Lords, established a republic, crushed the Irish, and vanquished the Scottish Covenanters. For Goodwin these astonishing events were proof positive of the providential hand of God behind the Independent cause. At no point during this extraordinary upheaval did he display the slightest hesitation or discomfort at the questionable legality or violence of the army's actions. On the contrary, he gloried in the triumphs of the army, and was one of the few ministers prepared to justify Pride's Purge and the regicide in print. He and his congregation were trusted servants of the ruling junta, and their writings reveal the mentality of the Puritan revolutionaries.

Independents and the Army Coup

At the height of the Second Civil War, Goodwin's congregation was actively involved in the struggle to keep London within Parliamentary control. Parliament appointed Philip Skippon as commander-in-chief of the City militia. A Norfolk man, he had fought under Sir Horace Vere in the Palatinate and the Netherlands, and may have known Goodwin through his Norfolk connections or through Lady Mary Vere.[1] He now developed an intelligence network that resulted in the arrest of many royalist agents between June and December.[2] Goodwin's followers already had a well-developed reputation for espionage, and they were certainly engaged in raising troops and horses. In July 1648 a royalist newsbook alleged that Goodwin ('the

---

1 R. Brenner, *Merchants and Revolution* (Princeton, 1993), 436–37.
2 I. Gentles, 'The struggle for London in the Second Civil War', *Historical Journal*, 26 (1983), 291–97.

Grand Conventicler'), Mark Hildesley and Thomas Patient (pastor of a Baptist church in Bell Alley) were using Coleman Street as a base for recruiting sectaries for the siege of Colchester.[3] In early August, another newsbook reported that a city officer had discovered 83 horses in Coleman Street, 'saddled and bridled with holsters and pistolls'.[4]

London's royalists, however, were equally active, recruiting men and collecting arms and horses to relieve their forces at Colchester. 'For the Cavaliers', writes Ian Gentles, 'London in the summer of 1648 was a powder keg, waiting for the flame which was never ignited'. With the defeat of the Scottish royalists at the battle of Preston on 17 August, and the fall of Colchester soon afterwards, a Parliamentarian victory became inevitable. By the end of the month, the Cavaliers were fleeing the City.[5]

In the wake of the Second Civil War, the Independent party sought a permanent solution to the nation's constitutional crisis. There were a series of meetings designed to draw up a new constitution, an Agreement of the People. Two members of Goodwin's congregation – Daniel Taylor and John Price – were heavily involved. At an initial meeting in the Nag's Head Tavern by Blackwell Hall, leading Independents (Taylor, Price, Colonel Tichborne, Dr Parker and Colonel White) met with the Leveller activists Lilburne and Wildman. Lilburne claimed that there was a sharp disagreement over priorities. While 'the Gentleman Independents' and army grandees wanted to execute the king and purge Parliament, the Levellers insisted that the new Agreement of the People must come first. However, they agreed to choose four representatives from each side to draw up the Agreement. Price was one of the Independents chosen, but he refused to sit on the same committee as Walwyn. Lilburne retorted that 'Mr Walwyn had more honesty and integrity in his little finger than John Price had in all his body!' After much debate, both Price and Walwyn stepped aside, and when the other six met at the Nag's Head on 15 November, no member of Goodwin's congregation was present.[6]

On 6 December 1648, Colonel Pride purged Parliament of Presbyterian MPs, thus instigating an Independent coup and opening the way for the trial of the king. Goodwin was well connected with the army leadership. According to one royalist newsbook, Cromwell had recruited him almost a year before to preach at army headquarters, along with other Independents like Thomas Goodwin, 'Symonds and Simpson', and Philip Nye.[7] Whether at the behest of the army leadership, or on his own initiative, Goodwin set to work on a tract to justify Pride's Purge. Meanwhile, the various factions in the Independent party continued to meet regularly at Whitehall to debate the Agreement and the future settlement of the

---

3 *Mercurius Elencticus*, 19–26 July 1648, 274. See also C. Walker, *Relations and Observations ... The History of Independency* (1648), 123, which refers to 'Skippon's secret Listing of Schimatiques in the City amongst the Congregations of Mr Goodwin, Mr Patience, and others'.
4 *Mercurius Melancholius*, 7–14 August 1648, 147.
5 Gentles, 'The struggle for London', 298–99.
6 John Lilburne, *The Legall Fundamentall Liberties of the People of England* (1649), in W. Haller and G. Davies, eds, *The Leveller Tracts, 1647–53* (New York, 1944), 415–17.
7 *Mercurius Elencticus*, 12–19 January 1648, 15.

nation. A group of sixteen was assembled, which included four soldiers (led by Ireton), four MPs (including the republicans Henry Marten and Thomas Chaloner), four Levellers (Lilburne, Walwyn, Wildman, Maximilian Petty), and four City Independents (including Daniel Taylor and Richard Price the scrivener from Goodwin's congregation). This working group met in Whitehall during the first ten days of December and considered a draft constitution drawn up by the Leveller committee members and Henry Marten. Their agreed text was then submitted to the Council of Officers on 11 December, which accepted most of the committee version but made some minor revisions.[8]

The main point of controversy was with Ireton, who disagreed with the radical Independents and Levellers over the role of the magistrate in religion. Ireton shared the view of the Westminster Independent divines that the magistrate did have a role in suppressing heresy, though there should be toleration for all orthodox Protestants of whatever church.[9] Lilburne recalled 'a long and tedious tug we had with Commissary-General Ireton only, yea sometimes whole nights together, principally about liberty of conscience and the Parliament's punishing where no law provides'. On 14 December, Goodwin and other divines joined the negotiators at Whitehall to discuss the religious clause in the Agreement. A full record of the debate survives, and it bears comparison with the famous Putney debates of the previous year. As Ian Gentles suggests, it is 'one of the finest debates on freedom of conscience ever recorded'.[10] On one side were the conservative Independents led by Ireton and Philip Nye, who defended the magistrate's power in religion; on the other side were the radical tolerationists, including Independent and Baptist preachers (Goodwin, Hugh Peter, Joshua Sprigge, Dr Parker and Thomas Collier), and laymen and soldiers (including Lilburne, Wildman, Richard Overton, and Colonel Thomas Harrison).[11]

Goodwin was one of the most vocal participants in the debate, and he got things started with a radical thesis: 'That God hath not invested any power in a civil magistrate in matters of religion'. This being the case, he wondered if the Army Council had any 'competence' to 'intermeddle' or 'interpose' on the issue. The Council should ask itself whether 'a business of this nature should be of your cognizance at all'. He could see the benefits of including a clause in the Agreement declaring 'that the magistrate has no coercive power in matters of religion'. But if the Council pronounced on the issue, 'then you go against your own principles, for you do assume and interpose in matters of religion'.[12]

---

8 B. Taft, 'The Council of Officers' Agreement of the People, 1648/9', *Historical Journal*, 28 (1985), 169–85.
9 See J. Coffey, 'The toleration controversy', in C. Durston and J. Maltby, eds, *Religion in Revolutionary England* (Manchester, 2006).
10 Ian Gentles, *The New Model Army, 1645–53* (Oxford, 1992), 287.
11 *The Clarke Papers: Selections from the Papers of William Clarke*, ed. C. H. Firth, Camden Society, new series, vols. 49, 54, 61, 62 (1891–1901), ii. 71–132. I have used the Royal Historical Society's reprint of *The Clarke Papers*, vols i and ii (Woodbridge, 1992), but the Whitehall Debates are also reprinted in A. S. Woodhouse, ed., *Puritanism and Liberty* (London, 1938), 125–78.
12 *Clarke Papers*, ii. 74–75.

Goodwin's speech provoked an anti-clerical tirade from a Mr Hewitt, who thought that the learned clergyman was trying to stop the laity discussing theological questions.[13] Hewitt had missed Goodwin's point, and the report in *Mercurius Pragmaticus* made the same mistake.[14] Goodwin was not questioning the right of the laity to discuss religious controversies. He was questioning the competence of magistrates and politicians to determine matters of religious controversy (including the current debate over the magistrate's power in matters of religion). If the Council really believed that civil magistrates had no authority in matters of religion, they should not seek to pronounce on this particular controversy, thus making it clear that their authority as rulers extended over civil matters, not over religion or theology.

Although this was a radical solution, it was hardly a practical one. The burning controversy over the magistrate's power in religion meant that the Agreement could not afford to ignore the issue, and Goodwin's proposal was soon set aside. The debate quickly evolved into a confrontation between Ireton and Nye and the radical tolerationists. Ireton had no problem with toleration for godly Protestants, for 'men really conscientious'. But he believed that the magistrate had a 'restrictive' and 'compulsive' power in matters of religion – he could restrain men from teaching false religion and heresy, and could compel men to attend Protestant worship. To support this conclusion, he appealed to two grounds: the light of nature (which enabled men to discern the evil of false religion) and the Old Testament (which obliged magistrates to restrain it).[15]

Goodwin intervened to rebut both arguments. Although 'men are capable by the light of nature to conceive that there is a God', it was very difficult for them 'to conceive this in a right and true manner'. Thus appeals to the light of nature could not demonstrate that the magistrate should punish idolatry and false religion. As for the Old Testament Law, Goodwin asserted that ancient Israel was an unparalleled 'type' of the New Testament church, not a model for 'lands and states under the Gospel'. Magistrates should not think that they had the same powers as the Old Testament kings, who were 'appointed, instituted and directed by God himself'. The power of contemporary magistrates, by contrast, was 'bestowed by man, by the people', and Goodwin rejected the designation theory that 'men present and God empowers'. The extent of magistrates' power varied, because 'Magistrates, I say, have so much power as the people are willing to give them'. But since the people have 'not a power in themselves' to restrain false worship, 'they cannot derive any such power from the magistrate'.[16]

This origins of government argument, drawn from natural law contract theory, was challenged by Philip Nye, but endorsed by the Leveller Wildman, who also backed Goodwin's arguments on the abrogation of the Old Testament Law and the limits of the light of nature. Ireton, however, was deeply uncomfortable with this

---

13 *Clarke Papers*, ii. 75.
14 *Mercurius Pragmaticus*, 12–19 December 1648, cited in *Clarke Papers*, ii. 75n.
15 *Clarke Papers*, ii. 78–83, 95–99, 112–15.
16 *Clarke Papers*, ii. 115–18.

minimalist account of the magistrate's powers. He asked his opponents if they believed that theft and murder should no longer be punished either, since the Gospel era was 'a time of mercy'. Goodwin, who was soon to defend the regicide, responded that capital punishment for murder was 'a rule of equity and justice' derived from 'the Law of Nature' not from the Law of Moses. But if power to punish false religion by death had been given to all magistrates, 'then every magistrate in the world had been bound to have put all his subjects to death'.[17]

The Whitehall Debates confirm Goodwin's status as one of the most significant tolerationists of the 1640s. As Gerald Aylmer has pointed out, 'it was the radical Independent John Goodwin, and not any of the Levellers, who gave Ireton ... his worst hammering'.[18] On this question at least, Goodwin's congregation lined up with the Levellers against the conservative Independents and Presbyterians. On the following day, 15 December, another meeting was due to be held at Colonel Tichborne's between representatives of both camps. The radical tolerationists (including Goodwin, Wildman, Collier and Daniel Taylor) were to face a group of Presbyterian and Independent divines (including Calamy, Ashe, Seaman, Burgess, Marshall and Nye).[19] Unfortunately, no record of this meeting has survived, but it underlines the radicalism of Goodwin's position – the learned divine was now allied with sectarian preachers and army radicals against a phalanx of respected ministerial colleagues.

Frustrated by the slow progress of negotiations, and suspicious that the grandees of the army would not honour the Agreement, Lilburne published a version of it on 16 December, under the title *Foundations of Freedom*. It was 'an exact copy of what the greatest part of the foresaid sixteen had agreed upon, I only mended a clause in the first reserve about religion to the sense of us all but Ireton'. Although Daniel Taylor and Richard Price had been involved in drawing up this second Agreement of the People, Price was furious at Lilburne for publishing it without the consent of the others, and the two 'had a good sharp bout at Colonel Tichborne's house within two or three days after'. Lilburne recorded that 'after that I came no more amongst them, but with other friends prepared a complaint against their dealing with us and a kind of protest against their proceedings', which he then presented to Cromwell on 28 December.[20] In the treacherous weeks ahead, the Levellers would come to see Cromwell and Ireton as new tyrants, whereas Goodwin and his followers were to be Cromwell's staunchest supporters. Although the Officers' *Agreement of the People* was published in December, and was debated into the middle of January, the Rump showed little interest in adopting it as the new constitution. Goodwin's followers themselves supported the revised *Second Agreement*, for it named Hildesley, Taylor and Richard Price as part of a twelve-man commission assigned with the task of redrawing electoral boundaries and collecting signatures to the *Agreement*. However, in the face of the Rump's indifference, neither the

---

17 *Clarke Papers*, ii. 122–24, 127–31.
18 G. E. Aylmer, ed., *The Levellers in the English Revolution* (London, 1975), 41.
19 *Clarke Papers*, ii. 72.
20 Lilburne, *Legall Fundamentall Liberties*, 423–24.

City Independents nor the army nor the Levellers did much to promote it. The remarkable constitutional deliberations of December 1648 were to come to nothing.[21]

The December Common Council elections, by contrast, marked a turning point in the politics of the City. Two-thirds of incumbents lost their seats on the council, and the City's 'moderate republicans' usurped its leadership.[22] James Farnell identified the 'Goodwin Independents' as a highly influential bloc within the new Common Council. Of its seventeen most active figures, no fewer than five were close associates of Goodwin – three were members of his gathered church (Hildesley, Taylor, Lacy), and two were parochial Independents from Coleman Street (Rowe, Russell).[23] Along with their allies, these men 'would not only dominate the City government in the first years of the republic, but share the Commonwealth's key administrative positions, especially in finance, the navy, and local military administration'.[24]

The Independent purges of Parliament and the Common Council provoked outrage among Presbyterians and royalists. Of the Independent clergy, only two were outspoken in their support for the army's action – Hugh Peter and John Goodwin.[25] Goodwin leapt to the army's defence in his *Right and Might Well Met*, dedicated to Lord General Fairfax and signed on 1 January 1649. He declared that 'the late garbling of the Parliament' had purged it of MPs who had 'given the right hand of fellowship' to the royalist enemy. He then defended the Purge against a series of common objections. To the accusation that the soldiers had 'acted out of their sphere' and beyond their calling, Goodwin replied (as he had in 1647) that 'necessity' had suspended 'the ordinary law of Callings'. The nation was in peril, and in fact the army did have a calling to protect 'the peace, liberty and safety of the Kingdome'. When chief magistrates created inferior magistrates or officers, they invested such men with 'power to punish themselves also, in case they prove evil doers'. The 'call of the Armie' came from 'the cries of the peoples Liberties' and lives, which were about to be sacrificed by renegade MPs.[26]

As for the charge that the army had 'resisted Authority', Goodwin maintained that the soldiers had neither disobeyed a lawful command nor sought to abolish political authority. The purged MPs 'were strangely struck with a political phrensie (as Plato tearmeth it) they acted as men bereaved of their senses, that had quite forgotten the businesse committed unto them'. The army had acted like a sane man who lawfully 'wrests a Sword out of the hand of a mad man, though it be never so legally his'. Although the soldiers did not have 'the explicit and expresse consent of the people therein', they did have men's tacit consent 'sufficiently expressed in their wants and necessities'. Even if the people objected to the purge,

---

21 Taft, 'The Officers' Agreement of the People'.
22 Brenner, *Merchants*, 542–44.
23 J. E. Farnell, 'The usurpation of honest Lordon householders: Barebone's Parliament', *English Historical Review*, 82 (1967), 24–46.
24 Brenner, *Merchants*, 544.
25 See Gentles, *The New Model Army*, 306.
26 *Right and Might Well Met* (1649), 2–8.

the army's intervention was still justified, for 'it is a deed of Charity and Christianity, to save the life of a lunatique or distracted person even against his will'. Pride's Purge was an emergency operation, and when physicians knew what was best for their patients, they had no need to wait for consent. Legal precedent was not necessary. Showing a characteristic disregard for positive law, Goodwin asserted that 'the Law of Nature, necessity, and of love to their Country and Nation' trumped 'all humane Lawes and constitutions whatsoever'. Even 'the Lawes of God' had 'to give place to their elder Sister, the Law of necessity'. Human laws and constitutions 'were all made with knees', wrote Goodwin, 'to bend to the Law of nature and necessity'. That this was so had been acknowledged by Aristotle, Cicero, Tully and Roman law itself.[27] The army's action was lawful, even if it was not strictly legal.

Nor should critics complain that the soldiers had no right 'to judge what such a necessity is'. In a clear echo of *Anti-Cavalierisme*, Goodwin asserted that 'Every man is bound to consider, judge, and determine, what is meet and necessary for him to doe'. The 'judging faculty' had been 'planted in the soules and consciences of men by God', and they should not neglect it by blindly following commands. They rightly saw that many MPs 'were become Renegadoes from their Trust', and were giving succour to royalists who could plunge the country into a third civil war, or subject it 'to the iron yoke of perpetuall tyranny and bondage'. Faced with 'the imminent danger of bloody combustions', the army had a duty to intervene even though they had no legal precedent for doing so. 'As Aquinas the Schooleman well observeth', laws were framed for the common good, and in the unusual cases where a law clashed with the public welfare, it should be suspended.[28]

The fact that the soldiers had sworn (when taking the Solemn League and Covenant) 'to preserve the rights and priviledges of Parliaments' was not a problem. Far from violating the rights and privileges of Parliament, the Purge had 'reduced the Parliament to the true nature, dignity and honour of a Parliament'. Whereas (in January 1642), Charles I had tried to pull MPs from the Commons by 'force and violence'; the army had displayed 'more civility' by merely denying admission. And whereas the five members of 1642 were 'the greatest Patrons and Protectors of the Kingdomes Interest', the purged MPs of 1649 were 'Proselytes to prerogative, and had renounced the Law and Doctrine of the peoples liberties'.[29]

In truth, the soldiers were heroes, who had taken lions by the beards, and prevented them from devouring the sheep. Their action called to mind 'the unparallelable example of the Lord Jesus Christ' in his harrowing of hell. Cicero, 'the Roman Orator', had observed that it was the custom of almost all nations 'to place the Assertors of their Countries liberties, next to the immortall Gods themselves, at the places of honour'. Once the English 'dranke a while of the sweet waters of that Well of liberty, which the Army have dig'd and opened with their Swords', they would rise up and bless their benefactors.[30]

---

27 *Right and Might*, 11–16, 33–35.
28 *Right and Might*, 16–24.
29 *Right and Might*, 27–33.
30 *Right and Might*, 43–44.

For Goodwin then, the army's coup was an act of liberation inspired by 'a Christianly-heroique Spirit'. On the one hand, it called to mind Christ's release of imprisoned souls from hell.[31] On the other, the soldiers were like the defenders of ancient republics who stood up for their nation's liberties. Their decisive intervention was at once godly and heroic, biblical and classical. Puritan concern to seize the providential moment merged with republican determination to 'seize the *occasione*'.[32] Goodwin praised the soldiers for taking the opportunity presented by 'the providence of God in a peculiar juncture of circumstances'.[33]

Goodwin's combination of idealism, opportunism and ruthlessness was what made him a true revolutionary. Convinced that the army was on the side of Right, he had no compunction about defending the use of Might, despite the absence of legal justification or popular consent. For Zagorin, Goodwin's dismissal of the need for express consent was 'the fatal flaw' in his argument and in the Rump's position. While invoking the principle of popular sovereignty, the revolutionaries were blatantly disregarding it. And by appealing to the concept of 'necessity' Goodwin was resorting to an expedient that could be used to justify anything.[34] More sympathetically, George Mosse has seen Goodwin as part of a broader tradition of religious casuistry, which adjusted Christianity to worldly wisdom and secular exigencies. 'With Goodwin,' he writes, '"necessity" has come to be an overriding argument; reason of state is triumphant, but not in the sense of a realism emancipated from Christian concerns'. Whereas Machiavelli maintained that Christian morality and expediency were incompatible, Goodwin and other casuists harnessed them together. By accepting 'the necessity for "policy" and reason of state in the world, [they] brought about the gradual acceptance of modern methods of politics'.[35]

Goodwin's shameless casuistry shocked contemporaries. The diplomat Sir Francis Nethersole argued that in trying to defend the indefensible, Goodwin had contradicted his earlier statements in *Anti-Cavalierisme* concerning the inviolability of the king's life, and thus condemned himself.[36] William Prynne denounced Goodwin as the army's 'S[y]cophant Chaplain'. Speaking on behalf of the purged MPs, he complained that 'this black-mouthed Chaplain of Colemanstreet bespatters us with his Saint-like Rhetorique'. If Goodwin and Peter had lived in 1605, the Gunpowder Plotters would had no trouble in finding 'an advocate or ghostly Father'.[37] The aged Presbyterian John Geree pointedly dedicated his reply – *Might Overcoming*

---

31 One is reminded of a much later example of civic millennialism, Julia Ward Howe's 'Battle Hymn of the Republic': 'As He died to make men holy/Let us die to make men free'.
32 See D. Norbrook, 'Republican Occasions in *Paradise Regained* and *Samson Agonistes*', Milton Studies, 42: *Paradise Regained in Context*, ed. A. Labriola and D. Loewenstein (Pittsburgh, 2003), 122–48.
33 *Right and Might*, 14.
34 Zagorin, *A History of Political Thought in the English Revolution* (1954), 82–83.
35 G. Mosse, *The Holy Pretence: A Study in Christianity and Reason of State from William Perkins to John Winthrop* (Oxford, 1957), 117–120, 151.
36 Sir Francis Nethersole, *Ho auto-katakritos. The Self-condemned* (1649).
37 William Prynne, 'Epistle to the Reader', in *The Substance of a Speech made in the House of Commons by Wil. Prynn* (1649).

Right – to Lady Mary Vere and her daughter Lady Fairfax, hoping that they could persuade General Fairfax to intervene to stop the king's trial. Lady Vere, of course, had once been a regular hearer of Goodwin, and Geree sought to embarrass him by noting that she was 'affectionately serious' against the actions of the army. Geree was appalled to see 'a Divine of note' defend 'the foulest actions'. He depicted 'this Champion of the Army' as an exponent of popish casuistry, who favoured 'the Jesuitical doctrine of deposing, or destroying Princes'.[38]

Regicide

The events of January 1649 can only have confirmed Geree's opinions. Goodwin was one of the few Puritan clergy to be openly associated with the king's trial. On 8 January, the High Court of Justice – established to preside over the trial – met for the first time in Westminster's Painted Hall. Apart from Goodwin and Hugh Peter, 'all except the judges and officers of the Court were kept out'.[39] One eyewitness later recalled that 'John Goodwin sat in the middle of the table, and he made a long speech or prayer'.[40]

Meanwhile, the City's political Independents were making their voices heard. On 13 January, led by Rowe and Tichborne, Common Council passed a motion urging the Commons to bring to trial 'all the grand and capital authors' of the Second Civil War 'from the highest to the lowest'. It also recommended that 'the militia, navy and all places of high office' be placed in the hands of those who were 'constant and uniform' adherents to the regime.[41] Among the twenty men chosen to present the petition at Westminster were four from Coleman Street: Rowe, Barnardiston, Hildesley, and Taylor. By accepting a petition which was not supported by the Lord Mayor and the aldermen, the Commons effectively sanctioned 'the Guildhall coup which sealed the supremacy of the Common Council in the government of the metropolis'.[42] It also appointed a new City Militia Committee, 'dominated by that radical leadership ... which had come to constitute the core of the City's newly empowered ruling group'. Among the thirty-seven men appointed were Owen Rowe, Mark Hildesley and Daniel Taylor.[43]

During the tense days of January, the City radicals threw their weight behind the revolutionary faction at Westminster. In mid-January, Rowe and Tichborne, leaders of the City radicals, helped to prepare the great hall at Westminster for the trial, against the wishes of moderates who wanted the trial to be held away from London at Windsor. Although many MPs shrank from the prospect of regicide,[44]

---

38 John Geree, *Katadynastes: Might overcoming Right, or a Cleer Answer to M. John Goodwin's Might and Right well Met* (1649), sigs. A2r-A3v, 1, 13, 33, 41.
39 *The Diurnal of Thomas Rugg, 1659–61*, ed. W. L. Sachse, *Camden Third Series*, 91 (1961), 118–119.
40 *A Complete Collection of State Trials*, ed. T. B. Howell, 34 vols (London, 1809–26), v. 1124.
41 Brenner, *Merchants*, 544–45.
42 S. Kelsey, 'The trial of Charles I', *English Historical Review*, 118 (2003), 590.
43 Brenner, *Merchants*, 551.
44 See Kelsey, 'The trial of Charles I', 583–616.

Goodwin and the City radicals were among the king's most implacable foes. Lilburne claimed that even before Pride's Purge, the London Independents had 'plainly told us' that the army's priorities were 'To cut off the Kings Head' and to purge Parliament.[45]

Goodwin may have encountered the king face to face on 15 January. Along with Hugh Peter and William Dell he (or Thomas Goodwin) was part of a trio of militant Independent chaplains who were sent to hold several conferences with Charles before his departure to Whitehall on 19 January.[46] Having failed to make any impression on the stubborn monarch, the three chaplains were commissioned by the Court of Justice to bring the king to London on 19 January.[47]

In the midst of all this, Goodwin found time to pen his own vindication in response to Sir Francis Nethersole, which he dated 18 January. It was printed for Henry Cripps, who was taking over the role of Goodwin's publisher after the death his former master, Henry Overton.[48] Goodwin denied Nethersole's charges. He was not 'a Selfe-condemned Heretique', and it was no heresy to hold that 'whosoever sheddeth mans blood, be he never so high, or never so low, his blood lawfully may be shed by man in a judiciary way'. *Right and Might Well Met* had not addressed the question of whether it was lawful 'to smite the lives of Tyrants, or King Tyrants', but even if it had defended tyrannicide this would hardly contradict *Anti-Cavalierisme*. In 1642, as in 1649, Goodwin had opposed the Jesuitical doctrine of killing kings by 'assassination, poisoning, and such extrajudicial and murtherous practices', but he had not written against 'any judiciarie triall of, or legall proceedings against Kings'. It is true that he had then described kings as 'consecrated corn', who could only be reaped by the hand of God itself. But 'whatsoever is done in a way of justice ... may in sufficient proprietie of speech, be said to be done by God himself'. The lawfulness of judicial proceedings against kings had been defended by Prynne, Calvin and Samuel Rutherford, whose *Lex, Rex* Goodwin 'would gladly recommend to your serious perusall'.[49]

The fact that Goodwin was keen to clear away objections to the king's execution is significant, for some recent scholarship has suggested that leading army figures were still looking for a way to avoid killing the king.[50] This may be so, but Goodwin (like Peter and Dell) was clearly trusted by Cromwell and other army politicians. Given the semi-official position he now enjoyed, he was probably doing more than expressing a purely personal opinion. By defending in theory the execution of

---

45 Lilburne, *Legall Fundamentall Liberties*, 415.
46 Both contemporary newsbooks and some modern historians record that it was Thomas Goodwin who accompanied Peter and Dell to Windsor. See *Moderate*, 9–16 Jan. 1649; *Moderate Intelligencer*, 11–18 Jan. 1649; *Perfect Occurences*, 12–19 Jan. 1649, 802; Kelsey, 'The trial of Charles I', 602. However, later accounts always associate John Goodwin (not Thomas) with Hugh Peter and the regicide.
47 See R. Stearns, *The Strenuous Puritan: Hugh Peter, 1598–1660* (Urbana, 1954), 333.
48 A Henry Cripps had lived as a servant in the home of Henry Overton. See T. C. Dale, transcriber, *The Poll Tax for London in 1641*, The Society of Genealogists (1935), 8. For an alternative account of what little is known about him, see H. R. Plomer, *A Dictionary of the Booksellers and Printers who were at work in England, Scotland and Ireland from 1641 to 1667* (London, 1907), 55–56, 119.
49 Ο κριτης ιης αδικιας. *The Unrighteous Judge* (1649), 4–6, 8–18.
50 See especially S. Kelsey, 'The death of Charles I', *Historical Journal*, 45 (2002), 727–754.

a king after a 'judiciarie triall', Goodwin was preparing the ground for regicide.

The trial opened on 20 January, and lasted for one week. Among the witnesses was Richard Price, the scrivener, a leading light in Goodwin's gathered church.[51] Price was 'sprung on the court unannounced' on 25 January, and gave evidence relating to the Ogle plot of 1644 which had been exposed by Goodwin and other Independents. His testimony was intended to highlight the king's duplicity, though Sean Kelsey suggests that it had little impact.[52] More significantly, one witness later reported that Price had acted in a clerical capacity at the court, and assisted in drafting the charge against the king.[53] Goodwin also knew a number of the judges personally. Isaac Pennington and Owen Rowe were friends and former parishioners; Augustine Garland had grown up in the parish before being educated at Emmanuel College; Miles Corbet was MP for Goodwin's old stamping ground of Great Yarmouth; William Heveningham was another member of the Norfolk Puritan gentry. Did Goodwin endeavour to pressurise these men and other judges into supporting the king's execution? If so, he had mixed success. Pennington and Heveningham refused to sign the death warrant, and the latter claimed at his trial in 1660 that he had 'protested against it' with 'courage and boldness'.[54] On the other hand, Rowe, Garland and Corbet were among the fifty-nine regicides, and their resolve may have been strengthened by Goodwin's reassurance.

In his capacity as an official chaplain, Goodwin was apparently hovering around the king himself during these final days. The royalist Clement Walker reported that the Council of War 'appointed that weather-cock John Goodwin of Colemanstreet (the Balaam of the Army that curseth and blesseth for hire) to be Superintendent both over King and Bishop, so that they could hardly speak a word together without being over-heard by the long-schismaticall-eares of blackmouthed John'.[55] Goodwin later claimed to be unimpressed by the royal intellect. Kings, he drily noted, 'have opportunities above other men' to acquire a good education, but there was little evidence of this in Charles I:

> By that houres discourse or more with him, whereunto both he (I conceive) as well as my self, were rather importuned by others, than led by either our respective desires, a few dayes before his death, I found an experiment of truth in that common saying,
> ... *minuit praesentia famam*, i.
> What fame makes great, presence finds lesse to be.[56]

Charles was sentenced to death on Saturday 27 January, condemned as a 'tyrant, traitor and murderer'. The execution took place outside the Banqueting

---

51 See *A List of the Names of those Pretended Judges who Sat, and Sentenced to Death, our Sovereign King Charles the First* (1649).
52 See S. Kelsey, 'Politics and procedure in the trial of Charles I', *Law and History Review*, 22 (2004), 1–26.
53 See *An Exact and Most Impartiall Account of the Indictment, Arraignment, Trial and Judgment (according to Law) of Nine and Twenty Regicides* (1660), 103–04.
54 *State Trials*, ed. Howell, v. 1219.
55 Clement Walker, *History of Independency* (1649), ii. 109.
56 Υβριστοδίκαι. *The Obstructors of Justice; or A Defence of the Sentence passed upon the late King* (1649), 96–97.

Hall at Whitehall on the afternoon of Tuesday 30 January. Many of the regicides were occupied with other business in the Commons or elsewhere in Whitehall. Hugh Peter was ill, but Goodwin himself was lurking in the background. According to one contemporary account, Goodwin was among the Puritan preachers who offered his services as a chaplain to the king on that fateful day, but was politely 'thanked and dismist'.[57] Although it was bitterly cold, a huge crowd assembled to watch the king's final moments. As in the trial, Charles carried himself with great dignity, and declared that he was dying 'a Christian according to the profession of the Church of England'. When the axe fell, the crowd groaned in horror.[58]

The regicide had been carried through by a small militant minority, and was deplored by Royalists and moderate Parliamentarians alike. Both the Scottish Covenanters and the London Presbyterian clergy published statements condemning the King's execution. With the legitimacy of the new regime in dispute even among the godly, a propaganda offensive was essential. In February 1649, the regicide was defended in a blizzard of pamphlets and newsbooks, in what Amos Tubb has recently called 'one of the most remarkable polemical campaigns in English history'. Working hand-in-hand with sympathetic printers and booksellers, radical pamphleteers 'set out to convince their countrymen that the single most unpopular political act of the civil wars was not only just, but the best thing ever to happen in England'.[59]

Mid-February witnessed the publication of John Milton's *Tenure of Kings and Magistrates*, and John Price's *Clerico-Classicum*. Matthew Simmons (who had printed *Right and Might*) was the printer of both tracts, and there are reasons to suspect a coordinated campaign. Both authors quoted sixteenth-century Protestant resistance theorists to justify the regicide, and sought to embarrass the Presbyterian clergy by turning their words against them. Price took particular delight in a sermon by Christopher Love in which the preacher had muttered darkly about the premature deaths of Prince Henry and King James, and practically accused Charles I of betraying the Huguenots and fomenting the Irish Rebellion. Price praised the army as 'the Lord's Battle-Axe' and declared the regicide to be 'the highest act of Justice that was ever performed in this land'. The King's execution was defended by reference to Numbers 35, and the idea of blood guilt, but Price was quick to deny that the regicides had been inspired by non-rational 'impulses of spirit'. 'Morall principles, and the written word of God saith, that the blood-guilty person must dye', and both reason and Scripture made it clear that governments should 'execute judgement and justice impartially'. It was opponents of the king's execution, not the regicides, who were 'steered by an *impulse of spirit & impressions of heart*.[60]

Thomason collected Price's tract on 19 February, and Milton's on 15 February. Two days before, he had acquired an anonymous pamphlet, Κολλουριον *[Kollourion]*:

---

57 This is taken from Thomas Herbert's account of the king's last days and recorded in A. Wood, *Athenae Oxonienses*, ed. Bliss, 4 vols (Oxford, 1813–20), iv. col. 29.
58 See Gentles, *The New Model Army*, 308–13.
59 A. Tubb, 'Printing the regicide of Charles I', *History*, 89 (2004), 500–24, quotations on 502, 518.
60 John Price, *Clerico-Classicum, or The Clergi-allarum to a Third War* (1649), 9, 8, 48–49.

or *An Eye Salve to Anoint the Eyes of the Ministers of the Province of London*, written 'By a Minister of the Gospel' and published by Henry Cripps. The author may well have been John Goodwin.[61] The tract suggested that God had used the army as his instrument 'to bring down that proud Nimrod, the KING that hunted after, not onely the Estates, but Liberties and precious lives of the best of his Subjects'. The Presbyterians were raising an outcry against the execution of 'a notorious enemy to the Lord Jesus Christ'.[62]

Goodwin's major defence of the regicide, *The Obstructors of Justice*, was eventually published in May, with his name and portrait emblazoned on the title page. As Samuel Wesley later remarked, Goodwin 'had the impudence to appear in print in defence of the Fact, with his brazen Picture in the Frontispiece'.[63] *Obstructors* expanded the arguments of *Kollourion*, drew on both Milton and Price, and responded to the counter-revolutionary writings of Henry Hammond and John Geree. In his dedication to the Rump, Goodwin praised the Commons for its 'zeal, and faithfulnesse, I mean, in that most exemplary act of Justice upon the late King'. He urged MPs not to be discouraged because 'the Nation is departed from you'. Men did not appreciate 'that Royal Act of Justice' because they were 'overshadowed with Prerogative Divinitie', unaccustomed to 'such Heroique transactions', and frightened by pessimists who predicted woeful consequences. Goodwin intended to put their minds at rest by justifying 'the said Action', and showing how it would heal rather than curse the nation. He had 'surveied' the public debate over the regicide, and this was his 'Report'.[64]

He began by castigating the Presbyterians for fomenting the Second Civil War and then making 'God himself a Patron and Protectour of murtherers'. Goodwin reminded them that God required that all murderers should be put to death. This was 'a Statute-Law unto all Flesh', given after the Flood: 'Whoso sheddeth mans bloud, by man shall his bloud be shed: for in the image of God made he him' (Genesis 9:6). To this universal law there were no exceptions. God was not 'an accepter of persons'; justice was impartial; all men were accountable and equal before the law. The law of the land might not specify that kings could be executed, but neither did it specify that 'moris-dancers' should be put to death for murder.[65]

'The Crown is but the Kingdoms, or peoples livery', wrote Goodwin. They could not be blamed for 'laying aside a King or Kingly Government'. 'Government by Kings' might be found to be 'a nuisance to the peace or liberties of the people', or 'over-burthensome to the State', especially when 'the Government we speak of is gotten into a race or bloud, that is unfit for Government, as that which for severall descents together, as in Father, in Sons, in Sons son &c, is either boyled up into, and breaks out in oppression and tyranny, or else turns to a water of naturall simplicity and weaknesse or froths into voluptuousnesse and luxurie'. In

---

61 See Appendix.
62 *Kollourion* (1649), 2, 4.
63 Samuel Wesley, *A Defence of a Letter concerning the Education of Dissenters* (1704), 18.
64 *Obstructors of Justice*, sig. A3r-v.
65 *Obstructors of Justice*, 1–11.

such a case, 'a people or State formerly Governed by Kings, may very lawfully turn these servants of theirs out of their doors; as the *Romans* of old, and the *Hollanders* of late (besides many nations more) have done, and are blameless'.[66]

Without claiming that monarchy was an illegitimate form of government, Goodwin was clearly implying the superiority of republics. Not content with making a specific charge against Charles I, he wished to censure the Stuart 'race' (including James I) and cast aspersions on the very institution of dynastic monarchy. Goodwin gave the impression that there was a systemic fault with a form of government so prone to producing tyrannical, stupid or degenerate rulers. The fatal flaws of dynastic monarchies were being implicitly contrasted with the virtuous republics of the ancient Romans and the Protestant Dutch.

Goodwin did not develop this republican line of argument, but concentrated instead on the natural law contract argument elaborated by Reformed resistance theorists. 'Kings are the manufacture, workmanship, or *creatures* of the people', he asserted, and the people could 'proportion, limit, and circumscribe' the power of their rulers, and call them to account if they exceeded the bounds and became tyrannical. The preachers of divine right monarchy were responsible for bringing 'a world of troubles, miseries and calamities upon the world'.[67]

Against the theorists of non-resistance, Goodwin presented a radically populist theory of resistance. The 'executions of just Laws' did not merely lie with magistrates. Both the Bible and the 'the greatest Rabbies in the Presbyterian School' (Prynne, Rutherford, Knox, Polanus) had identified a 'principle of Devolution' – when 'Superiour Magistrates' failed to execute justice, 'the right of these Executions accrue to the Inferiour'. If inferior magistrates faltered, the power and right of execution devolved 'upon the people', including 'private men'.[68]

To back up his case, Goodwin marshalled a good deal of biblical evidence. He appealed to the notorious examples of biblical assassins, including Eglon who had slain King Ehud. He also appealed to the concept of 'blood guilt',[69] explaining that when 'a land is polluted with bloud, [it] cannot be recovered from under that danger of divine displeasure, whereunto it is subjected by such a pollution, but onely by the capitall punishment of him, or them, who have so polluted it'. Since Charles I was 'the Supreme Actour also in the tragedie of bloud', and had practically confessed as much 'at the treaty in the Isle of Wight', it would be a mockery of justice if he were to be reprieved. The Presbyterian and Anglican divines were like King Saul who had 'so importunely' pressed for the sparing of the tyrant Agag.[70]

This profoundly biblical, providentialist account of the regicide stood in apparent tension with Goodwin's appeal to 'the Law of nature, and all principles of reason, equity, yea and common sence it self'.[71] Indeed, ever since Patricia

---

66 *Obstructors of Justice*, 12.
67 *Obstructors of Justice*, 22, 29.
68 *Obstructors of Justice*, 40–47.
69 P. Crawford, 'Charles Stuart: that man of blood', *Journal of British Studies*, 16 (1977), 41–61.
70 *Obstructors of Justice*, 43–45, 3, 61, 63, 66.
71 *Obstructors of Justice*, 60.

Crawford's seminal article on 'the man of blood', historians have associated the 'blood guilt' defence of the regicide with irrational fanaticism, 'scripture-laden hysteria', and 'savage, elemental forces'.[72] In Goodwin's case, however, the blood guilt argument was advanced with typical clarity and intelligibility. He employed biblical examples to illustrate rational principles, and argued that Christianity left states 'to the Regulation of the Law of nature, and nations'. He flatly rejected the theocratic notion that the Mosaic judicial law was binding on modern states – divines who argued this were trying to 'exauthorize States-men ... from legislation' so that 'Clergie-men' could dictate law. But the idea of blood guilt was not something unique to the Mosaic law, it was 'a Statute-Law unto all Flesh', part of the natural law given to all mankind after the Flood (Genesis 9:6). Capital punishment for murderers was a universal moral norm, accessible to reason but reiterated in the Scriptures.[73]

This view was, in fact, commonplace. The notion that those who shed the blood of others forfeited their own lives was axiomatic; it was the logic that undergirded the commonly accepted practice of capital punishment.[74] What was shocking about the case for regicide was the *application* of this logic to the king – the suggestion that murderous monarchs were no more immune from the death penalty than murderous 'moris-dancers'. Applying the concept of blood guilt to 'the Lord's Anointed' was not so much 'mystical' as profoundly demystifying.

Besides advancing a positive case for the king's execution, Goodwin also confronted all the major objections to the regicide – that it was illegal, without precedent, in violation of the Solemn League and Covenant, contrary to Romans 13 and so on. Each of these was dismissed one after the other as entirely lacking in substance. To Prynne's objection that Charles I had never killed anyone himself, Goodwin responded contemptuously:

> To murther with the hand is too servile, and small a game of wickednesse for Kings to play at ... the way and Method of murther appropriate unto Kings, is to murther thousands without striking a stroak, and whilst themselvs take their ease, onely by speaking a word, or subscribing a Commission: and in this sence the King may be said to have *murthered* many thousands of his poor Subjects, even *with his own hands*, inasmuch as he signed those Commissions ... [75]

A just war could 'conferre the honour of innocencie, upon the shedding of bloud'. But Charles I was 'the Architect and Master-work-man in raising an unnecessary, or unjust War', and he had thereby made himself 'the first-born of murtherers'. Goodwin was emphatic in his defence of the king's execution: 'Doubtlesse never

---

72 As is shown by M. Dzelzainis, 'Anti-Monarchism in English republicanism', in M. van Gelderen and Q. Skinner, eds, *Republicanism: A Shared European Heritage*, 2 vols (Cambridge, 2002), 27–41, esp. 32–34. Dzelzainis rightly emphasises the rationality of the case for regicide advanced by Goodwin, Price and Milton.
73 *Obstructors of Justice*, 33, 27, 3, 40–41.
74 See John Hales's sermon on Numbers 35 verse 33 in *The Golden Remains of John Hales* (1659), 74–96.
75 *Obstructors of Justice*, 92.

was there any person under heaven sentenced with death upon more equitable or just grounds in respect of guilt and demerit'.[76]

In his reply to the Presbyterian John Geree, appended to the *Obstructors*, he mocked the naïve faith that Charles would have compromised with Parliament. This was 'very anti-rationall', thought Goodwin, 'a ridiculous kind of *utopianisme*'. 'Kings never held themselves bound to keep any agreement made with their Subjects ... further or longer than they themselves pleased'. Even in Homer's days, 'This dissembling of feud till an opportune time for revenge' was 'a principle familiarly practiced by Kings' like Agamemnon. Charles I was a chronic case of this monarchical disease. 'The King was an old and known Practitioner in pretences and shifts, to evade any obligation whatsoever lying upon him, whether by promise, compact or oath, in order to the promotion of his tyrannicall ends'. He had 'resigned up himself (if Mr Prynns story be true) to the service of the Pope'. Goodwin also had it on good authority that the Stuart family had been nursing thoughts of revenge on the English nation ever since its part in the execution of Mary Stuart under Elizabeth. James I had hidden this desire well, 'being more timorous, and inclining to politick, clandestine, and underhand acts'. But it was 'conjecturable, if not demonstrable', that 'the mischief, ruin and destruction of the English Nation was become the hereditary engagement' of the Stuart dynasty. If Charles had been restored to power, he would have destroyed the army, closed Parliament and broken 'the bones of the Nation, that it could never have stood up more to defend it self against him'. Instead of lamenting his demise, the English should rejoice – he was 'the greatest enemy which they ever had', but he was now 'in such a condition' where he could inflict no further harm upon them. Pride's Purge and the regicide had been acts of 'Necessity'.[77]

With Milton, Goodwin was promoting an unapologetic revolutionary republicanism. His defence of the regicide was accompanied by a broader assault on the Stuart dynasty and on government by kings.[78] Goodwin realised that he was part of a tiny revolutionary minority – 'the Generality of the Nation', he admitted, 'inwardly hate' the regicides, 'and look upon [them] as enemies and disturbers of their peace'.[79] He was fully aware of the supreme irony that the revolution had been carried out in the name of 'the people' but against their wishes. Like Milton, Goodwin combined populist rhetoric with contempt for 'the Generality of the Nation'. Some of the regicides had hesitated over signing the death warrant, and even Cromwell was alleged to have muttered: 'Cruel necessity'. Goodwin, by

---

76 *Obstructors of Justice*, 97, 90.
77 *Obstructors of Justice*, 'A Brief Reply', 99–132.
78 On the lively current debate over the definition of republicanism see the essays in van Gelderen and Skinner, eds, *Republicanism*, and David Wootton's critique in the *English Historical Review*, 120 (2005), 135–39. I have labelled Goodwin a republican because of his anti-monarchism, but in Blair Worden's terms he was a 'negative republican' rather than a 'positive republican' (committed to the introduction of republican architecture). See Worden, 'Republicanism, regicide and republic: the English experience' in van Gelderen and Skinner, eds, *Republicanism*, 327 n.16.
79 *Obstructors of Justice*, 129.

contrast, 'not only justified the putting the king to death, but magnified it as the gloriousest action men were capable of'.[80]

Goodwin believed that the regicide had inaugurated the dawning of a new day. In politics, as in theology, he was exhilarated by the prospect of new light. In an age when 'novelty' was generally something to be avoided, Goodwin positively embraced it.[81] He explained that people were always startled at 'the first apparitions of things new and strange', but after 'a diligent enquiry ... the things themselves become the delight and great contentment of men'. The fact that the regicide was almost unprecedented did not trouble him, for 'every succeeding age hath an opportunity of being wiser than the former', and establishing 'new patterns' for future generations.[82]

The royalist newsbook, *Mercurius Elenticus*, expressed predictable revulsion at such views. Goodwin was a 'base villaine' who had taken the arguments of the Jesuit Mariana and 'published them to the World, to justifie the most horrid murther of the late King'. 'Good God!', exclaimed the journalist, 'what mischiefe is it such fellows will not doe?' Having murdered the king, 'they Triumph in it'. The newsbook printed a prayer allegedly uttered by 'the Coleman-streete Prophet' during morning service on the previous Sunday, in which he asked the Lord to honour 'thy faithfull Servants' for their 'zeale to thy Cause' and their patience under 'the late Tyrant':

> ... it is true Lord, and wee cannot but acknowledge, wee have no outward warrant from thee, for removing the late King, but the inward dictates of the spirit within us, crying and forcing us onward, for Justice against that Man of Blood, besides the necessities urging us thereunto for our owne preservations ... though Lord it bee not to bee Justified by thy written Word, yet let it be to our Consciences, by the free working of thy blessed spirit within us ...[83]

This is how royalists (and some modern historians) liked to think of the regicides – as men driven by irrational impulses who were uncomfortably aware that their shocking action lacked any legal or scriptural justification. In print, however, Goodwin was a very different sort of revolutionary, one who insisted on the rationality and equity of the act of regicide.

Securing the Commonwealth

As well as executing the king, the new regime instigated treason trials against other fomenters of the Second Civil War. In March 1649, three of Goodwin's

---

80 Gilbert Burnet, *A History of My Own Time*, ed. O. Airy, 2 vols (Oxford, 1897), i. 121.
81 On the negative connotations of 'novelty' see C. Condren, *The Language of Politics in Seventeenth-Century England* (Basingstoke, 1994), ch. 5. On the self-consciously innovatory agenda of radicals see J. Scott, *England's Troubles* (Cambridge, 2000), 233–35.
82 *Obstructors of Justice*, sig. A3, 78.
83 *Mercurius Elenticus*, 11–18 June 1649, 60–61.

associates – Rowe, Taylor and Hildesley – were appointed to the 34-person court set up to try the Duke of Hamilton, the Earl of Holland and several others.[84] Rowe, Taylor, Hildesley and Russell were also four of the five most active men in the Common Council throughout 1649. Russell was elected to serve on twenty-two committees, Rowe and Taylor sat on sixteen apiece, and Hildesley on fifteen.[85]

The Coleman Street Independents also played a key role in the downfall of the Levellers. Although the Leveller newsbook *The Moderate* supported the king's trial and execution, Lilburne had launched a fresh campaign against the country's new rulers by late February. His inflammatory tract *England's New Chains Discovered* was quickly followed in March by *The Second Part of Englands New-Chaines*. At the same time, Walwyn published *The Vanitie of the Present Churches*, a scathing critique of the Independent congregations that formed the regime's main support base in the City. The pamphlet named no names, but Goodwin and his followers must have recognised immediately that their church was Walwyn's prime target. The Leveller writer alluded unmistakeably to their learned pastor, their much acclaimed lay preachers, their long *ex tempore* sermons and 'bastard Scholastick knowledge', their 'foul aspersions' against those who 'joyne not with them', their new-found Arminianism, their economic prosperity and their activities as 'Spies' and 'Intelligencers'.[86]

The Leveller assault on the regime and its supporters met with a swift response. Three weeks after the publication of *Vanitie*, Walwyn was arrested in a pre-dawn raid on his home. Three other Leveller leaders – Lilburne, Overton, and Thomas Prince – were imprisoned with him in the Tower of London. According to *Mercurius Militaris*, Cromwell and Ireton turned to 'their friends in Coleman street' to help them against the Levellers. The newsbook reprinted the relation of a young man from Coleman Street, William Blanke. Blanke explained that he had been taken to a chamber in Whitehall, 'where there were many Officers of the Army, as also Capt. Stacy, Mr Lavender, Mr John Goodwin, Mr John Price, and M. Barrus Shoomaker, where they offereth to me and nine more an Oath of Secrecy'. The oath – 'by the four Evangelists' – would commit the swearer to seek and report 'Delinquents'. Sir Arthur Hesilrig had told Blanke that Walwyn and Lilburne must be 'taken off', because they were 'great Politicians'. But Blanke refused the oath, and was imprisoned.[87]

The Levellers were cornered. They had lost much of their support in the army and in the City's congregations, and in late April, seven leading Independents and Particular Baptists published *Walwins Wiles*, a character assassination of their sharpest critic. The tract was almost certainly written by John Price, but it was also signed by David Lordell and Richard Arnold, both members of Goodwin's gathered church.

---

84 Brenner, *Merchants*, 548.
85 Kirby, 'Parish', Appendix C: The Significance of the Goodwin Group on Common Council, 1649–52, 240.
86 *Walwyn*, esp. 312, 314, 316, 321–22, 326–27.
87 *Mercurius Militaris*, 8 May 1649, p 29–31; John Lilburne, *A Preparative Hue and Cry after Sir Arthur Haslerig* (1649), 7–8.

Their co-signatories included the Baptist William Kiffin, and the separatist Edmund Rosier, who had both been associated with Lilburne and with Goodwin's followers.[88] Price was able to draw on the dossier assembled three years earlier by the congregation's committee for investigating Walwyn's orthodoxy. The tract related various tales about Walwyn the scoffer, a man who mocked the idea of hell, denigrated the Scriptures and drove godly women to suicidal despair. It accused him of a design that would result in 'the utter and irrecoverable loss of Ireland, ruin of the Army, crushing the present Authority, dividing the honest party'. *Walwins Wiles* was dedicated to the army, and it implored the soldiers to unite around the new government.[89]

The army did not disappoint. Although there was a minor Leveller rebellion in mid-May, it was crushed at Burford. The Levellers were finished as an organised force in English politics, and the sense of disillusionment and betrayal they felt made their replies to *Walwins Wiles* all the more pointed. In *The Charity of Churchmen*, printed in late May, Humphrey Brooke defended the religious and political reputation of his close friend. He pointed out that Price's charges against Walwyn were remarkably similar to the Presbyterian allegations against Goodwin, and cited *Innocencies Triumph*, *Cretensis* and *Hagiomastix* to prove the point.[90] Thomas Prince issued his reply to 'these seven Vipers' from the Tower, and denied accusations that he was an ignorant dupe of Walwyn. Like Brooke, Prince was personally acquainted with Goodwin's congregation and had known Kiffin for nine years.[91]

Walwyn defended himself in two pamphlets. *The Fountain of Slaunder Discovered* (1649), contained a number of allusions to Goodwin's congregation, but *Walwyns Just Defence* was far more explicit. In this tract, Walwyn explained his love-hate relationship with the Goodwin Independents in great detail, depicting himself as an innocent man betrayed by erstwhile friends. He accused the congregation of idolising Goodwin, thirsting after material prosperity, engaging in espionage and other dubious practices, and slandering the reputation of innocent men. For all their much-vaunted piety, 'these seeming Saints' were worldly politicians who had violated Christian principles of love, honesty and simplicity.[92] Walwyn claimed that Lilburne had also expressed loathing at the 'ingratitude' displayed 'so exceeding all measure, in some of the subscribers of this pamphlet'.[93] In a later tract, Lilburne alleged that the hopman Richard Arnold, 'a Member of the Knavish Conspiracy called Mr John Goodwin's Congregation', was an 'agent' of Haselrig and Cromwell who had plotted 'to take away our lives'.[94]

---

88 It seems clear from the replies by Walwyn, Prince and Brooke that these five signatories were well known to the Levellers, but that Henry Foster and Henry Burnet were not.
89 *Walwins Wiles*, in W. Haller and G. Davies, eds, *Leveller Tracts, 1647–1653* (New York, 1944), 283–317.
90 H[umphrey] B[rooke], *The Charity of Church-Men* (1649), in Haller and Davies, eds, *Leveller Tracts*, 333–34, 338, 342, 346–47.
91 Thomas Prince, *The Silken Independents Snare Broken* (1649), 2, 10.
92 *Walwyns Just Defence*, passim, in *Walwyn*. Quotation on 429.
93 *Walwyn*, 405.
94 Lilburne, *A Preparative Hue and Cry*, 9.

The antagonism between the Levellers and Goodwin's followers would linger for some time. In 1651, John Price and Lilburne became involved on opposite sides of a dispute between Sir Arthur Haselrig and John Musgrave. Price leapt to Haselrig's defence in *Musgrave Muzled* (1651), in which he alleged that Lilburne's father and uncle had been implicated in financial corruption. An indignant Lilburne wrote to Price insisting on the integrity of his family, and visited him at his house in Coleman Street where the two men had 'a pretty large discourse'. When Price refused to yield, Lilburne published their correspondence and labelled Price 'Sir Arthurs Pen-Agent'.[95] The fact that the two men were even on speaking terms is remarkable, and it is noticeable that Lilburne's initial letter addressed Price 'as a friend, in a friendly way'.[96] A few months earlier, in December 1650, John Wildman had joined with Price to defend the rights of London's freemen in a debate before the Lord Mayor, Court of Aldermen and Common Council at the Guildhall.[97] Ideologically, old Levellers and radical Independents still had a good deal in common. Just as important were personal ties, for the Leveller leaders had known Goodwin's people for many years. Thomas Devenish had been Lilburne's landlord at Winchester House, Southwark, and one of the Leveller leader's complaints in 1649 was that the two men had been unjustly deprived of the freehold and inheritance of Winchester House.[98]

The Levellers, in fact, were never the main threat to the new republic. Trouble loomed in Scotland and Ireland, where the regicide had been roundly condemned, and in August 1649 Cromwell crossed the Irish Sea to deal with the royalist forces. The absence of their military hero was unnerving to supporters of the commonwealth, and Goodwin's congregation may have drawn up a petition for his return. A satirical pamphlet published in early August 1649 was entitled *Cromwell's Recall, or The Petition of the Zealous Fraternity ... at the house of John Goodwin Arch-Flamin of England*. The spoof petition expressed dismay that 'our most noble Lord and Brother Oliver Cromwell ... the Pillar of Heresie and Mammons Viceregent ... should leave us, before a perfect establishment of our Government'. It beseeched Parliament 'to call back Goliah from facing the Israelites', and was 'signed by many ill-affected in London' and presented by 'Goodwin, and

---

95 John Lilburne, *A Letter of Lieutenant Colonel John Lilburns, written to Mr. John Price of Colemanstreet London, (and a member of Mr. John Goodwins congregation) the 31. of March 1651... Unto which is annexed Mr. John Price his Answer Thereunto (1651)*; John Lilburne, *A Just Reproof to Haberdashers Hall* (1651), 5.

96 Lilburne, *A Letter*, 5.

97 *London's Liberties: or A Learned Argument of Law and Reason upon Saturday, December 14 1650* (1651). In September 1652, John Wildman joined with Richard Price to buy the fee farm of Fairburn Manor in Yorkshire (see More, 'New Arminians', 156).

98 Lilburne, *A Preparative Hue and Cry*, 5–6; Thomas Devenish, *To the Supreme Authority of England, the Commons Assembled in Parliament* (n.d.), 1–4. It is possible that even Walwyn rebuilt bridges with his former friends in Coleman Street – the vestry minute book for the parish records the presence of a 'Mr Wallwin', 'Mr Wallen', or 'Mr Wallin' at meetings of the General Vestry in December 1657 and April and November 1658. See GL MS 4458/1, ff. 233, 236, 243. This could, of course, be another Walwyn.

three of the chief'. The pamphlet reflected the perception that Goodwin and his followers were close allies of Cromwell, masters of godly cant, and financial beneficiaries of the revolution.[99]

1649 had been an *annus mirabilis* for Goodwin, and it culminated in November with his restoration to the vicarage of St Stephen's. In March 1649, Mark Hildesley's name had headed the list of parishioners present at a meeting of the vestry. Hildesley was made an auditor of the parish accounts, and John Price was appointed one of the collectors for the poor.[100] During the summer of 1649, Goodwin's supporters launched a concerted campaign for his return. On 9 July, the Commons read 'The humble Petition of several Inhabitants of the Parish of Stephen's, Coleman-street', which presumably called for Goodwin's restoration. The House referred the petition to the Committee of Plundered Ministers, and also appointed several MPs, including Henry Ireton, to withdraw, 'prepare and Vote, and present it to the House'.[101] The Presbyterian incumbent at St Stephen's, William Taylor, must have felt increasingly beleaguered. In August, he was called before the Council of State to answer charges made by 'a couple of Tub-preachers', including John Price. Taylor was charged with praying for 'the posterity and royall Consort of King CHARLES the First', and the 'conversion' of the new government. The Council of State thanked Price and his assistant for their loyal efforts, and proceeded to remove Taylor from the vicarage. To the Presbyterians, this was merely the beginning of an Independent campaign to purge the City's pulpits of 'all the Champions of Presbytery' and make way for 'the more glorious Revelations of Everard, Price, Pool, Fountain, Kiffin ... who exercise their gifts in the Bishop of London's Chapel at the Spittle, and Broken-Wharfe'.[102]

The way was now open for Goodwin's return. At a meeting of the General Vestry on 11 November, parishioners noted that 'it hath pleased the All-wise God by the hand of the present supreame authoritie of this Nation to reinstate his faithfull Servant Mr John Goodwin into his place in Colemanstreet'. Because they wished to restore their former vicar 'without preiudice to that church of Christ to whom he is united', the gathered congregation was to be given 'the same libertie and accomodation in the publike meeteing place of Colemanstreete, as with readynes was granted them by the people in Abchurchlane parish'. The parishioners agreed on five particulars concerning the members of the gathered church: (1) they would 'have the use of the meeteing-place to receive the Lords Supper soe oft as they see cause, after the sermon ended, and to make collections among themselves at such times for their own poore'; (2) during their times of communion, the gathered church 'may be intire of themselves, and none wthout their permission and fre consent may put themselves among them or offer to communicate with them'; (3) they could have the use of St Stephen's 'after sermon ended, to consult and determine

---

99 *Cromwells Recall, or The Petition of the Zealous Fraternity, convented Iniquity, at the House of John Goodwin* (1649), 1–3.
100 GL MS 4458/1, f. 158.
101 *CJ*, vi. 256.
102 *Mercurius Aulicus*, 28 August–4 September 1649, 20–22.

their other affaires for the well ordering their body, and bee therein intire of themselves'; (4) 'public collections' for the poor made on fast and thanksgiving days would be 'divided equally', with half given to the officers of the parish and half 'to the officers' of the gathered church; (5) parishioners should be encouraged 'to afford what accommadacion they can in the spare roome of their pewes to the members of the said Church and others who shall come to heare there', though the rights of the parishioner to 'accommodate whome he pleaseth' would still be recognised. The agreement was signed by twenty-six parishioners, headed by four of the City's most prominent political Independents: Pennington, Rowe, Hildesley, and Barnardiston.[103]

The arrangement offered the best deal imaginable for the gathered church. It would benefit from having full access to St Stephen's while retaining its own autonomy and integrity. But Goodwin's joy at his return was soon dampened. Taylor was no longer vicar, but he remained at St Stephen's throughout the 1650s, and the relationship between the Arminian/Independent/republican vicar and his Calvinist/Presbyterian/royalist colleague must have been uneasy, to say the least. It was worsened by the fact that Taylor apparently retained much of the income that had once been given to the vicar. As Goodwin later explained:

> ... at my return I found only a piece of a Skeleton or bare Anatomy of those Means, which at my enforced departure I left a fair and full Body. The chief men upon the place, during my absence, had (it seems) irrevocably transferred their devotion-benevolence, together with their devotion it self in hearing, upon him, who had all that while served their turns, and his own, in my Pulpit [i.e. William Taylor]; who, what he won in this kind, wears to this day. So that if I should estimate the damage and loss I sustained by the hard measure of my Sequestration (without valuing the disparagement and disrepute accompanying it) at 500*l*. I should (I believe) cut short the account by one half.[104]

Goodwin may have enjoyed the moral and financial support of leading parishioners like Pennington and Rowe, but conservative parishioners like Andrew Kendricke and Jeremy Sambrook (whose names were conspicuously absent from the agreement to restore Goodwin) would certainly have favoured Taylor. In March 1650, the vestry tried to deal with the situation by setting up a committee to investigate 'the arreares of Mr Goodwin and Mr Taylor and peruse the parish booke'. Goodwin also asked for a lecturer to be appointed to preach on Sunday afternoons, a request rejected by the vestry.[105]

Still, Goodwin had been restored to his parish, and the English commonwealth was enjoying great success against its foes. The Levellers had been destroyed as an organised movement, and Cromwell's expedition to Ireland was a triumphant (if bloody) success. Having broken the back of Irish resistance, Cromwell turned to Scotland in 1650, and won a crushing victory over the Covenanters at Dunbar on 3 September.

---

103 GL MS 4458/1, ff. 160–61.
104 *Peace Protected* (1654), 8.
105 GL MS 4458/1. f. 164.

For English Independents, Dunbar was final proof of God's favour. A thanksgiving day was appointed for 8th October, and the churches of the Independents rang out with praises. Goodwin composed a psalm of twenty-seven stanzas especially for the occasion. 'Sung by Mr. John Goodwin, in St Stephens Coleman-streete Church', it told the story of the Covenanters defeat in true Old Testament style, celebrating Jehovah's intervention on the side of the English. Goodwin depicted the Covenanters as 'Task-masters fierce and cruel' who had brought 'wheel/and chains ... Your Liberties to bind'. Characteristically, his providentialist hymn depicted the conflict as a war of liberation.[106]

Goodwin's providentialist vision of politics was in line with the Commonwealth's official ideology. As John Wallace has observed, 'its chief spokesmen abandoned for two or three years the high-minded claims of the revolution to represent the people, and fell back on the categorical assertion that the victors had a just title to rule by right of providence'.[107] However, triumphalist legitimation of the new regime fell flat among most contemporaries, who did not share the victors' sense of divine vindication. More successful was an altogether more moderate and secular argument presented by Francis Rous. Rous as much as admitted that the regime had no just title, but maintained that the lawfulness of a government was irrelevant to the lawfulness of obedience.[108] This de facto case for submission was vigorously debated between 1649 and 1652, especially after the Rump prescribed a new oath of allegiance or Engagement. 'The Engagement controversy' resulted in over seventy publications. In opposition were Anglicans like Robert Sanderson and Presbyterians like Prynne and Edward Gee. In favour were writers like John Dury, Anthony Ascham and Marchamont Nedham. Moreover, Hobbes's *Leviathan* (1651) has been plausibly interpreted as being a contribution to the debate.[109]

Goodwin contributed to the controversy by letter and by pamphlet. On 2 January 1650, he wrote to William Heveningham, who had attended thirteen sessions of the king's trial, but refused to sign the death warrant. Heveningham had raised various objections to the Engagement, and Goodwin wrote to reassure him. As usual, he declared that God 'by His Divine Providence' had 'decided the question' after 'so many soleme Appeales on both sides'. But his main goal was to advance the de facto case for the Engagement, and the letter adopted a brusquely unsentimental approach to the question of allegiance. As Goodwin's opening statement explained: 'It is most Just and True to be ffaythful to the Government that Gives protection'. He argued that 'the Cheat of Jure Divino ought to be hoysted out of Civill as well as out of Ecclesiastical' matters, for it prevented

---

106 *Three Hymns, or Certain Excellent New Psalmes, composed by those three Reverend, and Learned Divines, Mr John Goodwin, Mr Dasoser Powell, Mr Appletree* (1650). *A Dictionary of Hymnology*, ed. J. Julian (London, 1892), 348, recommends Goodwin's hymns to 'persons in search of the grotesque'.
107 J. M. Wallace, 'The Engagement controversy, 1649–1652: an annotated list of pamphlets', *Bulletin of the New York Public Library*, 68 (1964), 384–405.
108 Francis Rous, *The Lawfulnes of Obeying the Present Government* (1649).
109 See Wallace, 'The Engagement controversy'. On Hobbes see Q. Skinner, *Visions of Politics, iii: Hobbes and Civil Science* (Cambridge, 2002), chs. 8 and 10.

people from recognising that 'we are to call and acknowledge that a Lawful just poweir in whose Handes the Sword Restes'. The King of Spain had realised this – he had recognised the English government because 'His interest must looke after p[re]sent possessors' rather than 'inconsiderable pretenders'. The early Christians had acknowledged the authority of Augustus, even though his government was obtained 'by as slender a Tytell, as Great Usurpation, & as vast a profusion of Blood, as ever any man'. The Engagement oath called only for fidelity. Those who refused it were guilty of 'perversenes or a Conscience most Ridiculously Boggling'.[110]

A year or so later, Goodwin appears to have adopted a very different line in an anonymous pamphlet: *Englands Apology for its Late Change: or a Sober Perswasive of all Disaffected or Dissenting Persons to a Seasonable Engagement for the Settlement of this Common-wealth* (12 February 1651).[111] The tract was avowedly providentialist and chimed in with Goodwin's defence of the regicide and his victory hymn after Dunbar. It began by noting that 'Others have spoke enough of the argumentative part of our Affaires, and have proved by reason what God hath acted by providence', a clear reference to writers like Rous, Ascham and Nedham, whom he commended elsewhere. But the author was concerned that this concentration on secular arguments was legitimating cynicism and ingratitude among the English people. His tract would be 'a serious memorial of what God hath done for us', an unapologetic reassertion of the revolutionaries' claim that they had God on their side.[112]

Goodwin was under no illusions about the reception of his tract. Having been liberated from 'Pharoahs bondage', the English (like the Israelites before them) would rather return to Egypt 'then be led by providence under the conduct of Moses, through to Canaan'. Royalists had used Presbyterian discontent to divide the godly, and sow 'the foundations of our ruine'. Thus 'the great designe of this paper is but to minde us what God hath done for us', and to persuade people to take the Engagement and support the Commonwealth.[113]

Goodwin proceeded to give his version of Civil War events. Parliament's first principle 'was to bring Delinquents to condigne punishment'. In 1642, 'The King was first opposed universally in his personal capacity, and reserv'd in his publique ... and upon this we waged warre'. But despite the good start, things had quickly got bogged down as Parliament was held back by 'delayes in warre', 'the influences of the Court', and 'neutrall friends'. Only when the 'petty Royal Armie' of the Earl of Essex was replaced by the New Model Army, did God swing into action. The 'first testimony of God' had occurred at the battle of Naseby, an event 'written in marble', 'immortall to all posterity'. From that day to this, God had 'visibly appeared' with 'this poore (at first despised, though now envied) Army', testifying that he was 'so in love with Englands liberties'. In the Second Civil War, in Ireland, and now in Scotland, God had given the army 'an equall, and astonishing successe

---

110 Holkham MS 684, J[ohn] G[oodwin], 'A letter by a friend to W. Heveningham' (also available on MS Film 489 in the Bodleian library).
111 For Goodwin's probable authorship, see Appendix.
112 *Englands Apology* (1651), sig. A2r.
113 *Englands Apology*, 1–3.

against every party'. The victory over the Covenanters at Dunbar had crowned it all, for Scotland was 'a privileged place, and, one would thinke, holy ground'.[114]

These battles declared God's verdict on Britain's civil wars: 'How can a model of the workings of God for his people be drawn in fairer and clearer colours?' But faced with a new threat from the north, the English Presbyterians were equivocating, sympathising with 'a Scottish Tyrannie'. But surely they could see that 'God writes his mind sometimes in his Works, as well as in his Word'? God had vindicated the New Model Army 'from the smallest and contemtiblest of beginnings', in 'the greatest straits', 'against every party', and in the midst of numerous 'plots'. When the Covenanters and the New Model had both made their 'Appeal to God' – 'when prayers clash in heaven' – the Lord had closed his ears to Scottish pleas and sided with the English. Surely this was proof that God was doing something extraordinary, something eschatologically significant. 'All these workings have been in the latter days', wrote Goodwin, 'when God is throwing down the old heavens and earth'. God was appearing against both 'Popery and Antichristianisme' (represented by the Royalists) and 'Tyranny and Oppression' (represented by the Scots). The prophecies of 'Daniel and the Apocalypse' were being fulfilled before their eyes, and 'the destruction of Antichrist' was 'beginning first among his own people'.[115] Building to a crescendo, Goodwin added the vocabulary of classical and English liberty to the language of providence and apocalypse:

> God hath given us an opportunity against our wills to make our selves the freest and happiest Nation on this earth, and we are the first of so large a Continent that God hath advantaged with such a blessing; our Ancestors for these 500 yeers have bin struggling to get but the name of freedom and liberty, and have for this end deposed one King, and set up another, who had commonly a worse title and reign, but God hath given us our choice, whether royal bondage, or English liberty; were we never so nigh the regaining our conquer'd priviledges as now? What is there but a name between us and a Free-State ... [116]

It was now quite clear that 'Gods great design is to bring to nought the Princes of this world ... because they have bin the greatest shedders of the bloud of the Saints that cries under the Altar, and the only mighty upholders of the throne of the Beast'. In an extraordinary piece of hyperbole, Goodwin declared the regicide to be nothing less than 'the first cleer and thorow Act of Justice that ever was executed in the Western World'. The king was 'guilty of all the blood which hath been so prodigally spilt among us', and it was little short of miraculous that he had been put to death without 'the least tumult' 'in so populous and vast a City, among millions of his most intire and desperate friends'. Now was the time 'to wean our hearts from the flashy ravishments of Names and Titles', and make the English Commonwealth 'the freest and choisest in Europe'. Appealing to English history, Goodwin explained that 'never yet had we the happinesse to change into a Commonwealth, although our best histories tell us, that the first of this Nation

---

114 *England's Apology*, 3–16.
115 *Englands Apology*, 18–28.
116 *Englands Apology*, 28.

when they were most free, was without Kings'. The godly should not 'strive against the streame of providences', but throw themselves behind the Commonwealth, 'the only Bulwarke left us, both to keepe out tyranny, and preserve our liberties'.[117]

This was Goodwin's most powerful statement about the meaning and purpose of the Civil Wars. *Englands Apology* drew together themes he had touched on in earlier writings – God's providential hand in events, the final battle with Antichrist, the blood guilt of the king, the perfidy of the Presbyterians, the tyranny of the Scots, and the defence of English liberties. It also echoed other apologists for the Revolution. The emphasis on God's providential 'appearances' was a constant theme of Cromwell's letters and speeches; the declaration that in the latter days God was 'throwing down the heavens and the earth' was the grand claim of John Owen's apocalyptic sermon to the Rump in April 1649, *The Shaking and Translating of Heaven and Earth*; the claim about England's pre-monarchical history and the condemnation of 'flashy ravishments of Names and Titles' chimed with Milton's critique of a corrupt court; the language of the 'Free-State' shows that Goodwin had learnt from Nedham's republican political theory articulated in *The Case of the Common-Wealth of England Stated* (1650).[118] Goodwin had fused ideas of Anglo-Saxon liberties and classical liberty and placed them in a providentialist and apocalyptic framework. This was a curious jumble of ideas, but in the minds of Goodwin and some of his godly contemporaries it was a compelling synthesis. Goodwin thought that he could now grasp what God was up to in Western history. This was England's Exodus, and the godly were standing on the threshold of the Promised Land.

But Goodwin's fears about a return to Egypt were well founded. As the Commonwealth faced the prospect of a further war with the Scots, intelligence uncovered a conspiracy involving exiled royalists and London Presbyterians. On 2 May 1651, the regime arrested three London Presbyterian ministers, including Goodwin's critic, the 'Novice-Presbyter' William Jenkyn. In June, the High Court of Justice sentenced one of the ministers, Christopher Love, to death. The sentence sparked off weeks of argument between militants (like Sir Henry Vane) who supported the execution, and moderates (like John Dury) who wanted to promote healing between Presbyterians and Independents. Goodwin's congregation was firmly on the side of the hardliners. In mid-July, John Price wrote to Love, whom he had first met eleven years earlier. Addressing Love as 'a spiritual Brother', Price chastised him for 'projecting, promoting, actual producing a new bloody War, a War between Saints, a War against Saints, a War to restore a wicked, a bloody Family, so signally and eminently dethroned by the vindicative Justice of Almighty God'.[119]

Goodwin himself may well have called for the implementation of Love's sentence in an anonymous tract, *A Just Balance, or some Considerable Queres about Mr Love's Case, Tryal and Sentence* (28 July 1651).[120] It argued that the

---

117 *Englands Apology*, 29–33, 38.
118 Goodwin later recommended Nedham's book in *Peace Protected*, 75–76.
119 John Price, *The Wounds of a Friend: or A Letter mentioned by Mr Love upon the Scaffold* (1651), 6–8.
120 For the authorship, see Appendix.

Commonwealth 'hath now for these several years by-past, by many signal declarations from heaven, been owned, countenanced, confirmed and established herein by God himself'. Yet inexcusably, Love and his confederates had plotted the current war between Scotland and England. This 'embroyling of a Nation ... in blood' was a far more grievous sin than a single murder. Such blood-guilt could only be removed by the execution of those responsible. When Parliament had observed this principle and executed 'Justice on the Grand Delinquent himself [Charles I], and other Grandees', God had blessed it with 'Victories and Successes almost beyond belief given in an uninterrupted Series'. Love was 'an Arch-designer' of the latest war, and neither his clerical status nor his personal godliness could exempt him from justice. Even a retraction should not exempt him from the sentence of death. Numbers 35 was 'inflexible and express', and Romans 13 taught that the magistrate existed to punish the evildoer. Those who petitioned for Love's pardon would 'keep the land under pollution and defilement with blood'. If they had their way, they would encourage the enemy and provoke the army.[121]

If Goodwin was the author of this pamphlet, as seems likely, it is little wonder that he published it anonymously. In calling for the execution of a fellow minister he would have risked his reputation and further jeopardised the reception of his Arminian theology. His relationship with William Taylor, who had promoted Love's writings, would have been strained even further.[122] But he was far from isolated in believing that Parliament must carry out the sentence on Love. Although the execution was twice postponed, Love was finally put to death on 22 August. As Blair Worden points out, the execution broke the back of clerical resistance to the regime, and was swiftly followed by a grovelling retraction from William Jenkyn. But on the very day of Love's death, the Scottish army encamped at Worcester, ready for its final showdown with the English.[123]

Worcester was to be Cromwell's crowning victory, the battle which confirmed the Commonwealth's dominion over the whole of Britain. Parliament appointed Friday 24 October 1651 as a day of thanksgiving for the victory. Goodwin composed two hymns for the occasion, and had them sung by his congregation. He then published the hymns, together with a note 'To the Presbyterian Ministers, and others, who are unsatisfied with the Lawfulness of giving thanks to God for the shedding of blood'. Goodwin agreed that considered 'simply of it self, it is a sad thing, and a matter rather of sorrow then rejoicing, to see so Noble a Creature as man, to loose his life in such a manner'. But he asked his critics to remember that the enemy had sought to take away 'our Lives, Liberty, and Freedome'. Goodwin hoped – rather optimistically – that his Presbyterian brethren would stop carping and start singing.[124] Citing the model of battle hymns in the book of Psalms,

---

121 [John Goodwin?], *A Just Balance* (1651), 1–20.
122 Taylor was one of four Presbyterian ministers to recommend Love's *Grace* (1652), though their Epistle 'To the Christian Reader' stressed that 'This whole discourse is not about *State*, but about *Soul-affairs*', and contained no reproaches of the 'present Governours' (sig. A3).
123 Worden, *The Rump Parliament, 1648–53* (Cambridge, 1974), 247–48.
124 *Two Hymns, or Spirituall Songs* (1651), 1–3.

Goodwin's own compositions celebrated England's deliverance from the spiritual tyranny of the Scots:

> The mighty God hath once again
> Appear'd from Heaven high,
> His people to deliver from
> The house of slavery.
> The iron yoke he lately broke
> Which men prepared had,
> To put upon the necks of Saints,
> To make their hearts full sad ...
>
> Come let us tread them down (said they)
> Like clay and mire in street;
> Wee'l give them laws, and lords, and kings,
> And all as we think meet.
> Our sword shall teach them what to know
> Of God, what to believe:
> To worship God as they think meet,
> No longer will we give.[125]

For Goodwin then, the war with the Scots was above all a war for liberty of conscience. The Scottish Presbyterians had set out to dictate to England's independent believers. In response to their hubris, God had intervened to deliver his saints.

Saints in Power

By late 1651, Goodwin's saints were certainly riding high. They were a force to be reckoned with in City politics. Mark Hildesley was elected to the Court of Aldermen in 1649, and Daniel Taylor followed in 1651.[126] The Common Council was dominated by political Independents, led by Owen Rowe and supported by members of Goodwin's gathered church. No fewer than eight members of Goodwin's gathered church were elected to Common Council at some stage between 1649 and 1652 – Mark Hildesley, Nathaniel Lacy, Daniel Taylor, Henry Brandreth, Thomas Alderne, John Price, Richard Price and Thomas Lamb.[127] These men were repeatedly nominated by Common Council to sit on its committees, and worked closely alongside old allies like Robert Tichborne and Edmund Rosier. In June 1651, for example, four of the eighteen men nominated to organise the Lord Mayor's banquet were from the congregation – Hildesley, Brandreth, John Price, and Lamb.[128] By late 1651, the City's Militia Committee was also packed with eight members of

---

125 *Two Hymns*, 10–11.
126 See A. B. Beaven, ed., *The Aldermen of the City of London* (London, 1913), ii. 72, 79.
127 See Kirby, 'Parish', Appendix B, 238–39.
128 CLRO CCJ, vol. 41, ff. 54r–56r.

the congregation. Hildesley and Taylor had been appointed (alongside Rowe) in January 1649, Captain Lacy was added in February, and in August 1651 five more members joined the Committee.[129] Goodwin's congregation was playing an entirely disproportionate role in the City's defence.

Goodwin and his followers also benefited financially from the Revolution. Walwyn suggested that the congregation was 'of a near relation to those that hold prosperity a mark of the true Church'. He compared them to 'the Jews in Amsterdam', alleging that 'by buying, and selling and purchasing, and lending, they are able to enrich one another, so as they grow to a mighty interest'. He accused Daniel Taylor of using his political weight to reduce his Excise bill, and claimed that Lamb and Lacy 'have some hundreds of pounds in the Excise, which yeilds them good interest'.[130] Ellen More notes that at least six members of the congregation invested in the market for sequestered royalist estates or the Excise farm. Several sat on the Committee for Compounding of Delinquents' Estates, while others were Trustees for the Sale of Dean and Chapter Lands. Mark Hildesley and Daniel Taylor held lucrative posts on the Customs Commission between 1649 and 1653, and George Foxcroft was Treasurer of the Excise in 1654–55.[131] When Parliament's Committee for the Navy made a contract in November 1650 for provisions, four of the nine men listed were members of Goodwin's church.[132]

The prominence of Goodwin's congregation was such that the author of *A Model of a New Representative* singled it out for criticism in October 1651. The author expected an imminent millennium, and proposed that the gathered churches select all the MPs for a new representative. However, he went out of his way to exclude 'Mr John Goodwins Church', 'being they are so disrelished in the Nation'. Goodwin and his people were 'such high extollers of Reason' that they would allow no 'Act to pass the House, which should not be grounded upon Reason'. They were 'so well versed in the art of reasoning' that they could bamboozle 'a hundred honest men'. Moreover, there was no danger in debarring them, because they and their pastor had always displayed impeccable loyalty to the regime and would never desert it for royalism.[133] Austin Woolrych has suggested that the criticism of the congregation was 'clearly ironical', and that the author may have been a member of the church.[134] However, the gathered churches of London seem to have taken the pamphlet at face value, and they signed a joint statement repudiating its call for rule by the congregational churches and professing their loyalty to

---

129 *CJ*, vi. 136, 619. The new additions were: Captain Thomas Alderne, Henry Brandreth, Captain Richard Price, William Allen, Thomas Lamb.
130 *Walwyn's Just Defence* in *Walwyn*, 406, 429, 430.
131 See More, 'New Arminians', 153–58; More, 'Congregationalism', 228.
132 *CJ*, vi. 500–01 (22 November 1650). Captain Thomas Alderne, Henry Brandreth, Captain Nathaniel Lacy and Captain Richard Price were listed alongside men like Colonel Thomas Pride and the republican Slingsby Bethel.
133 *A Model of a New Representative* (1651), 5–6.
134 A. Woolrych, *Commonwealth to Protectorate* (Oxford, 1982), 17 n23.

the Rump.¹³⁵ *A Model* is best read as an early Fifth Monarchist contribution to the contemporary debate over a new representative to replace the Rump Parliament.

In response, Daniel Taylor issued *Certain Queries* (29 November 1651), a thirteen-point reform programme probably intended to clarify the principles and goals of 'Mr John Goodwins Church'. It was published by the radical bookseller Giles Calvert (who had published *A Model* a month previously), and was dedicated to Oliver Cromwell. Taylor reminded Cromwell that 'I have heard you so free of late to my self and others since Worcester Fight, how your heart was bent for the publique good, and I know your Genius runs full and fast that way'. Taylor urged Cromwell to throw his energies into reform.¹³⁶

A new representative was Taylor's first demand, for like many radicals he was dissatisfied with the Rump's sluggish progress on reform. Taylor was well aware that 'most men spirits stand still opposite to a real and sound reformation', and he believed that 'most men have lost that priviledge of being choosers' because they were 'helpers of the common Enemy', 'opposers of Reformation', or 'Non-ingagers'. For this reason, a key role in future elections should be given to 'those persons which have been constant friends to this Parliament'. This clearly meant 'the Party commonly called Congregational Churches', including those pastored by Sidrach Simpson, John Simpson, Thomas Goodwin, John Goodwin, Christopher Feak, Henry Jessey and William Kiffin. The franchise should not be restricted to congregational churches, but all across the land they could assist in determining who got to vote by identifying those 'that are honest, well-affected men to this present Power, and to real Reformation, though not in such Church waies'. Recent experience of London elections had shown that even those 'very guilty in publique acting' could 'make shifts to evade' franchise restrictions, a fact that underlined the necessity of vetting voters and finding 'a safe way' of electing a new representative. It might also be necessary to increase the number of MPs for London, and reduce the number for other places, such as 'Cornwall, and many inconsiderable Towns and places in the Land'. Anticipating the objection that all this was self-serving, Taylor emphasised that the work of establishing a new representative 'will prove rather a great work and burthen, then priviledge'.¹³⁷

Besides calling for a new representative chosen by those loyal to 'the republique', Taylor offered a raft of other suggestions for reform. MPs could be relieved of 'other offices' that distracted them from Parliamentary business; 'Acts against Adultery, Whoredom, Drunkenness, Swearing, Cursing, Blasphemy' could be enlarged to facilitate prosecution of offenders (including 'those called Ranters');

---

135 *A Declaration of Divers Elders and Brethren of Congregationall Societies in and about the City of London* (1651). This was signed by leading Congregationalists and Baptists including William Greenhill, John Simpson, Thomas Brooks, Christopher Feake (a future Fifth Monarchist!), Henry Jessey, Hanserd Knollys and William Kiffin. Although Goodwin's church was not mentioned, *A Declaration* may be read as an implicit rejection of its exclusion in *A Model*. Despite their differences over baptism and predestination, Goodwin associated with Jessey and Kiffin later in the 1650s.
136 Daniel Taylor, *Certain Queries* (1651), sigs. A2v-A3.
137 Taylor, *Certain Queries*, 7-9.

the handsome salaries paid to the commissioners for customs, excise and the sale of public lands could be reduced and the money used 'for the relief of the poor'; popish-style oaths could be replaced by 'lifting up the hand according to Scripture example'; the observance of 'every old Popish holy day' could be ended; the fifth of November anniversary (which had become the occasion of 'formality, and vanity, and much hurt and ryots') could be replaced by 'the third of September' to commemorate deliverance 'out of the hands of Tyrants, Bishops, and Scots'; doctors and lawyers could be prohibited from charging 'such vast and boundless Fees'; tithes could be abolished, and ministers paid from 'some publike bank'; parishes could be reduced to a manageable size so that the Gospel would be preached 'to poor dark Souls ... as in Wales and Cornwal, and the North of England'; 'Pauls London', the cathedral, could be made the new home of the public courts, or else used to house 'the noysome and troublesome market' which presently clogged up 'the best street in London, Cheapside'; City government could be reformed by getting rid of the expensive feasts which emptied the pockets of poor citizens; the monopolies of the East India Company and the cloth trade could be ended; legal procedure should be reformed to minimise the number of 'vexatious suits' and maximise access to justice; 'all Fairs' should be 'put down' and replaced by 'great Markets', for fairs were damaging to the wholesale trade, attracted disreputable types and fostered 'much drunkenness and uncleanness'; the Jews could be readmitted to England to prepare the way for their conversion; in accordance with biblical example, thieves should not be executed but could be asked to make restitution, a policy that would reduce recidivism and turn them into hardworking citizens.[138]

    This was very much a Londoner's reform programme – it ignored Ireland and Scotland, and viewed Cornwall, Wales and the North as dark corners of the land. It was also a radical programme, showing scant regard for established institutions and professional interest groups, and displaying a revolutionary's faith in the possibility of wholesale, sweeping change. Finally, it was a conspicuously godly programme, a call for national reformation. Goodwin was passionately opposed to persecution and religious uniformity, but without any sense of contradiction he and his congregation still held on to the Puritan dream of a godly nation. It was an extraordinary vision, at once narrow in its sympathies and immense in its scope. On one level, Taylor was a realist, who understood that only a small minority shared his dream and offered practical suggestions for implementing change. On another level, however, his was a utopian scheme, born out of the stunning ease with which the New Model Army had conquered the republic's foes. Not content with the abolition of monarchy and the House of Lords, Taylor was keen to promote a new series of jarring, divisive reforms. Cromwell, by contrast, wanted 'healing' as well as reformation. He would quickly find that peacetime civilian politics was more difficult than war, and he would plot an uneven course away from revolution to conservation and moderation. When he did so, Goodwin and his congregation would feel betrayed. The 1650s had begun with great promise. They were to end in disappointment.

138 Taylor, *Certain Queries*, 9–23.

7

'THE GREAT SPREADER OF ARMINIANISM'
1647–53

Goodwin's notoriety as a republican Independent was rivalled only by his reputation as a pugnacious proponent of Arminian theology. This chapter will tell the story of how and why he finally broke with Calvinism, going on to become (in the words of Milton's biographer, John Toland) 'the great Spreader of *Arminianism*'.[1]

Conversion to Arminianism

On 1 April 1645, George Thomason collected yet another pamphlet assailing the controversial vicar of St Stephen's, Coleman Street. It was entitled *A Vindication of Free-Grace in Opposition to this Arminian Position – Naturall Men may do such things as whereunto God hath by way of Promise annexed Grace and Acceptation – preached by John Goodwin*. The author, Samuel Lane, had been a devoted admirer of Goodwin and he compared the gathered church to 'a Garden of many excellent Flowers, whereof tis hard to pick the fairest'. He had, however, been greatly disturbed by some statements his pastor had made from the pulpit in April 1644. Goodwin had been preaching a series of sermons *against* the Arminians, but as one might expect from a protégé of Davenant and Preston, he had tried to make Arminianism redundant by modifying Calvinism to make it more acceptable. According to Lane, Goodwin's efforts had been 'greatly approved by many', who declared that he had 'cut the hair between other Divines and the Arminians' and urged him to publish the sermons.[2]

Lane disagreed. Far from finding a mediating position, Goodwin had fallen into Arminianism. Lane's fears were confirmed by a conversation with two members of a sizeable sect, presumably the General Baptists, who taught that 'God hath promised grace upon man's doing'. These men told Lane that 'in holding this Tenent, they held but that which Master John Goodwin maintaines, in whom they greatly glory'.[3]

---

1 John Toland, The *Life of John Milton* (1699), 125.
2 Samuel Lane, *A Vindication of Free Grace* (1645), sigs. A2r, A4r.
3 Lane, *A Vindication*, sig. A4r.

Lane was particularly disturbed by a sermon Goodwin had preached on 12 April 1644. Goodwin had been trying to answer the classic objection to the Calvinist doctrine of predestination – that it removed all incentive for human action.[4] Goodwin had responded by arguing that 'if naturall men' earnestly sought grace, 'they shall surely finde it'. Although in one sense men were 'dead in their sins', they still enjoyed 'a naturall life of reason, judgement, understanding, conscience, &c. in them: by reason of which excellent principles ... they may do such things whereunto God hath been graciously pleased to annex a promise of grace, there is a power in men to do such things ... '[5]

For Lane, this was an 'Arminian position', since Calvinists had classically insisted that men dead in their sins were simply unable to repent and believe until regenerated by God's saving grace. He wrote a lengthy letter to Goodwin expressing his concerns,[6] to which Goodwin responded in a sermon preached on 28 April 1644. Lane obtained a copy of the sermon from Thomas Rudyard, 'a very exact writer', verified it with several other hearers and note takers,[7] and printed it after his first letter. It demonstrated that, far from reneging on his earlier statements, Goodwin had reiterated them. It was very important, he had argued, that the godly did not present God as 'unreasonable and hard' or 'greivous and harsh in the eyes of flesh and bloud'. Instead, 'we should be very careful' to 'mollifie', 'qualifie and soften the hardness' of God's proceedings. Arminians were sure to triumph when their opponents 'make the saving tearms of the Gospell so hard and impossible to be performed by men'. They would have a tougher challenge if the orthodox set out 'to justifie God in point of equity' in the condemnation of sinners. God was not like a tyrannical prince who professed to love his subjects, but destroyed them for not doing something that was 'impossible for them to performe'. Instead he was a gracious, just and reasonable God, who never asked sinners to do what was beyond their ability. Sinners were condemned for failing to do what was within their power. However, this doctrine was not to be confused with 'the Arminian opinion of Free-will'. The Arminians did not merely insist that man had the power to believe, they also held man could of his own free will 'without any extraordinary hand of God' turn from a sinful way of life to the life of faith. By contrast, Goodwin insisted that while man had 'power' to repent and believe, he had no 'will' or 'inclination' to do so.[8]

Lane was not impressed by Goodwin's reply, and explained why in a second letter. On the one hand, Goodwin had misrepresented the Arminians in order to distance himself from them. Arminians did not deny that the will of natural man was defective, nor did they not deny the necessity of enabling supernatural grace. On the other hand, Goodwin's crucial distinction between man's 'power' to believe and his lack of 'will' to believe was simply incoherent. If the will of unregenerate

---

4 Lane, *A Vindication*, 22.
5 Lane, *A Vindication*, 2, 6–7.
6 Lane's first letter is printed in Lane, *A Vindication*, 1–21.
7 Lane, *A Vindication*, sigs. A3v-A4v, 36.
8 'A Sermon', in Lane, *A Vindication*, 22–36.

men was so defective, how could they be said to have the power to believe? Goodwin both affirmed and denied natural man's power to believe. By trying to stake out a middle way between classic Calvinism and Arminianism, he was trying to have it both ways.[9] Convinced that Goodwin was spreading dangerous error, Lane went into print with his two long letters to Goodwin, together with the minister's sermon.

Lane's charges stuck, and were merrily recycled by the Presbyterians. But they prompted Goodwin himself 'to search more narrowly and thoroughly, then formerly I had done, into the Controversies agitated'.[10] In *Hagiomastix*, he openly admitted that he had recently been studying the writings of Arminius and his followers 'about the bondage, and freedome of the will'.[11] Goodwin confessed that though he had read Arminius expecting to find expressions of 'rank import', he was surprised that 'a faire and reasonable construction' of the notorious Dutchman's words were 'fully reconcilable with the judgements and expressions of some reformed Churches'. He admitted that it was 'otherwise' with some later Arminians. He also noted that Melancthon and other Lutherans sympathised with Erasmus's defence of the freedom of the will. Moreover, even the Reformed were not unanimous: 'To my knowledge the Reformed Churches themselves do not generally, at least not universally agree, in condemning the Arminian free-will'.[12]

This programme of reading was no doubt in preparation for his reply to Lane. As Goodwin later explained, although Lane's *Vindication* was 'libellous enough, and full of broad untruths', it created such a stir in the City, and such 'applause' from his critics, that he 'drew up a competent Answer', which refuted Lane point by point.[13] However, the publication of the 'Answer' was long delayed, because 'Clergie-Classical Counsells' secured 'the denial (at least suspension) of the Presse for the publishing of this Tract'.[14] Henry Overton finally registered the tract by 'John Goodwyn' with the Stationers Company in February 1647, under the title *God Justified in the Condemnation of Man without the Helpe of the Arminian tenet of Free will.*[15] The title tells us that at this point, Goodwin still saw himself as anti-Arminian. Yet not a single copy of this book survives, and it seems certain that it was never published. Goodwin later recalled that he had planned to publish the 'Answer', but changed his mind on the grounds that 'a just and entire Treatise' would be more effective than a polemical pamphlet against Lane.[16] The 'just and entire Treatise' would eventually be published in 1651 as *Redemption Redeemed.*

---

9 Lane's second letter is printed in Lane, *A Vindication*, 37–68.
10 Απολυτρωσις, *Redemption Redeemed* (1651), 'Preface to the Reader',
11 *Hagiomastix* (1647), 104.
12 *Hagiomastix*, 104–05.
13 *Redemption Redeemed*, 'Preface to the Reader', a1r-v. See also *Anapologesiastes Antapologia* (1646), sig. e.
14 *Anapologesiastes*, sig. e; *Cretensis* (1646), 16.
15 *A Transcript of the Registers of the Worshipful Company of Stationers, 1640–1708*, 3 vols (London, 1913–14), i. 261.
16 *Redemption Redeemed*, 'Preface to the Reader', sig. a1r-v.

Once he had decided on this course of action, his ideas evolved rapidly. Looking back on these days in 1651, Goodwin explained that he was 'strengthened with further Light shining into my Heart dayly from the Father of Lights'.[17] The 'further light' that shone changed Goodwin's theology. In February 1647, Goodwin still considered himself a Calvinist. By December, he was an Arminian (though it was a tag he shunned on account of its pejorative connotations).

Prior to 1647, Goodwin had continued to adhere to the orthodox Reformed doctrine of absolute, unconditional predestination. As he noted in 1651, he had shared the standard Puritan position 'till some few years last past'.[18] But like his chief theological mentors, John Davenant and John Preston, he had tried to outflank the Arminians by presenting a soft-focus Calvinism. Davenant and Preston had rejected Beza and Perkins' doctrines of double predestination and limited atonement and emphasised the natural capacity of even the non-elect to repent and believe. Goodwin's surviving sermons suggest that he had taken a similar tack.[19]

There was, however, a serious problem with this moderate Calvinism. 'Universal atonement', 'sufficient means' and even 'natural ability' were all very well in theory, but in practice they never led anyone to salvation in the absence of electing grace. As Richard Baxter explained, the non-elect 'have sufficient power (which is not effectual through their own wilfulness)'. God had given the non-elect sufficient grace and means to render them 'inexcuseable',[20] but faith and repentance remained a purely theoretical possibility, since no non-elect person ever actually took it up. Such a position risked seeming disingenuous and incoherent. 'Sufficient' means seemed curiously insufficient, and natural 'ability' seemed oddly incapable.

The recognition that this was so seems to have hit Goodwin in 1647. The problem of man's ability and responsibility was the fulcrum on which the whole argument turned. Goodwin came to believe that 'the Arminian tenet of free will' was essential if God was to be justified in condemning man. Significantly, his new position was first expressed in *The Divine Authority of the Scriptures* (18 December 1647), a work of apologetics designed to justify the ways of God to men – a suspiciously Arminian project. In a key section on the equity and justice of God's plan of salvation, Goodwin declared that 'there is not the least touch of injustice, nor of any thing that is unequall or hard' in the Gospel. However, he accepted that some accounts of the Gospel did imply that God was unjust.[21] In order to make the point as forcefully as he could, Goodwin asked his readers to imagine a king speaking to a man whose legs had been amputated. The king speaks to the man 'with many expressions of love', promising him that if he finishes the race, he will receive 'exceeding great rewards'. Such a king, Goodwin concludes, would rightly

---

17 *Redemption Redeemed*, 'Preface to the Reader', sig. av.
18 *Redemption Redeemed*, 'Preface to the Reader', sig. ar.
19 Richard Baxter (heavily influenced by Ussher and Davenant) did the same throughout his career, leading to accusations that he preached up 'Arminianism, and Free-Will'. See J. I. Packer, *The Redemption and Restoration of Man in the Thought of Richard Baxter* (Vancouver, 2003), 226–35, 413.
20 Quoted in Packer, *Redemption and Restoration of Man*, 226–27.
21 *The Divine Authority of the Scriptures Asserted* (1647), 168.

be regarded as a cruel tyrant, for 'this would be a carriage savouring more of a bloudy and unmanlike insolencie over this poor wretch in his misery, then of any reall affection, grace, or respect towards him, or of any desire to his good'.[22]

Goodwin now drove his point home. Some Christians portrayed a God who spoke to sinners in 'moving and melting expressions of mercy', promising salvation 'if they will believe, repent, and turn unto him', while knowing full well that sinners were 'wholly destitute of all power to doe what he requires of them'. This was to represent 'the glorious God in his greatest expressions of mercy and grace ... as laughing the world to scorn' rather than being 'truly desirous' to save.[23] Against this distorted image, Goodwin set an alternative picture of a just God who did not demand the impossible. God had given men 'gracious, liberall and plentifull means' to be saved. Even pagans, he suggested, 'had sufficient means' to repent, believe and receive salvation.[24]

It was precisely because men were 'capable' of repentance and faith that they could be held accountable for unbelief. If people were incapable, they were also excusable. Of all the excuses that men used for not doing what they were commanded to do, 'there is none more plausible, none more reasonable or fair, then this, to say, that he was not able to doe it ... or that it was a thing impossible for him to doe'. Indeed, 'according to the strict rules of reason and equity, [incapacity] ought to exempt a man from all censure and punishment'. Man's moral responsibility was bound up with his ability. If he was unable to do something, he could not be held responsible for not doing it. And this meant that God, from whom human standards of justice and equity derived, could not be justified in condemning men who were incapable of obeying his command. This would be 'altogether unworthy of God ... the father of mercies, and God of all consolation'.[25]

At the same time, Goodwin rearticulated a distinctly Grotian theory of atonement.[26] In his death, Christ had not borne the exact punishment deserved by sinners. Instead, he had taken an exemplary punishment that bore testimony to the righteous wrath of a holy God against sin, and thus 'pacified and reconciled God unto the world', allowing him to 'offer terms of reconciliation and peace' to sinners without compromising the requirements of justice.[27] Crucially, this was a theory of atonement that did not lead inexorably towards either universal salvation or limited atonement. Traditional penal theory (in which Christ paid off the sinner's debt and took the sinner's punishment) seemed to imply that all those for whom Christ died would necessarily escape the punishment of hell – leading some to conclude that Christ had only died for the elect. The Grotian theory, by contrast, explained how Christ's universal atonement made salvation possible for all without making it inevitable.

22 *Divine Authority*, 169.
23 *Divine Authority*, 169.
24 *Divine Authority*, 182–86.
25 *Divine Authority*, 200–02.
26 Grotius had developed his governmental theory of the atonement as an alternative to both Socinian and mainstream Reformed theories in his treatise *De Satisfactione Christi* (1617).
27 *Divine Authority*, 194–99.

Goodwin anticipated the obvious objection to his emphasis on natural man's moral and spiritual capacity: 'viz. that it is an Arminian doctrine, and maintains free-will'. He replied that 'if it be a doctrine asserted by Paul and Peter (as most assuredly it is) it ought to suffer no disparagement for being found among the tenets of Arminius'. It was 'a common Papisticall trick, to nick-name truths and opinions' after 'some heretic or other, who asserted them'.[28]

This was not an answer calculated to satisfy his Calvinist critics. Unlike Richard Baxter, Goodwin made no attempt to reconcile his theory of atonement and natural capacity with the Calvinist doctrine of election.[29] His Presbyterian critics were in no doubt that he had fallen into serious 'errors about natural mans free will'.[30] William Jenkyn showed that Goodwin echoed 'your masters the Remonstrants' at a number of points, not least in comparing the Calvinist God to a cruel tyrant and comparing contra-Remonstrants to Manicheans.[31]

When Goodwin clarified his position in *Sion-Colledg Visited*, he employed the standard Arminian distinction between auxiliary grace and compulsory grace. Divine grace *assisted* the will and made it possible for men to repent and believe, but it did not *compel* the will. 'I never denied,' he wrote, 'but always have asserted the necessity of grace by way of adjutory; onely the necessitation or compulsion of grace, is no Article of my creed'. He alleged that the self-styled 'orthodox' among the Reformed had 'exchanged the Fathers *adjutorium*, into their own *compulsorium*'.[32] By denying 'the necessitation or compulsion of grace', Goodwin was destroying a central pillar of the Calvinist system. If the individual was able to resist or receive divine grace, then his personal destiny was determined by his own free response, and not by God's eternal decree. And this was the crucial dividing line between Calvinism and Arminianism.

Thus it is safe to conclude that *Divine Authority* marked a dramatic turning point in Goodwin's theological pilgrimage. In that work, he had mapped out a programme of future publications in which he would vindicate his new anti-Calvinist theology. He would offer a worthy conception of God, a true exposition of the biblical teaching on predestination, and an account of how Christ had conferred 'gracious abilities' of free will upon men. In addition, he also promised to deal with the salvation of pagans at greater length.[33] This theological programme came to fruition in *Redemption Redeemed, The Pagans Debt and Dowry*, and *An Exposition of Romans 9*, undeniably Arminian works.

---

28 *Divine Authority*, 202–03.
29 See Packer, *The Redemption and Restoration of Man*, 407–09, 213–26.
30 *A Testimony to the Truth of Jesus Christ* (1648), 11–15.
31 William Jenkyn, *The Busie Bishop* (1648), 30–32.
32 *Sion-Colledg Visited* (1648), 12–25. See also *Neophutopresbuteros* (1648), 42–68.
33 *Divine Authority*, 169–70.

Public Disputations

Having flagged his new theology in print, Goodwin now ventured into public debate. Between December 1649 and February 1650, he participated in three disputations over the doctrine of grace with his fellow Independent divines, Vavasour Powell and John Simpson. According to Powell, the first disputation arose out of 'some difference between Master Goodwins People and others', and was arranged for the purpose of 'Reconciliation, not for Contention'.[34] Powell and Goodwin agreed to discuss universal redemption, and Round One of the controversy took place on 31 December 1649, when the two men debated in Coleman Street. The moderators were Goodwin's follower, David Lordell, and (on the other side of the debate) the licenser and one-time ally of 'Gangraena Edwards', James Cranford.[35] But a series of other speakers contributed, including John Price; the respected Congregationalist pastors Joseph Caryll, Henry Jessey and John Simpson; and the Presbyterian Roger Drake. Round Two took place on 14 January 1650 in All Hallows the Great, Thames Street, and pitted Goodwin against John Simpson. It was moderated by the young Congregationalist preacher George Griffith and Mr Ames, probably the Baptist and future Quaker William Ames.[36] The third and final disputation between Goodwin and Simpson was held on 11 February, and was chaired by Cranford and Griffith.

Such public disputations had become a common feature of the Puritan scene in the 1640s,[37] but the Goodwin disputations were particularly significant. Conducted 'in the presence of divers Ministers of the City of London, and thousands of others',[38] they deserve to be recognised as a major episode in the history of London Puritanism, one that revealed the crumbling of the Calvinist consensus among the godly.

We are fortunate to have what looks like a verbatim record of these debates, published by Goodwin's follower, John Weekes, under the title *Truths Conflict with Error* (28 March 1650). The debates covered a variety of topics, including the nature of the divine decrees, the meaning of Romans 9, the notion of 'sufficient means' and the salvation of the heathen. Despite the controversial issues involved, they were different in tone to Goodwin's doctrinal spats with the Presbyterians in 1647–48. There was relatively little in the way of name-calling or heresy accusations, and Powell began the first debate by telling Goodwin, 'God knows how much I did love and respect you, and still do'.[39] These Independent preachers had fought

---

34 *Truths Conflict with Error* (1650), 110.
35 For Cranford's role in Edwards' crusade against heresy see A. Hughes, *Gangraena and the English Revolution* (Oxford, 2004), 139–42, 236–39.
36 On Griffith see R. L. Greaves, *Saints and rebels: Seven Nonconformists in Stuart England* (1985), 77–97; on Ames see *ODNB*.
37 A. Hughes, 'The pulpit guarded: confrontations between orthodox and radicals in revolutionary England', in A. Lawrence, W. R. Owens and S. Sim, eds, *John Bunyan and his England 1628–1688* (London, 1990), 31–50; A. Hughes, 'Public disputations, pamphlets and polemic', *History Today*, (February 1991), 27–33.
38 *Truths Conflict with Error*, Title Page.
39 *Truths Conflict with Error*, 2.

alongside each other in the trenches against royalists and Presbyterians. If Presbyterians could afford to disown Goodwin, Independents still saw him as one of their champions.

Yet the issues were too explosive to be easily defused. The second disputation ended in acrimony. Henry Jessey, the respected Baptist pastor, tried to play the peacemaker, reassuring the people 'That the difference between the two Opinions is not so great, but that men, whether they believe the one, or the other, they may be saved, through the Grace of God in Jesus Christ'. Simpson could not agree: 'Mr Jesse, Mr Jesse', he exclaimed, 'no more of that: for I conceive, that they that hold general Redemption, and Free-will, in opposition to Free-Grace, never had any experimental knowledge of the Grace of God in Jesus Christ'. Jessey was disappointed: 'I am sorry to hear such words from you'.[40] The third disputation also ended in bitterness, with Vavasour Powell pronouncing that 'Mr. Goodwin hath run himself [aground], (although a good Saylor) and lost his Ship in the Sands'.[41] In the eyes of most Puritans, Goodwin had fallen into grievous error.

Weekes noted that news of the debates had 'gone forth both far and neare'.[42] One member of the audience did present his own considered conclusions in *A Right Use made by a Stander By at the Two Disputations at Great All-hallows*. The 'Stander By' was John Graunt, possibly the irenic godly layman who later became a distinguished statistician and a founding member of the Royal Society.[43] Graunt's pamphlet shows that at least some listeners were prepared to follow these debates with an open mind and arrive at their own position. Although he defended absolute predestination, his main concern was to protest against the double predestinarianism of high Calvinists, which he said made God 'the Author of sinne'. And he agreed with Goodwin that the heathen were not without hope of salvation.[44]

Within a fortnight of the final debate with Simpson, Goodwin himself had written and published a fifteen-page pamphlet entitled *The Remedie of Unreasonableness*. It answered Simpson's charge that 'I maintain Free-Will in opposition to Free-Grace'.[45] Far from exalting 'Free-Will', Goodwin insisted had always asserted the necessity of divine grace.[46] He also maintained that his doctrine exalted 'Free-Grace', emphasising its freeness, its fullness and its power. God's grace was entirely *free*, because although God was under no obligation to save men, he had provided 'the gift of Jesus Christ', the means of salvation and divine assistance to enable them to repent and believe. It was also *full*, because it was

---

40 *Truths Conflict with Error*, 70.
41 *Truths Conflict with Error*, 112.
42 *Truth's Conflict with Error*, sig. A2v.
43 See *ODNB*. The other candidate is John Grant of Bucklersby, author of a number of theological tracts – but this seems unlikely since he was an intemperate heresiographer who had lambasted Arminius as 'that wicked heretic' in *Truths Victory against Heresie* (1645), 15.
44 John Graunt, *A Right Use Made by a Stander By at the Two Disputations at Great All-hallows between Mr Goodwin and Mr Symson* (1650), 1–7.
45 *The Remedie of Unreasonableness* (1650), 3, 5.
46 *Remedie of Unreasonableness*, 6.

these verses and texts affirming human responsibility drove him towards Arminianism.

Besides the Scriptural testimony, Goodwin and his congregation cited 'two main considerations and grounds', which 'commanded our judgements and Consciences'.⁴⁹ The first was that 'our Brethren's Doctrine ... hath in it a black thread of a manifest inconsistence with the nature and attributes of God'. It undermined divine 'immutability, simplicity, wisdom, Grace, goodness, justice and love to mankind'.⁵⁰ Goodwin had come to feel that Calvinism drew a distorted picture of God's character. The biblical God was loving and just towards all he had made, not willing that any should perish but that all should come to repentance. The high Calvinist God, by contrast, was not a loving parent but an unjust tyrant, who condemned the mass of mankind to perdition without giving them the means or opportunity of salvation. In his preface to *Redemption Redeemed*, he explained that although he had fed on a diet of Calvinist notions for many years, 'the truth is, I found it ever and anon gravellish in my mouth, and corroding and fretting in my bowels'.⁵¹ This sense of moral revulsion at predestinarian orthodoxy was arguably the crucial factor in Goodwin's conversion to Arminianism. It was the ethical critique of Calvinism that had fired him up in 1647, when he announced his new position with a passionate outcry against the perceived injustice of the Calvinist God.

The second of 'the two main considerations' was the fear that Calvinism produced antinomianism. Goodwin had come to believe that the teaching of absolute predestination was incompatible with 'the Interest or advancement of true godliness in the World'.⁵² He feared that predestinarianism engendered 'wilde Satyrs, lusts, sensual, and sinfull distempers'.⁵³ As he later told Joseph Caryl,

> your doctrine ... is accessory to far the greatest part of those abominations at this day raging amongst us, Antinomians, Enthusiasm, Familism, of the dangerous and vile opinions and practices of those called Seekers, and of those bred of the dregs and retirement of all these, the Ranters, and generally of all the coolings, declinings, backslidings, and of all other foul and sad miscarriages among Professors.⁵⁴

This accusation was not without substance. For several decades, the Puritan subculture had been troubled by antinomian teachers who portrayed themselves as the champions of 'free grace'.⁵⁵ By the mid-seventeenth century, antinomianism was being taken to extravagant extremes by 'Ranters' and other

---

49 *Eirenomachia: the Agreement and Distance of Brethren* (1652), 81 (see also sig. A3v).
50 *Eirenomachia*, 81.
51 *Redemption Redeemed*, 'Preface', sig. ar.
52 *Eirenomachia*, 81.
53 *Redemption Redeemed*, 'Preface', sig. a3r.
54 'Mr Goodwin's Letter to Mr Caryl' in *A Fresh Discovery of the High Presbyterian Spirit* (1655), 79.
55 For two very fine treatments see D. Como, *Blown by the Spirit: Puritanism and the Emergence of an Antinomian Underground in Pre-Civil-War England* (Stanford, 2004); T. D. Bozeman, *The Precisianist Strain: Disciplinary Religion and Antinomian Backlash in Puritanism to 1638* (Chapel Hill, NC, 2004).

given to all mankind, and was 'not imprison'd or confin'd, within the narrow Con of an handful of men'. And it was *powerful*, because every man who was converted was 'mightily strengthened and assisted by the supernatural, or sp Grace of God'. Indeed, because the converted person could not have repented believed without divine grace, 'the act of Conversion, or believing, is to be asc unto God'.[47]

Audaciously, Goodwin tried to turn the tables on his opponents. It wa high Calvinists, he suggested, who magnified man's will and denigrated grace. They exalted the will of man by implying that God's irresistible grace the regenerated human will 'free from all possibility of sinning', a view lader dangerous antinomian potential. And they reduced the scope of God's saving by restricting it to a small number of the elect. By denying universal reden they were rejecting the common opinion of the early Church Fathers (as ' and Beza themselves' acknowledged), and the generally accepted view Lutherans. To cap it all, the high Calvinists found it impossible to preach w resorting to 'these Theological truths, *That Christ dyed for all men, Th vouchsafeth sufficient means of Salvation unto all*. Calvin and his followe: 'palpable self-inconsistents' who constantly 'Arminianiz'd'.[48]

Reasons for Embracing Arminianism

Goodwin's conversion to Arminianism was the result of a variety of fact came together in his mind to form a cumulative case against Calvinist ort First among them was his reconsideration of the Scriptural witness. G(Calvinism ultimately ran aground on the rock of Scripture's universalist texts expressing God's love for all mankind, Christ's death for the whol and the free offer of salvation to everyone. He was also troubled, as his cont 1644 sermons indicate, by the numerous passages in Scripture where G(on sinners to repent, and held them responsible for failing to do so. He ci 13:34, in which Christ declares: 'O Jerusalem, Jerusalem, which killest the and stonest them that are sent unto thee; how often would I have gath children together, as a hen doth gather her brood under her wings, and not!' Initially, Goodwin felt that he could do justice to such texts while r a Calvinist – that is, he could teach that God loved all men and had give: the ability to repent and believe, while also affirming that God had rest saving grace to the elect who alone would be saved. Ultimately, ho\ concluded that this was a contradictory position. He gave up his soft but i1 Calvinism, and adopted a thoroughgoing Arminianism on the groun offered a more satisfying account of the biblical data. The bulk of *R Redeemed* was devoted to thorough exegesis of the key universalist texts that they made far more sense within an Arminian framework. His refl

47 *Remedie of Unreasonableness*, 6–8.
48 *Remedie of Unreasonableness*, 8–15.

radicals.⁵⁶ Even some of Goodwin's former hearers had fallen into practical antinomianism. Lawrence Clarkson had once been an Independent who admired the 'moderate' doctrine of 'Mr Goodwin'. But he then embraced the antinomian theology of Tobias Crisp, eventually becoming 'the Captain of the Rant' and indulging his 'filthy lust' with female followers.⁵⁷ Equally shocking was the case of the lace-seller Mary Gadbury, 'a frequent hearer of the Word' who 'chiefly' attended the sermons of Goodwin and Henry Jessey. In 1649, she fell in with the self-proclaimed 'son of God' William Franklin, and ended up giving birth to their illegitimate (and deformed) child.⁵⁸

For Goodwin the root cause was doctrinal not ecclesiastical. As was the case with Richard Baxter, the experience of antinomian Puritanism in the 1640s helped to reinforce his opposition to high Calvinist doctrines of justification and predestination.⁵⁹ Goodwin concluded that predestinarianism fostered presumption. Thinking themselves among the indefectible elect, justified from eternity and clothed in Christ's perfect righteousness, some Calvinists thought that nothing they did could affect their standing before God. They needed to be taught that good works mattered. Since predestination was conditional, there was no room for spiritual complacency. Since justification did not involve the imputation of Christ's righteousness, no one could be saved without living a godly life. Doctrine, Goodwin repeatedly argued, must pass the 'touchstone' test of Titus 1.1, where the Gospel was defined as 'the Truth which is according unto godlinesse'.⁶⁰

Thus ethical considerations were at forefront of Goodwin's mind when he adopted Arminianism – he had come to believe that Calvinism pictured an unjust God and produced immoral believers. But there were other factors too. While predestinarian teaching inspired presumption in some, it led others into severe depression. Error, Goodwin lamented in *Redemption Redeemed*, bred 'fears, sad apprehensions, disconsolate thoughts'.⁶¹ This point has been well established by recent scholarship, and Blair Worden has even written somewhat hyperbolically that 'The volume of despair engendered by Puritan teaching on predestination is incalculable'.⁶² In the course of his ministry Goodwin would have counselled tortured

---

56 See G. Huehns, *Antinomianism in English History: With Special Reference to the Period 1640–1660* (London, 1951); A. L. Morton, *The World of the Ranters* (London, 1970); N. Smith, *Perfection Proclaimed: Language and Literature in English Radical Religion, 1640–1660* (Oxford, 1989). For a useful corrective see J. C. Davis, *Fear, Myth and History: The Ranters and Historians* (Cambridge, 1986) and the ensuing debate in *Past and Present*, 129 (1990).
57 See Lawrence Clarkson, 'The Lost Sheep Found', in *John Bunyan, Grace Abounding with other Spiritual Autobiographies*, ed. J. Stachniewski and A. Pacheco (Oxford, 1998), 178–90. The editors suggest (268) that Clarkson was referring to Thomas Goodwin, but the *ODNB* article on Clarkson suggests John, who had a higher profile in the City.
58 See H. Ellis, *Pseudocristus* (1650), 8ff. See also Ariel Hessayon's *ODNB* article on William Franklin.
59 On Baxter see T. Cooper, *Fear and Polemic in Seventeenth-Century England: Richard Baxter and Antinomianism* (Aldershot, 2001).
60 *Redemption Redeemed*, 268–69.
61 *Redemption Redeemed*, sig. a3r.
62 Quoted in J. Stachniewski, *The Persecutory Imagination: English Puritanism and the Literature of Religious Despair* (Oxford, 1991), 1. For an alternative view, which persuasively highlights the softer side of Calvinism, see M. Davies, *Graceful Reading* (Oxford, 2002).

souls who feared that their damnation had been sealed from eternity. Indeed, Isaac Pennington junior – who would have sat under Goodwin's ministry and may have joined the gathered church – was tormented for 'many years' by the thought that he was among those whom God had passed over.[63] Arminianism offered a way out of such pastoral difficulties – the preacher could assure his hearers that God had not decreed their damnation. The Gospel was the good news of divine 'Philanthropy'.[64]

Another factor was Goodwin's feud with the Presbyterian clergy, which coincided with his theological paradigm shift. His clash with Edwards and the promoters of the blasphemy bill fuelled his disillusionment with clerical dogmatism and inclined him to question accepted 'orthodoxy'. In fact, *God Justified* was withdrawn from publication at the very time when Goodwin was being denounced as a heretic before Parliament itself. He had little to lose. At no time in his ministry was he more inclined to rethink his theological position. If his rejection of Calvinism was driven primarily by ethical and theological considerations, it was facilitated by his situation. Ejected from his parish, vilified by his Presbyterian foes, he may even have suspected that their fierceness was fostered by their vision of an implacable God. Whatever his inward thoughts, his break with Calvinism was a powerful way of repudiating conservative Reformed dogmatism, even if it estranged him from many of his fellow Independents at the same time. Had he been a Westminster divine, the constraints of collegiality would have probably restrained his theological speculation. As it was, he found himself at loggerheads with most of the London ministry, and was practically a free agent.

The political context was also significant. Goodwin had spent the 1640s arguing against arbitrary rule by kings, and it is striking how often political analogies crop up in his theological writings. In *Redemption Redeemed*, Goodwin made an explicit comparison between the absolutist political theory of the royalists and the absolutist picture of God drawn by some theologians. Royalists had attempted to flatter kings by vesting them with arbitrary prerogatives, such as the right to impose taxes at will, to take away men's estates, and to exempt malefactors from death. 'In like manner,' wrote Goodwin, 'some men desirous to commend themselves unto God, as men zealous for his glory more then others ... bestow upon him in the name of Prerogatives' actions and attributes which actually detract from his glory. These theologians depicted God as a sadistic tyrant, who had made an irreversible decree to cast his 'most excellent Creatures' into the endless torments of hell. Goodwin did not deny that 'God hath an absolute Sovereignty and Lordship over his Creature', but he did deny that God exercised his sovereignty 'upon the hardest terms, and most grievous unto his Creature'.[65] Despite his politics, he did not try to depict heaven as a republic – like Milton, he thought that heaven was the one place where republicanism was inapplicable. But though his God was a monarch,

---

63 Isaac Penington, *Observations on Some Passages of Lodowick Muggleton* (1668), 23–4.
64 Goodwin makes this point repeatedly in his writings from the early 1640s to the 1660s. See for example Ειρηνομαχια [*Eirenomachia*]. *The Agreement and Distance of Brethren* (1652), 11.
65 *Redemption Redeemed*, 66–68.

he was a constitutional monarch, addicted to the good of his subjects. God was not like the king who only 'loves two or three Favourites about his Court', but neglects the 'great Body of his Subjects' who are 'in imminent danger of perishing'. Instead, he was 'a lover of his Subjects', a lover of all men.[66] In this respect, Goodwin was keen to make his theology match his politics.

Finally, we need to consider Goodwin's intellectual sources. Crucially, his confidence in his new reading of the Bible was bolstered by support from tradition, above all from the early church Fathers. As he explained in 1652, 'We are much confirmed that we have truth on our side ... because as far as we have had opportunity, to understand the sence of Orthodox and learned Antiquity in the point, we find them generally ours'.[67] 'If the opinions commended by me for Truth ... be Arminian', he wrote elsewhere, 'certain I am that the ancient Fathers and Writers of the Christian Church were generally Arminian'.[68] In *Redemption Redeemed*, Goodwin would devote two whole chapters to demonstrating that universal redemption and the defectibility of the saints were doctrines unanimously embraced by the early theologians of the Christian church.

If patristic testimony weighed heavily in Goodwin's thinking, Laudian Arminianism was more a stumbling block than an inspiration. In *Redemption Redeemed* Goodwin had to go to some lengths to explain why Arminianism had been championed by 'the worst of our late Bishops, such as Romanized, and Tyrannized'. He suggested that 'the popish gang of Bishops' had latched onto Arminianism for essentially 'politique' reasons. The Laudians shrewdly understood that Puritan teaching was both unpopular and theologically problematic. Goodwin did admit that 'the Cathedrall Generation of Men throughout Christendome' were 'great admirers' of the Church Fathers.[69] But given his detestation of the Laudians, it seems unlikely that he was influenced by their theological writings. Indeed, one of his major achievements in the 1650s was to decouple Arminianism from Laudianism, and show that Arminianism was perfectly compatible with the hotter sort of Protestantism.

The Dutch Arminians are a far more likely influence. Goodwin admired the apologetics and biblical commentary of Grotius, and as we have seen, he openly admitted in 1647 that he had been reading Arminius and his 'followers'.[70] Critics were convinced that Goodwin was drawing on the Dutch Arminians. William Jenkyn told Goodwin, 'The Arminians were your schoolmasters'.[71] Richard Resbury had no doubt that 'Arminius and Mr Goodwin are Master and Scholar'. Goodwin had abandoned the great men of the Reformed tradition to follow 'obscure names' like Arminius, Bertius, Tilenus and Corvinus.[72] John Pawson wrote that 'The

---

66 *Redemption Redeemed*, 408.
67 *Eirenomachia*, 55.
68 *Redemption Redeemed*, sig. c4r.
69 *Redemption Redeemed*, 170–171.
70 Even in 1642, he was already citing a work by the Remonstrant Corvinus. See *Imputatio Fidei, or A Treatise of Justification* (1642), i. 177.
71 Jenkyn, *The Busie Bishop*, 30.
72 Richard Resbury, *The Lightless-Starre, or Mr John Goodwin proved a Pelagio-Socinian* (1652), 4.

substance and strength of what Arminius & others with him, have heretofore pleaded for ... is now Englished by the Reverend Author of *Redemption Redeemed*.[73] John Owen agreed that Goodwin had 'borrowed' his argument from the Remonstrants, and was keen 'to show it to the world in English dress'. The Remonstrants were 'his masters', and so much of *Redemption Redeemed* was 'purely translated from them' that Owen had even considered 'placing their Latin against his English in the margin'.[74]

Goodwin himself, however, hardly ever quoted Arminius or his followers, and he refused to accept the label 'Arminian' for his own position. He was covering his tracks, and downplaying his debt to the Dutch Remonstrants because the term 'Arminian' sent shivers down Puritan spines. As he later pointed out, his critics realised that 'the name of Arminius is the most forcible Engine (though made of nothing but air and wind) to batter the walls of those opinions, which they so cordially wish in the dust'.[75] In the minds of the godly, 'Arminianism' had been hopelessly discredited by its association with Laudianism. If the theological argument was to be won, it had to be disentangled from other issues. Thus Goodwin studiously avoided all references to Arminian works, though he was thoroughly familiar with the Remonstrant theologians.

He also refused to characterise the controversy as a debate between 'Calvinists' and 'Arminians'. Naming positions after individual theologians, he suggested, was misleading, since even his critics shared many of Arminius's beliefs (e.g. his Trinitarianism). Indeed, he once claimed that since Calvin, Musculus and Peter Martyr had all made statements favourable to general redemption, he could just as easily call his doctrine '*Calvinism, Musculism, Martyrism* or the like'.[76] Goodwin continued to refer to Calvin (particularly Calvin the commentator) with respect, while admitting that he was 'the Standard-Bearer Himself of this Brigade'.[77] The controversy was depicted as a debate over the five points discussed by Remonstrants and Contra-Remonstrants in the 1610s and at the Synod of Dort. In charitable mode, he referred to 'our Brethren's Doctrine';[78] in polemics he attacked 'the Contra-remonstrant party'.[79]

If a debt to Dutch Arminianism seems clear, what of the emergence of universal grace theology among England's hot Protestants? There had been a vigorous sect of 'freewillers' among England's evangelicals as early as the mid-sixteenth century,[80] and Goodwin did note that 'many of the learned Martyrs in Queene Maries dayes'

---

73 John Pawson, *A Brief Vindication of Free Grace* (1652), sig. A2r.
74 John Owen, *The Doctrine of the Saints Perseverance* (1654), in *The Works of John Owen*, ed. W. H. Goold, 24 vols (London, 1850–1855), 584, 595, 597, 600.
75 'Mr Goodwin's Letter to Mr Caryl' in *A Fresh Discovery*, 75.
76 *Confidence Dismounted, or a Letter to Mr Richard* Resburie (1651), 19.
77 *Redemption Redeemed*, 387. *An Exposition of the Nineth Chapter of...Romans* (1653), 112 describes Paraeus as one 'much devoted to Calvin's Doctrine' (i.e. absolute double predestination).
78 A phrase used throughout *Eirenomachia*.
79 See *The Banner of Justification Displayed* (1659), sig. a4v.
80 See T. Freeman, 'Dissenters from a dissenting church: the challenge of the Freewillers, 1550–1558' in Marshall and A. Ryrie, eds, *The Beginnings of English Protestantism* (Cambridge, 2002), 129–56.

leaned towards 'Arminian' positions.[81] Elizabethan Puritanism, by contrast, had been deeply influenced by high Calvinism, a fact that Goodwin blamed on William Perkins: 'The great worth of the Man otherwise, commended his Opinion unto many far above the worth thereof'.[82] Puritan attachment to absolute predestination had only been strengthened by the Dutch Arminian controversy and by the anti-Calvinism of the Laudians.

Although the General Baptists did break with Calvinism, their most famous leader in the 1640s, Thomas Lamb (pastor of the famous church in Bell Alley), combined a belief in general atonement with a belief in unconditional predestination. When Goodwin turned Arminian, Lamb wrote against him.[83] However, Arminian convictions were articulated by other radical Puritans, including Laurence Saunders, *The Fullnesse of Gods Love Manifested* (1643). A few non-sectarian Puritans were also defending Arminianism. Particularly influential was Thomas Moore senior, who published *The Universality of Gods Free Grace in Christ to Mankind* (1646), and was condemned by one Calvinist critic as the leader of the 'Morians'.[84] Goodwin may have known some of these figures personally. Saunders was a business partner of Clement Wrighter and a close friend of William Walwyn, both of whom were familiar with Goodwin's ministry.[85] Moore was a Norfolk man who had known John Cotton, and who (despite his lack of university education) had become a respected pastor.[86] But theological influence is more likely to have flowed from Goodwin to sectarian radicals than in the other direction.

There is another possible influence on Goodwin's thinking, albeit a more surprising one. In the course of his writings in the 1650s, he constantly cited orthodox Reformed theologians: Calvin, Musculus, Martyr and other sixteenth-century Calvinist exegetes. Goodwin was steeped in their writings, but as he considered the doctrine of grace, he began to notice a profound and unsustainable tension in their writing. On the one hand, they taught absolute (even double) predestination, the bondage of the will, and the inevitability of the saints' perseverance. On the other hand, they wrote as if God loved all his creatures and longed to save them; as if Christ had died for everyone; as if all sinners had the capacity to repent and believe; and as if people who had experienced genuine conversion could fall from grace. Goodwin noted the same feature in the preaching of English Puritan divines. This is the phenomenon which Richard Greaves dubbed

---

81 *Redemption Redeemed*, 169. See also *Treatise of Justification*, sig. e2r.
82 *Redemption Redeemed*, 169.
83 Lamb's moderate Calvinism is elaborated in the following works: *A Treatise of Particular Predestination* (1642); *Absolute Freedom from Sin...in Opposition to Conditional, set forth by Mr John Goodwin in his Book (hereby appearing falsly) entituled [Redemption Redeemed]* (1656).
84 See Theophilus Brabourn, *A Confutation of the Dutch-Arminian Tenent of Universal Redemption with relation in special unto certain Sectaries in England. By name, the Morians, or Revelators* (1651).
85 K. Lindley, *Popular Politics and Religion in Civil War London* (Aldershot, 1997), 394, 396–97.
86 See G. F. Nuttall, 'John Horne of Lynn', in P. Brooks, ed., *Christian Spirituality: Essays in Honour of Gordon Rupp* (London, 1975), 237–41.

'pastoral Arminianism'.[87] The ubiquity of such pastoral Arminianism explains why Goodwin was able to quote orthodox Reformed writers as leading witnesses in his case against Calvinist doctrine.

There were then, a range of factors that disposed Goodwin to reconsider his theology of grace – exegetical considerations, the problem of divine justice and love, the spectre of antinomianism, spiritual despair among the godly, hostility to clerical dogmatism and absolutist royalism, patristic testimony, Arminian writings, and the perceived inconsistency of orthodox Reformed theologians. All of these contributed to his change of mind in 1647, but the problem of justifying the Calvinist God was the decisive issue.

Redemption Redeemed

Goodwin's *magnum opus* was finally completed a year after his second disputation with Simpson, and its dedicatory epistle was signed on 22 February 1651. It was a book designed to impress. It was the first (and last) of Goodwin's works to be published in folio, a format reserved for major treatises. Its author wanted it to take its place in all good theological libraries, and his wish seems to have been fulfilled – it is the only one of his many publications to be found in the Bibliotheque Nationale in Paris.[88] It was expertly produced and handsomely bound by John Macock for Lodowick Lloyd and Henry Cripps, Goodwin's publishers since the death of Henry Overton. At six hundred pages, it was the longest and most substantial defence of Arminianism yet published in the English language.

Goodwin dedicated the book to Benjamin Whichcote and the other heads of the Cambridge Colleges. A number of these men were Westminster Divines drafted in as Masters and Heads of Colleges in the Parliamentarian purge of the University in 1644–45 – Anthony Tuckney (Emmanuel), Herbert Palmer (Queens'), Richard Vines (Pembroke Hall), Lazarus Seaman (Peterhouse), Thomas Hill (Trinity), and John Arrowsmith (St John's). But other college heads were drifting from Reformed orthodoxy into Platonist or latitudinarian styles of theology. Men like Ralph Cudworth (Clare), John Worthington (Jesus), and Richard Love (Corpus Christi) were not belligerent anti-Calvinists (they could not have remained in post if they were), but they could be called post-Calvinist. Whichcote himself was provost of King's College and Vice-chancellor of the University since 1650. His sister, Elizabeth, was married to George Foxcroft, a member of Goodwin's gathered church and a a signatory to the congregation's Arminian declaration in 1652.[89] The Foxcrofts' son, Ezekiel, was an undergraduate at King's, and was elected to a fellowship in the college in 1652. He was to be closely associated with Whichcote and the Cambridge Platonists.[90]

---

87 Richard Greaves, *Glimpses of Glory: John Bunyan and English Dissent* (Stanford, CA, 2002), 110–11, 149, 171, 213, 331, 583.
88 Bibliotheque Nationale, FR BN F30522903.
89 *Eirenomachia*, sig. Av.
90 See *ODNB* on 'Elizabeth Foxcroft [*née* Whichcote]'.

Thanks to the Foxcrofts, Goodwin seems to have been well informed about Whichcote's thinking. In 1648, he had claimed that an eminent university theologian had read *The Divine Authority of the Scriptures Asserted* and was appalled by the accusations against its author:

> It was the expression of a man, as eminent both for pietie, parts and place, as either of our Universities afford, and not of the abhorred order of Independency neither (as his preferment sufficiently testifieth), finding me charged by the testimony-mongers of Sion Colledge, with the foul crime of denying the authority of the Scriptures, & having seen my tractate upon that subject, that he wondered how ever it should come into the hearts of these men, to lay such a thing to my charge, how they durst traduce me as a man denying the authority of the Scriptures, when I had written so clearly, fully & effectually, in the defence and vindication thereof.[91]

In a later work, Goodwin told of 'one known to be as learned, grave, and judicious, as any English born at this day; who said it was as good a Book as any was written since the Apostles dayes'.[92] Goodwin's Calvinist critic, George Kendall, reported that he had been 'credibly informed' that the individual concerned was 'the Reverend Doctour Whichcote'.[93] Thus by dedicating the book to Whichcote and the heads of the Colleges, Goodwin was deliberately forcing Arminianism onto its agenda, in the knowledge that the institution would be unable to present a united front.

William Haller once suggested that if Goodwin had remained at Queens' he, and not Whichcote, might be remembered as 'the earliest Cambridge Platonist'.[94] As early as 1647, Goodwin referred to reason as the 'candle of the Lord' (Proverbs 20:27) that Christ 'lighted up in every mans soul'.[95] This was a favourite phrase of the Cambridge Platonists,[96] and Goodwin's use of it may indicate that he was already familiar with their teaching. He was definitely attracted to their claim that there was a 'correspondency' between the visible and the invisible world so that natural things were a 'representation' of the supernatural.[97] And although he later referred rather sniffily to men 'of the *Platonique* addiction',[98] he did share their desire to demonstrate the reasonableness of Christianity. In his 'Preface to the Reader', he defended rational religion against anti-intellectual enthusiasts and Calvinist theologians who denigrated natural reason. Christian doctrines like the Trinity, the Incarnation and the Virgin Birth were not 'against, or at least, above, and out of the reach and apprehension of Reason'. There was 'nothing in Christian

---

91 *Neophutopresbuteros*, 9.
92 *The Six Book-sellers Proctor Non-Suited* (1655), 28.
93 George Kendall, *A Verdict on the Case depending between Mr. Goodwin and Mr. Howe*, 3, printed in Obadiah Howe, *The Pagan Preacher Silenced* (1655).
94 W. Haller, *Liberty and Reformation in the Puritan Revolution* (New York, 1955), 147.
95 *Divine Authority*, sig. a2r.
96 See C. A Patrides, ed., *The Cambridge Platonists* (London, 1969), 11–12, 18, 50, 197, 334; G. R. Cragg, ed., *The Cambridge Platonists* (New York, 1968), 10, 18, 44, 53ff, 138, 141.
97 *Being Filled with the Spirit*, 123–24; *A Door opening unto the Christian Religion* (1662), ii. 13–16.
98 *A Door*, ii. 13.

Religion ... but what fairly and friendly comports with that Reason and Understanding which God hath given unto Man'.[99]

It was not surprising then, that in chapters 1 to 4, Goodwin laid the groundwork for his Arminianism by engaging in some philosophical theology. He began in chapter 1 by emphasising man's complete dependence on God. This was rhetorically important, for Arminians were constantly accused of exalting man's natural ability and robbing God of his glory. Thus Goodwin insisted that man was incapable of any action without the 'concurrence' and 'co-operative Presence of God'. Yet crucially, human actions were not 'determined, or necessitated' by God. 'The essentiall and characteristicall property' of the will was 'a liberty or freedom of chusing its own motions, or acts'. If God necessitated human actions, this distinctive property of the will would be 'destroyed', and God would be made 'the Author of Sin'.[100]

Having laid out his stall, Goodwin then used his second chapter to elaborate this libertarian concept of free will. The 'Dependance' of second causes on the first cause (God), did not mean that God had determined 'their motions, actions or operations'. To illustrate the point, Goodwin used several examples that would prove controversial among his critics. Parents were not 'determined, or necessitated' in their generation of children, and the lifespan of human beings was not 'peremptorily fixed, or determined' by God. This was 'Alcoran Divinity', 'a Great Article in the Turkish Creed'. Christians, by contrast, were not fatalists. Christianity taught that men and angels were 'rationall, voluntary, and free working causes', who were capable of 'deliberation' and making 'their owne proper and free election of what they act'. Goodwin even denied that 'God peremptorily decreed or determined before hand the Crucifying of Christ by Herod, Pilate, the Gentiles, or the Jewes'. He simply decreed that they 'should be at liberty to Perpetrate this great wickednesse' if they so chose. As Goodwin explained (a little later), 'No act of God, nor Co-operation of his with his Creature, imposeth any necessity upon any free-working cause', for 'the wills of men are left free by God, either to will, or not to will, things that are sinfull'. Even Judas 'was at as much liberty' as the other apostles. God might sway or incline the will, but he did not force or necessitate it.[101]

Calvinists objected that if history was determined by the choices of free agents, then the future must be uncertain, even in the mind of God. Goodwin denied that this was so. God was 'infinite in wisdom' and possessed exhaustive foreknowledge. He was 'able infallibly, without all possibility of error or mistake, to foresee' future events, not simply because he was conscious of his own 'intentions for the government of the world', but also because he was 'able to penetrate, calculate, and compute, all, and all manner of relations, and aspects, between all and all manner of causes and effects'. God even knew how men would act if they were placed in entirely different circumstances to their present ones. This was technically known as *scientia media* or 'middle knowledge'. The concept was originally deployed

---

99 *Redemption Redeemed*, sigs. br–dr.
100 *Redemption Redeemed*, 3–6.
101 *Redemption Redeemed*, 7–13, 21, 53–54.

against Dominican determinists by the Jesuit Luis de Molina and then against Calvinists by Arminius himself. For Goodwin it helped to reconcile divine foreknowledge of the future with human free will. He rejected the familiar objection that God's certain foreknowledge of future events made them inevitable – 'no knowledge, as such, hath any influence at all upon the object, or thing known, to cause it to be, or not to be'.[102]

After explaining his understanding of human free will and divine foreknowledge, Goodwin explained that God's decree was conditional and collective. It did not determine the fate of particular individuals, but established that 'whosoever believeth, shall be justified', and that 'He that believes not, shall be condemned'.[103] For Goodwin, this Arminian understanding of the divine decree cohered with the attributes of God as expressed in classical theism – especially divine goodness. By teaching that God had decreed the reprobation of men from eternity, theologians had dealt a fatal blow to the doctrine of divine goodness. And Goodwin was not impressed by moderate Calvinists 'who think to qualifie the harshness of the matter, with the softnesse' of the term 'Preterition'. Such theologians argued that God had simply passed over the non-elect and not included them in his decree of election. As Goodwin pointed out, the effect of this single predestination was identical to double predestination. Preterition 'tendeth every whit as infallibly, as unavoyably to the everlasting ruine and misery of the Creature, as a Positive Reprobation could do'. The 'doom-full preterition' of the Calvinists, was 'that blood which many wring out of the Scripture in stead of Milke'. 'But the Scripture every where abounds in giving testimony to the Love and Goodnesse of God towards all his Creatures'. God was called 'a Faithfull Creator', and compared to a loving 'Parent, Father, or Mother'. He was the Creator of all men, believers and unbelievers alike, and all were 'the workmanship of his hands'. He longed for all to be saved and only turned away from his creatures after severe provocation. Thus 'it manifestly appears, that such an hatred or rejection of the Creature by God from eternity, as is commonly taught, and received amongst us, is broadly and wholly inconsistent with that Love, Tendernesse, and Respect, which the Relation of a Creator to a Creature every where imports'.[104]

In chapters 5 to 8 and 16 to 19, Goodwin advanced his critique of Calvinist doctrine by setting out the case for 'Universall Attonement'. He began by quoting the Scottish high Calvinist, Samuel Rutherford: 'I know no Article of the Gospell, which this new and wicked Religion of Universall atonement doth not contradict'. Goodwin declared that this was 'one of the strangest and most importune sayings' he had ever heard from a learned man. Universal atonement was the ancient doctrine of the Christian church, and it was 'the Heart and Soul' of the Gospel.[105]

---

102 *Redemption Redeemed*, 21–23, 27. On the controversy over middle knowledge within Reformed theology see R. Muller, *Post-Reformation Reformed Dogmatics*, 4 vols (Grand Rapids, 2003), iii. 417–24.
103 *Redemption Redeemed*, 32–40.
104 *Redemption Redeemed*, 65–73.
105 *Redemption Redeemed*, 73.

In order to demonstrate this, he devoted five chapters to an exegesis of key texts. Chapter 5 examined texts which taught that Christ had died for the 'world'; chapter 6 dealt with texts which said that Christ died for 'all men' and 'every man'; chapter 7 surveyed verses promising salvation indifferently to 'Him' or 'Whosoever' shall believe; chapter 8 analysed places in which Christ was said to have died for those who actually perished; finally, chapter 16 presented miscellaneous texts which confirmed the doctrine of universal salvation. In expounding these verses, Goodwin applied the techniques of humanist scholarship, and endeavoured to close every loophole exploited by Calvinist theologians who wished to dodge the full force of Arminian proof texts.[106]

Once he had made the Scriptural case for universal redemption, and answered Calvinist objections to Arminian exegesis, Goodwin provided a full statement of his position in chapter 17. He emphasised that all men had 'a fair and gracious possibility' of salvation. Christ's atonement had 'put all Men without exception, into a capability of being saved (by believing)' and had 'wholly dissolved' the guilt and condemnation brought on all men by Adam. This meant that 'now no Man shall perish, or be condemned, but upon his own personall account' – God would only condemn sinners for their own voluntary sins, not for any original sin contracted from Adam. Every person had been given 'sufficient strength and means' to repent, believe and persevere unto salvation.[107] God (in other words) was justified in the condemnation of sinners, but only with the help of the Arminian tenet of free will.

Goodwin did not flinch from emphasising God's condemnation of sinners. He took great pains to stress that 'universal redemption' was not the same as 'universal salvation'. Origen's hope that all men (and even the devils) would eventually be saved was flat contrary to the teaching of the Scriptures. The New Testament repeatedly stressed 'the Paucity' of the saved, and the everlasting torments of the damned in hell fire. If Goodwin had become an optimist about the scope of God's grace, he was still a pessimist about how people in general would exercise their free will.[108]

He tried to clinch his argument for universal atonement with a set of logical arguments and a clutch of citations from authorities. Chapter 18 presented thirteen syllogistic arguments as 'Seconds, or Assistants' to 'Scripture-Authority', while chapter 19 set out to demonstrate that universal redemption was 'the Sence of Antiquity' and was supported by 'the variableness of Judgement in modern Writers'.

If the vindication of 'universal redemption' was the central purpose of Goodwin's treatise, he was also determined to present the Arminian position on a second key issue: the perseverance of the saints. Calvin and his followers had argued that believers who had experienced justification could never fall away from grace. Their perseverance was assured. The Remonstrants, however, had contended that there was 'a possibility of defection in the Saints themselves'. Goodwin set aside half of *Redemption Redeemed* (seven chapters, and 240 pages) to defending this

---

106 See for example his treatment of John 3:16 in *Redemption Redeemed*, 75–87.
107 *Redemption Redeemed*, 433.
108 *Redemption Redeemed*, 433–50.

view. The defectibility of the saints followed on ineluctably from his position on free will. Since men had libertarian free will (the power to do otherwise), divine grace was resistible and the perseverance of the saints was not inevitable.

The chief argument against the Arminian view was that it destroyed the comfort of the saints. Goodwin agreed that in some cases, Calvinist teaching did assure men that their salvation was irreversibly secure. But he thought this was dangerous presumption, which produced 'those frequent, daily and most sad apostasies' that had become all too evident among the godly. In such cases, Calvinist doctrine proved 'a great Benefactresse to the flesh'. Of course, respectable Calvinist theologians strenuously denied that apostates had ever been saved in the first place, but this exposed the fallacy of their claim to provide greater comfort to the believer. If apostates had been universally recognised as true believers before falling away, how could any believer be sure that his own faith was genuine and not fake? Since Calvinists insisted that saints engaged in 'extravagancies of sin' could not be assured of persevering to the end, how could they provide more comfort than Arminians? By their own confession, 'there is no such great difference between the two Doctrines, in Reference to the Peace or Comfort of the Saints'. In practice, neither Arminians nor Calvinists could give an 'absolute assurance of salvation'. But believers had no reason to be tormented by fear of spiritual suicide, since God had provided them with both the means and the capability to avoid it.[109]

The removal of this objection allowed Goodwin to proceed to the Scriptural arguments. He dealt first with the Calvinist proof texts (chapters 10–11), paying particular attention to texts in which God appeared to promise that all true believers would persevere to the end. He then turned in chapter 12 to the Arminian proof texts, such as 1 Corinthians 9.2 where the Apostle explains that he disciplines himself lest 'I myself should be a cast-away'. If Paul was in danger of becoming a reprobate, Goodwin argued, 'then may true believers fall away both totally and finally'. Arminians knew that a godly life was not an optional extra for the Christian: 'without holiness no man shall see God'. Too many Reformed divines had given the impression that 'a mans Justification may stay behinde, when his Holiness is departed'.[110]

In chapter 13, Goodwin advanced nine other arguments against 'the common Doctrine of peremptorily-decreed Perseverance'. He alleged that the doctrine made God a respecter of persons, 'implacably severe' towards the sins of the non-elect, but 'indulgent above measure' to his predestined elect. It rendered the ministry vain and void, since the exhortations, threats and promises of Gospel preachers made little sense if the fate of individuals was already predetermined. Calvinists had well rehearsed ripostes to this argument, so Goodwin devoted sixteen pages to countering them. He also argued that the Calvinist doctrine rendered 'the onely wise God strangely irrational', a deity who promised believers that their salvation was already sure, but then warned them against falling away. It failed to make sense of the biblical talk of rewards for the faithful, and could not account for other characteristic teachings of Scripture. Finally, it caused the saints to doubt

---

109 *Redemption Redeemed*, 111, 174, 115–16, 175–76.
110 *Redemption Redeemed*, 279, 273.

the integrity of other believers, wondering if their faith (which to all appearances was so genuine) was merely a forgery.[111]

The Arminian doctrine, Goodwin maintained, surmounted all of these problems, and was supported by compelling examples of true believers who had fallen away. In chapter 14, the cases of David and Solomon in the Old Testament were treated at length, and Goodwin also examined various New Testament apostates from Judas to Hymeneus and Philetus, who 'made shipwreck' of their faith. In chapter 15, he assembled a dozen pages of quotations to confirm that the possibility of falling from grace was 'the uniform and constant opinion of all Orthodox Antiquity'. Unfortunately, the true biblical doctrine of conditional perseverance had been 'opposed by a great party of the Reformers of Religion in these latter days'; in 'sweeping' the house clean with such haste, they had thrown out some gold and silver along with all the rubbish. But Goodwin took comfort in the fact that the Lutherans (including Melancthon and Chemnitius) had taught the traditional view, and he noted that despite themselves the Calvinists often implied that saints could fall away. Calvin was 'the Great Patron or Founder' of the predominant Reformed doctrine, but the Holy Spirit had led him to undermine his own teaching in his commentaries. Thus for all that was thrown against it, the doctrine of the saints' defectibility was supported by Scripture, reason, personal examples, orthodox antiquity, the Lutherans, and even 'its professed Adversaries'.[112]

Goodwin ended his great work by sketching out his future writing programme. In part two he would 'launch forth into the deep of the Great Question concerning Personal Election and Reprobation'. He would also maintain that no infant was doomed to hell 'before the commission of Actual Sin'. Goodwin flagged up two other projects: a discussion of 'Universal Grace', which would argue that God gives 'all Men without exception, a sufficiency of power or means, whereby to be saved', and a separate work on the key Calvinist proof text of Romans 9. He warned his readers that they may have to wait some time before these works saw the light of day, for he had 'a slow genius in writing' and was hindered by 'continual diversions'.[113] As things transpired, he did discuss 'Universal Grace' in *The Pagans Debt and Dowry* (1651) and he also published his promised *Exposition of Romans 9* (1653). But part two of his *magnum opus* never appeared – Goodwin's energies were consumed by other controversies, and by the need to answer the many critics of *Redemption Redeemed*.

The Reception of *Redemption Redeemed*

Goodwin's great book was published in the same year as a far more theologically subversive book by Thomas Hobbes. Yet during the first half of the 1650s,

---

111 *Redemption Redeemed*, ch. 13, quotations at 300–02, 319.
112 *Redemption Redeemed*, 367, 370, 383–84, 387–90, 395–97, 403.
113 *Redemption Redeemed*, 569–70.

Redemption Redeemed attracted more published replies than *Leviathan*.[114] Within weeks of its publication, it was clear that Goodwin had set the Arminian cat among the Calvinist pigeons.

In a sermon preached at St Paul's before the Lord Mayor and Aldermen of London, Dr Thomas Hill, Master of Trinity College, Cambridge, denounced the book for its 'Arminian' and 'Pelagian' errors. He claimed that it elevated 'carnal Reason', advanced fallen human nature above the grace of God, undermined God's sovereignty, ignored the clear teaching of Romans chapter 9, taught the miserable doctrine of falling away, and twisted the words of famous authors.[115] Hill's audience included Goodwin sympathisers, and Goodwin soon knew that he had been condemned *in absentia* before the City elite. On 9 May, he wrote a personal letter to Hill, denying his charges and demanding 'some Christian satisfaction from you'. He offered to meet with Hill, whom he had previously 'honoured' for his learning and 'meek, temperate, and Christian spirit'. When Hill failed to respond, Goodwin published *Moses Made Angry: Or, A Letter Written and Sent to Dr Hill* (1651).

Meanwhile, the impact of Goodwin's big book was being widely registered. On 16 June, Richard Baxter wrote to another moderate Calvinist, Richard Vines: 'I see now J[ohn] Goodwin is a flat Arminian: but that Condemneth not any charitable thoughts of him then nor is his Treat[ise] of Justificat[ion] any the worse'.[116] When the third edition of William Fenner's *A Divine Message to the Elect Soul* was published in 1651, Goodwin's epistle to the reader was retained, but his full name was replaced with the initials 'J.G', presumably because 'John Goodwin' might disturb readers of a nervous disposition.[117] In a letter to Joseph Caryl, Goodwin complained that his fellow Independent divine had been going around pointing out dangerous passages in *Redemption Redeemed*. This was distressing, for Goodwin admired Caryl 'as the glory of the London ministry'. He now feared that he was 'possibly looked upon by you, as by many others, as the reproach and shame of this Ministry'.[118]

Redemption Redeemed perturbed another old acquaintance of Goodwin, Thomas Fuller. He wrote to Bishop Joseph Hall, the last surviving member of the English delegation at the Synod of Dort, to check Goodwin's claim that the delegates had been bound by oath before the proceedings began to vote down the Remonstrants. Hall indignantly rejected the allegation as 'slanderous'.[119] Another distinguished Calvinist divine, Thomas Barlow, future Bishop of Lincoln, wrote to Goodwin

---

114 In the long run, of course, Hobbes's treatise was far more controversial. See S. I. Mintz, *The Hunting of Leviathan* (Cambridge, 1962) and Jon Parkin's eagerly awaited study of the reception of Hobbes, *Taming the Leviathan*.
115 Hill's sermon was never printed, but his main objections to *Redemption Redeemed* are listed in Goodwin's *Moses made Angry: or a Letter written and sent to Dr Hill* (1651).
116 *Correspondence of Richard Baxter*, ed. G. Nuttall and N. Keeble, 2 vols (Oxford, 1991), i. 69.
117 J. G., 'To the Reader', in William Fenner, *A Divine Message to the Elect Soul* (1651). This edition was reprinted in 1652, 1653 and 1657, but Goodwin's full name was restored in the fourth edition of 1676 when the initial shock of his conversion to Arminianism was long forgotten.
118 'Mr Goodwins Letter to Mr Caryl' in *Fresh Discovery*, 74–81.
119 *The Works of the Reverend Joseph Hall*, ed. P. Wynter, 10 vols (Oxford, 1863), x. 524–5.

personally in September. Barlow owned several of Goodwin's books and pamphlets including *The Treatise of Justification*,[120] and his letter commended Goodwin's intellectual clarity. However, he questioned Goodwin's claim 'that Christ died for all without exception'.[121]

Goodwin would respond to Barlow's challenge in *The Pagans Debt and Dowry*, but in the meantime he had to deal with a less respectful critic. Richard Resbury, a Northamptonshire minister, published a set of anti-Arminian sermons in September, and managed to get them advertised in the newsbooks.[122] Although they had been preached several years before, he had published them under the title, *Some Stop to the Gangrene of Arminianism, Lately Promoted by Mr John Goodwin in his Book entituled, Redemption Redeemed*. In his preface, he condemned Goodwin as 'that unhappy man' whose 'daring hand' had produced 'his wretched Treatise'. Under the influence of 'his great Masters Arminius and Corvinus', Goodwin had come to despise God's 'peculiar grace'. He had propounded 'monstrous Conclusions', 'wrested Quotations', 'uncouth Philosophy', and 'consequentiall Blasphemy'.[123] Once again, as in the case of Hill, Goodwin published an instant rebuttal, an open letter to his critic, entitled *Confidence Dismounted*.

But the most revealing exchange of 1651 was between two Cambridge heavyweights, Benjamin Whichcote and Anthony Tuckney. Tuckney was a former Westminster divine, Master of Emmanuel College. Like his close associate, Thomas Hill, he was deeply disturbed by *Redemption Redeemed* and its dedicatory epistle to Whichcote and the Cambridge Masters, and he wanted the University to sound the trumpet of doctrinal orthodoxy. He was increasingly worried, however, by theological drift, and concerned that the brilliant young Whichcote was too enamoured with the Anglicans, Thomas Jackson and Henry Hammond, and with Platonic 'Philosophy and Metaphysics'. He did not want his 'good friend' to come near the tents of the Arminians, 'though J. GOODWIN, like a colonel, can march up in the face of all such imputations'.[124]

Whichcote's letters in reply studiously avoided any mention of Goodwin, but Whichcote did mount an emphatic defence of the liberty of individual judgement, which he described as 'the foundation of Protestancy'. If the conscientious theologian was not allowed to 'think and beleeve as hee findes cause', he asked, 'wherefore do we study? Wee have nothing to do, but to gett good memories; and to learne by heart'. To insist that men must have implicit faith in what they were told was to go 'to ROME again'. In a possible allusion to Goodwin, Whichcote wrote: 'And I dare not blaspheme free and noble spirits in religion, who search after truth with indifference and ingenuitie: lest in so doing I should degenerate into a spirit of

---

120 Barlow's library can be found in the Bodleian under the classmark 'Linc.' His collection contains Goodwin's *Treatise of Justification, Anti-Cavalierisme, The Obstructors of Justice, The Pagans Debt and Dowry* and *Basanistai*.
121 *The Genuine Remains of That Learned Prelate Dr Thomas Barlow* (1693), 122–30.
122 *A Perfect Diurnall*, 15–23 September 1651, 1324; *Severall Proceedings in Parliament*, 18–25 September 1651, 1612.
123 *Some Stop to the Gangrene of Arminianism* (1651), A2r-v, A4.
124 B. Whichcote, *Moral and Religious Aphorisms*, ed. S. Salter (1753), 27–8, 36–8.

Persecution'. 'The destroying this spirit [of persecution] out of the Church, is a peece of the Reformation, which God, in these times of Changes, aims att'.[125] The arguments, so similar to those of Goodwin and Milton, showed that Whichcote had no stomach for going into battle against *Redemption Redeemed.*

Conservative Calvinists were disappointed. As Henry Jeanes noted, 'there was a generall, and (as I think) a just expectation, that some in the University of Cambridge' would answer Goodwin. Jeanes had gone into print only after 'their long silence'.[126] In a dedicatory epistle to Whichcote and the Heads of Colleges, George Kendall endeavoured to put the best gloss on the long silence. He suggested that 'it would have been too much Honour to one single Doctor, to have been confuted by a whole University'. Contemporaries had 'misconstrued your silence, as if it spake your approbation of him and his book'.[127] Of course, as Kendall knew, Whichcote's silence may have reflected 'approbation' of *Redemption Redeemed*, though other College Heads were staunchly Calvinist. Thomas Hill had made good progress on a refutation when his efforts were cut short by his death in 1653. Tuckney preached the funeral sermon, and told his Cambridge audience that Hill could be 'ill spared' at 'such a time'. If he had lived, he would have 'shortly confuted' the notorious Arminian.[128]

The silence of Cambridge was made good by Oxford in the form of George Kendall, a former fellow of Exeter College, and John Owen, Whichcote's opposite number as Oxford's Vice-Chancellor. According to Anthony Wood, Kendall was so 'eagerly bent' against Goodwin, that he left his Cornwall rectory for 'ministry of a church in Gracious-street in London, purposely that he might be in a better capacity to oppose him and his doctrine'.[129] Kendall's refutation of *Redemption Redeemed* came in two big volumes: *Theokratia* (1653) challenged Goodwin's doctrine of general redemption, and *Sancti Sanciti* (1654) tackled Goodwin's secondary claim that the saints could fall from grace. Both volumes were published in folio, and totalled more than 1000 pages of text. Kendall's massive refutation combined scholastic learning with cutting satire, and was commended by Joseph Hall, whose letters to the author were published in *Sancti Sanciti.* In 1654, John Owen published his own massive critique of *Redemption Redeemed,* chapters 9–15.[130] Of all the critics, Owen was the most celebrated and best connected. His close relationship with Cromwell gave him great influence within the Cromwellian church, and Goodwin was understandably worried that Owen and his allies were using their connections to stop the spread of Arminianism. Although Owen's *Doctrine of the Saints Perseverance* was respectful towards Goodwin, he offered an

---

125 Whichcote, *Moral and Religious Aphorisms*, 56–57, 113–16.
126 Henry Jeanes, '*A Vindication of D. Twisse from the exceptions of Mr. John Goodwin in his* Redemption Redeemed', in William Twisse, *The Riches of Gods Love* (1653), ii. 201.
127 Kendall, *Theokratia* (1653), 'To the Revered Doctor Benjamin Whichcote', sig. a.
128 Anthony Tuckney, *Thanatoktasia, Or Death Disarmed* (1654), 58, 66.
129 A. Wood, *Athenae Oxonienses*, ed. P. Bliss, 4 vols (Oxford, 1813–20), ii. col. 638.
130 *The Doctrine of the Saints Perseverance* (1654), in *The Works of John Owen*, ed. W. H. Goold, 24 vols (1850–53), vol. xi.

exhaustive rebuttal of the Arminian's arguments and exegesis.[131]

Besides Owen and Kendall's immense tomes, there were other shorter replies to Goodwin. In 1652, Richard Resbury returned to the fray with in *The Lightless-Starre, or Mr John Goodwin proved a Pelagio-Socinian*. The book contained a letter in reply to Goodwin's *Confidence Dismounted*, and a 185-page analysis of the preface and the four foundational chapters of *Redemption Redeemed*, which Resbury believed to be riddled with Pelagianism and Socinianism. Resbury also appended a brief Latin discourse by John Preston defending the irresistibility of converting grace. It was a sharp reminder that Goodwin deserted the path of his former mentor, and was soon published in English translation.[132] In 1653, the Presbyterian Henry Jeanes produced a new edition of William Twisse's classic, *The Riches of God's Love*, and appended a substantial reply defending the deceased theologian against Goodwin's criticisms.[133] Jeanes admired Goodwin's 'great gifts and parts', but chided him for approaching complex problems of philosophical theology as if he was Alexander cutting the Gordian knot.[134]

If Jeanes was writing for other divines, the Scottish Presbyterian, Robert Baillie saw the need to appeal to a wider audience. He responded to Goodwin's 'Great Book' by publishing *A Scotch Antidote against the English Infection of Arminianism* (1652). The substance of this book had first been delivered as 'a long and learned speech' before the Glasgow General Assembly in December 1638.[135] Baillie could hardly have foreseen that a lecture against Laudian Arminianism delivered at the outbreak of the British troubles would be reissued to combat Puritan Arminianism at their close. He now realised that the orthodox had been so preoccupied with 'purging of the ditches' of bishops and ceremonies, that they had failed to see that 'the gates of our great Towers' were being stormed by teachers of error. 'Little pocket Books' like his were vital weapons in the battle to defend the fortress of Protestant truth.[136]

Sermons were another weapon. In May 1652, the Calvinist John Pawson (a former fellow of St John's, Cambridge) preached against Goodwin's theology before the Lord Mayor and Aldermen of the City of London at St Paul's. The Court of Aldermen ordered the printing of the sermon, and it duly appeared under the title, *A Brief Vindication of Free Grace* (1652). The Court's Order angered Goodwin, for one of Pawson's dedicatees was Robert Tichborne, an old friend of Goodwin's congregation. Goodwin criticised the City's politicians for setting themselves up as 'a *Facultas Theologica* ... giving a definitive sentence in matters of such profound disputation'.[137] Pawson, however, stressed that he honoured Goodwin's 'piety, parts

---

131 Goodwin and Owen's divergent reading of Scripture is explored in H. M. Knapp, 'John Owen's interpretation of Hebrews 6:4–6: Eternal perseverance of the saints in Puritan exegesis', *Sixteenth-Century Journal*, 34 (2003), 29–52.
132 *The Position of Mr Preston...concerning the Irresistibleness of Converting Grace* (1654).
133 Henry Jeanes, *A Vindication of Dr Twisse* (1653), ii. 201–62.
134 Jeanes, *A Vindication of Dr Twisse*, ii. 201, 226.
135 See A. Peterkin, ed., *Records of the Kirk of Scotland* (Edinburgh, 1838), 160.
136 Robert Baillie, *A Scotch Antidote against the English Infection of Arminianism* (1652), A3r–v.
137 *Exposition of Romans 9*, 'The Epistle Dedicatory', sig. A2v.

and painfulness (during many years past) in the work of the Lord', and hoped 'to meet him in the bosome of Christ'.[138]

Perhaps the most surprising reply to Goodwin was Thomas Lamb's *Absolute Freedom from Sin* (1656). As we have already seen, Lamb was a paradoxical figure, a General Baptist who believed in absolute predestination. He feared that Goodwin was discrediting the doctrine of general redemption by tying it to notions of conditional election, free will and falling from grace. Lamb had noticed that other responses to Goodwin came from high Calvinists, those (like Owen) who limited Christ's atonement to the elect. By writing his book, he hoped to rebut Arminian doctrines while salvaging the great truth 'that Christ died for the sins of all and every man', a 'Gospel-truth I have preached and disputed for a long time, and been a great sufferer in witness thereof'. He dedicated his book to Oliver Cromwell on the grounds of 'the esteem I have of your abilities ... as a competent Judg of the state of the controversie'.[139]

The fact that such an open theological controversy could occur in print is a testimony to the extensive freedom of debate permitted under the commonwealth and Protectorate. But at least some of Goodwin's critics called for censorship of his book. In *A Second Beacon Fired* (1654), six Presbyterian booksellers, probably aided by clergy from Sion College, cited *Redemption Redeemed* among a variety of blasphemous and heretical works that should be suppressed by the magistrate.[140] Goodwin believed that his notorious book had been listed 'to serve the design of their Petition for the Restraint of the Press'.[141]

Assailed by this blizzard of sermons, pamphlets and learned treatises, Goodwin sometimes felt wearied and beleaguered. In February 1653 he complained of 'hard thoughts, and hard sayings, and hard writings, and hard dealings, and frowns'. Like the prophet Jeremiah, he had become 'a man of contention to the whole Earth'.[142]

Yet if Goodwin found the flack hard to take, he must have realised that he had accomplished his purpose. *Redemption Redeemed* had created something of a sensation among England's Reformed theologians. Having been thrown out with the Laudian bishops, Arminianism was back. Goodwin's book was widely read by his fellow divines who clearly regarded him as a force to be reckoned with. Confronted by his challenge, English theologians found they did not speak with one voice. While men like Hill, Tuckney, Kendall and Owen continued to defend a strict Calvinist orthodoxy, others like Baxter, Whichcote and even Barlow were less dogmatic. Although they may not have shared Goodwin's Arminianism, they were unwilling to expel him beyond the Pale. Even critics like Pawson, Owen, Jeanes and Powell expressed respect for Goodwin, and treated him as an erring brother rather than an untouchable heretic. Calvinism was losing its hegemony.

---

138 John Pawson, *A Brief Vindication of Free Grace* (1652), sig. A2v.
139 Thomas Lamb, *Absolute Freedom from Sin* (1655), sigs. A3r–A4v.
140 *A Second Beacon Fired* (1654), 4.
141 *A Fresh Discovery*, 'Epistle to the Reader'.
142 *Exposition*, 'Epistle to the Reader', sig. b3v–b4r.

Goodwin's book both epitomised and exacerbated the crisis of Calvinism. While it provoked numerous rebuttals, it would also win converts, not least at Cambridge.

The sense of disarray and panic at Cambridge was captured by a satire entitled, *Umbra Comitiorum, or Cambridge Commencement in Types* (1651). The author, apparently an Anglican royalist, clearly had a detailed knowledge of University politics, and he noted that 'the Spiritual Host' (the Calvinists led by Hill and Tuckney) were in 'Combat' with Vice-chancellour Whichcote. Commencement was now dominated by Westminster Divines and their young acolytes, 'such as deny John Goodwin, and all his Works'. Intemperate denunciations of Goodwin were all the rage. At one commencement, a pupil of Hill had risen to speak: 'His anger-quodled brain did so boyle against M. Goodwin, and the zeal of his tongue spat so much fire and faggot, as if the flat-pated Heads had appointed him executioner for the burning of his Book (which their illiterate Noddles are not able to answer)'. Another young Calvinist, 'a most Orthodox Cub of Immanuel', 'roars out ... against John Goodwin hanging forth in his very countenance the red flag of defiance against him. This pulpit Fire-man was a shining light in a dark Commencement'.[143]

Goodwin himself heard that *Redemption Redeemed* had been attacked from 'the University Pulpit at Cambridge' by an unnamed preacher who denounced its teachings as 'Godlesse, Christlesse, Spiritlesse, Gracelesse'.[144] John Arrowsmith, Goodwin's successor at King's Lynn in 1630, and now Master of Trinity College and Lady Margaret Professor of Divinity, made critical comments on *Redemption Redeemed* and other Arminian works in his lectures, which formed the basis for his major Latin work, *Tactica Sacra* (1657). In 1653, Tuckney described Goodwin as 'the great daring Champion of the contrary errours, whom the abusive wits in this University with an impudent boldness could say, none here durst adventure upon'.[145]

The furore at Cambridge suggests that something of a Goodwin fan club was developing in the early 1650s. It probably included Tobias Conyers, whose election to a fellowship at Peterhouse in 1651 was blocked by the Master, Lazarus Seaman, on the grounds that Conyers had maintained 'some Arminian tenent' in the Schools. Conyers' tutor, Charles Hotham, petitioned Parliament in protest, and published his own accounts of the case. Hotham was deprived of his fellowship by a Parliamentary committee on 29 May, but more than thirty Cambridge fellows signed a letter in his support, including the Cambridge Platonists, Henry More, Ralph Cudworth and John Smith.[146] After his ejection, Hotham caricatured Calvinists as those who painted God 'as a false-hearted, dissembling Hypocrite, and a self-seeking Tyrant'.[147] It is hardly surprising to find that when Conyers moved to London soon afterwards, he joined Goodwin's congregation.

---

143 *Umbra Comitiorum* (1651), 1, 4, 5. I owe this reference to Professor Sonoko Yamada.
144 'Mr Goodwin's Letter to Mr Caryl' in *A Fresh Discovery*, 74–5.
145 Tuckney, *Thanatoktasia*, 58.
146 See *The Petition and Argument of Mr Hotham* (1651), 106–38; *A True State of the Case of Mr Hotham, Late Fellow of Peter-house* (1651); J. Venn and J. A. Venn, *Alumni Cantabrigienses...Part I from the Earliest Times to 1751*, 4 vols (Cambridge, 1922–27), i. 382.
147 Charles Hotham, *Corporations Vindicated in their Fundamental Liberties* (1651), 1–46;

The controversy over Conyers and Hotham shows that Goodwin was sowing on fertile soil. Indeed, Cambridge in the early 1650s was home to a remarkable group of young divines who would promote Arminianism within the Church of England. William Sancroft was a fellow of Emmanuel until his ejection in 1651, and may well have been an admirer of *Redemption Redeemed*.[148] Besides Sancroft, there were other young men at Cambridge in the early 1650s who were to become influential Arminian Anglicans: Isaac Barrow (appointed fellow of Trinity College in 1649), John Tillotson (appointed fellow of Clare Hall in 1651), Simon Patrick (MA, Queens', 1651), Edward Stillingfleet (appointed fellow of St John's, 1653), Richard Kidder (BA, Emmanuel, 1652), Thomas Tenison (scholar of Corpus Christi, 1653). This cohort of students included no fewer than three future Archbishops of Canterbury (Sancroft, Tillotson and Tenison). Given their Arminian sympathies, they can hardly have missed the controversy over *Redemption Redeemed*. The most important influences on them were clearly the Cambridge Platonists, and the Anglican Arminian, Henry Hammond. But *Redemption Redeemed* may have helped to confirm their rejection of Calvinism. It is significant that when the well-informed Dutch Remonstrant historian, Geeraert Brandt, listed the leading English Arminian theologians in 1674, he included Goodwin among what was otherwise an entirely 'Anglican' group.[149]

As well as being read at centres of learning, Goodwin's Arminian works also found a ready audience among the godly laity. One of his converts was Christopher Salter, who wrote to Goodwin in May 1653, when he was working as a surgeon for the army's garrison on the Isles of Scilly. He explained that over the past twenty years he moved from conventional Church of England Puritanism to become a Presbyterian, an Independent, an Anabaptist, and then a Seeker. He attributed his spiritual fits to the anxieties induced by his 'depending upon the common notion of Election'. Eventually, for 'the space of two years', he adopted a rudimentary Deism – he 'rejected the Scripture', but still believed in God.[150]

Despite his loss of faith, Salter kept returning to the Bible, and gradually started to rebuild his spiritual life with the help of the writings of the General Baptist Richard Stooks and the Arminian Puritan John Horn.[151] Then God's providence 'brought your Book of Redemption to my hand'. Salter had 'read it over once and again'. With growing excitement, he realised that this was 'an house

---

148 Sancroft was certainly an anti-Calvinist, and one of the works often attributed to him (*Modern Policy* [1652]), describes Goodwin as 'an able divine'. However, as the *ODNB* article on Sancroft points out, there is no firm evidence that he was the author.
149 Geeraert Brandt, *The History of the Reformation and Other Ecclesiastical Transactions in and about the Low Countries*, 4 vols (1720–23), ii. xi. Brandt's dedicatory epistle was written in 1674, and cited the chief English Arminian sympathisers as Hammond, Heylin, Farrindon, Pearson, Goodwin, Chillingworth, Taylor, Gunning, Hales, Womack and Pierce.
150 Salter, *Sal Scylla, or A Letter written from Scilly to Mr John Goodwin* (1653), 5–6.
151 Salter, *Sal Scylla*, 4. Richard Stooks, *Truths Champion*, 2nd edn (1651). Salter says that he had read this and Horn's book against Owen four or five years earlier, but Horn, *The Open Door for Mans Approach to God*, was only published in 1650. He may have read the first edition of *Truth's Champion* in 1648–49.

wherein to shelter me from all winds and weather', built on 'that Foundation Truth' of universal redemption. As an Arminian he felt isolated, for 'I know but two or three in all these West-parts like-minded in this point, the rest (which are many and zealous) ... are bewitched by tradition'. The local Calvinists crowed about George Kendall's answer to Goodwin, but Salter was eagerly awaiting 'your Romans 9 volume' and 'your second part'.[152]

Others who had been Arminians for some time welcomed Goodwin as an eloquent new champion. The Arminian William Hartley did not know Goodwin personally, but he had attended the disputation with Simpson in 1650, 'where (notwithstanding the prejudice offered by the Moderators, and Mr Powel) the truth of Mr Goodwin's Position and his abilities in the management thereof was sufficiently demonstrated'. Hartley's sermon on God's universal love for mankind was 'printed by John Macock for Lodowick Lloyd and Henry Cripps' in 1650, possibly on Goodwin's recommendation.[153] Cripps and Lloyd also published a work by the Arminian rector of All Hallows in King's Lynn, John Horn, which included a reply to George Kendall.[154] Horn hoped to provide some nourishment 'to stay stomakes, till he [Goodwin] have prepared a fuller meal of Reply to him'. Although Horn wished that Goodwin would eschew 'Metaphysical weapons' and concentrate on biblical exegesis,[155] the two men were theological allies, and Kendall satirised Horn as Goodwin's 'Journey-man'.[156]

Goodwin's Arminianism also found a reception among General Baptists and Quakers. The Baptist Arminian Samuel Loveday had published a shorter Arminian tract on Romans 9 in 1650,[157] but when he published *Personal Reprobation Reprobated* (1676), it was essentially an amalgam of his earlier work and Goodwin's more scholarly commentary. He acknowledged Goodwin as 'a man of high esteem with most of the reformed Protestants'.[158] The erudite Quaker, Samuel Fisher, published a massive critique of the Calvinist clergy, with a section on 'universal redemption' that appears to draw heavily on the arguments and language of *Redemption Redeemed*.[159] Another learned Quaker, Benjamin Furly, owned Goodwin's *magnum opus* and the account of his debates with Powell and Simpson.[160]

Thus Goodwin's anti-Calvinist writings found wide acceptance among Anglicans, Independents, General Baptists and even Quakers, and made a significant contribution to the demise of the Calvinist consensus among the godly. In 1657,

---

152 Salter, *Sal Scylla*, 3–5, 7.
153 William Hartley, *Good news to all people. Glad tydings for all men. God good unto all, and Christ the saviour of the world (1650)*, 32.
154 See Nuttall, 'John Horne of Lynn', 231–47.
155 John Horn, *Diatribe peri paido-baptismou, or A Consideration of Infant Baptism... Together with a Digression in Answer to Mr Kendall* (1654), 155, 157.
156 Kendall, *Sancti Sanciti* (1654), 'Appendix', 149.
157 Samuel Loveday, *The Hatred of Esau, and the Love of Jacob Unfoulded, Being a Brief and Plain Exposition of the 9. Chapter of Pauls Epistle to the Romanes* (1650).
158 Loveday, *Personal Reprobation Reprobated* (1676), 65, which alludes to Goodwin's *Exposition of Romans 9*, 115.
159 Samuel Fisher, *Rusticus ad Academicos* (1660), 4th Exercitation, 87–152.
160 See below, p. 281.

Goodwin wrote that since the publication of *Redemption Redeemed*, he had good reason to believe that 'the Doctrine unjustly defamed' had 'gathered many thousands' in England alone.[161] By 1659, he could tell a Calvinist critic that he had received 'many Letters, and Messages otherwise' of thanks and encouragement 'from severall persons of considerable worth, for Godliness, and Knowledge, inhabiting in several parts of the Nation, some of them Ministers of the Gospel, and others of them Students in the University of good standing, &c'.[162]

The godly scientist, Robert Boyle, registered the shift in Puritan attitudes to Arminianism in his *Seraphic Love* (1659). In the original manuscript, written in the late 1640s, Boyle made no reference to Arminianism, but in the printed edition of 1659, he included a new section on 'the Controversies betwixt the Calvinists and the Remonstrants, about Praedestination and the Coherent Doctrines'. Without revealing his own position, he offered a strikingly impartial summary of the two views, and referred to 'The Godly of both Parties'. He suggested that absolute predestination was 'Detested as little less than Blasphemous', 'not onely by almost all the rest of Mankind, but by the rest of the Protestant Churches themselves, the Lutherans, and divers learned Divines of the Church of England'. Goodwin was probably one of the 'learned Divines' Boyle had in mind, for he owned a copy of *Eirenomachia* (discussed below) and echoed Goodwin's claim that Arminians did not denigrate God's grace or exalt human merit. Although Boyle had reservations about Arminianism, he advised his readers that 'the doctrine of predestination is not necessary to justify the freeness and greatness of God's love'.[163] For Boyle, and for increasing numbers of English Protestants, absolute predestination had ceased to be a non-negotiable doctrine. Arminianism was no longer heresy, but a legitimate option for evangelical Protestants.

Further Arminian Works

Goodwin's reputation as 'the great spreader of Arminianism' did not simply rest on *Redemption Redeemed*. Between 1651 and 1653, he produced several other Arminian works, each with a distinctive purpose.

The first was *The Pagans Debt and Dowry* (1651), written in response to the challenge of Thomas Barlow, who wondered if pagans throughout the ages and across the continents had really enjoyed sufficient means to repent and believe. As he observed, 'many Nations never heard of Christ. And some say there are whole Nations that worship no God'.[164] Goodwin replied that 'The Scriptures in severall places ... plainly insinuate a capacity in the Heathen, yea in all men by the light of Nature ... by such a regular and rational process of discourse, as that mentioned,

---

161 'Preface' to *Triumviri* (1658), sig. d4.
162 *Banner of Justification*, 'Epistle to the Reader', sig. av.
163 *The Works of Robert Boyle*, ed. M. Hunter and E. B. Davis, 14 vols (London, 1999–2000), i. 108–11; *The Early Essays and Ethics of Robert Boyle*, ed. J. T. Harwood (Carbondale, IL, 1990), 265.
164 *The Genuine Remains of That Learned Prelate Dr Thomas Barlow* (1693), 122–30.

to attain or make out this Evangelicall Conclusion, That some Mediation, some Attonement or other, hath been made, and accepted by God, for the sins of men'.[165] The 'vast magnitude of the heavens' and the glories of the natural world revealed a mighty creator, while storms and providential judgements revealed a just God 'infinitely bent in hatred and severity against sin'. But 'rain from heaven, and fruitful seasons' 'plainly show, that he that bestows them, is not extream, useth not extremity against those that do amiss; and consequently that he is by one means or other, taken off from the rigor of his Justice, and severity of his wrath against sinners'. The heathen might not be able to understand why God 'holds forth his white flag', nor could they name their Saviour, but by making the most of their natural light they could come to see that God would save them if they repented and trusted in him for salvation. Like the faithful Jews of the Old Testament they would be saved by Christ, even though they knew him only 'vertually and interpretatively', not 'explicitely, and directly'.[166]

The Pagans Debt and Dowry underlined once more the Arminian themes of God's reasonableness, love and impartiality, and man's natural capacity and moral responsibility. Predictably, the tract confirmed Calvinist suspicions that Goodwin exalted the capacity of 'natural man' and human reason, and demoted the importance of divine grace and special revelation. Obadiah Howe spoke for many when he entitled his reply, *The Pagan Preacher Silenced* (1655), and George Kendall sneered at Goodwin's 'licensing the Sun, Moon, and Stars to Preach the Gospel'. If Goodwin was correct, there was little reason to fear for the Roman Catholic laity who lacked the Scriptures in their own language, and there was little need to preach to the American Indians. Both groups could learn 'all the chief contents of the Gospel' from 'that grand Itinerant Preacher', the Sun.[167]

In May 1652, Goodwin and his gathered church published another book, *Eirenomachia: The Agreement and Distance of Brethren: or A Brief Survey of the Judgement of Mr. J. G. and the Church of God walking with him*. The account was signed by fourteen leading men from the congregation, including Thomas Lamb, John Price, Daniel Taylor, George Foxcroft and William Allen. They dedicated the work to Oliver Cromwell, who was on familiar terms with several of the signatories. They assured Cromwell of 'the longing desire of our soul to go hand in hand with our Brethren as far as ever ... we are able'. By dedicating the work to the Lord General, they were not seeking 'favour, countenance, or protection'; they were giving Cromwell 'an opportunity ... of honouring your self yet more' by countenancing and protecting the truth. Signing themselves 'Your Excellencies most cordially devoted Servants in Christ', they assured the great man that 'we have constantly followed you with our prayers' and would 'continue our wrastlings with God for you'.[168]

---

165 *The Pagans Debt and Dowry* (1651), 10. The texts he cited were Acts 14:7, Romans 1:18–23, Psalm 19:4, Hebrews 11:6.
166 *Pagans Debt*, 14, 25, 9, 13, 11, 37–38.
167 George Kendall, 'A Verdict in the Case depending between Master J. Goodwin and Master Howe', in Howe, *The Pagan Preacher Silenced* (1655), 2–6.
168 *Eirenomachia*, 'To his Excellency, Oliver Cromwell'.

Set in such a context, *Eirenomachia* was – as the title suggests – an irenic exercise. It emphasised the common ground between Calvinists and Arminians, and each chapter began with a list of points on which both sides agreed, before outlining the differences and giving reasons for the Arminian position. The five chapters dealt methodically with different topics: 1. Election and Reprobation, 2. The Death of Christ, 3. The Grace of God, 4. The Power of Man, 5. Perseverance. In these chapters, Goodwin and his congregation effectively declared their allegiance to classical Reformed Arminianism (though they studiously avoided any reference to the Dutchman). Their five points were a reiteration of the five articles of the Remonstrants: 1. Conditional election, 2. Universal atonement, 3. The necessity of prevenient grace, 4. The resistibility of prevenient grace, 5. The possibility of falling away.[169]

By touching on the five key points of the Calvinist–Arminian controversy, Goodwin was able to present the first overview of his own position.[170] At 82 pages, the work was clearly intended to be an accessible introduction to Arminianism, a primer that even Cromwell (who was no great reader) might work his way through. Ellis Bradshaw certainly saw the book as 'very dangerous', and published *A Compendious Answer* in reply. Bradshaw addressed the congregation as 'Your loving Brother', and in his dedication to Cromwell praised Goodwin's people as 'reall Practitioners' of godliness and 'reall Engagers' for the commonwealth. But he wanted Cromwell and others to 'see how farre it is possible for a whole Church to erre, and that in Fundamentalls'.[171]

Rather than reply to Bradshaw, Goodwin pressed ahead with *An Exposition of the Ninth Chapter of Romans*. Romans 9 was the great Calvinist proof text, and the Calvinist interpretation of the text was firmly embedded in popular Puritan consciousness. The Apostle had quoted a series of awe-inspiring Old Testament verses – 'Jacob have I loved, but Esau have I hated'; 'I will have mercy on whom I will have mercy'; 'Shall the thing formed say to him that formed it, Why hast thou made me thus?' God was the potter, argued Paul, and man was mere clay.

Goodwin argued that Calvinists had misread Romans 9. The letter had been dealing with the question of justification, and arguing that man was justified by faith not by works. Romans 9 was not introducing a new issue – the predestination of individuals – but carrying on the argument about justification. It was designed to show Paul's Jewish readers 'That that very Gospel, or Doctrine of Justification, which they so deeply abhorred, and desperately opposed, was anciently preached unto them in their forefathers, by God himself'.[172] Isaac and Jacob were cited as representative types or examples of those who had been justified by faith, while Ishmael and Esau were types of those who tried to be justified by works. The

---

169 Reprinted in H. Bettenson, ed., *Documents of the Christian Church* (Oxford, 1943), 374–76.
170 *Redemption Redeemed* had focused on two points – the extent of the atonement and the perseverance of the saints.
171 E. Bradshaw, *A Compendious Answer to a Book called A Brief Survay of the Judgement of Mr. John Goodwin and the Church of God Walking with Him* (1652), sigs. A2–A4.
172 *Exposition*, 10, 89–90, 6–7.

Apostle was not pronouncing on their eternal destiny.[173] His argument was that the sovereign God had every right to establish the terms of justification.[174]

Goodwin's understanding of the terms of justification was itself controversial. He explained that 'God of his free and meer grace accepteth such a mans faith, in the place or stead of a perfect and compleat observation of the whole Law'. But works were far from irrelevant – in the final justification on 'the great day', believers would be vindicated on the basis of their works (Romans 2:13, Matthew 7:21–27, Matthew 25:34–36). Only believers who persevered in good works to the end would be justified.[175] The key point was that even the best Christian failed to observe the law perfectly, and could not claim salvation by merit:

> Therefore when the Apostle excludeth works from justification, he excludeth them onely under the notion or conceit of merit ... There is no opposition, but a clear consistencie, between *grace* and *works*, unless by *works* we understand *merit*.[176]

Human faith and human works might have a part to play in justification, but only because a sovereign God had graciously decreed to accept them despite their lack of merit.

Although Goodwin was careful to insist on Protestant principles of justification by faith and salvation by grace, he had redefined *sola fides* and *sola gratia* along Arminian lines. Works were not meritorious, but final justification could not occur 'without some considerable concurrence of them'.[177] Salvation was by grace, but grace was sufficient and universal rather than irresistible and particular. These formulations were anathema to high Calvinists and struck at the root of English antinomianism. Moderate Calvinists like Baxter felt more ambivalent about Goodwin's new theology, accepting his points about works and universal grace, but wishing to hold on to the doctrine of absolute predestination. But in the second half of the seventeenth century, the Arminian theology that Goodwin had articulated so forcefully in the early 1650s would enter the mainstream of the Church of England.

---

173 *Exposition*, 89–120.
174 *Exposition*, 138–41.
175 *Exposition*, 128–31.
176 *Exposition*, 129.
177 *Exposition*, 128.

8

'A MAN OF STRIFE'
1652–59

By 1653, Goodwin's intellectual journey was largely complete. He had changed his mind on ecclesiology, politics and theology, but his new positions were now firmly set. His mission during the rest of the 1650s was to propagate his vision of a truly reformed Protestantism.

To begin with, Goodwin was optimistic. The republic's triumphs over its foes promised a new era of stability and freedom, when the godly could complete the reformation without fear of regal tyranny and clerical uniformity. But Goodwin (like so many other radical Puritans) was to be disappointed. The factionalism of the godly dogged the republic in the 1650s as it had troubled Parliamentarianism in the 1640s. Goodwin's own congregation was afflicted by a painful schism. Despite his vigorous efforts, the promotion of Arminianism proved an uphill struggle. Even Oliver Cromwell, who had promised so much, came to be viewed as a betrayer of the revolutionary cause.

The Rump and 'State Religion'

One reason for Goodwin's disillusionment lay in the persistent appeal of 'State Religion'. Although the advocates of Presbyterian uniformity had been defeated, liberty of conscience was still threatened by a conservative Calvinism that wanted the state to police the boundaries of orthodoxy. In February 1652, a group of influential Independent clergy (led by John Owen) drew up a petition to be presented to Parliament. Owen and his colleagues were profoundly disturbed by the publication of the Socinians' *Racovian Catechism* (1651), and were determined to push for a government crackdown on heresy. They were, however, committed to toleration for various kinds of orthodox Trinitarian Puritans, including Baptists, separatists and even Arminians. Determined to assemble a broad coalition behind their proposals, the Owen group approached Goodwin through his old friend Philip Nye. Nye persuaded both Goodwin and John Price to add their signatures to a petition calling for greater regulation of religion, and he indicated that the proposals would be submitted to the Commons for its consideration.[1] 'The Humble Petition of divers Ministers of the Gospel' was presented to the Commons by Owen and others on 10 February,[2] and *The Humble Proposals* was printed and collected by Thomason at the end of March.[3] Besides Owen and Nye, its key promoters were Goodwin's old friends Thomas Goodwin and Sidrach Simpson. Although Goodwin was not named in the printed document, he was one of the 'other Ministers' who had subscribed to it.

Goodwin's support for the Humble Proposals is one of the more puzzling episodes in his career. Throughout the 1640s, he had posed as an inveterate critic of the magistrate's power in religion. His opposition to state religion was such that in early 1652, a satirical pamphlet suggested that he should be the 'High Priest' ordained to preach the funeral sermon of 'the Publike Faith' 'from Tuthill Fields to Whitechappel'.[4] Yet the man who had clashed with Nye at the Whitehall Debates now seemed to be moving to Nye's side of the argument. The Humble Proposals urged Parliament to empower certain persons in each country to examine and approve candidates for the parish ministry, and to establish 'six Circuits' to examine and eject men unfit for the ministry. As Marchamont Nedham later pointed out, this was the genesis of the Cromwellian system of Triers and Ejectors against which Goodwin inveighed in 1657.[5] The Independent proposals went further still. They recommended that everyone 'be required to attend the publike Preaching of the Gospel every Lords day', either at parish churches or at independent congregations; that all non-parochial congregations be registered with magistrates; that Parliament suppress 'that abominable Cheat of Judiciiall Astrology'. Finally, the ministers proposed that no one 'be suffered to preach or promulgate any thing in opposition' to those fundamental principles of the Christian religion essential to salvation.[6] A list of sixteen *Principles of Christian Religion* was drawn up, which defined the 'fundamentals' of faith in Trinitarian and evangelical Protestant terms.[7]

Goodwin later protested that in signing the proposals he had never intended to give them his unqualified endorsement. He and Price had told Nye that they did not support the implementation of the proposals. But Nye persuaded them that 'we might lawfully subscribe them, as meet to be delivered unto, and to be taken into consideration, by the Committee'. Reassured, Goodwin and Price added

---

1 [Anon], *An Apologie for Mr John Goodwin* (1653), 1; John Goodwin, *The Apologist Condemned* (1653), 3–5; Marchamont Nedham, *The Great Accuser Cast Down* (1657), sig. b4v, 49; HMC, 13th Report, *The Manuscripts of His Grace the Duke of Portland* (1891), i. 671.
2 *CJ*. vii. 86.
3 E.658(12): *The Humble Proposals of Mr. Owen, Mr. Tho. Goodwin, Mr. Nye, Mr. Sympson, and other Ministers* (1652).
4 *Pauls Churchyard* (1652), 20.
5 Nedham, *The Great Accuser*, sig. b2, 49.
6 *The Humble Proposals*, 5–6.
7 Although the sixteen 'fundamentals' had been drawn up earlier in the year, they were only published in December 1652. See *Proposals for the Furtherance and Propagation of the Gospel ... As also, some principles of Christian religion, without the beliefe of which, the Scriptures doe plainly and clearly affirme, salvation is not to be obtained* (1652), 12.

their signatures, believing that the proposals were merely an innocuous discussion starter. Whether the two men were this naïve is doubtful. It is possible that Goodwin shared the feeling that something must be done about the new Socinian menace. It is more likely, however, that he signed for another reason. He was under heavy fire for *Redemption Redeemed*, and the fear of being ostracised from the fellowship of the godly and the corridors of power must have weighed heavily on his mind. He claimed that he and Price had signed because they wanted to go along with the other ministers.[8] By signing, he could maintain his bond with the other Independent divines and help to legitimise Arminianism. For in asking him to support the Humble Proposals, the conservative Independents were making a major concession – they were tacitly acknowledging the basic orthodoxy of godly Arminians, and confirming their place within the Commonwealth church. Indeed, the preamble to the proposals declared that the ministers 'had equall respect to all Persons fearing God, though of differing judgements'.[9] For Goodwin, this was an offer he could not refuse, even if grasping it meant backtracking on his earlier denials of the magistrate's power in religion.

Before long, however, Goodwin was forced to think again. The *Humble Proposals* provoked a storm of protest from radical Puritans like Milton, Vane and Roger Williams, old allies of Goodwin in the toleration controversy of the previous decade.[10] Goodwin remained silent throughout the ensuing controversy, but in March 1653 he published his most significant pamphlet on religious liberty since *Hagiomastix*.

Thirty Queries (1 March 1653) addressed the question of 'Whether the Civil Magistrate stands bound by way of Duty to interpose his Power or Authority in matters of Religion, or Worship of God'. Goodwin answered the question with an unambiguous negative, reflecting his serious concerns about the commonwealth's religious policy. Firstly, there was the threat of religious coercion against 'heretics'. Although Goodwin deplored Socinianism, he was equally hostile to the use of coercion against heretics. He warned that 'the blood of Heretiques is the seed of Heresie'. Secondly, there was the failure of the Rump to abolish tithes, despite years of radical clamour. Goodwin emphasised that God had already ordained sufficient means for the propagation of the Gospel, and did not need men to invent additional devices for doing the job. Thirdly, and most importantly, there was the looming threat of a centralised body of 'triers' who would vet men for parish ministry. Goodwin was implacably opposed to the idea of magistrates appointing men to be judges over the faith of others. Magistrates had 'little time to wade into the depths of controversial Divinity'. They were unlikely to be able to tell apart the 'Orthodox' from the 'Heterodox' just by looking at their faces! Their appointed judges would be fallible and biddable men, 'likely to be of a State Religion'. They would be men 'who wear soft raiment, and live in Kings Houses, who by

---

8 *Apologist Condemned*, 4–5.
9 *The Humble Proposals*, 3.
10 See C. Polizzotto, 'The campaign against "The Humble Proposals" of 1652', *Journal of Ecclesiastical History*, 38 (1987), 569–81.

ignoble artifices and compliances have insinuated themselves into the familiarity and friendship of the anointed Cherubs of the earth'.¹¹

Drawing on natural law contract theory, Goodwin presented a radically minimalist account of the magistrate's power. Because the power of the magistrate was derived from the people, he could only exercise the powers which the people entrusted to him. But the people 'have no right at all, nor colour of right, to delegate unto any man any authority or power to intermeddle or officiate in one kind or another in the affairs of Jesus Christ'. It followed that the civil magistrate had only received authority in civil matters. He could punish violations of 'the Law of Nature', but only if the offences directly harmed 'the welfare, honor, and prosperity of that community of men' for which the ruler was responsible. Spiritual matters were simply beyond his jurisdiction. The magistrate should not 'act out of his sphere' by meddling in matters 'spiritual or ecclesiastick'; instead he should restrict himself to matters 'politick or civil'.¹²

This involved a drastic curtailment of the power of magistrates, who had traditionally been charged within Christendom with enforcing both tables of the Decalogue, religious and civil. Goodwin, by contrast, was positing a sharp dichotomy between the two spheres, something akin to what later generations would call 'the separation of church and state'.¹³ Indeed, his first query made it clear that a Christian magistrate had no more power than a pagan magistrate. Since the magistrate qua magistrate was locked into the sphere of civil matters, 'nothing more accrues to him, by way of Duty, in his Office, by his being Christian', nor was anything 'diminished or taken off from him, by his being, or turning Pagan'.¹⁴

Unsurprisingly, Goodwin's forthright rejection of the magistrate's authority in religion called forth sharp responses. *Master John Goodwins Queries Questioned* (1653), condemned him for undermining magistracy and promoting a cruel clemency, and presented a very conventional restatement of the traditional Reformed ideal of the godly magistrate who enforced church attendance, required tithes and the maintenance of ministers, and punished heresy. Another book, entitled *The Establishment* (1653), did not mention Goodwin directly, but it took aim at his argument that Christian magistrates had no more power in matters of religion than pagans.¹⁵ The author of *An Apologie for Mr John Goodwin*, also collected by Thomason on 28 March 1653, offered a shrewder reply. He charged Goodwin with trying to turn the magistrate into 'a kind of Bat, that is confined to the

---

11 *Thirty Queries* (1653), 7, 12–15. This may be an allusion to John Owen, who was well known for his sartorial elegance as well as his access to Cromwell. See H. Trevor-Roper, *Religion, the Reformation and Social Change* (London, 1967), 218–19.

12 *Thirty Queries*, 6, 4, 16.

13 On the origins of this problematic phrase see P. Hamburger, *Separation of Church and State* (Cambridge, MA, 2002).

14 *Thirty Queries*, 3. Compare John Locke, *A Letter concerning Toleration*, ed. J. Tully (Indianapolis, 1983), 32: 'The Civil Power is the same in every place: nor can that Power, in the Hands of a Christian Prince, confer any greater Authority upon the Church, than in the Hands of a Heathen; which is to say, just none at all'.

15 *The Establishment* (1653), 67–69.

twilight of Nature'. His proposal was profoundly naïve. Religion and politics simply could not be neatly separated in the way he proposed. Every civilised commonwealth in the world made provisions for religion by establishing 'publique places and Revenues'. The civil magistrate had an unavoidable duty ('as a publique parent') to make provision for public religion in his territory.[16]

Goodwin had appealed to natural law to restrict the power of the magistrate to the civil sphere, but his critic pointed out some serious problems with the argument. In his Arminian works, such as *The Pagans Debt and Dowry*, Goodwin was keen to present a maximalist account of the light of nature – it could 'discover the way to Faith and Salvation'. But in his tolerationist writings, he suddenly reverted to a minimalist account, suggesting that since the magistrate's power was restricted to enforcing the law of nature, he could not have any authority over religion. The truth, argued the critic, was closer to the maximalist account, for 'the Law of Nature teacheth the magistrate to make Lawes against false worship and Idolatry'. The author cited Selden, Plato and the example of Romulus to show that Gentiles had a basic natural knowledge of God and made the establishment of divine worship their priority when setting up their commonwealths.[17]

In his reply, *The Apologist Condemned*, Goodwin referred to his critic as 'a Graceling of the Greatness of this World', known for 'his Democritical wit' and 'his Devotion to the Goddess Mendacina'.[18] The man who fitted this profile best was Marchamont Nedham, the republic's propagandist, who was later to write a lengthy reply to Goodwin's critique of the Triers. On that occasion, Nedham seems to have worked with Philip Nye, and in 1653 it was probably Nedham who defended Nye against Goodwin. However, he did so in his own way, offering a decidedly republican defence of both natural religion and civil religion, one that hardly matched the conservative Independent's traditional Reformed defence of the magistrate's role in religion.

In *The Apologist Condemned* (19 April 1653) Goodwin denied that the light of nature laid the basis for religious establishments. The light of nature knew nothing of 'the Christian Magistrate'. The fact that a magistrate bore 'the additional external denomination of Christian' did nothing to augment his power. The light of nature did not teach magistrates to make laws against false worship and idolatry, for on its own it was 'not sufficient to discover the worshipping of God in a false manner'. The example of Romulus only proved that 'Rulers of the Earth, have ... an itching humor, and love to be tampering in matters of Religious and Divine Worships of their own calculation and contrivance'.[19] Goodwin now feared that significant elements within the new regime strongly supported the imposition of tithes, Triers, compulsory worship and 'orthodoxy'. He concluded by reminding his readers of the ancient Sicilian tyrant, Phalaris, whose cruel servant Perillius had devised a brazen bull in which innocent victims could be roasted. If England ever acquired

---

16 *An Apologie for Mr John Goodwin*, 2–6.
17 *An Apologie for Mr John Goodwin*, 7–9.
18 *Apologist Condemned*, 3, 9.
19 *Apologist Condemned*, 11–12, 16–17, 21–25.

a Phalaris, Goodwin bitterly remarked, 'there would be found more than one Perillius to make him Brazen Bulls for the tormenting of such Christians, who are either too weak, or too wise, to swim down the stream of a State Religion, or to call men, Rabbi'.[20]

The regime's most ardent defender was clearly becoming rather jaundiced. But Goodwin balanced criticism with praise. When 12 April 1653 was set aside as an official Thanksgiving Day for England's naval victory in the first Anglo-Dutch war, 'an excellent Hymne' by Goodwin was printed in abbreviated form in *The Moderate Publisher*. Battle hymns were now becoming a Goodwin speciality, and he exulted over the defeat of the Protestant Dutch with the same passion as he had toasted the demise of the Protestant Scots at Dunbar and Worcester. Along with other English Puritans, he justified the Dutch War as a war on a Protestant nation corrupted by materialism.[21] The drama of the great three-day battle was depicted with some relish: sails were 'torn all to Rags', masts 'tumbled down', ships were ripped apart by 'Thunder-bolts of Iron', and the sea turned red with 'streaks of blood'. Goodwin's main concern, however, was to attribute the victory to God. Yet another divine intervention led him to conclude that fighting 'for us poor English men' was God's 'right hands occupation'.[22]

From Commonwealth to Protectorate

On 20 April 1653, just a week or so after the publication of Goodwin's hymn, Cromwell marched to Westminster and forcibly dissolved the Rump. Despite its triumphs over the Irish, the Scots and the Dutch, the Purged Parliament had not fulfilled hopes for domestic reform, and was accused of trying to perpetuate itself. For godly republicans like Henry Vane and Edmund Ludlow, the dissolution of the Parliament was a betrayal of the revolution. Goodwin, apparently, did not share their disillusionment, but he was noticeably silent throughout the dramatic months from April to November. Given Daniel Taylor's proposals for a new representative back in 1651, we can safely assume that Goodwin would have supported the Nominated Assembly (or Barebone's Parliament) that met in July. It was named after the lay preacher Praise-God Barebone (who had sat on Common Council alongside members of Goodwin's congregation), and it contained a high proportion of members from the gathered churches. None of Goodwin's known followers was a member, though several were appointed to the High Court of Justice set up in November.[23]

---

20 *Apologist Condemned*, 12, 15, 34.
21 See S. Pincus, *Protestantism and Patriotism: Ideologies and the Making of English Foreign Policy, 1650–1668* (Cambridge, 1996), Part i.
22 *The Moderate Publisher*, 8–15 April 1653, 803–04. Although Pincus stresses the apocalyptic context of the war, Goodwin's hymn is providentialist rather than apocalyptic, and contains no obvious eschatological references.
23 *CJ*, vii. 353. Among the thirty-three commissioners were Mark Hildesley, Daniel Taylor, Richard Arnold and Owen Rowe. The puzzling row over the High Court of Justice is discussed in A. Woolrych, *Commonwealth to Protectorate* (Oxford, 1982), 300–01.

Goodwin himself was soon disillusioned with the performance of the Parliament. He later wrote that 'one Reason why God took no more pleasure in the Parliament of the last sitting', was that it had passed civil marriage legislation vesting jurisdiction in matrimonial cases in Justices of the Peace. Goodwin complained that this would stigmatise legitimate children and honourable marriages which had not been solemnised by JPs.[24]

Goodwin did not state his other reasons 'why God took no more pleasure' in the Nominated Assembly, but when it was dissolved in December, and replaced by the Protectorate, he was quick to write in support of the new regime. His support was very welcome, because Cromwell was under fire from a vociferous minority of Fifth Monarchists, who had placed their hopes in the Nominated Assembly. Former associates of Goodwin like Vavasour Powell and John Simpson were denouncing the Protector from the pulpit. Goodwin's *Dis-satisfaction Satisfied* (22 December 1653) presented seventeen queries designed to reconcile men to the new government. It began, without any sense of irony, by invoking Romans 13, the classic text on obedience to 'the powers that be' that Goodwin had worked so hard to neutralise in previous writings. He now argued that since Paul taught Christians to submit to Nero, 'a Monster of men', the people should submit to governments even when they disapproved of how they come to power. The New Testament urged Christians to pray for those in authority, thus ending 'quarrelsome disputes about the Rights and Titles of those, who are in present possession of the Soveraign or ruling powers'. 'Private men' should not condemn rulers who sometimes had to 'act besides, or contrary to, the letter of the Law' in order to promote 'the publique Interest and Safety'. Goodwin reminded his hearers that Moses had been rejected by his own people, who failed to see him as a God-given 'Ruler and a deliverer'. The people should recognise Cromwell and his fellow rulers as 'the Preservers of their lives, liberties, and estates', men who had put their own lives in jeopardy on the battlefield for the sake of the nation.[25]

The Fifth Monarchist preachers were depicted as 'Back-biters', who made 'daring and bold speeches' against the 'worthy Assertors of the Liberties of the People'. Real prophets would not declaim against a ruler whom they acknowledged to be 'a person fearing God', a man of tender conscience who was especially sensitive to the welfare of the godly. But the Fifth Monarchists were false prophets, 'ecstatical and fierie' men out 'to make proselytes to Barrabas, in stead of Jesus Christ'. They talked about 'the fift Monarchy' as if they could 'accelerate or hasten' its coming, when the time of its arrival was 'unchangeably, unalterably, unremoveably fixed by God'. By predicting 'unto the people, how long the present Government shall stand', they imposed 'a kind of wretched necessity upon themselves to turn every stone for the raising of Tumults and Insurrections in the Land'.[26]

---

24 *Peace Protected and Discontent Dis-armed* (1654), 6. On the legislation see Woolrych, *Commonwealth to Protectorate*, 291–92.
25 Συγκρητισμος. Or *Dis-satisfaction Satisfied* (1653), 3–10.
26 *Dis-satisfaction Satisfied*, 10–17.

This aggressive defence of the Protectorate disappointed commonwealthsmen like Henry Marten, who alleged that Goodwin had turned against 'fighters & adventurers for ye Commonwealth'.[27] But the most aggrieved readers were the Fifth Monarchist preachers. Goodwin soon found himself condemned as a 'Time-Server; a Worshipper of the Greatness of this World'. He responded in March 1654 with a second, expanded edition of his tract, entitled *Peace Protected, and Discontent Dis-armed*. He confessed that 'from first to last' he had been 'a zealous Assertor' of 'the present Authority'. However, he had also been 'as zealously faithful in declaring and asserting the just and lawful bounds of this Authority'. His 'great design' in giving Ceasar his due, was 'to deny unto Caesar, or take from him, that which I know is not his, when ever he assumes it'.[28] Thus while Cromwell enjoyed Goodwin's support, it was neither unconditional nor uncritical. Goodwin was surely aware that the Protectorate was about to establish a panel of Triers to vet and approve new clergy for parish churches. 'From the first day that I heard of these Commissions', he later wrote, 'my heart was troubled within me'.[29] In 1657, his attack on the Triers would precipitate his break with Cromwell, but even in March 1654 he was warning the Protector against exceeding his bounds by assuming unlawful power in matters of religion.

If *Peace Protected* was still essentially supportive of the new regime, John Price's *Tyrants and Protectors* was more ominously ambivalent. Published in June 1654, three months after the establishment of the Triers, the tract could be read as an endorsement of Cromwell or as a warning shot across his bows. Price certainly had no truck with those who numbered Cromwell among the tyrants. He compared the regime's critics to the feckless Israelites 'murmuring' against Moses and Aaron. The English should be grateful that they enjoyed a liberty 'the like whereof is not in all the world, that liberty the like whereof the generations that are past did never understand'.[30]

The first half of the book depicted the character of the tyrant, using numerous historical examples. Price's tract reflected the resurgence of neo-classical political thought in the wake of the regicide. He and his pastor had clearly been reading Milton and Nedham, and they may well have turned to the works of Tacitus and other Roman historians. Alongside the usual list of biblical tyrants, there were tyrants from classical antiquity – Alexander the Great, Pompey, Hannibal, Methridates, Julius Ceasar, Nero, and Caligula. The fact that the greatest political figures of the ancient world were traduced as tyrants suggests a republican disdain for powerful rulers. The work reflected the moral values of Puritan republicans like Milton – austerity, simplicity, integrity. One purple passage lambasted the decadent courts of kings, and Price even nodded towards the neo-classical concept of liberty, complaining that the subjects of tyrants were utterly dependent on 'his

---

27 BL Add MS 71532, f. 17. On Marten's disillusionment with Cromwell see S. Barber, *A Revolutionary Rogue: Henry Marten and the English Republic* (Stroud, 2000), 38–39, 62.
28 *Peace Protected*, 4–10.
29 Βασανισται [Basanistai], *or the Triers or Tormentors Tried and Cast* (1657), 'To the Reader'.
30 J. P., *Tyrants and Protectors* (1654), sig. A4r.

meer discretion', and were thus enslaved 'as in a great Bridewell'. 'Where a Tyrant rules, the Estates, Lives and Liberties of the People are not theirs, but his; not at theirs, but at his commands'.[31]

The prime target of this character sketch was not Cromwell, but 'the late King of England of bleeding memory', who had 'acted so like a Devil, murthering and massacring his people with fire and sword, until the wrath of the Lord broke out upon him ... to the horror and amazement of all Princes round about'. For Price, Charles I was the last in a long line of biblical, classical and later European tyrants. Indeed, 'almost all Princes or Courts of Princes in Christendom' had been guilty of corruption. God had been angry at 'the pride, gluttony, drunkenness, wantonness, luxury, lasciviousness of the Kings and Courts of this Nation in their constant succession one after another, until the hand of Vengeance did put a full stop hereunto by that fatal Blow at White-hall Gate, 1648'. 'They are extinct, dead, and buried', declared Price, 'and I wish such an immoveable stone may be layd upon the mouth of their Sepulchres by our present and successive Governors, that they may never rise again'.[32]

Although he hoped that the age of hereditary, dynastic monarchies was gone for good, Price was not opposed in any doctrinaire fashion to the rule of a single person such as a Lord Protector. In the second half of his pamphlet, he depicted 'A Protector, or *Homo Homini Deus*', making it clear that rule by a Protector or 'a Christian Prince' was entirely lawful. But Price's 'Protector' was a figure of almost impossibly lofty ideals and standards, the polar opposite of Machiavelli's *Prince*.[33] Although Oliver Cromwell had once seemed like a new Moses to Goodwin's congregation, he was no longer 'the delight of their souls'. The tract made a point of praising 'the late Lord Ireton ... the very mention of whom melts the spirits of those that well knew him'. Cromwell's name was conspicuously absent. A true Protector, Price warned, would be ever alert to the temptation to 'pride and vanity' afforded by 'his valour, his victories, his greatness, his Highness, his Armies, his Navies, the crowchings of his enemies, the applications of the great Princes of other Nations, his great houses, his revenues'. The fear was that the Protectorate would slide from austere republican simplicity to imperial luxury and grandeur. Price shuddered at the thought that Whitehall might one day see another 'fool or Jester, which formerly Princes could not be without in this Nation'.[34]

Yet it was the coterie of Calvinist Congregationalists at Cromwell's court which most troubled Price. He explained that a true Protector was one who studied 'The Saints just liberty' and shunned 'men of persecuting principles'. Such men 'are always found defaming, vilifying and reproaching their dissenting brethren unto the Rulers', so that 'there are men of worth, learning, excellency, and holiness, whose names and reputations suffer shipwreck by the men of this Character'.[35]

---

31 J. P., *Tyrants and Protectors*, 1–21, quotations at 5, 6.
32 J. P., *Tyrants and Protectors*, 6, 15, 18.
33 J. P., *Tyrants and Protectors*, 27–52.
34 J. P., *Tyrants and Protectors*, 32, 45, 52.
35 J. P., *Tyrants and Protectors*, 37–42.

The reference to Goodwin and his conservative Independent critics was unmistakable. Price complained bitterly about the way Goodwin's congregation had been used and abused:

> when any knotty, painful, and laborious business (pertinent to their function) in times of straits, appear necessary to be done; the men of their quarrel are then in esteem, but when the cloud is over, and the work is done, and the Sun shines again, they have done with them, they are shut up again in darkness under their black reproaches, and if they have but the liberty of their private Confines, Societies, and Companies, it is reward sufficient, if not too much for all their labours.[36]

This is a revealing passage. Goodwin and his followers, who had played such an active role as agents and propagandists in 1649, now felt betrayed. Cromwell, who had once been so accessible and friendly towards Goodwin's followers, was remote and prejudiced against them. Their Arminianism had made them unwelcome at court, and they now feared that the Triers would prevent godly Arminians from entering the public ministry. Price emphasised that he was not opposed to the Triers in principle, but he feared what would happen if 'men of persecuting principles for conscience sake' became dominant once more. 'Kings, and Princes, and Parliaments have been dasht in pieces at this stone by too much complyance with the men of this Character'.[37] The Goodwin Independents were now unsure about Cromwell's commitment to religious liberty. Moreover, they were not content with 'the liberty of their private Confines, Societies, and Companies'. They wanted a piece of the action at Whitehall, and longed for the influence they had enjoyed back in 1649.

In many ways, their attitudes were similar to those of Milton, whose *Defensio Secunda* (published in May 1654) showed greater enthusiasm for the revolution than for the Protectorate. Like Price, Milton worried that Cromwell was backtracking on religious liberty, cosying up to Presbyterians and royalists, going silent on the regicide, abandoning the revolution, and in danger of succumbing to imperial ways. Price's *Tyrants and Protectors* and Milton's *Defensio Secunda* warned the Protector even as they defended him.[38]

Developments during the first Protectorate Parliament in late 1654 only intensified the concerns of radical Independents. In early October, the Parliament was presented with a pamphlet by six Presbyterian booksellers, entitled *A Second Beacon Fired*, which called for a crackdown on heresy. The booksellers deplored the publication of heretical books, and named Goodwin's *Redemption Redeemed* alongside works by Biddle, Dell, Feake and other radicals.[39] The Presbyterians clearly hoped that the days of an unfettered press were drawing to a close. They were no doubt encouraged when a Parliamentary committee appointed a group of divines to determine the fundamentals of the Reformed religion. The group included

---

36 J. P., *Tyrants and Protectors*, 40.
37 J. P., *Tyrants and Protectors*, 40–42.
38 See B. Worden, 'John Milton and Oliver Cromwell', in I. Gentles, J. Morrill and B. Worden, eds, *Soldiers, Writers and Statesmen of the English Revolution* (Cambridge, 1998), ch. 11.
39 *A Second Beacon Fired* (1654), 4.

the leading Congregationalist divines, Owen, Nye, Thomas Goodwin and Sidrach Simpson, as well as leading Presbyterians like Richard Vines, Francis Cheynell, Stephen Marshall and Richard Baxter. According to Baxter, 'The great doer of all that worded the Articles was Dr Owen: Mr Nye, and Dr Goodwin and Mr Syd. Symson were his Assistants; and Dr Cheynell his Scribe'.[40] Baxter himself fought a rearguard action against 'the over-Orthodox divines', but he could not prevent the group drawing up a list of twenty fundamentals, which was privately published for the benefit of MPs. Thomason managed to obtain a copy for his collection, and entitled it *A New Confession of Faith, or the First Principles of the Christian Religion* (1654).[41]

Although the main targets of *A New Confession* were Socinians, Quakers, and Ranters, it was also (as Michael Lawrence observes) 'an anti-Arminian confession' with clauses that Goodwin could hardly sign. Thus fallen man was 'disabled to all that is spiritually good' and salvation could only come by 'the Revelation of the Gospel'.[42] Shortly after receiving their copies, MPs debated the subject of heresy. On 7 December 1654, Parliament voted that 'the true reformed Protestant religion' should be 'the public profession of these nations'. A majority of MPs voted in favour of including 'damnable heresies' within Parliament's purview, and another vote required that such heresies 'be enumerated in a constitutional Act'.[43]

Goodwin feared that the ghost of enforced uniformity – apparently banished by the revolution – had returned to haunt the land. On 12 December he completed *A Fresh Discovery of the High Presbyterian Spirit,* an eloquent plea for liberty of conscience and freedom of the press.[44] It contained a letter he had written to the six booksellers on 9 November, and a sixty-page dissection of their reply. But the booksellers were a mere cover for Goodwin's real target – the Calvinist ministry with its desire to impose a narrowly defined 'orthodoxy'. Goodwin was convinced that while the booksellers had signed *A Second Beacon*, its real author was 'another Spirit, which some years since leapt upon me'.[45] He did not name anyone, but his pamphlet contained a number of references to William Jenkyn, the 'Novice Presbyter' who had attacked him in 1648. The booksellers' reply to Goodwin made detailed charges against his theology, just as Jenkyn had done. Goodwin once again defended his teachings on predestination, justification, and Scripture, and emphatically denounced the blasphemous teaching of John Biddle.

Yet his main burden was to defend 'liberty of Printing'. In his November letter to the booksellers, Goodwin advanced a set of strikingly Miltonic arguments

---

40 *Reliquiae Baxterianae* (1696), ii. 197–99.
41 Thomason Tracts: E.826[3].
42 M. Lawrence, 'Transmission and Transformation: Thomas Goodwin and the Puritan Project, 1600–1704', unpublished Ph.D. thesis, University of Cambridge (2002), 170–75. The confessions of 1652 and 1654 are reprinted side by side in Appendix A.
43 See Gardiner, *History of the Commonwealth and Protectorate*, 4 vols (London, 1903), iii. 220.
44 Thomason did not collect the tract until 5 January 1655.
45 *A Fresh Discovery of the High Presbyterian Spirit* (1655), 'To the Reader'.

in favour of a free press.[46] Christ had not authorised any person to appoint a few men 'whom they shall please to call Orthodox' to tell the Holy Ghost what he could and could not reveal to 'other men'. The 'Beacon-Firers', Goodwin complained, 'tempt men in authority to assume unto themselves such an exorbitant and prodigious power'. Yet there were no good grounds for investing particular individuals 'with a Nebuchadnezzarean power over the Press', to slay or spare books as they pleased. Such a power was inconsistent 'with the interest and benefit of a free commonwealth', and amounted to a monopoly that deprived the nation of the benefits of the gifts, parts, experiments, diligence and labours of many of her worthy members'. There was every possibility that the magistrate might appoint unsound 'Press Masters', particularly as he would choose men who instinctively 'comply with a State Religion'. Such fallible press masters would 'run an extream hazard of fighting against God'. And 'a power of gagging the Press' was opposed to the biblical injunction 'to try all things'.[47]

Moreover, the restraint of the press could not achieve its goal of stopping the spread of heresy. The proverb warned that 'stollen waters are sweet'; banning books would only increase their attractiveness and pique the curiosity of the common people. Heretics would be driven underground, where they would devise new and crafty ways of propagating their ideas. Such underground heresies were less likely to be vanquished by public argument. Attempting to suppress them by banning books was as futile as setting 'a company of armed men about an house to keep darknesse out of it in the night'. Spiritual darkness would only be dispelled by spiritual light. The restraint of printing and licensing of the press were not among God's appointed means for suppressing heresy. The Gospel flourished most when the church relied on spiritual means to vanquish error. But the booksellers were probably less interested in the Gospel than in their own trade, which would benefit greatly from their 'monopolizing of the Presse'.[48]

Besides attacking 'press masters', Goodwin also deconstructed the very notion of 'State Religion'. He was not sure what people meant when they talked about 'a Christian Commonwealth'. Nor was it clear whether 'the State' referred to the rulers and governors, or to 'the great Body it self, and Bulk of the Nation'. Either way, it was hard to tell what its religion was. 'A State Religion' was bound to be 'a many-headed Beast', since statesmen themselves disagreed over religion – 'as many men, so many minds'. If a State authorised 'a model of Religion, or Confession of Faith', one could only ascertain the 'State Religion' by asking 'each particular member of this State' to 'explain his sence touching every Article, or head of Doctrin therein'.[49] This was an unmistakeable reference to Owen's *New Confession of Faith*, and it revealed how sharply Goodwin had diverged from the conservative

---

46 See D. M. Wolfe, *Milton in the Puritan Revolution* (New York, 1941), 129–30. W. M. Clyde, *The Struggle for Freedom of the Press from Caxton to Cromwell* (St Andrews, 1934), 256–61, sets Goodwin's tract in context. An extract from *Fresh Discovery* is reprinted in Appendix F.
47 *Fresh Discovery*, 4–7.
48 *Fresh Discovery*, 8–11.
49 *Fresh Discovery*, 51–54. Compare again John Locke, *A Letter concerning Toleration*, 44: 'There is absolutely no such thing, under the Gospel, as a Christian Commonwealth'.

Independents since signing their Humble Proposals of 1652. Progressively sidelined on account of his Arminianism, he had become increasingly hostile to the Cromwellian state church. He was now opposed to any state regulation of religion.

The tract drew a sharp response from an anonymous Presbyterian. *An Apologie for the Six-Booksellers* lambasted Goodwin as 'this great Presbytero-Mastix, and Antisionita', and renewed the attack on Goodwin's orthodoxy. It condemned 'M. Goodwins great Diana, that accursed Idoll of Toleration', and claimed that he had even followed the Socinians in teaching that God was ignorant of future contingencies. Goodwin repudiated these allegations in *The Six Booksellers Proctor Non-Suited* (1655). He had plainly and 'upon all occasions' asserted God's exhaustive 'knowledg of all future contingencies, yea of all things whatsoever'. Moreover, he did not idolise toleration. Contrary to what his critics suggested, Goodwin was committed to fighting 'cursed or damnable Doctrines'. He believed in a 'Christian non-toleration' – heretics should be silenced by rational arguments. He rejected 'Antichristian non-toleration' – 'the battails of God' should not be fought with 'unhallowed weapons' like fining, imprisoning, burning or slaying. Liberty of conscience did not mean 'an exemption of any mans conscience, from subjection unto God, or Christ, or any of their lawes', but it did require 'an exemption of the conscience from subjection unto men, or their Doctrines'. In matters of religion, men should not be subject to the state or the clergy, but to God alone.[50]

Church Troubles: Socinians and Baptists

It has been suggested that Goodwin remarried in the early 1650s.[51] A John Goodwin did marry Mary Bradshaw at St Stephen's, Coleman Street, on 13 February 1652/53,[52] but this may well be Goodwin's oldest son, who was now in his mid-twenties. The parish registers of St Margaret, Lothbury, record that 'John Goodwin of Criple gate, & Sarah Carew both of Criple gate parish were married this 31st day of July 1653'.[53] Since Goodwin's will of 1658 shows that his wife was called Sarah, some have leapt to the conclusion that this was Sarah Carew. It is even tempting to speculate that Mary Bradshaw and Sarah Carew were related to the regicides, John Bradshaw and John Carew, though there is no evidence that this is so.[54] More problematically, there is no other contemporary reference to Goodwin living in Cripplegate, and no record of the death of Goodwin's first wife. Goodwin's will asks his sons John and Edward 'to be assistant unto my said wife their mother' in the execution of the will.[55] By 'their mother' Goodwin may have meant 'their

---

50 *The Six Book-sellers Proctor Non-Suited* (1655), 16, 12–13.
51 *Calamy Revised*, ed. A. G. Matthews (Oxford, 1934), 227; Tai Liu, 'Goodwin, John (c. 1594–1665)' in *ODNB*.
52 GL MS 4449/2, Parish Register of St Stephen Coleman Street.
53 GL MS 4346/1, Parish Register of St Margaret Lothbury. Henry Overton's brother? Valentine was a Registrar at St Margaret's.
54 The *ODNB* article on Carew and his father (Sir Richard) record no sister called Sarah, and Carew was too young to have a marriageable daughter; Bradshaw had no daughters.
55 NA PROB 11/320.

stepmother', but it remains more likely that Goodwin's first wife was still living.

At St Stephen's (or Stephen's as it was called under the Puritans), Goodwin continued to work alongside the Presbyterian William Taylor. They were both described as 'Ministers' in the parish minutes, and cajoled their parishioners into donating £155 2s for the relief of the persecuted Waldensians of Savoy in 1655.[56] Goodwin rarely attended vestry meetings, though he did audit the parish accounts. Several of his followers were prominent in parish affairs, especially Mark Hildesley, Thomas Alderne, John Price and Joseph Gallant (the parish registrar). As far as we know, the gathered congregation continued to meet in the parish church. However, its harmony was now disturbed by the dual impact of Socinianism and 'Anabaptism'.

The Socinian threat was highlighted by the defection of one of Goodwin's youngest followers, Thomas Firmin. Born in Ipswich in 1632 to Puritan parents, Firmin had come to London as an apprentice in his late teens. His master was 'an Arminian, a Hearer of Mr John Goodwin', and Firmin had accompanied his master 'to the elegant and learned Sermons of Mr Goodwyn'. Firmin quickly fell under Goodwin's sway, exchanging 'the opinions of Calvin, in which he had been educated, for those ... of Arminius and the Remonstrants'. He also learned 'to write Short-hand', so that he could take verbatim notes on Goodwin's sermons. However, at some point in the early 1650s, probably after he had established his own successful business, Firmin got to know John Biddle, who converted him to Socinianism.[57]

Firmin's defection and Biddle's influence prompted Goodwin to tackle Socinianism from the pulpit. In 1654, he declared that he had 'laboured, and this publickly, more abundantly' against Biddle's teachings than the Presbyterians themselves.[58] Several of his anti-Socinian sermons were eventually published posthumously in *A Being Filled with the Spirit* (1670).[59] This sermon series attracted a large audience, for many years later the publisher could state that 'there are many yet alive of those that heard it'.[60] The sermons offer one of the best entry points into Goodwin's mature theology and one of the best examples of his regular preaching. In them, he refuted Socinians and Seekers, refined his Arminianism,

---

56 GL MS 4458/1, f. 200.
57 *The Life of Mr Thomas Firmin* (1698), 5–10.
58 *Fresh Discovery*, 45.
59 Although this appears to constitute a single sermon series, it is difficult to date. At one point, Goodwin refers to his funeral sermon *Mercy in her Exaltation* (1655), 'opened unto most of you formerly upon another occasion' (82). However, this reference could have been added by Goodwin or his publisher when the sermons were being prepared for publication. In 1658, Eversden still had unsold copies of *Mercy in her Exaltation* in his bookshop in Pauls Church-yard (see *Triumviri* [1658] appendix), and he may still have been hoping to sell a few in 1670. Everything else in the volume points towards a date in the early fifties. Goodwin refuted Biddle's *Twelve Arguments* (1647), and commended a critique of Biddle published 'somewhile since', Nicholas Estwick's *Pneumatologia, or A Treatise of the Holy Ghost* (1648) – see 169, 177, 196–238, 374. Significantly, the sermons contained no reference to the flurry of anti-Biddle literature published in the mid-1650s.
60 Πληρωμα το πνευματικον. *Or A Being Filled with the Spirit* (1670), 'The Publishers to the Ingenuous and Christian Reader'.

and promoted practical Puritan divinity.

The critique of Biddle occupied most of chapters 7, 8 and 13 of *A Being Filled with the Spirit*. Alluding perhaps to Firmin, Goodwin warned his hearers 'that there are many young men that are able to puzle you'. An 'Antitrinitarian Spirit hath broken prison of late, and gotten abroad amongst us, very busie in making Proselytes'. Biddle's error in denying the deity of the Holy Ghost was a 'Plague', 'most dangerous', 'blasphemous', Satanically inspired and 'destructive unto the salvation of men'.[61]

Goodwin responded in detail to all twelve of Biddle's arguments against the divinity of the Spirit, and mounted arguments of his own from Scripture, reason and tradition in defence of orthodoxy. He recoiled from the idea that the Holy Ghost was 'some great Angel' or created spirit. He argued that the New Testament attributed things to the Holy Spirit that were attributed exclusively to Jehovah in the Old Testament. Texts like Matthew 28:19, where the disciples were commanded to baptise 'in the name of the Father, and of the Son, and of the Holy Ghost' were clearly Trinitarian, for it was 'altogether irrational' to think that the Spirit who inspired the Scriptures 'should couple the Name of an infinite and incomprehensible God and the name of a mear finite Creature together'. Indeed, it was beyond 'the limits or bounds of Reason' to believe that the Spirit (if he were a mere creature) had inspired the biblical writers to pen 'representations of himself' which would lead men so easily into Idolatry. If Biddle was right, the Spirit's inspiration of the Scriptures was a botched job. Orthodox Trinitarianism made far more sense, and it had been crisply articulated by those 'who are versed in the traversing of such curious questions'. The concepts of Essence and Being, Modus and Subsistence, could be effectively deployed to prove that Trinitarianism was 'most rational'.[62]

Goodwin's insistence that the doctrine of the Trinity made rational sense shows that he wished to reconcile his trenchant Trinitarianism with his earlier emphasis on fallibility, uncertainty and toleration. He explained that while 'a modesty and tenderness in Judgement' was appropriate on questions where the Christian world was deeply divided, he was no advocate of 'an absolute Scepticism, or meer Neutrality of Judgements'. 'In the Question of the Holy Ghost's being God, there is no place nor possibility for a neutrality of judgement or Opinion; but we must of necessity, at least in our practice or behaviour towards him conclude him either to be God, or not God'. However, he realised that some of his hearers were torn between the two sides of the argument: 'we are intangled and perplexed in our Judgements and Consciences'. In such a situation, one should take the safest course.[63]

On the question of the Trinity, it was safest to follow 'the whole Christian World, Fathers, Martyrs, Confessors, Pastors, Teachers, Bodies of Churches, ever since the Apostles daies'. It was 'the first-born of improbabilities' that the Church had 'for 1600 years and upwards' been 'wallowing in the horrid pollutions of idolatry' by worshipping a mere creature as God. How could Christ and the Holy Ghost

---

61 *Being Filled with the Spirit*, 143, 169, 179, 375.
62 *Being Filled with the Spirit*, 148, 155–56, 185–86, 172–73.
63 *Being Filled with the Spirit*, 376–79.

have tolerated such a 'sleep of death' in the Church? Biddle and his ilk made the entire Christian world out to be gross idolaters worthy of hell. But was this a remotely plausible verdict on holy men like 'Ignatius, Justin Martyr, Irenaeus, Epiphanius, Basil, Nazianzen, Chrysostome, Jerome, Austin' and many other 'famous lights of the Christian world'? The anti-Trinitarians were cutting themselves adrift from the church through the ages, and all for a 'Rhapsody or Fardle of old abhorrid Errors and Heresies of the Anthropomorphists, Arians, Macedonians, Origenists'. Goodwin's advice to those troubled by Biddle's arguments was to weigh up the risks and consider the probabilities. The balance of probability lay with the Trinitarians, and the greatest risks lay with their opponents. This approach was compatible with the anti-dogmatism of *Hagiomastix*, and Goodwin also finished his treatment of the issue by emphasising that he still supported civil toleration. 'There are men, and still have been, whose mouths must be stopped', he wrote; 'but not as some would interpret it, by Prisons, or by Sword: No, but stopped they must be, i.e. way-laid in their Judgments, Consciences, and Understandings by the Scriptures'.[64]

Goodwin's critique of the Socinians was combined with an equally robust assault on the Seekers, those radical Puritans 'who make it a matter of Conscience to turn their backs upon the Ministry of the Gospel'. This was 'a strange spirit' that 'walks up and down the streets of your City', and had even waylaid those who once loved 'the Assemblies of the Saints'. Once again, Goodwin was probably speaking from bitter experience of men like Nicholas Culpepper and Isaac Pennington junior, who no longer worshipped with the congregation. Goodwin had little sympathy for such disillusioned drifters. He accused them of being 'Sceptiques' and 'absolute Neutralists'. Seekers condemned the ministry as dry and unedifying, but many thousands could testify to the transformative power of the pulpit. A godly ministry had 'mighty Engines and Screws whereby to manage and command the hearts and consciences of men'. It was like 'a Conduit Pipe ... to convey the Holy Ghost into the hearts and souls of men'.[65]

Goodwin contrasted Spirit-filled believers with 'the generality of Professors', men whose religion was 'dull and heavie', 'lean and starveling', 'carnal' and 'formal'. Such men knew nothing of the 'soul-ravishing Consolations of the Gospel, and that joy in the Holy Ghost, which is unspeakable and full of glory'. The godly, by contrast, were inebriated with the 'New Wine' of the Gospel.[66] Goodwin's Arminianism had not dulled his spiritual fervour. His sermons were still stamped with the affectionate, practical divinity that was the hallmark of the Puritan preachers. He retained the characteristic Puritan emphasis on 'experimental' (i.e. experiential) faith, 'immediacy in communion with God', and 'the presence of the Holy Spirit in the believer'.[67] However much he stressed the reasonableness of Christianity, he remained one of 'the hotter sort of Protestants'.[68] If anything, his

---

64 *Being Filled with the Spirit*, 382–86.
65 *Being Filled with the Spirit*, ch. 14. Quotations at 387–88, 400, 411, 412, 415, 417.
66 *Being Filled with the Spirit*, 46, 78–79.
67 See G. Nuttall, *The Holy Spirit in Puritan Faith and Experience* (second edition, Chicago, 1992), 7, 171, 176.
68 P. Collinson, *The Elizabethan Puritan Movement* (Cambridge, 1967), 27.

Arminian belief in the universality of God's love for mankind had intensified his delight in the 'great bountifulness of God towards the Children of men'.[69]

Thus the Goodwin of the 1650s remained the model of an orthodox, godly divine. Determined to sail in the mainstream of the Western theological tradition, he was a champion of the learned ministry, and a purveyor of ardent spirituality. It is hardly surprising that irenic fellow ministers like Henry Jessey and Ralph Venning continued to believe that he was on the side of the angels, even though they disagreed with his Arminianism. Venning wrote the dedicatory epistle to the posthumously published edition of Goodwin's sermons on the Spirit, though he confessed that he was 'not of the same mind and opinion with the Learned Author in some other controverted Points'.[70] In fact, one section of the book sketched out a distinctively Arminian doctrine of the Spirit, emphasising the universality of his presence and the necessity of human cooperation with the Spirit's resistible influence.[71]

Goodwin's followers fully endorsed his Arminianism, his Trinitarianism and his Puritanism. But in 1653, the congregation experienced a schism over baptism. One of the leading members of the church, the merchant William Allen, had long been troubled by 'doubts about Infant Baptism', and he fell under the influence of the erudite General Baptist pastor, Samuel Fisher. Fisher was an admirer of Goodwin's Arminian and tolerationist writings, and recommended that magistrates should read *Thirty Queries* and *The Apologist Condemned*, 'neither of which ever will be answered solidly by their parish ministers'.[72] His arguments converted Allen to believer's baptism, and Allen in turn convinced another member of the church, Thomas Lamb. The two men were baptised by immersion and succeeded in winning others in the congregation to their principles. Goodwin was keen to accommodate them, and for a while 'part of the Church' continued to meet in Lamb's house on Monday nights, as was their custom. But after a sharp exchange between Lamb and Daniel Taylor, the non-Baptists stopped attending this meeting. Goodwin had 'some high words' with Lamb, and for reasons of principle the Baptists decided to leave the congregation. They had come to believe that 'for pure conscience' they must separate from the society on the grounds that it was not a properly constituted church, and that it was unlawful 'to communicate with unbaptised Persons'. The separation was agonising for both parties. Lamb later testified that 'Mr Goodwin and the Church were the dearly beloved of my soul ... fellowship therein, I reckoned one of the chiefest comforts of my life'. Having concluded that he must leave them, he wept day and night; his grief was such that death seemed sweeter than ever before. For the rest of the congregation, the split was so painful that 'they were not able to bear any publick discourses to the point in difference: Mr Goodwins teares, at the mention of something relating thereto,

---

69 See for example, *Being Filled with the Spirit*, 65–66, 71–72.
70 *Being Filled with the Spirit*, sig. a3v.
71 *Being Filled with the Spirit*, 18–41.
72 Samuel Fisher, *Christianismus Redivivus, Christendom both un-christened and new-christ'ned* (1655), 547.

went to my heart'. The breakaway group did not join an existing General Baptist church because none provided 'such means of Edification' as they had enjoyed with Goodwin. Instead, they formed a new congregation in Lothbury with 'about Twenty that came off by their means from the same Fellowship'.[73]

Although face-to-face communication had broken down between the two groups, they did engage in a protracted exchange of pamphlets. William Allen explained his position in *Some Baptismal Abuses Briefly Discovered*, written in May 1653.[74] Goodwin quickly replied in *Philadelphia, or XL Queries* (22 June 1653), to which Allen responded in *An Answer to Mr J. G. his Forty Queries* (23 September). Goodwin then issued *Water-Dipping no Firm Footing for Church-Communion* (December 1653), arguing that even if the Baptists were correct on baptism, they had an obligation to remain in communion with true believers who had not received believer's baptism. In *Truth Prevailing against the Fiercest Opposition* (1655), Thomas Lamb offered a much more personalised response to Goodwin. He wrote with much 'regret of spirit', because his former pastor was 'right dear and precious in my sight'. But he had to vindicate the Baptists from the aspersions of Goodwin, who had represented them as persons who had 'metamorphosed' from 'Lambs to Wolves, Tygers, or Serpents'.[75]

Lamb maintained that the Baptists were following their former pastor's teaching through to its logical conclusion. Believer's baptism was congruent with gathered churches of visible saints, whereas infant baptism agreed with 'the National Church … which you have renounced'. Goodwin had always taught that 'every man should judge for himself, what was according to the Word of God' rather than bowing to human authorities; the Baptists had simply taken him at his word. In refusing communion with unbaptised believers, they had done what Goodwin had done to 'the godly Presbyterians of Coleman-street'. Goodwin, however, had forgotten 'his brave old sayings'. He had 'come to shake hands with the old enemy of the truth, *Gangraena*'.[76]

Goodwin had been planning to write a second volume of *Redemption Redeemed*, but he was now thoroughly distracted from his real passion.[77] He devoted much of his time to writing a major work on the baptismal controversies. It was finally published in July 1655 under the title *Cata-Baptism: or New Baptism, Waxing Old, and Ready to Vanish Away*. In the Epistle Dedicatory, Goodwin expressed his affection for his Baptist brethren, but complained that 'Some of your Churches esteem all others no better then Heathen and Publicans'. In no uncertain terms, he urged the Baptists to think again. Why were they forsaking the mainstream of Christianity in both 'Antiquity' and 'modern times'? Was there anyone of note 'in all the golden Regiment of Reformed Divines' who agreed with them? Did not the Papists have

---

73 Letter from Barbara Lamb to Richard Baxter, *Reliquiae Baxterianae* (1696), Appendix iii, 51–52; Thomas Lamb, *Truth Prevailing against the Fiercest Opposition* (1655), 93–97.
74 The dedicatory epistle was dated 11 May 1653, though Thomason did not collect the tract until 23 June.
75 Lamb, *Truth Prevailing*, sigs. A2r–v.
76 Lamb, *Truth Prevailing*, sig. a3v, a4v–br; 2, 48, 85–91.
77 See *Cata-Baptism* (1655), sigs. gv–g2r.

'many subtle Agents' working for the ruin of the Protestant religion by 'secretly incouraging you in your way'? And did not history show that Anabaptism always led to wickedness in the long run?[78]

Goodwin explained that he had three leading Baptist apologists in his sights: John Tombes, Samuel Fisher and William Allen. He lavished praise on Richard Baxter, '*whose memorial throughout all Ages may well be* Malleus Anabaptismi, T*he Maul of Anabaptism*'. Baxter had done 'more real service unto Jesus Christ, and the precious souls of men, then all the Anabaptists' in the land. His *Plain Scripture Proof* (1651) should have been sufficient to extinguish 'the fire of Anabaptism', but since it was still alive, and had been kindled in Goodwin's own house of God, 'by one of the houshold' (i.e. Allen), Goodwin had written his own treatise. Part I would set out fifty-eight considerations designed to settle common scruples touching baptism, while Part II would answer Allen's *Some Baptismal Abuses*.[79]

The schism depressed Goodwin, and he had penned a gloomy and somewhat paranoid 'Admonition' to the 'remainder' of his 'Flock'. He explained that he was an old man, and this might be his last book, so he wanted to warn them against contemporary perils. He listed 'the principal Sects' that threatened to waylay the godly. First and foremost were the Quakers, 'that late Diabolical Sect'. Under 'a pretence and shew of mortification', they taught people to follow the light within, without examining 'whether this light be darkness'. Then there were the Anabaptists, who majored in pride, 'turbulency of spirit', and 'the despising of those that are good'. Antinomianism was 'a Schole of Lawless Liberty' that had logically issued in 'Ranting', for 'a Ranter is nothing but an Antinomian sublimated'. Seekers disregarded Scripture 'upon pretence of looking after something higher'. Quinto-Monarchians were men of a 'fierce and restless spirit', who used 'unhallowed methods and wayes' to bring in the rule of Christ 'before the times of the other Monarchies be fulfilled'. Behemites or Mysterialists would 'allegorize quite away' the authority of the Scriptures, and tempt them away with 'mysteries' and strange expressions. Contra-Remonstrancie would foster 'carelessness and security' and plant 'hard thoughts' about the God of grace. Arians would deny the deity of the Holy Ghost. And High-Presbyterians would tell you that 'you must submit your faith to the test of men, and be content to be at a classical, or Synodical allowance for what you shall beleeve'. Lurking in the shadows were 'cunning Emissaries of the Romish faction, Jesuites, and others' who 'insinuate themselves with all, or most, of the prementioned Sects'. Against such enemies, the congregation had to stand firm in its faith, supporting each other and 'not suffering any person to straggle'. They should always prize the ordinances of God and value 'the language, phrases and terms of the Scriptures'.[80]

If Goodwin was sounding more conservative and wary than in the 1640s, the reason lay with the context rather than with the preacher. He had always warned his congregation against heresies, and he was as hostile as ever to high Presbyterians

---

78 *Cata-Baptism*, sigs. a2r–a3r, b2r, c2r–v.
79 *Cata-Baptism*, sigs. cr, dr–v, e2v, e4v.
80 *Cata-Baptism*, 'An Admonition', sigs. ir–k4v.

and high Calvinists. But the major challenges to his congregation came from radical Protestants like the Socinians and the Baptists, and Goodwin's response highlighted his residual conservatism. He was determined to keep within the 'main current' of the Christian tradition on the Trinity and infant baptism. The Baptists, like the Socinians, were going out on a limb and rejecting centuries of Christian consensus. Goodwin was more cautious, more self-consciously mainstream, and more respectful of churchly tradition.

Catabaptism was read and pondered by Thomas Lamb, who also studied the anti-Baptist works of Baxter and Nathaniel Homes. By 1658, both Lamb and Allen were having serious doubts about their separatist and Baptist principles. Their congregation now had over one hundred members, but their former mentor, Samuel Fisher, had shaken their confidence by joining the Quakers. Lamb and Allen started to question the wisdom of 'unchurching all besides themselves'. Both men entered into correspondence with Richard Baxter, who encouraged their new direction. When Lamb raised the possibility of returning to Goodwin's congregation, Baxter demurred. He raised no objection to Goodwin's theology, but queried his ecclesiology. If Goodwin's congregation was 'disorderly gathered out of many Parishes without necessity', Lamb would be better to join his local parish church, since 'Cohabitation is the Aptitude requisite to Church-Membership'. Lamb wrote to Baxter in January 1659, explaining that he had 'been at Mr. G's Congregation ... to acknowledge my Sin in separating from them upon such silly Grounds'. But he had also told the church that two things hindered him from becoming a member: he was still obligated to 'the poor People I now serve' at Lothbury, and he had 'Scruples' about the schismatic tendencies of Independency itself. He told Baxter that Goodwin's church had 'made a Vote to receive me when my Spirit should be free to return, and indeed always have manifested much love to me'. Although Goodwin was 'for Free Communion', and was willing to endorse Baxter's ecumenical 'Uniting Draught', Lamb was now deeply suspicious of 'Independant Principles'.[81] The Lothbury General Baptist church was dissolved in mid-1659.[82] Lamb returned to the parish church rather than to Goodwin's congregation, and Allen composed *A Retraction of Separation* (1660).

The Baptist schism had delivered a severe blow to Goodwin's congregation, and the church was furthered depleted by a series of bereavements. Henry Overton had died in 1648, and at least ten more prominent members passed away in the 1650s.[83] Other members moved out of London to the suburbs or the country, and even if they continued to commute to the church, their involvement must have diminished.[84] The congregation attracted new members like Tobias Conyers, and

---

81 *Reliquiae Baxterianae*, Appendix iii, 51–53, 57, 64–65.
82 See the letter from Thomas Lamb in *The Correspondence of Richard Baxter*, ed. G. Nuttall and N. Keeble, 2 vols (Oxford, 1991), i. 395.
83 Bartholomew Lavender (1650); Nathaniel Lacy (1652); Thomas Devenish (1654); Daniel Taylor, William Godfrey and Joseph Gallant (1655); and John Dye, Thomas Alderne, George Cook and Thomas Morris (1657). Evidence from wills and St Stephen's parish records.
84 See More, 'Congregationalism', 232.

threatened by 'the fearfull apostacy, which is endeavoured by some to be fastened upon you, with plausible pretences'. The plotters were 'such who for the most part had neither heart nor hand to engage with you, and the good people of the nation, in the day of straights and extremities'. Now that things were easy, they were trying to persuade Cromwell 'by plausible pretences' to rebuild 'that old structure of government, which God by you and them [the godly], had signally borne testimony against, and destroyed'. The office of king had been abolished in March 1649, and condemned by 'the honest party'. If Cromwell was talked into resurrecting the title by 'your new pretending friends', then 'blasphemy, ruine and confusion, would inevitably follow'. Out of 'faithfulnesse to the good old cause', the pastors were obliged to bear 'our testimonies against this retrogradation'. Echoing Cromwell's famous letter to the Scottish Covenanters, the signatories wrote: 'We beseech you, in the bowels of Jesus Christ, remember what God did for you and us, at Marston Moore, Naseby, Penbrook, Preston, Tredah, Dunbarr and Worcester'. To forget such deliverances and take up the Crown would be to 'return unto Egipt'. If the Protector ignored 'the sighes, groanes, and teares' of the faithful, 'deliverance will arise to his forsaken cause, and people, some other way'.

This was a warning of the most serious kind. If he took the crown, England's Moses would be held personally responsible for reversing England's Exodus. In the face of such petitions from both the army and the gathered churches, the Protector was left little choice. In May 1657 Cromwell accepted the Humble Petition and Advice, which allowed him to nominate his successor, but he refused the Crown. However, his investiture under the new constitution, which took place in a grand ceremony in Westminster Hall on 26 June, was hardly calculated to reassure his critics. Clarendon later noted that there was 'nothing wanting to a perfect formal coronation but a crown and an archbishop'.[92]

Goodwin never commented on the ceremony but his disillusionment with Cromwell was now complete. In late June or early July, perhaps to coincide with the investiture, he published a stinging attack on the Cromwellian church settlement, entitled Βασανισται [Basanistai]. Or the Triers or Tormentors Tried and Cast.[93] For some time, he had been concerned that the Triers were preventing young Arminians from securing parish livings, and according to Marchamont Nedham he had even made a formal appeal against the Commissioners, 'on behalf of another, to his Highness the Lord Protector, before whom the Appeal was admitted, and the Business heard'.[94] This may be the encounter with Cromwell which Goodwin had referred to in *The Six Book-Sellers*: 'I not long since plainly expressed my self to the chief Ruler of the land, that my sence was not to have any *Toleration* granted by the Magistrat, to any sort, or sect, of erroneous men whatsoever; yea and further, that it was not in the Magistrate's power to grant any'.[95] Goodwin seems to have

---

92 See R. Sherwood, *Oliver Cromwell: King in all but Name, 1653–58* (Stroud, 1997), 95–104.
93 Thomason's copy is dated 23 July, but Marchamont Nedham's reply has a dedicatory epistle to Cromwell dated 8 July 1657.
94 Nedham, *The Great Accuser Cast Down*, 60.
95 *Six Book-Sellers*, 5.

felt that Cromwell needed a lesson on the limits of his authority: toleration was not a privilege granted by a powerful Lord Protector, for the magistrate could have no lawful power to intrude in matters of religion. But if Goodwin's record of service could still secure him a one-to-one meeting with Oliver, he was frustrated by his lack of regular access to the Protector and the Council of State. He later complained that the Triers had 'the daily opportunity of access to their ear, whereof I am as good as wholly deprived'.[96] Excluded from the heart of the action in Whitehall, he made his voice heard through the press.

Significantly, *Basanistai* was issued by Henry Eversden. Like Goodwin's previous publishers (Henry Cripps and Lodowick Lloyd), Eversden had a shop in Popes Head Alley. He had previously published Goodwin's funeral sermon for Daniel Taylor, but it is not clear why Goodwin switched allegiance from Cripps and Lloyd, who had served him well since 1649 and were still in business. The most plausible explanation is that the two booksellers had gone their separate ways after 1655. Lloyd started to publish mystical works by Jacob Boehme and Isaac Penington junior. Cripps continued to sell Independent books, but was perhaps unwilling to sell pamphlets attacking Cromwell. Whatever the reasons, Eversden was to act as Goodwin's publisher from 1657 to 1660 and beyond, for it was he who published *A Being Filled with the Spirit* in 1670.

Goodwin presented his critique of the Triers as an old man's final testimony. Before he passed on, he was determined to bequeath a solemn warning against the evil of state power in religion.[97] He admitted that the Triers themselves were often 'men of conscience and worth'. He had no vendetta against those who appointed them, for it had been 'the great contest and strife of my soul' to defend 'the Parliamentary and present Government'. Yet he had fundamental objections to the 'office' itself. There had been 'a kind of fatal unhappinesse incident to the Rulers of the Earth professing Christianity' – almost invariably, these rulers thought that they could give the Gospel a helping hand by using 'that Authority and power which is vested in them, for other [i.e. civil] purposes'. Making the false assumption that Christ's provisions for his church were insufficient, they had supplemented them with 'new Laws and Ordinances ... to regulate the judgements or Consciences of men, in matters of Faith, or things appertaining unto God, which is his appropriate Sovereigntie'. Wresting the 'golden scepter' from Christ's hands, rulers had seized dominion over men's faith and Christ's church.[98]

The Triers were the latest manifestation of Christendom's tragic flaw, and the main body of the tract presented eighteen arguments against the institution. Most fundamentally, Goodwin rested his case on a rigorous New Testament primitivism. Christ had provided the church with everything it needed for the propagation of the Gospel. He had given no warrant whatsoever to the civil magistrate 'for the erecting of any such authority in the Church', and he had never granted power to a few men 'to exercise any such dominion over the faith, judgements, or consciences

---

96 *Triumviri*, sig. a4.
97 *Basanistai*, 'To the Reader'.
98 *Basanistai*, 'To the Reader'.

of far greater numbers of men'. State-erected institutions like the Triers were an 'affront' to Christ, since they implied that he had not been wise or careful enough to establish them himself. Christ had given individual congregations 'a liberty or power to chuse for themselves ... a spiritual shepherd', so the Triers 'entrench upon the spiritual rights and priviledges of the people of God', as well as undermining the rights of lay patrons.[99]

The Triers had been 'mounted upon thrones of power and authority' far above their predecessors the bishops. Though they were fallible men, and drawn from a single faction (the high Calvinists), they had been granted dominion over all other parties, 'contrary to all approved principles of State-policy, and much more Christian piety'. It was well known that they would veto any young man for simply professing 'those great and important truths' of universal redemption and sufficient saving grace. An ex-thief or former murderer was more likely to win their approval than a godly Arminian. Their dominion over others amounted to an assault on English liberty: 'never was there the like insufferable yoak of slavery fastened about the necks of the free born people here'. The Triers were like the 'Spanish Inquisition', for they 'act so Inquisition-like'; they 'grinde the faces, and break the bones of men of signall piety and worth, who know more of God, and of his Gospell, and Grace here, than themselves'. The power of the Triers was 'of the house and lineage of the Papall'.[100]

The logic of the argument was driving Goodwin towards a flat denial of the power of civil magistrates in matters of religion. He chastised 'the professing powers of this world' for their 'itching desires to be officious unto Jesus Christ' by offering to supplement his provisions with 'projections and inventions of their own'. Indeed, civil magistrates had no more power 'than what hath been regularly vested in them, or conferred upon them by the people'. If a people conferred a power over conscience on their rulers, they were being spiritually irresponsible, and giving away something that was not theirs to give. 'God reserves the legislative power over the consciences of men unto himself alone', Goodwin insisted. Thus 'any donation of what is not the givers own, or which he hath no right to give, is a nullity, or nothing passes to another by vertue of it'.[101]

Goodwin was aware of the objections people would raise to his position. If 'the Parochicall Congregations' were allowed to choose their own minister, surely most would elect 'either Popish, or ignorant, or ungodly, or malignant persons'? Faced with this problem, Goodwin refused to compromise his insistence on devolution, decentralisation and subsidiarity. The 'hyper-archepiscopall' and 'super-metropolitan' power of the Triers should be dismantled, and each parish should choose its own minister. 'Let their Kingdome be divided', concluded Goodwin, 'and given to the Congregations of the Land'.[102]

This was a challenge the Protectorate could not afford to ignore. The regime was disturbed by 'how industriously this Book of Mr Goodwin hath been dispersed,

---

99 *Basanistai*, n.p.
100 *Basanistai*, n.p.
101 *Basanistai*, n.p.
102 *Basanistai*, n.p.

and how high a prejudice arose among the more undiscerning sort' because of it.[103] Almost immediately, the government propagandist Marchamont Nedham was set to work on a reply, *The Great Accuser Cast Down: Or a Publick Trial of Mr John Goodwin at the Bar of Religion and Right Reason*. It was an abusive satire, strikingly reminiscent of John Vicars' *Coleman-Street Conclave Visited* (1648). In his dedicatory epistle to Cromwell and throughout the tract, Nedham mocked and vilified his quarry. 'The Great Accuser' was 'a Turbulent man', 'another Hector', a man who wished to 'usurp the Papal Chair', 'a meer Brat of Arminius', a 'Mongrel-Politician'. It was customary to bring 'a strange creature' before princes for their entertainment, said Nedham, and he was exhibiting 'one of the strangest'. Goodwin was 'a leader of that savage Herd, which would make the Prince or Magistrate but a Man of Straw'.[104]

Nedham poured cold water on Goodwin's primitivism. Christ had not detailed each and every means to be used in the propagation of the Gospel, and magistrates were at liberty to use their discretion in this area. The Triers did not have authority over every congregation in the land, but only over the public churches and public preachers. Gathered churches had been given unprecedented liberty under Cromwell.[105] Goodwin's real concern, alleged Nedham, was 'to let in Arminians into a few Parishes', and he hardly cared if his policy allowed in lots of popish, superstitious and malignant clergy at the same time. He was 'very angry on the behalf of those of his Sons, whom he hath begotten through his perverting of the Gospel'.[106]

Goodwin was also deeply confused. Where exactly did the right of choosing and approving ministers lie – with the parishioners, the gathered churches, local presbyteries, or county commissioners? All of these were mentioned in the tract, and Goodwin did not seem able to choose between them. In lambasting the Triers he was contradicting himself, for back in February 1652 he and John Price had signed the original petition to Parliament calling for the establishment of 'two such Ordinances as you now write against'. Now, however, he was at one with those who espoused 'Fifth Monarchy Principles', and he was at least as daft as 'his Brother [Roger] Williams' who called for the abolition of tithes and the toleration of Jews, Turks, Papists and Pagans.[107] It was hard to believe that 'the man was ever acquainted with the Schools of Reason'.[108]

Nedham's attack infuriated Goodwin. In his preface to *Triumviri*, he admonished the Triers for employing 'that infamous and unclean character' to defend them. But he detected another hand behind the book, that of the Cromwellian Independent Philip Nye. Nye and Nedham had combined to traduce him.[109] In late August, Goodwin's camp struck back. Henry Eversden issued a bitter

103 Nedham, *The Great Accuser*, 'To his most serene Highness, Oliver, Lord Protector'.
104 Nedham, *The Great Accuser*, sigs ar–b2v, 54, 88, 118.
105 Nedham, *The Great Accuser*, 1–18.
106 Nedham, *The Great Accuser*, 44, 54–56, 70.
107 Nedham, *The Great Accuser*, 47–49, 64–65. See also 124 for another comparison with Williams.
108 Nedham, *The Great Accuser*, 130.
109 *Triumviri*, sigs. a3v–a4.

indictment of Cromwell, *A Letter of Addresse to the Protector*. It was published under the initials 'D.F.', but we know from a later catalogue that its author was Goodwin's protégé Tobias Conyers.[110] He wasted no time laying into Cromwell: 'I have stood by you as an Idle spectator upon this deck of State ever since your Lordship laid hold on the Helm of English affairs, and have seen you for your own safety and interest unhappily constrained to cast over board the most considerable rights and priviledges of the people'. By employing Nedham, 'that mercenary soul', the regime had brought discredit on itself.[111]

A Letter of Addresse went on to develop some remarkable arguments. According to Conyers, the unjust politics of the Protectorate flowed from its narrow, inequitable and elitist Calvinist theology. Believing that only the elect had any chance of salvation, the Calvinist Cromwell neglected 'the great heape of your Subjects'. Like the God he worshipped, he cared only for the elect few. A better politics would emerge from a more generous Arminian theology, for if God loved everyone, then his worshippers were obliged to pursue policies that were inclusive, impartial and equitable.[112] Alongside this strikingly theological analysis of politics, Conyers also advanced a classical republican critique of the Protector, using an example cited years earlier by Henry Parker.[113] Cromwell was compared to Alexander the Great, who set out to 'vindicate the provinces from the Persian Luxury and Tyranny, [only] to fall himself into the same evils'. Goodwin was the contemporary equivalent of 'good Calisthenes', one of Alexander's faithful counsellors who were troubled 'to see their general in the Persian garbe, forgetting his own severe virtue and discipline, to prefer the manners and customs of the conquered to those of his own victorious followers'. The author commended Goodwin for 'his known abilities', 'his Republick-interest and good affection to the government', and his willingness to appear 'for the common cause of liberty which men began to give up for lost'. The regime's disdain for Goodwin was indicative of its corruption.[114]

A Letter of Addresse was collected by Thomason on 25 August 1657. Two days later, Cromwell's spy chief John Thurloe brought the pamphlet to the attention of the Council of State. The Council noted that it was 'very derogatory of his Highness's honour', and ordered the publisher, Henry Eversden, to be taken 'into custody', though he 'denies any knowledge of the author'. Five members of the Council (Thurloe, Wolseley, Jones, Strickland and Sydenham) were appointed to 'consider the business and report'.[115] Goodwin himself was twice hauled before the Council after the Triers 'turned Informers against me, and accused me ... to the secular powers'. His accusers had excerpted 'certain innocent passages ... transcribed out of my book', and presented them to 'my Judges'. They had even asked 'to be admitted to stand by and hear with what severity I should be reproved for their

---

110 Tobias Conyers, *A Pattern of Mercy* (1660). The appended catalogue of 'Books worth Buying' lists 'A Letter of Address to the late Protector Oliver, by D. F. *alias, Tobias Conyers*'.
111 [Tobias Conyers], *A Letter of Addresse to the Protector* (1657), 1–3.
112 [Conyers], *A Letter of Addresse*, 6–7.
113 See Henry Parker's reference to Alexander and Calisthenes in *Jus Populi* (1644), 49.
114 [Conyers], *A Letter of Addresse*, 20–22.
115 *CSPD* (1657–58), 83, 550.

sakes'. The whole thing reminded Goodwin of the trial of Christ, when the chief priests plotted his downfall.[116]

In the wake of the Triers controversy, Eversden published another work by Conyers, a translation of Arminius, *The Just Mans Defence*.[117] The translation had been completed in 1655, and the manuscript sent to Cromwell. In a dedication dated 5 June 1655, Conyers had styled himself 'Your Highness's most humble servant', and praised Cromwell as one 'in whom so many princely virtues are constellated'. But he had reminded the Protector that as 'a man of War, Liberty was that Motto in your Ensign which encouraged the Soldiers of Christ to fight and pray under you'. Conyers had urged Cromwell to defend 'Christian Liberty' within the Church of England, by defending the right to godly Arminians to take up clerical livings. Instead of being subjected to 'a few unpremeditated Questions ... of some particular men' (the Triers), prospective clergy should simply be asked to subscribe 'a known Confession of Faith drawn up in Scripture terms & phrases'.[118]

By publishing this dedication along with the translation in 1657, Conyers was offering an implicit rebuke to Cromwell, one that reinforced the explicit attacks of *Basanistai* and *A Letter of Address*. But for all their complaints, the Puritan Arminians continued to occupy parish pulpits and enjoy freedom of the press. In late 1657 or early 1658, Goodwin finally published his long-awaited reply to his Calvinist critics, *Triumviri*. The main text (some 372 pages) responded to his three leading adversaries, Resbury, Pawson and Kendall, but in a very long preface (of 143 pages) he also settled scores with Owen, Lamb, Jeanes, Howe and Nedham. He explained that much of the reply to Kendall had been written in 1653–54, before his critic was awarded an Oxford DD and became Dr Kendall. But the publication had been delayed by 'sundry and various interruptions' and the 'infirmities of age'. On 'the advice of friends and Physicians, interdicting me the use of pen and paper', he had been forced to set aside his studies for 'a good part of the year'.[119]

Triumviri was an eagerly awaited book. Henry Oldenburg, a key figure in the Hartlib circle, may have been referring to this title when he wrote to Hartlib from France in January 1658: 'Mr Goodwins book, mentioned by us, I wish we had already in our hands; for yt person useth to have no vulgar conceptions in matters divine'.[120] However, unlike Goodwin's earlier works, *Triumviri* provoked no

---

116 See *Triumviri*, sig. a4; *The Clarke Papers*, ed. C. H. Firth, iii. 118.
117 In a catalogue of books at the end of the tract, Eversden noted that Goodwin's reply to Kendall, Resbury and Pawson was 'in the Press and ready to Publish'. Since Goodwin wrote his Preface to *Triumviri* on 18 November 1657, this suggests that *A Just Mans Defence* was published between September and November and after *A Letter of Address*.
118 *The Just Mans Defence, or The Declaration of the Judgement of James Arminius ... Translated for the Vindication of Truth, by Tobias Conyers* (1657), sigs. A3r–a4v.
119 *Triumviri*, sigs. ar–br.
120 *The Correspondence of Henry Oldenburg*, ed. A. R. Hall and M. B. Hall, vol. i (Madison and Milwaukee, 1965), 150. On 151 n. 5 the editors suggest that Oldenburg was 'probably' referring to John Goodwin, whose *Basanistai* had been published in 1657. John Goodwin certainly seems to be the likeliest candidate. Thomas Goodwin was Dr Goodwin and had not published a significant volume in 1657; Philip Goodwin's *Mystery of Dreames* was collected by Thomason in February

significant reply. John Owen was insulted by the fact that 'after two or three years consideration, in answer to a book of neer 140 sheets of paper, [Goodwin] returnes a scoffing reply to so much of it, as was written in a quarter of an hour'.[121] Moreover, by 1658, orthodox Calvinists were increasingly preoccupied by the challenge of Anglican Arminians like Thomas Pierce, Jeremy Taylor and Peter Heylin. Calvinists like Henry Hickman charged directly at Pierce but glanced at Goodwin. Hickman trundled out the tired old clichés about 'the Ishmael in Coleman street', and took Goodwin to task for his 'vanity, arrogance and ignorance hardly to be equall'd'. Ironically, as Pierce quickly pointed out, Hickman was guilty of mining Goodwin (and others) for learned quotations while failing to acknowledge his sources.[122]

In January 1658, two months after completing his reply to his critics, Goodwin drew up his last will and testament.[123] He styled himself 'John Goodwin of Hackney in the County of Middlesex' which suggests that he had moved his residence out of the City and was commuting back to Coleman Street to preach. It is significant that his preface to *Triumviri*, was not signed (as usual) 'From my study in Coleman Street', but simply 'From my study'.[124] Goodwin's involvement in the day-to-day running of the parish was clearly minimal, and many of the pastoral duties seem to have been carried by the Presbyterian incumbent, William Taylor. Of thirty marriages recorded in the parish register between April 1656 and November 1660, Taylor conducted seventeen and Goodwin only four.[125] Intriguingly, Hackney was also the residence of Mark Hildesley, Thomas Alderne, Owen Rowe and of Goodwin's ancient patron Lady Mary Vere. Moreover, in October 1651, Goodwin had baptised Daniel Taylor's daughter at Hackney.[126] It is likely that his supporters had helped their pastor retire to this pleasant and healthy village, just three miles north-east of the City.[127]

Despite his age, Goodwin declared that he was 'in perfect health and memory'. He bequeathed £10 to the poor of his Independent congregation (to be distributed by Richard Arnold and Samuel Sowden), and £5 to the poor of the Coleman Street parish. The difference between the two donations says much about the closeness of Goodwin's ties to his gathered church, and casts doubt on the assumption that it only attracted the affluent middling sort. Goodwin also

---

1658, and while it may have interested the Hartlib circle, it was not strictly about 'matters divine'. Oldenburg may have been referring to *Basanistai*, but it had been published six months earlier in June/July 1657, whereas *Triumviri* would have been hot off the press.

121 John Owen, *Of the Divine Originall* (1658), 'Epistle Dedicatory'.
122 Thomas Pierce, *The New Discoverer Discover'd* (1659), 285–87, 296–97.
123 NA PROB 11/320.
124 *Triumviri*, 'Preface', sig. q4r.
125 GL MS 4449/2 St Stephens Parish Register. The remaining marriages were conducted by Alderman Andrews and Alderman Atkins (three each), and Mr Offspring, Mr Hopwood and Mr Sheaffield (one each).
126 NA PROB 11/297, Will of Mark Hildesley; NA PROB 11/265, Will of Thomas Alderne; *ODNB* articles on Owen Rowe and Mary Vere; GL MS 4449/2.
127 On the popularity of Hackney as a place of retirement see *The Diary of Samuel Pepys*, ed. R. Latham and W. Matthews, 11 vols (London, 1970–83), x. 165–66.

remembered his old parish, leaving £5 for 'the poore people of the Parish of East Raynham ... whereof I was sometyme Rector'.

But most of the will concerned his family. Several years earlier, in his comments on the death of Daniel Taylor, Goodwin had emphasised that the main purpose of a will was to provide for one's dependents, not to distribute largesse to all and sundry.[128] He left 40 shillings to his brother William. His oldest sons were in considerable debt to their father, and Goodwin promised to cancel John's £400 debt, and Edward's debt of £200. Samuel Goodwin, by contrast, was bequeathed £300, as well as 'All my lands lyeing in the Barrony of Leinster in Ireland'. Goodwin's two unmarried daughters, Sarah and Elizabeth, were also left £300 each to be paid to them either on their twenty-first birthdays or on their marriages. Goodwin's married daughter, Mary Mountague, was left just £5, as were two female servants. What remained ('my goods chattells ready money plate bookes houshould stuffe and personall estate') was bequeathed to his wife Sarah, who was to be executrix of the will, assisted by John and Edward. In total, Goodwin bequeathed £935, cancelled £600 of debts, and left land in Ireland. If making ends meet had been difficult in the late 1640s, he had clearly prospered (if only modestly) since the revolutionary events of 1648–49. With financial income from his Independent congregation, his parish, the sale of his books, (and possibly the state), he was well able to provide for his family.

After Oliver

For all his health problems and anticipations of mortality, Goodwin's career was far from over. The Lord Protector, however, was in his final months. He died on 3 September 1658, the anniversary of his great victories at Dunbar and Worcester. With him gone, the future was uncertain. His son and successor Richard had Presbyterian sympathies and was unlikely to have much time for an Arminian Independent like Goodwin. Moreover, Richard's Protectorate Parliament was dominated by religious conservatives, and in April 1659, it called a public day of fasting and humiliation on account of the 'many blasphemies and damnable heresies' in the land. Alarmed by this threat to toleration, the army rallied to what they now termed 'the Good Old Cause' of civil and religious liberty. In April 1659, an army coup forced the dissolution of Parliament, and shortly afterwards Richard resigned as Protector and the Rump was restored. The leader of the April coup was Oliver Cromwell's brother-in-law, Desborough, a friend of Thomas Alderne.[129] There can be little doubt that Goodwin and his congregation welcomed the army coup, as did most radical Puritans.[130] Their joy was to be short-lived. In October, the army expelled the Rump as it had done in 1653, frustrated at its conservatism. A

---

128 *Mercy in her Exaltation*, 'To the Reader', sig. a4v–br.
129 NA PROB 11/265, Will of Thomas Alderne.
130 See R. Mayers, *1659: The Crisis of the Commonwealth* (Woodbridge, 2004). See also B. Manning, *Revolution and Counter-Revolution in England, Ireland and Scotland, 1658–1660* (London, 2004).

'A MAN OF STRIFE'

Committee of Safety was established under Charles Fleetwood – among its members was Goodwin's follower, Henry Brandreth. It was a short-lived experiment. In December 1659, London apprentices rioted against the army. Samuel Pepys observed that when their petition was read out in Common Council, Brandreth 'inveighed highly against the Insolence of the boys', only to be 'hissed down by the whole Council'.[131] By the close of the month, the Committee of Safety had collapsed, and the Rump Parliament was recalled.

Surprisingly, we know nothing about Goodwin's reaction to these dramatic and chaotic happenings. His silence during the political turmoil of 1659–60 is one of greatest puzzles of his career. His voice had been heard at every moment of crisis during the revolutionary years – in 1642, 1647, 1649, 1653 and 1657. But now, when the Revolution itself was at stake, Goodwin had nothing to say. It is tempting to conclude that he was once more under doctor's orders to desist from pamphleteering, but (as we shall see) he did publish a substantial theological pamphlet in 1659. Perhaps he was, for the first time, genuinely perplexed by events and unclear about the way forward. Having defended the expulsion of the Rump, he could not join the Commonswealthmen who clamoured for its recall. Having clashed with the Protectorate, he could not support the Cromwellians. Having never shown much interest in constructing new constitutional models, he could not add to the proposals made by Harrington and others. But one still might have expected him to speak out on his favourite theme of religious liberty, a hot topic once again in 1659–60, as Presbyterians, Independents and sectarians struggled for control of the political agenda. His silence may reflect the declining influence of his pen and his congregation. From 1640 to the mid-1650s, Goodwin had been one of the most important Puritan pamphleteers, but his days on the frontlines were now over.

What we do hear instead are condemnations of Goodwin. His old foe, William Prynne, denounced *The Obstructors of Justice* in his tract *The Re-publicans and others spurious Good Old Cause*, published in May. Goodwin, Milton, Cook and Bradshaw had gloried in the regicide, 'as the Highest Act of Justice, the Best of Causes, the Greatest Mercy and Deliverance that ever befell the English Nation'.[132]

Goodwin himself stuck with theology. In *The Banner of Justification Displayed* (1659), he used his Epistle to the Reader to reflect on his own theological reputation. To those who called him 'that Ishmael of Colemanstreet', he retorted that Jeremiah was 'a man of strife, and a man of contention to the whole Earth', but was still 'a true Prophet'. Goodwin admitted that if he had capitulated to Owen or Kendall ('great Doctors, and men of Renown, famous in the Congregation of the Contra-Remonstrants'), this would have 'restored me to the Synagogue of the *Orthodox*, out of which I was cast long since, and have remained an Out-cast several years'. The Arminian tenets he had defended had 'divided between the world, and me,

---

131 See C. Tomalin, *Samuel Pepys: The Unequalled Self* (London, 2002), 77–78.
132 William Prynne, *The Re-publicans* (1659), 10. See also William Prynne, *A True and Perfect Narrative of what was done, spoken by and between Mr Prynne, the old and newly Forcibly late secluded Members, the Army Officers, and those now Sitting* (1659), 50.

and kept many good things thereof from me', because they were not favoured by 'the great men' who 'exercise Dominion' over the faith of others 'under the importune claim of being *Orthodox*'.[133] Goodwin admitted that 'now and then' he may 'have taken a step or two out of the common Road', but he had not taken 'this kind of digression' for profit or pleasure. Indeed, 'in matter of Doctrine I never leave the way that is most occupied by pious, sober, and learned men, unless it be either to carry some stumbling stone out of it, or else to fetch in somewhat to make it more smooth and pleasant'.[134]

The book itself was devoted to the theology of justification. It was now seventeen long years since Goodwin had addressed the subject in his first major work, *Imputatio Fidei* (1642). Since then the debate had moved on. Richard Baxter's 'neonomian' theology had reasserted the necessity of good works and obedience in the justification of the sinner, and Anglican theologians like Henry Hammond were travelling even further in the direction of 'moralism'. Many feared that both Baxter and Hammond were undercutting the essential Reformation principle of justification by faith alone (*sola fide*). By the late 1650s, Goodwin wanted to make his own contribution to this debate.

Goodwin argued that the New Testament used the term 'justification' in two different ways.[135] Firstly, 'justification properly so called' was simply *remission of sins*. The Pauline teaching was clear – remission of sins came by faith alone, not by works. The Reformers had been right to teach that justification in this narrow sense (i.e. forgiveness) was by faith alone. Good works, no matter how impressive, could never make atonement for past sins. Such atonement could only be made by Christ's death, and could only be claimed by faith. Christian preachers should have no reservations 'to deliver this positively for a Doctrine of Evangelical Truth, that men are justified by Faith, yea or by Faith alone'. By contrast, Goodwin expressed his 'dislike' of the moralist preachers who taught 'that men are not justified by Faith, or by believing'. This doctrine was 'diametrically opposite to the frequent, cleer, and express words of the Scripture'. Yet Goodwin (like all the mainstream Reformers) had to add two riders: justifying faith was 'spiritfull, lively and active' and would bear fruit in good works; and justifying faith was always 'accompanyed with an unfeigned Repentance'.[136]

The second (broader) way in which the term 'justification' was used in the New Testament was to indicate God's *approbation or commendation* of the saints for their progress in righteousness. Good works were essential for this kind of justification. When the Apostle James wrote that Abraham was 'justified by works' he was not contradicting the Apostle Paul who taught that Abraham was 'justified by faith'. Paul was explaining that Abraham received *forgiveness of sins* on the basis of faith alone, while James was declaring that Abraham received *God's approval* or

---

133 *The Banner of Justification Displayed* (1659), sigs. a3r–a4r.
134 *Banner of Justification*, sig. b4r.
135 Arguably, his doctrine of double justification was similar to that of Martin Bucer. See D. Steinmetz, *Reformers in the Wings* (Oxford, 2001), 89–90.
136 *Banner of Justification*, n. p.

commendation on the basis of his obedience. By distinguishing clearly between these two senses of justification, one could do justice to the New Testament witness. If the mistake of antinomians was to emphasise faith at the expense of repentance and the fruit of good works, the mistake of moralists was to imply that forgiveness of sins was achieved by a good life rather than by faith in Christ's atonement alone.[137]

At both the outset and the close of the English Revolution, Goodwin had published books on the doctrine of justification by faith. It is a reminder that for this most political of divines, matters of eternal salvation still mattered most.

---

137 *Banner of Justification*, n. p.

9

'INFAMOUS FIREBRAND'
1660 AND BEYOND

The Restoration marked the destruction of Goodwin's dreams. Yet as this chapter shows, he somehow escaped with his life despite a royal proclamation against him. He continued to publish significant works and was under surveillance by the authorities. Although his followers were scattered, his books remained in circulation after his death and former disciples continued to promote his principles. And thanks to John Wesley (whose father Samuel had called Goodwin 'that *Infamous Firebrand*'), our subject was to be rescued from obscurity, and hailed as the 'Wycliffe of Methodism'.

Restoration

In February 1660, General Monck marched into London and reinstated the MPs excluded from Parliament in 1648. This decisive reversal of Pride's Purge effectively ended the revolution. Increasingly, the old monarchy seemed to offer the best prospect for a permanent political settlement.[1]

Tobias Conyers was now minister at St Ethelbert's. In a controversial sermon before General Monck and the Lord Mayor in February 1660, on the very eve of the Restoration, he preached eloquently on the text 'Be ye therefore merciful, as your heavenly Father is merciful' (Luke 6.36). Conyers could see which way the wind was blowing. With Presbyterians and Episcopalians poised to regain their former dominance, the prospects for dissenters looked bleak. He urged his listeners to imitate the 'almost incredible clemency and mercy' of God. The Lord was 'a tender-hearted Father', 'full of bowels, pitiful and compassionate towards the children of men ... the Father of Compassions'. 'Let us imitate God in his bounty and liberality', admonished Conyers. Christians should not persecute others for matters of conscience, for 'there is nothing more tender than a mans conscience; the Grasshopper is a burden to it'. Civil magistrates had no authority under the Gospel

---

1 See R. Hutton, *The Restoration: A Political and Religious History of England and Wales, 1658–1667* (Oxford, 1986), chs. 3–4.

to punish men for conscientious opinions 'wholly remote from secular consideration'. However, they should ensure that everyone attended some form of Christian worship on the Lord's Day, and they should punish swearing, 'all immodesty, and violation of the Laws of Nature'. They could even punish blasphemy, if they could find a person 'who could infallibly determine' what blasphemy was.[2]

Conyers' sermon provoked 'the great cry of the City', as Presbyterians and Episcopalians accused him of being 'Schismatical, an Enemy to the Church' and heretical to boot. In an 'Author's Apology' attached to the published sermon, Conyers confessed that 'it is true that I hold communion with, and observe the laws of Piety and holy Charity with that Christian people to whom Mr John Goodwin is Pastour'. But he added that this did not make him a sectarian, because 'in that congregation are persons of greater wisdom, moderation and latitude, then to confine the administration of Ordinances within their own precinct'. Far from being an exclusive sect, Goodwin's gathered church was open and inclusive, freely allowing its members to attend parish churches and giving Conyers 'permission' to perform his ministerial duties. As for being heretical, Conyers was simply being attacked for his Arminian vision of a God who was compassionate towards all his creatures, a theology shared by the Church of England's 'most learned and best beloved children, as Dr. Hamond, Dr. Taylor, Mr. Thorndike, Mr. Thrucross, Mr. Gunning, Mr. Pierce'.[3]

If Conyers was keen to placate his Episcopalian critics, he remained defiantly supportive of toleration for 'all those that dissent in Religion', provided they were peaceable. That Rome, with its pretence to 'high infallibitie' should persecute was understandable; but that Protestants should do so was incomprehensible. As for his brief comment on blasphemy, which had aroused more protest than anything else, Conyers maintained that it was very difficult 'to state the Nature of Blasphemy'. The judicial law of Moses was no longer binding, infallible judges were no longer available, and only in heaven would 'diversity of Opinions' be replaced with 'absolute and entire Love and Unity'.[4]

Conyers' sermon gave powerful expression to two central convictions of his mentor Goodwin – his Arminian belief that God was a great lover of his creature man, and his opposition to coercive uniformity. But the reaction to the sermon showed that the tide had turned decisively against the Independents and the republic. For more than a decade, a small and unrepresentative minority had managed to dominate English politics. Their time was over.

When the Rump finally dissolved itself in March 1660, elections followed, and a new Convention Parliament met in April. It was firmly in favour of a restoration of the monarchy, and heavily stocked with Presbyterians and moderate Anglicans. In mid-May, it passed an attainder of treason against the most notorious deceased regicides – Cromwell, Bradshaw, Ireton and Pride.[5]

---

2 Tobias Conyers, *A Pattern of Mercy: Opened at St Pauls before the Right Honourable the Lord Mayor, and the Lord General Monck, February 12 1659* (1660), 7, 10–11, 29, 8, 27–28.
3 Conyers, *A Pattern of Mercy*, 'The Authors Apology', sigs. A3v–A4v.
4 Conyers, *A Pattern of Mercy*, 'The Authors Apology', sigs. a–a4.
5 Hutton, *The Restoration*, 132–34.

For Goodwin, these were frightening weeks. Next to Hugh Peter, he had been the most ardent clerical champion of the regicide, and he now faced the prospect of execution for treason. Captain John Clarke wrote to John Davenport in New England saying that he thought Goodwin, Nye and Peter would all lose their lives.[6] On Saturday 16 June, Parliament asked the King to issue a proclamation, calling in two books by John Milton (*Eikonoklastes* and *Defensio*), and John Goodwin's *The Obstructors of Justice*, 'written in Defence of the traitorous Sentence against his said late Majesty'. Confiscated copies were to be 'burnt by the Hand of the common Hangman', and both men were to be arrested by the Commons sergeant-at-arms.[7] Two days later, on Monday 18 June, the Commons resolved that Goodwin and his fellow Independent Philip Nye were to be among the twenty persons excepted from the Act of General Pardon and Oblivion, though each would only face 'such Pains, Penalties and Forfeitures (not extending to life), as shall be thought fit to be inflicted on him by another Act'. The unfortunate Hugh Peter, who had lobbied for Charles I's execution, was also excluded from the Act, but was given no such assurance that he would be exempt from capital punishment. Milton, by contrast, was not even named, meaning that he would benefit from the Act despite his forthright defence of the regicide and his bitter attack on *Eikon Basilike*.[8]

On 27 June, the king's council ordered that the proclamation against Milton and Goodwin be issued, though this was not done until August. In July, royalist pamphleteers denounced the two men. George Starkey declared that Peter and Goodwin were 'more punishable' than other men for their part in the regicide, for 'they had a hand in the whole, from beginning to end'. They had 'counselled, contrived, and incouraged these villainies, which ended in murther, and vouched the holy Writ for their warrant, to provoke to the attempt, and defended the fact afterward, both by preaching and writing'.[9] A satirical poem on Cromwell's followers mentioned Goodwin alongside Milton and Peter as one of 'those Black Chaplains that preach'd up Nolls Nose'.[10] The *Devils Cabinet Councell Discovered* pictured Goodwin and Peter sitting in a conspiratorial circle chaired by the Devil – also among the eleven revolutionaries seated with Satan were Cromwell, Saye, John Bradshaw, Thomas Harrison and the republican MP Thomas Scott. The author repeated Clement Walker's allegation that in January 1649 Goodwin had been appointed to eavesdrop on the private conversations of the King and Bishop Juxon.[11] With publicity like this, Goodwin's prospects looked bleak.

When the proclamation against Goodwin and Milton was finally issued on 13 August 1660, it noted that the two men had 'both fled, or so obscure themselves,

---

6 *Letters of John Davenport, Puritan Divine*, ed. I. M. Calder (New Haven, 1937), 177n.
7 *CJ*, viii. 65–66. Parliament's order was printed in *Mercurius Politicus*, 14–21 June 1660, 391.
8 *CJ*, viii. 68.
9 George Starkey, *Royal and Other Innocent Blood Crying Aloud to Heaven* (1660), 19.
10 Colonel Baker, *The Blazing-Star ... Or Nolls Nose* (1660).
11 *The Devils Cabinet-Councell Discovered: or the Mystery and Iniquity of the Good Old Cause* (1660), 39. Intriguingly, the title is identical to the subtitle of Acontius's work, *Satans Stratagems, or the Devils Cabinet-Council Discovered* (1648).

4 John Goodwin and Hugh Peters seated in Cromwell's hellish council, frontispiece to *The Devils Cabinet Councell* (1660).

that no endeavours used for their apprehension can take effect, whereby they might be brought to Legal Tryal, and deservedly receive condigne punishment for their Treasons and Offences'. But sheriffs, magistrates, JPs and university officials were ordered to confiscate all copies of the offending books, and have them 'publickly burnt' by the hangman.[12] The books were duly burnt at the Sessions House in the Old Bailey in August and September, and there may have been similar book-burning ceremonies elsewhere.[13] On 13 August, the very day on which the proclamation against Goodwin and Milton was issued, the Commons decided that Goodwin and Nye would face no further penalties if they agreed never to accept or exercise 'any Office, Ecclesiastical, Civil or Military, or any

12 By the King, *A Proclamation for calling in, and suppressing of two Books written by* John Milton ... *And also a third Book Intituled,* The Obstructors of Justice, *written by* John Goodwin (1660).
13 See *The Life Records of John Milton*, ed. J. M. French, 5 vols (New Brunswick, NJ, 1949–58), iv. 334–38: *Parliamentary Intelligencer*, September 3–10 1660, 589; *Mercurius Publicus*, September 6–13 1660, 578. See also *The Diary of Bulstrode Whitelocke, 1605–1675*, ed. R. Spalding (Oxford, 1990), 613.

other publick Employment' anywhere in England or Wales.[14] Accordingly, on 6 September, a general vestry at St Stephen's elected William Taylor vicar of the parish, 'the vicaradge beinge voide by act of Parliament'.[15]

Contemporaries were astonished at the relative good fortune of Goodwin and Milton. According to Gilbert Burnet, 'the sparing of these persons was much censured', for the two men had defended the regicide with as much zeal and to greater effect than Hugh Peter, who was condemned to death. As Burnet explained, 'Goodwin had so often not only justified but magnified the putting the king to death, both in his sermons and books, that few thought he could have been either forgot or excused: for Peter and he were the only preachers that spoke for it in that strain'. Burnet speculated on the reasons for Goodwin's escape: 'But Goodwin had been so zealous an Arminian, and how sown such division among all the sectaries upon these heads, that it was said this procured him friends. Upon what account soever it was, he was not censured'.[16]

Goodwin's relief at his own survival was mixed with despair at the destruction of the republic. He must have watched in dismay as former allies crumbled in the face of resurgent royalism. Owen Rowe made an abject apology for his part in the regicide.[17] He was imprisoned in the Tower of London alongside his old friend and ally Isaac Pennington who had not signed the death warrant. Pennington, who was in his seventies, died in the Tower in 1660, and Rowe, now in his sixties, died the following year. Goodwin's bookseller, Henry Eversden, rushed out at least four royalist tracts in 1660, though whether he did so willingly or under duress is unclear. Two years later he published a book by John Gauden, the probable author of *Eikon Basilike*, entitled *Stratoste Aiteutikon: A Just Invective against those of the Army and their Abettors, Who Murthered King Charles I* (1662). Unsurprisingly, Goodwin's books were conspicuously absent from the appended catalogue of Eversden's publications.[18]

Goodwin, who had trumpeted the regicide as an act of the highest justice, now lived through the trial and execution of his fellow revolutionaries. In mid-October, ten regicides were put to death for treason, including Hugh Peter, John Cook, Thomas Harrison and Miles Corbet. According to Pepys, Harrison's execution was greeted with 'great shouts of joy'.[19] The gruesome spectacle of public punishment inflicted on these men was a graphic demonstration of the power of the Restoration state and the destruction of the revolutionary cause. On 30 January 1661 (the anniversary of the regicide), the corpses of Cromwell, Ireton, Pride and

---

14 *CJ*, viii.118.
15 GL MS 4458/1, f. 255.
16 Gilbert Burnet, *The History of My Own Time*, ed. O. Airy, 2 vols (Oxford, 1897), i. 283.
17 *State Trials*, v. 1204–05.
18 The 1660 tracts were R. W., *The Originall of the Dominion of Princes ... or the Kings Prerogative instituted by God, and proved from the Holy Scriptures to be Jure Divino*; *The History of his Sacred Majesty Charles the II ... Begun from the Murther of his Royall Father*; *The Subjects Joy for the Kings Restoration*; *A Knot Untied, or The Allegiance Sworn to the King, no Breach of Allegiance due unto God*.
19 See H. Nenner, 'The trial of the regicides: retribution and treason in 1660', in Nenner, ed., *Politics and the Political Imagination in Later Stuart Britain* (Woodbridge, 1997), 21–42.

Bradshaw were disinterred, desecrated and hanged at Tyburn.[20] Although this marked the climax of the recriminations, old republicans could not sleep secure in their beds. As late as June 1662, Sir Henry Vane was put on trial, despite having neither signed the death warrant nor publicly defended the regicide.[21]

Vane's execution reflected persistent fears of a sectarian coup. In January 1661, the Fifth Monarchist Thomas Venner had caused panic across London, when he led a minor uprising of fellow zealots. The revolt was crushed, and Venner and thirteen of his followers executed, but royalists were petrified of another rising of Baptists, Quakers and republicans. The fact that Venner was associated with a congregation in Coleman Street meant that Goodwin and his followers were lumped together with the rebels. Six leading members of Goodwin's church (which was obviously still functioning) hastily issued a *Declaration* explaining that their own principles were 'diametrically repugnant' to those of Venner. They accused the Fifth Monarchy Men of three fundamental errors. Firstly, they had tried 'to accelerate and hasten' Christ's Second Coming 'by force and violence', rather than accepting that no man could predict the timing of his Return. Secondly, Goodwin's people rejected the Fifth Monarchists' 'unchristian and unman-like principle, after the custome of Mahomet, to propagate Religion by the sword: The Gospel we own and profess, is not *Evangelium armatum*, an armed Gospel; the weapons of that warfare, wherein we serve as Christians, are not carnal, but spiritual'. Thirdly, Goodwin's congregation declared, 'we are far from disowning the present Powers and Dominions of the earth, and in particular that of his Majesty, utterly renouncing that principle, whether appropriately Papal, or by whomsoever owned or professed, That all temporal power is founded in grace'.[22]

Despite the clarity of the *Declaration*, and Goodwin's earlier denunciations of the 'Quinto-Monarchians',[23] the dirt stuck, and Gilbert Burnet later confidently pronounced that Goodwin 'headed' the Fifth Monarchy Men.[24] The *Declaration* is the last we hear from the gathered church, but there is reason to think that the congregation continued to meet. As we shall see below, Goodwin lived in the suburb of Bethnal Green after the Restoration, and he and his wife maintained links with an active network of sympathisers.

Moreover, the parish of St Stephen's continued to be a hotbed of sectarian activity, with the congregations of Thomas Lamb and Henry Jessey still meeting there. Abraham Cowley's anti-sectarian satire, performed before the court in 1663, was naturally titled *Cutter of Coleman Street*.[25] Goodwin's followers were still active

---

20 See L. L. Knoppers, *Historicizing Milton: Spectacle, Power and Poetry in Restoration England* (Athens, GA, 1994), 42ff.
21 On Vane's execution see J. Coffey, 'From apocalyptic Witness to Whig hero: the death of Sir Henry Vane the younger', in Thomas Freeman and Thomas Meyer, eds, *Martyrdom and Sanctity in Early Modern England* (Woodbridge, 2007).
22 *A Declaration on the Behalf of the Church of Christ usually meeting in Coleman-street, in Communion with Mr John Goodwyn, against the Late Insurrection made in the City of London* (1661), 3–4.
23 John Goodwin, 'An Admonition to the Sheep of Christ', section 10, *Cata-Baptism* (1655).
24 Burnet, *History of my Own Time*, ed. O. Airy, i. 120–21.
25 See Kirby, 'Parish', 223–27.

in parish affairs. John Price, Captain Stacy and Samuel Sowthen continued to attend vestry meetings after the Restoration, and in March 1661 the general vestry voted against Theophilus Alford, whom the Bishop of London had proposed as the new vicar to replace the deceased William Taylor. A serious attempt was made to recruit Goodwin's Arminian protégé, Tobias Conyers, instead. In May 1661 the general vestry ordered the churchwardens to draw up 'a Petition to present to the bishop for the induction of Mr Conyers: May the 20th 1661'.[26] The lobbying did not succeed, for Alford was inducted on 29 May. But he was never popular, and eventually resigned in 1664.[27]

Despite losing his living, Goodwin quickly returned to the fray. His post-Restoration output has been almost entirely neglected by scholars, but it is substantial and revealing. His first publication, in 1661, was a commendatory epistle to a short work by Thomas Goad, one of the English commissioners to the Synod of Dort. Goad had died in 1638, but before his death he had written a disputation 'concerning the Necessity and Contingency of Events in the World'. Goodwin, writing under his initials, explained that he had acquired the author's unpublished manuscript 'by buying some of the Books of his deceased Amanuensis'. This was quite a coup, for the disputation showed that before his death Goad had abandoned the Calvinism of Dort. It condemned Calvinist necessitarianism and the compatibilist concept of free will. High Calvinists taught that God had necessarily determined events by 'an irresistible Decree' such that 'they should inevitably come to pass'. This, Goad argued, was the Heathen doctrine of necessity beloved by Stoics and Muslims, and (whatever its proponents might claim) it made God the author of sin. Goad himself favoured the Arminian view that 'God hath decreed that many things should be done voluntarily by his creatures', and that men had 'a liberty of contradiction, to do, or not to do'. Because God had given man this libertarian free will, there was a significant element of 'contingency' in events.[28]

Goad's disputation was printed by William Leak, and was also appended to a separate work by the Anglican Arminian, Laurence Womock.[29] It was another indication that despite their profound political and ecclesiological differences, Goodwin and the Anglican Arminians could join forces against Calvinist predestinarianism. Yet Goodwin was deeply uneasy about other trends within Anglican theology. In 1662, he wrote a fourteen-page 'Advertisement to the Reader' for Zachary Mayne's book on the doctrine of justification. Mayne was an Oxford protégé of Thomas Goodwin, but he had felt the lure of Biddle's anti-Trinitarianism and was enamoured with Baxter's views on justification. In the preface to his work, he distinguished four positions on justification. At one extreme stood Luther and the Antinominans (and presumably most high Calvinists) who 'banish all consideration of works' from justification; at the other extreme stood an unnamed

---

26 GL MS 4458/1, f. 261.
27 See Kirby, 'Parish', 215–20, and G. Hennessey, *Novum Repertorium Ecclesiasticum Parochiale Londinense* (London, 1898), 385.
28 Thomas Goad, *Stimluus Orthodoxus; sive Goadus Redivivus* (1661).
29 Laurence Womock, *The Result of False Principles* (1661).

group (the Anglican moralists) who taught that 'the righteousness of faith is an holy temper of heart, or a Christ-like Nature in a mans soul'. Mayne rejected both of these views, and praised Goodwin and Baxter for developing mediating positions. Alluding to Goodwin's *Banner of Justification*, he noted that 'Mr Goodwin allowes Evangelical Works a share in Justification, but then it is only in that part or Kinde of Justification which consists in the divine approbation, but excludes them out of that part or that kinde of Justification which consists in remission of sins, which yet he affirmes is the strict Gospel-justification; and for this, he makes faith alone to be the condition of it'. Baxter, by contrast, was closer to the Anglican moralists, for he made 'Faith and Evangelical Works together the compleat condition of that Justification which consists in pardon of sins, as well as of the divine approbation'.[30]

Goodwin's 'Advertisement' explained his latest thinking on the issue. 'I know no Doctrine greater than that of justification', he declared, 'within the whole Hemisphere of Christian Profession'. Goodwin was concerned that some Protestant divines seemed to be returning to the old doctrine of justification by inherent righteousness. Mayne had rightly torn into 'so Anti-Evangelical a notion' with Pauline 'passion'. The Anglican moralists seemed to forget that sins needed to be forgiven – or did they actually believe that God forgave our sins because of our 'inherent righteousness'? To teach this would be to 'wholly evacuate … the propiatory sacrifice of Christ'. Godliness met with God's moral approval, *sensu morali*, but it did not legally acquit the individual of sin, *sensu forensi*. God declared believers to be forgiven simply because they had faith in Christ's atoning death, not because they were morally righteous. Good works were necessary for justification in the *secondary* sense of divine approbation (God's final 'well done!' to the godly person), but they had no part in justification in its *primary* sense of remission of sins. The greatest threat to the doctrine of justification came from theologians 'of a Legal spirit'.[31]

By attacking 'Legalism' like this, Goodwin was distancing himself from Anglicans in the mould of Hammond and Taylor. He may have agreed with their Arminianism (a vital reform of the Reformation), but he disagreed with their doctrine of justification (a betrayal of the Reformation). Written against the background of the Anglican royalist triumph, Goodwin was in no mood for compromise. The newly fashionable theology was 'anti-Evangelical' and therefore anti-Protestant. In their theology, as in their ecclesiology, their worship and their coercive uniformity, the high Anglicans were beating a path back to popery.

Goodwin's major post-Restoration work was an anonymous 500-page catechism, *A Door Opening unto the Christian Religion* (1662), sold in Popes head alley (where Cripps and Lloyd had a shop), at the Gray-hound in Pauls Churchyard (where Eversden was based), and in Fleet Street (possibly by William Leak).[32]

---

30 Zachary Mayne, *St Pauls Travailing-pangs with his Legal-Galatians or A Treatise of Justification* (1662), 'Preface', sigs. A3-A7.
31 J.G., 'An Advertisement to the Reader', in Mayne, *St Pauls Travailing-pangs*, sigs. c-c7v.
32 On the authorship, see Appendix.

Goodwin may have been working on the catechism prior to the Restoration, but some passages – if not the whole work – were clearly written after 1660. The book followed the normal pattern of catechisms by addressing the three major elements of Christian identity – doctrine, ethics and worship. It broke from the normal catechetical pattern by not using the Apostles Creed (an indication, perhaps, of Goodwin's radical Protestant suspicion of creeds), but it did contain substantial sections on the Lord's Prayer and the Decalogue. The format dictated that this was a work light on apparatus, and Goodwin did not cite authorities or attack opponents by name. The references were overwhelmingly Scriptural. However, the author did allow himself to quote some of his favourite authors, like Brightman and Grotius, and the genre enabled him to make polemical points.[33] The work had three obvious purposes: theological, pastoral and political. It would summarise Goodwin's mature theology; offer spiritual counsel; and critique the Restoration settlement.

Because of its length and scope, the catechism allowed Goodwin to recapitulate many of his key theological emphases on Trinitarianism, Arminianism, the salvation of heathens, justification, millenarianism, paedobaptism, and congregationalism. At numerous points, he echoed his earlier works. Thus in defending Arminianism, he deployed the theological and ethical arguments he had been using since the late 1640s. 'God is a great lover of that Creature of his, which is called Man', Goodwin insisted. To deny that men had 'sufficiency of power' to repent and believe was to turn God into a tyrant and give the unrepentant the perfect excuse for their behaviour. God's actions were always 'reasonable' and in accordance with 'equity'. He was 'zealously, rejoycingly, triumphantly addicted to do good unto his poor Creatures'. So it was that every human being had a realistic opportunity to repent and believe, even pagans who had never heard of Christ. 'The glory of the Gospel doth not stand in this, that there was no Salvation in the world before that [i.e. Christianity] entered into it'.[34]

As well as being a summation of Goodwin's theological progress, *A Door* also allows us to listen to Goodwin the Puritan pastor. The godliness that Goodwin preached had lost none of its rigour or passion. He waxed eloquent on mortification and self-denial, and defended extemporary prayer against set liturgy. 'A prayer newly conceived by the help of the Spirit of God,' wrote Goodwin, 'comes warm from the heart'. By comparison, 'the womb of memory, and much more of a book, is but a cold place'. Extemporary prayer gave the Holy Spirit 'full liberty'; 'a set form of words' confined him. God required 'fervency' in prayer, not dull routine.[35]

This defence of Puritan piety, with its stress on the motions of the Spirit and the zeal of the believer, was politically loaded. Goodwin was endeavouring to stoke the flames of godly fervour in a Restoration culture that was overtly hostile to 'enthusiasm'.[36] His book was a rebuke to courtly hedonists and churchly formalists,

---

33 Grotius was cited on the title-page.
34 *A Door opening unto the Christian Religion* (1662), 95, 122–26, 261, 181.
35 *Door*, 186, 188, 219.
36 See S. Achinstein, *Literature and Dissent in Milton's England* (Cambridge, 2003), ch. 6: 'Enthusiasm'.

and he inveighed against immorality and idolatry. Moreover, he placed contemporary events within an explicitly millenarian framework, and saw three signs of the last days around him: firstly, 'an extraordinary Spirit of security, sensualitie, and earthly-mindednesse working at an high rate in the generality of men'; secondly, 'A great despondency and fainting of heart in the generality of the Saints, and people of God, by reason of that low and most sad condition, unto which they shall be brought by their enemies'; and thirdly, 'a triumphant confidence amongst the enemies of the Saints and Servants of God, that ... the world is now become theirs'. Yet once again, Goodwin was reluctant to push speculation too far – he affirmed his faith in a coming millennium, but warned that dating the end 'is a matter of very great difficulty, and which hath not prospered in the hand of any undertaker, that I know of'.[37]

A Door does contain the occasional defiant aside attacking kings, as when Goodwin writes 'That God ... is altogether unlike the generality of those that are called Gods upon Earth, Kings, Princes, Potentates, and Grandees of the World, who are more ready to tread and trample upon, to grind the faces, and to break the bones of those that are beneath them, and under their power; especially, if they have at any time provoked them, or been disobedient to them, than to commiserate or relieve them in their distresse'. But when Goodwin came to discuss the crucial Fifth Commandment, he urged his readers to submit rather than fight. If Christians cannot in good conscience obey a law, he advised, they should patiently subject themselves to the punishment imposed on non-observers. 'The persons of their Magistrates, yea though they be none of the best, they ought to reverence and honour, as being set over them by the providence of God, under him to rule and govern them for their good'.[38]

Despite such political quietism, Goodwin was vehement in his attacks on the established church. His anonymous pamphlet, *Prelatick Preachers None of Christ's Teachers* (1663), reveals that his polemical axe was as sharp as ever.[39] In apocalyptic tones, he denounced 'the Babylonish Ministry' as an ally of 'the Beast, Babylon, the False Prophet, and Scarlet Whore'. He called on the godly to come out of Babylon by boycotting the parish churches. Those who attended the services of the priests were 'being a great offence, and stumbling, to their weak Christian Brethren'. Their presence at these 'Congregations of a Politique Construction, and worldly complexion' lent credibility to the new order and effectively condoned 'all the outrages of persecution and cruelty' being perpetrated by the bishops.[40] The *jus divinum* claims of Episcopalians were without foundation, and Goodwin 'most heartily and seriously' recommended an 'elaborate and learned Discourse' by his old rival, William Prynne, to prove the point.[41] Indeed, episcopal ordination was simply invalid. This was a surprising

---

37 *Door*, 72–76.
38 *Door*, 95–96, 432.
39 For the authorship, see Appendix.
40 *Prelatick Preachers none of Christs* (1663), 52, 72–75, 79.
41 *Prelatick Preachers*, 70–71 (see also 2–3, 67). The treatise was Prynne's *The Un-Bishopping of Timothy and Titus*, 2nd edn (1660).

argument from one who had himself been ordained by a bishop and had served as a parish minister for many years, but Goodwin went to some length to explain that there was 'a very great difference between times of ignorance and times of knowledge'. It was one thing to be ordained by a bishop in the 1620s, quite another to do so in the 1660s, after 'the times of Reformation'.[42]

For Goodwin, the Restoration church settlement was a denial of all that God had done in 'the times of Reformation', and an appalling regression to the dark days of the 1630s. He was no doubt particularly pained that some of his own erstwhile followers were now – as we shall see – nestled within the bosom of the Restoration Church. He chastised those who 'turn Renegadoes from the holy Assemblies of the Saints', and lamented the degeneration of 'good men, zealously addicted to the purity of Gods worship, haters of all superstition, and flesh-devised Ceremonies brought into this worship, lovers of the Saints, asserters of their liberties'. Such men had now 'lost their native shapes', like hens 'trodden by Crowes' in 'unnatural copulation'.[43]

As well as condemning conformists and the episcopal clergy, Goodwin authored an unpublished tract, 'Some further considerations about Common Prayer'.[44] In doing so, he was rejecting the compromises of moderate Puritans like Richard Baxter and Edmund Calamy, and concurring with other Independents like John Owen and Vavasour Powell.[45] In *Prelatick Preachers* he had denounced 'The Idolatrous madness of the Common-Prayer-Book-worship', describing it as 'a menstrous rag of Popish devotion'.[46] In his unpublished paper, he declared that the liturgy 'smells rank of the mass book'. Those who used the Anglican service may not have committed 'broad faced idolatry', but they were guilty of 'trifling dalliance or wanton compliance' with popish superstition. There was not a word in the New Testament requiring 'a set forme of liturgy', especially such a form as the Prayer Book, with its 'needless repetition', 'tautologies' and confused mixture of 'canonicalls & Apocriphalls'.[47]

Yet what bothered Goodwin most deeply about the restored church was its Antichristian usurpation of Christ's authority over conscience. Having spent two decades defending the liberty of individuals and congregations from the dictates of ecclesiastical and civil authority, Goodwin found himself answering the standard arguments in favour of enforced uniformity all over again.[48]

---

42 *Prelatick Preachers*, 51–61.
43 *Prelatick Preachers*, 23–24.
44 [John Goodwin], 'Some further considerations about Common Prayer', CUL Add. 44 (7), 1–3. For the authorship, see Appendix.
45 See Vavasour Powell, *Common-Prayer-Book No Divine Service* (1661); [John Owen], *A Discourse concerning Liturgies* (1662). On Congregationalist and Baptist opposition to liturgies see R. Greaves, *Glimpses of Glory: John Bunyan and English Dissent* (Stanford, CA, 2002), 154–56; G. Nuttall, *The Holy Spirit in Puritan Faith and Experience*, second edition (Chicago, IL, 1992), ch 4: 'The Spirit and Prayer'.
46 *Prelatick Preachers*, 1.
47 'Some further considerations', 1–3.
48 'Some further considerations', 21–31.

In *Prelatick Preachers*, he arraigned the bishops for teaching 'the importune doctrine of *blind Obedience* to Superiours, both Ecclesiastical and Civil'. Turning their back on Protestant principle, 'they leave no liberty or freedom of judgement, or conscience, to inferiours, to judge of the lawfulness, and unlawfulness of the Superiours command'. Their impositions were 'derogatory unto the Royalties of Jesus Christ, as Sole King, and Law-giver unto his Church'.[49] Goodwin pictured them (as he had pictured the Covenanters) plotting to 'enslave' believers and 'set task-masters over them'. The clerical hierarchy was bent on burdening the godly with 'Liturgies, Letanies, Collects, and other devices', to make them 'pray, when we say, pray; bow, when we say, bow; kneel, when we say kneel'. Churchmen who claimed 'a power of imposing upon men what they please in matters of Religion' were 'Antichrists of an inferiour order'.[50] Yet despite the apparent triumph of episcopacy, Goodwin refused to be downcast. This was merely 'a lightning before Death ... the lifting up of our Bishops from the gates of death, is like to prepare the way to their second death, or fall, from whence there will be no redemption'.[51]

The bitter rhetoric of *Prelatick Preachers* jarred with more moderate Dissenters. Richard Baxter (who identified Goodwin as the author) disapproved.[52] John Tombes wrote that when he came across *Prelatick Preachers*, 'I perceived, that the seeds of most rigid separation were well sown, and did spread themselves much among many'.[53] Goodwin was speaking for a wide constituency of Nonconformists – people who had been actively involved in the parochial system for decades, but were so alienated by the Restoration church and its imposed uniformity that they adopted unequivocal separatism. Like Bunyan's *I Will Pray with Spirit* (1662), *Prelatick Preachers* was 'an openly oppositional tract', more radical and confrontational than the writings of Owen and other leading Congregationalist ministers.[54]

Anglican polemics downplayed the internal divisions among Dissenters, and depicted Nonconformists as united in conspiracy against church and state. One satirical pamphlet of 1663, *Cabala*, claimed to provide *An Impartial Account of the Non-Conformists Private Designs, Actings and Ways*. John Goodwin was named alongside Philip Nye, Ralph Venning and George Griffith, as a member of 'a close-Committee of the well-affected and ejected Ministers', commissioning John Vicars and William Prynne 'to exercise their gift of History' by writing an account of the ejection. Tobias Conyers was listed as one of six 'Messengers to the Several Churches', and William Allen also appeared as a Nonconformist activist. Richard Baxter was implausibly shown recommending the republication of 'most of Milton and Mr Goodwyn's Papers'.[55] While the pamphlet is misleading in depicting Goodwin

---

49 *Prelatick Preachers*, 11, 18.
50 *Prelatick Preachers*, 40–41, 77.
51 *Prelatick Preachers*, 16.
52 *Reliquiae Baxterianae* (1696), iii. 19, §41.
53 John Tombes, *Theodulia* (1667), 'Preface'.
54 Neil Keeble, quoted in R. Greaves, *Glimpses of Glory: John Bunyan and English Dissent* (Stanford, CA, 2002), 157–59.
55 *Cabala, or an Impartial Account of the Non-Conformists Private Designs, Actings and Ways from August 24, 1662 to December 25 in the same Year* (1663), 1–2, 5, 17, 21, 12.

hand-in-hand with former foes, it does show that Goodwin and his followers continued to enjoy a certain notoriety.

Indeed, letters from Goodwin to his wife in late 1663 and early 1664 indicate that he had recently been forced to leave London, probably because the authorities had got wind of his seditious tracts.[56] The letters reveal a man under pressure, but not 'a man by himself'. As always, Goodwin was sustained by faithful friends and supporters. In September 1663, he wrote that he and his son Samuel were benefiting from the 'good aire' of their new location, and were 'bettered in our healths & come degrees above ye ordinarie pitch of Bednall Green'. They had moved away from the London suburbs, where Sarah and the rest of the family remained, and had relocated, probably to Leigh in Essex, from where Goodwin addressed a later letter. This was a place closely associated with the Puritan Earl of Warwick, and Goodwin was enjoying the hospitality of old companions, Mr and Mrs Luddington.[57] However, he was keen to find a more permanent home, and wanted to take advice from Sarah and 'my friends about thee, & in ye citie'. He had his eye on a house, the best bargain within a hundred miles, but was willing to emigrate to Holland if his friends thought it best – a clear sign that he had been subject to government harassment. He apologised to Sarah for not writing more 'to fortifie thy spirit against thy present troubles & feares'. His hand was so weak that he could not compose long letters, but he urged her to 'stirr up ye guift of God yt is in thee', and signed himself 'yors above what y[o]u think, & as much as y[o]u can well desire, you know who'.[58]

A month later, on 24 October, Goodwin told Sarah that his friend 'Mr Firmin' (probably the Essex minister Giles Firmin) was raising his case with Dr O[wen]. He took some encouragement from this, though his long-standing suspicions of the conservative Congregationalists remained – 'I believe ye man [i.e. Owen] to be as politiquely addicted, as Mr Nye himself'. Goodwin's daughter had been visiting him, and he wanted to return with her to see the family again, if only for 'a day or two'. But he would only come if Sara and their friends thought it 'convenient & safe'. He had 'submitted my self all along hitherto unto thee, & thy Counsellors', and would make no decisions without Sara's consent.[59]

By January 1664, Goodwin was itching to move to his own house, and he asked Sarah to allay the fears of his son John, who worried that by purchasing a property his father would attract unwelcome attention. Goodwin explained that there was no reason for concern – his friends had concocted a 'plot' so that 'my name is not to be so much as mentioned in any transaction about ye purchase'. In any case, he believed that he was 'much more taken notice of in the place of my present abode, by reason of a continuall recourse of persons of all sorts hither, then I shall be at least for a long time, in yt other house, wch will be a place of

---

56 The letters are summarised in *CSPD* (1663–64), 272, 313, 437, 445.
57 The will of Thomas Alderne (NA PROB 11/265) referred to 'my good friend Thomas Loddington', and a 'Mr Luddington' also attended some vestry meetings at St Stephen's in the 1650s.
58 NA SP 29/80/62 (15 September 1663).
59 NA SP 29/82/39 (24 October 1663).

privacie & retirement'. It was a 'weatherbeaten, forlorn, & forsaken house', and its owner would pull it down if he did not find a buyer soon; his purchase of such a cheap property was unlikely to attract much notice or resentment. Goodwin thought it safer for him to find 'an hole for the hideing of his head in theise parts, then to be adventured on Bednall Green', and he hoped that the family would delay no longer. His scrapes with the authorities had clearly created tensions with his wife and sons, and he complained that he was 'still in ye same scrubbing condition, wch thou leftest me, when thou rannest away so fast from me'. He confessed to 'a feminine longing, to be somewhere wth thee in our own', but he was conscious of how much he was responsible for Sarah's present woes and 'former trouble'. Signing himself in a clear but unsteady hand – 'Thy poore husband, yet rich in love to thee' – he prayed that God would compensate and reward her.[60]

In his final letter, dated 16 January 1664, he again urged Sarah to lose no time 'in getting me into an house of mine owne'. 'For since thy going from me', he complained, 'I am ill bested here, neither dareing to adventure to put on a clean shirt, for feare of taking cold, nor able to put on a clean band, not knoweing where to find strings to tie it'. In the past week, he had had 'a dangerous cold', only soothed by '2 or 3 small doses of burnt brandie, & 2 evening recipes of Mrs Lodintons butterd ale (ye blessing of God accompanyeing all)'. He was an old man, who needed his wife, and he prayed that God would 'keep us for a better world than this'.[61]

Despite his decrepitude and low spirits, Goodwin was still perceived as a threat by a government that did not appreciate his vitriolic tracts or the 'continuall recourse of persons of all sorts' to his residence. In March 1664, Roger L'Estrange obtained a warrant to apprehend Goodwin, with all his papers and writings.[62] It may be that Sarah was searched too, since government agents seized the letters she had received from John. A year later, in March 1665, a government informer, 'A. W.', reported an alleged conspiracy 'to murder ye King' involving some soldiers and 'ye chiliasts'. The informer claimed that Goodwin – 'whom he believe writt *Mene Tekeel*' – was 'wrighting another peece of the same nature', which was 'almost ready for press'.[63] Although the misattribution of *Mene Tekel* to Goodwin does not inspire confidence in the report's veracity, it does show that the septuagenarian pastor was still seen as a potential threat. To his dying days, he was a man to be watched.

We know nothing about the circumstances of his death. In the early eighteenth century, Edmund Calamy recorded that Goodwin had died in 1665 at the age of seventy-two.[64] Subsequent accounts have followed Calamy, though he was a year out on Goodwin's age, and Goodwin's will was not proved until 3 May 1666. The likelihood is that he died in late 1665 or in early 1666. It has been speculated that

---

60 NA SP 29/110/61 (11 January 1664).
61 NA SP 29/110/102 (16 January 1664).
62 *CSPD* (1663–64), 519.
63 NA SP 29/114/11; *CSPD* (1664–65), 234.
64 Edmund Calamy, *A Continuation of the Account*, 2 vols (London, 1727), i. 78.

he died of the plague, for the parish burial register of St Stephen's for 1665 does record that 'John Goodwin in Whites Alley vitler was buried the 3d day of Septem'.[65] There is something appealing about the idea of the preacher returning to his old parish, living through the plague with his former parishioners, and being buried on Oliver Cromwell's auspicious day (the anniversary of Dunbar, Worcester and Cromwell's own death). But Goodwin had moved out of the City in the 1650s, and away from London in 1663, and he is very unlikely to have returned as a vitler. The parish registers probably specify the residence and profession of this John Goodwin in order to distinguish him from his notorious namesake.

Goodwin's wife Sarah did not remarry, but she did have the support of the couple's remaining children. When she made her own will in September 1677, she named her sons Edward and Samuel, but not her oldest son John who may have died some time after 1664 when he was mentioned in his father's letters. The three daughters named in John Goodwin's will were still alive in 1677, and were now called Mary Mountagu, Sarah Smartfoot and Elizabeth Mountagu.[66] Sarah and Elizabeth had obviously wed at some stage after 1658, and Elizabeth may well have married into the same family as Mary, whose husband was probably the Coleman Street baker, William Montague, a member of Goodwin's gathered church. For Sarah, the family must have helped to make life bearable during the difficult years after 1660. We know too little about her. She was not an educated woman—her will contains 'the marke of Sarah Goodwin', not her signature, though she was apparently able to read, a skill usually taught separately before writing. Sarah was clearly part of the community of the godly. When Goodwin wrote to her in 1663–64, he expected her to know about Dr Owen and Mr Firmin, and used her to pass on news to friends and supporters. John's letters to Sarah suggest that theirs was an affectionate relationship, and if he lived up to his own advice to husbands, he must have been a benign patriarch.[67] Yet like so many clerical wives in these years – Anglican and Dissenter – Sarah Goodwin had suffered much for her husband's principles.

Legacy

In the years following his death, Goodwin's reputation gradually diminished. He remained sufficiently notorious to merit a mention in the famous 'Judgement and Decree' issued by the University of Oxford in 1683. The document condemned twenty-seven 'damnable doctrines' taught by the Parliamentarian rebels, and cited Goodwin for defending a contract theory of government and praising the regicides as 'blessed instruments of God's glory in their generation'. The 'pernicious books' of the authors listed – including one assumes *Anti-Cavalierisme* and *The Obstructors of Justice* – were to be banned and publicly

65 GL MS 4449/2.
66 NA PROB 11/355, Will of Sarah Goodwin.
67 See *Door*, 439–40.

burned at the University.⁶⁸ Goodwin's sermons on the Holy Spirit fared rather better. They were published posthumously by Henry Eversden in 1670, and two of his Arminian tracts were republished in 1671 by Peter Parker, the printer of *Paradise Lost* and various Nonconformist writings.⁶⁹ But in the eighty years thereafter, not a single one of Goodwin's writings was reprinted.

Yet Goodwin's works were to be found in numerous private libraries. John Locke owned a copy of *Anti-Cavalierisme*.⁷⁰ The Presbyterian Lazarus Seaman, whose library of five thousand books was one of the first to be sold through a published auction catalogue, owned seven of Goodwin's books, including *Anti-Cavalierisme* and *Redemption Redeemed*.⁷¹ The library of Benjamin Worsley, a close associate of Hartlib and a one-time resident of Coleman Street, contained thirty-five copies of Goodwin works, including all his major theological books and numerous 'small tracts'.⁷² Goodwin's parishioner, Nathan Paget, owned seven tracts published by his vicar in the 1640s, as well as the posthumous *A Being Filled with the Spirit*.⁷³ The Whig lawyer, William Petyt, or his brother Silvester, possessed thirteen of Goodwin's books, including works on politics, theology, and toleration.⁷⁴ The Anglican divine, Thomas Plume, whose remarkable library of 7–8000 volumes remains intact to this day in his hometown of Maldon, Essex, had acquired around twenty-five of Goodwin's books and pamphlets.⁷⁵ Unsurprisingly, Goodwin's Calvinist opponent, John Owen, owned seven of his books, including the major theological tomes.⁷⁶ The erudite Quaker, Benjamin Furly, owned *Redemption Redeemed* and a copy of Goodwin's debate on universal redemption with John Simpson and Vavasour Powell.⁷⁷ The library of Samuel Pepys contained a copy of *Theomachia*.⁷⁸ The radical Independent, Samuel Jeakes, had bought 70% of his collection of 2100 volumes secondhand, and he owned four Goodwin pamphlets.⁷⁹ Finally, the vast library of the Deist, Anthony Collins, had eight titles by Goodwin, including theological writings and *Anti-Cavalierisme, Hagiomastix* and *Right and Might Well Met*.⁸⁰

68 *The Judgement and Decree of the University of Oxford, passed in their Convocation, July 21, 1683 against Certain Pernicious Books and Damnable Doctrines, Destructive to the Sacred Persons of Princes, their State and Government, and of all Humane Society* (1683), 2–3, 6.
69 *Pleroma to Pneumatikon, or, A Being Filled with the Spirit* (London: Printed by E. C. for Henry Eversden, 1670); *Eirenomachia, The Agreement and Distance of Brethren* (London: Printed for Peter Parker, 1671); *The Pagans Debt and Dowry* (London: Printed by T. J. for Peter Parker, 1671).
70 J. Harrison and P. Laslett, *The Library of John Locke* (Oxford, 1965), no. 1285b.
71 *Catalogus Variorum & Insignium Librorum ... Lazari Seaman* (1676), 15, 54, 57, 60–61, 63.
72 *Catalogue Librorum ... D. Doctoris Benjaminis Worsley* (1678).
73 *Bibliotheca Medica viri Clarissmi Nathanis Paget*, M. D. (1681), 35, 36, 38, 42.
74 *A Catalogue of the Petyt Library at Skipton, Yorkshire* (Gargrave, 1964), 156–57.
75 S. G. Deed, ed., *Catalogue of the Plume Library at Maldon, Essex* (Maldon, 1959), 75. Several of Goodwin's books in Plume's library were accidentally omitted from the catalogue. I am grateful to the librarians for allowing me to see these.
76 See the sale catalogue of Owen's books: *Bibliotheca Oweniana* (1684), 1, 5, 21.
77 *Bibliotheca Furliana, sive catalogues librorum* (Rotterdam, 1714), 55, 88.
78 *Catalogue of the Pepys Library at Magdalene College Cambridge* (Cambridge, 1978), i. 78.
79 M. Hunter, G. Mandelbrote, R. Ovenden, and N. Smith, eds, *A Radical's Books: The Library Catalogue of Samuel Jeake of Rye, 1623–90* (Woodbridge, 1999), 10–13, 98–99, 108, 190–91.
80 *Bibliotheca Anthonij Collins: or a Catalogue of the Library of Anthony Collins* (1731), 75, 89.

Each of these collections was made available for use by other readers. The Petyt brothers' bequeathed their books to their old grammar school in Skipton; the Plume Library in Maldon was established for the use of local clergy; Furly's personal library was used by a remarkable coterie of intellectuals that included the Arminians, Philip van Limborch, Jean le Clerc and John Locke; Jeakes' books were also borrowed by a circle of friends; the libraries of Seaman, Owen, Worsley, Paget and Collins were auctioned after their deaths, and such secondhand sales were an ideal opportunity to purchase affordable old books. The publisher's copy of the sale catalogue for Samuel Jacombe's library indicates the prices paid for secondhand books. Jacombe was a distinguished Presbyterian divine, who owned a dozen copies of books by John Goodwin. At the auction of his library in 1687, *Redemption Redeemed* was purchased for 5s 6d, *A Being Filled with the Spirit* for 2s, *The Divine Authority of the Scriptures* for 1s 5d, and *An Exposition of Romans 9* for 1s; other works like the *Pagans Debt and Dowry*, *Triumviri*, *Catabaptism* and *Basanistai* sold for less than a shilling.[81] Mid-seventeenth century books remained available for decades after publication.

If Goodwin's books were still in circulation, so were some of his friends and associates. The Coleman Street Independent church had probably folded when he left London or after his death, but the parish of St Stephens was still haunted by ghosts from Goodwin's past. Thomas Lamb, who had returned to the parish church after his spell with the General Baptists, became a prominent and respected parishioner. He wrote against Nonconformists like Richard Baxter in *A Stop to the course of Separation* (1672), and *A Fresh Suit against Independency* (1677). His funeral took place at St Stephen's in 1686, when the vicar, Richard Lucas, preached the sermon.[82] Some years earlier, in 1672, Goodwin's old associate John Horn had preached another funeral sermon at St Stephen's for the venerable Puritan Arminian, Thomas Moore senior. Remarkably, both Horn and Moore were ejected ministers, but they were irenic Dissenters and Arminian theologians, and Moore may have been a parish resident.[83] Years after Goodwin's own death, St Stephens was still a centre of Arminianism.

The Restoration careers of members of Goodwin's gathered church are for the most part shrouded in obscurity. But of those we can trace, the majority moved on from Independency. An exception is Samuel Sowthen (or Southen) – when he died in July 1665, a broadside elegy acclaimed his stubborn nonconformity in verse.[84] But in contrast to Sowthen, others who had sat under Goodwin's ministry struck out in their own directions even while retaining many convictions instilled by their former pastor. Several embraced Quakerism, which shared Goodwin's doctrine of universal redemption but emphasised the 'inner light' rather than Scripture and the Cross. Isaac Pennington junior became a Quaker in 1657.

---

81 *Bibliotheca Jacombiana* (1687), 51, 56, 73, 105.
82 Richard Lucas, *A Sermon preacht at the Funeral of Mr. Thomas Lamb, 23 July 1686* (1686).
83 John Horn, *Reward of the Wise* (1672). A 'Tho: Moore' attended vestry meetings from 1664: GL MS 4458/1 ff. 282, 284, 287, 289.
84 *An Elegy upon the Death of that able and faithful Servant of God, Mr Samuel Sowthen, who died the 2d of July, 1665* (1665).

During the Restoration, he was one of the sect's most prolific pamphleteers, and an eloquent critic of persecution.[85] John Fenwick, who had attended Goodwin's congregation in 1649, also converted to Quakerism at a later date, and emigrated to the Quaker colony of New Jersey.[86] Luke Howard, who had joined Goodwin's congregation for a brief period in 1642–43, became a leading Particular Baptist before converting to the Quakers in the mid-1650s.[87] Howard published a number of Quaker pamphlets from 1658 onwards, and in his dispute with the Baptists he was defended by Thomas Rudyard – possibly the same man who had been an avid note-taker at Goodwin's sermons in the early 1640s.[88] Rudyard himself wrote around a dozen Quaker tracts, including attacks on tithes, religious persecution and the London Baptists.

In contrast to the Quakers, Thomas Firmin declined the sectarian option during the Restoration. He became a wealthy merchant and a personal friend of a host of leading moderate Anglicans, including John Tillotson, John Wilkins, Benjamin Whichcote, Matthew Hale, Robert Boyle and John Locke.[89] His anti-Trinitarianism and Anglicanism represented a departure from his former pastor, but in other respects he faithfully echoed Goodwin. According to one posthumous account, Firmin was 'a hearty Assertor of the Liberties of his Native Country' who deplored 'the perpetual Bellowing of *Passive Obedience*, and *Non-Resistance*, from the Pulpits'. He shared Goodwin's conviction that pagans were capable of salvation through 'the Natural Knowledge which all Men have of God'. 'He always looked upon Liberty of Conscience to be the Birth-Right of every Christian', and chided the Anglican ministry for their 'unnatural Persecution against the Dissenters'. Finally, he despised implicit faith, always endeavoured to convince men 'by calm and sober Arguments', and thought that 'Conviction and not Authority ought to influence Mankind'.[90] In these respects, if not in his unitarianism, Firmin was relaying the lessons taught him by John Goodwin.

In making his peace with the Restoration church, Firmin was joined by other former disciples of Goodwin, including Tobias Conyers, the Foxcrofts, William Allen and Thomas Lamb. Having had his appointment as vicar of St Stephen's blocked by the Bishop of London in 1661, Conyers was then ejected from St Antholin's in 1662. However, he quickly found a parish in York, and from 1670 to

---

85 *ODNB*. The most recent study is M. E. Halvorsen, '"The day of small things": The Quaker understanding of conversion and the inner light in the writings of Isaac Pennington the Younger', Ph.D. dissertation, University of Washington (2002).
86 See *ODNB*.
87 See Luke Howard, *Love and Truth in Plainness Manifested* (1704), 5–8; Luke Howard, *A Looking-Glass for Baptists* in *The Seat of the Scorner Thrown Down* (1673), 28; L. V. Hodgin, *The Shoemaker of Dover: Luke Howard, 1621–99* (1943); *ODNB*.
88 See Luke Howard, *The Seat of the Scorner Thrown Down ... to which is added a Further Answer by T[homas] R[udyard]* (1673), 58; Samuel Lane, *A Vindication of Free Grace* (1645), sig. A3v.
89 Firmin made it into the *DNB* and the Oxford *DNB*, but the last major study was H. W. Stephenson, 'Thomas Firmin, F. R. S. (1632–1697)', D.Phil. dissertation, University of Oxford (1949).
90 *The Charitable Samaritan: or A Short and Impartial Account of that Eminent and Publick-spirited Citizen Mr. Tho. Firmin ... by a Gentleman of his Acquaintance* (1698), 4, 8–9, 10, 14.

his death in 1687, he was prebendary of York.[91] In 1680, he published two anonymous Whig tracts, entitled *The Plotters Doom* and *Popery and Hypocrisy*. Lamenting the 'Hellish Plot against the life of our King, Government and Protestant Religion', he also denounced the 'inhumane rage against our dissenting brethren'.[92] Like Firmin, he was a voice for toleration within the Restoration Church.

The Foxcrofts became acquainted with Henry More through Elizabeth's brother Benjamin Whichcote and their son Ezekiel, a fellow of King's who was associated with the Cambridge Platonists. During George Foxcroft's absence abroad with the East India Company from 1666 to 1672, Elizabeth lived with the philosopher Lady Anne Conway and served as her amanuensis. She shared Conway's mystical bent, and was an admirer of Jacob Boehme. Ezekiel was a friend of John Worthington, as well as of Hartlib and Boyle, and was famed for his translation of Johann Valentin Andreae's Rosicrucian text, *The Hermetick Romance, or, The Chemical Wedding* (1690). He has also been identified as a likely source of Isaac Newton's knowledge of alchemy.[93]

William Allen had returned to the bosom of the established church at the Restoration, and Baxter recorded that he and Thomas Lamb were 'now more zealous than other men against Independency and Separation, by how much the more they smarted by it'.[94] Although never ordained, Allen the Anglican published over a dozen books and pamphlets, including attacks on the Quakers, Roman Catholicism, and the high Calvinist doctrine of justification. His debt to Goodwin can be discerned at many points, not least in *A Discourse of Divine Assistance* (1679), which continued Goodwin's theological project by providing an Arminian account of how God's 'Preventing [i.e. prevenient'] Grace' gave 'Preparatory Assistance' enabling all men to repent and believe. A 1693 tract complained that the classic Protestant doctrine of justification was being undermined by 'New Methodists' who smuggled works back into justification – the chief culprits named were 'the great Champion *J. G.*', Baxter and Allen.[95] Among Anglicans, Allen was highly regarded by Archbishops Sancroft and Tillotson, and the distinguished scholar Bishop William Lloyd. In 1707, his works were republished in a folio volume of 754 pages, introduced by John Williams, Bishop of Chichester, and concluded with a funeral sermon on Allen by Richard Kidder, Bishop of Bath and Wells.[96]

Allen, Lamb, Conyers, Firmin and the Foxcrofts were all associated with latitudinarian Anglicans who preached universal redemption and stressed individual judgement. As Baxter explained, 'those called *Latitudinarians* ... were mostly

---

91 J. Venn and J. A. Venn, *Alumni Cantabrigienses* ... *Part I from the Earliest Times to 1751*, 4 vols (Cambridge, 1922–27), i. 382.
92 [Tobias Conyers], *Popery and Hypocrisy* (1680), 28–29, 34–36.
93 Sarah Hutton, 'Foxcroft [Whichcote], Elizabeth (1600–1679)', *ODNB*. Numerous references to the Foxcrofts can be found in *Conway Letters: The Correspondence of Anne, Viscountess Conway, Henry More, and their Friends, 1642–1684*, ed. M. H. Nicolson (New Haven, 1930).
94 *Reliquiae Baxterianae*, ii. 81, iii. 180.
95 *A War among the Angels of the Churches* (1693), 6–9.
96 *The Works of William Allen, Consisting of Thirteen Distinct Tracts on Several Subjects* (1707), sig. a2v; William Allen, *Certain Select Discourses* (1699), 'Preface', sig. Ar–v.

Cambridge-men, *Platonists* or *Cartesians*, and many of them *Arminians* with some Additions, having more charitable Thoughts than others of the Salvation of Heathens and Infidels ... These were ingenious Men and Scholars, and of Universal Principles, and free ... '[97] It is not hard to see why people who had sat under Goodwin's ministry for many years could be attracted to Whichcote, Tillotson or More.

The independence and intellectual confidence of Goodwin's followers bears eloquent testimony to the effectiveness of what Marchamont Nedham called 'the Divinity-School in Coleman-University'.[98] Firmin and Allen had become articulate lay theologians, recognised and valued as discussion partners by some of the most eminent intellectuals of the established church. Their development owed much to their former pastor. Goodwin had repeatedly denounced the popish doctrine of 'implicit faith', and had attacked clergy for '*dictating* like Emperors, instead of *arguing* like Teachers'. As he told Richard Resbury, 'My frequent and free advice to all my Friends and Hearers, is known to be this: Not to believe any thing, whether from me, or any other man, but what they see sufficient ground and reason why they should believe'.[99] Eschewing pretensions to personal infallibility, he had taught his followers to search the Scriptures and think for themselves. He was, no doubt, dismayed by some of the results – he lived to see erstwhile followers become Baptists, Quakers, Socinians and Anglicans. But even though they abandoned some of his most cherished positions, they also continued to bear his imprint. All maintained his Arminian view of grace and free will, and most retained his hostility to imposed uniformity.

However, the careers of these men do underline Goodwin's institutional failure. In contrast to Richard Baxter and John Owen, he had not been able to build a coherent and lasting movement. Although Goodwin could inspire intense loyalty among his closest followers, he was not well placed to build bridges and assemble coalitions. By defending unpopular causes, like toleration, regicide and Arminianism, he had made many enemies. Those who agreed with him on politics often took exception to his theology, while those attracted to his theology often deplored his politics. And by urging his followers to think for themselves he reduced his chances of forming a regimented third force of Arminian Independents. Despite (or because of) his notoriety, he did not leave behind a party of 'Goodwinians' to compare with the 'Baxterians'. Without a group of dedicated followers to keep his memory alive, Goodwin came to be seen as a singular and isolated figure. By the early eighteenth century, Edmund Calamy could get away with describing Goodwin as 'a man by himself'.

Goodwin and the Methodists

Although Goodwin's fame receded in the decades after his death, he was not entirely forgotten. He was awarded an entry in James Granger's *Biographical History*

---

97 *Reliquiae Baxterianae*, ii. 387.
98 Marchamont Nedham, *The Great Accuser Cast Down* (1657), 42.
99 *Confidence Dismounted* (1651), 8, 14.

of England (2nd edition, 1775), where he was described as 'a man who made more noise in the world than any other person of his age, rank, and profession'. Granger noted that 'he had the hardiness to introduce Arminianism among the Calvinists, which he bravely and zealously defended', but added that 'no man more eagerly promoted, or more zealously defended the murder of the king'.[100] Goodwin's notorious *Defence of the Murther of Ch. I*, as one catalogue entitled it, may even have become a collector's item, since it is the only one of his works to appear in a number of private libraries.[101] His radical political writings were cited in *The Dissenters Memorial* (1711), an Anglican compilation of incriminating quotations from seventeenth-century Puritans. But the compiler also quoted his attacks on Presbyterian bigotry.[102] Theologians occasionally cited Goodwin too – the Anglican Arminian Daniel Whitby pointed readers towards *Redemption Redeemed* and the *Treatise of Justification*; the Socinian Dissenter Thomas Emlyn used a quotation from *Water-Dipping* in a book against the Baptists; the commentator Matthew Henry had read *An Exposition of Romans 9*; and James Fraser of Brea condemned the *Treatise of Justification* as 'very grosse, and intirely subversive of the Gospel'.[103]

In the second half of the eighteenth century, Goodwin was discovered and championed by the Wesleyan Methodists. Wesley's own Arminianism was derived from the seventeenth-century Anglican theologians, including Richard Lucas, vicar of St Stephen's Coleman Street from 1678, author of influential devotional works and friend of Thomas Lamb.[104] The young Wesley had probably never encountered the writings of Lamb's former pastor, though Wesley's father had denounced 'that *infamous Firebrand*, John Goodwin, who had been one of the cursed Cabal for taking away the Life of the Lords Anointed'.[105] But Wesley's contests with Calvinists led him to familiarise himself with a wide range of seventeenth-century Arminian literature. It is not clear when he and other Methodist leaders first came across Goodwin, but when they did they immediately recognised a kindred spirit.

Between 1755 and 1758, Wesley was engaged in a theological controversy with the Calvinist James Hervey over the doctrine of justification. Although Hervey died in 1758, the dispute simmered on, and in 1765, Wesley published an abridged version of Goodwin's *Treatise of Justification*. Wesley explained that he had 'submitted ... to the importunity of my friends, who have long been soliciting me to abridge

---

100 James Granger, *A Biographical History of England*, 4 vols (London, 1775), iii. 41–42.
101 A Catalogue of the Library, Antiquities &c of the Late Learned Dr. Woodward (1728), 8; A Catalogue of the *Books of the Right Honourable Charles Viscount Bruce of Ampthill* (1733), 36; *A Catalogue of the Large and Vendible Library of the Late Learned and Ingenious Mr Michael Maittaire* (1749), 188.
102 *The Dissenters Memorial* (1711), 15, 16, 30, 31, 39.
103 D. Whitby, *Reflections on Some Assertions and Opinions of Mr Dodwell* (1707), 43; Whitby, *A Discourse* (1710), 457; T. Emlyn, *Mr Wall's History of Infant Baptism Improv'd* (1709), title page; M. Henry, *An Exposition of the Several Epistles*, 6 vols (1721–25), vi. 39; J. Fraser, *A Treatise concerning Justifying Faith* (1723), sig. ii.
104 See H. B. McGonigle, *Sufficient Saving Grace: John Wesley's Evangelical Arminianism* (Carlisle, 2002), chs. 2–4. On Lucas see *ODNB*. On his friendship with Lamb, see Lucas, *An Enquiry after Happiness* (1685), 'To the Reader', sig. a3v.
105 Samuel Wesley, *A Defence of a Letter concerning the Education of Dissenters* (1704), 18.

and publish the ensuing treatise'. He believed that 'I could not either draw up or defend better than I found it done to my hands by one who, at the time he wrote this book, was a firm and zealous Calvinist'.[106] The republication of Goodwin's controversial treatise provoked a storm of criticism from Calvinists like the Scottish Presbyterian, Dr John Erskine, who accused Wesley of teaching justification by works and condemned him for denying predestination. The result was a profound setback to the Methodist cause in Scotland, where Calvinism was still dominant among Evangelicals.[107]

The debate over Wesley's theology intensified after 1770, when the Methodist Conference approved a set of *Minutes* that stressed the necessity of good works for (final) salvation. The 'Minutes Controversy' revived earlier arguments over the Wesleyan teaching on justification and predestination. In 1771, Charles Wesley wrote to his brother suggesting that this might be a good time for John to publish a short extract from *Redemption Redeemed*.[108] Wesley had previously encouraged Sellon to produce a new edition of the book, together with answers to John Owen's 'evasions'.[109] In the following year, Sir Richard Hill published a *Review of all the Doctrines Taught by The Rev John Wesley*, in which he listed the contradictions between Wesley's own teaching and Goodwin's *Treatise of Justification*. Wesley responded by explaining that 'John Wesley is not John Goodwin ... I am no way engaged to defend every expression of either John Goodwin, or Richard Baxter's *Aphorisms*. The sense of both I generally approve, the language many times I do not.'[110] Calvinists continued to believe, however, that these two heterodox Puritans had led Wesley astray. The Independent William Shrubsole treated his readers to a Bunyanesque allegory involving travellers tempted to wander from the true path into 'Freewill Forest', 'Arminian Wood', '*Goodwin's-Sand*' and '*Baxter's Heath*'.[111] Another attack on Wesley and Goodwin came from the Anglican Calvinist, Augustus Toplady, in his *Historic Proof of the Doctrinal Calvinism of the Church of England* (1774). Toplady had dubbed Wesley 'the John Goodwin of the present age'. Now in an attempt to discredit his Arminian foes, he portrayed Goodwin as a treasonous regicide, and a 'ranter' and 'leveller' to boot. The Arminian lay-preacher was a 'cunning' Machiavellian 'fox' who had managed to flatter Cromwell even while being the 'grand ringleader' of the Fifth Monarchists.[112] This thoroughly muddled account suggests that Toplady knew little about Goodwin, and relied on misleading sources such as Burnet. But his focus on Goodwin 'the Arminian rebel' was well calculated to irritate the loyalist Wesley in the mid-1770s.

The Wesleyans responded indignantly to Toplady's allegations. Walter Sellon, an Anglican Methodist clergyman, suggested that Toplady 'could hardly have said

---

106 *The Works of John Wesley*, 14 vols (London, 1872), x. 317.
107 McGonigle, *Sufficient Saving Grace*, 235–36.
108 McGonigle, *Sufficient Saving Grace*, 276.
109 *The Letters of the Rev. John Wesley*, ed. J. Telford, 8 vols (London, 1931), v. 96.
110 *The Works of John Wesley*, x. 384. See also 385–91.
111 William Shrubsole, *Christian Memoirs, or a Review of the Present State of Religion in England* (1776), 206, 230, 234, 237, 241.
112 *The Works of Augustus Toplady*, 6 vols (London, 1825), i. 200–07; ii. 320, 343–44.

any thing greater in his commendation' of Wesley than to call him 'the John Goodwin of the present age'. Goodwin was 'a glorious champion for the truth of the Gospel, and genuine doctrines of the Church of England'. 'His *Redemption Redeemed* will ever remain as a monument of his great reading, clear reasoning, and sound judgement in the points we contest about'. His politics may have been wrongheaded, but he was a worthy 'theologist'.[113] When Sellon confronted the errors of Calvinists, he urged his readers to turn to Goodwin's *Treatise of Justification, Redemption Redeemed* and *An Exposition of Romans 9*.[114] Wesley's own respect for Goodwin as a theologian was undiminished by Toplady's attack, and in the third volume of *The Arminian Magazine* (1780), he republished Goodwin's paraphrase of Romans 9 and several further extracts.[115] He explained that he had done so because the book had become so scarce, and because 'many of my friends have long desired to see' it.[116]

Goodwin's texts were still changing people's minds. Having been a moderate Calvinist, the Yorkshire preacher Thomas Taylor moved towards Arminianism through reading Wesley. However, he 'held fast by Calvinian Imputed Righteousness, and Calvinian Final Perseverance'. He had 'never so much as heard' of John Goodwin, he wrote, 'and no wonder, for he was a condemned heretic among the Calvinists'. But when he read Wesley's abridgement of the *Treatise of Justification*, he was convinced: 'I saw the truth as clear as the shining sun. I saw Calvinian Imputed Righteousness is downright Antinomianism'. He then read *Redemption Redeemed* on the perseverance of the saints, and found that Goodwin answered Calvinist objections 'in so masterly a manner, as has not left the shadow of a doubt upon my mind'.[117]

Methodists continued to read and republish Goodwin well into the nineteenth century. An abridged version of *Redemption Redeemed* appeared in 1806, and in 1822 Thomas Jackson produced his substantial biography, *The Life of John Goodwin*. The Methodists' leading systematic theologian, Richard Watson, lent heavily on Goodwin's 'masterly' *Treatise of Justification* in his treatment of that topic in his *Theological Institutes*.[118] In 1835, Methodists republished three of Goodwin's theological tracts: *An Exposition of Romans 9, The Banner of Justification Displayed* and *The Agreement and Distance of Brethren*. In the following year, the prolific evangelist and theologian, Samuel Dunn, published a 450-page anthology entitled *Christian Theology by John Goodwin*. This was followed in 1840 by an unabridged edition of *Redemption Redeemed*. Thanks to such publications, Goodwin's renown among the Methodist cognoscenti even spread to the United States. The prime spokesman of American Methodism, Daniel Whedon, penned two leading articles

---

113 'The Church of England Vindicated', in *The Works of the Reverend Walter Sellon*, 2 vols (1814–15), i. 376–77, 415.
114 *The Works of the Reverend Walter Sellon*, i. 11, ii. 308–09.
115 *The Arminian Magazine*, 3 (1780), 9–19, 65–81, 121–37, 177–94.
116 *The Works of John Wesley*, xiv, 287; *The Arminian Magazine*, 3 (1780), 9–19.
117 Thomas Taylor, *Redeeming Grace Displayed to the Chief of Sinners* (1781), 47–48.
118 *The Works of the Rev. Richard Watson*, 12 vols (London, 1834–37), xi. 180–83, 190–210, 350, 421.

on Goodwin in the *Methodist Quarterly Review*, describing him as 'a remarkable divine'.[119] Indeed, American Methodists adopted the same combination of positions as Goodwin and Milton. They enrolled 'those two Arminian Puritans' in their list of heroes, and presented Arminianism as a theology with 'a peculiar affinity' with republicanism and liberty of conscience.[120] Back in England, *A Being Filled with the Spirit* was republished in 1867, and Jackson – now a venerable Methodist patriarch nearing ninety – issued his extended biography of Goodwin in 1872. As one writer noted, Goodwin had been reclaimed as 'the Wycliffe of Methodism'.[121]

Despite receiving the enthusiastic endorsement of Methodist theologians, Goodwin never became a household name among Evangelicals. As Jackson admitted in 1872, Goodwin was 'a man comparatively unknown'.[122] In part, this was because he had not written a popular devotional classic to compare with Rutherford's *Letters*, Baxter's *Saints Everlasting Rest*, or Bunyan's *Pilgrim's Progress*.[123] Moreover, after 1872, Goodwin's writings once again fell into disuse. When Henry Clark published a short *Life of John Goodwin* (1913), he noted that 'one of Congregationalism's great men' was largely forgotten.[124]

Although many Puritan works were republished in the second half of the twentieth century, the publishers (like the Banner of Truth Trust) were staunch Calvinists. Books that strayed from the path of Reformed orthodoxy were avoided like the plague. As in the 1650s, Thomas Goodwin was a respectable figure, but John was beyond the pale. One lecture at the Calvinist 'Westminster Conference' was devoted to Goodwin, but it was subtitled 'the Unorthodox Puritan'.[125] Among evangelical Protestants, Goodwin was almost completely forgotten. When W. W. Biggs published a short account of Goodwin in the Nonconformist 'Heritage Biography' series in 1961, he admitted that 'The name of John Goodwin is virtually unknown today, and his voluminous tracts and treatises lie unread on library shelves'.[126]

By the early twenty-first century, however, Goodwin was making a modest comeback. Disputes over predestination and freewill had returned with a vengeance among American Evangelicalism, especially after the emergence of 'Open Theists'

---

119 D. D. Whedon, 'John Goodwin', *Methodist Quarterly Review*, 45 (July 1863), 357–81; 'Memorabilia of John Goodwin', *Methodist Quarterly Review*, 51 (October 1869), 486–505, quotation at 487. On Whedon's theology, which moved away from classical Reformed Arminianism, see M. Noll, *America's God* (New York, 2002), 354–59.
120 See the article on 'Arminianism and Arminius' in the July 1879 edition of the *Methodist Quarterly Review*.
121 W. H. Goold, 'Prefatory note', *The Works of John Owen*, 24 vols, ed. W. H. Goold (London, 1850–53), xi. 2. The phrase was also used by the Methodist G. Wakefield, *Puritan Devotion* (London, 1957), 24.
122 Jackson, *The Life of John Goodwin* (London, 1872), iii.
123 For a useful survey of such classic texts see R. Gleason and K. Kapic, eds, *Invitation to the Puritan Classics* (Downers Grove, IL, 2004).
124 H. W. Clark, *The Life of John Goodwin* (London, 1913), 7.
125 J. G. Stringer, 'John Goodwin: the Unorthodox Puritan', *Westminster Conference, 1955: Issues and Approaches* (2002), 12–20.
126 W. W. Biggs, *John Goodwin* (London, 1961), 3, 20.

who denied God's foreknowledge of future events. One classical Arminian, John D. Wagner, republished an abridged version of *Redemption Redeemed*, 'Goodwin's master work' – in order to counter the resurgence of Calvinism.[127] An expanded second edition was published in 2004.[128] It was a telling reminder of the deep continuities within evangelical Protestantism. For if John Goodwin remained almost unknown within the tradition, his theological heirs and their opponents were as vigorous as ever.

---

127 John Goodwin, *Redemption Redeemed: A Puritan Defense of Unlimited Atonement*, ed. John D. Wagner (Eugene, OR, 2001).
128 John Goodwin, *Redemption Redeemed: A Puritan Defense of Unlimited Atonement: Expanded Edition*, ed. John D. Wagner (Eugene, OR, 2001).

Conclusion

'A Harbinger of the Lockean Age'

We began this book by highlighting two dominant images of our subject – Goodwin 'a man by himself', and Goodwin 'a harbinger of the Lockean age'. We have seen that the first image is seriously misleading. Goodwin had many enemies, but he also had numerous allies. Although he developed a distinctive intellectual profile that did not fit neatly into any of the major ideological blocs of his day, there was nothing eccentric or unintelligible about his ideas. Many contemporaries shared his congregationalism, tolerationism, Arminianism and republicanism, though few combined them all at once. Anglicans who warmed to his theology deplored his politics; Independents who liked his ecclesiology blanched at his doctrine.

But far from being an isolated maverick, Goodwin was always well connected to significant networks. In his Cambridge days, he was inducted into the spiritual brotherhood of Puritan clergy. For the best part of three decades, he was one of the major voices of Puritan London, a man with many ties to merchants and politicians, intellectuals and artisans. Throughout the revolutionary years, he enjoyed the passionate support of a large and gifted congregation that played an active role in the events of 1648–49 and was a significant force in City politics. He and his followers worked closely with the Saye-St John faction at Westminster and with other City Independents, and endured a troubled relationship with the Levellers. In the 1650s, Goodwin's anti-Calvinist books created a stir at Oxford and Cambridge, and he was at the heart of a developing network of Arminian Puritans. Despite his radicalism, he continued to cooperate with other godly clergy against Baptists, Quakers and Socinians. His skill as a theologian was admired by men like Richard Baxter, Benjamin Whichcote and John Wilkins, and he was widely acknowledged (by different camps) as a champion of Independency and Arminianism. Even in the dark days of the Restoration, he was still collaborating with other divines and publishers, and entertaining a steady stream of visitors. He was never 'a man by himself'.

But what of the second image of Goodwin: the liberal rationalist and forerunner of John Locke? For American historians like William Haller, W. K. Jordan, Perez Zagorin and Ellen More, Goodwin was a man of the future, a progressive who articulated the emerging values of tolerance, liberty, rational enquiry, and individualism. On this account, Goodwin's biography is part of a larger narrative, the story of 'How Toleration Came to the West', or of 'How the Enlightenment came to Calvinist England'.

At one level, this book has tried to correct the Whiggish image of Goodwin by emphasising his own self-image as a godly, learned Reformed theologian. In his treatises on justification and predestination, he believed that he was retrieving the doctrine of the Apostle Paul and the Church Fathers. Although Haller and More stressed his fondness for Castellio and Acontius, he spent far more time immersed in the biblical commentaries of Calvin, Musculus and Piscator. Although he highlighted textual issues in biblical scholarship, he had no doubts about the authority and infallibility of Scripture. For all his alleged rationalism, he accepted unquestioningly the great ages of the biblical patriarchs and the miracles recorded in Scripture. For all his supposed heterodoxy, he was resolutely opposed to Socinianism. For all his humanism, he employed the categories of scholastic Aristotelianism. Goodwin may have extolled 'new light' and 'novelty', but on the issues of baptism and the Trinity he thought it safest to keep to the old paths. Ellen More argued that Goodwin looked forward to a new age, the age of Pepys and Locke. But the Restoration marked the destruction of much that Goodwin held dear and the triumph of the things he hated – dynastic monarchy with its dissolute court, ecclesiastical hierarchy and conformity, the immorality and profanity of the theatres, lukewarm religion. Goodwin's austere Puritan republicanism had become outdated, unfashionable and seditious. Pepys revelled in this new world; Goodwin did not.

Yet despite its obvious flaws, the Whiggish picture of Goodwin cannot be dismissed out of hand. The very fact that his career could be construed in these terms is telling, for it is difficult to imagine such a story being told about someone like Samuel Rutherford.[1] Admirers of Rutherford's work of resistance theory *Lex, Rex* tried to squeeze it into a liberal mould, but much of his oeuvre remained stubbornly resistant to such treatment.[2] Goodwin looks very different. Rutherford saw the Covenanter Revolution as a chance to impose true religion on the British Isles; Goodwin saw the English Civil War as a war of liberation from regal and clerical slavery. Rutherford assailed 'pretended liberty of conscience'; Goodwin valorised it. Rutherford cried for the enforcement of strict Reformed orthodoxy; Goodwin mocked fallible 'Clergy-men' who stifled theological debate. Rutherford propounded an awe-inspiring vision of an utterly sovereign God who predestined most of humanity to hell for his own glory; Goodwin taught that God was equitable, reasonable and benevolent, 'a great lover of his creature man'. Rutherford depicted man as enslaved to sin and incapable of faith or repentance without the overpowering grace of God; Goodwin argued that God's universal grace gave 'natural men' the

---

1 Having said that, Rutherford (not Goodwin) is honoured alongside Milton as a writer in 'The Liberal Tradition' on the website of the neoconservative Acton Institute: http://www.acton.org/research/libtrad
2 See J. Coffey, *Politics, Religion and the British Revolutions: The Mind of Samuel Rutherford* (Cambridge, 1997).

capacity to repent and believe, so that even pagans could be saved. It is easy to see why Rutherford has been depicted as a hardline reactionary and Goodwin as a forerunner of the moderate Protestant Enlightenment. It is hardly surprising that Goodwin has attracted the attention of American liberal historians and been largely ignored by anti-Whig revisionists.

Moreover, the Whiggish representation of Goodwin coincides with at least part of his own self-image. If Goodwin saw himself as a godly Reformed divine, he also imagined himself an explorer of new worlds and a prophet of liberation. In his mind, Western Christendom was poised on the verge of historic transformations. This conviction was underpinned by a humanist faith in the value of intellectual enquiry and debate. It was also grounded in Goodwin's millenarianism, which was more muted than in some other radical Puritans, but emerges unmistakably in a number of his writings. Goodwin helps us to see how a new style of English Protestantism emerged from the fusion of radical Reformation and Renaissance humanism during the English Revolution.[3]

At the heart of his vision of the future were two motifs – intellectual exploration and liberation from slavery. The first was set out in his great programmatic statement in the preface to *A Treatise of Justification* (1642). Goodwin shared the Hartlib circle's Baconian belief that the discovery of the Americas was a prelude to a host of intellectual advances that could transform human society.[4] His own openness to intellectual change – especially in matters theological – was connected to his belief that theologians were like oceanic explorers. Like Milton, he was committed to 'revolving new motions and ideas' and 'the reforming of Reformation itself'.

The second motif in Goodwin's vision of the future was the notion of liberation from slavery. It was first articulated in *Anti-Cavalierisme* (1642), and reverberated through all of his political and ecclesiastical writings in the revolutionary era. For Goodwin, as for so many radical Puritans, the civil war and its aftermath was England's Exodus from Egyptian bondage. The English had been enslaved under 'cruel taskmasters' who exercised dominion over them. Bishops and presbyters alike were intent on binding the people of God, and robbing them of their independent judgement. But the tide of history was flowing against them. God was acting to liberate his people through the Independents and the New Model Army. Intermediate authorities who presumed to interpose between the individual and God were being overthrown. The state was being taught its limits, and learning not to domineer over conscience.

For Goodwin, England's new reformation was to be a voyage of discovery and a trek towards freedom. Inspired by Columbus the explorer and Moses the liberator, the English could set out in search of new continents of knowledge and a Promised Land of civil and religious liberty. This conception of historical change was shaped

---

3   The confluence of radical Reformation and Renaissance humanism during the English Revolution is examined in J. Scott, *England's Troubles: Seventeenth-Century English Political Instability in European Context* (Cambridge, 2000), chs. 10–14.
4   It is not surprising that Goodwin's statement was highlighted in C. Webster, *The Great Instauration: Science, Medicine and Reform, 1625–1660* (London, 1975), 8–9, 11, 19, 34.

by classical and humanist sources as well as by theological ones, and it constituted a profound reconfiguration of the Reformed tradition. Conservative Calvinists, like Samuel Rutherford, predicted with some prescience that the craze for 'liberty of conscience' would end in unbridled individualism, licentiousness and scepticism. But for Goodwin and Milton, this vision of new light and liberty was anything but godless. Theirs was not a modern secular liberalism, but it was a kind of early modern liberation theology.

In Goodwin, as in Milton, we can see the forging of a primitive version of the Whig interpretation of history, one that couples Protestantism with liberty and progress. Of course, traditional Protestants had seen the Reformation as liberation from popish tyranny, but with Goodwin and his ilk we have a broader conception – the times of ignorance and servility were drawing to a close, and God was redeeming his people from all forms of domination. This was a story about civil liberty, liberty of conscience and intellectual discovery. It was a profoundly political, even worldly vision. While Goodwin (and to a lesser extent Milton) still remained self-consciously Reformed, they had undertaken a subtle but powerful re-conceptualisation of Protestant religion.[5]

Goodwin's eschatology of exploration and liberation was distinctly radical, but it allowed him to be swept along by the main currents of intellectual change. By undermining intellectual conservatism, it fostered openness to fresh ideas, and contributed to the erosion of Calvinist orthodoxy. Goodwin modified and softened received Reformed theology in much the same way as his Anglican contemporaries. It is no surprise that some of his former followers felt at home in the company of Whichcote and More, Tillotson and Locke. On point after point, Goodwin adopted positions that would enjoy great appeal in Anglophone Protestant theology for the next two centuries. One thinks of his accent on the reasonableness of Christianity, evidentialist apologetics, religious toleration, the right to private judgement, universal redemption, the Grotian theory of atonement, the place of good works in (final) justification, and the salvability of the heathen.[6] Ideas that sounded dubious in the 1640s had become thoroughly conventional a century or so later. The Arminianism that Goodwin so eagerly promoted would be characteristic of the moderate Protestant Enlightenment.[7]

Nothing illustrates this transformation of attitudes better than the writings of eighteenth-century Presbyterians. In the 1640s, Presbyterians had excoriated the radical Independents and their 'accursed toleration'. By the early eighteenth

---

5 For further reflections on the transition from Puritanism to Whiggism see M. Goldie, 'Priestcraft and the birth of Whiggism', in N. Phillipson and Q. Skinner, eds, *Political Discourse in Early Modern Britain* (Cambridge, 1993), pp. 209–31.
6 See Brooks Holifield, *Theology in America: Christian Thought from the Age of the Puritans to the Civil War* (New Haven, 2003).
7 On the connections between Arminianism and Enlightenment see H. Trevor-Roper, 'The religious origins of the Enlightenment', in his *Religion, the Reformation and Social Change* (London, 1967), ch. 4; J. G. A. Pocock, *Barbarism and Religion*, vol. i: *The Enlightenments of Edward Gibbon* (Cambridge, 1999); D. Sorkin, 'Geneva's "enlightened orthodoxy": the middle way of Jacob Vernet (1698–1789)', *Church History*, 74 (2005).

century, the Nonconformist historian Edmund Calamy, grandson and namesake of Goodwin's colleague and Presbyterian critic, was defining Protestant dissent in terms that would have disturbed his grandfather and gratified Goodwin.[8] Under the influence of Locke, Presbyterians capitulated to the seductive new ideas with remarkable alacrity, softening (or even abandoning) their Calvinism and embracing voluntarist ecclesiology and tolerationist politics. In the eighteenth century, many Presbyterians throughout the English-speaking world spoke the language of their erstwhile Independent foes.[9]

But if many of the ideas Goodwin promoted became mainstream, aspects of his agenda remained irreducibly oppositional, at least in an English context. Unlike the Anglican latitudinarians, Goodwin had challenged the very notion of 'State Religion', repudiated tithes, castigated 'domineering' clergy and 'monopolizing' printers, denigrated set forms of prayer, rejected episcopacy, and cast doubt on the value of dynastic monarchy. He had promoted lay preaching, voluntary self-governing congregations, armed resistance to tyranny, and a free state. In England, these ideals remained distinctly counter-cultural, but they were kept alive by radical Dissenters.[10]

What was marginal in England became central in North America. By the mid-eighteenth century, the Congregationalist preachers of Puritan New England were becoming fluent in the idiom of 'civil and religious liberty'. Historians have commented on 'the Lockeianization of Protestant politics' in America, noting that divines like Elisha Williams defended religious liberty by appealing to natural law contract theory and a distinctively Protestant notion of the right of private judgement.[11] Yet remarkably similar arguments had been advanced by Goodwin a century before in the Whitehall Debates and various tracts. Like their English ancestors, radical American Whigs interpreted Protestant history as a story of liberation from 'ecclesiastical and civil tyranny', a tale of expanding knowledge discovered through 'freedom of inquiry and examination'. They deplored 'the execrable race of the Stuarts' and the 'dominion' of clerical hierarchies, but admired 'the spirit of liberty ... which severed the head of Charles the First from his body'.[12] Radical Protestant eschatology with its expectation of new light and liberation from slavery was to reach its apogee in the 'civic millennialism' of the

---

8   See E. Calamy, *A Defence of Moderate Non-Conformity*, 3 vols (London, 1703–05).
9   See J. Bradley, 'The religious origins of radical politics in England, Scotland, and Ireland, 1662–1800', in J. Bradley and D. van Kley, eds, *Religion and Politics in Enlightenment Europe* (Notre Dame, 2001), ch. 4; J. S. Tiedemann, 'Presbyterianism and the American Revolution in the Middle Colonies', *Church History*, 74 (2005).
10 See J. Bradley, *Religion, Revolution and English Radicalism: Non-conformity in Eighteenth-Century Politics and Society* (Cambridge, 1990), chs. 4–5; K. Haakonssen, ed., *Enlightenment and Religion: Rational Dissent in Eighteenth-Century Britain* (Cambridge, 1996).
11 M. P. Zuckert, 'Natural rights and Protestant politics', in T. S. Engeman and M. P. Zuckert, eds, *Protestantism and the American Founding* (Notre Dame, IN, 2004), 21–75.
12 The quotations are taken from a classic statement of the radical Whig interpretation of Protestantism: John Adams, 'A Dissertation on the Canon and Feudal Law' (1765) in *The Political Writings of John Adams*, ed. G. W. Carey (Washington, DC, 2000), 3–21.

American Revolution.[13] As Ruth Bloch argues in her study of this phenomenon, 'It can scarcely be overemphasized that radical whig ideology grew out of the experience of the English Revolution and Commonwealth of the 1640s and 1650s'.[14] If Goodwin had done much to popularise this new Protestant politics during the Puritan Revolution, it was the writings of Milton, Locke and Sidney that transmitted it to future generations.[15]

So was Goodwin a harbinger of the Age of Reason, a man of 'enlightened' views, a Locke before Locke? The answer is yes and no. No, because much of what passed for Enlightenment in the eighteenth century would have left Goodwin cold. To his dying days he remained a 'Puritan', an enemy of 'Anti-evangelicall' moralism and tepid religion. In doctrine and devotion (though not in politics), he had more in common with John Wesley than with John Locke.[16] Yet like Goodwin, Wesley was a 'reasonable enthusiast' who married ardent piety to Arminian sensibilities.[17] The founder of Methodism can be depicted as a man of the Counter-Enlightenment, but along with fellow-Evangelicals Isaac Watts and Philip Doddridge, he could act as an intellectual middleman, selectively mediating Enlightenment values and inculcating hot Protestant religion at the same time.[18] In his *Arminian Magazine*, for example, Wesley published an eclectic mix of extracts from such works as Locke's *Essay concerning Human Understanding*, Castellio's anti-Calvinist *Dialogues*, Goodwin's *Exposition of Romans 9*, Nye's *Life of Thomas Firmin* and Baxter's *Certainty of the World of Spirits*.[19] His relationship with the Enlightenment was ambivalent.

Goodwin, of course, had no 'Enlightenment' to relate to. He was immersed in the intellectual and religious culture of an earlier age, and we should not treat him as a maverick loner born in the wrong century, 'a man by himself' 'in advance of his time'. But equally, it would be foolish to deny that Goodwin reflected and reinforced intellectual and religious trends that would come to fruition in 'the Lockean age'. In the long term, Goodwin's writings were far less influential those

---

13 A point made by S. Yamada, 'Two ways toward the millennium: John Goodwin vs. the Fifth Monarchists', *The Hiroshima Law Journal*, 23 (1999), 41, who refers to N. Hatch, *The Sacred Cause of Liberty* (New Haven, 1977).
14 R. Bloch, *Visionary Republic: Millennial Themes in American Thought, 1756–1800* (Cambridge, 1985), p. 3.
15 See G. Sensabaugh, *That Grand Whig, Milton* (Stanford, 1952); *Milton in Early America* (Princeton, 1964); D. Armitage, A. Himy, and Q. Skinner, eds, *Milton and Republicanism* (Cambridge, 1995), part iv; A. P. F. Sell, *John Locke and the Eighteenth-Century Divines* (Cardiff, 1997); M. Goldie, 'Introduction' to *The Reception of Locke's Politics*, 6 vols (London, 1999), vol. i.; A. Houston, *Algernon Sidney and the Republican Heritage in England and America* (Princeton, 1991).
16 On Locke's Socinian tendencies, see J. Marshall, *John Locke: Resistance, Religion and Responsibility* (Cambridge, 1994).
17 See H. Rack, *Reasonable Enthusiast: John Wesley and the Rise of Methodism* (London, 1989).
18 On Methodism and Enlightenment see D. Hempton, *Methodism: Empire of the Spirit* (New Haven, 2005), ch. 2. See also B. Semmel, *The Methodist Revolution* (London, 1974); D. Bebbington, *Evangelicalism in Modern Britain* (London, 1989), 47–74; and G. Himmelfarb, *Roads to Modernity: The British, French and American Enlightenments* (New York, 2004), ch. 5.
19 See *Arminian Magazine*, vol. 5 (1782).

of his contemporaries Milton and Sidney. But during the middle decades of the seventeenth century, few had done so much to redefine the theology, ecclesiology and politics of English Protestantism.

Appendix

Anonymous Works Attributed to Goodwin

Few problems are more vexing for the intellectual biographer than the problem of attribution. In Goodwin's case, more than a dozen anonymous works have been attributed to him by contemporaries or by modern scholars. The anonymous works vary in length and significance, but in many cases their identification makes a difference to the way we tell Goodwin's story.

Broadly speaking, we can adduce two types of evidence in our attempt to ascertain authorship. *External evidence* includes any contemporary attribution of authorship, whether by another pamphleteer, a diarist or informant, or a reader who wrote the name of the supposed author on their own copy. In a number of cases discussed below, there is no such evidence available. Even where it is available, one cannot automatically assume that the contemporary attribution is accurate. *Internal evidence* includes vocabulary and phraseology; concepts and ideas; the printer and publisher of the work; and incidental references to people, places, books or events. One can ask whether a pamphlet bears a close stylistic resemblance to other writing by the author, and whether it contains characteristic ideas and expressions familiar from his other works.

Having analysed the dozen or so anonymous works attributed to Goodwin, I have tried to assess the likelihood of his authorship, assisted by the standard reference works of Wing and Halkett/Laing.[1] Since I have not 'arriv'd at the beautiful haven of infallibilitie', my judgements are open to revision in the light of fresh evidence or a different assessment of the existing data.

---

1 Donald Wing, *A Short-Title Catalogue of Books printed in England, Scotland, Ireland, Wales and British America and of English Books printed in Other Countries, 1641–1700*, 2nd edition, 4 vols. (New York, 1982–98); Samuel Halkett and John Laing, *Dictionary of Anonymous and Pseudonymous English Literature*, 9 vols (Edinburgh, 1926–1962).

Appendix

Arguments against Bowing at the Name of Jesus (1641).

Wing: W2083

The title page explains that the document was 'Composed about five yeares since, By A Reverend Minister of the City of London for his own defence'. The number of Puritan clergy in the City of London in the 1630s was substantial, so there are a variety of possible candidates. Henry Burton was the author of another (more aggressive) tract on the same subject, *Jesu-Worship Confuted, or Certaine Arguments against Bowing at the Name of Jesus* (1640), so he can be safely ruled out. Wing and Halkett and Fisher suggest that the author was one William Wickins (1614–99), but Wickins was clearly too young to be a 'Reverend Minister' in the mid-1630s.[2]

John Dury may have alluded to Goodwin's authorship of such a paper, when he wrote in 1640 that 'I have not seen any reasons putte to paper by Mr Cotton or Mr Goodwyn against the bowing at the name of Jesus'.[3] However, he may have been referring to Thomas Goodwin, or simply wishing that Cotton and Goodwin would address the topic. Ellen More attributes the pamphlet (tentatively) to Goodwin largely on the grounds that it argues against the imposition of *adiaphora*, but this is hardly unique to Goodwin.[4] The main argument for Goodwin's authorship lies in the fact that he was 'a Reverend Minister of the City of London' who had been reported in 1636 ('five yeares since') for administering communion on Easter Day to parishioners who were sitting rather than kneeling.[5] But kneeling at communion was a quite different issue to 'bowing at the name of Jesus', and the author of the tract defends kneeling as 'naturall, and sutable, and sufficiently licenced, and warranted in Scripture' (pp. 8–9). This does not necessarily rule Goodwin out, since he may have accepted kneeling at communion while not enforcing it, but it does make his authorship a little less likely. The style of the tract, with its scholastic logic and references to New Testament Greek, is what one would expect from 'A Reverend Minister of the City of London', though Goodwin did not usually rely as heavily on syllogistic argument. He remains one of a number of possible candidates (i.e. Puritan ministers in the City of London in the mid-1630s).

Author: Possibly Goodwin

M.S. to A.S. Printed by F. N. for Henry Overton (1644).

Wing: G1180 (cancelled); S116A.

The Reply of Two of the Brethren to A.S ... formerly called M.S. to A.S. Printed by M. Simmons for H. Overton (1644).

Wing: G1198 (cancelled); R1048B.

Wing originally attributed these works to Goodwin, but then backtracked. The original attribution is correct. '*M.S. against A.S* is John Goodwin of Coleman

---

2 The attribution was presumably made because Wickins wrote a later tract attacking the ritual: *The Warrant for Bowing at the Name of Jesus* (1660).
3 HP 2/2/33B, Letter from Dury to Samuel Hartlib (7 August 1640).
4 More, 'New Arminians', 39–42.
5 NA SP16/339/53, Information concerning the Diocese of London, 1636.

Street', Robert Baillie asserted in May 1644.[6] The tract was also confidently attributed to Goodwin by George Thomason, William Prynne and Thomas Edwards.[7] Goodwin himself cited and defended the tract in other works, which suggests that he was indeed the author.[8] Moreover, both editions were published by Henry Overton, Goodwin's follower and his main publisher in the 1640s. It is true that Goodwin refers to this work as if it was by someone else,[9] but since the tract was anonymous he may well have wished to maintain the formal anonymity. The external evidence for Goodwin's authorship is decisive.

There is still a puzzle over the identity of 'M.S.' and the 'Two Brethren' of the second edition. 'M.S.' may be Matthew Simmons, who printed *The Reply*, but the first edition was printed by 'F.N.'. The reason for calling the tract *M.S. to A.S.* remains unclear. As for the 'Two Brethren', Ellen More plausibly suggested that Goodwin wrote the work with John Price, his right-hand man and already an established pamphleteer.[10] There is no external evidence for this, but it would explain the title of the second edition. Whatever the case, Goodwin was clearly the main author of both editions, and oversaw their composition even if he had a co-author.

Author: Definitely Goodwin, but who was the co-author?

A Paraenetick or Humble Addresse to the Parliament and Assembly for (Not Loose, But) Christian Liberty. Printed by Matthew Simmons for Henry Overton (1644).

Wing: W2768, W2769

Wing attributes this to Roger Williams, but it was omitted from the standard edition of his *Complete Writings* and Williams' scholars have not regarded it as part of his oeuvre.[11] Given the printer, the publisher, and the explicit congregationalism, the author is far more likely to be Goodwin. George Gillespie certainly seems to attribute the pamphlet to him: 'Upon the same foundation doth M. Goodwin build in his Theomachia, and the Paraenetick for Christian Liberty, pag. 2 and 11, supposing the credit and authority of Gamaliels speech'.[12] The tract defends the 'Congregational Way', lay preaching and Christian liberty, and warns Parliament against being 'fighters against God' (a clear echo of *Theomachia*). It contains characteristically Goodwinian references to Gamaliel, 'domineering' prelates, and

---

6   Robert Baillie, *Letters and Journals* (3 vols, 1841–42), ii. 180–81.
7   Thomason dated his copy 3 May 1644 and wrote 'By Mr John Goodwin Colm-street' on the title page; Prynne, *The Sword of Christian Magistracy Supported* (1647), 152, 164; Edwards, *The Casting Down ... or A Treatise against Toleration* (1647), 117.
8   *Innocencies Triumph* (1644), 4; *Innocency and Truth* (1645), 12–13, 40–41.
9   *Innocencies Triumph*, 4.
10 More, 'New Arminians', 74.
11 *The Complete Writings of Roger Williams*, 7 vols (New York, 1963). The tract is not even mentioned in Edwin Gaustad's biography, *Liberty of Conscience: Roger Williams in* America (Grand Rapids, 1991).
12 [George Gillespie], *Wholesome Severity reconciled with Christian Liberty* (1645), 28.

a providential 'juncture of times'. There is a Latin quotation from Goodwin's former colleague and friend, John Stoughton of St Mary Aldermanbury.

If Goodwin was the author, the anonymity of the tract is not surprising. This was a stinging critique of both Parliament and the Assembly of Divines, published at a time (November 1644) when Goodwin was fighting to hold on to his parish living. He wished to vent his frustration at Westminster's assault on 'Christian Libertie', without paying the costs of owning up to authorship.

Author: Probably Goodwin

Certain Briefe Observations and Antiquaeries on Master Prins Twelve Questions (1644).
Wing: G1155, R1667

A Moderate Answer to Mr. Prins Full Reply. Printed for Benjamin Allen (1645)
Wing: G1181, R1676

These two tracts can be considered together, since the title page of *A Moderate Answer* announces that it is 'By the same Author' as *Certain Briefe Observations*. Ignoring this, Halkett and Laing attribute the first to Robinson and the second to Goodwin. Wing hedges its bets by listing them under both Goodwin and Henry Robinson, but Robinson was favoured by W. K. Jordan.[13]

Internal evidence is indecisive, since the arguments employed can also be found in Goodwin's writings. However, external evidence confirms that Goodwin was not the author. Later in 1645, he declared that he had 'put forth only one book (and that a very small one too …)' between the publication of *Theomachia* (Thomason: 2 September 1644) and Prynne's *Truth Triumphing over Falshood* (Thomason: 2 January 1645).[14] The 'very small' book was clearly *Innocencies Triumph* (Thomason: 26 October), and Goodwin's statement rules out *Certaine Brief Observations* (Thomason: 4 October). In 1646, Goodwin explained that he had written 'three severall tracts' against Prynne – i.e. *Innocencies Triumph, Innocency and Truth*, and *Calumny Arraigned*. The first two were responses to Prynne's *A Full Reply*, and it is very unlikely that Goodwin would have thought it necessary to write yet another retort to Prynne's *Full Reply* (i.e. *A Moderate Answer*).[15] The author may have been Henry Robinson, though another possibility is Goodwin's follower, John Price.

Author: Not Goodwin, but possibly by an associate

---

13 W. K. Jordan, *Men of Substance* (Chicago, 1942), 90–92; Jordan, *The Development of Religious Toleration in England*, 4 vols (London, 1932–40), iv. 140–76.
14 *Calumny Arraigned* (1645), 5.
15 *Anapologesiastes* (1646), 'Preface', §13.

A Short Answer to A.S. (1645)

Wing: G1201

This is attributed to Goodwin by Wing, and William Prynne identified Goodwin as the 'supposed' author.[16] It is attributed to Henry Robinson in the British Library Catalogue and by W. K. Jordan.[17] Prynne was clearly not certain of this attribution (hence the 'supposed'), and his attributions were not always accurate. He suggested Henry Robinson as the author of *The Arraignment of Mr Persecution* (though we now know it was Richard Overton), and he had been mistaken before in assuming that Goodwin was the author of *Certaine Brief Observations*. Goodwin himself never cited *A Short Answer*, whereas he did cite and defend the anonymous *M.S. to A.S./Reply of Two of the Brethren*. When in 1646 Thomas Edwards charged him with not responding to Adam Steuart's *Duply* to 'the two brethren', Goodwin did not deny the charge, though his comment is perhaps cryptic enough to leave a little room for doubt.[18]

In terms of internal evidence, the most striking feature of the pamphlet is its appendix: 'Twenty six difficult questions easily answered concerning a toleration of differing opinions'. The author follows through on the logic of radical tolerationist argument, by frankly stating that Roman Catholics cannot be forced to attend Protestant services. Toleration of 'Jesuited Papists and other subtle Hereticks' 'may gaine some to Sathan', but since truth will also be 'published and improved' many more will be gained to God. Elsewhere, the author quotes Roger Williams' *Bloudy Tenent* and [Robinson's] *John Baptist*. All this suggests that he was a more radical and sectarian writer than Goodwin. At times, the arguments of *A Short Answer* are very close to those found in Goodwin's tracts (e.g. the stress on fallibility, the attack on implicit faith), but these were common currency among radical tolerationists. And while a Goodwin reply to A.S.'s *Duply* to M.S. would make sense, he was preoccupied in early 1645, and had only just published his response to Prynne a few days earlier (Thomason collected *Calumny Arraigned* on 31 January, and *A Short Answer* on 3 February).

The evidence suggests, therefore, that Goodwin was probably not the author, and Henry Robinson is the most obvious candidate. However, it should be noted that there appears to be a contradiction between *A Moderate Answer* (also often attributed to Robinson) and *A Short Answer*. The former insists that toleration for Catholics does not follow from tolerationist premises, for 'they differ in fundamentals, and are properly another Religion'.[19] It may be that Robinson was the author of *A Short Answer*, but not of the two earlier pamphlets against Prynne.

Author: Probably not Goodwin

---

16 William Prynne, *A Fresh Discovery of some Prodigious New Wandring-Blasing-Stars, & Firebrands, Stiling themselves New-Lights* (1645), 4.
17 Jordan, *Men of Substance*, 91–92; Jordan, *Development of Religious Toleration*, iv. 140–76.
18 Thomas Edwards, *Gangraena*, ii. 58; Goodwin, *Anapologesiastes*, 'Preface to the Reader', sig. cr: 'As for my *nil-respondes* to Mr *Robrough*, and *Adam Steuart*, I shall account honestly unto Mr *Edwards*, when he and I reckon about the arrears, of *Gangraena* the younger'.
19 *A Moderate Answer* (1645), 45, 38.

Appendix

***Some Modest and Humble Queries concerning a Printed Paper*. Printed by Matthew Simmons for Henry Overton (1646).**

Wing: G1204

Goodwin confirmed his authorship of this anonymous pamphlet by defending the queries at length in *Hagiomastix ... A Vindication of some printed Queries published some moneths since by Authority* (1647). His congregation also acknowledged the *Queries* as his work, and Thomas Edwards took it for granted that Goodwin was the author.[20]

Author: Definitely Goodwin

***The Army Harmlesse*. For John Pounset (1647).**

Wing: G1150

An anonymous pamphlet normally attributed to Goodwin. The McAplin Catalogue suggests 'attribution uncertain', but notes that it appears 'bound in a volume marked "Goodwin's Tracts"'. None of Goodwin's known works were published by John Pounset, but Pounset did have a pamphlet printed by Matthew Simmons in 1647. Moreover, Goodwin is identified as the author in *A Model of a New Representative* (1651), 6. As a defence of the army's revolt, *The Army Harmlesse* was of a piece with Goodwin's other works of political casuistry, especially *Anti-Cavalierisme* and *Right and Might Well Met*. Like them, it appealed to 'the Law of necessity', pointed to a providential 'juncture of time', and defended the right of private men to judge in cases of necessity. And like his other political tracts, it depicted revolutionary events as a liberation from 'servitude and vassalage'.

Author: Almost certainly Goodwin

J. G., B.D., *Independencie Gods Veritie*. Printed for William Ley (1647).

Wing: G1173

Although this pamphlet has always been attributed to Goodwin, there are some oddities about it. First and foremost, the title page gives the author as '*J.G.* B.D.' Goodwin was never awarded a B.D., but I have not been able to find an Independent with the initials J. G. who was. The tract is published by William Ley, rather than for Goodwin's usual publishers, and it contains uncharacteristic references to 'S. Paul' and an absence of learned quotations. None of these features count decisively against Goodwin's authorship, and given the lack of any obvious alternative, it is reasonable to conclude that the 'B.D.' after Goodwin's name is merely a publisher's error. The arguments in favour of Independency and toleration are entirely consonant with Goodwin's own position.

Author: Probably Goodwin

---

20 *An Apologeticall Account* (1647), 6–7; Edwards, *The Casting Down*, 117.

Κολλούριον: Or Eye Salve to Anoint the Eyes of the Ministers of the Province of London. **Printed by G. Dawson for Henry Cripps (1649).**
Wing: K746
This single sheet, eight-page pamphlet was written 'By a Minister of the Gospel' and sold by Henry Cripps, Goodwin's publisher after the death of Henry Overton. The *ODNB* attributes the pamphlet to the Congregationalist minister, William Bartlet, who did have other books published by Henry and Elizabeth Overton and shared Goodwin's liking for Greek titles. But Bartlet's known writings do not include any political tracts. The case for Goodwin is stronger because the arguments of *Kollourion* are very closely paralleled in his other political works and reappear in amplified form in *The Obstructors of Justice*, published several months later in May. For example, we find the army hailed as God's 'instruments' 'bringing the grand incendiaries ... to condigne punishment (2–3); Numbers 25 cited to justify the execution of judgement by private persons (3; *Obstructors*, 43–45); an injunction to 'adore the glorious and wonderful actings of God' in the regicide (3); the regicide justified on the grounds that God is no 'respecter of persons' (6; *Obstructors*, 5–7); and a characteristic reference to 'bloody Cavalierisme' (6).
Author: Probably Goodwin

Englands Apology. **Printed by Matthew Simmons for Livewell Chapman (1651).**
Wing: E2942, E2943
Gerald Aylmer first attributed this pamphlet to John Goodwin in a footnote to a *Past and Present* article in 1968, but did not give his reasons.[21] He was presumably following a seventeenth-century reader who included the tract in a volume of Goodwin's writings now held by the Bodleian Library. It is inscribed 'Diverse Treatises written by John Goodwin', and includes twelve well-known works by Goodwin followed by 'three others' – attacks on Goodwin by Kendall and Lane, and *Englands Apology*.[22] Although Livewell Chapman did not print any of Goodwin's other works, the printer, Matthew Simmons, had worked regularly with Goodwin since 1644.

Internal evidence lends support to the attribution. The tract is a contribution to the Engagement Controversy (on which Goodwin was otherwise surprisingly silent), and its arguments and positions are strikingly similar to those employed in his other political tracts. It emphasises the 'blood guilt' of Charles I and extols the regicide as 'the first cleer and thorow Act of Justice that ever was executed in the Western World'.[23] It chimes with Goodwin's hymns on England's liberation from

---

21 G. Aylmer, '*Englands Spirit Unfoulded, or an Incouragement to take the Engagement*: A Newly Discovered pamphlet by Gerrard Winstanley', in C. Webster, ed., *The Intellectual Revolution of the Seventeenth Century* (London, 1974), 110–11. Originally published in *Past and Present*, 40 (1968).
22 Bodl., Shelfmark: 4º X 42(2) Jur.
23 Cf. *Obstructors of Justice* (1649), sig. A3v ('that Royal Act of Justice'); Price, *Clerico-Classicum*, 48 ('the highest act of Justice that was ever performed in this land').

clerical domination and 'Scottish Tyrannie'. It employs once again the example of Haman and Mordechai.[24] The emphasis on God going 'out of his ordinary course' is closely paralleled elsewhere in Goodwin's sermons.[25]

Author: Probably Goodwin

A Just Balance, or Some Considerable Queries about Mr Love's Case, Tryal and Sentence. **By Ja. Cottrell for Giles Calvert (1651).**

Wing: J1229

According to a contemporary inscription on the title-page of the copy held in the Routh Collection of Durham University Library, the author was 'John Goodwin of Colemanstreet'.[26] Its format (thirty-two queries) is similar to that used elsewhere by Goodwin, and it refers to his favourite biblical commentators, Peter Martyr, Junius and Musculus. The tract was a contribution to the debate over Christopher Love, a Presbyterian minister found guilty of plotting against the Commonwealth. Its call for Love's execution was controversial, but entirely in keeping with Goodwin's hard line towards malignants. The providentialist logic and the appeal to the notion of bloodguilt are reminiscent of *Right and Might Well Met* and *The Obstructors of Justice*. The anonymity of the tract is not surprising if Goodwin was the author – he wanted to call for 'justice' to be done on Love, but wanted to do so anonymously, so that he could not be accused of baying for Presbyterian blood.

Author: Probably Goodwin

A Door Opening to Salvation, or A Brief Account, by Way of Question and Answer, of some of the Principal Heads of the Great Mystery of Christian Religion **(1662).**

Wing: D1909

This major catechism has been omitted from previous studies of Goodwin, though in the early eighteenth century, Edmund Calamy's list of Goodwin's works included 'His Catechism, or the Principal Heads of the Christian Religion'.[27] More recently, Ian Green tentatively identified Goodwin as the author.[28] Comparison with Goodwin's other writings provides ample confirmation for this attribution. *A Door* recapitulates many of Goodwin's key theological emphases on Trinitarianism, Arminianism, the salvability of pagans, justification, millenarianism, paedobaptism, and congregationalism. At numerous points, it echoes his earlier works, especially *A Treatise of Justification*, *The Divine Authority of the Scripture*, and *Redemption*

---

24 Cf. *Butchers Blessing* (1642), 4.
25 See *A Being Filled with the Spirit* (1670), 28–41.
26 Durham University Library, Shelfmark: Routh 63T.13/11.
27 Edmund Calamy, *An Account of the Ministers ... Ejected by the Act of Uniformity*, 2 vols, second edition (London, 1713), i. 53.
28 I. Green, *The Christian's ABC: Catechisms and Catechizing in England, c. 1530–1740* (Oxford, 1996), 638–39, 654–55.

Redeemed. It also cites favourite authors like Grotius and Brightman. The style and distinctive set of positions indicate that Goodwin was definitely the author.

Author: Definitely Goodwin

Prelatick Preachers None of Christ's (1663).
Wing: G1192

Attributed to John Goodwin by Richard Baxter.[29] Although the NUC notes 'Ascription to John Goodwin very doubtful', numerous internal features of the tract confirm Goodwin's authorship: characteristic phrases such as 'the Holy Ghost taketh notice', 'the best Interpreters', 'our English proverb'; the polemic against blind obedience; the learned references to Greek and Latin texts; the citations from Brightman, Mede, Hammond, Prynne and Grotius; the quotation from Minut. Felix (69), also used on the title page of *Eirenomachia*; the attempt to explain why early Stuart Puritan ministers were not 'prelatick preachers' even though they accepted episcopal ordination; the congregationalist assertion that Christ is 'the Sole Lawgiver' to his church, and that the people should choose their own pastor.

Author: Definitely Goodwin

'Some further considerations about Common Prayer'
Cambridge University Library MS

The seventeenth-century owner of this manuscript made a note on the back page: 'This Libell I take to have been Mr John Goodwins; and is in Print if I remember right'. Despite an extensive search, I have been unable to find a published version of this 31-page paper. However, the internal evidence confirms that Goodwin probably was the author of the 'Libell'. The uncompromising stance matches that of *Prelatick Preachers None of Christ*; the author condemns imposed uniformity as an enslavement of conscience and a usurpation of God's prerogative; he assumes the value of a learned ministry and opposes set forms of prayer; he argues against the magistrate's authority in religion using arguments familiar from Goodwin's earlier tracts; there are characteristic expressions like 'veines of Scripture'; the paper cites Augustine, Tertullian and Calderinus. Moreover, one passage very closely parallels a similar one in *A Being Filled with the Spirit* (1670), 191: Goodwin says that God is like a husband whose 'jealousie' over his wife is aroused not only by adultery but by 'any familiarity or correspondencie' she has with other men.

Author: Probably Goodwin

---

29 *Reliquiae Baxterianae* (1696), iii. 19, §41.

Appendix

Laophilus Misotyrannus, *Mene Tekel, or The Downfall of Tyranny* (1664).
Wing: J988

Attributed to Goodwin by a government informer in 1665, who claimed that Goodwin – 'whom he believe writt *Mene Tekeel* – was 'wrighting another peece of the same nature'.[30] However, other informers attributed the tract to Roger Jones, an attribution endorsed by Wing and other authorities.[31] The militant advocacy of armed resistance contrasts sharply with Goodwin's circumspection in *A Door*, and the stress on the magistrate's duty to suppress idolatry and blasphemy is at odds with Goodwin's denial of the magistrate's power in matters of religion.

Author: Not Goodwin

The Errours of the Carelesse by Necessitie Confuted (c. 1800)

This was published as a Goodwin tract around 1800 by H. Bradford of Thame, and introduced with the following note: 'The Publisher ... has every reason to believe it to be the work of the celebrated John Goodwin. It bears the signature J. G. and is dated 1648, and the subject is such as would flow from the pen of this distinguished divine'. The publisher adds nothing about whether the item was a rare tract or a manuscript, or where it was found.

In fact, as Professor Sonoko Yamada has pointed out to me, both the title and the content are very similar to that of an anonymous and unpublished treatise: 'The Confutation of Errours of the Careless by Necessity'. This tract was written against the Calvinist, John Careless, and refuted by John Knox in 1559.[32] We can safely conclude that Goodwin was not the author. It is conceivable that he acquired a copy of the reconstructed treatise in 1648 and initialled it 'J.G.', which would explain why Bradford thought that Goodwin was the author.

Author: Not Goodwin

---

30 NA SP 29/114/11; *CSPD* (1664–65), 234.
31 *CSPD* (1664–65), 329; *CSPD* (1666–67), 537, 545. See R. Greaves, *Enemies under his Feet: Radicals and Nonconformists in Britain, 1664–77* (Stanford, CA, 1990), 17, 35, 107, 211.
32 Knox's reply can be found in *The Works of John Knox*, ed. D. Laing, 6 vols (Edinburgh, 1846–64), v. 15ff. It contained lengthy extracts from the 'Confutation', and these were reprinted in the *Transactions of the Baptist Historical Society*, 4 (1914), 89ff. For background see D. A. Penny, *Freewill or Predestination* (Woodbridge, 1990), pp. 160–90.

A Goodwin Bibliography

1   Unpublished Manuscript Sources
2   Works by John Goodwin
3   Works against Goodwin and his Congregation
4   Works by Goodwin's Followers
5   Posthumously Republished Works by Goodwin
6   Secondary Sources on Goodwin
7   Unpublished Theses on Goodwin

1   Unpublished Manuscript Sources

Bodleian Library, Oxford

Ashmolean MS 436, no. 8, fols. 47–48, 'Sermon by Mr John Goodwin at Abchurch 1648, Octobr 22 M.'
Pococke MS 429, fols. 3–7, Letter from Thomas Barlow to John Goodwin
Rawlinson MS G.117 fols. 1r–3r, Letter from Goodwin to John Davenant

British Library, London

Add. MS 15,669, Proceedings of the Committee for Plundered Ministers
Add. MS 34,599, Correspondence of Henry Spellman containing seals of various scholars, including the simple floral seal of 'John Goodwin'
Add. MS 71,532, f. 17, Henry Marten's critical comment on Goodwin's Συγκρητισμος. *Or Dis-satisfaction Satisfied* (1653)
Harleian MS 837/151 fos.48r–59r, Goodwin's position paper on justification, 1639

Cambridge University Library

Add. MS 44(7), John Goodwin, 'Some further considerations about common prayer'
CUA Matriculation Book, vol. 1 (1544–1613)

CUA Supplicats
Queens' College Journale, vol. 5 (1587–1621)
Queens' College Journale, vol. 6 (1622–1691)
Queens' College Bursars Books, no. 24 (c. 1614)
Queens' College Bursars Books, no. 25 (1625–26)
Queens' College Bursars Books, no. 26 (1624–25)

Corporation of London Record Office
Common Council Journal, vols 40 and 41

Guildhall Library, London
MS 3891/1 St Mary Abchurch, churchwardens' accounts
MS 4346/1 St Mary Lothbury, parish register
MS 4449/1 St Stephen Coleman Street, parish register (1558–1636)
MS 4449/2 St Stephen Coleman Street, parish register (1636–1717)
MS 4457/2 St Stephen Coleman Street, churchwardens' accounts (1586–1640)
MS 4458/1 St Stephen Coleman Street, vestry minutes (1622–1694)

Holkham Hall, Norfolk
Holkam MS 684, Letter from Goodwin to William Heveningham

National Archives, Kew
SP 16/339/53 Information concerning the Diocese of London (1636)
SP 16/351/100 Account of the Visitation of the Diocese of London (March 1637)
SP 16/371/39 Information concerning the Diocese of London (November 1637)
SP 29/80/62 Letter from Goodwin to Sarah Goodwin (15 September 1663)
SP 29/82/39 Letter from Goodwin to Sarah Goodwin (24 October 1663)
SP 29/110/61 Letter from Goodwin to Sarah Goodwin (11 January 1664)
SP 29/110/102 Letter from Goodwin to Sarah Goodwin (16 January 1664)
SP 29/114/11 (March 1665), Informers report on Goodwin
PROB 11/320, Goodwin's will

Norfolk Record Office
ANW 13 Archdeacon's Parish Register Transcripts
DN/REG 16, book 22, Institution Book (1604–29)
DN/VSC 2/3A Visitation Consignation Books for the Diocese of Norwich (1633)
KL/C 7/0 King's Lynn Hall Book (1611–37)
MF 27/3 Papers sent to the Bacon/Townshend Families (1556–1638)
PD 368/1 Helloughton Parish Records (1539–1653)
PD 369/1 St Mary's, East Rainham Parish Records (1627-)
Townshend 62 MS 1481 Townshend Estates Account Book
Y/C 19/6 Great Yarmouth Assembly Book (1625–42)

2 Works by John Goodwin

Pre-1640

Epicedium Cantabrigiense (1612). Cambridge University verses in honour of Prince Henry. Includes an acrostic poem by 'I. Goodwin. Coll. Reginalis' on pages 48–49.

Lacrymae Cantabrigienses (1619). Cambridge University verses in honour of QueenAnne. Includes a poem by 'Ioan. Goodwin Coll. Reginal. Soc.' on pages 31–32.

'Epistle to the Reader' in Henry Ramsden, *Gleaning of God's Harvest* (1639).

'Epistle Dedicatory to the Right Honourable Sir Maurice Abbot' and 'Epistle of the Reader' in Richard Sibbes, *An Exposition of the Third Chapter of the Epistle of St Paul to the Philippians* (1639).

1640

The Saints Interest in God. Printed by M. F[lesher] for Henry Overton. 12mo. [60], 341, [1] p. November 5th sermons. Dedication to Isaac Pennington, Sr., signed 7 August 1640. STC: 12031

God a Good Master and Protector. Printed by T. Cotes, and are to be sold by W. Harris. 12mo. [36], 294, 199 p.
Wing: G1168. Dedication to Elizabeth Hampden signed 14 October 1640.

The Christians Engagement for the Gospel. Printed by T. Cotes for P. Cole. 12mo. 334pp.
Wing: G1159. Dedication to John Pym signed 4 December 1640.

1641

The Returne of Mercies, or The Saints Advantage by Losses. Printed by M.F. for R.D. and H. Overton. 12mo. [22], 383 p.
Wing: G1199. Registered 21 November 1640. Dedication to Lady Clark of Reading signed 18 May 1641. Epistle to the Reader signed 24 May.

Christ Lifted Up, or The Heads of the chief Controverted Points, Preached by Mr John Goodwin, Pastor of Colman-street London, Which hath been the pretended grounds of the opposition that he hath had, by some other Ministers. 4to. [14] p.
Wing: G1157.

Impedit ira Animum, or Animadversions upon some of the looser and fouler passages in a Written Pamphlet intituled, A Defence of the true sense and meaning of the words of the Holy Apostle. 4to. [4], 15, 106 p.
Wing: G1171.

Ireland's Advocate. A Sermon preached to promote the contributions for the reliefe of the Protestants in Ireland. Printed for William Larnar. 4to. [2], 36 p.
Wing: G1178. Thomason: E.149(2): 14 November.
1642

Imputatio Fidei; or a Treatise of Justification. Printed by R. O. and G. D. for Andrew Crooke. 4to. [58], 210, 231 p.

Dedication dated 24 January. Engraved portrait of Goodwin, and engraved title page.
Wing: G1172. Thomason: E.139(1): 24 January.

Anti-Cavalierisme; or, Truth pleading for the Suppression of that butcherly brood of Cavaliering Incendiaries. Printed by G. B. and R. W. for H. Overton. 4to. Pp. [2], 51.
Wing: G1146, G1146A, G1147. Thomason: E.123(25): 21 October.

The Butcher's Blessing. Printed for Henry Overton. 4to. [2], 6 p.
Wing: G1152. Thomason: E242(8): 4 November.

1643

Os Ossarianum, or a Bone for a Bishop to Pick. A Vindication of a treatise called Anti-Cavalierisme from the exceptions of Gr. Williams, Bishop of Ossory. Printed by Henry Overton. 4to. 64 p.
Wing: G1185. Thomason: E96(1): 11 April.

'A Letter sent from I.G. to T.G' in *A Quarie concerning the Church-Covenant practiced in Separate Congregations*. Printed for John Bellamie and Ralph Smith. 4to. [2], 14 p.
Wing: G1195.

1644

[John Goodwin], *M.S. to A.S. With a plea for Libertie of Conscience in a Church Way against the cavils of A.S., and observations on his Considerations upon the Apologeticall Narration*. Printed by F. N. for Henry Overton. 4to. [2], 110 p.
Wing: G1180 (S116A). Thomason: E.45(3): 3 May.

[John Goodwin], *A Reply of Two of the Brethren to A.S. ... formerly called M.S. to A.S.* Printed by M. Simmons for H. Overton. 4to. [4], 112 p.
Wing: G1198 (R1048B). Thomason: E.54(18): 3 May.

Θεομαχια *[Theomachia], or the Grand Imprudence of Men running the Hazard of Fighting against God in suppressing any Way, Doctrine, or Practice concerning which they know not certainly whether it be from God or no. Being the Substance of two sermons preached in Colemanstreet upon occasion of the Late Disaster sustain'd in the West*. Printed for H. Overton. 4to. Pp. [iv], 52.
Wing: G1206, G1207. Registered 24 September. Thomason: E.12(1): 2 September.

Innocencies Triumph; or, an Answer to the back-part of a discourse by W. Prynne, intituled, A Full Reply. Printed for Henry Overton. 4to. [2], 22 p.
Wing: G1174, G1175. Thomason: E14(10): 26 October.

[John Goodwin?], *A Paraenetick or Humble Addresse to the Parliament and Assembly for (Not Loose, But) Christian Liberty* (1644). Printed by Matthew Simmons for Henry Overton. 4to. [2], 14 p.
Wing: W2768, W2769. Thomason: E.19(10): 30 November.

Innocency and Truth Triumphing Together; or, the latter part of an answer to a discourse by William Prynne, called A Full Reply. Printed by Matthew Simmons for Henry Overton. 4to. [8], 99 p.
Wing: G1176. Thomason: E24(8): 8 January.

1645

Calumny Arraigned and Cast; or, A Briefe Answer to William Prynne, in a Discourse, entituled, Truth Triumphing over Falsehood. Printed by M. Simmons for H. Overton. 4to. [8], 55 p.
Wing: G1153. Registered 13 January. Thomason: E26(18): 31 January.

'Epistle to the Reader' in William Fenner, *A Divine Message to the Elect Soul* (1645). Edmund Calamy also recommends the book. Republished in 1647, 1650, 1651 and 1676.

1646

Twelve Serious Cautions very necessary, to be observed in and about a Reformation. Printed by M.S. for Henry Overton. 4to. [4], 8 p.
Wing: G1211. Registered 12 February. Thomason: E.322(31): 17 February.

Cretensis: or a Briefe Answer to an Ulcerous Treatise lately published by Mr. Thomas Edwards, intituled, Gangraena. Printed by M.S. for Henry Overton. 4to. [2], 50 p.
Wing: G1161, G1162. Registered 7 March. Thomason: E.328(22): 19 March.

Anapologesiates Antapologias. Or the Inexcuseablenesse of that Accusation of the Brethren called Antapologia. Printed by Matthew Simmons for Henry Overton. 4to. [45], 253, [11] p.
Wing: G1145. Registered 2 July 1645. Thomason: E.353(5): 27 August.

[John Goodwin], *Some Modest and Humble Queries concerning a Paper intituled, An Ordinance presented to the House of Commons for preventing Heresies.* Printed by Matthew Simmons for Henry Overton. 4to. [2], 8 p.
Wing: G1204. Registered 19 September. Thomason: E.355(1): 22 September.

1647

Hagiomastix, or the Scourge of the Saints displayed in his colours of Ignorance and Blood, or a vindication of some Queries published in way of answer to certaine Anti-papers of Syllogismes entituled Vindication of a Printed Paper. Printed by Matthew Simmons for Henry Overton. 4to. [34], 134, [2] p.
Wing: G1169. Thomason: E.374(1): 5 February.

'Epistle to the Reader' in William Fenner, *Practicall Divinitie: or Gospel Light Shining Forth in severall choice Sermons.* Signed by John Goodwin, 5 February 1647.

A Candle to see the Sunne; or, a further clearing up of some passages mis-apprehended by some in a Treatise intituled Hagiomastix displayed. Printed by M.S. for H. Overton. 4to. 4 p.
Wing: G1154. Thomason: E.377(6): 18 February.

God Justified in the Condemnation of Man without the Helpe of the Arminian tenet of Freewill. Registered 30 February. Not published.

A Post-script or Appendix to a Treatise lately published intituled Hagio-mastix. Printed for H. Overton. 4to. [10], 28, [2] p.
Wing: G1191. Registered 4 March. Thomason: E.383(10): 2 April.

[John Goodwin], *The Army Harmlesse: or, a dispasionat discussion of the proceedings of the Army under Sir Thomas Fairfax.* Printed for John Pounset. 4to. [2], 29 p.
Wing: G1150. Thomason: E.398(27): 16 July.

J[ohn] G[oodwin], B.D., *Independencie Gods Veritie, or the Necessitie of Toleration. Unto which is added the chief Principles of the Government of Independent Churches.* Printed for W. Ley. 4to. 8 p.
Wing: G1173. Thomason: E. 410(24): 14 October.

The Divine Authority of the Scriptures Asserted, or the Great Charter of the Worlds Blessednes Vindicated. Printed by A. M. for Henry Overton. 4to. [22], 377, [9] p. Engraved portrait of Goodwin.
Wing: G1163. Registered 3 April. Thomason: E.420(1): 18 December.

1648

Sion-Colledg Visited; or, some Animadversions upon a pamphlet under the title of A Testimonie to the Truth of Jesus Christ, subscribed, as it is pretended, by Ministers of London. Printed by M. S. for Henry Overton. 4to. [2], 29 p.
Wing: G1202. Registered 26 January. Thomason: E.425(2): 1 February.

'Epistle of the Reader' in Jacob Acontius, *Satans Stratagems; or the Devils Cabinet-Councel discovered.* Printed by John Macock and are to be sold by John Hancock. 4to. [16], 136 p. Thomason: E.428(19): 24 February. Reissued in 1651 as *Darkness Discovered, or the Devils Secret Stratagems Laid Open.* Printed by J[ohn] M[acock]; sold by William Ley.

Νεοφυτοπρεσβυτερος *[Neophutopresbuteros], or The Yongling Elder or Novice-Presbyter. Complied especially for the Christian Instruction of William Jenkin.* Printed for Henry Overton. 4to. [8], 139 p.
Wing: G1183. Thomason: E.447(27): 15 June.

1649

Right and Might Well Met. Or a Briefe Enquiry into the Proceedings of the Army. Wherein the said Proceedings are Vindicated. Printed by Matthew Simmons for Henry Cripps. 4to. [4], 44 p.
Wing: G1200. Thomason: E.536(28): 2 January.

Ο κριτης της αδικιας *[Okrites tes Adikias]. The Unrighteous Judge, or an Answer to a Paper, pretending a Letter to Mr Jo Goodwin by Sir Francis Nethersole.* Printed by G. Dawson for Henry Cripps. 4to. [2], 18 p.
Wing: G1179. Thomason: E.540(1): 25 January.

[John Goodwin?], Κολλουριον *[Kollourion]: Or Eye Salve to Anoint the Eyes of the Ministers of the Province of London.* Printed by G. Dawson for Henry Cripps. 4to. [2], 6 p.
Wing: K746. Thomason: E.542(16): 13 February.

Υβριστοδικαι *[Hybristodikai]. The Obstructors of Justice; or A Defence of the Sentence passed upon the late King. Opposed chiefly to the Serious Representation of some of the Ministers of London; as also to the Humble Addresse of Dr Henry Hammond; together with a brief reply to Mr John Geree's book intituled Might Overcoming Right.* Printed for Henry Cripps and Lodowick Lloyd. 4to. [8], 146 p. Engraved portrait of Goodwin.
Wing: G1170. Thomason: E.557(2): 30 May.

'Recommendation' in Hezekiah Woodward, *Of the Childs Portion, viz: Good Education* (1649). The recommendation was signed by Edmund Calamy, John Goodwin, Joseph Caryll, Jeremiah Burroughs, and William Greenhill.

1650

The Remedie of Unreasonableness; or the substance of a speech intended at a conference or dispute, in Al-hallows the Great, London. Feb. 11. 1649. Exhibiting the heads of John Goodwins Judgement concerning the Grace of God. Printed by John Macock for Lodowick Lloyd and Henry Cripps. 4to. 15 p.
Wing: G1197. Thomason: E.594(1): 22 February.

Truths Conflict with Error; or, Universal Redemption Controverted in three publike disputations. The first between John Goodwin and Vavasour Powell, the other two between John Goodwin and John Simpson. Printed by Robert Austin. 4to. [4], 118 p.
Wing: T3167B. Thomason: E.597(2): 28 March. Edited for publication by John Weekes.

Three Hymnes, or certain excellent new Psalmes, composed by those three reverend, and learned divines. Mr. John Goodwin, Mr. Dasoser [sic] Powel, and Mr. Appletree. Sung in their respective congregations, at Stephens Coleman-streete, London, and at Mary Abchurch, on Thursday the 8. of October, 1650. being a day set a part for the total routing of the Scots army in Musleborough-field, by his Excellency the L. Gen. Cromwel. Printed for John Clowes. 4to. [2], 11 p.
Wing: T1093C. Thomason: E.1300(3): 8 October.

1651

[John Goodwin?], *Englands Apology for its Late Change, or A sober perswasive, of all disaffected or dissenting persons, to a seasonable engagement, for the settlement of this common-vvealth. Drawne from the workings of providence. The state of affaires. The danger of division.* Printed by M. S. for Livewell Chapman. 4to. [4], 38 p.
Wing: E2942, E2943. Thomason: E.623(12): 12 February

Απολυτρωσις Απολυτρωσεως *[Apolytrosis Apolytroseos], Redemption Redeemed. Wherein the most glorious work of the redemption of the world by Jesus Christ, is by expressness of scripture, clearness of argument, countenance of the best authority, as well ancient as modern, vindicated and asserted in the just latitude and extent of it, according to the counsel and most gracious intentions of God, against the incroachments of later times made upon it, whereby the unsearchable riches and glory of the grace of God therein, have been, and yet are, much obscured, and hid from the eyes of many.* Printed by John Macock for Lodowick Lloyd and Henry Cripps. Fol. [38], 570, 16 p. Engraved portrait of Goodwin in 1641.
Wing: G1149. Dedication to Benjamin Whichcote and Heads of Cambridge Colleges signed 22 February.

Moses made Angry: or, A Letter written and sent to Dr Hill, Master of Trinity Colleg in Cambridg, upon occasion of some hard passages that fell from him in a Sermon preached at Pauls, May 4 1651. Printed by J. M. for Henry Cripps and Lodowick Lloyd. 4to. 12 p.
Wing: G1182.

[John Goodwin?], *A Just Balance, or Some considerable querees about Mr Love's case, tryal, & sentence, as likewise, about those that appeared petition-wise on his behalf. Tending, without partiality, to discover what grounds there are, or may be, either in conscience and religion, or in reason and policie of state, to proceed, either with the execution, or perpetual suspension of the said sentence.* Printed by Ja: Cottrell for Giles Calvert. 4to. [2], 18 p.
Wing: J1229. Thomason: E.638(6): 28 July.

Confidence Dismounted, or a Letter to Mr Richard Resburie of Oundle in Northamptonshire, upon occasion of a treatise of his concerning Election and Reprobation. Printed by John Macock for Henry Cripps and Lodowick Lloyd. 4to. 21pp.
Wing: G1160. Thomason: E.643(18): 17 October.

Two Hymns, or Spirituall Songs. Sung in Mr Goodwins Congregation on Friday last being the 24 of Octob. 1651, which was a day set apart by Authority of Parl. for a solemn Thanksgiving unto God by this Nation, for that most wonderfull and happy successe of the English Army. Printed by F. N. 8vo. [2], 12 p.
Wing: G1212.

The Pagans Debt and Dowry. Printed by J. Macock for H. Cripps and L. Lloyd. 4to. 66 p.
Wing: G1186.

1652

'Epistle to the Reader' in *Foure Pious, Godly and Learned Treatises ... by a late Faithfull and Godly Minister of Jesus Christ.* Printed by Thomas Slater.

Ειρηνομαχια *[Eirenomachia]. The Agreement and Distance of Brethren, or a brief survey of the judgement of Mr J G touching important heads of Doctrine.* Printed by J. Macock for H. Cripps and L. Lloyd. 4to. [12], 82 p.
Wing: G1164. Thomason: E.664(8): 17 May.

1653

Thirty Queries modestly propounded in order to a Discovery of the Truth in that Question; Whether the Civil Magistrate stands bound to interpose his Authority in matters of Religion. Printed by J.M. for Henry Cripps and Lodowick Lloyd. 4to. 16 p.
Wing: G1208. Thomason: E.689(4): 1 March.

'Hymn on the Dutch War'. Printed in *The Moderate Publisher*, 8–15 April 1653.

The Apologist Condemned; or a Vindication of the Thirty Queries concerning the Power of the Civil Magistrate in matters of Religion. By way of answer to An Apologie for Mr John Goodwin and Mr J. Goodwin's Queries Questioned. Printed by J. M. for Henry Cripps and Lodowick Lloyd. 4to. 34 p.
Wing: G1148. Thomason: E.691(16): 19 April.

An Exposition of the Nineth Chapter of the Epistle to the Romans: wherein is proved that the Apostles scope therein is to maintain his great doctrine of justification by faith. Printed by John Macock for Henry Cripps and Lodowick Lloyd. 4to. [44], 408, [20] p.
Wing: G1166. Thomason: E.709: 5 August.

Philadelphia, or XL Queries peaceably and inoffensively propounded for the discovery of truth in this question, or case of conscience; whether persons baptized (as themselves call baptism) after a profession of faith, may, or may not, lawfully, and with good conscience, hold communion with such churches, who judg themselves truly baptized, though in infancy, and before such a profession? Together with some few brief touches about infant, and after-baptism. Printed by J. M. for Henry Cripps and Lodowick Lloyd. 4to. 32pp.
Wing: G1189. Thomason: E.702(7): 22 June.

Water-Dipping no Firm Footing for Church-Communion. Proving it necessary for persons baptized after the new mode of Dipping to continue Communion with those Churches of which they were Members before the said Dipping. Printed by J.M. for Henry Cripps and Lodowick Lloyd. 4to. 90 p.
Wing: G1213. Thomason: E.723(15): 12 December.

Συγκρητισμος *[Synkretismos]. Or Dis-satisfaction Satisfied. In seventeen Queries tending to satisfie the scruples of persons dis-satisfied about the late Revolution of Government in the Commonwealth.* Printed by J. Macock for H. Cripps and L. Lloyd. 4to. 20 p.
Wing: G1205. Thomason: E.725(7): 22 December.

1654

Peace Protected, and Discontent Disarmed. Wherein the seventeen Queries lately published to allay the discontents of some about the late Revolution of Government are reinforced. Printed by J. Macock for H. Cripps and L. Lloyd. 4to. 78 p.
Wing: G1188. Thomason: E.732(27): 11 April.

1655

A Fresh Discovery of the High Presbyterian Spirit. Or the Quenching of the Second Beacon Fired. Declaring the un-Christian dealings of the authors of a pamphlet entituled A Second Beacon Fired, &c in presenting a falsified passage out of one of Mr John Goodwins books. Printed for the Author, and sold by H. Cripps and L. Ll[oyd]. 4to. [10], 84 p.
Wing: G1167. Thomason: E.821(18): 5 January.

The Six Booksellers Proctor Non-Suited. Printed for H. Cripps and L. Lloyd. 4to. 23 p.
Wing: G1203.

Mercy in her Exaltation; or, a soveraigne antidote against the fear of the second death in a sermon preached at the funeral of Daniel Taylor. Printed by J. Macock for H. Eversden. 4to. [12], 56 p.
Wing: G1181. Thomason: E.848(24): 20 July.

Cata-Baptism; or, New Baptism waxing old and ready to vanish away. Considerations touching the subject of Baptism, and an Answer to a discourse against Infant-Baptism by W[illiam] A[llen]. Printed for H. Cripps and L. Lloyd. 4to. 96, 406, [18] p.
Wing: G1155. Thomason: E.849: 21 July.

'Recommendation' in John Toldervy, *The Foot out of the Snare* (1655).
An anti-Quaker pamphlet commended by Thomas Brooks, Thomas Jacomb, George Cokayn, William Adderley, John Goodwin, John Tombes, William Jenkyn and Matthew Poole.
Thomason: E.861(13): 24 December.

1657

Βασανισται *[Basanistai]. Or The Triers or Tormentors Tried and Cast, by the Laws both of God and of Men.* Printed for Henry Eversden. 4to. [16], 33, [3] p.
G1151. Thomason: E.910(12): 23 July.

'Address of the Anabaptist Ministers in London to the Lord Protector'. Signed by Goodwin and eighteen other leaders of Baptist and Independent churches . Reprinted in *Original*

Letters and Papers of State Addressed to Oliver Cromwell, ed. John Nickolls (London, 1743), 142–3.

1658

Triumviri, or the Genius, Spirit and Deportment of the Three Men, Mr Richard Resbury, Mr John Pawson, Mr George Kendall in their late Writings against the Free Grace of God in the Redemption of the World, and vouchsafement of Means of Salvation unto Men; briefly described in their nature and true colours. Printed for Henry Eversden. 4to. [142], 371, [2] p.
'Preface to the Reader' signed 18 November 1657.
Wing: G1210.

1659

The Banner of Justification Displayed: or A Discourse concerning the Deep, and Important Mystery of the Justification of a Sinner. Printed by E.C. for H. Eversden. 4to. [20], 66, [2] p.
Wing: G1150A.

1661

'Epistle to the Reader', in Thomas Goad, *Stimluus Orthodoxus, sive Goadus Redvivus.* Printed for William Leak.

1662

[John Goodwin], *A Door Opening unto the Christian Religion.* 4to. [2], 479, 139.
Wing: D1909.
'An Advertisement to the Reader' in Zachary Mayne, *St Pauls Travailing-pangs with his Legal-Galatians: Or A Treatise of Justication.*

1663

[John Goodwin], *Prelatique Preachers none of Christs.* 4to. [2], 85 p.
Wing: G1192.

1670

Πληρωμα το πνευματικον *[Pleroma to Pneumatikon]. Or A Being Filled with the Spirit.* Printed by E. C. for Henry Eversden. 4to. [22], 555, [12] p. Sermons preached in early 1650s. Foreword by Ralph Venning.
Wing: G1190.

3 Works Against Goodwin and his Congregation

1641

George Walker, *A Defence of the True Sense and Meaning of the Words of the Holy Apostle Roms*

Chap 4 vers 3. 5. 9. The first edition was anonymous; a second edition was subsequently published under Walker's name by one of Goodwin's followers along with Goodwin's *Animadversions*.

George Walker, *Socinianisme in the Fundamentall Point of Justification Discovered and Confuted.*

1643

Griffith Williams, *Vindiciae Regum; or, The Grand Rebellion. That is a Looking-Glasse for Rebels.* Thomason: E.88(1): 2 February. Reply to *Anti-Cavalerisme* and other Parliamentarian writings.

Henry Hammond, *Of Resisting the Lawfull Magistrate under Colour of Religion*. Pages 7–20 critique *Anti-Cavalierisme*. Republished in 1644 and 1647.

Griffith Williams, *Os, Ossis and Oris: or, a collection of the most remarkable passages in a book, intituled: Os Ossorianum, or a bone for a bishop to pick*. Thomason: E.96(15). This is ascribed to Goodwin in Wing (G1184) but it is actually a collection of Goodwin's statements made by his critic, Griffith Williams.

Henry Roborough, *The Doctrine of Justification Cleared*. Republished 1650. A reply to Goodwin's *Animadversions* and *Treatise of Justification.*

1644

William Prynne, *A Full Reply to Certaine Brief Observations ... Together with Certaine Briefe Animadversions on Mr John Goodwins Theomachia* (1644).

[George Gillespie], *Faces About. Or, a Recrimination upon Mr John Goodwin, with animadversions upon his late book Theomachia* (1644). This twelve page tract is attributed to William Prynne by Wing (P3952), but Prynne was not one for anonymity and he replied to *Theomachia* elsewhere (see *A Full Reply* below). A more plausible suggestion is that the author was George Gillespie (Rev. J. C. Johnston, *Treasury of the Scottish Covenant*, [Edinburgh, 1887], 303. William M. Campbell, 'George Gillespie', *Records of the Scottish Church History Society*, 1949). Thomason's copy has a note saying that it was by 'a Scots-man' and the author refers to his onerous 'imployments' (3); the tract contains Gillespie's favourite terms of abuse such as 'adieophorit, neutralist, Nullifidian' (4); finally, a passage in Gillespie's *Wholesome Severity* may allude to his authorship of *Faces About*: 'In this sir, you have *faced about*, sure you are not *As You Were*, for Mr. Goodwin himself (*Theomaxia*, p. 11), says that ... '

1645

[George Gillespie], *Wholesome Severity Reconciled with Christian Liberty*. Replies to several tolerationist tracts, including Goodwin's *M.S. to A.S.*, *Theomachia*, *Innocencies Triumph* and *A Paraenetick*.

William Prynne, *Truth Triumphing over Falshood, Antiquity over Novelty ... in refutation of Mr John Goodwins Innocencies Triumph, Burtons Vindication of Churches commonly called Independent &c.*

A[dam] S[teuart], *Zerubbabel to Sanballat and Tobiah, or the first part of the Duply to M.S.*

alias Two Brethren.

A[dam] S[teuart], *The Second Part of the Duply to M.S. alias Two Brethren.*

John Vicars, *To his Reverend ... Friend.* Defends Prynne against Goodwin's charges in *Innocencie and Truth triumphing together.*

Samuel Lane, *A Vindication of Free Grace in Opposition to this Arminian Position – Natural Men may do such things whereunto God hath by way of promise annexed Grace and Acceptation – preached by John Goodwin.*

1646

Thomas Edwards, *Gangraena.*
Issued in three parts (February, May, December). In Part II, pages 30–140 (half the tract) are devoted to an attack on Goodwin's pamphlet, *Cretensis.*

Josiah Ricraft, *A Nosegay of Rank-Smelling Flowers such as grow in Mr John Goodwins Garden.*

A Vindication of a Printed Paper, entituled An Ordinance ... against the irreligious and presumptious exceptions call'd Some Humble and Modest Queries. By a Westminster Divine, possibly Samuel Rutherford or George Gillespie.

1647

Moro-Mastix: Mr John Goodwin whipt with his own Rod. Or The dis-secting of the sixteenth section of his Book truly nam'd by himself Hagio-Mastix: so far as it falsly and frivolously mentions a late disputation in Christ-Church-Parish, concerning the lawfulness of paying tythes.

William Walwyn, *A Still Small Voice from the Scriptures, Witnessing them to be the Word of God.* April. Walwyn's response to the heresy trial against him conducted by Goodwin's congregation.

John Lilburne, *Jonahs Cry out of the Whales Belly; or certain Epistles writ by Lieu. Coll. John Lilburne unto Lieu. Generall Cromwell and Mr John Goodwin.*

Thomas Edwards, *The Casting Down of the last and strongest hold of Satan. Or a Treatise against Toleration and pretended Liberty of Conscience.* Replies to Goodwin's tolerationist tracts, especially *M.S. to A.S., Theomachia* and *Hagiomastix.*

1648

John Vicars, *Coleman-Street Conclave Visited, and that Grand Impostor, the Schismaticks Cheater in Chief, discovered. Containing a Display of Mr John Goodwins Self-conviction and of the Heresies and Hypocrisie of this Gargantua.* Includes a satirical portrait of Goodwin.

William Jenkyn, *The Busie Bishop; or the Visitor Visited.* Reply to *Sion Colledg Visited.*

C[ornelius] B[urgess], *Sion College, what it is and what it doeth. With a Vindication of that Society from the diffamations of two Satyres, the one called Sion College Visited, the other The Pulpit Incendiary.*

William Jenkyn, *The Blind Guide, or the Doting Doctor.* Reply to *Neophutopresbuteros*, but refers to other Goodwin writings.

1649

Francis Nethersole, *The Self Condemned. Or a Letter to Mr Jo Goodwin.* Reply to *Right and Might Well Met.*

John Geree, *Might Overcoming Right. A Cleer Answer to Mr John Goodwins Might and Right well met.*

William Prynne, 'Epistle to the Reader', in *The Substance of a Speech Made in the House of Commons by Wil. Prynn.* The Epistle is signed 22 January and includes an attack on Goodwin's *Right and Might Well Met.*

Christopher Love, *A Modest and Clear Vindication ... of the Ministers of London from the Aspersions of John Price.* A reply to Price's *Clerico-Classicum.*

[William Walwyn], *The Vanitie of the Present Churches.* This tract does not mention any churches by name, but at numerous points it appears to be condemning Goodwin's congregation.

William Walwyn, *The Fountain of Slaunder Discovered.* Once again, without mentioning any names, Walwyn's main target seems to be Goodwin and his followers.

H[umphrey] B[rooke], *The Charity of Church-Men, or a Vindication of Mr William Walwyn.* A reply to *Walwins Wiles* containing direct attacks on John Goodwin and John Price.

William Walwyn, *Walwyn's Just Defence against the Aspersions Cast upon Him in a Late Un-Christian Pamphlet Entituled, Walwyns Wiles.*

Samuel Rutherford, *A Free Disputation against Pretended Liberty of Conscience.*

A Vindication of Hammond's Addresse from the exceptions of Eutactus Philodemiuss together with a Reply to Mr John Goodwins ... As far as concernes Dr Hammond. Replies to Goodwin's attack on Hammond in *The Obstructors of Justice.*

Alethophilus Basiuluphilus Britannophilus, *Cromwell's Recall: or the Petition of the Zealous Fraternity at the House of John Goodwin, the Arch-flamin of England, to the House of Common Traytors assembled in Parliament, with a Declaration of the said House for the recall of Cromwell from his dangerous expedition to sit with them and vote that which he dare not doe.* A satire.

1650

John Graunt, *A Right Use made by a Stander-by at the Disputations between Mr Goodwin and Mr Symson concerning the points of Generall Redemption.* Not so much an attack on Goodwin, as a thoughtful reflection on his disputations with Calvinist divines.

1651

Richard Resbury, *Some Stop to the Gangrene of Arminianism lately promoted by M. John Goodwin in his book entituled Redemption Redeemed.*

1652

Robert Baillie, *A Scotch Antidote against the English Infection of Arminianism.* Not a direct attack on Goodwin, but issued in response to *Redemption Redeemed.*

Richard Resbury, *The Lightlesse Starre; or Mr John Goodwin discovered Pelagio-Socinian by the examination of his Preface to his book entituled Redemption Redeemed*. Replies to *Confidence Dismounted* and critiques the preface and first four chapters of *Redeemed Redeemed*.

John Pawson, *A Brief Vindication of Free Grace ... relating to several positions asserted by M. John Goodwin in his late book entituled, Redemption redeem'd, and in his former treatise of justification : delivered in a sermon before the Right Honourable, the Lord Mayor and aldermen of the city of London, at Pauls, May 30, 1652*.

Ellis Bradshaw, *A Compendious Answer to ... A brief survey of the judgement of Mr J G* (1652). A reply to *Eirenomachia*.

1653

William Allen, *Some Baptismal Abuses briefly Discovered*.

William Allen, *An Answer to Mr JG his Forty Queries*.

Master John Goodwins Queries Questioned. Reply to *Thirty Queries*.

An Apology for Mr John Goodwin. Reply to *Thirty Queries*.

Henry Jeanes, *A Vindication of D. Twisse from the exceptions of Mr. John Goodwin in his Redemption Redeemed*, in William Twisse, *The Riches of Gods Love*.

George Kendall, *Theokratia, or, A vindication of the doctrine commonly received in the reformed churches ... from the attempts lately made against it, by Master John Goodwin in his book entituled Redemption redeemed*.

1654

George Kendall, *Sancti Sanciti, or, The common doctrine of the perseverance of the saints ... vindicated from the attempts lately made against it by Mr. John Goodwin*. A further reply to *Redemption Redeemed*.

John Owen, *The Doctrine of the Saints Perseverance ... Vindicated in a Full Answer to the discourse of Mr. John Goodwin against it, in his book entituled Redemption Redeemed*.

1655

An Apologie for the Six Book-sellers, subscribers of the second Beacon fired. Reply to *A Fresh Discovery of the High Presbyterian Spirit*.

Robert Crosse, *Logou Alogia sev Excertatio Theologica*. An Oxford disputation against Arminianism, published partly in response to Goodwin's *Redemption Redeemed*.

Obadiah Howe, *The Pagan Preacher Silenced*. Includes an 11-page paper by George Kendall, *A Verdict in the Case depending between Master J. Goodwin and Master Howe*. Replies to *The Pagans Debt and Dowry*.

Thomas Lamb, *Truth Prevailing against the Fiercest Opposition*. Reply to *Water-Dipping*.

1656

Thomas Lamb, *Absolute Freedom from Sin ... in Opposition to Conditional, set forth by Mr*

John Goodwin in his Book (hereby appearing falsly) entituled [Redemption Redeemed]. The author was another Thomas Lamb, the famous pastor the General Baptist church in Bell Alley.

1657

George Kendall, *Fur Pro Tribunali.* The final section of this work is directed against 'D. Johannes Godwinus eloquentissimus ... & Haereticorum omnium fidelissimus Patronas' (ii. 145).

Marchamont Nedham, *The Great Accuser Cast Down. Or a publick trial of Mr John Goodwin at the bar of Religion and Right Reason.* Reply to *Basanistai.*

1663

R. R., *David's Appearance in the behalf of Israel, against J.G. the Goliath of the Philistins against his* Redemption Redeemed, *so called.*

4 Works by Goodwin's Followers

This section lists works written by members of Goodwin's congregation or other supporters during the time when they were associated with Goodwin. I have not included pamphlets by individuals like William Allen and Nicholas Culpepper who published after they had left Goodwin's congregation.

Thomas Devenish, *Certaine Observations concerning the Duty of Love, and of the contrary Evill, Uncharitablenesse* (1641).

*J[ohn] P[rice], *Some Few and Short Considerations on the Present Distempers* (1642). Wrongly attributed to John Price of Coleman Street. It does not read like John Price, and Thomason attributes it to 'Dr Price'.

John Price, *A Spiritual Snapsacke for the Parliament Souldiers* (1643).

John Price, *Honey out of the Rock, or, Gods Method in Giving the Sweetest Comforts in Sharpest Combates* (1644).

P.P. [Hezekiah Woodward?], *As you Were: or A Reducing (if possibly any) seduc't ones, to facing about, turning head, front against God) by the Recrimination (so intended) upon Mr. J.G. (Pastor of the church in Colmanstreet) in point of fighting against God* (1644). The author describes himself as 'an unworthy Auditor' of Goodwin, and replies to *Faces About* (1644) which had attacked *Theomachia* (1644).

Daniel Taylor, *Vicars Letter and Answer* (1645). Reply to John Vicars by a leading member of Goodwin's gathered church.

John Price, *Unity our Duty* (1645).

J[ohn] P[rice], *Independency Accused by Nine Severall Arguments written by a Godly Minister to a Member of Mr John Goodwins Congregation, and Acquitted by Severall Replyes to the said Arguments by a Member of the Same Church* (1645).

John Price, *A Moderate Reply to the Citie-Remonstrance* (1646).

John Price, *The City-Remonstrance Remonstrated* (1646).

Robert Smith et al., *An Apologeticall Account of some Brethren of the Church whereof Mr Goodwin is Pastor why they cannot execute that Unchristian Charge, viz. of delivering up their said Pastor unto Sathan, which is imposed upon them in a Booke called A Vindication of a Printed Paper* (1647).

[John Price], *The Pulpit Incendiary, or, The Divinity of Mr Calamy, Mr Case, Mr Cauton, Mr Cranford, and Other Sion-Colledge Preachers in their Morning Exercises* (1648).

John Price, *Clerico-Classicum, or, The Clergi-Allarum to a Third War* (1649).

John Price et al., *Walwins Wiles: or The Manifestators Manifested* (1649). Probably written by Price, and signed by two other members of Goodwin's congregation, David Lordell and Richard Arnold.

John Price, *The Cloudie Clergie: or A Mourning Lecture for our Morning Lecturers* (1650).

David Brown, *Two Conferences between some of those that are called Separatists and Independents, concerning their Tenents: One whereof, was appointed with Mr Burton, and a number of his Church, and the other with Mr Goodwin, and some of his Church* (1650).

[John Price], *Musgrave Muzl'd: or The Mouth of Iniquitie Stoped* (1651).

John Price, *The Wounds of a Friend: or A Letter mentioned by Mr Love upon the Scaffold in his Speech a little before his Death* (1651).

D[aniel] T[aylor], *Certain Queries, or Considerations presented to the View of All that Desire Reformation of Greivances* (1651).

Eirenomachia; the Agreement and Distance of Brethren, or a brief survey of the judgement of Mr J G touching important heads of Doctrine (1652). Although written by Goodwin, thirteen members of his congregation also signed this theological statement.

Christopher Salter, *Sal Scylla: or a Letter written from Scilly to Mr J G* (1653).

J[ohn] P[rice], *Tyrants and Protectors set forth in their Colours, or The Difference between Good and Bad Magistrates* (1654).

D. F. [Tobias Conyers], *A Letter of Address to the Protector, occasioned by Mr Nedham's Reply to Mr Goodwins Book against the Triers* (1657).

Tobias Conyers, *A Pattern of Mercy: Opened in a Sermon at St Pauls before the Right Honourable the Lord Mayor and the Lord General Monck* (1660).

A Declaration on behalf of the Church of Christ usually meeting in Coleman-street in Communion with Mr John Goodwyn against the Late Insurrection made in the City of London (1661).

5 Posthumously Republished Works by Goodwin

Eirenomachia, or The Agreement and Distance of Brethren (London: Printed for Peter Parker, 1671).
The Pagans Debt and Dowry (London: Printed by T. J. for Peter Parker, 1671).
A Treatise on Justification: Extracted from John Goodwin by John Wesley (Bristol: William Pine,

1765).

Extract from *An Exposition to Romans 9* published in *The Arminian Magazine*, ed. John Wesley (1780).

Redemption Redeemed, a little modernised and abridged by John Bates (Halifax, 1806).

A Treatise on Justification: Extracted from John Goodwin by John Wesley, second edition (London: George Story, 1807).

An Exposition of Romans 9 with A Banner of Justification Displayed by John Goodwin, to which is added Eirenomachia, The Agreement and Distance of Brethren, with a Preface by Thomas Jackson (London: Baynes & Son, 1835).

A Treatise on Justification. Extracted from Mr J. Goodwin by Rev. J. Wesley, third edition (London: J. Mason, 1836).

Christian Theology by John Goodwin selected and systematically arranged, with a Life of the Author, by S. Dunn (London: Thomas Tegg & Son, 1836).

Christian Theology by John Goodwin selected and systematically arranged, with a Life of the Author, by S. Dunn (Dublin: Tegg, 1837).

Redemption Redeemed, unabridged (Thomas Tegg, 1840).

Trefn Duw yn cyfiawnhau dyn euog. Traethawd ar gyfiawnhad pechadur, trwy ffydd yn Nghrist; wedi eu gymeryd allan o waith y Parch John Goodwin, abridged by John Wesley, translated by Robert Humphreys (Caernarfon: H. Humphreys, 1843).

Redemption Redeemed, abridged (London: Wesleyan Office, 1846).

A Being Filled with the Spirit (Edinburgh: James Nicholls, 1867).

Anti-Cavalierisme in W. Haller, ed., *Tracts on Liberty in the Puritan Revolution*, 3 vols (New York, 1933–34), ii. 217–69.

Theomachia in W. Haller, ed., *Tracts on Liberty in the Puritan Revolution*, 3 vols (New York, 1933–34), iii. 3–52.

A Fresh Discovery of the High-Presbyterian Spirit (extracts) in W. M. Clyde, *The Struggle for Freedom of the Press from Caxton to Cromwell* (St Andrews, 1934), 328–37.

Independency God's Verity (extract) in A. S. P. Woodhouse, ed., *Puritanism and Liberty* (London, 1938), p. 186.

Right and Might Well Met (extracts) in A. S. P. Woodhouse, ed., *Puritanism and Liberty* (London, 1938), 212–20.

Right and Might Well Met (extracts) in A. Sharp, ed., *Political Ideas of the English Civil Wars, 1641–1649* (Harlow, 1983), pp. 223–31.

Right and Might Well Met, in Joyce Malcolm, ed., *The Struggle for Sovereignty: Seventeenth-Century English Political Tracts*, 2 vols (Indianapolis, 1999), i. 307–58.

Redemption Redeemed: A Puritan Defense of Unlimited Atonement, ed. John Wagner (Wipf and Stock, 2001). An abridgement, based on the 1846 edition.

The Divine Authority of the Scriptures Asserted (Kessinger Publishing, 2003). A facsimile of the original edition.

Redemption Redeemed: A Puritan Defense of Unlimited Atonement, ed. John Wagner (Wipf and Stock, 2004). An abridgement, which includes material not in the 2001 edition.

A Being Filled with the Spirit (Tentmaker Publications, 2004). A reprint of the 1867 edition.

6 Published Secondary Sources on Goodwin

Biggs, W. W., *John Goodwin* (London, 1961).
Clark, H. W., *The Life of John Goodwin* (London, 1913).
Freshfield, E., 'Some remarks upon the Book of Records and History of the Parish of St Stephen, Coleman Street, in the City of London', *Archaeologia*, 50 (1887), 17–57.
Jackson, T., *The Life of John Goodwin ... with a Review of Several Public Transactions in Great Britain, during the Civil Wars and the Inter-regnum* (London, 1822)
Jackson, T., *The Life of John Goodwin: Comprising an Account of the Controversies in which he was Engaged in Defence of Universal Toleration in Matters of Religion*, second edition (London, 1872).
Kirby, D., 'The Radicals of St Stephen's, Coleman Street, London, 1624–42', *Guildhall Miscellany*, 3 (1969–71), 98–119.
More, E., 'John Goodwin and the origins of the new Arminians', *Journal of British Studies*, 22 (1982), 50–70.
More, E., 'Congregationalism and the social order: John Goodwin's gathered church, 1640–60', *JEH*, 38 (1987), 210–35.
Stringer, J. H., 'John Goodwin: the Unorthodox Puritan', *Westminster Conference 1955: Issues and Approaches* (2002), 12–20.
Webster, T., 'Strange bedfellows: Oliver Cromwell, John Goodwin and the crisis of Calvinism', *Cromwelliana* (1990), 7–17.
Whedon, D. D., 'John Goodwin', *Methodist Quarterly Review*, 45 (1863), 357–81.
Whedon, D. D., 'Memorabilia of John Goodwin', *Methodist Quarterly Review*, 51 (1869), 486–505.
Williams, D. A., 'London Puritanism: the Parish of St Stephen's, Coleman Street', *The Church Quarterly Review*, 160 (1959), 464–82.
Yamada, S., *Igirisu Kakumei no Shukyo Siso [John Goodwin: His Thought and Career in the 1640s]* (Tokyo, 1994).
Yamada, S., *Igirisu Kakumei to Arminius Shugi [John Goodwin and the Doctrine of Universal Redemption]* (Saitama, 1997).
Yamada, S., 'John Goodwin against the Cromwellian Church Scheme', in H. Tamura, ed., *Oliver Cromwell and the English Revolution* (Saitama, 1999).
Yamada, S., 'Two ways toward the Millennium', in H. Tamura, ed., *The Millennium in the English Revolution* (Tokyo, 2000), translated in *The Hiroshima Law Journal*, 23 (1999).

7 Unpublished Theses on Goodwin

Burgess, J. P., 'The problem of Scripture and political affairs as reflected in the Puritan Revolution: Samuel Rutherford, Thomas Goodwin, John Goodwin and Gerrard Winstanley', Ph.D. thesis, University of Chicago (1986).
Hinson, W. J., 'The theological thought of John Goodwin, 1593–1665', Ph.D. thesis, University of Edinburgh (1953).
Kirby, D., 'The parish of St Stephen's Coleman Street, London: A study in radicalism, c. 1624–1664', B. Litt. thesis, University of Oxford (1968).

More, E., 'The new Arminians: John Goodwin and his Coleman Street congregation in Cromwellian England', Ph.D. thesis, University of Rochester (1979).

Sommerville, M., 'Independent Thought, 1603–49', Ph.D. thesis, University of Cambridge (1981).

Strickland, W. J., 'John Goodwin as seen through his controversies, 1640–60', Ph.D. thesis, Vanderbilt University (1967).

Zimdars, D. E., 'John Goodwin and the development of rationalism in seventeenth-century England', Ph.D. thesis, University of Chicago (1967).

INDEX

Abbott, George (Archbishop) 37, 44, 48
Abbott, Morris 2, 48
Abbott, Mrs 50–51
Abelard, Peter 69
Acontius, Jacopo 7, 12, 38–39, 132, 160–61, 292
Agreement of the People 168–73
Ainsworth, Henry 31, 37
Alderne, Thomas 125–27, 195, 246, 261, 262
Aldersley, Samuel 48
Alford, Theophilus 272
Allen, J. W. 39, 89
Allen, William 55, 125–27, 230, 249, 250, 251, 252, 277, 283–85
Allison, C. 75
Alsted, Johannes 71
Ambrose 34
Ames, William (Puritan theologian) 37, 41, 58
Ames, William (Quaker) 205
Anabaptists 26, 80
Anderson, Mr 102
Andrae, Johann Valentin 284
Andrewes, Lancelot 28
Anglicans (see also bishops, Episcopacy) 2, 75, 272–73, 283–85
Anselm 36
antinomianism 54–55, 72, 131, 138, 141, 155, 208, 209, 251, 265, 272
anti-popery 70–71, 76, 77–78, 80–81, 85, 87, 91, 113, 114, 120, 275–76, 285
anti-scripturism 131, 136, 138, 146, 154, 165
anti-Trinitarianism (see also Socinianism) 21, 39, 144, 283
apologetics 38, 52, 132, 156–58, 159, 202, 294
Apuleius, Lucius 32
Aquinas, Thomas 18, 36, 157, 174

Archer, John 58
Arianism 112, 119, 136, 156, 248, 251
Ariosto 41
Aristotle, Aristotelianism 18, 19, 32–34, 41, 292
Arminianism 1, 3, 8, 9, 11, 10, 24–28, 30, 38–39, 45, 55, 62, 68, 112, 115, 131, 136, 153, 155, 158, 185, 199–232, 235, 242, 243, 246, 248–49, 253, 255, 257, 258, 259, 260, 263–64, 267, 270, 272–73, 274, 281, 282, 285, 286–90, 294
Arminius, Jacobus 25–26, 32, 34, 38–39, 69, 74, 204, 211–12, 217, 222, 246, 258, 260
Armstead, William 39–40
Arnold, Richard 126, 127, 140, 185–86, 261
Arrowsmith, John 21, 30, 43, 102, 214, 226
Ascham, Anthony 190–91
Ashe, Simeon 20, 102, 172
Ashurst, Richard 105, 122
Ashmole, Elias 166
astrology 166–67, 234
Athanasius 119
atonement 69, 70, 141
  extent 24–26, 36, 217–18
  Grotian theory 38–39, 73–74, 203, 294
Augustine 34, 35–36, 248, 306
Avery, Samuel 82–83, 92, 104, 122
Aylmer, G. 60, 172, 304

Bachelor, John 99, 121
Bacon, Francis 16, 33, 293
Bacon, Nathaniel 14, 16, 39, 41
Baillie, Robert 107, 111, 166, 224, 300
Ball, Thomas 29
Balmford, James 55
Bancroft, Richard 22

INDEX

Baptists 1, 9, 49, 131, 139, 140, 170, 206, 227, 233, 249–52, 254–55, 271, 285, 291
  General 10, 199, 213, 225, 228, 249–52, 282
  Particular 185, 283
Barebone, Praise God 238
Barebone's Parliament 238–39
Barksdale, Clement 75
Barlow, Thomas 1, 221–22, 225, 229–30
Barnardiston, Thomas 48, 82, 84, 122, 126, 176, 189
Baro, Peter 25
Barrett, William 25
Barrington, Sir Thomas 79
Barrow, Isaac 227
Barrus, Mr 185
Bartlet, William 112, 304
Basil 35, 248
Bastwick, John 49, 54
Baxter, Richard 11, 37, 74, 100, 158, 202, 204, 209, 221, 232, 243, 252, 264, 272–73, 276–77, 282, 284, 285, 287, 289, 291, 296, 306
Bayly, Lewis 41, 55
Baynes, Paul 41
Bede, The Venerable 36
Bellamy, John 99–100, 138
Bernard of Clairvaux 35, 36
Bertius 26, 211
Best, Paul 21, 136, 141, 146, 158, 159
Beza, Theodore 23, 25, 37, 38, 132, 202, 207
Bible 31, 55, 131–32
  authority 144–49, 154–58, 162, 163, 198
  interpretation 31, 50, 52, 53, 60, 69–70, 71–72, 110, 113, 133, 143, 145, 146–47, 166, 171–72, 179, 181–82, 207–08, 218, 219, 220, 231–32, 239, 247, 264–65, 266
Biddle, John 158, 242, 243, 246–48, 272
Biggs, W. W. 7, 289
bishops 2, 17, 22, 27–28, 42, 44, 45, 56, 58, 78, 80, 93, 109, 154, 211, 257, 275–77, 284
Blanke, William 185
blasphemy ordinance 131, 141–47, 165, 210
Boehme, Jacob 251, 256, 284
Book of Common Prayer 80, 276
Boye, Rice 49
Boyle, Robert 229, 284
Bradshaw, Ellis 231
Bradshaw, John 263, 267, 268
Bramhall, John 90
Brandreth, Henry 126, 141, 148–49, 195, 263

Brandt, Geeraert 227
Brawardine, Thomas 35
Bremer, F. 21
Brend, Hammond 126
Brenner, R. 6, 78, 82, 83, 92, 93, 94, 127
Bridge, William 21, 58, 80, 90, 102, 103, 108, 166
Bridgeman, Orlando 21
Bright, Francis 47, 48
Brightman, Thomas 59, 274, 306
Brinsley, John 42
Bristol, Earl of 107
Brook, Humphrey 131, 186
Brooke, Lord 71, 84
Brooks, Thomas 152, 253
Bruce, William 45
Bucer, Martin 31, 37
Buchanan, George 23
Buckingham, Duke of (George Villiers) 40, 45
Bullinger, Heinrich 37
Bunyan, John 277, 289
Burgess, Cornelius 1, 161, 165–66, 172
Burgess, G. 94
Burgess, J. 8
Burnet, Gilbert 270, 271, 287
Burroughs, Jeremiah 21, 43, 58, 80, 84, 90, 92, 94, 99, 102, 108, 112, 132, 135–37
Burton, Henry 22, 49, 58, 78–79, 99, 102, 121, 129, 134, 299

Calamy, Edmund (Sr) 21, 45, 80, 102, 103, 132, 158, 163, 172, 253, 276
Calamy, Edmund (Jr) 3, 4, 279, 285, 295, 305
Calderinus 306
Calvert, Giles 160, 197, 305
Calvin, John 31, 34, 35, 37, 72, 98, 114, 132, 133, 139, 142, 160, 177, 207, 212, 213, 220, 246, 292
Cambridge Platonists 214, 215, 222–23, 226
Cambridge University 14, 15–30, 33–34, 214–15, 221, 222–23, 224, 226–27
  Emmanuel College 20, 21, 29, 39, 42, 214, 222
  Queens' College 10, 15–30, 39–40, 102
Canne, John 60, 152
Capel, Arthur 21
Caryl, Joseph 132, 205, 208, 221, 253
Cartwright, Thomas 59
Castellio, Sebastian 38–39, 132, 160, 292, 296
Cato, Marcus Porcius 32, 64
Cawdry, Daniel 114
Cawton, Thomas 15, 20, 24, 158, 163
Celsi, Mino 38–39
censorship 49, 61, 66, 145, 242–44

Chaloner, Thomas 170
Chamier, Daniel 35, 37
Chaplain, Thomas 126, 141
Chapman, Livewell 304
Chappell, William 18
Charles I 16, 20, 23, 28, 64, 85, 93, 107–08, 136, 137, 147, 165, 173, 176–84, 188, 193–94, 241, 268, 270, 295, 304
Charron, Pierre 33, 41
Chemnitius 37, 220
Cheynell, Francis 161, 243
Chidley, Samuel 36
Chillingworth, William 161
Chrysostom, John 35, 248
Cicero, Marcus Tullius 19, 31, 32, 41, 173
Clarendon, Edward Hyde, Earl of 78
Clark, H. 7, 289
Clarke, John 268
Clarkson, Lawrence 209
classical learning 16, 18, 19, 30–33, 41, 89–90, 237–38, 240, 259
Cleere, Elizabeth 57
Clyde, W. 7
Cockcroft, Caleb 82–83, 92, 102
Collier, Thomas 170, 172
Collins, Anthony 281, 282
Collinson, P. 22, 51, 100
Comenius, Jan Amos 66, 71
Como, D. 54–55, 72
Compton, Spencer 21
Congregationalism (see also Independents) 1, 3, 7, 21, 45, 58–59, 98–130, 132–33, 143, 205, 274, 277, 278, 289
Conway, Anne 284
Conyers, Tobias 126, 226, 252, 259–60, 266–67, 272, 277, 283–84
Cook, George 126, 130
Cook, John 263, 270
Coornhert, Dirck Volckertszoon 39
Coppe, Abiezer 11
Corbet, Richard 94
Corbet, Miles 21, 42, 43, 84, 93, 178, 270
Corvinus 211, 222
Cotton, John 17, 20, 29–30, 44, 58, 84, 129, 133, 213, 299
Covenanters, Scottish 64, 101, 136, 144–45, 168, 179, 189–90, 191–92, 194–95, 224, 277, 292
Cowley, Abraham 271
Cox, William 17–18, 23
Cradock, Walter 129
Cragg, G. 7, 10
Crane, Robert 48
Cranford, James 205

Crawford, P. 181–82
Cripps, Henry 128, 177, 180, 214, 228, 253, 256, 273, 304
Crisp, Tobias 158, 209
Cromwell, Oliver 3, 11, 22, 80, 84, 96, 117, 121, 122, 127, 140, 149, 160, 172, 185–86, 187–88, 189, 193, 197, 198, 225, 230–31, 233, 238, 239, 240–42, 254–60, 262, 267, 268, 270–71, 280
Cromwell, Richard 261
Cudworth, Ralph 214, 226
Culpepper, Nicholas 2, 166
Cyprian 35

Davenant, Edward 18
Davenant, John 17, 22–23, 25–29, 37, 44–45, 48, 58, 64, 108–09, 199, 202, 268
Davenport, John 41, 84
Davies, S. 135
Decius, Emperor 63, 64
Dell, William 129, 177, 242, 253
Denison, Stephen 41
Dent, Arthur 41
Dering, Edward 41
Dering, Sir Edward 48
Desborough, John 262
Descartes, Rene 33
Devenish, Thomas 107–08, 126, 146, 149, 187
D'Ewes, Simonds 20, 26, 43, 79, 84, 129
Diggers 11
Digges, Dudley 91
Dod, John 41
Doddridge, Philip 296
Donne, John 16
Dort, Synod of 25–26, 42, 102, 212, 221, 272
Downham, John 37, 55, 165, 166
Drake, Roger 205
Dunbar, battle of 189–92, 238, 255, 262, 280
Dunn, Samuel 288
Dury, John 71, 160, 161, 190, 193, 299
Dutch War 238

Earle, Walter 79
Eaton, John 158
Eaton, Nathaniel 129
Eaton, Samuel 253
Eaton, Theophilus 48, 58
Edwards, Thomas 1, 2, 29, 31, 37, 38, 40, 43, 59–60, 80, 98, 123, 125, 130, 132, 134–35, 138, 140, 144, 162, 250, 300, 302, 303
Elizabeth I 13, 22, 183
Ellis, John 129

329

INDEX

Emlyn, Thomas 286
Engagement Controversy 304–05
Enlightenment 8, 292–96
Epiphanius 248
Episcopacy, Episcopalians (see also Anglicans, bishops) 1, 37, 79, 80, 108–09, 266–67, 275–76
Episcopius, Simon 39
Erasmus, Desiderius 113, 160, 201
Erskine, John 287
Essex, Robert Devereux, Third Earl of 95–96, 101, 122, 132, 191
Estius 36
Euripides 34
Evelyn, Sir John 82
Everard, Robert? 188
Eversden, Henry 253, 256, 258–59, 270, 273, 281
Exodus 90, 95, 151, 163–64, 168, 191, 193, 240, 255, 293

Fairclough, Samuel 20
Fairfax, Lady 176
Fairfax, Thomas 122, 148, 150, 160, 173
Familism 131, 139, 208
Farnell, J. 6, 173
Farrington, Caldwell 48, 83
Fathers, Church 72, 87, 204, 207, 211, 217, 220, 247–48, 292
Feake, Christopher 148, 197, 242
Feingold, M. 18
Fenner, William 21, 50, 132, 221, 253
Fenwick, George 21
Fenwick, John 283
Feoffees for Impropriations 44–45, 48
Ferne, Henry 90, 91
Fiennes, Nathaniel 79, 84, 148
Fifth Monarchists 124, 197, 239–40, 251, 258, 271, 287
Firmin, Giles 278, 280
Firmin, Thomas 246–47, 283, 284, 285, 296
Fisher, Samuel 15, 228, 249, 251, 252
Fleetwood, Charles 263
Fletcher, Giles 14, 16, 32, 33
Fludd, Robert 49
Fonseca 36
Fountain, Mr 188
Fox, George 154
Foxcroft, Elizabeth 124, 214, 283–84
Foxcroft, Ezekiel 214, 283–84
Foxcroft, George 48, 92, 105, 126, 196, 214, 230, 283–84
Foxe, John 8
Franck, Sebastian 37, 136

Franklin, William 209
Fraser of Brea, James 286
Frederick V, Elector 28
Freshfield, E. 5
Fuller, Thomas 14–15, 17, 24, 253
Furly, Benjamin 228, 281–82

Gadbury, Mary 209
Gallant, Joseph 126, 127, 130, 246
Garland, Augustine 178
Gataker, Thomas 1, 37, 41, 55, 71, 76, 135
Gauden, John 270
Gaulter, Rudolph 31, 37
Gee, Edward 190
Gentles, I. 169, 170
George, David 37, 136
Geree, John 1, 175–76, 180, 183
Gillespie, George 111, 115, 121, 144, 145, 157–58, 300
Goad, Thomas 272
Gomarus, Franciscus 25, 26
Goodman, John 79
Goodson, Mrs 124
Goodwin, John
  affection for 4–5, 59, 76, 119, 146, 249, 250
  Anti-Cavalierisme (1642) 67, 85–89, 132, 174, 175, 177, 280, 281, 293, 303
  Basanistai (1657) 255–58, 282
  Being Filled with the Spirit (1670) 246–49, 281, 306
  Cata-baptism (1655) 37, 250–52, 253, 282
  death 279–80
  education 15–24, 30–39
  Divine Authority (1647) 1, 32–33, 131, 154–58, 159, 202–04, 215, 282, 305
  Door Opening (1662) 273–75, 305–06
  Exposition of Romans 9 (1653) 36, 37, 204, 220, 228, 231–32, 282, 286, 288
  family 13–15, 39–41, 47, 116, 134–35, 245–46, 262, 278–80
  finances 16, 23–24, 40, 42, 45, 84, 116, 127, 152–53, 261–62, 278–79
  gathered church 5–6, 83, 98–101, 104–07, 112–13, 115–17, 121, 122, 123–30, 134, 135, 139–41, 146, 147–49, 151–54, 168–69, 172, 178, 185–89, 195–98, 199, 230, 246, 249–53, 261, 267, 271, 282–85
  Hagiomastix (1647) 131, 142–47, 148, 156, 159, 160, 186, 201, 248, 281, 303
  hymns and verse 15–16, 190, 194–95, 238
  ill health 260, 278–79
  lay preaching 60–61, 128–29

Index

M.S. to A.S. (1644) 108–112, 113, 299–300, 302
Obstructors of Justice (1649) 180–84, 268, 269, 280, 286, 304, 305
ordination 27–28
plays cards and bowls 20, 28, 134, 135
portraits 70, 154, 161–62, 180
public disputations 59–60, 146, 170–72, 205–06
Puritan piety 50, 51, 248–49, 274–75
Redemption Redeemed (1651) 1, 31, 201–02, 208, 209, 210, 211, 212, 214–29, 235, 250, 254, 281, 282, 286, 287, 288, 290, 305–06
revolutionary ruthlessness 80, 175, 193–94
Right and Might Well Met (1649) 173–76, 177, 179, 281, 303, 305
sarcasm, satire 15, 31–32, 68, 69, 76, 134, 135, 261
self-image 4, 9, 70, 166, 292
sermons 49–52, 61–65, 67–68, 77–78, 85, 113–15, 116, 127–28, 138, 139–40, 199–200, 246–49
tears 249–50
Theomachia (1644) 113–115, 121, 281, 300, 301
Treatise of Justification (1642) 1, 31, 34, 67, 68, 70–76, 89, 103, 143, 221, 264, 286–87, 288, 293, 305
Triumviri (1658) 260–61, 282
will 261–62
Goodwin, Sarah 245–46, 278–79
Goodwin, Thomas 15, 18, 21, 30, 42, 43, 49, 51–52, 58–59, 61, 80, 98, 99, 102, 104, 108, 112, 133, 169, 177, 197, 234, 243, 272, 289, 299
Gorton, Samuel 146, 159
Gouge, William 45, 55, 102, 132, 158
Granger, James 285–86
Graunt, John 206
Greaves, R. 213
Green, I. 305
Greenhill, William 102, 132, 136
Gregory the Great 36
Griffith, George 205, 277
Grotius, Hugo 12, 31, 35, 37, 38–39, 73–74, 157, 203, 274, 294, 306
Gunning, Peter 267
Gurney, Sir Richard 82

Hakewill, George 33, 71
Hale, Matthew 283
Hall, Joseph 31, 41, 42, 221, 223
Haller, W. 3, 7, 9, 38, 85, 215, 291–92

Hamilton, James, First Duke of 185
Hammond, Henry 1, 30–31, 75, 90–91, 158, 165, 180, 222, 227, 264, 267, 273, 306
Hampden, Elizabeth 77
Hampden, John 22, 77–79, 84, 101–02
Hancock, John 160
Harrington, James 263
Harrison, Thomas 170, 268, 270
Harsnett, Samuel 27, 28
Hartley, William 228
Hartlib, Samuel 2, 38, 49, 51–52, 71, 97, 121, 160, 161, 260, 281, 284, 293
Haselrig, Arthur 79, 84, 127, 185–87
Haymo of Faversham 36
Henry, Matthew 286
Henry, Prince 15–16, 179
heresy 24, 55, 68, 69, 76, 110, 131–67, 177, 235, 236, 242–45, 247–48, 267
Herle, Charles 90
Herbert, George 16
Hervey, James 286
Heveningham, William 40, 178, 190–91
Hewitt, Mr 171
Heylyn, Peter 90, 261
Hickes, William 55
Hickman, Henry 261
Hilary of Poitiers 35
Hildesley, Mark 83, 84, 92, 121, 122, 126–27, 129–30, 140, 146, 151, 169, 172–73, 176, 185, 188–89, 195–96, 246, 252, 261
Hill, C. 2, 10
Hill, Richard 287
Hill, Thomas 1, 21, 214, 221, 222, 225, 226
Hinson, J. 9
Hobart, Peter 29
Hobbes, Thomas 9, 155, 190, 220–21
Hobson, Paul 129, 158, 253
Holland, Earl of 185
Holles, Denzil 79, 147, 151
Homer 34
Homes, Nathaniel 99, 102–03, 107, 129
Hooker, Thomas 44, 52, 84
Horace 32
Horn, John 227–28, 282
Horton, Thomas 102–03
Hotham, Charles 226
Hotman, 23
How, Samuel 60–61, 128
Howard, Luke 100, 126, 283
Howe, Obadiah 230, 253, 254, 260
Hughes, A. 29, 136
humanism 8, 9, 12, 19, 30–33, 38, 41, 71, 293

Humble Proposals 233–35
Hunt, J. 3, 7
Hunter, M. 11
Hunton, Philip 90
Hus, Jan 109
Hutchinson, Joseph 126

Ignatius 35, 248
Independents (see also Congregationalism)
  political 22, 77, 83, 102, 107–08, 117, 121–22, 123, 127, 132, 136–38, 140, 141, 147, 148, 150–51, 163, 169–70, 176–79, 185–88, 195, 267–71, 291, 293
  religious 1, 2, 5, 6, 21, 43, 98–130, 131–67, 169–73, 177, 205, 233–35, 241–42, 243, 252, 253, 254–55, 276, 282, 285, 287, 291, 295
Irenaeus 248
Ireton, Henry 151, 170–72, 185, 188, 241, 267, 270–71
Irish rebellion (1641) 80–81, 84, 86, 179
Islam 109–110, 111, 112, 216, 272

Jackson, T. 3, 6, 288–89
Jackson, Thomas 222
Jacob, Henry 61
Jacombe, Samuel 282
James I 18, 20, 23, 28, 30, 179, 183
Jeakes, Samuel 281
Jeanes, Henry 224, 225, 260
Jenkyn, William 1, 159, 161, 163–64, 165–67, 193–94, 204, 211, 243, 253, 254
Jerome 248
Jessey, Henry 21, 49, 129, 197, 205–06, 209, 249, 253, 254, 271
Jews, Judaism 109–110, 111, 112, 198
Jones, Inigo 40
Jones, Philip 259
Jones, Roger 307
Jordan, W. K. 7, 291, 301, 302
Joyce, Cornet 147
Junius, Franciscus 31, 305
justification by faith 52, 66–67, 68–76, 103–04, 134, 135, 162, 231–32, 264–65, 272–73, 274, 284, 286–87, 294
Justin Martyr 157, 248
Juvenal 34, 41
Juxon, Bishop 56, 61, 268

Kelsey, S. 178
Kendall, George 215, 223, 225, 228, 230, 254, 260, 263, 304
Kendrick, John 83, 189

Kidder, Richard 284
Kiffin, William 2, 49, 52–53, 133, 186, 188, 197
Kirby, D. 5
Knollys, Hanserd 254
Knox, John 41, 98, 181, 307

Lactantius 35, 142
Lacy, Nathaniel 84, 126, 173, 195, 196
Lamb, Barbara 100, 124
Lamb, Thomas (merchant) 100, 104, 106, 125, 140, 195, 196, 230, 249–50, 252, 282, 283–84, 286
Lambe, Thomas (preacher) 146, 213, 225, 260, 271
La Motte, John 50, 84
Lane, Samuel 199–201, 304
La Peyrere, Isaac 155
Lapide, Cornelius à 35
Larner, William 80
Laud, William 28, 30, 44, 56–57, 80
Laudians 28, 30, 37, 44, 56–57, 61, 62, 63–64, 80, 91, 211, 212, 213, 224
Lavender, Bartholomew 126, 185
Lawrence, M. 243
Leake, William 272, 273
Lecler, J. 7
Le Clerc, Jean 282
Leigh, Edward 122, 145, 157
Leighton, Alexander 57
Leo the Great 36
Lessius, Leonhard 36
L'Estrange, Roger 279
Levellers 11, 90, 127, 131, 139–41, 147–49, 151, 154, 169–73, 185–87, 287, 291
Ley, William 303
liberty, liberties 6–8, 137, 150, 151, 240–41, 259, 260, 294, 295
  civil 7, 67, 87–88, 89–90, 117–18, 132, 173–74, 180
  religious 1–2, 6–8, 67, 88, 108–11, 117–18, 132, 235–38, 242, 260, 276–77, 283, 292
Lightfoot, John 21, 103
Lilburne, John 2, 11, 83, 121–22, 130, 135, 139–40, 146–48, 169–70, 172, 177, 185–87
Lilly, William (astrologer) 167
Lily, William (grammarian) 32
Limborch, Philip van 282
Lindley, K. 6, 83
Liu, T. 5
Lloyd, Lodowick 128, 214, 228, 253, 256, 273
Lloyd, William 284

INDEX

Locke, John 6–9, 12, 281–82, 283, 291, 292, 294, 295, 296
London 35, 44–49, 66, 71, 74, 78–84, 91–93, 96, 97–98, 125–26, 127, 130, 137, 140, 146, 147–48, 149, 151, 152–53, 158, 163, 165, 166–67, 169, 173, 176, 177, 188, 192, 197, 198, 205, 224, 238, 255, 261, 262–63, 266–72, 273, 278, 280, 291
   Bethnal Green 271, 278–79
   Common Council 78, 79, 81, 82, 93, 96, 137, 173, 176, 185, 187, 195, 238, 263
   Court of Aldermen 79, 81, 96, 195, 224
   Hackney 261
   Militia Committee 82, 93, 96, 151, 176, 195–96
   population 46
   St Mary, Abchurch 125, 152–53, 166–67
   St Stephen's, Coleman Street 2, 4, 5–6, 15, 44–49, 51, 57, 67, 76–77, 78–84, 98–101, 102, 104–07, 112–13, 115–17, 119–20, 122–23, 125–27, 129–30, 146, 151–52, 188–89, 245–6, 261, 271–72, 280, 282
   Sion College 35, 98, 159, 161–64, 165, 225
   strategic importance 91–92
   Tower 46, 80, 92, 96, 165
London, William 253–54
Lordell, David 185, 205
Love, Christopher 164, 179, 193–94, 253, 305
Love, Richard 214
Lucas, Richard 282, 286
Luddington, Mr and Mrs 278–79
Ludlow, Edmund 238
Luther, Martin 35, 36, 70, 75–76, 109, 114, 139, 142, 272
Lutherans 36–37, 201, 207, 220, 229

Machiavelli, Niccolo 175, 241
Macock, John 160, 228
Manchester, Earl of 101
Mansell, John 18–19, 28–29
Mariana, Juan 184
Marprelate tracts 69
Marshall, Stephen 21, 172, 243
Marten, Henry 79, 84, 170, 240
Martin, Edward 30
Mary I 212
Mary Stuart 183
Mather, Richard 129
May, Thomas 16
Mayne, Zachary 272–73
McConica, J. 19

Mede, Joseph 37, 71, 306
Melancthon, Philip 36–37, 139, 201, 220
Methodism 3, 6–7, 266, 286–89, 296
millenarianism 9, 71, 77, 87, 88–89, 90, 91, 192, 271, 274–75, 293–94, 295–96
Milton, John 6, 10, 11, 16, 32, 33, 71, 97–98, 109, 115, 147, 158, 159, 160, 179, 180, 183, 193, 199, 223, 235, 240, 242, 243–44, 263, 267–70, 277, 293, 294, 296, 297
Mollerus 37
Molina, Luis de 36, 217
Moline, Andrew 56
Monck, George 266
Montague, William 105, 122, 126, 129, 151, 280
Montaigne 33, 41
Moore, J. 25, 26
Moore (Sr.), Thomas 213, 282
More, E. 5, 8, 38, 105, 124, 126, 127, 196, 291–92, 299, 300
More, Henry 226, 284, 285, 294
Mornay, Philippe du Plessis 41, 157
Morrill, J. 11
Morris, Thomas 152
Mosely, Lt-Col 107–08
Mosse, G. 175
Mountain, George 17
Muller, R. 34
Musculus 35, 37, 157, 212, 213, 292, 305
Musgrave, John 187

Naseby, battle of 132, 135, 191, 255
natural law theory 9, 86, 89, 94, 120–21, 143, 149, 171–72, 181–82, 236–37, 267
Nazianzen 248
Nedham, Marchamont 1, 2, 4, 12, 33, 98, 190–91, 193, 234, 237, 255, 258, 260, 284
Netherlands 24, 25–26, 29, 58, 61, 99, 102, 109, 111, 115, 139, 152, 181, 238, 278
Nethersole, Francis 1, 175, 177
New England 15, 21, 45, 48, 54–55, 58, 84, 99, 109, 130, 133, 139, 295
New Model Army 131, 138, 147, 149–51, 163, 165, 169–70, 173–76, 189, 191–92, 198, 293
Newton, Isaac 284
Nonconformists, Restoration 277, 281, 282, 289
Norfolk 13–15, 20, 21, 29, 39–43, 95, 130, 168, 213, 261
   Great Yarmouth 41–42
   Helloughton 13–14, 21

INDEX

King's Lynn 18, 20, 21, 41, 42–43, 102
Norwich 13, 30, 27, 43, 46
Rainham 13–15, 21, 35, 39–43, 261
Nye, Philip 58, 80, 98, 102, 107–08, 109, 169–72, 233–34, 237, 243, 258, 268–70, 277, 278

Oates, Samuel 146
Ockham, William of 18
Oecolampadius 35, 37
Ogle, Thomas 107–08, 178
Oldenburg, Henry 260
original sin 73
Origen 35, 157
Overall, John 25
Overton, Elizabeth 124, 304
Overton, Henry 48–49, 84, 85, 95, 104, 113, 121, 126–29, 137, 145, 177, 201, 252, 299, 300, 303, 304
Overton, Richard 61, 83, 114, 147, 158, 159, 170, 185, 302
Ovid 32, 34
Owen, David 23
Owen, John 1, 2, 11, 31, 157, 193, 212, 223–24, 225, 233–34, 243, 244–45, 254, 260–61, 263, 276, 278, 280, 281–82, 285, 287
Oxford University 223, 280–81

pagans, salvability of 162, 204, 206, 229–30, 274, 283, 285, 293, 294
Paget, Nathan 2, 35, 38, 97, 122, 281–82
Paine, Thomas 128
Palmer, Herbert 1, 21, 29–30, 90, 102, 214
Paracelsus 38
Paraeus, David 23, 31, 35, 37, 135
Parker, Dr 169–70
Parker, Henry 84, 90, 95, 259
Parker, Peter 281
Parliament 23, 41, 65, 76–96, 101–02, 107–08, 109, 113, 117–118, 121, 122–23, 127, 131, 132, 136–37, 138, 141, 145, 146, 147, 148, 150–51, 163, 165, 169, 172–75, 183, 187, 188, 197, 233–34, 238–39, 242–43, 258, 262–63, 268, 269–70
Patient, Thomas 169
Patrick, Simon 227
Paul, R. S. 103
Pawson, John 211–12, 224, 225, 260
Pearl, V. 2, 6, 93
Pennington, Isaac (Sr) 2, 48, 58, 65, 76–84, 92, 93, 96, 98, 101, 123, 137, 151, 178, 189, 270

Pennington, Isaac (Jr) 97, 210, 248, 282–83
Pepys, Samuel 8, 270, 281, 292
Perkins, William 8, 24–26, 37, 41, 202, 213
Perne, Andrew 30
Peter, Hugh 21, 43, 84, 92, 99, 121, 137, 170, 173, 175, 176, 177, 179, 268, 270
Petty, Maximilian 170
Petyt, Silvester 281, 282
Petyt, William 281, 282
Pierce, Thomas 261, 266
Pinson, M. 74
Piscator 37, 292
Plato 7, 32–33, 41, 173, 215, 237
Plume, Thomas 281–82
Plutarch 32–33
Polanus, Amandus 181
Pool, Mr 188
Pounset, John 303
Powell, Vavasour 152–53, 205–06, 225, 228, 239, 276, 281
Power, William 18
prayer 15, 19, 22, 28, 51, 85, 99, 100, 123, 163, 184, 274, 276–77
preparationism 52–53
Presbyterians, Presbyterianism 1, 2, 3, 4, 9, 21, 24, 37, 98, 101–30, 131–67, 172, 175–76, 179, 180, 181, 186, 188, 189, 191–95, 201, 210, 225, 242–45, 250, 251, 253, 266–67, 286, 294–95, 295
Preston, John 10, 17–30, 41, 44, 50, 199, 202, 224
Price, John 32, 83, 99–100, 121–22, 125–30, 138, 140, 148–49, 165, 169, 179, 180, 185–87, 188, 193, 195, 230, 233–35, 246, 252, 272, 300, 301
  writings of 95, 113, 119–20, 128, 133, 137, 163–64, 183–84, 240–42
Price, Richard (mercer) 83, 93, 126
Price, Richard (scrivener) 83, 93, 98, 107, 126, 127, 152, 170, 172, 178, 195
Pride, Thomas 267, 270–71
Prideaux, John 36, 37
Pride's Purge 168, 266
Prince, Thomas 185–86
Prynne, William 49, 57, 58, 78–79, 95, 105, 115–16, 118, 119–22, 162, 175, 177, 181, 182, 183, 190, 263, 275, 277, 300, 301, 302, 306
Ptolemy 63
Puritan Revolution 8, 10–11, 43
Pym, John 65, 66, 77–78, 80–81, 101–02
Pythagoras 32

Quakers 228, 243, 251, 252, 253, 271, 282–

334

83, 285, 291
Quartermayne, Roger 137, 162
Queens' College (see Cambridge University)
Quintillian 19, 32

Ramus, Peter 18
Ranters 11, 197, 208, 243, 251, 253, 287
Raymond, J. 143
reason (see also apologetics) 7, 8, 9, 75, 132, 162, 179, 181–82, 196, 203, 215–16, 221, 230, 247, 291, 292, 294, 296
regicide 33, 42, 78, 85, 168, 176–84, 191, 192, 241, 263, 267, 268, 270, 271, 280, 286, 295, 304
republicanism 3, 32–33, 91, 94, 181, 183–84, 210–11, 237, 240–42, 259, 263, 271, 289, 291, 292
Resbury, Richard 1, 211, 222, 224, 254, 260, 285
resistance theory 23, 85–91, 93–95, 173–75, 179–84, 295
Rich, Nathaniel 47, 57
Richardson, John 25
Ricraft, Josiah 135, 254
Rivers, I. 75
Rivetus, Andreas 157
Roberts, William 30
Robinson, Henry 83, 109, 145, 301, 302
Roborough, Henry 1, 74–76, 99, 253, 254
Rogers, Samuel 51
Roman Catholicism 36, 79, 109–110, 111, 112, 139, 143, 250–51, 302
root and branch petition 79, 81–82
Rosier, Edmund 186, 195
Rothwell, John 253
Rous, Francis 129, 190–91
Rowe, Owen 48, 51, 58, 82, 84, 92, 96, 122, 123, 151, 173, 176, 178, 185, 189, 195–96, 261, 270
Rudyard, Thomas 126, 200, 283
Russell, James 82–83, 92, 96, 105, 123, 126, 151, 173, 185
Rutherford, Samuel vi, 2, 144–45, 147, 166, 177, 181, 217, 289, 292–93, 294

St John, Oliver 22, 43, 83, 101–02, 117, 122, 148, 291
St Stephens, Coleman Street (see London)
Sadler, John 148
Salter, Christopher 227–28
Saltmarsh, John 134, 146, 158
Saltonstall, Richard 48
Sambrook, Jeremy 189
Sancroft, William 227, 284

Sanderson, Robert 190
Saunders, Laurence 158, 213
Saunders, Robert 126, 146, 147
Saye and Sele, William Fiennes, First Viscount 22, 84, 101–02, 121–22, 148, 268, 291
scepticism 113, 115, 139, 142, 144–45, 154, 156, 161–62, 247, 248
scholasticism 18, 19, 30, 33–34, 72, 185
Scott, D. 101, 132, 138
Scott, Thomas 268
Scotus, Duns 18, 36
Seaman, Lazarus 102, 172, 214, 226, 281–82
Seaver, P. 5, 45
Second Civil War 168–69, 176
Seekers 131, 138, 146, 155, 208, 227, 246, 248, 251
Selden, John 237
Sellon, Walter 287
Seneca 32–34
separatism 59–60, 80, 140
Servetus, Michael 38, 69, 133, 160
Shrubsole, William 287
Sibbes, Richard 8, 19–20, 44, 50, 54
Sidney, Algernon 296, 297
Sidney, Philip 31, 41
Simmons, Matthew 97, 121, 128, 129, 179, 300, 303, 304
Simon, Richard 155
Simpson, John 125, 197, 205–06, 214, 228, 239, 281
Simpson, Sidrach 21, 29, 56, 58, 80, 99, 108, 152–53, 169, 197, 234, 243
Slingsby, Henry 21
Skinner, Q. 12, 89
Skippon, Philip 84, 168
Smith, John 226
Smyth, Robert 104–05, 126, 146
Socinians, Socinianism 9, 39, 55, 68–69, 74, 107, 112, 115, 131, 136, 141, 160–61, 224, 233–35, 243, 245, 246–48, 252, 253, 285, 286, 291, 292
Socinus, Faustus 32, 69, 73, 136
Socrates 32
Solemn League and Covenant 30, 101, 105, 134, 182
Sommerville, M. 9
Sowthen, Samuel 126, 261, 272, 282
Sparrow, Anthony 30
Spenser, Edmund 16
Spilsbery, John 254
Spinoza, Benedict 155
Sprigge, Joshua 170
Spurr, J. 10
Spurstow, William 77, 82, 83, 84

Index

Stacy, Capt. 126, 185, 272
Stanton, Dr 102
Stapleton, Philip 22, 101–02, 147
Starkey, George 268
Steel, William 130
Steuart, Adam 108, 111, 302
Stillingfleet, Edward 227
Stooks, Richard 227
Stoughton, John 45, 56, 57, 166, 301
Stow, John 46
Strafford, Earl of 79–80
Strickland, W. 8,
Strickland, Walter 259
Strickland, William 21
Suetonius 41
Swenckfeld, Caspar 38
Sydenham, William 259
Symonds, Joseph 58, 135, 152–53, 169

Tacitus 41, 240
Taylor, Daniel 5, 48, 70, 81–84, 92, 119, 125–28, 169, 170, 172, 173, 176, 185, 195–98, 230, 238, 249, 256, 261, 262
Taylor, Jeremy 6, 145, 261, 266, 273
Taylor, Thomas 288
Taylor, William 123, 129, 158, 163, 188, 189, 194, 246, 261, 270, 272
Tenison, Thomas 227
Terence 19, 31, 32
Tertullian 35, 87, 306
Thales 32
theatre 20, 50
Thirty Years War 28, 30, 41
Thomason, George 85, 109, 134, 151, 199, 236, 243, 258, 300, 301, 302
Thompson, Maurice 83
Thorndike, Herbert 267
Thurscross, Timothy 267
Thucydides 34
Thurloe, John 259
Tichborne, Robert 83, 151, 169, 172, 176, 195, 224
Tilenus, Daniel 211
Tillotson, John 227, 283, 284–85, 294
tithes 115, 116, 126, 139, 146, 152–53, 198, 235, 236, 237, 283, 295
Toland, John 199
Toldervy, John 253
toleration (see also liberty) 1–2, 37, 38–39, 107–08, 109–12, 113–15, 116, 117–18, 131–32, 133–34, 136, 138, 139, 141–47, 153–54, 160–61, 162, 164, 170–72, 235–38, 243–45, 255–58, 266–67, 283, 284, 285, 291, 292, 294–95

Tolmie, M. 5
Tombes, John 158, 251, 253, 277
Toplady, Augustus 287–88
Towers, John 30
Towne, Robert 158
Townshend, Roger 14–16, 28, 33, 39–43, 45
Trajan, Emperor 63, 64
Travers, Walter 41
Trevor-Roper, H. 28
Triers 234, 235, 237, 240, 242, 254, 254–58
Trinity, doctrine of 133, 134, 141, 144, 146, 155, 161, 215, 233–35, 247–48, 252, 274, 292
Tubb, A. 179
Tuckney, Anthony 20, 43, 214, 222–23, 225, 226
Twisse, William 75, 76, 224
Tyacke, N. 33
Tyndall, Humphrey 17

Underhill, Thomas 145
Ursinus, Zacharias 37, 157
Ussher, James 18, 25, 27, 41

Vane (Jr), Sir Henry 79, 84, 101, 121, 148, 193, 235, 238, 271
Venner, Thomas 271
Venning, Ralph 249, 277
Vere, Horace 41, 45, 84, 168
Vere, Mary 2, 40–41, 45, 49, 51, 168, 176, 261
Vermigli, Peter Martyr 31, 37, 114, 139, 212, 213, 305
Vicars, John 2, 24, 79, 119, 145, 161–63, 165, 258, 277
Viner, John 56
Vines, Richard 21, 76, 103–04, 214, 221, 243
Virgil 32, 34, 48

Waldensians 246
Wagner, J. 290
Walker, Clement 178, 268
Walker, George 1, 4–5, 31–32, 55–56, 66, 68–76, 102, 103, 107
Wallace, J. 190
Wallington, Nehemiah 49
Walton, Valentine 84
Walwyn, William 5, 83, 92, 98, 108, 109, 111, 121, 124, 128, 134, 139–41, 145, 154, 158, 159, 169–70, 185–87, 196, 213
Walzer, M. 90
Ward, Robert 20
Warwick, Robert Rich, Second Earl of 84, 278

Index

Watson, Richard 288
Watts, Isaac 296
Webster, T. 8, 49
Weekes, John 126, 141, 205
Wesley, Charles 287
Wesley, John 266, 286–88, 296
Wesley, Samuel 180, 266, 286
Westminster Assembly 3, 20–22, 29, 43, 76, 98, 101, 102, 107, 108, 111, 114, 115, 117, 121–22, 135, 136, 139, 142, 161, 164, 165, 166, 210, 226, 301
Wharton, Philip 101, 108
Whately, William 41
Whedon, D. 6–7, 288–89
Whichcote, Benjamin 214–15, 222–23, 225, 226, 283, 284–85, 291, 294
Whig history 7–8, 291–96
Whitaker, Jeremiah 21
Whitby, Daniel 286
White, Col. 169
White, Edmund 48
White, John 103
Whitehall debates 2, 144, 169–72, 234, 295
Whitfield, Mr 42
Whitgift, John 22, 27, 37
Whiting, Samuel 39
Wickins, William 299
Wightman, John 126
Wildman, John 169–72, 187
Wilkins, John 75, 283, 291
Williams, D. 5
Williams, Elisha 295

Williams, Griffith 1, 90, 91, 93–95
Williams, John 284
Williams, Roger 60, 109, 110, 115, 146, 158, 235, 258, 300, 302
Winstanley, Gerrard 11, 154
Winthrop, John 48, 49
Wolfe, D. 97
Wollaston, John 96
Wolseley, Charles 259
women, godly 41, 45, 47–48, 49, 50–51, 57, 77, 114, 124–25, 214
Womock, Laurence 272
Wood, Anthony 2, 223
Woodford, Robert 49
Woodward, Hezekiah 121, 132
Woolrych, A. 165, 196
Wootton, Anthony 37, 55–56, 69, 135
Worden, B. 194, 209
Worsley, Benjamin 281–82
Worthington, John 214, 284
Writer, Clement 154, 156, 213
Wroth, Thomas 47, 56, 77
Wyclif, John 109

Yamada, S. 9, 307
Yates, Mr 104
Yelverton, Christopher 21

Zagorin, P. 3, 7–8, 175, 291
Zimdars, D. 8
Zwingli, Ulrich 35, 37, 114

www.ingramcontent.com/pod-product-compliance
Lightning Source LLC
Chambersburg PA
CBHW071228230426
43668CB00011B/1352